PEARSON
myMISlab™

PEARSON
myMISlab™

LEARN ABOUT | BOOKS AVAILABLE | HELP

Welcome to MyMISLab, where learning and technology meet!

MyMISLab is a state-of-the-art, interactive, and instructive online solution for management information systems. Designed to be used as a supplement to a traditional lecture course, or to completely administer an online course, MyMISLab combines multimedia, tutorials, tests, and quizzes to make teaching and learning fun. Learn more...

First-time users
Register here

Students

Instructors

Returning users

Students

Instructors

Log In Here

ANNOUNCEMENTS

Students, using MyMISLab this semester? Give us your feedback!

Learn more about MyMISLab Try It!

BOOKS AVAILABLE

Here's a sampling of books available with MyMISLab. See the complete list of books, with ordering information.

AUTO-GRADED TESTS & ASSIGNMENTS

PERSONALIZED STUDY PLAN

ETEXT

MyMISLab is an **online learning system** for MIS. This fun and **easy-to-navigate** site enhances *Experiencing MIS*, Canadian Edition, with a variety of learning resources.

MyMISLab is found at **www.pearsoned.ca/mymislab.** Follow the simple registration instructions on the Access Code card bound into this text.

PEARSON
Education Canada

PEARSON

myMISlab™

In MyMISLab you are treated as an individual with specific learning needs.

GET A BETTER GRADE!

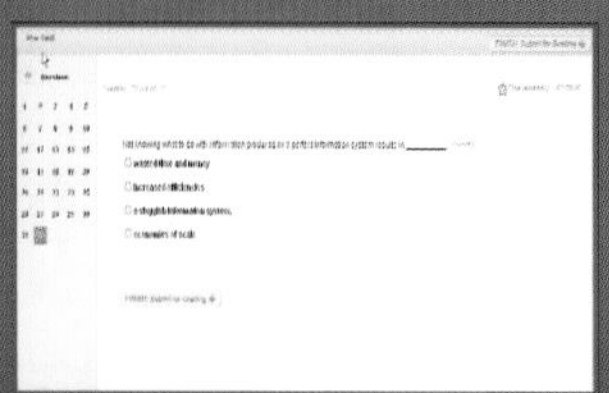

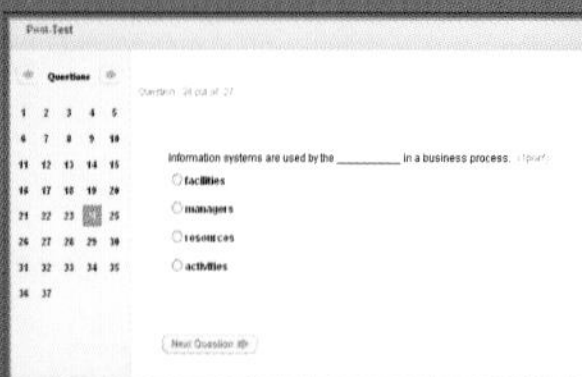

Auto-Graded Tests and Assignments

MyMISLab comes with two preloaded sample tests per chapter (Pre-Test and Post-Test). Work through these tests to identify areas you don't fully understand.

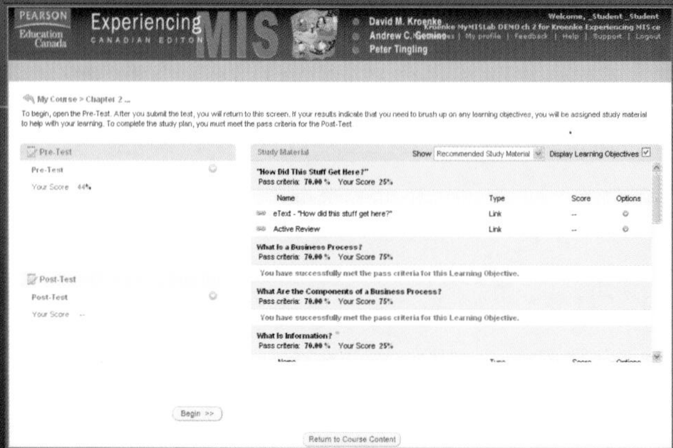

Personalized Study Plan

When you use MyMISLab, you're treated as an individual with specific learning needs. A personalized Study Plan is generated from your results on sample tests. You can clearly see which topics you have mastered and, more importantly, which ones you still need to work on.

eText

Each problem links to the eText page discussing the very concept being applied. You have access to the text material without leaving the online environment!

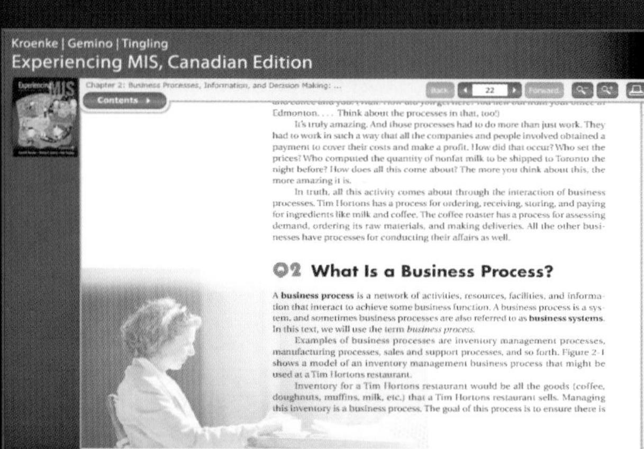

ADDITIONAL RESOURCES IN MYMISLAB

- Student PowerPoint® slides
- Glossary flashcards
- Research Navigator™
- Annotated figures and weblinks
- Chapter extensions of key concepts
- Author tutorial videos

www.pearsoned.ca/mymislab

Dear Student:

You have chosen to begin a career as a business professional by majoring in a business discipline. If your experience is anything like that of the authors of this Canadian edition of *Experiencing MIS*, you will not regret your choice. Working in business leads to fulfilling and enjoyable experiences and relationships with interesting, quality people. Working in a company you admire that sells products or services in which you believe will enable you to feel positive about yourself, your contributions, and your professional life.

The overall purpose of this book is to help you prepare for success in your business career. In writing the book, we kept in mind three goals:

1. To explain how you can use information systems to solve problems and make better decisions in business.
2. To show you how to increase your utility (and marketability) in business by applying knowledge of information systems.
3. To describe, in the context of management information systems (MIS), how you can become a better business professional.

Notice the emphasis is on you. It's up to you to prepare yourself. No particular book, no course, no professor, no T.A. can do it for you. However, many people have worked hard to structure this book so you can maximize the benefit from your study time.

To help you achieve your goals, we have included four unique features in this book. First, we have organized the material in every chapter around a set of questions. Use these questions to manage your study time. Read until you can answer the questions.

Second, every part and every chapter begins with a real-life scenario of a student or business professional who needs knowledge of information systems. Use these scenarios to understand how you can apply the knowledge of information systems to gain a personal competitive advantage.

Third, read the MIS in Use case included in each chapter. These cases provide real life examples of how organizations deal with information systems issues. You can also find a second case near the end of each chapter for additional insight.

Finally, read the two-page What Do YOU Think? feature found at the end of each chapter. The exercises often include ethical issues and ask you to develop opinions about important issues in information systems. If possible, discuss the questions in these guides with other people. Such discussions will give you a chance to develop your own opinions about important topics.

Like all worthwhile endeavours, this course takes work. That's just the way it is. No one succeeds in business without sustained focus, attention, desire, effort, and hard work. It won't always be easy, it won't always be fun. On the other hand, you will learn concepts, skills, and behaviours that will serve you well throughout your business career.

We wish you, as an emerging business professional, the very best success!

Sincerely,

David Kroenke
Seattle, Washington

Andrew Gemino
Peter Tingling
Vancouver, British Columbia

Experiencing MIS

CANADIAN EDITION

David M. Kroenke
University of Washington

Andrew Gemino
Simon Fraser University

Peter Tingling
Simon Fraser University

PEARSON
Prentice Hall

Toronto

Library and Archives Canada Cataloguing in Publication

Kroenke, David
Experiencing MIS / David M. Kroenke, Andrew C. Gemino, Peter Tingling. — Canadian ed.

Includes bibliographical references and index.
ISBN 978-0-13-239620-2

1. Management information systems. 2. Business—Data processing. I. Gemino, Andrew C. (Andrew Carlo), 1962– II. Tingling, Peter M. (Peter Maxwell), 1960– III. Title.

T58.6.K767 2008a 658.4'038011 C2008-901226-7

ISBN-13: 978-0-13-239620-2
ISBN-10: 0-13-239620-3

Vice President, Editorial Director: Gary Bennett
Acquisitions Editor: Don Thompson
Marketing Manager: Leigh-Anne Graham
Senior Developmental Editor: John Polanszky
Production Editor: Cheryl Jackson
Copy Editor: Kelli Howey
Proofreaders: Karen Alliston, Claudia Forgas
Production Coordinator: Andrea Falkenberg
Compositor: Nelson Gonzales
Photo Researcher: Amanda McCormick
Art Director: Julia Hall
Cover and Interior Designer: Anthony Leung
Cover Image: Veer inc.

1 2 3 4 5 12 11 10 09 08

Printed and bound in the United States of America

This book is dedicated to my wife, Kathy, and to Christina and Matthew who waited patiently while Dad finished his writing. AG

This book is dedicated to those who continue to teach me great things. My partner, Susanne, our children, my parents, colleagues, and, of course, my students, who never fail to astound and inspire me. PT

Brief Contents

Contents

Preface

When we agreed to take on the job of developing a Canadian version of David Kroenke's *Experiencing MIS*, we decided we would let three principles guide our development effort. The first principle was that the Canadian edition had to offer something new to the introductory MIS textbook market. Like many schools, our school has been facing a decline in MIS enrolment. We had also found that students were telling us that the more traditional MIS textbooks were not engaging enough for students to read. We recognized that the introductory MIS course might spur enrolment in upper division MIS classes if we could better engage students. To this end, David's U.S. edition was a breath of fresh air. The organization of material around questions (as opposed to topic headings), the engaging writing style, the focus on interactive student exercises, and the message that MIS knowledge is important for any business professional all pointed to the potential for a dynamic textbook that could engage students.

The second principle was that we were not simply "Canadianizing" the book by replacing "Seattle" with "Vancouver," "New York" with "Toronto," and the "U.S. dollar" with "loonies." Our editors at Pearson Education Canada gave us full freedom to utilize the material in David's original book, along with our own material, in any way we saw fit. This freedom allowed us to pick and choose from the 12 chapters, 24 chapter extensions, and well over 600 pages in the U.S. edition.

Our third principle: Small is beautiful. We decided right off the bat that the Canadian edition had to be substantially smaller than its U.S. counterpart. This led us to reconsider not only how to incorporate extension material, but also how to best arrange chapters and questions within them. What resulted was a Canadian edition of Kroenke's *Experiencing MIS*, but with some substantial differences.

- The Canadian book is smaller by over 200 pages.
- There is one completely new chapter — Chapter 9: IT Governance, Audit, and Ethics.
- Eight of the chapters have been substantially reorganized and rewritten (Chapters 1, 3, 4, 6, 7, 8, 10, and 11).
- The Canadian edition includes 16 new Canadian cases and several chapter discussions that include small- and medium-sized Canadian companies from a variety of industries, including
  - The Running Room (Edmonton, AB)
  - Active.com (BC)
  - Edoc (Victoria, BC)
  - ICS Courier (Toronto, ON)
  - Stantec (BC)
  - Winterborne Bicycles (ON)
  - Never Miss Your Bus (BC)
  - Vancity (BC)
  - Open Text (Waterloo, ON)
  - Blast Radius (Vancouver, BC)
  - Pacific Blue Cross (BC)

We took on this endeavour because we are passionate about our beliefs in the importance of MIS education. We hope that you will take the opportunity this course provides to experience MIS today, so that you are ready to participate in the incredible adventures coming your way. Information systems will have a profound impact on business organizations during your career. In the coming years, technologies will radically change how people relate to each other. Organizations will become more virtual and people will work to other people they may never meet face to face. Many jobs that are here today will be eliminated and new jobs will take their place. All of this change will be driven by people who experience MIS. So start your experience today. Turn to page 2 and read about Madison and her decision to sign onto a social networking site. And remember to have some fun experiencing MIS now!

Key Features

Experiencing MIS is the title and the theme of this book. In creating this book, we have worked to provide opportunities for students to experience MIS from their own personal perspective. We have organized the material around key questions and provided real life cases that support the ideas in these questions. At the end of the chapter, we ask students to review the original questions and what they have learned. We also provide exercises and cases that encourage students to develop their own opinion about important MIS topics. The features in this book are designed to encourage students to take an active role in developing their understanding of MIS and how it relates to their own business career. We believe that when we experience MIS from our own personal perspective, we realize the importance that information systems play in our lives now and in our future careers.

Opening Scenarios

Each of the four parts in the book begins with a real life scenario that students can relate to. The scenario runs throughout the three chapters included in each part, providing a story that links the material in the three chapters. The scenario provides an example that can be used in class. Each chapter ends by considering how the knowledge in the chapter helped to answer questions related to the opening scenario.

Chapter Study Questions

Instead of being organized around topics, every chapter is organized around a group of seven or eight questions. The questions provide a built-in set of learning objectives that are designed to engage students in reading the material. Students can organize their thoughts around the questions and the answers they develop.

Active Review

The chapter study questions are supported by Active Review questions near the end of each chapter. These questions provide a set of more detailed questions that offer an opportunity for students to see how much they have learned. If students are unable to answer the Active Review questions, they can turn back and review the appropriate section earlier in the chapter. This reinforces learning and provides feedback to students so they can better target their study.

What Do YOU Think?

These exercises are a unique feature of *Experiencing MIS* because they are designed to encourage students to develop their personal perspectives on issues in MIS. Several of the exercises (Chapters 2, 3, 5, and 10) focus on ethical issues, but a variety of issues are covered. These exercises can be used in class for discussion or can be used as personal assignments. The answers to these exercises aren't "hard and fast" — they require students to develop their own opinions. This forging of opinions creates further engagement in the material. We encourage instructors to find ways to incorporate these exercises into their classes so that students can experience MIS in a personal way.

MIS in Use

Each chapter includes an MIS in Use mini-case that provides a real-life example that highlights the questions discussed in the chapter. Each MIS in Use mini-case also comes with a set of questions that can be used in the lecture or as hand-in assignments. The mini-case and questions provide further opportunity to highlight important issues and create student engagement with the material.

Using Your Knowledge

At the end of each chapter, we have included a number of "Using Your Knowledge" questions. These questions provide opportunity for written assignments or discussion questions that often integrate the various issues raised in the chapter. The Using Your Knowledge questions provide another mechanism for engaging students in developing their own ideas about what MIS means to them.

Case Studies

A case study near the end of each chapter highlights issues covered in the chapter. Each case study has a set of questions that can be used to develop discussions or written assignments. The case studies provide an additional oppor-tun-ity for students to see how MIS affects real organizations. We have worked to provide case studies about small, medium, and large companies so that students are aware of the differences across these types of organizations.

We believe the key to creating an effective experience for students in this course is to provide opportunities for students to engage with the material and develop their own personal perspective on MIS. The features provided in this book are designed to support this development while at the same time providing a stimulating introduction to the world of Management Information Systems. We believe this book effectively presents information that students will need to be successful in their careers. We trust that this book demonstrates that the field of MIS remains as important in the coming decade as it was in the past and that our success in developing students with knowledge of MIS will play a critical role in our future economic development.

Topic Comparison: *Experiencing MIS* Canadian and U.S. Editions

The table on page xxi offers a quick guide to how the Canadian edition differs from the U.S. edition. The first column indicates the chapter in the Canadian edition; the second column identifies where the primary material from the chapter can be found in the U.S. edition; the third column shows the new cases added to each chapter in the Canadian edition; and the fourth column indicates topics not originally covered in the U.S. edition, but covered in the Canadian edition. The fifth column indicates any chapter extensions that were used in creating the Canadian chapter. Note that only a select amount of the information available in each chapter extension was used. In some cases, the chapter extensions were not used at all. A list of the unused chapter extensions is provided beneath the table. They are available online through the MyMISLab that accompanies this text. They provide additional topics of interest and are formatted in the same way as the text so they can be easily integrated into your course.

Supplements

The Canadian edition of *Experiencing MIS* is accompanied by a range of supplementary material available to both instructors and students.

Teaching Tools for Instructors

Instructor's Resource CD-ROM

This supplement includes the complete Instructor's Resource Manual, the TestGen testbank, PowerPoint® Presentations, and an Image Library. Instructors can also download some of these supplements from Pearson Education Canada's online catalogue at http://vig.pearsoned.ca.

Instructor's Resource Manual

This valuable resource features numerous teaching tools to help instructors make the most of the textbook in the classroom. Chapter objectives, chapter outlines, and answers to the questions are provided for each chapter.

TestGen

This computerized testbank contains over 1000 questions including multiple choice, true/false, fill-in-the-blanks, and essay questions. Questions can be searched and sorted by question type, level of difficulty, and chapter study question. This software package allows instructors to custom design, generate, and save classroom tests. The test program permits instructors to edit, add, or delete questions from the testbank and organize a database of tests and student results.

MyTest

The MyTest is a powerful assessment generation program that helps instructors easily create and print quizzes, tests, and exams, as well as homework or practice handouts. Questions and tests can all be authored online, allowing instructors ultimate flexibility and the ability to efficiently manage assessments anytime, anywhere.

PowerPoint® Presentations

These presentations combine lecture notes with images from the textbook. The lecture presentations for each chapter can be viewed electronically in the classroom or printed as black-and-white transparency masters.

Image Library

This library contains .gif or .jpg versions of figures from the textbook.

Chapter in Canadian Edition	Coverage in U.S. Edition	New Cases Added to Canadian Edition	New Material in Canadian Chapter	*Chapter Extensions Incorporated into Canadian Edition*
Chapter 1: Information Systems and You	Chapter 1	Running Room, Canadian Gun Registry	The Canadian ICT Industry	
Chapter 2: Business Processes, Information, and Decision Making	Chapter 2*	Edoc, Vancity	Decision making	*Incorporates: CE-2 Information Systems and Decision Making*
Chapter 3: Organizational Strategy, Information Systems, and Competitive Advantage	Chapter 3*	Winterborne Bicycles, ICS Courier	Productivity paradox; disruptive technologies	
Chapter 4: Hardware and Software	Chapter 4*	Stantec	Short history of computing systems	
Chapter 5: Database and Content Management	Chapter 5	Vancity, Active.com	Open text	*Includes chapter extensions: CE-5a Database Design, CE-5b Using Microsoft Access*
Chapter 6: Networks and Communications Technology	Chapter 6*	Never Miss Your Bus	Web crawlers and search engines	*CE-7 How the Internet Works Includes CE-6a Small Office, Home Office (SOHO) Networks*
Chapter 7: Information Systems for Competitive Advantage	Chapters 7 and 8	John Deere		*CE-9 Functional Information Systems, CE-10 Cross-functional Systems, CE-11 E-commerce, CE-12 Supply Chain Management*
Chapter 8: Decision Making and Business Intelligence	Chapter 9*	Pro Hockey Scouting	The information challenge	*CE-15 Reporting Systems and OLAP*
Chapter 9: Information Systems Strategy, Governance, and Ethics	Not in U.S. edition	Pacific Blue Cross	IS Auditing; IT governance; alignment	
Chapter 10: Understanding the IS Department: Operations and Projects	Chapters 10 and 11*		Operations vs. IT projects; how the Web has affected IS jobs; ITIL	
Chapter 11: IT Projects and Acquiring Information Systems	Chapters 10 and 11*	Simon Fraser University	IT project management; risks in IT project management	*CE-20 Outsourcing, CE-17 Small-Scale System Development*
Chapter 12: Managing Information Security and Privacy	Chapter 12	What is my real name? Spam Management		

** Material in chapter has been substantially changed. ** New material has been added to the chapter.*

Chapter Extensions not used in developing material for this book: CE-1 Information Systems for Collaboration; CE-3 Knowledge Management and Expert Systems; CE-4 Preparing a Computer Budget; CE-13 Information Technology for Data Exchange: EDI and XML; CE-14 Database Marketing; CE-16 Information Systems and Counterterrorism; CE-18 Large-Scale Systems Development; CE-19 Alternative Development Techniques; CE-21 Financing and Accounting for IT Projects; CE-22 Managing Computer Security Risk; CE-23 SSL/TLS and https; CE-24 Computer Crime and Forensics

Acknowledgments

We have many people to thank for their help in developing this textbook. Our first thanks go to David Kroenke, who sold us on his teaching approach when he visited Vancouver in 2006 and gave us the material from which to develop this text. We would also like to acknowledge our colleagues at Simon Fraser University, and in particular Kamal Masri, for helping to develop our introductory MIS course. We would also like to thank Zorana Svedic for her teaching and WebCT design and support. Zorana also provided the PowerPoint® slides for the textbook. Our thanks also go to the amazing Anthony Chan who worked on the testbank and provided ideas for material. Of course, our thanks would not be complete if we did not recognize the input from the many students we have had the pleasure of teaching in our introductory course. Their feedback played a big role in how the Canadian edition was developed.

We would also like to acknowledge the input from colleagues from other Canadian schools who provided their comments and ideas while the book was being developed. These include Anita Beecroft, Ed Bosman, John Bryant, Richard Crothers, Nelson Eng, Debbie Gorval, David Horspool, Jai-Yeol Son, Peter Thesiger, Robert Wood, and Jock Wylie.

Thank you to the following reviewers whose comments on various chapters and aspects of the entire project helped us to understand the needs of both instructors and students.

Hanadi Alnawab, Humber College Institute of Technology and Advanced Learning
Frank Anatol, Wilfrid Laurier University
James D. Clark, University of Lethbridge
Sylvia de Vlaming, Red River College
Michael E. Doucet, University of Ottawa
Albert Ersser, Mohawk College
Al Fukushima, Nicola Valley Institute of Technology
Frank Fusca, Humber College Institute of Technology and Advanced Learning
Franca Giacomelli, Humber College Institute of Technology and Advanced Learning
Myron Gordon, University of Northern British Columbia
Dennis Kira, Concordia University
Saroj Koul, Acadia University
Scott Laing, Saint Mary's University
Rick Menking, Trinity Western University
Jennifer Percival, University of Ontario Institute of Technology
Al Pilcher, Carleton University
Ylber Ramadani, George Brown College
E. Roventa, York University
Robert Riordan, Carleton University
Sheilagh Seaton, Okanagan College
Majid Shahidi, Vanier College
Roy Sinn, Langara College
Curt Soderstrom, College of the Rockies
Christopher Street, University of Manitoba
Ibrahim Sumrain, Grant MacEwan College
Cameron Welsh, University of Calgary

Thanks to all of the talented and patient people at Pearson Education Canada who helped to guide us through the process of creating this book. Our thanks go to Don Thompson, who oversaw the process; John Polanszky, our developmental editor, whose patience we tested on more than one occasion; Kelli Howey, our copy editor, and Cheryl Jackson, our production editor, who worked with us from rough Word documents to smooth page proofs. We would also like to say a special thanks to Ewan French, who introduced us to Pearson as potential co-authors and helped us to meet other colleagues who teach the introductory MIS course.

Most importantly, we would like to thank our families for providing us with the love, patience, and time necessary to create this Canadian edition.

Andrew Gemino
Peter Tingling

PART 1

MIS and You

This could happen to you

Knowledge of information systems will be critical to your success in business. If you are majoring in accounting, finance, marketing, human resources, or international business, you may not yet know how important such knowledge will be for you. The purpose of Part 1 of this textbook is to demonstrate why this subject is so important to every business professional today.

We begin by considering a student, Madison, and the choices she has to make as she considers building a personal profile on the web. Madison's personal profile is the collection of information about her that is available through the web. The information might include personal information (name, age, city, etc.) along with pictures, videos, music, and other files. These personal profiles are often organized in a social networking site such as MySpace (www.myspace.com), Nexopia (www.nexopia.com), or Facebook (www.facebook.com). These sites are called social networking sites because they provide Madison with the ability not only to create her own personal profile, but also to link herself to friends, family, team members, and other web acquaintances with similar sites. If you are not familiar with these sites you might want to take a look at one of them now.

Social networking sites are often offered free to the people who join. The businesses that operate these sites generate revenue primarily through advertisement. These advertisements are located throughout the site. The larger the number of people in the network, the larger the potential number of people viewing advertisements and the more valuable the site is to advertisers. The most successful sites have millions of personal profiles from people across the globe. This can be an attractive market for many firms, such as music and movie distributors, looking for opportunities to raise the profile of their products.

Quite a few of Madison's student friends already have profiles on one or more of these sites. She has heard about the sites and is intrigued about the profiles. She has even seen a few of the pages that her friends have. One day, Madison gets an email from one of her good friends inviting her to build a personal profile and link to her friend's page. She knows the person who sent the invitation really well. Since many people she knows have already joined the site, it seems like a fun idea. So Madison faces a decision: Should she build her personal profile on the web?

In Part 1 of this book we are going to look at three different aspects of Madison's decision to put her personal profile on a social networking website. The first aspect is to consider her initial decision about joining the site. What should she include? Whom would she link to? We will also consider what might surprise her about publishing her profile.

The next time we meet Madison, in Chapter 2, she will be graduating and busy developing her résumé and applying for jobs. We will look at the hiring process, an important business process for many firms. We then consider her web-based personal profile and how this might impact the hiring process. We find that Madison is in for a few more surprises.

We meet Madison again in Chapter 3, this time hard at work as a manager in the human resources department of a medium-sized high-technology company. We will explore how Madison uses information systems (including the web) to gain competitive advantage over other companies recruiting highly skilled workers. We will find that Madison relies heavily on information systems and the information they provide to consistently find talented people to work for her company.

Madison's journey illustrates why the knowledge in this class is so vitally important to business professionals today. Madison is a business manager. In college she majored in human resources. She is not an information systems professional, and she never thought she'd need to know how to manage the use of information systems. Yet that is exactly what her job requires her to do.

Keep thinking about Madison as you read this text. This could happen to you!

1 Information Systems and You

This
could happen
to you

Madison decided that it would be fun to have her personal profile on the web. She accepted her friend's invitation to join the social networking site. She then got busy collecting photographs of her friends and some of her favourite places from her trips. She used a template provided by the site to fill in her name, age, country, and city. She included a little bit of information about her family, the soccer team she played with in high school, her interests in music, and her favourite movies. She also linked her site to a few friends so they could share information.

Madison may not have realized it at the time, but when she published her personal profile on the social networking site she became part of a worldwide information system. She did not build the system herself. She never bought any hardware, nor did she hook it up. She won't buy or write any computer programs. She did, however, provide information about herself and her friends that is stored electronically and is made available to anyone on the Internet. That may be a more important issue than Madison initially considered.

A few weeks after publishing her personal profile, Madison went to look at her site and found that she had been linked to a larger number of friends. Some of them were people she didn't even know. She had recently received emails from some people who found her information on the site, but whom she had never even seen. She clicked on one of the friends links and was surprised to see pictures of people who were very clearly partying. Some of the pictures bordered on inappropriate. Others went past that. Madison had just finished sending an invitation to her aunt to visit her site. She hoped her aunt wouldn't see the friends link, but she had no control.

Madison started to think more carefully about her profile. What was her original objective? She thought it would be fun, but it didn't seem like fun any more. In the days that followed, Madison began to be more careful of whom she linked to. She also started to worry about who was viewing the site. She heard a story on the radio about someone who "borrowed" pictures of a celebrity from one website and then altered the pictures with a computer application and published them on another site. Madison thought, "If they can do that to her, they can do that to me." She started to think about taking her page down, but she wasn't sure even how to do that. She noticed that the social networking site had a link on the main page called "Privacy Protection." She wished she had read that earlier. Madison was realizing there were important issues to consider before becoming part of an information system. Who would have thought setting up a profile on the web would be so complicated?

Study Questions

Q1 What is an information system?

Q2 What is MIS?

Q3 How does IS differ from IT?

Q4 How important are IS to our economy?

Q5 How do successful business professionals use IS?

Q6 What new opportunities for IS are developing today?

Q7 What is this class about?

How does the knowledge in this chapter help Madison and you?

As you have seen, Madison was confronted with some surprising developments. She had a need for knowledge that she may not have possessed when she first published her profile. Madison's lack of knowledge could hurt her. Her lack of foresight is understandable, but improved knowledge of issues in MIS (management information systems) would have improved her ability to foresee some of these issues and limit her risk. Her lack of knowledge may lead her to a few sleepless nights worrying about her personal profile, but it doesn't have to be that way. Madison just needed some of the knowledge you are about to obtain in this course.

In this chapter we start with the basic questions. What is an information system? What are management information systems? How important are information systems in our economy? What opportunities open up if I learn more about information systems? You should have a good idea, by the end of this chapter, why knowledge about information systems is critical to your success as a future business professional.

Q1 What Is an Information System?

A *system* is a group of components that interact to achieve some purpose. As you might guess, an **information system (IS)** is a group of components that interact to produce information. That sentence, although true, raises another question: What are these components that interact to produce information?

Figure 1-1 shows the **five-component framework** of **computer hardware, software, data, procedures**, and **people**. These five components are present in every information system—from the simplest to the most complex. For example, when you use a computer to write a class report, you are using hardware (the computer, storage disk, keyboard, and monitor), software (Word, WordPerfect, or some other word-processing program), data (the words, sentences, and paragraphs in your report), procedures (the methods you use to start the program, enter your report, print it, and save and back up your file), and people (you).

In the past, the term *software* was used to refer to computer components that were not hardware (e.g., programs, procedures, and user manuals). Today, the term *software* is used more specifically to refer only to programs, and that is how we use the term throughout this book.

Consider a more complex example—an airline reservation system. It, too, consists of these five components, even though each one is far more complicated. The hardware consists of dozens or more computers linked together by telecommunications hardware. Further, hundreds of different programs coordinate communications among the computers, and still other programs perform the reservations and related services. Additionally, the system must store millions upon millions of characters of data about flights, customers, reservations, and other facts. Hundreds of different procedures are followed by airline personnel, travel agents, and customers. Finally, the information system includes people—not only the users of the system, but also those who operate and service the computers, those who maintain the data, and those who support the networks of computers.

The five components in Figure 1-1 are common to all information systems. For example, the social networking site Madison joined requires hardware and software and internet connections to operate. People adding their personal information, pictures, videos, and other files provide the data. The procedures for joining the site, making links, and protecting privacy are part of the site. Some of these procedures are embedded in the software; other procedures, such as privacy protection, are written down to guide users on appropriate use of the site. Procedures do not have to be written down. In many information systems people are assumed to know at least some of the procedures. Finally, people are involved throughout the system. There are the people who use the site. There are the IS professionals who build and maintain the site, and there are the people who sell advertising on the site. All these people are part of the system. An important point to learn in this class is that people are often the most critical part of an information system. Information systems are not just computers and data.

Before we move forward, note that we have defined an information system to include a computer. Some people would say that such a system is a **computer-based information system**. They would note that there are information systems

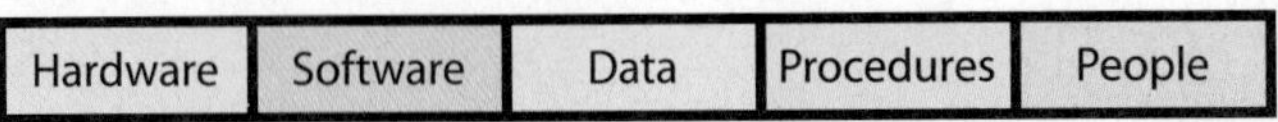

Figure 1-1
Five Components of an Information System

that do not include computers, such as a calendar hanging on the wall outside a conference room that is used to schedule the room's use. Such systems have been used by businesses for centuries. Although this point is true, in this book we focus on computer-based information systems. To simplify and shorten the book, we will use the term *information system* as a synonym for *computer-based information system.*

Q2 What Is MIS?

There are thousands, even millions, of information systems in this world. Not all relate to business. In this textbook, we are concerned with **MIS**, or **management information systems**. MIS is the development and use of information systems that help businesses achieve their goals and objectives. This definition has three key elements: *development and use, information systems,* and *business goals and objectives.* We just discussed information systems. Now let's consider development and use and business goals and objectives.

Development and Use of Information Systems

Information systems do not pop up like mushrooms after a hard rain; they must be constructed. You may be saying, "Wait a minute. I'm a finance (or accounting, or marketing) major, not an information systems major. I don't need to know how to build information systems."

If you are saying that, you are like a lamb headed for fleecing. Throughout your career, in whatever field you choose, you will need information systems. To have an information system that meets your needs, you need to take an *active role* in that system's development. Without active involvement on your part, it will only be good luck that causes the new system to meet your needs.

To that end, throughout this text we will discuss your role in the *development* of information systems. In addition, we devote all of Chapter 11 to this important topic. As you read this text and think about information systems, you should ask yourself questions like, "How was that system constructed?" and "What roles did the users play during its development?" If you start asking yourself these questions now, you will be better prepared to answer them once you start a job—when financial, career, and other consequences will depend on your answers.

In addition to development tasks, you will have important roles to play in the *use* of information systems. You will need to learn how to employ the system to accomplish your goals, and you will also have important ancillary functions. For example, when using an information system, you will have responsibilities for protecting the security of the system and its data. You may also have tasks for backing up data. When the system fails (most do, at some point), you will have tasks to perform while the system is down, as well as tasks to accomplish to help recover the system correctly and quickly.

Achieving Business Goals and Objectives

The last part of the definition of MIS is that information systems exist to help businesses achieve their *goals and objectives.* First, realize that this statement hides an important fact: Businesses themselves do not "do" anything. A business is not alive, and it cannot act. It is the people within a business who sell, buy, design, produce, finance, market, account, and manage. So information systems exist to help people who work in a business achieve the goals and objectives of that business.

Information systems are not created for the sheer joy of exploring technology. They are not created so that the company can be "modern" or so that the company can claim to be a "new-economy company." They are not created because the information systems department thinks they need to be created, or because the company is "falling behind the technology curve."

This point may seem so obvious that you wonder why we mention it. Every day, however, some business somewhere is developing an information system for the wrong reasons. Right now, somewhere in the world, a company is deciding to create a website for the sole reason that "every other business has one." This company is not asking questions like, "What is the purpose of the website?" or, "What is it going to do for us?" or, "Are the costs of the website sufficiently offset by the benefits?"—but it should be!

Even more serious, somewhere right now a business person has been convinced by some vendor's sales team or by an article in a business magazine that his or her company must upgrade to the latest, greatest high-tech gizmo. This person is attempting to convince his or her manager that this expensive upgrade is a good idea. We hope that someone somewhere in the company is asking questions like, "What business goal or objective will be served by the investment in the gizmo?"

Throughout this text, we will consider many different information system types and underlying technologies. We will show the benefits of those systems and technologies, and we will illustrate successful implementations of them. *MIS in Use* cases, such as the one about the Canadian Firearms Registry in *MIS in Use 1,* discuss IS implementations in specific real-world organizations. As a future business professional, you need to learn to look at information systems and technologies only through the lens of *business need.* Learn to ask, "All this technology may be great in and of itself, but what will it do for us? What will it do for our business and our particular goals?"

Again, MIS is the development and use of information systems that help businesses achieve their goals and objectives. Already you should be realizing that there is much more to this class than buying a computer, writing a program, or working with a spreadsheet.

Q3 How Does IS Differ from IT?

Information technology and *information system* are two closely related terms, but they are different. **Information technology (IT)** refers to methods, inventions, standards, and products. As the term implies, IT refers to raw technology, and it concerns only the hardware, software, and data components of an information system. In contrast, an information system is a system of hardware, software, data, procedures, and people that produce information.

IT, by itself, will not help an organization achieve its goals and objectives. It is only when IT is embedded into an IS—only when the technology within the hardware, software, and data is combined with the people and procedure components—that IT becomes useful.

Think about these statements from the standpoint of the information systems at your university. Do you care that the university network uses the latest, greatest technology to send messages across campus? Do you care that the university's website uses the latest, fastest hardware to show you available classes? Not really. It is only when the humans at the university (including you) use

Increasing Costs for the Canadian Firearms Registry System

In December 2002, the Auditor General of Canada, Sheila Fraser, reported that the Canadian Firearms Registry system costs were running well above initial estimates. At the start of the program in 1995, the Department of Justice reported to Parliament that the system would cost approximately $119 million to implement, and that the income generated from licensing fees would be $117 million. These figures suggested a net cost of $2 million for the program. The revised estimates from the Department of Justice in 2002 suggested that the actual cost of the program would be more than $1 billion by 2004–05 and that the income from licensing fees in the same period would be $140 million.

The Canadian Firearms Program is a government-run registry of legally owned guns in Canada. The program was established in December 1995 when Parliament passed the *Firearms Act* and associated Criminal Code amendments. The Criminal Code amendments came into force in January 1996, creating mandatory minimum prison sentences for firearms offences. The government announced that it would delay proclamation of the act until January 1997 so that the Department of Justice could design, develop, and implement the information technology and service delivery systems needed to manage the licensing and registration program.

The Department of Justice recognized that the program presented significant challenges due to its political, technical, and organizational complexities. To support the efficient collection and distribution of gun registry information, the Canadian Firearms Registry system was planned and approved for an initial cost of approximately $119 million.

The information on cost recovery provided to the government changed as the program developed. At the start of the program in 1995 the government was told that the program would be self-financing by 1999–2000. However, in 1996 the department told the government that it would take more than 10 years (from 1995–96 to 2005–06) for the program to become self-financing. By April 1998, the department had again revised its estimated break-even point. The government was told that it would take until 2012–13 for revenues from fees to cover all costs associated with developing, implementing, and operating the program since 1995–96. The revised break-even point was based on the assumptions that the program would collect about $419 million in fees by 2002–03 and about $828 million by 2007–08.

The Auditor General's report showed that the implementation of the firearms registry program by the Department of Justice had significant strategic and management problems. The report stated that estimated program costs often excluded program costs incurred by other agencies, such as the RCMP and provincial governments, giving a false impression of real cost. Up to 70 percent of the funds requested from Parliament came through "supplementary estimates," a method intended for unanticipated expenditures and requiring only a one-line statement to Parliament on the purpose of the request.

The Department of Justice offered several reasons for the cost escalation, including major delays in making regulations, provinces opting out of the program, the need for additional initiatives, incorrect assumptions about the rate it would receive applications for licences and registrations, and an excessive focus on regulation and enforcing controls.

The firearms registry program was an effort intended to reduce crime by making every gun traceable. The future of the Canadian Firearms Registry remains uncertain. While the legislation is still in place, as of May 17, 2006, the government is no longer asking long gun owners for a registration fee and will not prosecute long gun owners who do not register. The bottom line: Well over a billion dollars and more than a decade of work have been spent and the government is considering cancelling the entire program.

Source: The Canadian Auditor General report "Department of Justice—Costs of Implementing the Canadian Firearms Program," December 2002, www.oag-bvg.gc.ca/domino/reports.nsf/html/20021210ce.html.

procedures to do something—to enroll in a class, for example—that the IT becomes useful to you.

Consider Madison and her original objectives to set up her personal profile. She will use IT, but that is not her primary interest. Her goal is to combine the hardware, software, data, and procedures with people to make her experience on the social networking site enjoyable. The people are the most important part of the system for users like Madison.

Successful business people understand this crucial difference between IT and IS, and they take advantage of it, as we show next.

Q4 How Important Are IS to Our Economy?

Information systems are an increasingly important part of the Canadian economy. Industry Canada[1] is the federal government agency responsible for categorizing industry sectors and collecting information about them. The industry sector most closely related to the development and use of information systems is the Information and Communications Technology (ICT) sector.[2] This industry sector includes companies involved in software and computer services, cable and other program distributors, telecommunications services, ICT manufacturing, and ICT wholesaling. Figure 1-2 provides the percentage of total revenues associated with these sector categories.[3]

The Canadian ICT sector in 2006 included nearly 32 000 companies. Most of these companies, more than 97 percent, had fewer than 100 employees. In 2006, 80 percent of companies in the industry had 1 to 9 employees, 14.3 percent had 10 to 49 employees, and 2.6 percent had 50 to 100 employees. Despite the small percentage of companies with more than 100 employees (2.4 percent), these larger companies have a big impact on revenues for the sector. There are approximately 120 companies with more than 500 employees.[3]

The ICT sector in 2006 contributed $65 billion to Canadian GDP (as measured in $1997). This accounts for 5.9 percent of Canadian output. This percent-

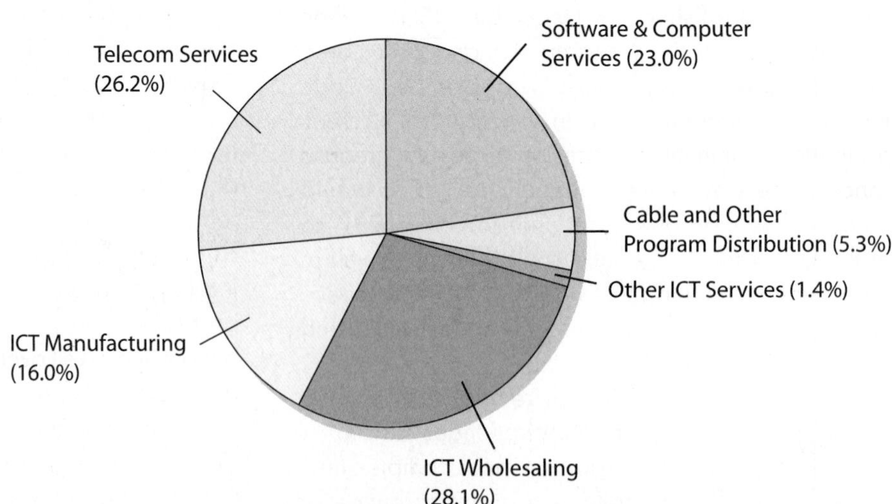

Figure 1-2
Revenues by ICT Sub-Sector, 2006

Source: Industry Canada, Canadian ICT Statistical Overview, "Revenues by ICT Sub-Sector, 2006," www.ic.gc.ca/epic/site/ict-tic.nsf/en/h_it07229e.html, February 25, 2008. Reproduced with the permission of the Minister of Public Works and Government Services, 2008.

1. www.ic.gc.ca.
2. http://strategis.ic.gc.ca/epic/site/ict-tic.nsf/en/Home.
3. The facts and graphs provided in this section come from the Canadian ICT Sector Profile, updated July 2007 and located at http://strategis.ic.gc.ca/epic/site/ict-tic.nsf/en/h_it07229e.html.

age has increased from 4.0 percent in 1997. The average annual growth in the ICT sector has been 8.0 percent since 1997, more than twice as fast as the overall economy (+3.4 percent). This faster growth means that the ICT industry sector has accounted for 11.5 percent of the Canadian GDP growth since 1997. This growth is displayed in Figure 1-3.

So what should all these numbers mean to you? One word: JOBS. The total number of workers in the ICT industry rose from 442 510 to 572 107 between 1997 and 2006. This is an increase of 30 percent. In 2006, 3.6 percent of all Canadian workers were employed by the ICT sector.

So where are the jobs? Most of the employment gains have occurred in the software and computer services industries, where the number of workers was 71 percent higher in 2006 than in 1997. Employment in the telecommunications services industries was 20 percent higher than in 1997. By contrast, employment in the ICT manufacturing industries has declined by 24 percent.

What we learn from these employment numbers is that there will be more jobs in service industries, where companies need help coping with their information systems, and fewer jobs in making the actual information technology used in systems. So, understanding how to use information technology effectively is an increasingly important skill to have.

You might be asking yourself, "Who are these people getting jobs in this industry, and what do they earn?" Employment in the ICT sector is characterized by a high level of education. In 2006, 41 percent of all workers had a university degree. The national average is 23 percent. The software and computer services industries have the most educated workforce, with 55 percent of employees reporting they have a degree.

Figure 1-4 shows that employees in the ICT sector are relatively well paid. According to Industry Canada, workers in ICT industries earned on average $54 315 in 2006, which is well above the economy-wide average of $37 865. Employees in the software and computer services industries were the most highly paid, with average earnings of $60 643 in 2006.

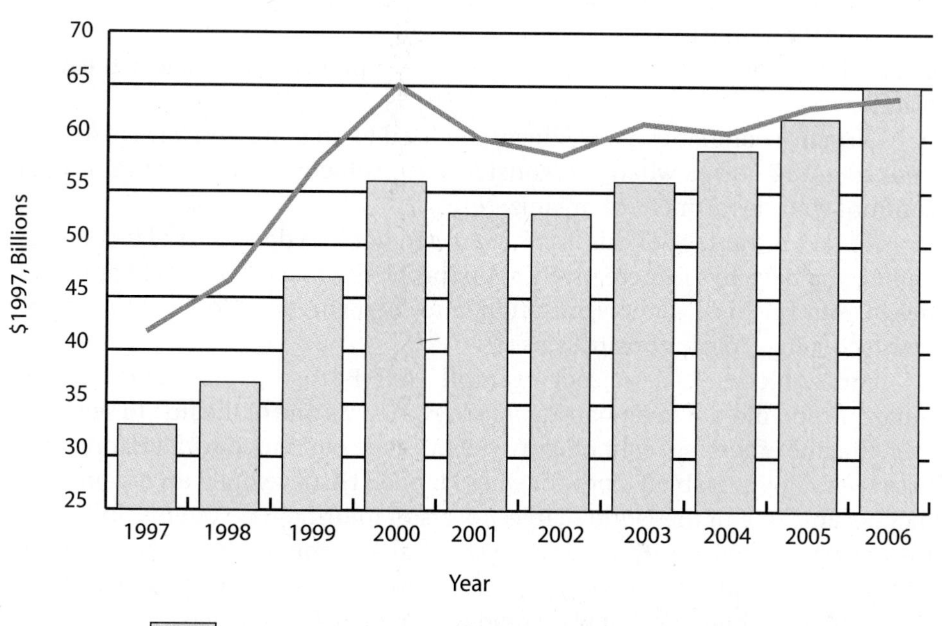

Figure 1-3
ICT Sector GDP, 1997–2006

Source: Industry Canada, Canadian ICT Statistical Overview, "ICT Sector GDP, 1997–2006," www.ic.gc.ca/epic/site/ict-tic.nsf/en/h_it07229e.html, February 25, 2008. Reproduced with the permission of the Minister of Public Works and Government Services, 2008.

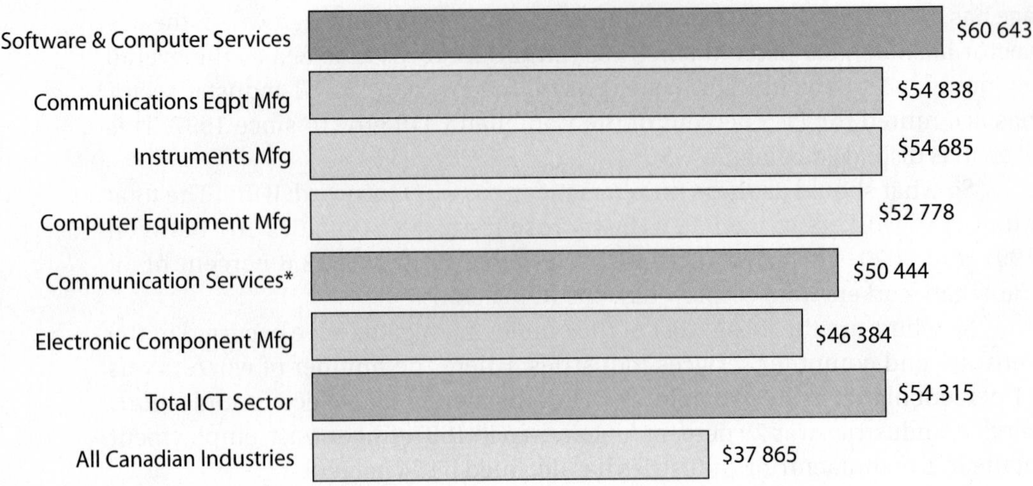

Figure 1-4 Average Annual Earnings by Major ICT Industry, 2006

Source: Industry Canada, Canadian ICT Statistical Overview, "Average Annual Earnings by Major ICT Industry, 2006," www.ic.gc.ca/epic/site/ict-tic.nsf/en/h_it07229e.html, February 25, 2008. Reproduced with the permission of the Minister of Public Works and Government Services, 2008.

So what should all this mean to you? The information presented in this section should help you to understand that information systems are an increasingly important part of our economy. In particular, the delivery of services (where people serve people) is a growing area of employment. The employment can be financially rewarding, with larger than average salaries, but it is a very knowledge-intensive industry where approximately half of all workers possess university degrees. Students in the Canadian economy who are working toward becoming business professionals cannot ignore the importance of understanding and working with information systems.

Q5 How Do Successful Business Professionals Use IS?

Today, every business professional uses numerous information systems. Some people do little more than write email, access web pages, and do instant messaging. While the ability to use such basic information systems is essential, that level of knowledge and use does not give anyone a competitive advantage in the workplace.

To gain a competitive advantage, you need to do more. You have to learn to think about IT and IS when you consider the problems and opportunities that confront your department or organization.

To take advantage of this trend, you need not be a developer of technology. Rather, you have to think creatively about problems, challenges, and opportunities in your business and organization, and then you need to be able to apply new technology to your business needs.

Amazon.com is a perfect example. Jeff Bezos, founder and CEO of Amazon.com, did not invent any technology. He was one of the first to see, however, that the emerging technology of the Internet, combined with existing database technology, enabled a new business model. He developed an organization that became one of the world's largest users of information systems. In fact, on December 14, 2005, the information systems at Amazon processed an average of 41 items per second for 24 hours. Truly, Amazon represents an innovative application of the technology that was emerging when Bezos founded the company.

Q6 What New Opportunities for IS Are Developing Today?

"That's fine," you might be saying. "That was then, and this is now. The Internet is old news. All the good opportunities are gone." If you think this way, you are wrong. In fact, there are great opportunities right now.

For example, read the news item in Figure 1-5. On October 9, 2006, Google bought YouTube for $1.65 billion in stock. Amazingly, this company was founded in the summer of 2005, and in August 2006 it had attracted 19.1 million customers. All 67 YouTube employees shared in the $1.65-billion buyout price! Consider two other such opportunities as well, which are discussed in the section that follows.

Two Opportunities, Right Now

Information technology has developed in such a way that, for all practical purposes, data storage and data communication are free. Of course, no business resource is free, but the costs of storage and data transmission are so low that, when compared to other business expenses, they are essentially zero.

Whenever an important business resource becomes free, new opportunities for using that resource abound. In the case of free data storage and free data transmission, consider Getty Images (www.gettyimages.com). Getty Images sells pictures over the Internet. The pictures are electronic; they are made of binary digits (see Chapter 4). Because the cost of both data storage and data transmission is essentially zero, the variable cost of production of a new image to Getty is zero. (See the Getty image in Figure 1-6.)

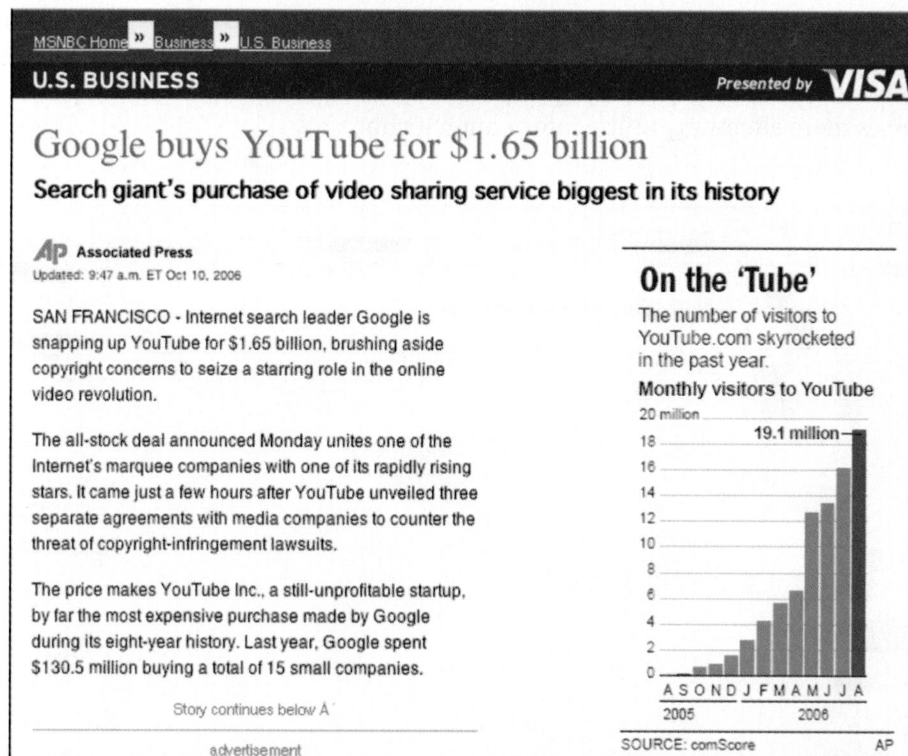

MSNBC Home » Business » U.S. Business

U.S. BUSINESS — Presented by VISA

Google buys YouTube for $1.65 billion

Search giant's purchase of video sharing service biggest in its history

Associated Press
Updated: 9:47 a.m. ET Oct 10, 2006

SAN FRANCISCO - Internet search leader Google is snapping up YouTube for $1.65 billion, brushing aside copyright concerns to seize a starring role in the online video revolution.

The all-stock deal announced Monday unites one of the Internet's marquee companies with one of its rapidly rising stars. It came just a few hours after YouTube unveiled three separate agreements with media companies to counter the threat of copyright-infringement lawsuits.

The price makes YouTube Inc., a still-unprofitable startup, by far the most expensive purchase made by Google during its eight-year history. Last year, Google spent $130.5 million buying a total of 15 small companies.

Story continues below

advertisement

On the 'Tube'

The number of visitors to YouTube.com skyrocketed in the past year.

Figure 1-5
A Great IS Opportunity—Google's Purchase of YouTube for $1.65 Billion

Figure 1-6
Another IS Opportunity—Getty Images Supplies Photographic Images Electronically

Reflect on that statement, "The cost of production is zero." Any revenue that Getty makes on an image goes straight to the bottom line. Truly, this is a business that has found an innovative application of IT.

Information systems can also extend the services provided by a traditional business. For example, consider The Running Room (www.runningroom.com). This retail business has grown from a one-room shop in a renovated living room in Edmonton, Alberta, to a chain of 96 stores located throughout Canada and the United States. The Running Room sells top-name running shoes and apparel and offers services such as clinics in walking, learning to run, and 10K training, half marathons, and marathons. A website was added in 1995 to support the retail stores. The website has extended services by providing discussion groups, online purchasing, clinic information, and updates for local events and races, and has an online membership of 348 000 users. The website not only provides information more efficiently to customers, it has also become the training ground for over 800 staff members. This close contact and customer support provides The Running Room with a competitive advantage over competitors that do not have a website. Many opportunities still exist to help traditional businesses more effectively utilize information technology.

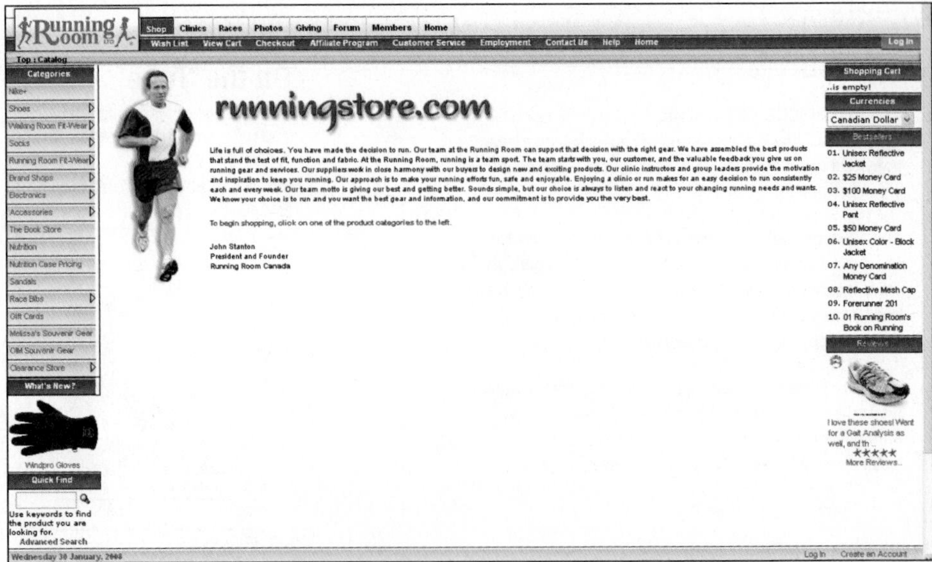

Figure 1-7
Running Room

Source: www.runningroom.com.

These opportunities are real, right now, but the best news is that there is no sign technology development is slowing down. New opportunities like this will continue to emerge, as predicted by Moore's Law.

Moore's Law

Gordon Moore is the co-founder of Intel Corporation, the world's leading manufacturer of computer chips and other computer-related components. In 1965 he declared that, because of technology improvements in electronic chip design and manufacturing, "The number of transistors per square inch on an integrated chip doubles every 18 months." This observation is known as **Moore's Law**. Moore's prediction has proved generally accurate in the more than 40 years since it was made.

The density of transistors on a computer chip relates to the speed of the chip, and so you will sometimes hear Moore's Law expressed as "The speed of a computer chip doubles every 18 months." This is not exactly what Moore said, but it comes close to the essence of his idea.

Dramatic Reduction in Price/Performance Ratio

As a result of Moore's Law, the price/performance ratio of computers has fallen dramatically for years (see Figure 1-8). As a result, computers have shrunk from multimillion-dollar, room-filling machines in 1968 to $300 small desktop devices in 2007. Along the way, the availability of increased computing power has enabled developments such as laser printers, graphical user interfaces like Windows and OS X, high-speed communications, cell phones, PDAs, email, and the Internet.

Moore's Law is the principal reason why data storage and data transmission are essentially free today. All indications are that the price/performance ratio of IT products will continue to fall. Opportunities for applying new technology will continue to emerge; you just need to learn to look for them!

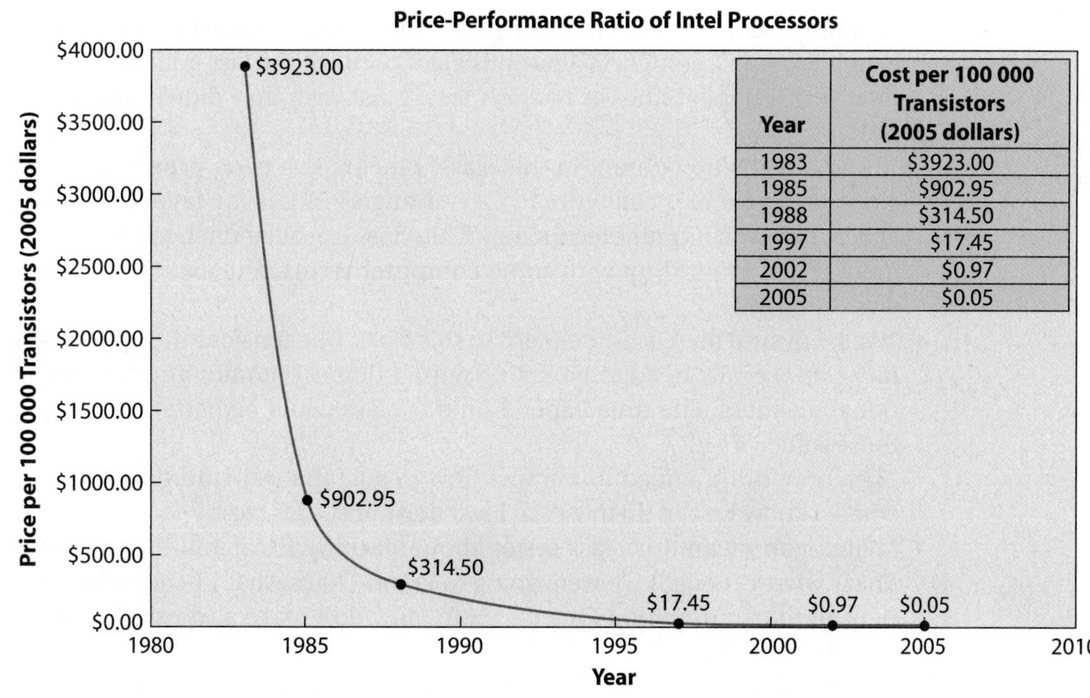

Year	Cost per 100 000 Transistors (2005 dollars)
1983	$3923.00
1985	$902.95
1988	$314.50
1997	$17.45
2002	$0.97
2005	$0.05

Figure 1-8
Computer Price/Performance Ratio Decreases

Q7 What Is This Class About?

Many students enter this class with an erroneous idea of what they will study. Often, students think of it as a computer class—or at least a class that has something to do with computers and business. Many students think that this class is about learning how to use Excel or Access or FrontPage. Figure 1-9 lists a number of reasons students have given us when explaining why they don't need to take this class. As you can see, opinions vary on what the class is about.

By now, you should have an idea that this class is much broader than just learning how to use Excel or Access. You may, in fact, use those programs in this class, but the focus will not be on learning what keys to push to make the program work as you want. Instead, the focus will be on *learning to use* those tools to accomplish a business purpose.

Consider again the definition of MIS: the development and use of information systems that help organizations (and the people who work in them) accomplish their goals and objectives. Thus, to understand MIS, you need to understand both business and technology, and you need to be able to relate one to the other.

The table of contents of the chapters in this book will give you an idea of how we will proceed. In the next two chapters, we will discuss the relationship of business processes and information systems, and we will show how information systems can be used to gain competitive advantages. Then in Chapters 4–6, you will learn about hardware, software, content and databases, and data communications technology. With that foundation, in Chapters 7–9 we will show how

Figure 1-9
Student Thoughts about "Why I Don't Need This Class"

- "I already know how to use Excel and Word. I can build a website. OK, it's a simple website, but I can do it. And when I need to learn more, I can. So let me out of this class!"
- "We're going to learn how to work with information systems? That's like practising the stomach flu. If and when the time comes, I'll know how to do it."
- "I'm terrified of computers. I'm a people person, and I don't do well with engineering-like things. I've put this class off until the last quarter of my final year. I hope it's not as bad as I fear; I just wish they didn't make me take it."
- "There's really no content in this class. I mean, I've been programming since high school, I can write in C++, though PERL is my favourite language. I know computer technology. This class is just a bunch of management babble mixed up with some computer terms. At least it's an easy class, though."
- "Well, I'm sure there is some merit to this class, but consider the opportunity cost. I really need to be taking more microeconomics and international business. The time I spend on this class could be better spent on those subjects."
- "The only thing I need to know is how to surf the web and how to use email. I know how to do those, so I just don't need this class."
- "What, you mean this class is not about learning Excel and FrontPage? That's what I thought we were going to learn. That's what I need to know. Why all this information systems stuff? How do I make a website? That's what I need to know."

technology can be used to gain a competitive advantage. Finally, in Chapters 10–12 you will learn about how IT departments work, how the IT architecture is managed, the management of systems development, and security. The Exercise "Duller Than Dirt?" at the end of this chapter on pages 20–21 shares our opinion about why these chapters—and this book—matter to you.

How does the knowledge in this chapter help Madison and you?

This chapter should encourage Madison. She now realizes that information systems are more than just computers and that she can play a large part in making information systems work for her. She understands that procedures are an important part of any information system that helps people work effectively. Knowing the proper procedures will help Madison use other sites more safely and effectively. She also realizes how quickly information can move, how easily it can be collected, and how important it is to protect important information.

Madison's reaction to her situation can be guided by considering the five components. She has no control over the hardware and software used on the website, but she does have control over the data she includes about herself. She can also read and follow recommended procedures so that she uses the site wisely. Finally, she can carefully select the people she wants to link to so that she limits her risk of using the site.

She should also realize that this site is not the end of the story. Technology will continue to develop and improve, and she'll need to think constantly about how she can use technology in other systems to accomplish her goals and objectives. Information systems are increasingly important to our economy. As a business professional, Madison will almost certainly have to interact regularly with information systems. She has to learn to understand these systems so that she can work more effectively.

Active Review

Use this Active Review to verify that you understand the material in the chapter. You can read the entire chapter and then perform the tasks in this review, or you can read the material for just one question and perform the tasks in this review for that question before moving on to the next one.

Q1 What is an information system?

List the components of an information system. Explain how knowledge of these components will guide Madison's work as she builds her information system.

Q2 What is MIS?

List the three elements of MIS. Why does a non-technical business professional need to understand all three? Why are information systems developed? Why is part of this definition misleading?

Q3 How does IS differ from IT?

Define *IS*. Define *IT*. Does IT include IS or does IS include IT? Why does technology, by itself, not constitute an information system?

Q4 How important are IS to our economy?

What does ICT stand for? What percentage of GDP do ICT industries account for? Is the ICT sector growing faster than the Canadian economy? How knowledge-intensive are these industries? What can an employee in the ICT industry expect to earn?

Q5 How do successful business professionals use IS?

Explain the employment trend involving emerging technology. How does this trend pertain to Jeff Bezos, CEO of Amazon.com?

Q6 What new opportunities for IS are developing today?

Explain what IT resources are essentially free today. Describe two opportunities for taking advantage of those free resources.

Q7 What is this class about?

In your own words, state what this class is about. Look at the table of contents of this book. What major themes does it address? How will those themes relate to you as a business professional? If you were (or are) employed and if you had to justify the expense of this class to your boss, how would you do it?

Key Terms and Concepts

Computer hardware 6
Computer-based information system 6
Data 6
Five-component framework 6
Information system (IS) 6
Information technology (IT) 8
Management information systems (MIS) 7
Moore's Law 15
People 6
Procedures 6
Software 6

Using Your Knowledge

1. Using your own knowledge and opinions as well as those listed in Figure 1-9 (page 16), describe three misconceptions of the purpose of this class. In your own words, describe what you think the purpose of this class is.

2. Describe three to five personal goals for this class. None of these goals should include anything about your final grade. Be as specific as possible, and make the goals personal to your major, interests, and career aspirations. Assume that you are going to evaluate yourself on these goals at the end of the quarter or semester. The more specific you make these goals, the easier it will be to perform the evaluation.

3. Consider costs of a system in light of the five components: costs to buy and maintain the hardware; costs to develop or acquire licences to the software programs and costs to maintain them; costs to design databases and fill them with data; costs of developing procedures and keeping them current; and finally, human costs both to develop and use the system.
   a. Over the lifetime of a system, many experts believe that the single most expensive component is people. Does this belief seem logical to you? Explain why you agree or disagree.
   b. Consider a poorly developed system that does not meet its defined requirements. The needs of the business do not go away, but they do not conform themselves to the characteristics of the poorly built system. Therefore, something must give. Which component picks up the slack when the hardware and software programs do not work correctly? What does this say about the cost of a poorly designed system? Consider both direct money costs as well as intangible personnel costs.
   c. What implications do you, as a future business manager, recognize after answering questions (a) and (b)? What does this say about the need for your involvement in requirements and other aspects of systems development? Who will eventually pay the costs of a poorly developed system? Against which budget will those costs accrue?

Case Study 1

Canadian Firearms Registry Program: Increasing Costs Revisited

Read "Increasing Costs for the Canadian Firearms Registry System" on page 9. The Auditor General's report made many recommendations in response to the problems identified, two of which were that:

> "The Department of Justice should provide Parliament annually with complete and accurate information on all past, current, and forecasted expenditures and revenues relating to the Program; and it needs to disclose and explain any major changes in the Program."

Questions

1. This chapter introduced a five-component framework for understanding information systems: hardware, software, data, procedures, and people. Which of these components do you believe is most responsible for the challenges faced by the firearms registry system?
2. Why did the Auditor General's report place the leadership and ownership on the entire Department of Justice and not the IT group that was responsible for building and implementing the information system?
3. Do you think that the challenges faced by the firearms registry system will be overcome by improved reporting of financial information to Parliament?
4. If you answered no, why do you think improved reporting is not enough?
5. What recommendations would you make to address the challenges faced by the firearms registry system?
6. Think back to the original goals and objectives of the Canadian firearms registry system. Do you think the current system has met these goals? Do you think the system will eventually be able to achieve these goals? Discuss why or why not.

What Do YOU Think?

Duller Than Dirt?

Yes, you read that title correctly: This subject can seem duller than dirt. Take the phrase "development and use of IS in organizations."

Read just that phrase and you start to yawn, wondering, "How am I going to absorb 400+ pages of this?"

Stop and think: Why are you reading this book? Right now in the Sea of Cortez, the water is clear and warm, and the swimming and diving are wonderful. You could be kayaking to Isla San Francisco this minute. Or somewhere in the world, people are skiing. Whether in Whistler, B.C., or Portillo, Chile, people are blasting through the powder somewhere. You could be one of them, living in a small house with a group of friends, having good times at night. Or whatever it is that you like to do, you could be doing it right now. So why are you here, where you are, reading this book? Why aren't you there?

Waking up should be one of your goals while in college or university. We mean waking up to your life. Ceasing to live according to someone else's plan and beginning to live your own plan. Doing that requires you to become conscious of the choices you make and the consequences they have.

Suppose you take an hour to read your assignment in this book tonight. For a typical person, that is 4320 heartbeats (72 beats times 60 minutes) you have used to read this book—heartbeats you will never have again. Despite the evidence of your current budget, the critical resource for humans is not money; it is time. No matter what we do, we cannot get more of it. Was your reading today worth those 4320 heartbeats?

For some reason, you chose to major in business. For some reason, you are taking this class, and for some reason, you have been instructed to read this textbook. Now, given that you made a good decision to major in business (and not to kayak in Baja), and given that someone is requiring you to read this text, the question then becomes, "How can you maximize the return on the 4320 heartbeats you are investing per hour?"

The secret is to personalize the material. At every page, learn to ask yourself, "How does this pertain to me?" and "How can I use this material to further my goals?" If you find some topic irrelevant, ask your professor or your classmates what they think. What's this topic for? Why are we reading this? What am I going to do with it later in my career? Why is this worth 1000 (or whatever) heartbeats?

MIS is all-encompassing. To us, that's one of its beauties. Consider the components: hardware, software, data, procedures, and people. Do you want to be an engineer? Then work the hardware component. Do you want to be a programmer? Write software. Do you want to be a practising philosopher, an applied epistemologist? Learn data modelling. Do you like social systems and sociology? Learn how to design effective group and organizational procedures. Do you like people? Become an IS trainer or a computer systems salesperson. Do you enjoy management? Learn how to bring all of those disparate elements together.

We've worked in this industry for many years. The breadth of MIS and the rapid change of technology have kept us fascinated for every one of those years. Further, the beauty of working with intellectual property is that it doesn't weigh very much; moving symbols around won't wear you out. And you do it indoors in a temperature-controlled office. They may even put your name on the door.

So wake up. Why are you reading this? How can you make it relevant? Jump onto Google and search for MIS careers or use some other phrase from this chapter and see what you get. Challenge yourself to find something that is important to you personally in every chapter.

You just invested 780 heartbeats in reading this editorial. Was it worth it? Keep asking!

Discussion Questions

1. Explain what it means to "wake up to your life."
2. Are you awake to your life? How do you know? What can you do once a week to ensure that you are awake to your life?
3. What are your professional goals? Are they yours, or are they someone else's? How do you know?
4. How does this class pertain to your professional goals?
5. How are you going to make the material in this class interesting?

2 Business Processes, Information, and Decision Making

This
could happen
to you

We now return to Madison, who has worked her way through most of the courses required for her degree. She is looking forward to graduating next semester. She has set herself the important task of looking for a great job. She has been developing skills through her student experience, including volunteering and taking advantage of international exchanges. She has even dropped into the career advancement centre in her school to help her with her résumé and where to start looking for work.

She has spent the last month polishing her résumé. Madison has made extensive use of the Internet in helping her with her job search. She has viewed job sites and listened to podcasts from employers to see what skills they are looking for. She has read many articles on the web about getting a great job. One day she came across an article entitled "10 Things to Do to Lose Your Job." She was interested in the title and read through the article. She was surprised to see number 6 on the list as "Post a personal profile." She had largely forgotten about the personal profile she had placed a few years ago on the social networking site. How could that get you fired?

Madison started following links and found out that there were several cases where people had lost their jobs because of what they had posted on their personal profiles. She read that companies no longer looked only at résumés. Companies were Googling current and prospective employees to gather more information. Some employees had personal profiles that indicated where they worked and had placed what the company thought were inappropriate pictures or writing. Madison had never thought about that.

Madison did not have any information on her profile that could be considered inappropriate, and if she had she could delete it quickly. But some of her friends' sites were closer to the edge. Thinking back, she remembered that one of her friends had posted some pictures on her own site that were taken during spring break in Florida. Madison had no control over those pictures, and she was in some of them. Those pictures were linked to her page. Are employers going to see THOSE photos?! Madison was learning that what is on the web is accessible to almost everyone. What was she going to do now? How would her personal profile affect her job hunting process?

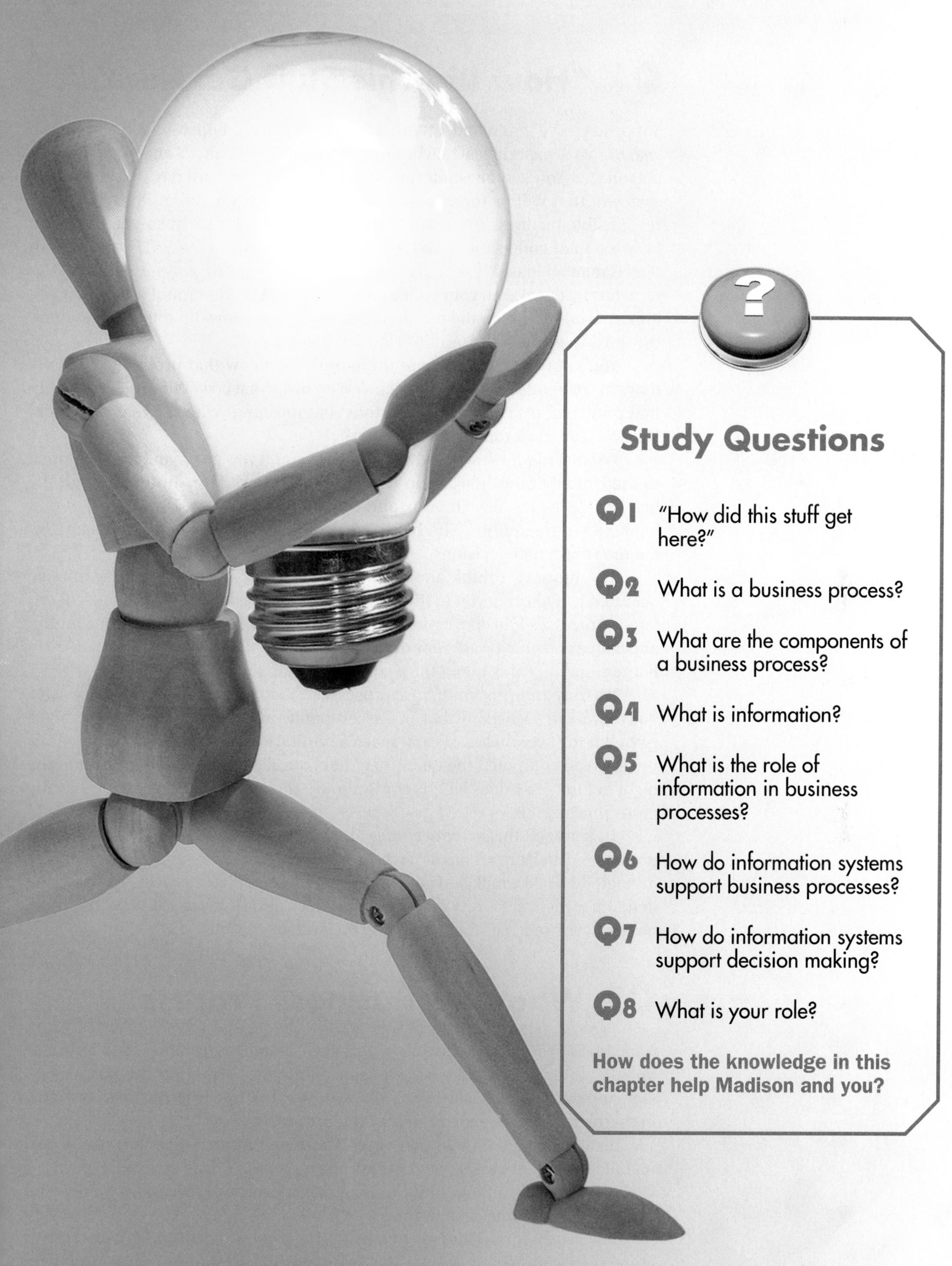
Study Questions
Q1 "How did this stuff get here?"
Q2 What is a business process?
Q3 What are the components of a business process?
Q4 What is information?
Q5 What is the role of information in business processes?
Q6 How do information systems support business processes?
Q7 How do information systems support decision making?
Q8 What is your role?
How does the knowledge in this chapter help Madison and you?

Q1 "How Did This Stuff Get Here?"

Suppose you've graduated, attained just the job you'd hoped to get, and have a year or two of experience. Maybe you're an auditor, a financial analyst, or a salesperson. . . . You can be whatever you want to be. One April day, your company asks you to travel to Toronto for a meeting at First Canadian Place. Like any responsible business professional you've arrived a bit early, so you decide to have a cup of coffee and a muffin at the Tim Hortons in the PATH underneath First Canadian Place.

Sitting down with your coffee and muffin, you let your mind wander. As you look around the room, the question occurs to you: "How did this stuff get here? the milk? the coffee? the muffin? How did it get here?"

You know that somewhere there must be a cow that produced the milk that's in your coffee. Where is that cow? Who owns that cow? Who decided to ship that particular milk to the Tim Hortons that morning? Who delivered the milk? How was the truck routed to customers?

For that matter, how did the coffee get here? It was grown in Kenya, shipped to the United States, roasted in Rochester, New York, distributed through the head office in Oakville, Ontario, and delivered to the store. How did all of that happen? Or the muffin? Who baked it? How many muffins did they bake? How did they make that decision?

The more you think about it, the more you realize that a near miracle occurred just to bring you to this experience. Hundreds, if not thousands, of different processes had successfully interacted just to bring together your muffin and coffee and you. (Wait! How did *you* get here? You flew out from your office in Edmonton. . . . Think about the processes in that, too!)

It's truly amazing. And those processes had to do more than just work. They had to work in such a way that all the companies and people involved obtained a payment to cover their costs and make a profit. How did that occur? Who set the prices? Who computed the quantity of nonfat milk to be shipped to Toronto the night before? How does all this come about? The more you think about this, the more amazing it is.

In truth, all this activity comes about through the interaction of business processes. Tim Hortons has a process for ordering, receiving, storing, and paying for ingredients like milk and coffee. The coffee roaster has a process for assessing demand, ordering its raw materials, and making deliveries. All the other businesses have processes for conducting their affairs as well.

Q2 What Is a Business Process?

A **business process** is a network of activities, resources, facilities, and information that interact to achieve some business function. A business process is a system, and sometimes business processes are also referred to as **business systems**. In this text, we will use the term *business process.*

Examples of business processes are inventory management processes, manufacturing processes, sales and support processes, and so forth. Figure 2-1 shows a model of an inventory management business process that might be used at a Tim Hortons restaurant.

Inventory for a Tim Hortons restaurant would be all the goods (coffee, doughnuts, muffins, milk, etc.) that a Tim Hortons restaurant sells. Managing this inventory is a business process. The goal of this process is to ensure there is

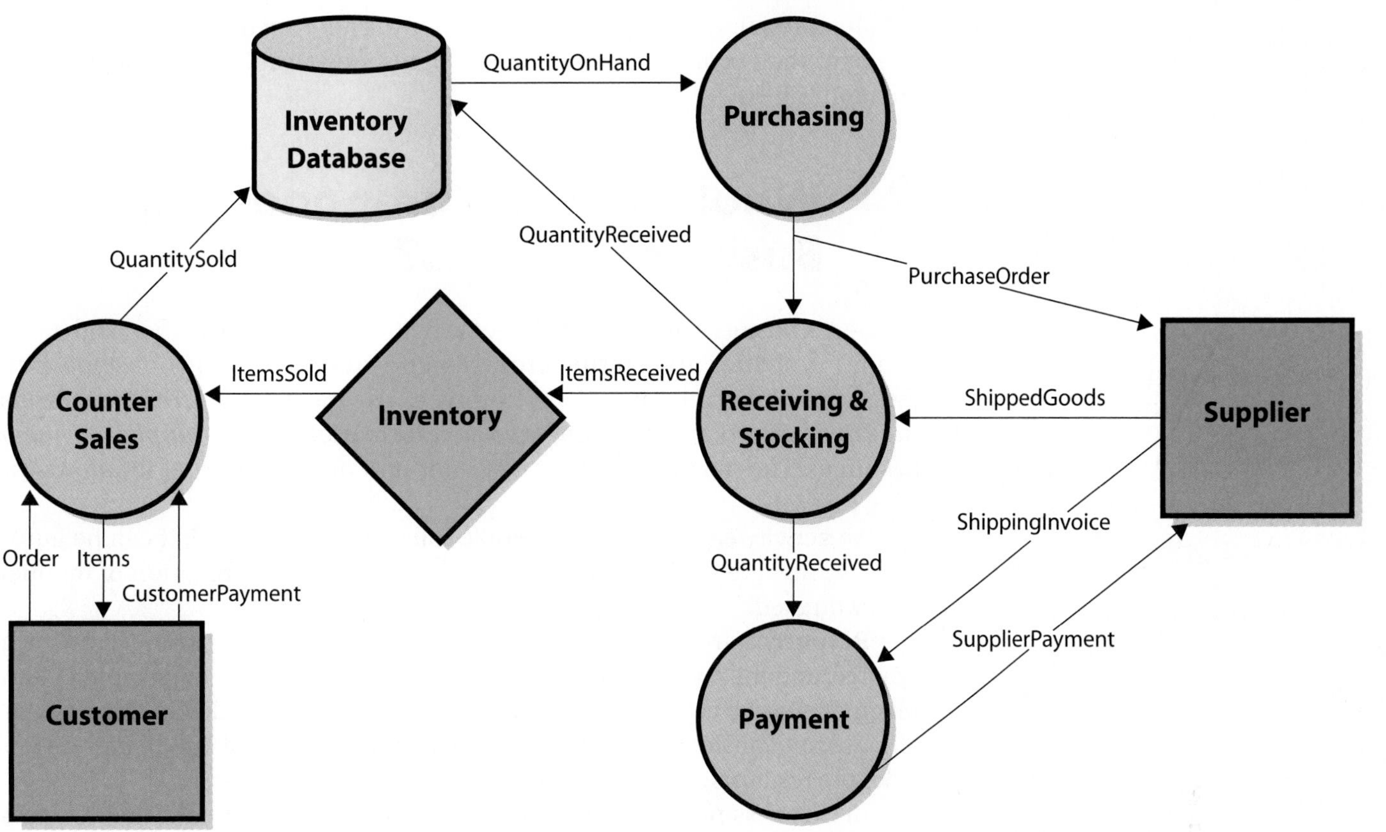

Figure 2-1
Portion of Inventory Management Business Process

enough inventory to fulfill customers' requests, while at the same time making sure there is not too much inventory (otherwise goods will spoil).

The inventory management process works to balance the demands from customers with the inventory purchased from suppliers. Purchasing is therefore an important activity in the inventory management process. But how can a manager at a Tim Hortons restaurant know how much coffee to purchase?

This is where the inventory management system comes in. The inventory management system supports the process by collecting information. An inventory database keeps track of what the customers have ordered (*QuantityOrdered*) and what is currently in inventory (*QuantityOnHand*). As customers make purchases, stock moves out of inventory. At some point, stock in inventory hits a critical point, often called the *reorder point.* When a good in stock hits this point, the system lets the manager of the restaurant know that it is time to order new supplies. Since goods are bought and sold at different rates, each good can have its own reorder point.

To order new inventory the manager creates a *PurchaseOrder.* A purchase order lists the items ordered and quantity desired. This purchase order is sent to the supplier. The supplier receives the purchase order and then ships the appropriate goods along with the *ShippingInvoice* to the restaurant. The *ShippedGoods* are first checked to make sure that the restaurant received what was ordered. The newly received goods are then placed in inventory and the inventory database is updated with the *QuantityReceived.* The supplier is then paid for the goods the supplier has shipped.

Consider the diagram in Figure 2-1 as a snapshot of the system. It does not show logic; it does not show what causes what. It is just a picture of the elements of the business process and how they interact. Also, there are many different ways of representing a business process. Many vendors of business process software have their own documentation standards. Any clear and consistent representation will do.

Q3 What Are the Components of a Business Process?

As stated, a business process consists of activities, resources, facilities, and information. **Activities** transform resources and information of one type into resources and information of another type. The payment activity transforms *QuantityReceived* and *ShippingInvoice* information into a *SupplierPayment* (resource). The payment activity has rules and procedures that it follows for doing this.

An activity can be manual (people following procedures), it can be automated (hardware directed by software), or it can be a combination of manual and automated.

Resources are items of value. A case of milk is a resource, a cheque is a resource, and the customer's cash is a resource. In Figure 2-1, both supplier and customer are also considered resources because they have value in this process. They are not considered activities, because they are external and hence are not under the restaurant's direction and control.

In business processes, **facilities** are structures used within the business process. Typical facilities are inventories and databases (as in Figure 2-1). Other examples of facilities are factories, pieces of equipment, trucks, file cabinets, and the like.

Information is knowledge derived from data. Activities use information to determine how to transform the inputs they receive into the outputs they produce. Because this book is about *information* systems, understanding the nature of information and ways of defining it are crucial.

Q4 What Is Information?

Information is one of those fundamental terms that we use every day but that turns out to be surprisingly difficult to define.

In this text, we will avoid the technical issues of defining *information* and will use common, intuitive definitions instead. Probably the most common definition is that information is *knowledge derived from data,* where *data* is defined as recorded facts or figures. Thus, the facts that employee James Smith earns $17.50 per hour and that Mary Jones earns $25.00 per hour are *data.* The statement that the average hourly wage of all employees in the Garden Department is $22.37 per hour is *information. Average wage* is knowledge that is derived from the data of individual wages.

Another common definition is that information is *data presented in a meaningful context.* The fact that Jeff Parks earns $10.00 per hour is data.[1] The statement that Jeff Parks earns less than half the average hourly wage of the Garden Department, however, is information. It is data presented in a meaningful context.

[1] Actually, the word *data* is plural; to be correct, we should use the singular form *datum* and say, "The fact that Jeff Parks earns $10.00 per hour is a datum." The word *datum*, however, sounds pedantic and fussy, and we will avoid it in this text.

Another definition of information you will hear is that information is processed data, or sometimes, information is *data processed by summing, ordering, averaging, grouping, comparing, or other similar operations.* The fundamental idea of this definition is that we do something to data to produce information.

There is yet a fourth definition of information, presented in the Exercise at the end of this chapter on pages 42–43. There, information is defined as *a difference that makes a difference.*

For the purposes of this text, any of these definitions of information will do. Choose the definition of information that makes sense to you. The important point is that you discriminate between data and information. You also may find that different definitions work better in different situations.

Characteristics of Good Information

All information is not equal: Some information is better than other information. Figure 2-2 lists the characteristics of good information.

Accurate

First, good information is **accurate information.** Good information is based on correct and complete data, and it has been processed correctly as expected. Accuracy is crucial; managers must be able to rely on the results of their information systems. The IS function can develop a bad reputation in the organization if a system is known to produce inaccurate information. In such a case, the information system becomes a waste of time and money as users develop workarounds to avoid the inaccurate data.

A corollary to this discussion is that you, a future user of information systems, ought not to rely on information just because it appears in the context of a web page, a well-formatted report, or a fancy query. It is sometimes hard to be skeptical of information delivered with beautiful, active graphics. Do not be misled. When you begin to use an information system, be skeptical. Cross-check the information you are receiving. After weeks or months of using a system, you may relax. Begin, however, with skepticism.

Timely

Good information is **timely information**—produced in time for its intended use. A monthly report that arrives six weeks late is most likely useless. An information system that tells you not to extend credit to a customer after you have shipped the goods is unhelpful and frustrating. Notice that timeliness can be measured against a calendar (six weeks late) or against events (before we ship).

When you participate in the development of an IS, timeliness will be part of the requirements you will request. You should be able to provide appropriate and realistic timeliness needs. In some cases, developing systems that provide

- Accurate
- Timely
- Relevant
  - To context
  - To subject
- Just sufficient
- Worth its cost

Figure 2-2
Characteristics of Good Information

information in near real time is much more difficult and expensive than producing information a few hours later. If you can get by with information that is a few hours old, it is important to say so during the requirements-specification phase.

Consider an example. Suppose you work in marketing and you need to be able to assess the effectiveness of new online ad programs. You want an information system that will not only deliver ads over the web, but will also enable you to determine how frequently customers click on those ads. Determining click ratios in near real time will be very expensive; saving the data and processing it some hours later will be much easier and cheaper.

Relevant

Information should be **relevant** both to the context and to the subject. Considering context, you, the CEO, need information that is summarized to an appropriate level for your job. A list of the hourly wage of every employee in the company is unlikely to be useful. More likely, you need average wage information by department or division. A list of all employee wages is irrelevant in your context.

Information should also be relevant to the subject at hand. If you want information about short-term interest rates for a possible line of credit, then a report that shows 15-year mortgage interest rates is irrelevant. Similarly, a report that buries the information you need in pages and pages of results is also irrelevant to your purposes.

Just Barely Sufficient

Information needs to be **sufficient** for the purpose for which it is generated, but **just barely so.** We live in an information age; one of the critical decisions that each of us has to make each day is what information to ignore. The higher you rise into management, the more information you will be given, and because there is only so much time, the more information you will need to ignore. So information should be sufficient, but just barely.

Worth Its Cost

Information is not free. There are costs for developing an information system, costs of operating and maintaining that system, and costs of your time and salary for reading and processing the information the system produces. For information to be **worth its cost,** there must be an appropriate relationship between the cost of information and its value.

You need to be ready to ask, "What's the value of the information?" or "What is the cost?" or "Is there an appropriate relationship between value and cost?" Information systems should be subject to the same financial analyses to which other assets are subjected.

Q5 What Is the Role of Information in Business Processes?

The discussion about information may seem overly theoretical. What does it have to do with realistic business processes?

Look again at the inventory management process in Figure 2-1. Consider the payment process, which compares the *QuantityReceived* (from receiving and stocking) to the *ShippingInvoice* (from the supplier). If the goods received match the goods billed, then payment generates a *SupplierPayment.*

Now let's apply some of the definitions from the last section. Is *QuantityReceived* an example of data, or is it information? By itself, it is just data, a recorded fact or figure: "We received these items from that supplier on this date." Similarly, the *ShippingInvoice* could also be considered to be just data: "We, Supplier X, delivered these items on this date."

When we bring these two items together, however, we generate information. Consider Bateson's definition of information: "Information is a difference that makes a difference." If the *QuantityReceived* says we received five cases of milk but the *ShippingInvoice* is billing us for eight cases, we have a difference that makes a difference. By comparing records of the amount we received to records of the amount we were billed, we are presenting data in a meaningful context, which is another definition of information.

Thus, the business process generates information by bringing together important items of data in a context. However, it also generates information at an even higher level. Over time, this process will generate information that will be useful for management and strategy decisions. For example, we could use the information produced by the process in Figure 2-1 to determine which are the cheapest, or fastest, or most reliable suppliers. We could use the information in the inventory database to assess our inventory ordering strategy.

Q6 How Do Information Systems Support Business Processes?

Information systems are used by the activities in a business process, but the particular relationship varies among business processes. In some processes, several activities use one information system. In other processes each activity has its own information system, and in still other processes some activities use several different information systems.

During systems development, the systems designers determine the relationship of activities to information systems. You will learn more about this topic in Chapters 10 and 11.You can read more about how information systems support business processes in *MIS in Use 2* later in this chapter. The case describes how an information system, Edoc, was used in the tugboat industry to support several manual business processes.

What Does It Mean to Automate a Process Activity?

We will consider the role of information systems for several of the activities in Figure 2-1, but before we do that, think about the five components of an information system that we introduced in Chapter 1. Notice the symmetry of components in Figure 2-3. The outermost components, hardware and people, are both *actors;* they can take actions. The software and procedure components are both sets of *instructions:* Software is instructions for hardware, and procedures are instructions for people. Finally, data is the bridge between the computer side on the left and the human side on the right.

When an activity in a business process is handled by an **automated system**, it means that work formerly done by people following procedures has been moved so that computers now do that work by following instructions in software. Thus, the automation of a process activity consists of moving work from the right-hand side of Figure 2-3 to the left.

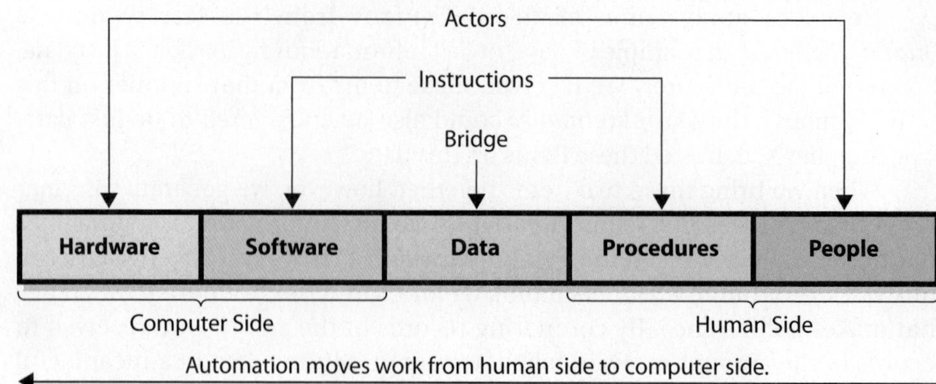

Figure 2-3
Characteristics of the Five Components

An Information System to Support Counter Sales

According to Figure 2-1, the counter sales activity interacts with the customer. It receives the customer's order, takes the items from inventory, and receives the customer's payment. This is just a model of the familiar process of ordering coffee and a muffin at a restaurant.

Counter sales uses the information system shown in Figure 2-4. This system is automated, however, and the cashiers do not even know they are using an information system. The cash registers contain a computer that communicates with another computer that hosts the inventory database. Programs in the cash register record sales and make appropriate changes to the inventory database whenever the cashier rings up a sale. The cashiers need to be trained only in how to use the cash register; they never need to work directly with the sales-recording programs on the computer.

The designers of this system decided to fully automate it because the cashier's job is a low-skill-level position with high turnover. The designers did not want the cashiers to have to receive training to use the cash registers.

An Information System to Support Payment

Now consider the payment activity in Figure 2-1. Payment receives the *QuantityReceived* and the *ShippingInvoice*, and it produces *SupplierPayment*. (In actuality, payment does not generate the cheque to the supplier. Because of accounting controls, no single person should approve a payment and generate the cheque.) Instead, payment generates an authorization and sends it to someone else to cut the cheque. These details are omitted here for simplicity—they are important, however!

Figure 2-4
Sales Recording Information System, Used by Counter Sales in Figure 2-1

Hardware	Software	Data	Procedures	People
- Cash register computer - Database host computer	- Sales-recording program on cash register	- Sales data - Inventory database	- Operate cash register	- Cashier

Mostly an automated system.
Almost all work is done by computers and software.

Hardware	Software	Data	Procedures	People
- Personal computer	- Adobe Acrobat Reader - Email	- *QuantityReceived* - *ShippingInvoice*	- Reconcile receipt document with invoice. - Issue payment authorization, if appropriate. - Process exceptions.	- Accounts payable

Mostly a manual system.
Little work is done by computers and software.
Most work is done by Accounts Payable clerk.

Figure 2-5 Payment System, Used by Payment Activity in Figure 2-1

As you can see in Figure 2-5, the information system that supports the payment activity is a mostly **manual system**. The accounts payable clerk receives both the *QuantityReceived* and the *ShippingInvoice* as Adobe Acrobat pdf files (the same sort of pdf files that you receive over the Internet). He or she then reads those documents, compares the quantities, and issues the payment authorization as appropriate. If there is a discrepancy, the accounts payable clerk investigates and takes action as appropriate.

The designers of this system chose to leave it as a manual system because processing exceptions is complicated. There are many different exceptions, and each requires a different response. The designers thought that programming all of those exceptions would be expensive and probably not very effective. The designers decided it would be better to let humans deal with such varied situations. This means, by the way, that the accounts payable clerks will need much more training than the cashiers.

An Information System to Support Purchasing

Now consider the information system that supports the purchasing activity in Figure 2-1. This system, shown in Figure 2-6, balances the work between automation and manual activity. The person doing the purchasing has a personal computer that is connected to the computer that hosts the database. Her computer runs an inventory application program that queries the database and identifies items that are low in stock and need to be ordered. That application produces a report that she reads periodically.

She then decides which items to order and from which suppliers. In making this decision, she is guided by the inventory management practices. When she decides to order, she runs a purchasing program on her computer. It is that program that generates the *PurchaseOrder* shown in Figure 2-1.

The designers of this information system decided to balance the work between the computer and the human. Searching the inventory database for items that are low in stock is a perfect application for a computer. It is a repetitive process that humans find tedious. On the other hand, selecting which supplier to use is a process that can require human judgment. The clerk needs to balance a number of factors: quality of supplier, recent supplier experience, the need to have a variety of suppliers, and so forth. Such complicated balancing is better done by a human. Again, this means that the purchasing clerks will need much more training than the cashiers.

Figure 2-6 Purchasing Information System, Used by Purchasing Activity in Figure 2-1

Hardware	Software	Data	Procedures	People
- Personal computer - Database host computer	- Inventory application program - Purchasing program	- Inventory database	- Issue *PurchaseOrder* according to inventory management practices and guidelines.	- Purchasing clerk

Balance between computer and human work.

The three different information systems at the restaurant support the needs of users in the company's various business processes—counter sales, payments, and purchasing.

Before we leave these five components, it is important for you to understand how YOU will relate to information systems. One of the most important tasks a business manager has is making decisions. Information is often a critical part of any decision-making process. We therefore consider how information systems support business decisions next.

Q7 How Do Information Systems Support Decision Making?

Making decisions is central to managing organizations. We found earlier in this chapter that data are an important part of any information system and that data can be transformed into information. Information is an important starting point for decision making in many organizations. So the first point we can make is that information systems support decision making by providing the information—the raw material—for many decisions.

Decision making in organizations is varied and complex, and before discussing the role of information systems in supporting decision making we need to investigate the characteristics and dimensions of decision making itself.

Decisions Vary by Level

- Decision level
  - Operational
  - Managerial
  - Strategic
- Decision process
  - Structured
  - Unstructured

Figure 2-7 Decision-Making Dimensions

As shown in Figure 2-7, decisions occur at three levels in organizations: *operational, managerial,* and *strategic.* The types of decisions vary depending on the level. **Operational decisions** concern day-to-day activities. Typical operational decisions are: How many widgets should we order from vendor A? Should we extend credit to vendor B? Which invoices should we pay today? Information systems that support operational decision making are called **transaction processing systems (TPS)**.

Managerial decisions concern the allocation and utilization of resources. Typical managerial decisions are: How much should we budget for computer hardware and programs for department A next year? How many engineers should we assign to project B? How many square feet of warehouse space do we need for the coming year? Information systems that support managerial decision making are called **management information systems (MIS)**. (Notice that the term *MIS* can be used in two ways: broadly, to mean the subjects in this entire book, and narrowly, to mean information systems that support managerial-level decision making. Context will make the meaning of the term clear.)

Strategic decisions concern broader-scope, organizational issues. Typical decisions at the strategic level are: Should we start a new product line? Should we open a centralized warehouse in Calgary? Should we acquire company A? Information systems that support strategic decision making are called **executive information systems (EIS)**.

Notice that, in general, the decision time frame increases as we move from operational to managerial to strategic decisions. Operational decisions normally involve actions in the short term: What should we do today or this week? Managerial decisions involve longer time frames: What is appropriate for the next quarter or year? Strategic decisions involve the long term; their consequences may not be realized for years.

Decisions Vary by Structure

Figure 2-8 shows levels of information systems with two decision processes: *structured* and *unstructured*. These terms refer to the method by which the decision is to be made, not to the nature of the underlying problem. A **structured decision** is one for which there is an understood and accepted method for making the decision. A formula for computing the reorder quantity of an item in inventory is an example of a structured decision process. A standard method for allocating furniture and equipment to employees is another structured decision process.

An **unstructured decision** process is one for which there is no agreed-on decision-making method. Predicting the future direction of the economy or the stock market is a famous example. The prediction method varies from person to person; it is neither standardized nor broadly accepted. (As one wit put it, "If you laid all the economists in the world end to end, they still would not reach a conclusion.") Another example of an unstructured decision process is assessing how well suited an employee is for performing a particular job. Managers vary in the manner in which they make such assessments.

Again, keep in mind that the terms *structured* and *unstructured* refer to the decision process, not to the underlying subject. Weather forecasting is a structured decision because the process used to make the decision is standardized among forecasters. Weather itself, however, is an unstructured phenomenon, as tornadoes and hurricanes demonstrate every year.

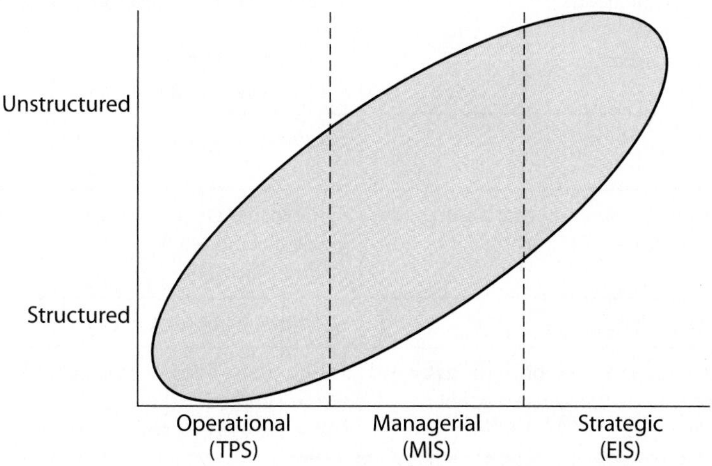

Figure 2-8
Relationship of Decision Level and Decision Process

Supporting Decision Making

The decision type and decision process are loosely related. As shown by the grey oval in Figure 2-8, decisions at the operational level tend to be structured, and decisions at the strategic level tend to be unstructured. Managerial decisions tend to be both structured and unstructured.

We use the words *tend to be* because there are exceptions to the relationship illustrated in Figure 2-8. Some operational decisions are unstructured (e.g., "How many taxicab drivers do we need on the night before the homecoming game?"), and some strategic decisions can be structured (e.g., "How should we assign sales quotas for a new product?"). In general, however, the relationship shown in Figure 2-8 holds.

Another way to examine the relationship between information systems and decision making is to consider how an information system is used during the steps of the decision-making process. The first two columns of Figure 2-9 show the typical steps in the decision-making process: intelligence gathering, formulation of alternatives, choice, implementation, and review. During **intelligence gathering**, the decision makers determine what is to be decided, what the criteria for the decision will be, and what data are available. **Alternatives formulation** is the stage in which decision makers lay out various alternatives. They analyze the alternatives and select one during the **choice step**, and then they implement the decision in the **implementation step**. Finally, the organization reviews the results of the decision. The **review step** may lead to another decision—and another iteration through the decision process.

As summarized in the right column of Figure 2-9, each of these decision-making steps needs a different type of information system. During intelligence gathering, email and videoconferencing facilitate communication among the decision makers. Also, during the first phase, decision makers use query and reporting systems as well as other types of data analysis applications to obtain relevant data. Decision makers use email and videoconferencing systems for communication during the alternatives-formulation step. During the choice step, analysis applications such as spreadsheets and financial and other modelling applications help decision makers to analyze alternatives. The implementation stage again involves the use of communications applications, and all types of information systems can be used during review.

Figure 2-9 Decision-Making Steps

Decision Step	Description	Examples of Possible Information Systems
Intelligence gathering	• What is to be decided? • What are the decision criteria? • Obtain relevant data	• Communications applications (email, video-conferencing, word processing, presentation) • Query and reporting systems • Data analysis applications
Alternatives formulation	• What are the choices?	• Communications applications
Choice	• Analyze choices against criteria using data • Select alternative	• Spreadsheets • Financial modelling • Other modelling
Implementation	• Make it so!	• Communications applications
Review	• Evaluate results of decision; if necessary, repeat process to correct and adapt	• Communications • Query and reporting • Spreadsheets and other analysis

Q8 What Is Your Role?

You are part of every information system that you use. When you consider the five components of an information system, the last component, *people,* includes you. Your mind and your thinking are not merely *a* component of the information systems you use; they are *the most important* component.

Consider an example. Suppose you have the perfect information system, one that can predict the future. (No such information system exists, but assume that it does for this example.) Now suppose that on December 14, 1966, your perfect information system tells you that the next day, Walt Disney will die. Say you have $50 000 to invest; you can either buy Disney stock or you can short it (an investment technique that will net you a positive return if the stock value decreases). Given your perfect information system, how do you invest?

Before you read on, think about this question. If Walt Disney is going to die the next day, will the stock go up or down? Most students assume that the stock will go down, so they short it, on the theory that the loss of a company's founder will mean a dramatic drop in the share price.

In fact, the next day, the value of Disney stock increased substantially. Why? The market viewed Walt Disney as an artist; once he died, he would no longer be able to create more art. Thus, the value of the existing art would increase because of scarcity, and the value of the corporation that owned that art would increase as well.

Here's the point: Even if you have the perfect information system, if you do not know what to do with the information that it produces you are wasting your time and money. The *quality of your thinking* is a large part of the quality of the information system. Substantial cognitive research has shown that although you cannot increase your basic IQ, you can dramatically improve the quality of your thinking. You cannot change the computer in your brain, so to speak, but you can change the way you have programmed your brain to work.

Edoc: Software Making Waves

Tugboats might seem like the last place to look for innovative information systems. But Edoc Systems Group (www.edoc.ca), a company with headquarters in Victoria, B.C., recognized the potential of information technology to automate business processes in this industry.

Tugboat companies are often family businesses that have been running for more than 100 years using a paper-based system. Things don't change quickly in this industry. For example, an Edoc employee visiting an Oregon company found that the dispatch log sheet the company was currently using had been in use with the same format since 1952! How can information technology help this industry?

The first step is to understand the challenge the tugboat companies face. Each company has a fleet of vessels, a set of crews that run the vessels, and a list of jobs from various customers that need to be done. The dispatcher is the person at the centre of the business process that matches jobs with crews and vessels. It is a complicated process where new jobs come in daily, vessels and crews have different capabilities, and customers have different priorities. Tugboats are also expensive (a tugboat can cost upward of $5 million and require thousands of dollars per day to run). Dispatchers require years of experience before they

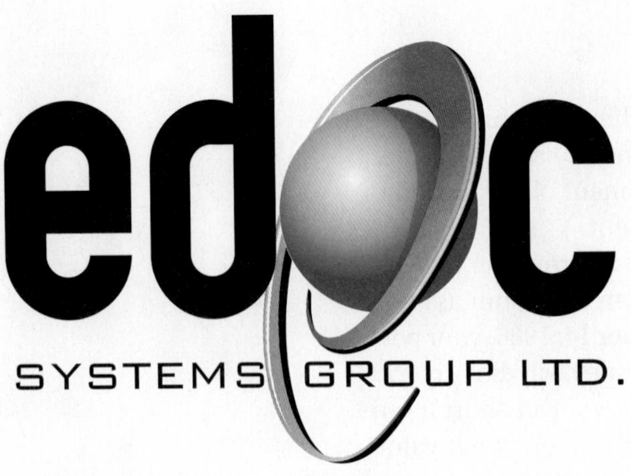

Figure 2-10
Edoc Logo

are ready to balance these factors and make efficient scheduling decisions.

The paper-based system worked for decades, but it was relatively inefficient and prone to error. Why? To understand this, you need a more detailed view of the process. The process would start with a customer order (usually from phone or fax). An employee at the tug company would write down the work needed to be done; it would get rewritten and handed to tug captains as a job to do; dispatchers would copy it again onto the dispatch log sheet. When the job was completed the captains would hand their log sheets back to the dispatchers. Dispatchers would review the sheets and send a delivery notice to their customer. The log sheets would then get passed to accounting staff, who would rewrite (or retype) the entire job into an invoice and send it out. Finally, the accountant would have to re-enter all the invoicing details into the accounting system. That means each job was handwritten seven different times by at least four different people. Each written entry not only takes time but also has the potential for copying errors.

Several years of work with tugboat companies resulted in Edoc developing HELM Marine Operations Software. HELM supports the dispatch process first by equipping each vessel with a computer that runs the HELM software. The software is used to keep track of the jobs assigned to the tugboat, details about each job, and information about when the job is completed. This information from each of the tugs is linked, through a computer network, with a central computer at the company's main office. This electronic linkage reduces the reliance on tug dispatch sheets and automates the job-completion notices that dispatchers need to send to their customers. The software also automatically produces invoices and links with the accounting system—thereby reducing even more data entry. HELM therefore provides more accurate and timely information. The hardware and software are used to save time for the dispatchers, captains, and accounting staff. The HELM software has eliminated up to 60 percent of the steps involved in the invoicing process and saved companies tens of thousands of dollars each year by reducing errors. Reporting times have also been decreased up to 90 percent—from 7 hours to 30 minutes in some cases. Edoc now has customers in B.C., Hawaii, Alaska, and the U.S. East Coast, and is expanding to include the U.S. West Coast and Gulf Coast as well.

Questions

1. Draw the paper-based process described in the case above. Now draw the process after HELM was introduced. What are the major differences between the diagrams?
2. The HELM software automates processes and saves time and money. Could HELM also result in increased revenue?
3. Can you think of other benefits that might arise from the use of the software? For example, experienced dispatchers in the industry are difficult to find. Can the system help with this challenge?

Source: EDOC Systems Group.

How does the knowledge in this chapter help Madison and you?

Madison has spent a month working on her résumé. But she is worried that the people who might be hiring her will look at other sources of information that she had little or no control over. The Intenet and social networking sites have changed the processes people use to evaluate employees. In thinking about her challenge, Madison decided that taking control of her web profile and making the Internet work in her favour was the best strategy to take. She paid more attention to whom she was linking with and also spent more time viewing her profile and removing links that might provide inappropriate information. She looked at her site from an employer's perspective and worked to leave a great impression with employers. Rather than trying to hide her page, Madison decided to use her page to launch and support her job-hunting campaign.

In taking control of her page, Madison was able to leverage the power of a large information system for her job search. She used her page as an additional information source and as a way to demonstrate her organizational and networking abilities. She also used the social networking sites and other search engines to look more closely at the companies where she received job interviews. She discovered that there is a wealth of information on the web for those who are willing and able to explore.

Her knowledge of the company and her sophisticated use of her networking page became important tools in Madison's job search. Madison realized that she could use information systems as a competitive advantage in her search. In using the web and social networking sites, she was able to distribute her résumé more quickly, to more people, and for less money than mailing her résumé. And her résumé became even more effective when she pointed prospective employers to her page, where she could highlight her skills. Madison learned that information systems can be an effective tool when you're able to use them to your advantage. Like Madison, the knowledge you are gaining in this course will help you make better use of information systems.

Active Review

Use this Active Review to verify that you understand the material in the chapter. You can read the entire chapter and then perform the tasks in this review, or you can read the material for just one question and perform the tasks in this review for that question before moving on to the next one.

Q1 "How did this stuff get here?"

Imagine yourself at a hockey or football game, or at some concert. What business processes are involved in producing that event? How did you buy a ticket? What processes were involved in that activity? What processes are needed to print the ticket? Who cleaned the stadium? What processes are involved in hiring, managing, and paying the cleaning staff?

Q2 What is a business process?

What is the definition of a business process? Consider one of the processes in your answer to Q1, and make a diagram similar to the one in Figure 2-1.

Q3 What are the components of a business process?

List the components of a business process. Define each component. Identify each type of component on your diagram in your answer to Q2.

Q4 What is information?

Give four definitions of information. Rank those definitions in order of usefulness in business. Justify your ranking.

Q5 What is the role of information in business processes?

Explain how information is created in the payment activity in Figure 2-1. Describe three different types of information that could be produced from the data in the inventory database.

Q6 How do information systems support business processes?

Explain the meaning of each cell in Figures 2-4, 2-5, and 2-6. Explain the differences in the balance between automated and manual systems in these three information systems. Summarize the justification that the systems' designers used for constructing systems with the balance shown.

Q7 How do information systems support decision making?

Describe the differences among operational, managerial, and strategic decision making. What are the steps in a decision process? Explain how information systems can support these steps.

Q8 What is your role?

Explain why the quality of your thinking has a lot to do with the quality of the information system.

Key Terms and Concepts

Using Your Knowledge

1. Consider the four definitions of information presented in this chapter. The problem with the first definition, "knowledge derived from data," is that it merely substitutes one word we don't know the meaning of (*information*) for a second word we don't know the meaning of (*knowledge*). The problem with the second definition, "data presented in a meaningful context," is that it is too subjective. Whose context? What makes a context meaningful? The third definition, "data processed by summing, ordering, averaging, etc.," is too mechanical. It tells us what to do, but it doesn't tell us what information is. The fourth definition, "a difference that makes a difference," is vague and unhelpful.

   Also, none of these definitions helps us to quantify the amount of information we receive. What is the information content of the statement that every human being has a navel? Zero—you already know that. On the other hand, the statement that someone has just deposited $50 000 into your chequing account is chock-full of information. So, good information has an element of surprise.

   Considering all these points, answer the following questions:

   a. What is information made of?
   b. If you have more information, do you weigh more? Why or why not?
   c. If you give a copy of your transcript to a prospective employer, is that information? If you show that same transcript to your dog, is it still information? Where is the information?
   d. Give your own best definition of information.
   e. Explain how you think it is possible that we have an industry called the information technology industry, but we have great difficulty defining the word *information*.

2. The text states that information should be worth its cost. Both cost and value can be broken into tangible and intangible factors. *Tangible* factors can be directly measured; *intangible* ones arise indirectly and are difficult to measure. For example, a tangible cost is the cost of a computer monitor; an intangible cost is the lost productivity of a poorly trained employee.

   Give five important tangible and five important intangible costs of an information system. Give five important tangible and five important intangible measures of the value of an information system. If it helps to focus your thinking, use the example of the class scheduling system at your university or some other university information system. When determining whether an information system is worth its cost, how do you think the tangible and intangible factors should be considered?

3. Suppose you manage the purchasing department for a chain of coffee shops. Assume that your company is in the process of developing the requirements for a new purchasing application. As you think about those requirements, you wonder how much autonomy you want your employees to have in selecting the supplier for each purchase. You can develop a system that will make the supplier selection automatically, or you can build one that allows employees to make that selection. Explain how this characteristic will impact the following:

   a. The skill level required for your employees
   b. The number of employees you'll need

c. Your employee hiring criteria
d. Your management practices
e. The degree of autonomy for your employees
f. Your flexibility in managing your department

Suppose management has left you out of the requirements-definition process. Explain how you could use the knowledge you developed in answering this question to justify your need to be involved in the requirements definition.

4. Singing Valley Resort is a top-end (rooms cost from $400 to $2500 per night), 50-unit resort located high in the mountains of Colorado. Singing Valley prides itself on its beautiful location, its relaxing setting, and its superb service. The resort's restaurant is highly rated and has an extensive list of exceptional wines. The well-heeled clients are accustomed to the highest levels of service.
   a. Give an example of three different operational decisions that Singing Valley personnel make each day. Describe an information system that could be used to facilitate those decisions.
   b. Give an example of three different managerial decisions that Singing Valley managers make each week. Describe an information system that could be used to facilitate those decisions.
   c. Give an example of three different strategic decisions that Singing Valley's owners might make in a year. Describe an information system for each.
   d. Which of the decisions in your answers to questions a, b, and c are structured? Which, if any, are unstructured?

Case Study 2

High Touch—High Tech

Formed in 1945, Vancity (www.vancity.ca) is Canada's largest credit union with more than $13 billion in assets and 350 000 customers. The company is different from many of the other financial institutions because it is owned by its member customers rather than shareholders; Vancity's 2500 employees pride themselves on providing outstanding service that is personal and professional while at the same time demonstrates innovation and responsibility.

Like most financial institutions, Vancity offers its customers traditional banking products such as savings and chequing accounts, loans, and credit cards, as well as mutual funds and other investment and financial planning services. However, this increase in the number of products and services is not without its challenges, particularly when coupled with increased customer access. The days when customers could transact business only while in a branch are now long in the past. Although a branch visit is still a cornerstone of banking, modern customers are just as likely to connect and do business with Vancity over the telephone or Internet. Banking is now anywhere and any time, and customers are supported by sophisticated computer systems that are safe and secure. However, it is not just high technology for the sake of high technology. Instead, as Tony Fernandes, Vice President Technology Strategy, puts it, "High tech is used to create high touch."

While many people still visit their local branch and have developed a relationship with the customer service representatives (CSR), this is not always possible and is increasingly the least frequent way that customers transact business. Staff changes, growth in the number of customers, and the fact that people are increasingly mobile mean that the in-branch staff are less likely to recognize their customers, or even if they do may simply not be aware of the complete relationship the customer has with Vancity. Addressing this problem, Vancity has implemented Customer Information File (CIF) technology to keep track of all the various types of business a customer has. Now, when customers visit the branch and present their customer card to the CSR, the CIF searches all the system records, identifies the services used, and develops a profile of the complete consolidated relationship between the client and Vancity. As a result, each customer receives the same high level of personal service even if it is their first time inside a particular branch, and Vancity is able to tailor or customize the experience specifically for them. For example, rather than ask all customers if they would like information on one of the new credit cards that Vancity is developing, the system can advise the customer service representative if the customer already has the card or should be offered something else. Alternatively, seeing that the customer has an investment plan already set up, the CSR could be prompted to ask the customer about a new retirement product being launched by Vancity's mutual fund department.

Source: Vancity. Used with permission.

Questions

1. What challenges are created when providing anywhere, any time services? (*Hint:* How and when did you conduct your last banking transaction?)
2. What business and technology issues would be faced by an organization that wants to have a complete view of its customers? (*Hint:* What are the benefits and costs of cooperation, and are there any privacy issues?)
3. Can you think of any examples where a lack of information or failure to consider the information could affect the profitability of a business?
4. If a customer has more than one account at a particular organization, should they receive separate mailings or all pieces in the same envelope?
5. Does being a credit union rather than a share corporation affect Vancity's structure?

Visit MyMISLab at **www.pearsoned.ca/mymislab**. MyMISLab is a state-of-the-art, interactive, online solution that combines multimedia, tutorials, and quizzes. Use MyMISLab for *Experiencing MIS* to prepare for tests and exams, and go to class ready to learn!

What Do YOU Think?

Ethics of Misdirected Information Use

Consider the following situations:

Situation A: Suppose you are buying a condo and you know that at least one other party is bidding against you. While agonizing over your best strategy, you stop at a local Starbucks. As you sip your latte, you overhear a conversation at the table next to yours. Three people are talking so loudly that it is difficult to ignore them, and you soon realize that they are the real estate agent and the couple who is competing for the condo you want. They are preparing their offer. Should you listen to their conversation? If you do, do you use the information you hear to your advantage?

Situation B: Consider the same situation from a different perspective—instead of overhearing the conversation, suppose you receive that same information in an email. Perhaps an administrative assistant at the agent's office confuses you and the other customer and mistakenly sends you the terms of the other party's offer. Do you read that email? If so, do you use the information you read to your advantage?

Situation C: Suppose that you sell computer software. In the midst of a sensitive price negotiation, your customer accidentally sends you an internal email that contains the maximum amount the customer can pay for your software. Do you read that email? Do you use that information to guide your negotiating strategy? What do you do if your customer discovers that the email may have reached you and asks, "Did you read my email?" How do you answer?

Situation D: Suppose a friend mistakenly sends you an email that contains sensitive personal medical data. Further, suppose you read the email before you know what you're reading and you're embarrassed to learn something very personal that truly is none of your business. Your friend asks you, "Did you read that email?" How do you respond?

Situation E: Finally, suppose that you work as a network administrator and your position allows you unrestricted access to the mailing lists for your company. Assume that you have the skill to insert your email address into any company mailing list without anyone knowing about it. You insert your address into several lists and, consequently, begin to receive confidential email that no one intended for you to see. One of those emails indicates that your best friend's department is about to be eliminated and all of its personnel fired. Do you forewarn your friend?

Discussion Questions

1. Answer the questions in situations A and B. Do your answers differ? Does the medium by which the information is obtained make a difference? Is it easier to avoid reading an email than it is to avoid hearing a conversation? If so, does that difference matter?
2. Answer the questions in situations B and C. Do your answers differ? In situation B, the information is for your personal gain; in C, the information is for both your personal and your organization's gain. Does this difference matter? How do you respond when asked if you have read the email?
3. Answer the questions in situations C and D. Do your answers differ? Would you lie in one case and not in the other? Why or why not?
4. Answer the question in situation E. What is the essential difference between situations A through D and situation E? Suppose you had to justify your behaviour in situation E. How would you argue? Do you believe your own argument?
5. In situations A through D, if you access the information you have done nothing illegal. You were the passive recipient. Even for item E, although you undoubtedly violated your company's employment policies, you most likely did not violate the law. So for this discussion, assume that all these actions are legal.
   a. What is the difference between legal and ethical? Look up both terms in a dictionary, and explain how they differ.
   b. Make the argument that business is competitive and that if something is legal, then it is acceptable to do it if it helps to further your goals.
   c. Make the argument that it is never appropriate to do something unethical.
6. Summarize your beliefs about proper conduct when you receive misdirected information.

3 Organizational Strategy, Information Systems, and Competitive Advantage

This could happen to you

Madison finished her business degree and landed a great job working in the human resources department for a high-technology firm in Ottawa's Kanata district. The company grew rapidly. In a few short years, Madison had demonstrated her ability to find and retain highly skilled employees. Her success had been recognized and she was now the manager of employee recruitment and selection for the company. Employees are a big source of the competitive advantage for the firm,[1] and Madison's job is central to the company's strategic objectives.

On an early evening skate down the Rideau Canal, one of Madison's friends asked her how she had become so successful so quickly. Madison shrugged it off with a "Just lucky, I guess," but later that evening she thought more about it. Why was she getting good results? She had always had a good sense of people and that was clearly an important skill. But lots of other people in her department had good people skills too. She thought about colleagues at other companies who did the same kind of work. When she looked closely, she started to realize that her advantage might come from information technology.

She noticed that many of the people in her department were more people-oriented and did not like using the computer. They weren't used to creating spreadsheets and analyzing data they found on the web. Some people shied away from posting jobs on Internet job sites like Monster.ca (www.monster.ca). They would say *"It's too complicated"* or *"You get WAY too many responses. We can't handle that."* Madison recognized that she had learned quite a bit during her degree about how to handle information technology and how to make it work for her. For example, she used her experience with social networking sites to full advantage: she Googled all her candidates and checked out their web presence before every interview. Information technology was a big part of her daily work.

Madison did not consider herself a computer geek. She was focused on people. What she had learned was how to use information technology to gain a competitive advantage.

1. See Huselid, Mark A., "The Impact of Human Resource Management Practices on Turnover, Productivity, and Corporate Financial Performance," *Academy of Management Journal* 38, no. 3 (June 1995): 635–672.

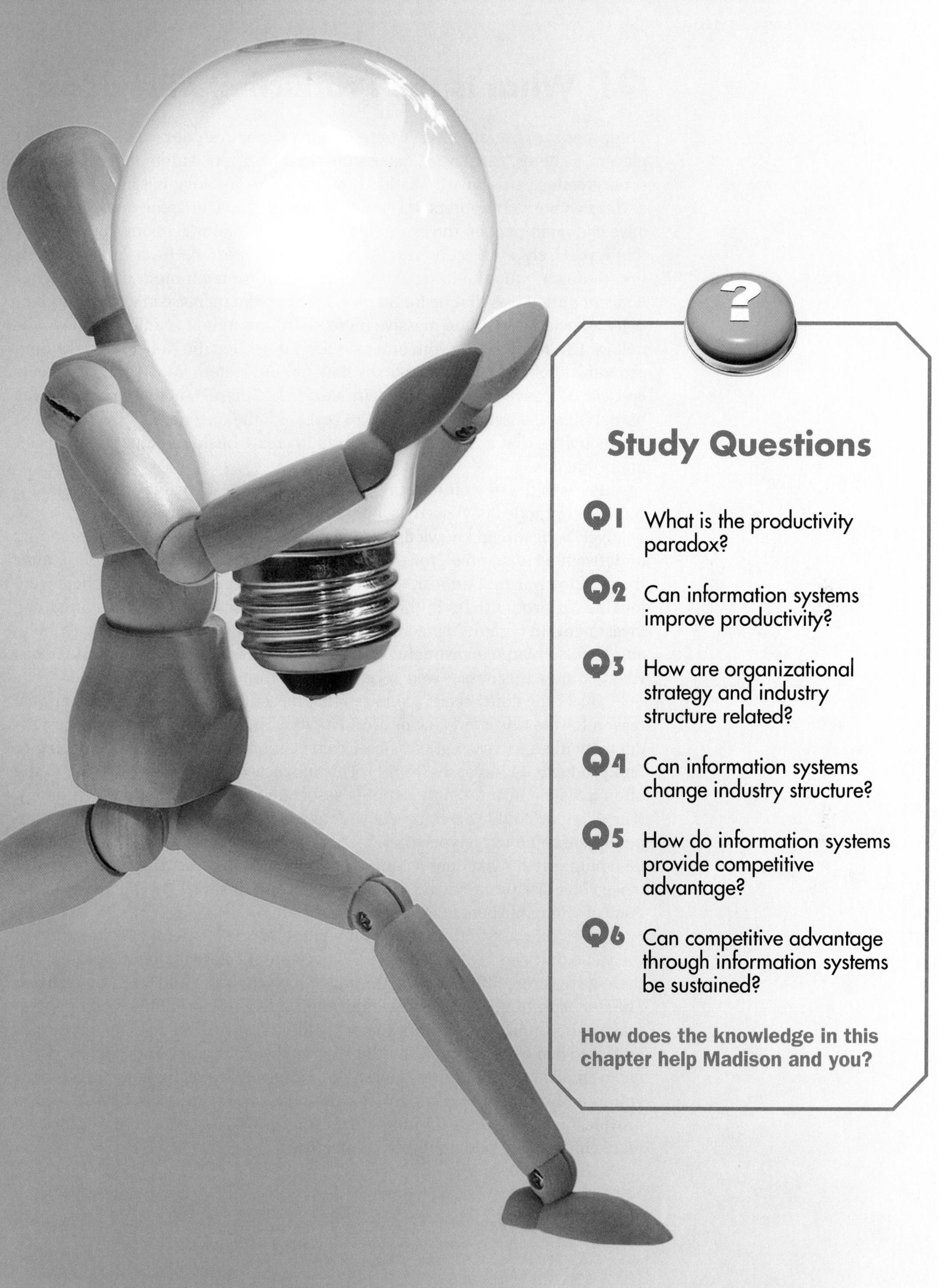

Study Questions

Q1 What is the productivity paradox?

Q2 Can information systems improve productivity?

Q3 How are organizational strategy and industry structure related?

Q4 Can information systems change industry structure?

Q5 How do information systems provide competitive advantage?

Q6 Can competitive advantage through information systems be sustained?

How does the knowledge in this chapter help Madison and you?

Q1 What Is the Productivity Paradox?

Computers are literally everywhere in our society. Watches, cell phones, MP3 players, cameras, calculators, televisions, cash registers, automobiles, and even some greeting cards have embedded computing technology. It is hard to think of a world without computers. It is even harder, perhaps, to argue that computers have had no impact on the economic productivity of our economy. But in 1989, that is precisely what economist Stephen Roach reported.[2] It was not his intention to downgrade the importance of information technology. Instead, what Roach reported was that he found no evidence of an increase in worker productivity associated with the massive increase in investment in information technology. This result, along with other similar studies, led the Nobel Prize–winning economist Robert Solow to make the now-famous statement, *"We see computers everywhere except in the productivity statistics."* The **productivity paradox** was born. While this issue is more than 20 years old, the question of how IT adds to productivity—that is, how IT can be used to create business value—remains an important one.

Perhaps the most interesting fact about the productivity paradox is that it was never practically viewed as a paradox for most organizations. Despite the relatively widespread knowledge of the paradox, the North American economy underwent a substantial growth in investment in information technology after the paradox was first published. While economists and other researchers were looking for productivity in the statistics, businesses were busy making huge investments in computing technology. The majority of businesses seemed to be able to justify large investments in IT. The important question to consider was whether these businesses were receiving value from their investments.

Over time it has been recognized that measurement error may be a critical reason for the observed lack of productivity.[3] The difficulty in measuring productivity in an increasingly service-based economy has made it challenging to find productivity increases from IT. This mismeasurement is in part due to the often invisible or intangible benefits associated with information technology. (For example, could you complete your latest essay assignment without a computer? You could use a typewriter. You still have to type the words, so there is little typing saved. What does a computer add to this process? Does the computer make you more productive? How much time does it save?) We will return to the issue of intangible benefits later in this chapter.

One response to the productivity paradox was a careful consideration of the value that can be derived from IT investment.[4] Researchers suggested that there were three different ways through which the value of IT can be realized. The first is through productivity. Information technology allows a company to make either more output from the same inputs, and/or to make better output and/or to make the output faster than before the technology. For example, if you had a small accounting firm, investing in information technology might allow you to add more customers, to automate basic tasks (like tax forms), and to provide more up-to-date information for clients. This investment makes the firm more efficient and potentially more effective.

2. Roach, S. S., "America's White-Collar Productivity Dilemma," *Manufacturing Engineering* (August 1989): 104.

3. See Brynjolfsson, E., "The Productivity Paradox of Information Technology: Review and Assessment," *Communications of the ACM* 36, no. 12 (December 1993): 67–77; and King, John L., "IT Responsible for Most Productivity Gains," *Computing Research News* 15, no. 4 (September 2003): 1–6, www.cra.org/CRN/articles/sept03/king.html (accessed March 21, 2007).

4. Hitt, L., and E. Brynjolfsson, "Productivity, Profit and Consumer Welfare: Three Different Measures of Information Technology's Value," *MIS Quarterly* 20, no. 2 (June 1996): 121–142.

The second way in which IT value is realized is through the structure of competition. Information technology can alter the way corporations compete. For example, when a rival accounting firm invests in information technology, it is often the case that other firms will follow suit to keep up with the competition. The accounting firms now compete on the software they offer and the technical support they can provide. The competitive structure changes because of information technology.

The final way that IT investment value is realized is by the end customer. Information technology helps make processes more efficient and changes the nature of competition. With increased competition, the reduction of costs associated with new processes is often transferred to the final consumer. The consumer may therefore see cheaper and better goods and services as a result of information technology. For example, accounting firms now offer their clients more services and perhaps even lower prices on services after investing in information technology. The consumer often reaps the benefit of higher investment in information technology.

Some controversy remains in regard to how productive information technology investments are. We will look more carefully in the remaining sections of this chapter at how information systems impact productivity, industry structure, and organizational strategy.

Q2 Can Information Systems Improve Productivity?

We saw in Chapter 2 that companies organize work through business processes. Business processes use resources, facilities, and information to accomplish activities. Business processes are therefore an important consideration in productivity. Productivity for organizations can be increased either through increased efficiency or effectiveness.

Increasing efficiency means that business processes can be accomplished either more quickly or with fewer resources and facilities (or both). Efficiency is usually relatively easy to measure. When organizations focus on efficiency they are working toward "doing things right." Doing things right often means using just the right amount of resources, facilities, and information to complete the job satisfactorily.

When companies focus on increasing effectiveness, they are interested in "doing the right things." Increased effectiveness means that the company considers offering either new or improved goods or services that the customer values. Doing the right things often requires companies to consider changing their business processes to deliver something new and improved.

Sometimes "doing the right things" and "doing things right" can be in conflict in a company. For example, Company A could be so focused on increasing efficiency that it misses the fact that customers have changed and no longer value Company A's product. Company A might be doing things right, but it is not doing the right things. Company B might be so focused on changing its product for customers that it does not spend enough time doing things right. Company B might operate inefficiently and would be at a disadvantage to other firms that are more efficient. While we might argue about whether "doing things right" or "doing the right things" is more important, it is clear that companies with long-term success are focused on both effectiveness and efficiency.

Business Processes and Value Chains

Business processes are closely related to the concept of a value chain. A **value chain** is a network of activities that improve the effectiveness (or value) of a good or service. A value chain is therefore made up of at least one and often many business processes. For example, a customer in Canada does not see much value in a large blob of natural rubber harvested at a rubber plant farm in Vietnam. But when a tire manufacturing company ships that blob to a factory, designs a tire, and sends the blob through the various processes required to make a tire, the blob of rubber has gained some value. Even more value is gained when the tire is shipped to a tire store close to the customer, and even more when a mechanic at the store installs the tire. Each business process adds more and more value. This is why we refer to this chain of events as a value chain.

In general, the more value a company adds to a good or service in its value chain, the higher the price the company can charge. The difference between the price the customer is willing to pay and the cost the company incurs in moving the goods or services through the value chain is defined as the **margin**. The greater the margin, the greater the profit (per unit) for the company.

The concept of a value chain was formalized by Porter. He identified two types of activities that support value chains. **Primary activities** are activities where value is added directly to the product. In our example above, shipping raw materials, designing the tires, manufacturing the tires, shipping finished tires, and installing the tires are all primary activities. Each of these primary activities adds value for the customer.

But there are a whole range of activities in companies that do not add value directly to the product. For instance, who pays the workers in the factory? Who bought the machines at the factory that make the tires? Who maintains the machines inside the factory and keeps the lights and heat working? Who schedules the shipping of the finished tires? Who keeps track of the mechanics' hours? These activities, and many more, are referred to as **support activities,** because they support the primary activities.

Support activities add value only indirectly. For example, nobody buys a tire because a company has a great payroll system. But a company could not run a factory without a payroll system. A great payroll system might make the company more efficient and allow the company to offer a lower price than competitors. The benefit of the payroll system may not directly add to the value as seen by the customer, but these support activities are critical to the success of the organization. Figures 3-1 and 3-2 summarize the concepts we have just discussed. You can use *MIS in Use 3* to further develop your ideas about the value chain.

Understanding the value chain helps us understand how information systems can increase productivity. Information systems increase productivity when they enable the development of more efficient support activities. These systems include applications such as financial accounting systems, human resources systems, production systems, and customer relationship management systems. Increasing the efficiency and effectiveness of these support systems increases the margin enjoyed by the company.

Information systems also increase productivity by offering new and improved services such as customer shopping through the web, 24-hour customer support through online discussion boards and frequently asked questions, online package tracking for the courier business, and airline ticket and hotel reservations through the web. Providing these new or improved services adds value for the customer and contributes to the company's margin.

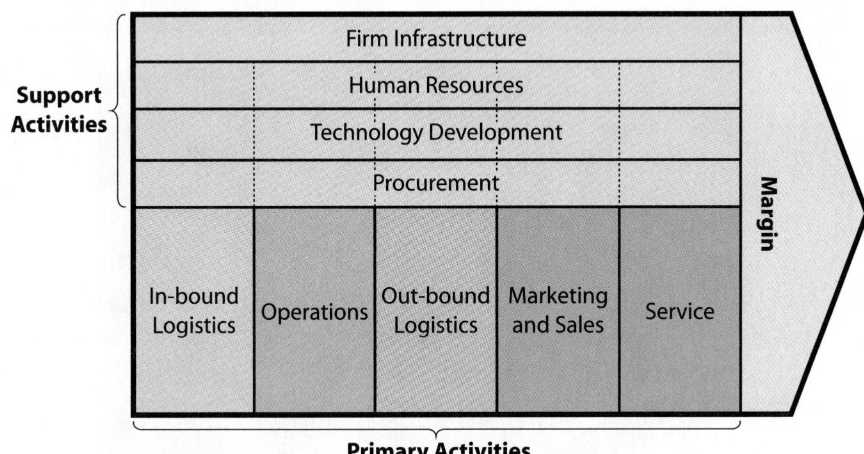

Figure 3-1
Porter's Value Chain Model

Source: Adapted with the permission of The Free Press, a Division of Simon & Schuster Adult Publishing Group, from *Competitive Advantage: Creating and Sustaining Superior Performance* by Michael E. Porter. Copyright © 1985, 1998 by Michael E. Porter. All rights reserved.

Q3 How Are Organizational Strategy and Industry Structure Related?

You will learn in your strategy class that an organization's strategy reflects its goals and objectives. A company's strategy is influenced by the competitive structure of the industry the company is in. In theory, a company's information systems strategy should support, or be aligned with, the overall company strategy. In the real world, it is possible for the organizational strategy and information systems strategy to be somewhat out of alignment. We will address this alignment in Chapter 7.

Organizational strategy begins with an assessment of the fundamental characteristics and structure of an industry. One model used to assess an industry structure is Porter's **five forces model**,[5] shown in Figure 3-4. According to this model, five competitive forces determine industry profitability: bargaining power of customers, threat of substitutions, bargaining power of suppliers, threat of new entrants, and rivalry among existing firms. The intensity of each of the five forces determines the characteristics of the industry, how profitable it is, and how sustainable that profitability will be.

Primary Activity	Description
In-bound logistics	Receiving, storing, and disseminating inputs to the product
Operations	Transforming inputs into the final product
Out-bound logistics	Collecting, storing, and physically distributing the product to buyers
Marketing and sales	Inducing buyers to purchase the product and providing a means for them to do so
Service	Assisting customer's use of the product and thus maintaining and enhancing the product's value

Figure 3-2
Task Descriptions for Primary Activities of the Value Chain

Source: Adapted with the permission of The Free Press, a Division of Simon & Schuster Adult Publishing Group, from *Competitive Advantage: Creating and Sustaining Superior Performance* by Michael E. Porter. Copyright © 1985, 1998 by Michael E. Porter. All rights reserved.

5. Porter, M., *Competitive Strategy: Techniques for Analyzing Industries and Competitors* (New York: Free Press, 1980).

Winterborne Bicycles: Building the Biking Experience

Winterborne Custom Bicycles (www.winterbornebikes.com) was founded in 2001 by Jason Filer in picturesque Guelph, Ontario. A small company, Winterborne's typical customer was a cycling enthusiast—a serious rider who knew bicycles and was ready to move up to a high-quality custom-designed and hand-built bicycle.

The main parts of a custom bike were the frame and the wheels, and the company offered a number of choices in the type, style, and price range. Extensive bike-fitting sessions were part of the design process. The customer could also specify the paint finish and component set that would complete the bike build.

Recently, in conjunction with a local college, Winterborne had also begun to offer intensive courses so that customers and current and aspiring bicycle mechanics could gain practical knowledge and experience with all major bicycle components, including frames, bearings, wheels, drive trains, brakes, and shifting systems, on a variety of bicycle styles and vintages.

Many customers came to the shop looking to purchase a custom bike or wheels, or to upgrade pieces for their current bike such as forks, suspension, handlebars, pedals, gearing, shifting, brakes, saddles, and seatposts. The company offered a number of brands in a wide range of styles and sizes.

Jason and his business partner, retired information systems executive Alan Medcalf, both considered Winterborne more of a vocation than a business and helped customers make the best possible choices for their cycling wants and needs. Both Jason and Alan were well-trained technicians who set up each bike and offered services including customization and bike repairs. Customers also relied on Jason and Alan for recommendations on a wide range of biking accessories such as helmets, riding gear, lighting, gloves, and shoes.

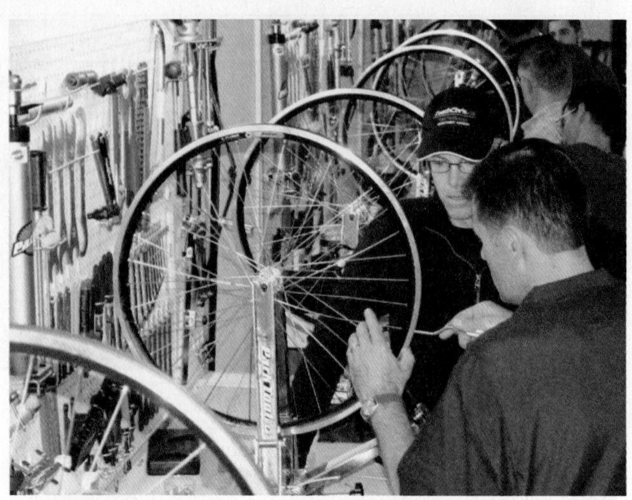

Figure 3-3
Winterborne Custom Bicycles

The company's website provided customers with information about products, and promoted events such as weekend maintenance clinics, the advanced maintenance course, group rides and clubs, trail maintenance days, and educational seminars.

Source: Winterborne Bicycle Institute. Used with permission.

Questions

1. Identify the value chain involved in a obtaining a new bicycle from Winterborne Custom Bicycles. Can you identify the primary activities that create value for the customer when purchasing a new bike?
2. What information systems do you think could be used to support these primary activities?
3. Consider the company's website (www.winterbornebikes.com). Does the website fill the role of a primary activity or is it more appropriately considered a support activity? Justify your answer.

To understand this model, consider the strong and weak examples for each of the forces in Figure 3-5. A good check on your understanding is to see if you can think of different forces of each category in Figure 3-5. Also, take a particular industry—say, auto repair—and consider how these five forces determine the competitive landscape of that industry.

Organizations examine these five forces and determine how they intend to respond to them. That examination leads to competitive strategy.

An organization responds to the structure of its industry by choosing a **competitive strategy**. Porter followed his five forces model with the model of four competitive strategies shown in Figure 3-6.[6] According to Porter, a firm can

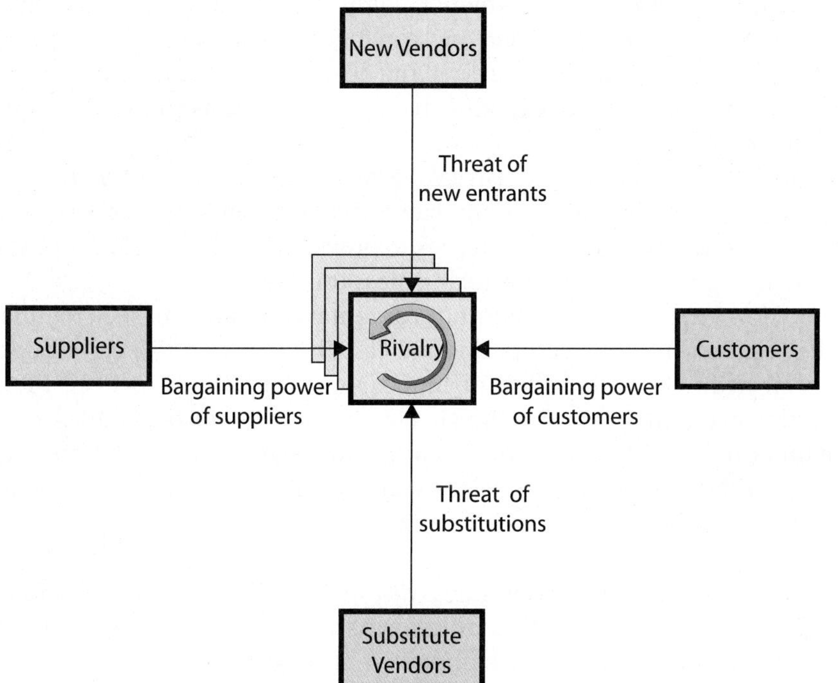

Figure 3-4
Porter's Model of Industry Structure

Source: Adapted with the permission of The Free Press, a Division of Simon & Schuster Adult Publishing Group, from *Competitive Advantage: Creating and Sustaining Superior Performance* by Michael E. Porter.

Force	Example of Strong Force	Example of Weak Force
Bargaining power of customers	Toyota's purchase of auto paint	Your power over the procedures and policies of your university
Threat of substitutions	Frequent-traveller's choice of auto rental	Patients using the only drug effective for their type of cancer
Bargaining power of suppliers	Students purchasing gasoline	Grain farmers in a surplus year
Threat of new entrants	Corner latte stand	Professional football team
Rivalry	Used car dealers	Canada Revenue Agency

Figure 3-5
Examples of Five Forces

6. Porter, M., *Competitive Strategy* (New York: Free Press, 1985).

Figure 3-6
Porter's Four Competitive Strategies

	Cost	Differentiation
Industry-wide	Lowest cost across the industry	Better product/service across the industry
Focus	Lowest cost within an industry segment	Better product/service within an industry segment

engage in one of these four fundamental competitive strategies. An organization can focus on being the cost leader, or it can focus on differentiating its products from those of the competition. Further, the organization can employ the cost or differentiation strategy across an industry, or it can focus its strategy on a particular industry segment.

Consider the car rental industry, for example. According to the first column of Figure 3-6, a car rental company can strive to provide the lowest-cost car rentals across the industry, or it can seek to provide the lowest-cost car rentals to an industry segment—say, domestic business travellers.

As shown in the second column, a car rental company can seek to differentiate its products from the competition. It can do so in various ways—for example, by providing a wide range of high-quality cars, by providing the best reservations system, by having the cleanest cars or the fastest check-in, or by some other means. The company can strive to provide product differentiation across the industry or within particular segments of the industry, such as domestic business travellers.

According to Porter, to be effective the organization's goals, objectives, culture, and activities must be consistent with the organization's strategy. To those in the MIS field, this means that all information systems in the organization must facilitate the organization's competitive strategy.

Q4 Can Information Systems Change Industry Structure?

Changes to industry structure often occur through innovation. Over the last 100 years, technology has enabled much of the innovation we have seen in our economy. This technological innovation is all around us today. One hundred years ago there was little electrical power. There were few telephones. Automobiles were just beginning to be produced. The world had just witnessed the first powered flight. Radio was still being developed and television was just a dream. Now we take these innovations for granted and wonder how people lived without them.

When considering technological innovation, Bower and Christensen[7] suggested that there are two general types of technology innovations. **Sustaining technologies** are changes in technology that maintain the rate of improvement in customer value. For example, the vulcanization of rubber allowed tire manufacturers to produce tires that rode more quickly and comfortably. This

7. Bower, J., and C. Christensen, "Disruptive Technologies: Catching the Wave," *Harvard Business Review* 73, no. 1 (Jan/Feb 1995): 43–53.

innovation improved the experience of driving a car and helped sustain the original innovation.

In contrast, **disruptive technologies** introduce a very new package of attributes to the accepted mainstream products. For example, in the music industry the advent of MP3 was a disruptive technology because it offered the ability to store and play music through digital devices. People moved from buying CDs and tapes to listen to in their SONY Walkman to downloading MP3s and listening to music through their Apple iPod.

Information technology has been an important part of technological innovations since the 1950s. From the first electronic computer in 1939 to the first personal computer in 1980 and the commercialization of the Internet in the early 1990s, the rate of innovation in information technology has been staggering. In some instances, information technology acts as a sustaining technology. Improved size and speed of memory helps us store and retrieve data more quickly. Faster processors help the computer accomplish more in the same amount of time. Sustaining technologies help make processes more efficient (and often more effective), and hence create value for organizations.

In other cases, information technology acts as a disruptive technology. For example, when the Royal Bank offered a national automated banking machine network in Canada in 1980[8] it presented customers with new choices. The other chartered banks in Canada quickly responded with machines of their own. Similarly, when the Canadian company Research In Motion (www.rim.net), operating out of Waterloo, Ontario, launched the first BlackBerry™ in 1999, it provided worldwide customers with new communication options. Wireless companies around the globe had to respond to these new sets of choices.

Both of these companies gained competitive advantage by employing information technology. When a company gains competitive advantage using a disruptive technology, there is the potential to alter the structure of an industry. Competing companies must react to the new conditions or risk losing margin and customers. Both large and small companies within the industry must react to these changes. You can learn more about how small companies react to a disruptive technology by reading the case about ICS Courier found at the end of this chapter.

In some cases the competitive advantage is so large that it leads to a new industry. Such was the case for the microcomputer. The advent of the microcomputer led to the development of the microcomputer industry and the creation of new companies such as Microsoft, Intel, Apple, Oracle, and Dell. Amazon, eBay, and Google resulted from the commercialization of the Internet. More recently, wireless network technology has led to the development of such Canadian companies as Waterloo's Research In Motion and Sierra Wireless (www.sierrawireless.com) based in Richmond, B.C.

Q5 How Do Information Systems Provide Competitive Advantage?

In your business strategy class, you will study the Porter models in greater detail than we have discussed here. When you do so, you will learn numerous ways that organizations respond to the five competitive forces. For our purposes, we can distill those ways into the list of principles shown in Figure 3-7. Keep in mind

8. www.rbc.com/history/anytimeanywhere/self_service-detail.html#2.

Figure 3-7
Principles of Competitive Advantage

Product Implementations
1. Create a new product or service
2. Enhance products or services
3. Differentiate products or services

System Implementations
4. Lock in customers and buyers
5. Lock in suppliers
6. Raise barriers to market entry
7. Establish alliances
8. Reduce costs

that we are applying these principles in the context of the organization's competitive strategy. (You can also apply these principles to a personal competitive advantage, as discussed in the Exercise "The Digital Divide" at the end of this chapter.)

Some of these competitive techniques are created via products and services, and some are created via the development of business processes. Consider each and how these techniques might result in a competitive advantage, which is a defined level of above-average returns for a company.

Competitive Advantage via Products

The first three principles in Figure 3-7 concern products or services. Organizations gain a competitive advantage by creating *new* products or services, by *enhancing* existing products or services, and by *differentiating* their products and services from those of their competitors. As you think about these three principles, realize that an information system can be part of a product or it can provide support for a product or service. *MIS in Use 3* discusses how a company that builds bikes uses the Internet to provide additional services to the customer. This adds value to customer interactions with the company.

Consider, for example, a car rental agency like Hertz or Avis. An information system that produces information about the car's location and provides driving instructions to destinations is part of the car rental and thus is part of the product itself. In contrast, an information system that schedules car maintenance is not part of the product, but instead supports the product. Either way, information systems can achieve the first three objectives in Figure 3-7.

The remaining five principles in Figure 3-7 concern competitive advantage created by the implementation of business processes.

Competitive Advantage via Business Processes

Organizations can *lock in customers* by making it difficult or expensive for customers to switch to another product. This strategy is sometimes called establishing high **switching costs.** Organizations can *lock in suppliers* by making it difficult to switch to another organization, or, stated positively, by making it easy to connect to and work with the organization. Finally, competitive advantage can be gained by *creating entry barriers* that make it difficult and expensive for new competition to enter the market.

Another means to gain competitive advantage is to *establish alliances* with other organizations. Such alliances establish standards, promote product awareness and needs, develop market size, reduce purchasing costs, and provide other benefits. Finally, organizations can gain competitive advantage by *reducing costs.* Such reductions enable the organization to reduce prices and/or to increase profitability. Increased profitability means not just greater shareholder value, but also more cash, which can fund further infrastructure development for even greater competitive advantage.

Q6 Can Competitive Advantage through Information Systems Be Sustained?

We have noted that information technology can provide a competitive advantage for companies. But can these advantages be sustained? Competitors often react to innovations by replicating the technology. Since the effect of information technology can be readily seen, it is hard to hide the innovation. Hardware and software can be purchased or developed. It is therefore almost impossible to keep competitors from developing competing technology.

Banks that produced the first automated banking machines were quickly followed by competitors. While patents can provide some protection for technologies (such as the BlackBerry), patents are difficult and expensive to enforce and they are not permanent. Does this mean that all information technology innovations are doomed to be temporary?

In his *Harvard Business Review* article "IT Doesn't Matter,"[9] Nicholas Carr suggested that the evolution of information technology in business follows a pattern similar to earlier disruptive technologies like railroads and electric power. As these disruptive technologies are being developed, the technologies open opportunities for companies to gain strong competitive advantages. But as the availability of the technologies increases, and their cost decreases, these technologies become more like commodities. From a strategic standpoint, the technologies become invisible and no longer provide advantages. In other words, the more ubiquitous—existing everywhere—information technology becomes, the less competitive advantage information technology provides.

We have noted above that this is true to a certain degree. But it is important to understand clearly what we are talking about. If we are talking about information technology (hardware, software, and networks), then what Carr has said is largely true. Hardware and software have become readily accessible to almost all companies and, while not entirely a commodity, they have largely become commoditized.

However, if we consider information systems (which also include procedures and people along with hardware and software), then what Carr notes is less convincing. The same information technology installed into different organizations might result in very different outcomes. While the machines and software may be a commodity, organizational procedures and the people in organizations are not standardized. Some companies (and some people) might be able to quickly adopt new technology. Other companies (or people) might be less willing or able to do so. It is important to recognize that long-term competitive advantage lies not with the technology but rather in how the company and people adopt the technology. If you learn one thing from this chapter, it should be that when it comes to information technology, people make all the difference. So while IT may not matter, information systems certainly do.

So how should we understand long-term competitive advantage? Sustained competitive advantage requires companies to find a distinctive way to

[9] Carr, N., "IT Doesn't Matter," *Harvard Business Review* 81, no. 5 (May 2003): 41–49.

compete. This way of competing will change over time. The emphasis should be placed on developing increasingly sophisticated integration between information technology and the people and procedures in the organization. Companies with sustainable competitive advantage work to integrate lots of activities: their marketing, customer service, product design, and product delivery. When a company successfully integrates many technology systems with its people and procedures, competitors have to match the whole system. While competitors might be able to purchase the technology, it takes time for people to gain the necessary experience and skill. Matching the entire set of information systems can be a steep hill to climb for companies with less experience and success in integrating people and technology.

How does the knowledge in this chapter help Madison and you?

This chapter provides several important ideas about the impact of information technology. First, knowledge of how information technology affects productivity provides Madison with an understanding of where technology can be used to increase her effectiveness and efficiency. This enables Madison to carefully decide what technologies make sense for her job. Her knowledge of business processes helps her understand where technology can add value for the customer. This makes Madison a more effective employee.

The second idea is that information technology can change industry structure. Madison therefore keeps her eyes open for disruptive technologies in her area of work. Internet job sites are just one form of disruptive technology that Madison has learned to use effectively. Her use of information technology helps improve her choices about employees and makes the company more efficient and effective in the long run.

Finally, Madison has learned that it is important not only to incorporate information technology into her work but also to continue to look for ways to grow even more effective. Long-term advantage is not provided by technology but rather by people learning how to incorporate new technology into company procedures. People make the difference. Learning how to integrate information technology into the way we work can provide a real long-term competitive advantage both for Madison and for her company.

There is just one caution. Integrating technology into the way you work is an important skill. However, it is important to remember that the technology must add value to the process. We will discuss value further in Chapters 7 and 9.

Active Review

Use this Active Review to verify that you understand the material in the chapter. You can read the entire chapter and then perform the tasks in this review, or you can read the material for just one question and perform the tasks in this review for that question before moving on to the next one.

Q1 What is the productivity paradox?

Explain what is meant by the productivity paradox. Can you explain how using the computer makes you more productive than simply using a typewriter? List three ways in which information systems can create value.

Q2 Can information systems improve productivity?

Explain the relationship between business processes and value chains. What are the differences between primary and support activities? How does information technology impact value chains?

Q3 How are organizational strategy and industry structure related?

Name and briefly describe the five forces. Give your own examples of weak and strong forces. What are the four main types of competitive strategy as identified by Porter?

Q4 Can information systems change industry structure?

Explain the differences between sustaining and disruptive technologies. Provide examples where information technology is a sustaining technology and where information technology is a disruptive technology.

Q5 How do information systems provide competitive advantage?

List and briefly describe eight principles of competitive advantage. Consider the bookstore at your school. List one application of information technology that takes advantage of each of these principles.

Q6 Can competitive advantage through information systems be sustained?

Describe what is meant by sustained competitive advantage. Explain why information technology does not generally provide sustained competitive advantage. Explain why information systems can provide sustained competitive advantage.

Key Terms and Concepts

Competitive strategy 51
Disruptive technologies 53
Five forces model 49
Margin 48
Primary activities 48
Productivity paradox 46
Support activities 48
Sustaining technologies 52
Switching costs 54
Value chain 48

Using Your Knowledge

1. Apply the value chain model to a retailer such as the Hudson Bay Company (HBC). What is its competitive strategy? Describe the tasks HBC must accomplish for each of the primary value-chain activities. How does HBC's competitive strategy and the nature of its business influence the general characteristics of HBC's information systems?

2. Apply the value chain model to a mail-order company such as L.L.Bean (www.llbean.com). What is its competitive strategy? Describe the tasks L.L.Bean must accomplish for each of the primary value chain activities. How does L.L.Bean's competitive strategy and the nature of its business influence the general characteristics of its information systems?

3. Suppose you decide to start a business that recruits students for summer jobs. You will match available students with available jobs. You need to learn what positions are available and what students are available for filling those positions. In starting your business, you know you will be competing with local newspapers, Craig's List (www.craigslist.org), and your college or university. You will probably have other local competitors as well.
   a. Analyze the structure of this industry according to Porter's five forces model.
   b. Given your analysis in (a), recommend a competitive strategy.
   c. Describe the primary value chain activities as they apply to this business.
   d. Describe a business process for recruiting students.
   e. Describe information systems that could be used to support the business process in (d).
   f. Explain how the process you describe in (d) and the system you describe in (e) reflect your competitive strategy.

4. Consider two different bike rental companies: One rental company provides low-priced rental bikes for students. The other company offers high-service rentals to executives at a conference resort. Think about the bikes they rent. Clearly, the student bikes will be just about anything that can be ridden out of the shop. The bikes for the business executives, on the other hand, must be new, shiny, clean, and in tip-top shape.
   a. Compare and contrast the operations value chains of these two businesses as they pertain to the management of bicycles.
   b. Describe a business process for maintaining bicycles for both businesses.
   c. Describe a business process for acquiring bicycles for both businesses.
   d. Describe a business process for disposing of bicycles for both businesses.
   e. What roles do you see for information systems in your answers to the earlier questions? The information systems can be those you develop within your company or they can be those developed by others, such as Craig's List.

5. Samantha Green owns and operates Twigs Tree Trimming Service. Samantha graduated from the forestry program of a nearby university and worked for a large landscape design firm, performing tree trimming and removal. After several years of experience she bought her own truck, stump grinder, and other equipment and opened her own business in Winnipeg.

   Although many of her jobs are one-time operations to remove a tree or stump, others are recurring, such as trimming a tree or groups of trees every year or every other year. When business is slow, she calls former clients to remind them of her services and of the need to trim their trees on a regular basis.

   Samantha has never heard of Michael Porter, nor of his theories. She operates her business "by the seat of her pants."

a. Explain how an analysis of the five competitive forces could help Samantha.
b. Do you think Samantha has a competitive strategy? What competitive strategy would seem to make sense for her?
c. How would knowledge of her competitive strategy help her sales and marketing efforts?
d. Describe, in general terms, the kind of information system she needs in order to support sales and marketing efforts.

6. FiredUp, Inc. is a small business owned by Curt and Julie Robards. Based in Brisbane, Australia, FiredUp manufactures and sells a lightweight camping stove called the FiredNow. Curt, who previously worked as an aerospace engineer, invented and patented a burning nozzle that enables the stove to stay lit in very high winds—up to 140 kilometres per hour. Julie, an industrial designer by training, developed an elegant folding design that is small, lightweight, easy to set up, and very stable. Curt and Julie manufacture the stove in their garage, and they sell it directly to their customers over the Internet and via phone.
   a. Explain how an analysis of the five competitive forces could help FiredUp.
   b. What does FiredUp's competitive strategy seem to be?
   c. Briefly summarize how the primary value chain activities pertain to FiredUp. How should the company design these value chains to conform to its competitive strategy?
   d. Describe business processes that FiredUp needs in order to implement its marketing and sales and also its service value chain activities.
   e. Describe, in general terms, information systems to support your answer to question (d).

Case Study 3

ICS Courier: Keeping Up with the Joneses

What happens to smaller companies when larger companies in the same industry invest heavily in information systems? How can smaller firms expect to "keep up with the Joneses"? A good example is provided by the courier industry. In Canada, the courier industry is large and competitive. The industry distributes more than 2.1 million packages per day with estimated annual revenue of \$4.7 billion.[10] FedEx gained a competitive advantage in 1994 when the company enabled customers to view the status of their packages using the Internet. Dominant firms in the industry, such as Purolator Courier, DHL Courier, UPS, and Canada Post responded to FedEx's move by providing customer access to their own tracking systems. Barcoded packages, handheld scanners, and a complex network of information systems enabled these large companies to provide package status to customers in a timely fashion.

But how could smaller courier companies respond to this technology investment? Smaller companies do not usually have the ability to pay for large and complex information systems. ICS Courier (www.ics-canada.net; see Figure 3-8), for example, is a relatively small courier business with annual revenues of

[10] Source: Transport Canada, "Canadian Courier Market Size, Structure and Fleet Analysis Study," www.tc.gc.ca/pol/en/Report/Courier2001/C2.htm.

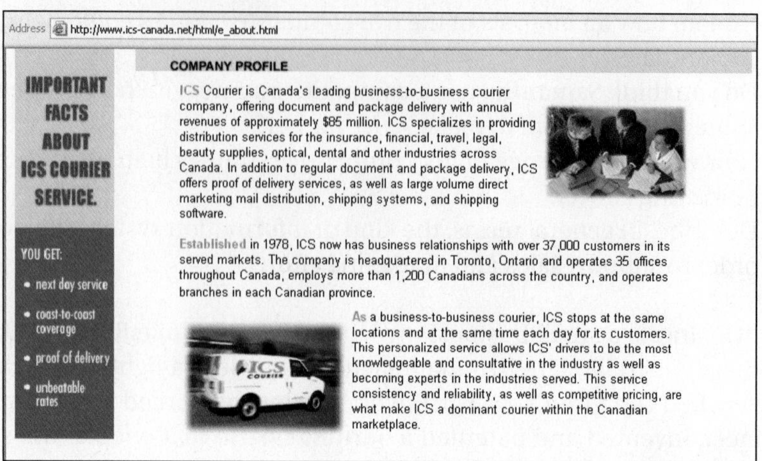

Figure 3-8
ICS Courier Van

$85 million. The company, headquartered in Toronto, was established in 1978, operates 35 offices, and employs more than 1200 people.

ICS Courier did not have the resources in place in 1994 to provide customers with access to package tracking. How could this company survive? ICS Courier recognized that as a smaller company it could specialize its services. The company focused on business-to-business courier services. ICS made sure that its drivers stopped at the same locations and at the same time each day for its customers. This personalized service allowed ICS drivers to be the most knowledgeable in the industry. The drivers became experts in the industries they served. The service consistency and reliability, as well as competitive pricing, helped to keep ICS growing in the Canadian marketplace.

By specializing, ICS Courier also bought some time before it had to make larger information systems investments. Its customers continued to demand package tracking, and the company made a significant investment in information systems. The company upgraded many of its support systems and successfully delivered an online package tracking service. This was not an easy, or inexpensive, process for ICS Courier. Often, smaller companies risk losing the entire business if their investments in an information technology project are not successful.

When large companies invest heavily in information systems, the bar is raised for the entire industry. Some companies cannot compete and they exit the industry. Other companies do find a way to compete. ICS Courier is an example of a smaller company that made a difficult transition in response to a change in information technology. The successful transition required a strong commitment to a company strategy focused on specialization and a successful implementation of information systems to support the strategy.

Source: ICS Courier. Used with permission.

Questions

1. ICS Courier focused on business-to-business customers, servicing law firms, insurance companies, and accounting and medical offices. How did the fact that drivers arrived consistently at the same place and time support the strategy of specialization?
2. Why would offering package tracking via the web support the specialization strategy for ICS? Given the companies that ICS serves, do you think ICS Courier could survive long term without making this technology investment?

3. Do you think package tracking through the web is a disruptive technology? Justify your answer.
4. Can you think of another disruptive technology for the courier industry?-

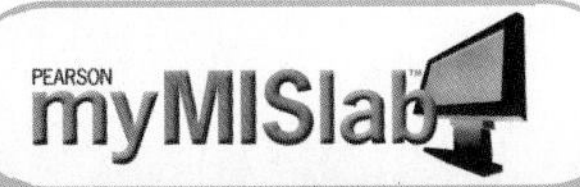

Visit MyMISLab at **www.pearsoned.ca/mymislab**. MyMISLab is a state-of-the-art, interactive, online solution that combines multimedia, tutorials, and quizzes. Use MyMISLab for *Experiencing MIS* to prepare for tests and exams, and go to class ready to learn!

What Do YOU Think?

The Digital Divide

An adage of investing is that it's easier for the rich to get richer. Someone who has $10 million invested at 5 percent earns $500 000 per year. Another investor with $10 000 invested at that same 5 percent earns $500 per year. Every year, the disparity increases as the first investor pulls farther and farther ahead of the second.

This same adage applies to intellectual wealth as well. It's easier for those with considerable knowledge and expertise to gain even more knowledge and expertise. Someone who knows how to search the Internet can learn more readily than someone who does not. And every year, the person with greater knowledge pulls farther and farther ahead. Intellectual capital grows in just the same way that financial capital grows.

Searching the Internet is not just a matter of knowledge, however. It's also a matter of access. The increasing reliance on the web for information and commerce has created a digital divide between those who have Internet access and those who do not. This divide continues to deepen as those who are connected pull farther ahead of those who are not.

Various groups have addressed this problem by making Internet access available in public places, such as libraries, community centres, and retirement homes. The Bill and Melinda Gates Foundation has given more than $262 million to public libraries for the purchase of personal computers and Internet access for them. Such gifts help, but not everyone can be served this way, and even with such access there's a big convenience difference between going to the library and walking across your bedroom to access the Internet—and in your bedroom you don't have to stand in line.

The advantages accrue to everyone with access, every day. Do you want directions to your friend's house? Want to know when a movie is playing at a local theatre? Want to buy music, books, or tools? Want convenient access to your chequing account? Want to decide whether to refinance your condo? Want to know what TCP/IP means? Use the Internet.

All of this intellectual capital resides on the Internet because businesses benefit by putting it there. It's much cheaper to provide product support information over the Internet than on printed documents. The savings include not only the costs of printing, but also the costs of warehousing and mailing. Further, when product specifications change, the organization just changes the website. There is no obsolete material to dispose of and no costs for printing and distributing the revised material. Those who have Internet access gain current information faster than those who do not.

What happens to those who do not have Internet access? They fall farther and farther behind. The digital divide segregates the haves from the have-nots, creating new class structures. Such segregation is subtle, but it is segregation nonetheless.

Do organizations have a responsibility to address this matter? If 98 percent of our market segment has Internet access, do we have a responsibility to provide

Discussion Questions

1. Do you see evidence of a digital divide on your campus? In your hometown? Among your relatives? Describe personal experiences you've had regarding the digital divide.
2. Do organizations have a legal responsibility to provide the same information for unconnected customers as they do for connected customers? If not, should laws be passed requiring organizations to do so?
3. Because it may be impossible to provide equal information, another approach for reducing the digital divide is for the government to enable unconnected citizens to acquire Internet access via subsidies and tax incentives. Do you favour such a program? Why or why not?
4. Suppose that nothing is done to reduce the digital divide and that it is allowed to grow wider and wider. What are the consequences? How will society change?

non-Internet materials to that other 2 percent? On what basis does that responsibility lie? Does a government agency have a responsibility to provide equal information to those who have Internet access and those who do not? When those who are connected can obtain information nearly instantaneously, 24/7, is it even possible to provide equal information to the connected and the unconnected?

It's a worldwide problem. Connected societies and countries pull farther and farther ahead. How can any economy that relies on traditional mail compete with an Internet-based economy?

If you're taking MIS, you're already connected; you're already one of the haves, and you're already pulling ahead of the have-nots. The more you learn about information systems and their use in commerce, the faster you'll pull ahead. The digital divide increases.

PART 2

Using Information Technology

This could happen to you

Dee Clark is the hospital sales marketing director for the Academic and Hospital Division of Emerson Pharmaceuticals, a $4-billion company.[1] Emerson employs 450 salespeople to present its drugs and information about their effectiveness to doctors in many different settings. Dee's job is to ensure that all her sales representatives have the information they need to succeed in this competitive industry.

In the fall of 2007, Dee was looking for better ways to connect with her salespeople. She was discussing this with one of her college friends, who suggested she use a blog to communicate the latest product news. A **blog**, or **weblog**, is an online journal that makes use of information technology to publish information over the Internet. She liked the idea of a blog and brought the idea to her manager. Her manager was happy to hear of Dee's innovative thinking. However, he wanted more specifics and told her that before he approved it he needed to know what the expected benefits would be.

Luckily, Dee had taken an introductory course in management information systems and was able to suggest that the blog would provide Emerson with a competitive advantage by helping her team differentiate its drugs from those of competitors, and it would also raise the barriers to entry against new pharmaceutical companies. Her boss was interested, but he

[1] The people and events in this case are real. Everything related here actually happened. However, to protect the innocent, the guilty, and the publisher of this text, the name of the company and the company's industry have been changed. Dee does exist and she works for a 450-person sales force.

wanted to know approximately how much it would cost before he gave his final approval.

How much will it cost? It depends. The cheapest solution would be to use one of the commercial sites that sponsor blogs, like MSN and Yahoo!. She can't do that, however, because she needs to restrict access to Emerson employees. A public blog would be accessible by the competition.

So she needs to set up her own blog. But how? What's involved? She knows she has to think about hardware, software, data, procedures, and people. The people will be both the sales force and herself. The sales force will need procedures for accessing the blog and leaving comments; Dee will need procedures for posting entries to the blog. Although she's never done that before, she's confident that she can learn the procedures required.

The hardware, software, and data components, however, have her flummoxed. When she talked with her IT staff, she met a barrage of questions that she didn't understand, let alone know how to answer. Questions included, "Are you going to run it on a Windows or Linux server? What blog software will you use? Are you going to put it on the Emerson network? If so, how are you going to get the software set up? Emerson uses Oracle, but what does your blog software require? Will you run it within the VPN, or will you use some private set of accounts and passwords?"

And finally: "You want it WHEN? By early January!?? You've got to be kidding! This is early December, and the holidays are coming up. There's no way."

Dee, however, is not easily put off. As a salesperson, she believes that the sale starts when the customer says no. She brought that same attitude to this project, and she wasn't about to quit. Through professional acquaintances, she learned about Don Gray, a consultant who specializes in setting up blogs and similar sites.

When she contacted him, Don responded more positively. Even he, however, asked her questions that she couldn't understand.

Dee needed the knowledge in the three chapters in this part. She needed a basic understanding of hardware; she needed to know the basics of database processing; and she needed to know about computer networks, firewalls, and something called a VPN. Had she possessed this knowledge, it would have taken her half as much time as it did—or even less time than that. She also would have had much less worry, anxiety, and stress.

4 Hardware and Software

This could happen to you

Because of the short time available, Dee decided to hire Don Gray, a consultant who specializes in setting up systems like blogs. Don has many years of experience working with people like Dee, and he knew not to throw a barrage of technical questions at her. However, before he could help her develop a cost estimate, he needed answers to a few basic questions:

- **"Will you run your blog on an internal Emerson site or contract with an outside hosting service?"**
- **"Either way, will your site use a Windows or Linux server?"**
- **"What blog software do you want to use?"**
- **"How do you want to code your entries? Are you going to use OpenSource, or do you want me to build in an html editor in your blog software?"**
- **"What browsers do you want to support? IE? Firefox? Netscape? Others?"**
- **"Do you care if your blog doesn't render perfectly in all browsers?"**

Dee was in a bind. She didn't know the answers to these questions (she didn't even know what some of them meant—such as "render perfectly in all browsers"). She really had nowhere to turn. The people in her internal IT department had told her there was no way the project could be done on time, and they were dismissive of her requests for help—even just to answer the questions above. She could ask Don to help her with the answers, but he had a potential conflict of interest: As a consultant, he might want to pad his bill with features she didn't need. While Don's references indicated that this was unlikely, she was reluctant to ask him to answer the very questions he was asking her. In short, Dee needed the knowledge in this chapter.

As a future business professional, you may find yourself in the same spot. You may not be creating a blog, but you may be creating some other information system and need to answer questions similar to those Don posed. As you read this chapter, think about these kinds of questions, and focus on gaining a foundation in hardware and software terms and concepts. The discussion is not highly technical; it focuses on knowledge that a future manager will need.

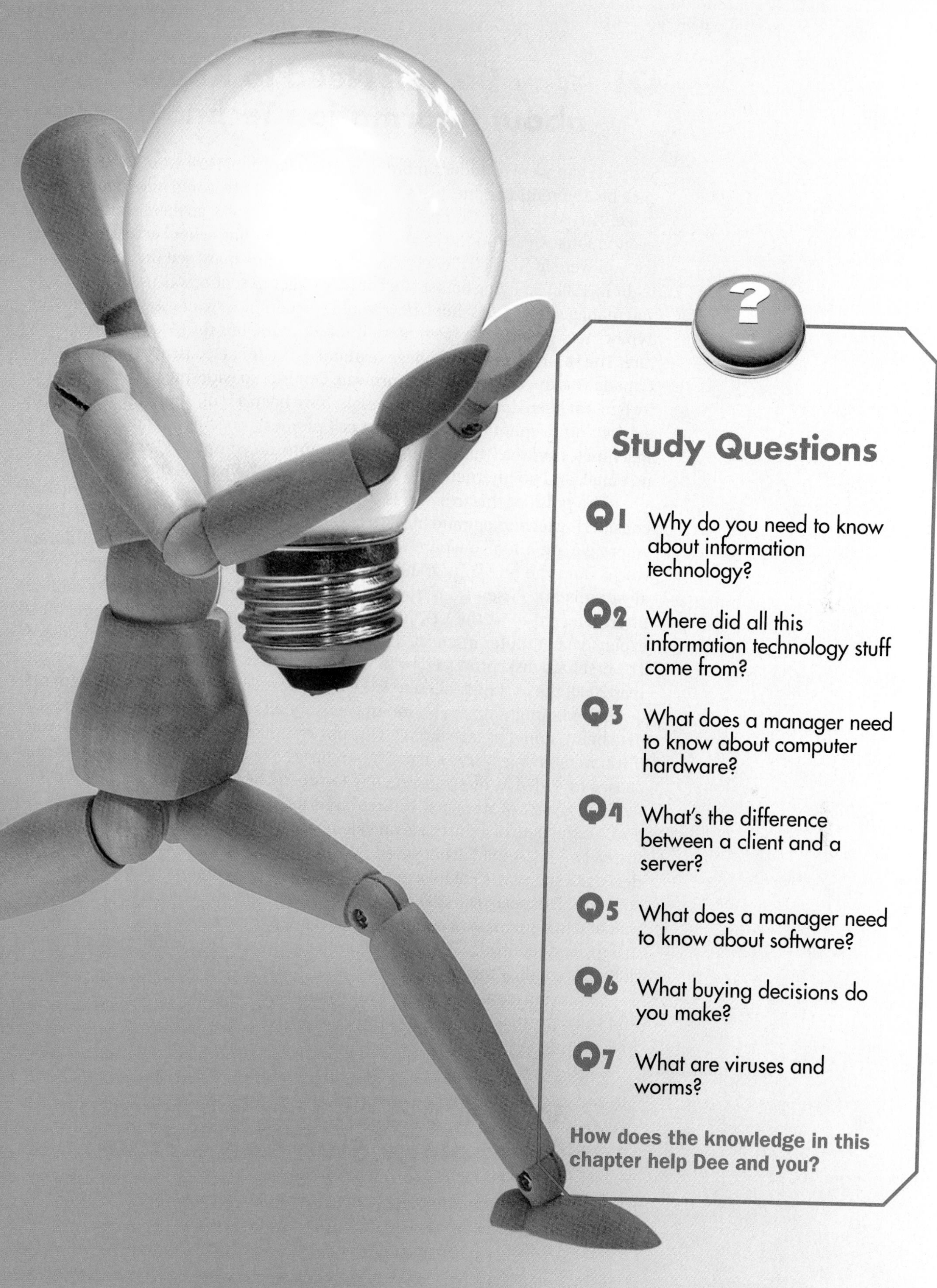
?
Study Questions
Q1 Why do you need to know about information technology?
Q2 Where did all this information technology stuff come from?
Q3 What does a manager need to know about computer hardware?
Q4 What's the difference between a client and a server?
Q5 What does a manager need to know about software?
Q6 What buying decisions do you make?
Q7 What are viruses and worms?
How does the knowledge in this chapter help Dee and you?

Q1 Why Do You Need to Know about Information Technology?

Suppose you were a student more than 100 years ago. How would your experience be different? For one, just getting to the university would have been a challenge. The Ford Motor Company sold its first car in 1903, so there wouldn't have been too many cars on the roads. If you were attending school across the country, you were in for a challenge. The Wright brothers managed the first powered flight in 1903. So flying across the country to get to school was not an option. If you managed to get to school, how would you complete your essay assignments? Typewriters would have been around for 20 years, but they were still relatively rare. The same was true of college textbooks. The first electrical lighting plant in Canada was opened in 1883 in Cornwall, Ontario, so widespread use of electricity had not been developed. There might have been a radio, but there was no television, no telephones (forget about cell phones), no shopping malls, no bank machines, no drive-thru fast food restaurants, no computers, no video games, no email, and no Internet. How did people survive? What did they do?

The point of this exercise is to draw your attention to the fact that when considering technology and how we use it, it is important to understand not only where we are but also where we have come from. You live in a very different world from the one your grandparents lived in. However, technology cannot always distance itself from its past. Take, for example, the year 2000 problem, often referred to as the Y2K problem. This problem was largely the result of expensive computer memory in the early days of computing. How expensive? The first hard disk, produced by IBM, had a cost of $10 000 per megabyte. (By the year 2000, the cost had fallen to less than 10 cents!) When computers were first developed, programmers had to make every effort to minimize the amount of data being stored to save money. One obvious place to save data was in the year. If you were saving the date of many purchases—say, for example, millions of purchases recorded at the Hudson's Bay Company in 1965—then you could eliminate quite a bit of storage if you removed the first two characters (19) from the year. So the date of a purchase on Valentine's Day 1965 would look like 02/14/65 instead of 02/14/1965. That saved money. But why is that a problem? It's no big deal until the year 1999 rolls around and you realize that you're using the same software. The next year (2000), the year would read 00! While it might not seem that bad to humans, to a computer that change could cause all sorts of problems in logic and reporting.[2] That's why companies around the world spent billions of dollars upgrading their systems for Y2K.

Knowing a small bit about information technology, including hardware and software, makes us more knowledgeable consumers of technology now and in the future.

Q2 Where Did All This Information Technology Stuff Come From?

The history of information technology is rich and recent. The first digital computing devices were invented in the 1940s. The first commercial computers were

2. You can read more about this at http://en.wikipedia.org/wiki/Y2K.

available in the 1950s, the first personal computers in the early 1980s, and the Internet came into wide use only in the 1990s. The section below provides a brief history of the development of the networked personal computer. The discussion is summarized in three points at the end of the section.

Early Computers: 1939–1952

The first patent on a digital computer was filed on June 26, 1947, by Eckert and Mauchly for developing the ENIAC computer.[3] Years later, the patent was overturned when a 1972 U.S. Supreme Court case (*Sperry Rand vs. Honeywell, 1973*) voided the ENIAC patent as a derivative of the Atanasoff-Berry Computer (ABC) conceived at Iowa State University before 1942.[4] See Figure 4-1.

Figure 4-1
The ENIAC Computer

Source: Collections of the University of Pennsylvania Archives.

The early computers were complex and expensive. A single user interacted with the computer, and only one program could run at a time. These computers were housed at universities and only a small number of people had access to them. These early machines were slowly improved and commercialized. The ENIAC, for example, was housed at the University of Pennsylvania and later gave rise to the Sperry-Rand Corp. The Mark I was developed jointly with Ferranti Ltd. at the University of Manchester in England. The first digital computer in Canada, the FERUT at the University of Toronto in 1952, was a copy of the Mark 1 and one of only a small number of digital computers in North America at the time.[5]

Mainframes: 1952–Present

Mainframes grew from the commercialization of early computers. **Mainframes** were the first digital computing machines used in business and government. The first-generation mainframes were based on vacuum tube technology such as the IBM 650. It cost between \$200 000 and \$400 000 and could add or subtract about 16 000 numbers per second. Second-generation mainframes introduced in the late 1950s used transistors, which made them smaller, easier to maintain, and more reliable. These first- and second-generation machines were often sold without software. The assumption was that companies themselves would develop the programs they wanted to use on the computer. See Figure 4-2.

Figure 4-2
The IBM 360

Source: Creative Commons Attribution 2.5. Photo by Ben Franske. www.creativecommons.org/licenses/by 3.0.

The third generation of mainframe machines introduced in the mid-1960s included operating systems and multiprocessing. This was a big step and these computers cost millions of dollars. The multiprocessing allowed for timesharing, where many users could share the main processor at the same time. Prior to multiprocessing, generally only one user could

[3] Read about the history of the ENIAC here: http://ei.cs.vt.edu/~history/ENIAC.Richey.HTML.

[4] Controversy remains regarding the first digital computer. You can read more about the ABC here: http://inventors.about.com/library/weekly/aa050898.htm.

[5] You can read more about the history of computing in Canada in the IEEE Annals of the *History of Computing* archive, Vol. 16, no. 2, June 1994.

interact with the computer at a time. Time sharing would eventually lead to more sophisticated networks among computers. These mainframes tended to be smaller than earlier models and were sometimes referred to as "mini-computers." This term is rarely used today. Mainframes have been a mainstay of business computing since the early 1960s, and models such as the IBM Z9[6] continue to be produced today. Contrary to popular opinion, a large amount of code running in larger organizations still rests on mainframe systems. Mainframes are designed for fast processing and massive storage, and for this reason they are likely to continue to be used far into the future as our need for information continues to grow.

Figure 4-3
The Altair 8800
Source: Photo by Michael Holley.

Microcomputers: 1975–Present

Early mainframes were relatively large machines. A typical second-generation mainframe would often include a central processing unit (one closet-sized machine), short-term memory (another closet), and long-term memory (several closets). People wanted something smaller. The microprocessor was developed in the early 1970s by Texas Instruments and Intel. It incorporated the central processing unit and some short-term memory into a single silicon "chip" using integrated circuits (ICs). The microprocessors were small and originally used in items such as handheld calculators. The microprocessors quickly became the critical piece in the development of the microcomputer.

The first **microcomputers,** like the MITS Altair 8800 (see Figure 4-3) and Datapoint 2200,[7] were developed in 1975. These early microcomputers often had no monitor and required users to develop their own programs. As the hardware technology developed, companies such as Microsoft wrote programming

THE FIRST VIDEO GAME

Steve Russell is credited with leading the team of 25-year-olds that produced what is often considered the world's first video game, called SpaceWar.[a] The game was conceived in 1961 by Wayne Witanen, J. Martin Graetz, and Steve Russell. The three unofficially formed the Hingham Institute Study Group on Space Warfare and, with inspiration provided by the novels *Skylark* and *Lensman* by Edward E. Smith, PhD, the group developed the concept. The game was developed in 1962 when Steve Russell was asked to create a demonstration program for the PDP-1, a mainframe computer developed by Digital Equipment Company (DEC).

In SpaceWar, two players go head-to-head. Each player controls a ship in combat; a sun is placed in the centre of the playing field. The sun exerts a force on all objects on the screen. Players manoeuvre with rockets and aim their torpedoes to blow up the other ship. While the program had little to do with any practical application, it was enormously popular and could apparently be found on almost all research computers in the United States throughout the 1960s.[b]

a. You can find more references about Spacewar at http://wheels.org/spacewar/index.html.
b. Source: http://inventors.about.com/library/weekly/aa090198.htm.

6. For more information, see www-03.ibm.com/systems/z/z9ec.
7. For more information, see www.islandnet.com/~kpolsson/comphist.

languages (BASIC) and operating systems (DOS) that could be used by microcomputers. By 1981, the microcomputer had developed enough for companies such as IBM, Apple, Compaq, and Texas Instruments to launch the personal computer (PC). These microcomputers had monitors, keyboards, portable floppy disks, word processors, spreadsheets, and other software. They were easier to use than mainframes and were immediately popular with many users. The PC revolution was born.

Networking Personal Computers: 1985–Present

Microcomputers were easy to use; however, they were largely stand-alone. Sharing data across two computers required saving data on a floppy drive and transferring the floppy drive to another machine. This was cumbersome. It also did not enable sharing of company data that was largely contained on mainframe systems. The next important development in computing was the development of local area networks.

Local area networks (LANs), exemplified by Ethernet, the most popular LAN,[8] provided the ability to hook many personal computers together. The LAN provided each computer with a specific address and then was able to deliver requests for data to appropriate addresses (see Chapter 6). The LAN revolutionized business computing by providing shared access to data, printers, and other peripheral devices. LANs normally served approximately 30 people; however, network technologies soon provided users to share access across different LANs.

The LAN revolution that occurred in the 1980s was followed in the 1990s with the commercialization of wide area networks (WANs). These networks, exemplified by the Internet, were originally developed in the late 1960s to hook together mainframe systems (stay tuned for more about WANs in Chapter 6). With the Internet came email, web browsing, and access to a worldwide network of computers often facilitated by mainframe computers. This is the technology we now live and work in.

Summary

What can we learn from this whirlwind technological tour? There are many things to learn, but three important lessons can be extracted from our discussion:

1. *Technology advances:* Information technology is continuously improving. This is exemplified by Moore's Law,[9] credited to Gordon Moore, a co-founder of Intel, who suggested that the number of transistors on a chip doubles about every 18 months. This rate of advancement has been maintained for almost three decades. As we learned earlier, some of these changes are sustaining and maintain the rate of improvement, while others are disruptive and cause rapid change. There are winners and losers when technology advances. Paying close attention to technological change may help you take better advantage of the changes coming your way.
2. *Small is powerful:* The history of computing can be viewed as an effort to make information technology small and powerful enough to be used almost anywhere. This trend is not likely to stop, as the advancement of

8. For more information, see www.cisco.com/univercd/cc/td/doc/cisintwk/ito_doc/ethernet.htm.
9. For more information, see www.intel.com/technology/mooreslaw/index.htm.

nanotechnology[10] proves. The difficulty with smaller and smaller machines remains in the ability to interface with the machines in a meaningful way.

3. *The network is the thing:* The value of information technology can be measured not only in the power of the processor, but also in the power of the network that can be accessed through the machine. All computing machines have inevitably moved toward networks for communication and collaboration. The interesting question to ponder is, After microcomputers and the Internet, what's next?

Q3 What Does a Manager Need to Know about Computer Hardware?

As discussed in the five-component framework, **hardware** consists of electronic components and related gadgetry that input, process, output, and store data according to instructions encoded in computer programs or software. The essential knowledge you need in order to be an effective manager and consumer of computer hardware is summarized in Figure 4-4.

One important idea that we will consider only briefly here is the notion of **e-cycling**, which is the recycling of electronic hardware. Managers are finding that companies cannot dispose of their computers and electronic equipment as they would their other waste. While there are no federal standards for e-cycling, many municipalities are working to address the issue. For example, a drive through e-cycling depot was opened in the old Currie Barracks in southwest Calgary. Companies such as Ecycling Canada (www.ecyclingcanada.com) have started to market their services to deal more appropriately with electronic waste. This issue will become increasingly important for managers to consider.

Students vary in the hardware knowledge they bring to this class. If you already know the terms in this grid, skip to the next question on page 77: "What is the difference between a client and a server?"

Figure 4-4
Input, Process, Output, and Storage Hardware

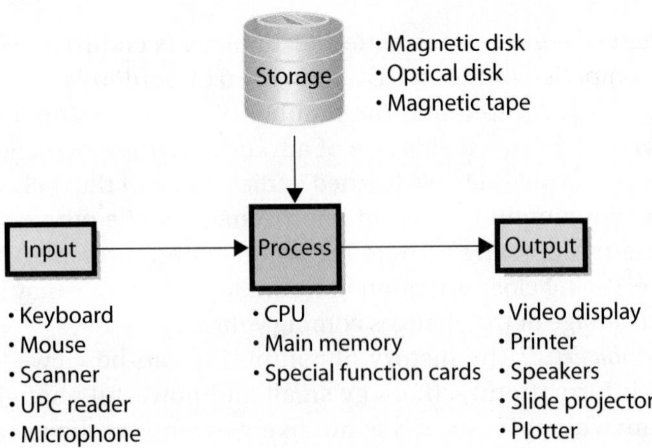

10. Learn more about nanotechnology at http://science.howstuffworks.com/nanotechnology.htm.

Input, Processing, Output, and Storage Hardware

Figure 4-4 shows the components of a generic computer. Notice that basic hardware categories are input, process, output, and storage. The table in Figure 4-5 provides a summary of this diagram.

As shown in Figure 4-4, typical **input hardware** devices are the keyboard, mouse, document scanners, and barcode (universal product code) scanners like those used in grocery stores. Microphones also are input devices; with tablet PCs, human handwriting can be input as well. Older input devices include magnetic-ink readers (used for reading the ink on the bottom of cheques) and scanners like the Scantron test scanner shown in Figure 4-6. *Processing devices* include the **central processing unit (CPU),** which is sometimes called the "brain" of the computer. Although the design of the CPU has nothing in common with the anatomy of animal brains, this description is helpful because the CPU does have the "smarts" of the machine. The CPU selects instructions, processes them, performs arithmetic and logical comparisons, and stores results of operations in memory. CPUs vary in speed, function, and cost. Hardware vendors such

Figure 4-5
What a Manager Needs to Know about Hardware

Component	Performance Factors	Beneficial for:	Example Application
CPU and data bus	• CPU speed • Cache memory • Data bus speed • Data bus width	• Fast processing of data once the data reside in main memory	• Repetitive calculations of formulas in a complicated spreadsheet • Manipulation of large picture images
Main memory	• Size • Speed	• Holding multiple programs at one time • Processing very large amounts of data	• Running Excel, Word, Paint Shop Pro, Adobe Acrobat, several websites, and email while processing large files in memory and viewing video clips • 3D games
Magnetic disk	• Size • Channel type and speed • Rotational speed • Seek time	• Storing many large programs • Storing many large files • Swapping files in and out of memory	• Store detailed maps of provinces and territories in Canada • Large data downloads from organizational servers • Partly compensate for too little main memory
Optical disk—CD	• Up to 700 MB • CD-ROM • CD-R (recordable) • CD-RW (rewritable)	• Reading CDs • Writable media can be used to back up files	• Install new programs • Play and record music • CD being replaced by DVD • Back up data
Optical disk—DVD	• Up to 4.7 GB • DVD-ROM • DVD-R (recordable) • DVD-RW (rewritable)	• Process both DVDs and CDs • Writable media can be used to back up files	• Install new programs • Play and record music • Play and record movies • Back up data
Monitor—CRT	• Viewing size • Dot pitch • Optimal resolution • Special memory?	• Limited budgets	• Nongraphic applications, such as word processing • Less-used computers
Monitor—LCD	• Viewing size • Pixel pitch • Optimal resolution • Special memory?	• Crowded workspaces • When brighter, sharper images are needed	• More than one monitor in use • Lots of graphics to be processed • Continual use

Figure 4-6
Scantron Scanner

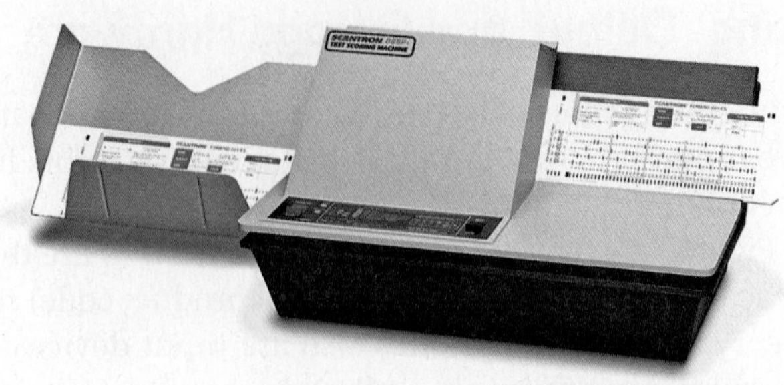

as Intel, Advanced Micro Devices, and National Semiconductor continually improve CPU speed and capabilities while reducing CPU costs (as discussed under Moore's Law in Chapter 1). Whether you or your department need the latest, greatest CPU depends on the nature of your work. The CPU works in conjunction with **main memory.** The CPU reads data and instructions from memory, and it stores results of computations in main memory. We will describe the relationship between the CPU and main memory later in the chapter. Finally, computers also can have **special function cards** (see Figure 4-7) that can be added to the computer to augment the computer's basic capabilities. A common example is a video card that provides enhanced clarity and refresh speed for the computer's video display. **Output hardware** consists of video displays, printers, audio speakers, overhead projectors, and other special-purpose devices, such as large flatbed plotters. **Storage hardware** saves data and programs. Magnetic disk is by far the most common storage device, although optical disks such as CDs and DVDs are also popular. In large corporate data centres, data are sometimes stored on magnetic tape.

Computer Data

Before we can further describe hardware, we need to define several important terms. We begin with binary digits.

Binary Digits

Computers represent data using **binary digits**, called **bits.** A bit is either a zero or a one. Bits are used for computer data because they are easy to represent physically, as illustrated in Figure 4-8. A switch can be either closed or open. A computer can be designed so that an open switch represents zero and a closed switch represents one. Or the orientation of a magnetic field can represent a bit; magnetism in one direction represents a zero, magnetism in the opposite direction represents a one. Or, for optical media, small pits are burned onto the sur-

Figure 4-7
Special Function Card

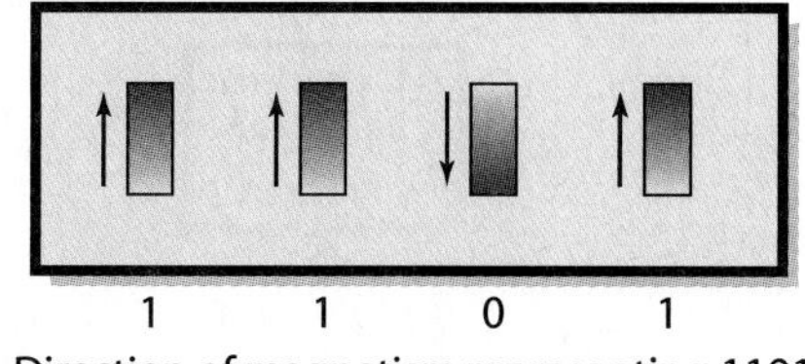

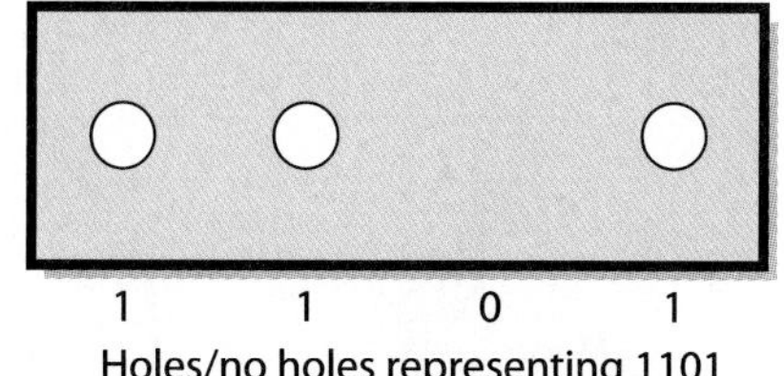

Figure 4-8
Bits Are Easy to Represent Physically

face of the disk so that they will reflect light. In a given spot, a reflection means a one; no reflection means a zero.

Sizing Computer Data

All computer data are represented by bits. The data can be numbers, characters, currency amounts, photos, recordings, or whatever. All are simply a string of bits.

For reasons that interest many but are irrelevant for future managers, bits are grouped into 8-bit chunks called **bytes.** For character data, such as the letters in a person's name, one character will fit into one byte. Thus, when you read a specification that a computing device has 100 million bytes of memory, you know that the device could hold up to 100 million characters.Bytes are used to measure sizes of non-character data as well. Someone might say, for example, that a given picture is 100 000 bytes in size. This statement means the length of the bit string that represents the picture is 100 000 bytes or 800 000 bits (because there are 8 bits per byte). The specifications for the size of main memory, disk, and other computer devices are expressed in bytes. Figure 4-9 shows the set of abbreviations that are used to represent data-storage capacity. A **kilobyte (K)** is a collection of 1024 bytes. A **megabyte** (**MB**) is 1024K. A **gigabyte** (**GB**) is 1024MB, and a **terabyte** (**TB**) is 1024GB.

Sometimes you will see these definitions simplified as 1K equals 1000 bytes and 1MB equals 1000K. Such simplifications are incorrect, but they do ease the math. Also, disk and computer manufacturers have an incentive to propagate this misconception. If a disk maker defines 1MB to be 1 million bytes—and not the correct 1024K—the manufacturer can use its own definition of MB when specifying drive capacities. A buyer may think that a disk advertised as 100MB has space for 100 × 1024K bytes, but in truth the drive will have space for only 100 × 1 000 000 bytes. Normally the distinction is not too important, but be aware of the two possible interpretations of these abbreviations.

In 293 Words, How Does a Computer Work?

Figure 4-10 shows a snapshot of a computer in use. The CPU (central processing unit) is the major actor. To run a program or process data, the CPU must first

Term	Definition	Abbreviation
Byte	Number of bits to represent one character	
Kilobyte	1024 bytes	K
Megabyte	1024 K = 1 048 576 bytes	MB
Gigabyte	1024 MB = 1 073 741 824 bytes	GB
Terabyte	1024 GB = 1 099 511 627 776 bytes	TB

Figure 4-9
Important Storage-Capacity Terminology

Figure 4-10
Computer Components

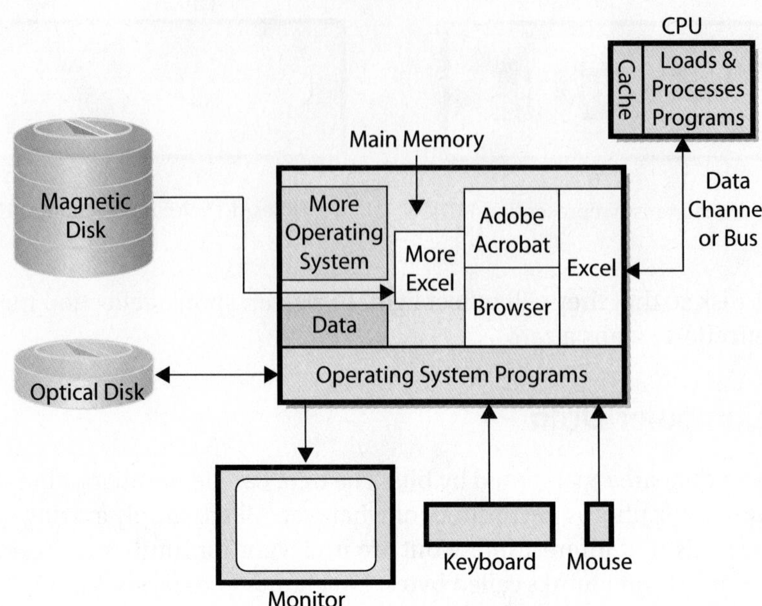

transfer the program or data from disk to *main memory*. Then, to execute an instruction, it moves the instruction from main memory into the CPU via the **data channel** or **bus**. The CPU has a small amount of very fast memory called a **cache**. The CPU keeps frequently used instructions in the cache. Having a large cache makes the computer faster, but cache is expensive.

Main memory of the computer in Figure 4-10 contains program instructions for Excel, Acrobat, and a browser (Internet Explorer or Firefox). It also contains instructions for the **operating system (OS),** which is a program that controls the computer's resources as well as a block of data. Main memory is too small to hold all the programs and data that a user may want to process. For example, no personal computer has enough memory to hold all the code in Microsoft Word, Excel, and Access. Consequently, the CPU loads programs into memory in chunks. In Figure 4-10, one portion of Excel was loaded into memory. When the user requested additional processing (say, to sort the spreadsheet), the CPU loaded another piece of Excel. If the user opens another program (say, Word) or needs to load more data (say, a picture), the operating system will direct the CPU to attempt to place the new program or data into unused memory. If there is not enough memory it will remove something, perhaps the block of memory labelled more Excel, and then it will place the just-requested program or data into the vacated space. This process is called **memory swapping.**

Why Does a Manager Care How a Computer Works?

You can order computers with varying sizes of main memory. An employee who runs only one program at a time and who processes small amounts of data requires very little memory—256K would be just fine. On the other hand, an employee who processes many programs at the same time (say, Word, Excel, Firefox, Access, Acrobat, and other programs) or an employee who processes very large files (pictures, movies, or sound files) needs lots of main memory, one or two megabytes. If that employee's computer has too little memory, then the computer will constantly be swapping memory, and it will be slow. (This means, by the way, that if your computer is slow and you have many programs open, you can likely improve performance by closing one or more programs.) Depending on your computer and the amount of memory it has, you might also be able to add more memory to it.

You can also purchase computers with CPUs of different speeds. CPU speed is expressed in cycles called *hertz*. In 2007, the CPU of a fast personal computer had a speed of 3.0 gigahertz (GHz); a slow computer has a speed of less than 1 GHz. As predicted by Moore's Law, CPU speeds continually increase. An employee who does only simple tasks such as word processing does not need a fast CPU. On the other hand, an employee who processes large, complicated spreadsheets or who manipulates large database files or edits large picture, sound, or movie files needs a very fast CPU—say, 3 GHz or more. One last comment: The cache and main memory are **volatile,** meaning their contents are lost when power is off. Magnetic disk and optical disk are **nonvolatile,** meaning their contents survive when power is off. If you suddenly lose power, the contents of unsaved memory—say, documents that have been altered—will be lost. It is a good idea to get into the habit of frequently saving documents or files that you are changing.

Q4 What Is the Difference between a Client and a Server?

Before we can discuss computer software, you need to understand the difference between a client and a server. Figure 4-11 shows the environment of the typical computer user. Users employ **client** computers for word processing, spreadsheets, database access, and so forth. Most client computers have software that

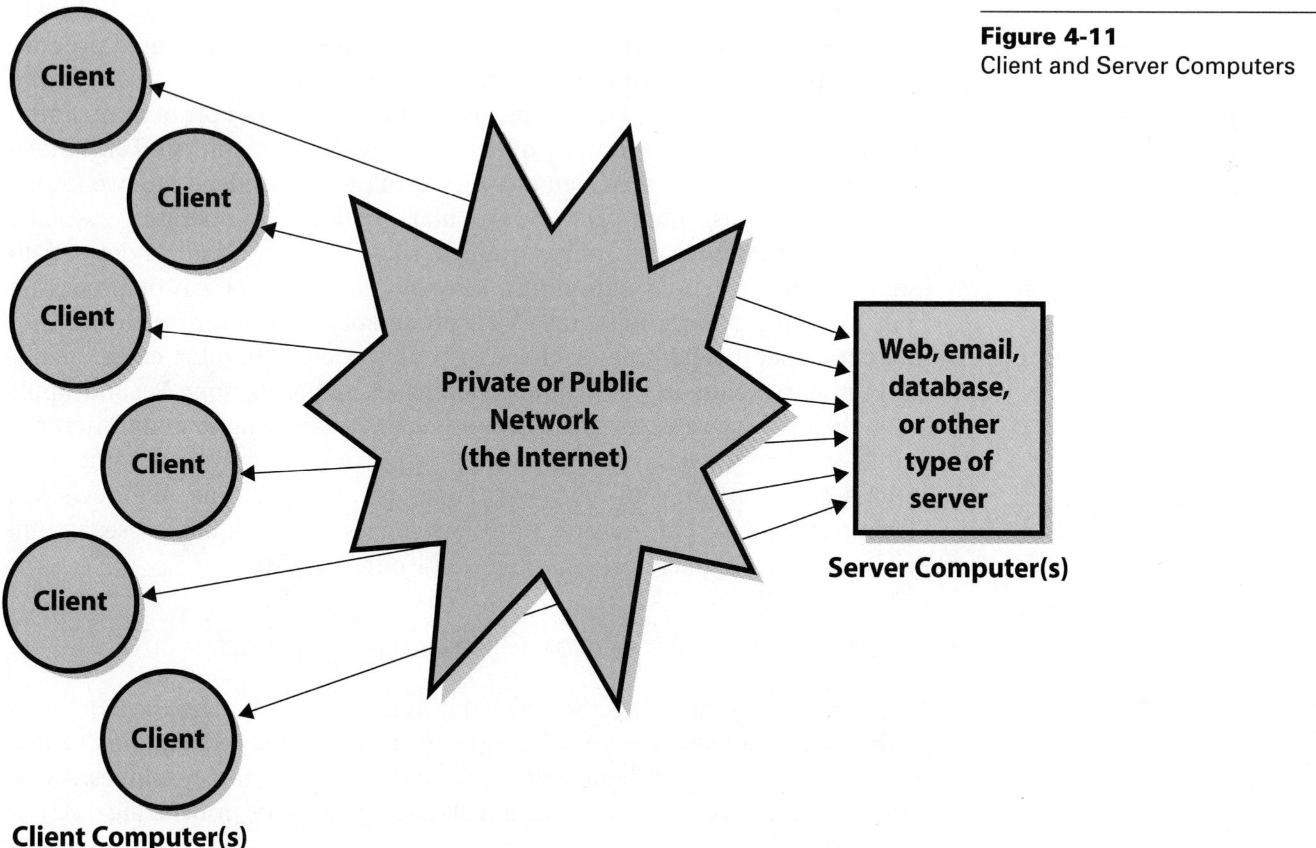

Figure 4-11
Client and Server Computers

enables them to connect to a network. It could be a private network at their company or school, or it could be the Internet, a public network. (We will discuss networks and related matters in Chapter 6. Just wait!)

Servers, as their name implies, provide some service to client computers. File servers allow clients to share files. Database servers provide access to data for clients and web servers provide Internet access to clients. Dee will use a server to run her blog. As you might expect, server computers often need to be faster, larger, and more powerful than client computers. Servers usually have very simple video displays, and some servers have no display at all because they are accessed only from another computer via the network. For large commerce sites such as Amazon.ca, the server is actually a large collection of computers that coordinate all activities (called a **server farm**). (By the way, the phrase *coordinate all activities* hides an incredibly sophisticated and fascinating technology dance: hundreds, possibly thousands, of transactions coming and going per minute as well as dozens of computers handing off partially completed transactions to one another, keeping track of data that has been partially changed, picking up the pieces when one computer fails—all in an eye-blink, with the user never needing to know any part of the miracle underway. It's absolutely incredible engineering!)

Q5 What Does a Manager Need to Know about Software?

The essential knowledge that you need to know about computer software is summarized in Figure 4-12. If you already possess this knowledge, skip to the next question—"What buying decisions do you make?"—on page 83.

Consider the two fundamental types of software. We have already spoken briefly about the *operating system,* which is a large and complicated program that controls the computer's resources, but there is also *application software,* which are programs that perform specific user tasks. An example of an operating system is Windows, and examples of applications are Microsoft Word and Oracle Customer Relationship Management. Also, you need to understand two important software constraints. First, a particular version of an operating system is written for a particular type of hardware. In some cases, such as Windows, there is only one commercially important version. Windows works only on processors from Intel and companies that make processors that conform to the Intel **instruction set** (the commands that a CPU can process). In other cases, such as Linux, many versions exist for many different sets of instructions. Second, application programs are written to use a particular operating system. Microsoft Access, for example, will run only on the Windows operating system. Some applications come in multiple versions. There are, for example, Windows and Macintosh versions of Microsoft Word. But unless informed otherwise, assume that a particular application runs on just one operating system.

What Are the Four Major Operating Systems?

An operating system (OS) is the heart of a computer system and the IS must be loaded before a user can interact with the system. The OS responds to user requests by allocating and managing tasks and internal system resources. An OS performs such tasks as controlling and allocating memory, prioritizing user and

Category	Operating System (OS)	Instruction Set	Common Applications	Typical User
Client	Windows	Intel	Microsoft Office: Word, Excel, Access, PowerPoint, many other applications	Business. Home.
	Mac OS (pre-2006)	Power PC	Macintosh applications plus Word and Excel	Graphic artists. Arts community.
	Mac OS (post-2006)	Intel	Macintosh applications plus Word and Excel. Can also run Windows on Macintosh hardware.	Graphic artists. Arts community.
	Unix	Sun and others	Engineering, computer-assisted design, architecture	Difficult for the typical client, but popular with some engineers and computer scientists.
	Linux	Just about anything	Open Office (Microsoft Office look-alike)	Rare—used where budget is very limited.
Server	Windows	Intel	Windows server applications	Business with commitment to Microsoft.
	Unix	Sun and others	Unix server applications	Fading...Linux taking its market.
	Linux	Just about anything	Linux & Unix server applications	Very popular—promulgated by IBM.

Figure 4-12
What a Manager Needs to Know about Software

system requests, controlling input and output devices (like the mouse or printers), and facilitating networking and managing the filing systems. Operating systems come with a user interface for managing the operating system, usually a graphical user interface. The operating system serves as a basic platform for all the other application software loaded into the system. The four major operating systems listed in Figure 4-12—Windows, Mac OS, Unix, and Linux—are very important. We describe them in the following sections.

Windows

For business users, the most important operating system is Microsoft **Windows** (the current version at the time of publication is Windows Vista). Some version of Windows resides on more than 85 percent of the world's desktops, and considering just business users, the figure is more than 95 percent. There are many different versions of Windows; some versions run on user computers and some support server computers for websites, email, and other processes (discussed in Chapter 6). Windows runs the Intel instruction set.[11]

Mac OS

Apple Computer, Inc. developed its own operating system for the Macintosh, **Mac OS**. The current version is Mac OS X Leopard. Macintosh computers are used primarily by graphic artists and workers in the arts community. Mac OS was designed originally to run the line of CPU processors from Motorola. In 1994, Mac OS switched to the PowerPC processor line from IBM. As of 2006, Macintosh computers are available for both PowerPC and Intel CPUs. A Macintosh with an Intel processor is able to run both Windows and the Mac OS.

11. There are versions of Windows for other instruction sets, but they are unimportant for our purposes here.

Most people would agree that Apple has led the way in developing easy-to-use interfaces. Certainly, many innovative design ideas have first appeared in a Macintosh and then later been added, in one form or another, to Windows.

Unix

Unix is an operating system that was developed at Bell Labs in the 1970s. It has been the workhorse of the scientific and engineering communities since then. Unix is generally regarded as being more difficult to use than either Windows or the Macintosh. Many Unix users know and employ an arcane language for manipulating files and data. However, once they surmount the rather steep learning curve, most Unix users swear by the system. Sun Microsystems and other vendors of computers for scientific and engineering applications are the major proponents of Unix. In general, Unix is not for the business user.

Linux

Linux is a version of Unix that was developed by the **open-source community**. Open source refers to software in which the source code, the actual program code, is published and therefore open for others to view. This community is a loosely coupled group of programmers who mostly volunteer their time to contribute code to develop and maintain Linux. The open-source community owns Linux, and there is no fee to use it. Linux can run on client computers, but it is most frequently used for servers, particularly web servers.

IBM is the primary corporate proponent of Linux. Although IBM does not own Linux, IBM has developed many business systems solutions that use Linux. By using Linux, IBM does not have to pay a licence fee to Microsoft or another vendor. Apache web server (www.apache.org) is another example of widely used open source software that is used in a majority of web servers around the world. Open source software has had a considerable effect on the software industry and will continue to play an important role in the future of software development.

Own versus License

When you buy a computer program, you are not actually buying that program. Instead, you are buying a **licence** to use that program. For example, when you buy Windows, Microsoft is selling you the right to use Windows. Microsoft continues to own the Windows program.

In the case of Linux, no company can sell you a licence to use it. It is owned by the open-source community, which states that Linux has no licence fee (with certain reasonable restrictions). Companies such as IBM and smaller companies such as RedHat can make money by supporting Linux, but no company makes money selling Linux licences.

What Types of Applications Exist, and How Do Organizations Obtain Them?

Application software consists of programs that perform a business function. Some application programs are general purpose, such as Excel or Word. Other application programs are specific. QuickBooks, for example, is an application program that provides general ledger and other accounting functions. We begin by describing categories of application programs and then move on to describe sources for them.

What Categories of Application Programs Exist?

Horizontal-market application software provides capabilities common across all organizations and industries. Word processors, graphics programs, spreadsheets, and presentation programs are all horizontal-market application software. Examples of such software are Microsoft Word, Excel, and PowerPoint. Examples from other vendors are Adobe Acrobat, Photoshop, and PageMaker and Jasc Corporation's Paint Shop Pro. These applications are used in a wide variety of businesses, across all industries. They are purchased off-the-shelf, and little customization of features is necessary (or possible). **Vertical-market application** software serves the needs of a specific industry. Examples of such programs are those used by dental offices to schedule appointments and bill patients, those used by auto mechanics to keep track of customer data and customers' automobile repairs, and those used by parts warehouses to track inventory, purchases, and sales. Vertical applications can usually be altered or customized. Typically, the company that sold the application software will provide such services or offer referrals to qualified consultants who can provide this service. **One-of-a-kind application** software is developed for a specific, unique need. The IRS develops such software, for example, because it has needs that no other organization has. Some application software does not neatly fit into the horizontal or vertical category. For example, customer relationship management (CRM) software is a horizontal application because every business has customers. But it usually needs to be customized to the requirements of businesses in a particular industry, and so it is also akin to vertical market software. You will learn about other examples of such dual-category software in Chapter 7 when we discuss enterprise resource planning (ERP), and other such applications. In this text, we will consider such applications to be vertical market applications, even though they do not fit perfectly into this category.

What Is Firmware?

Firmware is computer software that is installed into devices like computers, printers, print servers, and various types of communication devices. The software is coded just like other software, but it is installed into special, read-only memory of the printer or other device. In this way, the program becomes part of the device's memory; it is as if the program's logic is designed into the device's circuitry. Users do not need to load firmware into the device's memory. Firmware is not volatile, as it exists even when the power is turned off.

The **Basic Input/Output System (BIOS)** is an important piece of firmware. BIOS is used when a computer is initially booted up. BIOS is required because all volatile memory was lost when the computer was shut down. The only way to get the computer running again is to provide a set of instructions in non-volatile read-only memory (ROM). The first thing the computer does when starting up is to load BIOS from ROM and run through the commands provided by the firmware. BIOS checks to make sure that the memory and input devices are functional. Once these are working, the operating system will be loaded. Firmware can be changed or upgraded, but this is normally a task for IS professionals. The task is easy, but it requires knowledge of special programs and techniques that most business users choose not to learn.

What Is the Difference between a Thin and Thick Client?

When you use applications such as Word, Excel, or Acrobat, those programs run only on your computer. You need not be connected to the Internet or any other network for them to run.

Other applications, however, require code on both the client and the server. Email is a good example. When you send email, you run a client program such as Microsoft Outlook on your computer, and it connects over the Internet or a private network to mail server software on a server. Similarly, when you access a website, you run a browser (client software) on your computer that connects over a network to web server software on a server. An application that requires nothing more than a browser on the client is called a **thin client.** An application such as Microsoft Outlook that requires programs other than a browser on the user's computer is called a **thick client.** The terms *thin* and *thick* refer to the amount of code that must run on the client computer. All other things being equal, thin client applications are preferred to thick client applications because they do not require the installation and administration of client software. On the other hand, the thick client application may provide features and functions that more than compensate for the expense and administration of its installation. In addition, a thick client does not need access to the network to run. So if your network goes down, the thick client will still be available, whereas your thin client will be unable to run software.

Figure 4-13
Thin and Thick Clients

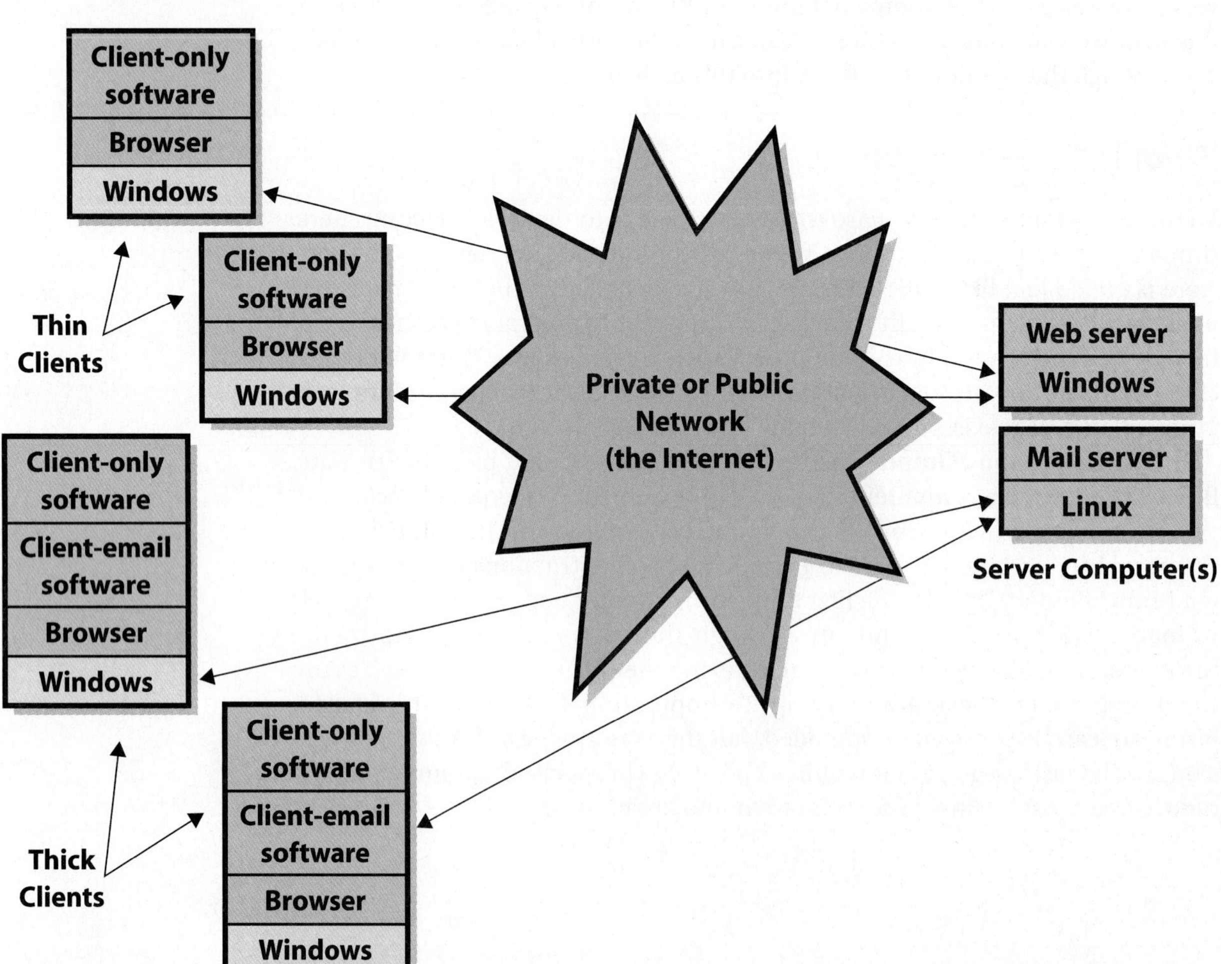

Client and server computers can run different operating systems. Many organizations have standardized on Windows for their clients and Linux for their servers. Figure 4-13 shows an example. Two thin clients are connecting via browsers to a web server that is running Windows. Two thick clients are connecting via an email client to an email server that is running Linux. Those two clients are thick because they have client email software installed.

Over the course of your career, application software, hardware, and firmware will change, sometimes rapidly. The Exercise "Keeping Up to Speed" at the end of this chapter challenges you to *choose* a strategy for addressing this change.

Q6 What Buying Decisions Do You Make?

In general, most business professionals have some role in the specification of the client hardware and software they use. Business managers also play a role in the specification of client hardware and software for employees whom they manage. The particular role depends on the policy manager's organization. Large organizations will have an IS department that is likely to set standards for client hardware and software. You will learn more about such standards in Chapter 11.

In medium to small organizations, policies are often less formal, and managers will need to take an active role in setting the specifications for their own and their employees' computers. Figure 4-14 lists the major criteria for both hardware and software.

Except in rare circumstances, medium to small organizations will usually standardize on a single client operating system because the costs of supporting more than one are unjustifiable. Most organizations choose Windows clients. Some arts and design businesses standardize on the Macintosh, and some engineering firms standardize on Unix. Organizations that have limited budgets

Category	Hardware	Software
Client	Specify: • CPU speed • Size of main memory • Size of magnetic disk • CD or DVD and type • Monitor type and size	Specify: • Windows, Mac, or Linux OS. May be dictated by organizational standard. • PC applications such as Microsoft Office Adobe Acrobat, Photoshop, Paint Shop Pro. may be dictated by organizational standard. • Browser such as Internet Explorer, FireFox, or Netscape Navigator. • Requirements for the client side of client-server applications. • Need for thin or thick client.
Server	In most cases, a business manager has no role in the specification of server hardware (except possibly a budgetary one).	• Specify requirements for the server side of client-server applications. • Work with technical personnel to test and accept software.

Figure 4-14
A Business Manager's Role in Hardware and Software Specifications

might choose to use Linux on the clients, but this is relatively rare. Managers and their employees may have a role in specifying horizontal application software such as Microsoft Office or other software appropriate for their operating systems. They will also have an important role in specifying requirements for vertical market or custom applications. We will say more about this role in Chapter 10. Concerning the server, a business manager typically has no role in the specification of server hardware, other than possibly approving the budget. Instead, technical personnel make such decisions. A business manager and those who will be the clients of a client-server application specify the requirements for vertical and custom-server software. They will also work with technical personnel to test and accept that software. In addition, business managers may be called on to provide unusual support involving IS, as *MIS in Use 4* describes.

Q7 What Are Viruses and Worms?

A **virus** is a computer program that replicates itself. Unchecked replication is like computer cancer; ultimately, the virus consumes the computer's resources. Furthermore, many viruses also take unwanted and harmful actions.

The program code that causes unwanted activity is called the **payload.** The payload can delete programs or data—or, even worse, modify data in undetected ways. Imagine the impact of a virus that changed the credit rating of all customers. Some viruses publish data in harmful ways—for example, sending out files of credit card data to unauthorized sites.

Macro viruses attach themselves to Word, Excel, or other types of documents. When the infected document is opened, the virus places itself in the startup files of the application. After that, the virus infects every file that the application creates or processes. A **worm** is a virus that propagates using the Internet or other computer network. Worms spread faster than other virus types because they are specifically programmed to spread. Unlike non-worm viruses, which must wait for the user to share a file with a second computer, worms actively use the network to spread. Sometimes, worms so choke a network that it becomes unusable. In 2003, the Slammer worm clogged the Internet and caused Bank of America ATM machines and the information systems of hundreds of other organizations to fail. Slammer operated so fast that 90 percent of the vulnerable machines were infected within 10 minutes. You can take several measures to prevent viruses. First, most viruses take advantage of security holes in computer programs. As vendors find these holes, they create program modifications, called **patches,** that fix the problem. To keep from getting a virus, check Microsoft and other vendor sites for patches frequently and apply them immediately. A patch for the Slammer worm was available from Microsoft several months before Slammer occurred. The worm did not infect any site that had applied the patch. When you think about it, it is not surprising that the problem occurred some time after the patch appeared. As soon as a vendor publishes the problem and the patch, every computer criminal in the world can learn about the hole. Virus developers can then write code to exploit the hole, and any machine that does not apply the patch is then doubly vulnerable. Therefore, the first rule in preventing viruses is to find and apply patches to the operating system and to applications. Other prevention steps are as follows:

- Never download files, programs, or attachments from unknown websites.
- Do not open attachments to emails from strangers.

Network Effects, Increasing Returns, and Lock In

How do the choices made by others affect your own options, and how should you evaluate new software? Those were two of the questions facing Brent North, managing partner of Stantec's Vancouver office, as he considered the use of a new three-dimensional drafting tool.

Founded in 1954, Stantec was an architectural and engineering firm that had evolved from a single-person consultancy through a combination of acquisitions and natural growth into a publicly traded corporation with more than 100 offices worldwide and 6500 employees. The Vancouver office, which had recently been acquired by Stantec, had approximately 125 professional staff and was largely focused on architecture.

Architecture had changed a great deal in 50 years. While grounded in creativity and design, architects today were far more proficient in computer technology; although some of Stantec's senior architects still looked fondly upon the slide rules and Mylar plastic that had been used to create early original designs, modern-day architects were far more likely to turn to their computers and use computer-assisted design, manufacturing, or engineering tools (CAD, CAM, CAE). There was a large and growing market for these products, and numerous suppliers delivered a variety of tools. However, in much the same way as in other software markets, it seemed that one or two suppliers had the majority market share and the other products occupied niches that, while perhaps important, lacked widespread adoption. For example, CATIA (Computer Aided Three Dimensional Interactive Application), from Dassault Systems, was widely used in manufacturing at Chrysler, General Electric, and Airbus (and had been used by Frank Gehry at the Guggenheim Museum in Bilbao, Spain).

Several years ago, Stantec had adopted AutoCAD® by Autodesk. Essentially a *de facto* standard, AutoCAD had approximately 80-percent adoption among architectural firms. Virtually all new architects had been taught how to use it while in university, and provided they were using the same version, cooperating firms working on large projects could share and transfer files knowing that they were compatible and interchangeable.

Although Brent was generally satisfied with Stantec's existing software tools, he had recently become aware of a product with features and capabilities that he thought could change the way Stantec competed. What concerned Brent, however, was the level of training required to make the change and the advantages of remaining with the industry standard. Not only would the new product require education and adjustment among the architects, but it was also incompatible with AutoCAD. While it could open files created by AutoCAD, once-processed files that it created could not be used by AutoCAD. This meant that if he brought the new product in for a trial he would no longer be able to easily cooperate with other firms on joint projects and, perhaps more importantly, it could reduce the level of cooperation and sharing within the firm. At the same time, he knew that pushed to the limit this line of thinking would keep Stantec hostage and could prevent all change. Was it worthwhile considering a new and incompatible product—and if he brought it in for a trial, how should he proceed?

Source: Stantec. Used with permission.

Questions

1. How do the challenges faced by Stantec differ from those faced by other industries? (*Hint:* Think about sharing files among students for group projects.)
2. What are the implications of this case for companies that develop new software tools? How could adoption barriers be reduced? (*Hint:* Think of "disruptive" technologies.)
3. Are there any examples of "inferior" technologies that have achieved "lock in" or would be hard to improve? (*Hint:* You probably have used one already today.)
4. How do the ideas of "switching costs" and "networks effects" relate to high technology, or do they exist in other industries? (*Hint:* Consider the railroad industry, for example.)
5. How should new software be evaluated? How important is market share? Are these factors more or less important to smaller firms?

- Do not open unexpected attachments to emails, even from known sources.
- Do not rely on file extensions. A file marked MyPicture.jpg is normally a picture (because of the .jpg file extension). For a variety of reasons, however, this file may be something else—a virus.
- Companies such as Symantec, Sophos, McAfee, Norton, and others license products that detect and possibly eliminate viruses. Such products can operate in proactive mode by checking attachments as you receive them. They can also operate retroactively by checking memory and disk drives for the presence of viral code. You should run a retroactive antivirus program at regular intervals—at least once a week.

Such **antivirus programs** search the computer's memory and disk for known viruses. Obviously, if a virus is unknown to the antivirus software, then that virus will remain undetected. You should periodically obtain updates for the latest virus patterns from the vendor who produces the antivirus product. Additionally, realize that even though you use antivirus software you are still vulnerable to viruses that are unknown to the virus detection company. Now for the ugly news: What do you do if you have a virus? Most antivirus products include programs for removing viruses. If you have a virus, you can follow the instructions provided by that software to remove it. However, it is possible that the virus may have mutated into a different form. If so, then the antivirus product will not see the mutated version, and it will remain on your computer. Unfortunately, the only sure way to eliminate a virus is to delete everything on your magnetic disk by reformatting it. Then you must reinstall the operating system and all applications from known, clean sources (e.g., the original CD from the vendor). Finally, one by one, you must reload data files that you know are free of the virus. This is a laborious and time-consuming process, and it assumes that you have all your data files backed up. Because of the time and expense involved, few organizations go through this process. However, reformatting the disk is the only sure way of removing a virus. Viruses are expensive. To protect your organization, you should ensure that procedures exist to install patches as soon as possible. Also, every computer should have and use a copy of an antivirus program. You and your organization cannot afford not to take these precautions. We will discuss other problematic programs, such as spyware, in more detail in Chapter 12.

Figure 4-15
Stantec Logo

How does the knowledge in this chapter help Dee and you?

Dee has been asked to develop a plan for launching a blog to support her salespeople. The information in this chapter is a good start for Dee in developing this plan. First, this chapter suggests that Dee will need to consider both hardware and software issues related to the blog. She will also need to make sure that access to the blog will be secure within the Emerson network. You will learn more about that in Chapter 6. After you read Chapter 11, you'll know more about how information systems are acquired, and some of the challenges of running this type of information technology project. You will learn in Chapter 10 why the IT department may not be as excited about supporting the blog as Dee originally intended. Dee is going to have a battle here, and she does not yet know it. Some additional information would be useful before she gets fully engaged in the project.

While you may not intend to become an MIS major, it is safe to say that sometime in your career you will find yourself in a situation similar to the one Dee finds herself in. Your best defence in this situation is to have basic information about how information systems work, and some knowledge about the hardware and software these systems rely on. With this chapter, you are well on your way to having the knowledge you need to sponsor a project like Dee's.

Active Review

Use this Active Review to verify that you understand the material in the chapter. You can read the entire chapter and then perform the tasks in this review, or you can read the material for just one question and perform the tasks in this review for that question before moving on to the next one.

Q1 Why do you need to know about information technology?

How has information technology changed the way you live? Think about what you would do if you did not have access to computers or the Internet.

Q2 Where did all this information technology stuff come from?

Explain why you should be interested in advancements in information technology. Explain some trends in computing technology that are likely to continue.

Q3 What does a manager need to know about computer hardware?

List the categories of hardware. Describe memory swapping. Explain situations in which more main memory is needed. Explain situations in which a faster CPU is needed. Define each of the hardware terms in Figure 4-1.

Q4 What is the difference between a client and a server?

Explain the difference between a client and a server. Describe the differences in hardware requirements for clients and servers. Describe a server farm.

Q5 What does a manager need to know about software?

Explain the difference between an operating system and an application program. Describe the constraint on an operating system imposed by a computer's instruction set. Describe the constraint on applications and an operating system. Describe the difference between a thin and a thick client. When would you use one or the other? Explain the terms in Figure 4-9.

Q6 What buying decisions do you make?

Explain the terms in Figure 4-12.

Q7 What are viruses and worms?

Define *virus* and *payload*. Explain the differences between macro viruses and worms. Explain the importance of applying patches promptly. Describe other prevention steps. Explain the use of anti-virus software. Describe actions to take to eradicate a virus from a computer.

Key Terms and Concepts

Using Your Knowledge

1. Assume that you have been asked to prepare a computer hardware budget. Your company has identified three classes of computer user. Class-A employees use the computer for email, web browsing, Internet connectivity, and limited document writing. Class-B employees use the computer for all the activities of class A, plus they need to be able to read and create complicated documents. They also need to be able to create and process large spreadsheets and process small graphics files. Class-C employees are data analysts who perform all the tasks that class-A and class-B employees do; they also analyze data using programs that make extensive computations and produce large and complicated graphics.
   a. Using the Internet, determine two appropriate alternatives for each class of employee. Search dell.com, lenovo.com, hewlett-packard.com, and any other sites you think appropriate.
   b. Justify each of the selections in your answer to part (a).
   c. Specify the cost of each of the selections in part (a).

2. Search the Internet for the term *OpenOffice*. Explain what OpenOffice is. How do users obtain it? How much does it cost? Given this information, why do you think companies use Microsoft Office rather than OpenOffice? Why do you?

3. Describe the three categories of applications software. Give an example of each. Explain Figure 4-10. Search the Internet for an example of horizontal and vertical market software, other than those mentioned in this chapter. Search the Internet for the product QuickBooks. Briefly describe the functions of that product. What operating system(s) does it require? Suppose you wish to install and use QuickBooks, but you need some functions to be altered. Search the Internet for vendors or consultants who could help you. List two or three such vendors or consultants.

Case Study 4

Computerizing the Ministry of Foreign Affairs

In 1994 the Ministry of Foreign Affairs of a West African country embarked on an ambitious program to computerize its internal services and communications. The project began slowly, with limited funding, and it relied on donated hardware and software. In 1999 the goals of the project were revised to include the development of web-based applications, and at that point the project received internal budget allocations. Between 1999 and 2002, a total of $650 000 was allocated.

The system's purpose was to make the organization dynamic and modern via the use of information technology. For example, the United Nations provides data and documents electronically, and the Foreign Affairs Ministry wanted to participate in the use of this new technology. Another project goal was to facilitate communication between the Ministry of Foreign Affairs home office and its diplomatic missions abroad. In particular, the new system would use an external website and email to distribute information and facilitate discussions and decision making between geographically separated participants. A specific objective was to reduce travel costs by half. Unfortunately, by 2002 the project had delivered few benefits. Data continued to be stored on paper, a local computer network within the Ministry of Foreign Affairs was inoperative, and the diplomatic correspondence bag remained the primary means of exchanging paper-based information. Diplomats continued to travel, and travel expenses were not reduced by the new system. In short, the project was a failure. In his case study of this application, Kenhago Olivier identified three factors behind the failure of this system:

1. Vendor contracts were awarded not on the basis of competence, but rather on personal relations between Ministry of Foreign Affairs officials and vendor personnel.
2. The major application threatened the perquisites ("perks") of diplomats. Travel is an important source of revenue for headquarters personnel; they compensate for their low salaries by travel compensation and by the opportunity to trade goods.
3. The computing infrastructure was limited; there were a maximum of two personal computers per department at headquarters and only 35 computers in a building housing more than 300 officials.

Source: Olivier, K. T., "Problems in Computerising the Ministry of Foreign Affairs," *Success/Failure Case Study No. 23, eGovernment for Development*, www.egov4dev.org/mofa.htm (accessed October 2004).

Questions

1. The purpose of this system was for the Ministry of Foreign Affairs "to become a more dynamic, modern organization via the use of information technology." What are the dangers of stating the purpose of a system in this way? How could this statement be improved?
2. Why was the goal of reducing travel costs not achieved? What steps would need to be taken before this goal could ever be achieved? What is the likely outcome in any system in which the goals of the system conflict with the interests of important users? Which is stronger—the momentum of the new system or the resistance of the users?
3. When the features of new information systems conflict with the needs and desires of important user groups, what should be done? Should system development be stopped? If not, should the features be changed? What can be done to reduce the users' resistance? Who is in a position to resolve the conflict—the development team? The business users? Someone else?
4. This case description implies that the project was severely underfunded. Attempting to modernize a department with donated equipment sounds desperate, and trying to change communication patterns using email when 300 officials share 35 personal computers is probably impossible. The desire to use the UN's computer-based systems to reduce travel and to enable email communication are appropriate goals for a governmental organization today. But the limited funding is a reality. If you were placed in charge of a project that was underfunded like this one, what would you do?

5. In most cases, the costs of an information system are not known at the beginning of a project. It is only after specifying requirements and identifying alternative solutions that costs can be approximated. Knowing this, how would you proceed if you were given the responsibility for managing a new development project? What would you do if you found that the funding available is not nearly enough? What would you do if you found that the funding is 10 to 20 percent too low? What would you do if the funding appeared to be adequate, but you sensed that the cost estimates were optimistically low? In each of these cases, what is the best strategy for your organization? For your career?

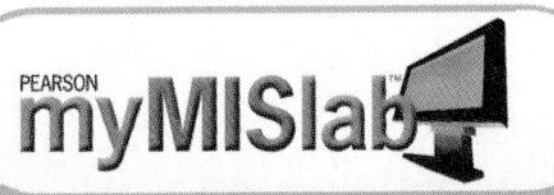

Visit MyMISLab at **www.pearsoned.ca/mymislab**. MyMISLab is a state-of-the-art, interactive, online solution that combines multimedia, tutorials, and quizzes. Use MyMISLab for *Experiencing MIS* to prepare for tests and exams, and go to class ready to learn!

What Do YOU Think?

Keeping Up to Speed

Have you ever been to a cafeteria where you put your lunch tray on a conveyor belt that carries the dirty dishes into the kitchen? That conveyor belt reminds us of technology. Like the conveyor, technology just moves along and all of us run on top of the technology conveyor, trying to keep up. We hope to keep up with the relentless change of technology for an entire career without ending up in the techno-trash.

Technology change is a fact, and the only appropriate question is, "What am I going to do about it?" One strategy you can take is to bury your head in the sand: "Look, I'm not a technology person. I'll leave it to the pros. As long as I can send email and use the Internet, I'm happy. If I have a problem, I'll call someone to fix it."

That strategy is fine, as far as it goes, and many business people use it. Following that strategy won't give you a competitive advantage over anyone, and it will give someone else a competitive advantage over you, but as long as you develop your advantage elsewhere, you'll be OK—at least for yourself.

What about your department, though? If an expert says, "Every computer needs a 500 GB disk," are you going to nod your head and say, "Great. Sell 'em to me!" Or are you going to know enough to realize that that's a big disk (by 2008 standards, anyway), and ask why everyone needs such a large amount of storage? Maybe then you'll be told, "Well, it's only another $100 per machine from the 60GB disk." At that point you can make a decision using your own decision-making skills, and not by relying solely on the IS expert. The prudent business professional in the twenty-first century has a number of reasons not to bury his or her head in the technology sand.

At the other end of the spectrum are those who love technology. You'll find them everywhere—they may be accountants, marketing professionals, or production-line supervisors who not only know their field, but also enjoy information technology. Maybe they were IS majors or had double majors that combined IS with another area of expertise (e.g., IS with accounting). These people read CNET News and ZDNet most days, and they can tell you the latest on IPv6 addresses. Those people are sprinting along the technology conveyor belt; they will never end up in the techno-trash, and they will use their knowledge of IT to gain competitive advantage throughout their careers.

Many business professionals are in between these extremes. They don't want to bury their heads, but they don't have the desire or interest to become technophiles (lovers of technology) either. What to do? There are a couple of strategies. For one, don't allow yourself to ignore technology. When you see a technology article in the *Globe and Mail,* read it. Don't just skip it because it's about technology. Read the technology ads, too. Many vendors invest heavily in ads that instruct without seeming to. Another option is to take a seminar or pay attention to professional events that combine your specialty with technology.

For example, when you go to the bankers' convention, attend a session or two on "Technology Trends for Bankers." There are always sessions like that, and you might make a contact in another company with similar problems and concerns.

Probably the best option, if you have the time for it, is to get involved as a user representative in technology committees in your organization. If your company is doing a review of its CRM (customer relationship management) system, for instance, see if you can get on the review committee. When there's a need for a representative from your department to discuss needs for the next-generation help-line system, sign up. Or, later in your career, become a member of the business practice technology committee, or whatever they call it at your organization.

Just working with such groups will add to your knowledge of technology. Presentations made to such groups, discussions about uses of technology, and ideas about using IT for competitive advantage will all add to your IT knowledge. You'll gain important contacts and exposure to leaders in your organization as well.

It's up to you. You get to choose how you relate to technology. But be sure you choose; don't let your head fall into the sand without thinking about it.

Discussion Questions

1. Do you agree that the change of technology is relentless? What do you think that means to most business professionals? To most organizations?
2. Think about the three postures toward technology presented here. Which camp will you join? Why?
3. Write a two-paragraph memo to yourself justifying your choice in question 2. If you chose to ignore technology, explain how you will compensate for the loss of competitive advantage. If you're going to join one of the other two groups, explain why, and describe how you're going to accomplish your goal.
4. Given your answer to question 2, assume that you're in a job interview and the interviewer asks about your knowledge of technology. Write a three-sentence response to the interviewer's question.

5 Database and Content Management

This
could happen
to you

Working with her consultant, Dee selected an application program called Movable Type for her blog. While that program was a bit more difficult to use than other programs, it had certain advanced features that gave her greater control over the look and feel of the blog. Her consultant said it was a professional-grade product.

Shortly after selecting the product, Don, the consultant, mentioned that she would need to install MySQL as well. "You need a DBMS to store your blog entries," he explained. "A what?" asked Dee. "Oh, right," explained Don, "a database management system—a DBMS."

Dee had decided that her blog needed to run within the Emerson network (you'll learn why in the next chapter), and Don told her to check with her IT department to see if they already had MySQL. When she asked her IT department, she was told, "No, we've standardized on Oracle. We don't run any other DBMS products."

When Dee reported this news to Don, he said that this would be a problem. He told her that Oracle is difficult to work with, even though it generates terrific performance on large databases. He would have to revise his labour estimates for the project if they were going to use Oracle. Also, he said he'd have to determine if an Oracle version of Movable Type existed. If not, they'd have to pick another application. That meant backing up to reconsider the decisions they'd already made.

Meanwhile, time was ticking away. It was now the second week in December, and Dee needed the blog up and running by the first week in January.

"Look," Don advised, "talk to them again. Installing MySQL isn't that hard. We're not talking about running the business on it, we're just going to run your blog. I can install it, and you can work out the licence issues yourself. It won't be that expensive or hard."

When Dee called the IT department back, she was met with strong resistance and a barrage of terminology she didn't understand. She needed the knowledge in this chapter.

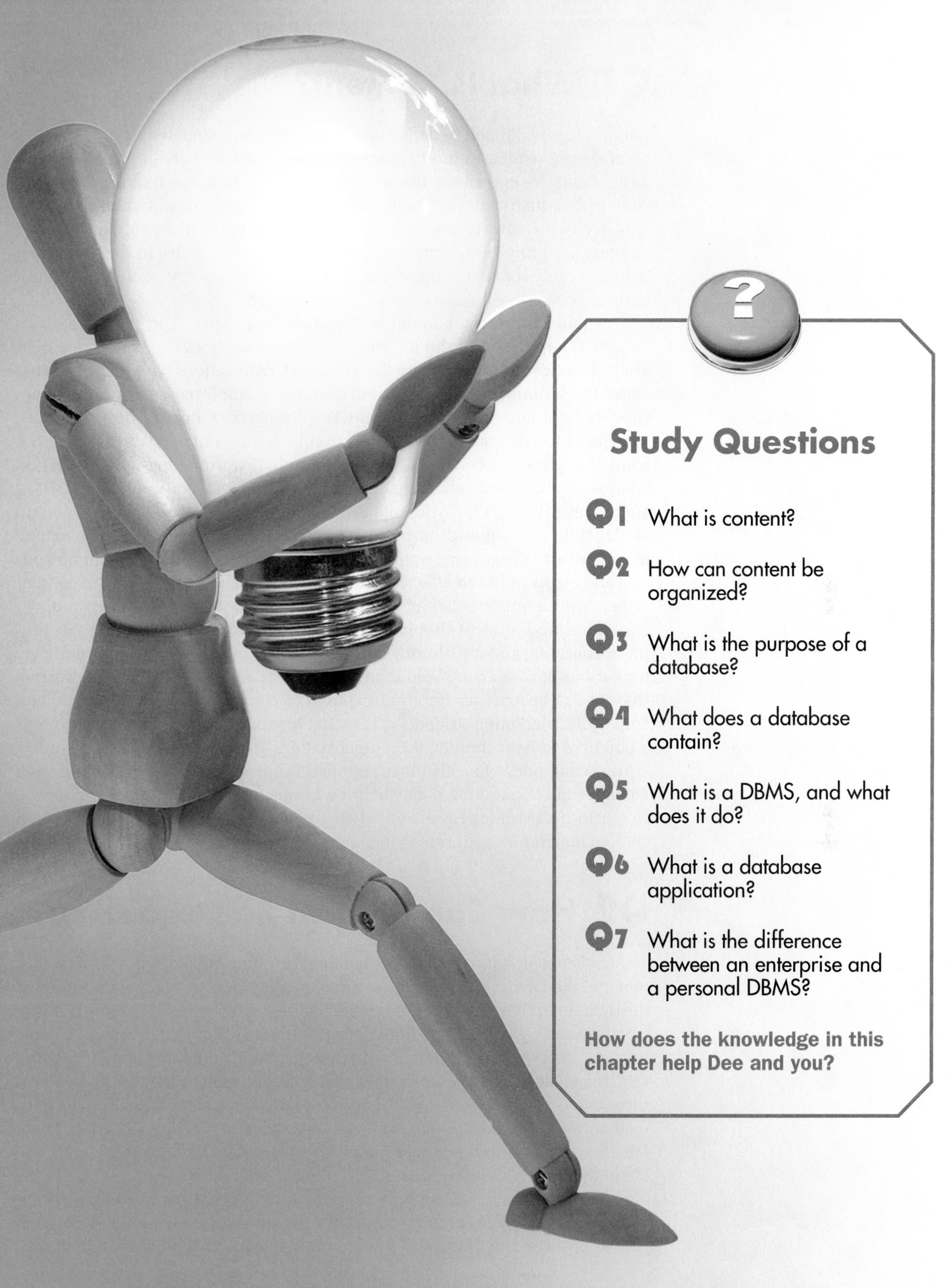

Study Questions

Q1 What is content?

Q2 How can content be organized?

Q3 What is the purpose of a database?

Q4 What does a database contain?

Q5 What is a DBMS, and what does it do?

Q6 What is a database application?

Q7 What is the difference between an enterprise and a personal DBMS?

How does the knowledge in this chapter help Dee and you?

Q1 What Is Content?

Content can be difficult to define. In the broadest sense, content is property. It is often closely related to **intellectual property,** which in Canada is defined as a form of creative endeavour that can be protected through a trademark, patent, copyright, industrial design, or integrated circuit topography.[1] Content varies by industry. In the advertising industry content refers to the pictures, commercials, and text used to promote ideas about products and services. In the publishing industry, content refers to the words. In the banking industry, content is account information.

Before computers, content was available on paper or in photographs or movies. Computers and the Internet have increased both the types of content available as well as the access to this content. Organizations have databases that store large amounts of data related to customers, employees, orders, and so on. Organizations also store other content. Word-processing documents (.doc, .pdf), spreadsheets (.xls), and presentations (.ppt) are a part of everyday work. Other content might include web pages (.htm, .html), text from blogs and discussion boards, graphics (.jpg, .gif, .bmp, .png, etc.), video files (.WMV, .AVI, and .MPG), audio files (.WAV, .MP3, .ACC, and .WMA), and even geographical information available through applications such as Google Earth™. The expanding volume of content and the growing number of formats for it make it difficult for individuals and corporations to effectively utilize content. The management of content is therefore an important challenge for any business student to understand.

A business student should also realize that the challenge today is not simply in collecting and distributing content, but also in presenting it appropriately for various stakeholders inside and outside the organization. The company's website has become an important source of content for both customers and employees. Marketing students realize that organizations view their websites as a potential to help "brand" their organization. The website has also become a critical component for customer support. People in information systems had enough trouble handling data when it was meant only for internal employees. How can organizations keep up when the volume, format, and presentation choices for content continue to increase?

Q2 How Can Content Be Organized?

The challenge in content management is processing and storing the right content and then getting the right content to the right person in the right format at the right time. One way of thinking about content management is to separate the management of content data from the presentation of content. We learned in the previous chapter that all data in computing systems are represented by bytes. Data management focuses on how to efficiently and effectively store and process these bytes. The management of many types of data has traditionally been handled through organizational database management systems (DBMS). These DBMS are central to the management of content data, and we will learn more about them later in the chapter.

The presentation of content has gone through changes as company websites have matured. In the early days of the Internet, employees might have been able to post content directly to a company's website. This practice did not pro-

[1] Read more about intellectual property at http://strategis.gc.ca/sc_mrksv/cipo/welcome/welcom-e.html.

vide a consistent look and feel and left the company at risk if incorrect data was posted. As organizational websites became more complex, employees could not be expected to keep up with all the changes. The presentation of content in organizations today is increasingly handled through a series of steps supported by software. Web content management systems have been developed to help companies organize this process.

When an employee wants to place some content on the organization's website, he or she will access the web **content management system (CMS).** The web CMS is usually located on the company's website server. The employee typically loads the raw content into the web CMS. Copy editors then review the document and make changes. They then pass the content on to layout editors, who prepare how the content will be presented. The content and presentation are stored with the help of a DBMS. The manager in charge of the website will then review the content and presentation and publish the work to the live website. The web CMS helps manage each step of this process and enables a company to standardize the look and feel of a website and control information available for customers and employees.

CMS's have also evolved. They have grown beyond just organizing documents for corporate websites. These systems now actively seek out documents located across an organization and organize access to this content. Media files, word-processing documents, html pages, and many other documents can all be categorized and searched by CMS. This provides increased organization for a wider range of a corporation's data assets. Current CMS, also handle document archiving and the increased use of electronic files for document management. OpenText (see box), a Canadian company located in Waterloo, Ontario (www.opentext.com), and EMC, a U.S. company (www.emc.com), are examples of these CMS.

OPEN TEXT: FROM SPINOFF TO MARKET LEADER

How does a small spinoff company from the University of Waterloo grow to be the world leader in enterprise content management systems? It all started with a project to drag the *Oxford English Dictionary (OED)* into the computer age. The *OED* had become so large that it was unwieldy to update. Researchers at the University of Waterloo, with funding help from the Canadian government, worked to build a full-text indexing and string-search technology for the *OED*. The project resulted in a product that was close to a web-based search engine—in 1989, years before web search engines were well known. Open Text was started in 1991. The company continued to develop increased functionality in the search engine through 1995. When the market for search engines no longer looked promising, the company turned to document management systems. Web-based document management systems proved to be a lucrative market, and Open Text grew from a company with 20 employees in 1995 to a company of more than 1000 employees and $147 million in 2001. The company has continued its rapid growth and celebrated its 15th anniversary as the market leader in enterprise content management.

Source: You can find more references about Open Text at www.opentext.com/corporate/our_history.html (accessed May 2007).

Q3 What Is the Purpose of a Database?

The purpose of a database is to keep track of things. When most students learn that, they wonder why we need a special technology for such a simple task. Why not just use a list? If the list is long, put it into a spreadsheet.

Many professionals do keep track of things using spreadsheets. If the structure of the list is simple enough, there is no need to use database technology. The list of student grades in Figure 5-1, for example, works perfectly well in a spreadsheet.

Suppose, however, that the professor wants to track more than just grades. The professor may want to record email messages as well. Or perhaps the professor wants to record both email messages and office visits. There is no place in Figure 5-1 to record that additional data. Of course, the professor could set up a separate spreadsheet for email messages and another one for office visits, but that awkward solution would be difficult to use because it does not provide all the data in one place.

Instead, the professor wants a form like that in Figure 5-2. With it, the professor can record student grades, emails, and office visits all in one place. A form like the one in Figure 5-2 is difficult, if not impossible, to produce from a spreadsheet. Such a form is easily produced, however, from a database.

The key distinction between Figures 5-1 and 5-2 is that the list in Figure 5-1 is about a single theme or concept. It is about student grades only. The list in Figure 5-2 has multiple themes—it shows student grades, student emails, and student office visits. We can make a general rule from these examples: Lists that involve a single theme can be stored in a spreadsheet; lists that involve multiple themes require a database. We will learn more about this general rule as this chapter proceeds.

To summarize, the purpose of a database is to keep track of things that involve more than one theme.

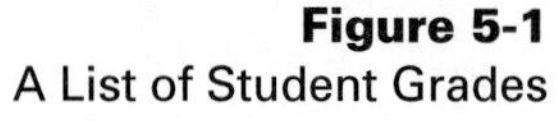

Figure 5-1
A List of Student Grades

Microsoft Excel - Student Grades.xls

File Edit View Insert Format Tools Data Window Help

G13

	A	B	C	D	E
1	**Student Name**	**Student Number**	**HW1**	**HW2**	**MidTerm**
2					
3	BAKER, ANDREA	1325	88	100	78
4	FISCHER, MAYAN	3007	95	100	74
5	LAU, SWEE	1644	75	90	90
6	NELSON, STUART	2881	100	90	98
7	ROGERS, SHELLY	8009	95	100	98
8	TAM, JEFFREY	3559		100	88
9	VALDEZ, MARIE	5265	80	90	85
10	VERBERRA, ADAM	4867	70	90	92

Sheet1 / Sheet2 / Sheet3 /

Reply with Changes... End Review...

Ready

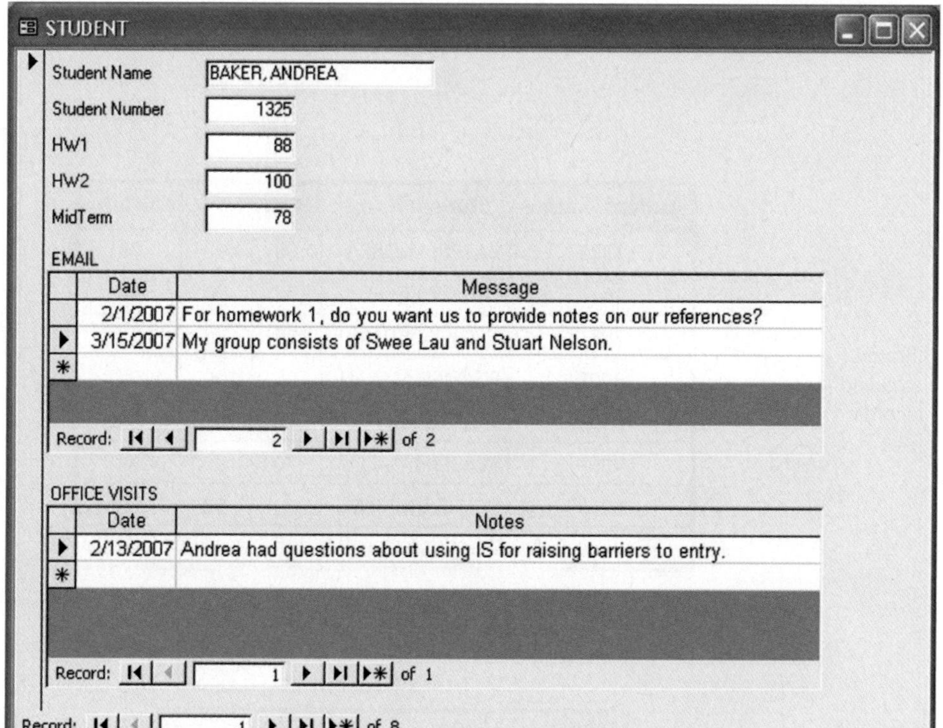

Figure 5-2
Student Data Shown in Form of a Database

Q4 What Does a Database Contain?

The design of databases is a specialized skill that a person in MIS should understand. Any business student who plans to work with corporate data should also be familiar with the basic design of databases. You will learn the basics in this chapter. In addition, two technical appendices (Chapter Extension 5a, "Database Design" and Chapter Extension 5b, "Using Microsoft Access") are provided for more in-depth coverage of this topic.

A **database** is a self-describing collection of integrated records. To understand this definition, you first need to understand the terms illustrated in Figure 5-3. As you learned in Chapter 4, a **byte** is a character of data. Bytes are grouped into **columns**, such as *Student Number* and *Student Name.* Columns are also called **fields**. Columns or fields, in turn, are grouped into **rows**, which are also called **records**. In Figure 5-3, the collection of data for all columns (*Student Name, Student Number, HW1, HW2,* and *MidTerm*) is called a row or a record. Finally, a group of similar rows or records is called a **table** or a **file**. From these definitions, you can see that there is a hierarchy of data elements, as shown in Figure 5-4.

It is tempting to continue this grouping process by saying that a database is a group of tables or files. This statement, although true, does not go far enough. As shown in Figure 5-5, a database is a collection of tables *plus* relationships among the rows in those tables, *plus* special data, called *metadata,* that describes the structure of the database. By the way, the cylindrical symbol represents a computer disk drive. It is used in diagrams like that in Figure 5-5 because databases are normally stored on magnetic disks.

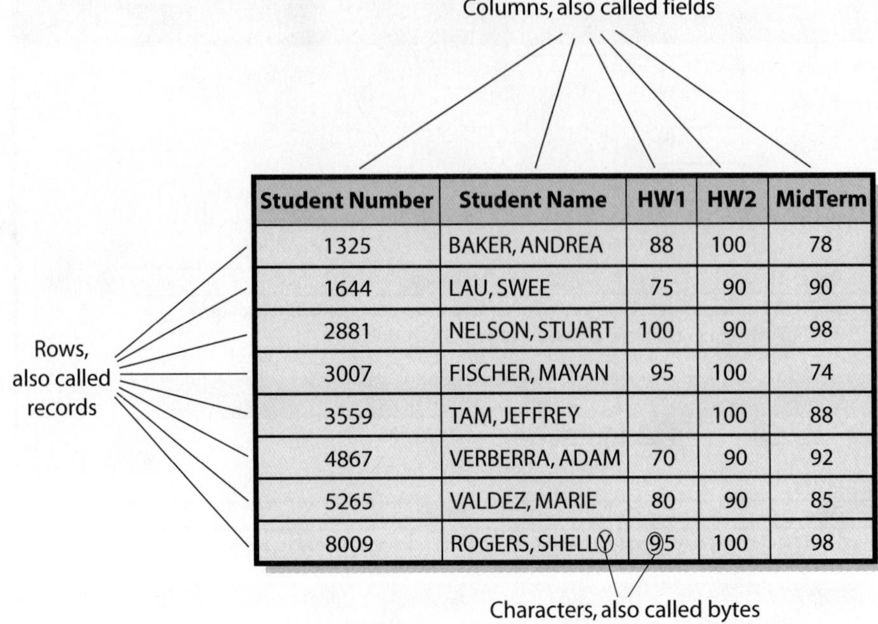

Student Number	Student Name	HW1	HW2	MidTerm
1325	BAKER, ANDREA	88	100	78
1644	LAU, SWEE	75	90	90
2881	NELSON, STUART	100	90	98
3007	FISCHER, MAYAN	95	100	74
3559	TAM, JEFFREY		100	88
4867	VERBERRA, ADAM	70	90	92
5265	VALDEZ, MARIE	80	90	85
8009	ROGERS, SHELLY	95	100	98

Figure 5-3
Student Table (also called a file)

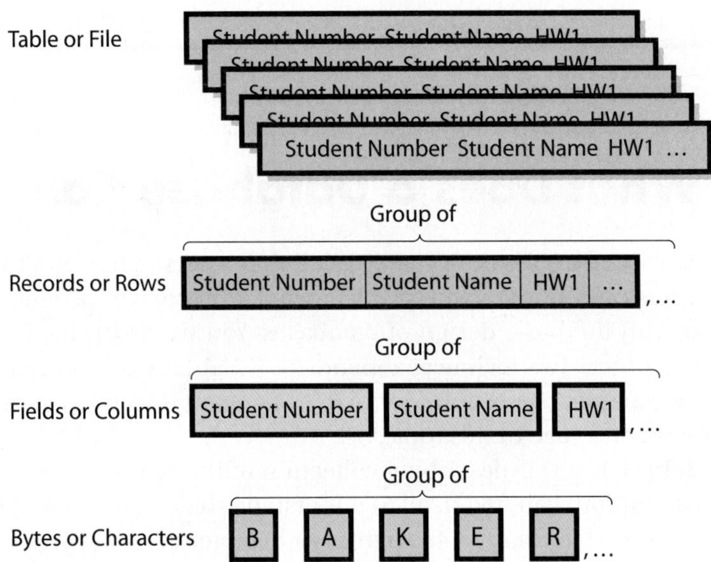

Figure 5-4
Hierarchy of Data Elements

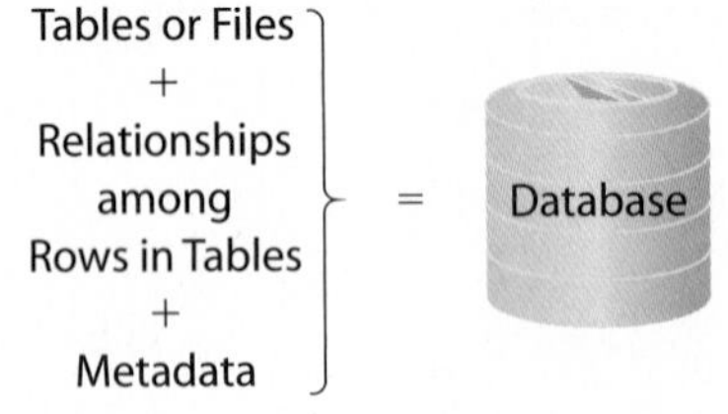

Figure 5-5
Components of a Database

Relationships among Records

Consider the terms on the left-hand side of Figure 5-5. You know what tables are. To understand what is meant by *relationships among rows in tables,* examine Figure 5-6. It shows sample data from the three tables *Email, Student,* and *Office_Visit.* Notice the column named *Student Number* in the *Email* table. That column indicates the row in *Student* to which a row of *Email* is connected. In the first row of *Email,* the *Student Number* value is 1325. This indicates that this particular email was received from the student whose *Student Number* is 1325. If you examine the *Student* table, you will see that the row for Andrea Baker has this value. Thus, the first row of the *Email* table is related to Andrea Baker.

Now consider the last row of the *Office_Visit* table at the bottom of the figure. The value of *Student Number* in that row is 4867. This value indicates that the last row in *Office_Visit* belongs to Adam Verberra.

From these examples, you can see that values in one table relate rows of that table to rows in a second table. Several special terms are used to express these ideas. A **key** is a column or group of columns that identifies a unique row in a table. *Student Number* is the key of the *Student* table. Given a value of *Student Number,* you can determine one and only one row in *Student.* Only one student has the number 1325, for example.

Every table must have a key. The key of the *Email* table is *EmailNum,* and the key of the *Student_Visit* table is *VisitID.* Sometimes more than one column is needed to form a unique identifier. In a table called *City,* for example, the key would consist of the combination of columns (*City,Province*), because a given city name can appear in more than one province.

Student Number is not the key of the *Email* or the *Office_Visit* tables. We know that about *Email* because there are two rows in *Email* that have the *Student Number* value 1325. The value 1325 does not identify a unique row; therefore, *Student Number* is not the key of *Email.*

Nor is *Student Number* a key of *Office_Visit,* although you cannot tell that from the data in Figure 5-6. If you think about it, however, there is nothing to prevent a student from visiting a professor more than once. If that were to happen, there would be two rows in *Office_Visit* with the same value of *Student Number.* It just happens that no student has visited twice in the limited data in Figure 5-6.

Figure 5-6
Example of Relationships among Rows

Email Table

EmailNum	Date	Message	Student Number
1	2/1/2007	For homework 1, do you want us to provide notes on our references?	1325
2	3/15/2007	My group consists of Swee Lau and Stuart Nelson.	1325
3	3/15/2007	Could you please assign me to a group?	1644

Student Table

Student Number	Student Name	HW1	HW2	MidTerm
1325	BAKER, ANDREA	88	100	78
1644	LAU, SWEE	75	90	90
2881	NELSON, STUART	100	90	98
3007	FISCHER, MAYAN	95	100	74
3559	TAM, JEFFREY		100	88
4867	VERBERRA, ADAM	70	90	92
5265	VALDEZ, MARIE	80	90	85
8009	ROGERS, SHELLY	95	100	98

Office_Visit Table

VisitID	Date	Notes	Student Number
2	2/13/2007	Andrea had questions about using IS for raising barriers to entry.	1325
3	2/17/2007	Jeffrey is considering an IS major. Wanted to talk about career opportunities.	3559
4	2/17/2007	Will miss class Friday due to job conflict.	4867

Columns that fulfill a role like that of *Student Number* in the *Email* and *Office_Visit* tables are called **foreign keys**. This term is used because such columns are keys, but they are keys of a different (foreign) table from the one in which they reside.

Before we go on, we will note that databases that carry their data in the form of tables and that represent relationships using foreign keys are called **relational databases**. (The term *relational* is used because another, more formal name for a table is **relation**.) In the past, databases existed that were not relational in format, but such databases have nearly disappeared. Chances are you will never encounter one, and we will not consider them further.[2]

Metadata

Recall the definition of database again: A database is a self-describing collection of integrated records. The records are integrated because, as you just learned, relationships among rows are represented in the database. But what does *self-describing* mean?

It means that a database contains, within itself, a description of its contents. Think of a library. A library is a self-describing collection of books and other materials. It is self-describing because the library contains a catalogue that describes the library's contents. The same idea also pertains to a database. Databases are self-describing because they contain not only data, but also data about the data in the database.

Metadata are data that describe data. Figure 5-7 shows metadata for the *Email* table. The format of metadata depends on the software product that is processing the database. Figure 5-7 shows the metadata as they appear in Microsoft Access. Each row of the top part of this form describes a column of the *Email* table. The columns of these descriptions are *Field Name, Data Type,* and *Description. Field Name* contains the name of the column, *Data Type* shows the type of data the column may hold, and *Description* contains notes that explain

Figure 5-7
Example of Metadata (in Access)

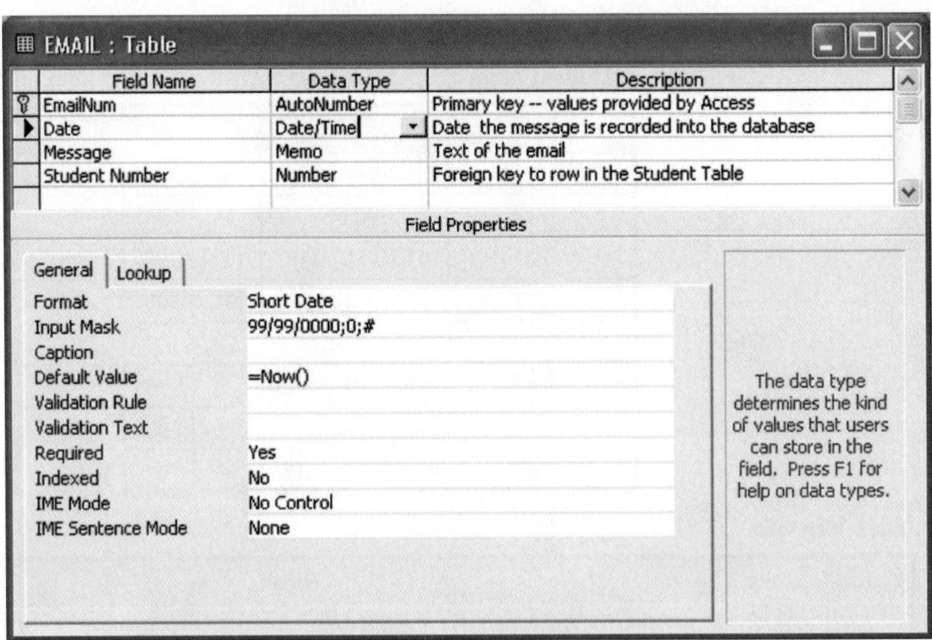

2. Another type of database, the object-relational database, is rarely used in commercial applications. Search the web if you are interested in learning more about object-relational databases. In this book, we will consider only relational databases.

the source or use of the column. As you can see, there is one row of metadata for each of the four columns of the *Email* table: *EmailNum, Date, Message,* and *Student Number.*

The bottom part of this form provides more metadata, which Access calls *Field Properties,* for each column. In Figure 5-7, the focus is on the *Date* column (note the filled-in right-face pointer next to its name, like the one shown here ►). Because the focus is on *Date* in the top pane, the details in the bottom pane pertain to the *Date* column. The *Field Properties* describe formats, a default value for Access to supply when a new row is created, and the constraint that a value is required for this column. It is not important for you to remember these details. Instead, just understand that metadata are data about data and that such metadata are always a part of a database.

The presence of metadata makes databases much more useful than spreadsheets or data in other lists. Because of metadata, no one needs to guess, remember, or even record what is in the database. To find out what a database contains, we just look at the metadata inside the database. Metadata make databases easy to use—for both authorized and unauthorized purposes, as described in the Exercise "Nobody Said I Shouldn't" at the end of this chapter.

Q5 What Is a DBMS, and What Does It Do?

A database, all by itself, is not very useful. The tables in Figure 5-6 have all the data the professor wants, but the format is unwieldy. The professor wants to see the data in a form like that in Figure 5-2 and also as a formatted report. Pure database data are correct, but in raw form they are not pertinent or useful.

Figure 5-8 shows the components of a **database application system**. Such applications make database data more accessible and useful. Users employ a **database application** that consists of forms (like that in Figure 5-2), formatted reports, queries, and application programs. Each of these, in turn, calls on the database management system to process the database tables. We will first describe database management systems and then discuss database application components.

The Database Management System

A **database management system (DBMS)** is a program used to create, process, and administer a database. As with operating systems, almost no organization develops its own DBMS. Instead, companies license DBMS products from vendors like IBM, Microsoft, Oracle, and others. Popular DBMS products are **DB2** from IBM, **Access** and **SQL Server** from Microsoft, and **Oracle** from the Oracle Corporation. Another popular DBMS is **MySQL**, an open-source DBMS product

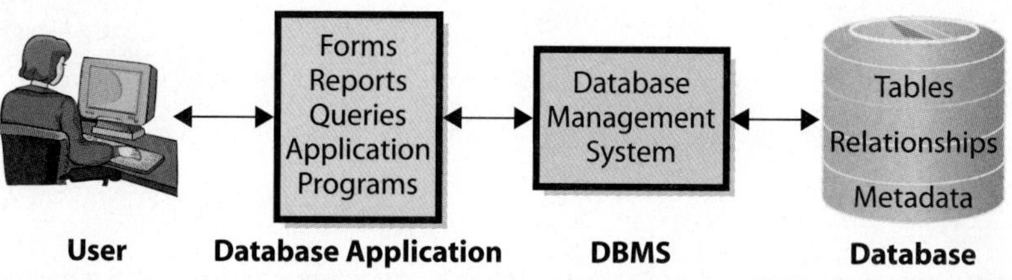

Figure 5-8
Components of a Database Application System

that is free for most applications. Other DBMS products are available, but these five process the great bulk of databases today.

Note that a DBMS and a database are two different things. For some reason, the trade press and even some books confuse the two. A DBMS is a software program; a database is a collection of tables, relationships, and metadata. The two are very different concepts.

Creating the Database and Its Structures

Database developers use the DBMS to create tables, relationships, and other structures in the database. The form in Figure 5-7 can be used to define a new table or to modify an existing one. To create a new table, the developer just fills out a new form like the one in Figure 5-7.

To modify an existing table—for example, to add a new column—the developer opens the metadata form for that table and adds a new row of metadata. For example, in Figure 5-9 the developer has added a new column called *Response?* This new column has the data type *Yes/No,* which means that the column can contain only one of the values—yes or no. The professor will use this column to indicate whether he has responded to the student's email. Other database structures are defined in similar ways.

Processing the Database

The second function of the DBMS is to process the database. Applications use the DBMS for four operations: to *read, insert, modify,* or *delete* data. The applications call upon the DBMS in different ways. From a form, when the user enters new or changed data a computer program that processes the form calls the DBMS to make the necessary database changes. From an application program, the program calls the DBMS directly to make the change.

Structured Query Language (SQL) is an international standard language for processing a database. All five of the DBMS products mentioned earlier accept and process SQL (pronounced "see-quell") statements. As an example, the following SQL statement inserts a new row into the *Student* table:

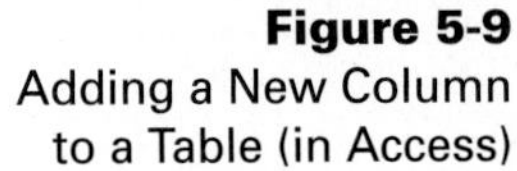
Figure 5-9
Adding a New Column to a Table (in Access)

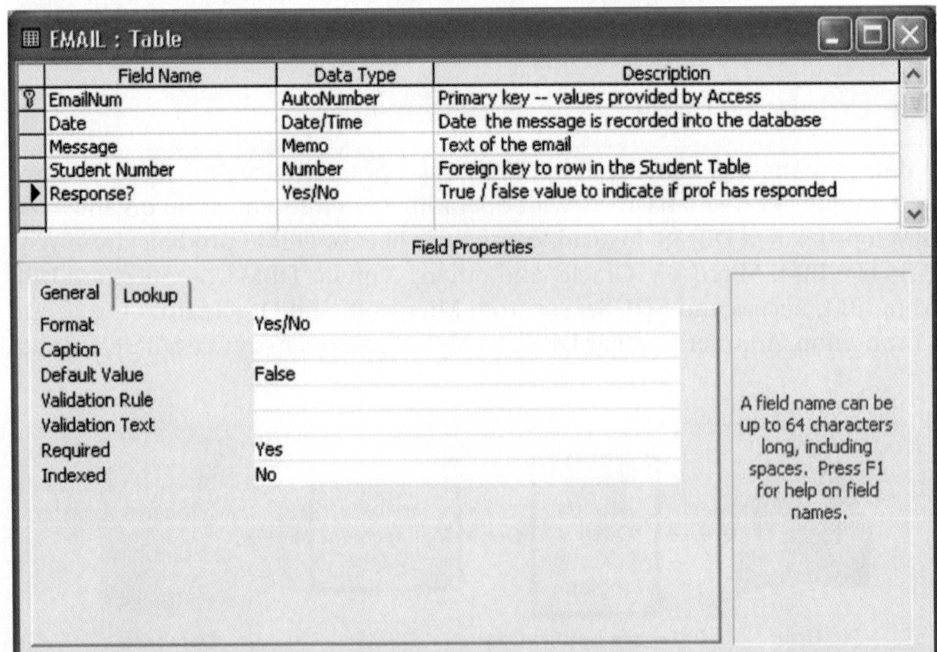

```
INSERT INTO Student
   ([Student Number], [Student Name], HW1, HW2, MidTerm)
   VALUES
   (1000, 'Franklin, Benjamin', 90, 95, 100)
```

Statements like this one are issued "behind the scenes" by programs that process forms. Alternatively, they can also be issued directly to the DBMS by an application program.

You do not need to understand or remember SQL language syntax. Instead, just be aware that SQL is an international standard for processing a database. Also, SQL can be used to create databases and database structures. You will learn more about SQL if you take a database management class.

Administering the Database

A third DBMS function is to provide tools to assist in the administration of the database. Database administration involves a wide variety of activities. For example, the DBMS can be used to set up a security system involving user accounts, passwords, permissions, and limits for processing the database. To provide database security, a user must sign on using a valid user account before she can process the database.

Permissions can be limited in very specific ways. In the *Student* database example, it is possible to limit a particular user to reading only *Student Name* from the *Student* table. A different user could be given permission to read the entire *Student* table, but limited to update only the *HW1, HW2,* and *MidTerm* columns. Other users can be given still other permissions.

In addition to security, DBMS administrative functions include backing up database data, adding structures to improve the performance of database applications, removing data that are no longer wanted or needed, and similar tasks. One of these tasks involves setting up a system for dealing with database growth, as discussed in *MIS in Use 5.*

Q6 What Is a Database Application?

A *database application* is a collection of forms, reports, queries, and application programs that process a database. A database may have one or more applications, and each application may have one or more users. Figure 5-10 shows three applications; the top two have multiple users. These applications have different purposes, features, and functions, but they all process the same inventory data stored in a common database.

Forms, Reports, and Queries

Figure 5-2 (page 99) shows a typical database application data entry **form**, and Figure 5-11 shows a typical **report**. Data entry forms are used to read, insert, modify, and delete data. Reports show data in a structured context.

Some reports, like the one in Figure 5-11, also compute values as they present the data. An example is the computation of *Total weighted points* in Figure 5-11.

The Many Names of One Customer

Founded in 1945, Vancouver-based Vancity is Canada's largest credit union, with more than $13 billion in assets. By a combination of organic (natural) and inorganic (acquisition) growth, Vancity now has more than 40 branches in the lower mainland and 350 000 individual and business customers.

The majority of Vancity's member customers did not have just a single product or service, but rather a variety that could include savings and chequing accounts, loans and credit cards, and mutual funds and other investment products. Indeed, further complicating the relationship was that customers not only had multiple products, but could also have multiple instances of individual products. That is, a customer could have two savings accounts, multiple credit cards, and a number of mutual funds in a variety of ownerships (such as registered retirement savings programs [RRSPs], registered education savings plans [RESPs], and non-registered investment plans), and these could be held or have been set up at different branches.

This diversity of products and services—while attractive to both Vancity and its member customers—created a major data-quality headache for Tony Fernandes. As Vice President Technology Strategy, one of his responsibilities was the overall quality of information. His challenge was to ensure that the data in the customer information file (CIF), the database that held all customer data, was accurate and identified customers uniquely and completely. As he put it, "My job is to manage similarities and differences. We need to know if the Jon Doe who lives on Victoria Street and has a savings account is the same Jonathan Doe who has a business account and a residence on Boundary Road."

The challenge was significant. In many cases names were not unique and were complicated by short forms or by people having a variety of legal, given, and familiar names.

Vancity attempted to resolve many of these problems as customers activated each new product or service, but it was not always feasible. Something as relatively simple as spelling an address could result in duplicate entries that had to be reconciled. For example, the address 35 Westforest Trail could also be entered as 35 Westforest Tr. At the lowest level these types of entries caused inefficiencies such as sending duplicate information. More troubling to Tony, of course, were problems of incomplete customer information or more complicated issues such as misidentification of financial records.

Source: Vancity. Used with permission.

Questions

1. How serious a problem is this to the financial services industry? Is it more serious for some industries than others? (*Hint:* How much of an issue is it for the health industry?)
2. Are there any other costs to Vancity when duplicate information is sent to customers? (*Hint:* What impression would you have if you received duplicate marketing information from various organizations?)
3. What are the various challenges in cleaning and grooming data? (*Hint:* Are there reasons why customers may have separate or changing information?)
4. Would the problem be solved by identifying customers numerically? How would customers perceive this? Are there legal issues?

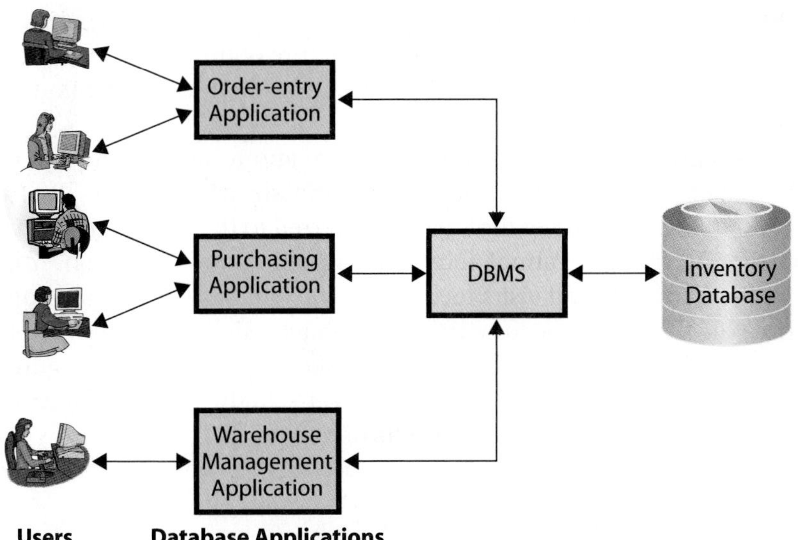

Figure 5-10
Use of Multiple Database Applications

Student Report with Emails

Student Name	*BAKER, ANDREA*	*HW1*	*88*	
		HW2	*100*	
Student Number	*1325*	*MidTerm*	*78*	*(53 homeworks)*
		Total weighted points:	*422*	

Emails Received

Date	*Message*
2/1/2007	For homework 1, do you want us to provide notes on our references?
3/15/2007	My group consists of Swee Lau and Stuart Nelson.

Student Name	*LAU, SWEE*	*HW1*	*75*	
		HW2	*90*	
Student Number	*1644*	*MidTerm*	*90*	*(53 homeworks)*
		Total weighted points:	*435*	

Emails Received

Date	*Message*
3/15/2007	Could you please assign me to a group?

Figure 5-11
Example of a Student Report

Recall from Chapter 2 that one of the definitions of information is "data presented in a meaningful context." The structure of this report creates information because it shows the student data in a context that will be meaningful to the professor.

DBMS programs provide comprehensive and robust features for querying database data. For example, suppose the professor who uses the *Student* database remembers that one of the students referred to the topic *barriers to entry* in an office visit, but she cannot remember which student or when. If there are hundreds of students and visits recorded in the database, it will take some effort and time for the professor to search through all office visit records to find that event. The DBMS, however, can find any such record quickly. Figure 5-12(a) shows a **query** form in which the professor types in the keyword for which she is looking. Figure 5-12(b) shows the results of the query.

Database Application Programs

Forms, reports, and queries work well for standard functions. However, most applications have unique requirements that a simple form, report, or query cannot meet. For example, in the order entry application in Figure 5-10, what should be done if only a portion of a customer's request can be met? If someone wants 10 widgets and we have only 3 in stock, should a backorder for 7 more be generated automatically? Or should some other action be taken?

Application programs process logic that is specific to a given business need. In the *Student* database, an example application is one that assigns grades at the end of the term. If the professor grades on a curve, the application reads the breakpoints for each grade from a form and then processes each row in the *Student* table, allocating a grade based on the breakpoints and the total number of points earned.

Another important use of application programs is to enable database processing over the Internet. For this use, the application program serves as an intermediary between the web server and the database. The application program responds to events, such as when a user presses a submit button; it also reads, inserts, modifies, and deletes database data.

Figure 5-13 shows four different database application programs running on a web server computer. Users with browsers connect to the web server via the

Figure 5-12
Example of a Query

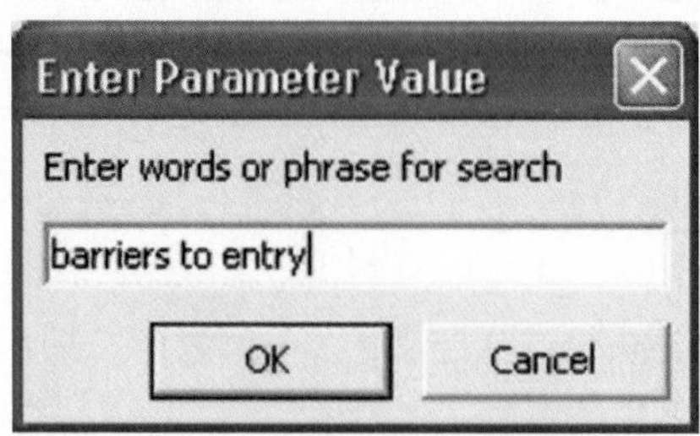

a. Form used to enter phrase for search

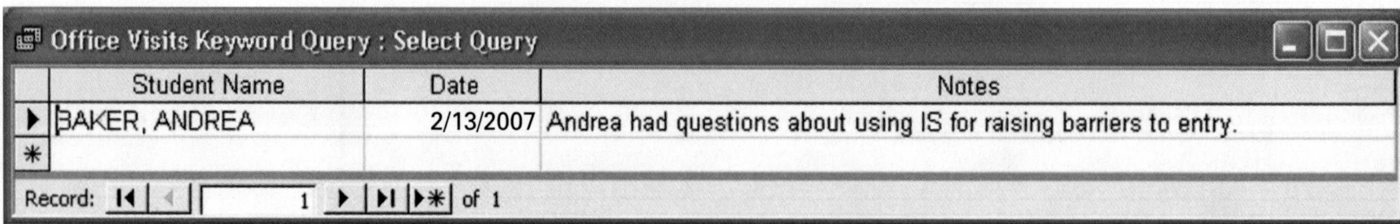
Office Visits Keyword Query : Select Query

Student Name	Date	Notes
BAKER, ANDREA	2/13/2007	Andrea had questions about using IS for raising barriers to entry.

Record: 1 of 1

b. Results of query operation

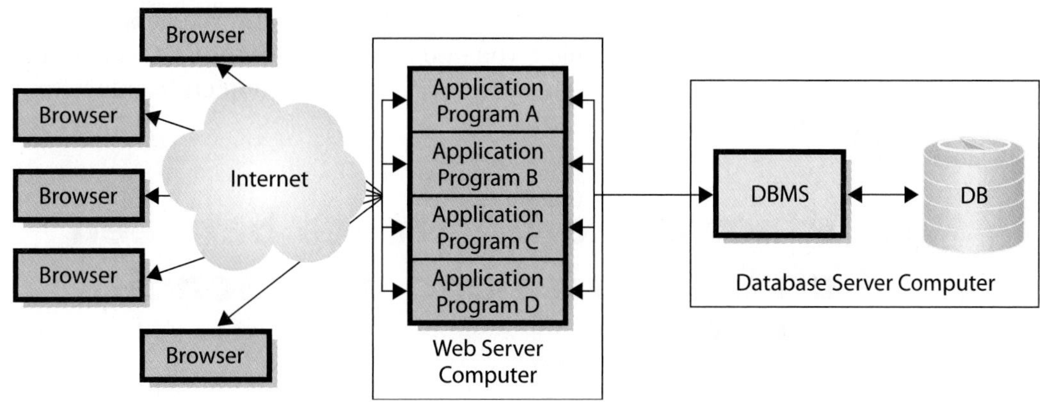

Figure 5-13
Four Application Programs on a Web Server Computer

Internet. The web server directs user requests to the appropriate application program. Each program then processes the database as necessary.

Multiuser Processing

Figures 5-10 and 5-13 show multiple users processing the database. Such **multiuser processing** is common, but it does pose unique problems that you, as a future manager, should know about. To understand the nature of those problems, consider the following scenario.

Two users, Andrea and Jeffrey, are clerks using the order-entry application in Figure 5-10. Andrea is on the phone with her customer, who wants to purchase 5 widgets. At the same time, Jeffrey is talking with his customer, who wants to purchase 3 widgets. Andrea reads the database to determine how many widgets are in inventory. (She unknowingly invokes the order entry application when she types in her data entry form.) The DBMS returns a row showing 10 widgets in inventory.

Meanwhile, just after Andrea accesses the database, Jeffrey's customer says she wants widgets, and so he also reads the database (via the order entry application program) to determine how many widgets are in inventory. The DBMS returns the same row to him, indicating that 10 widgets are available.

Andrea's customer now says that he'll take 5 widgets, and Andrea records this fact in her form. The application rewrites the widget row back to the database, indicating that there are 5 widgets in inventory.

Meanwhile, Jeffrey's customer says that he'll take 3 widgets. Jeffrey records this fact in his form, and the application rewrites the widget row back to the database. However, Jeffrey's application knows nothing about Andrea's work and subtracts 3 from the original count of 10, thus storing an incorrect count of 7 widgets in inventory. Clearly, there is a problem. We began with 10 widgets, Andrea took 5 and Jeffrey took 3, but the database says there are 7 widgets in inventory. It should show 2, not 7.

This problem, known as the **lost-update problem**, exemplifies one of the special characteristics of multiuser database processing. To prevent this problem, some type of locking must be used to coordinate the activities of users who know nothing about one another. Locking brings its own set of problems, however, and those problems must be addressed as well. We will not delve further into this topic here, however.

Realize from this example that converting a single-user database to a multiuser database requires more than simply connecting another user's computer. The logic of the underlying application processing needs to be adjusted as well.

Be aware of possible data conflicts when you manage business activities that involve multiuser processing. If you find inaccurate results that seem not to have a cause, you may be experiencing multiuser data conflicts. Contact your MIS department for assistance.

Q7 What Is the Difference between an Enterprise and a Personal DBMS?

DBMS products fall into two broad categories. **Enterprise DBMS** products process large organizational and workgroup databases. These products support many (perhaps thousands) of users and many different database applications. Such DBMS products support 24/7 operations and can manage databases that span dozens of different magnetic disks with hundreds of gigabytes or more of data. IBM's DB2, Microsoft's SQL Server, and Oracle's Oracle are examples of enterprise DBMS products. **Personal DBMS** products are designed for smaller, simpler database applications. Such products are used for personal or small workgroup applications that involve fewer than 100 users, and normally fewer than 15. In fact, the great bulk of databases in this category have only a single user. The professor's *Student* database is an example of a database that is processed by a personal DBMS product.

In the past, there were many personal DBMS products—Paradox, dBase, R:base, and FoxPro. Microsoft put these products out of business when it developed Access and included it in the Microsoft Office suite. Today, the only remaining personal DBMS is Microsoft Access.

To avoid one point of confusion for you in the future, note that the separation of application programs and the DBMS shown in Figure 5-10 is true only for enterprise DBMS products. Microsoft Access includes features and functions for application processing along with the DBMS itself. For example, Access has a form generator and a report generator. Thus, as shown in Figure 5-14, Access is both a DBMS and an application development product.

Figure 5-14
Personal Database System

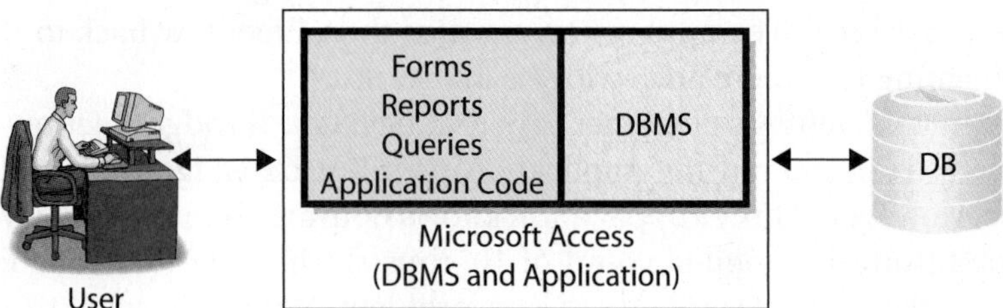

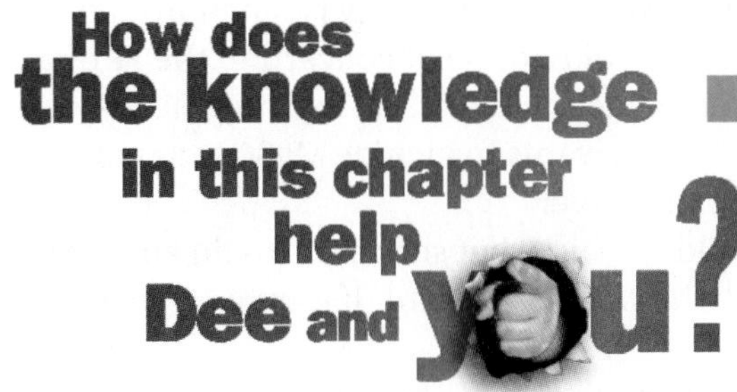

The knowledge in this chapter would have helped Dee understand how the blog could be used to manage important content that was previously not available. She might also realize why the IS department would be hesitant in being responsible for additional content and the presentation of that content. Dee might also have realized that there is some risk in allowing content in the blog that is not edited.

In addition, information in this chapter would have helped Dee to know what a DBMS is and what role it plays. She would have been able to understand the diagram in Figure 5-15 (and perhaps even draw it herself). This is the same diagram that you saw in Figure 4-8, page 77, except now we have filled in the software that runs on the server computer. The application is Movable Type, and it calls the DBMS MySQL, which processes the database. Of course, like every computer, the server also has an operating system, like Windows or Linux.

Figure 5-15
Role of DBMS for Dee's Blog

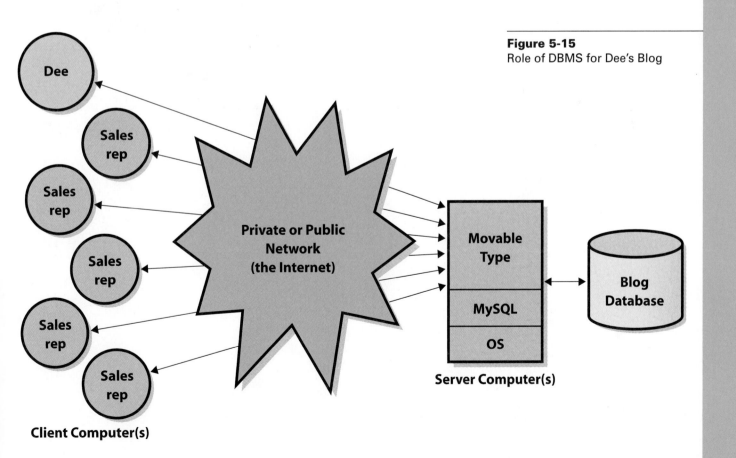

Dee
Sales rep
Sales rep
Sales rep
Sales rep
Sales rep
Client Computer(s)
Private or Public Network (the Internet)
Movable Type
MySQL
OS
Server Computer(s)
Blog Database

While this system does run a DBMS, it is completely isolated from the rest of the Emerson databases and really should not be of concern to the IT department. Dee is not proposing to replace Oracle with MySQL for things like processing orders or paying salespeople. She just wants to include MySQL, as part of the functionality of her application, on the server.

With this knowledge, Dee could explain what she wants to do and that her project is no threat or exception to the Oracle standard. It is an isolated system that needs MySQL to run.

Ultimately, Don made that exact argument to the IT department. Once the department understood Dee's plan, they had no problem with Dee's use of MySQL—as long as she paid any required licence fees for it out of her own budget. Unfortunately, without knowledge of database concepts, Dee was unable to make that argument herself, so she was forced to hire her consultant to make that argument for her. Doing this meant a delay of another few days as well as an additional expense. Still, she had passed another hurdle on the way to developing her system.

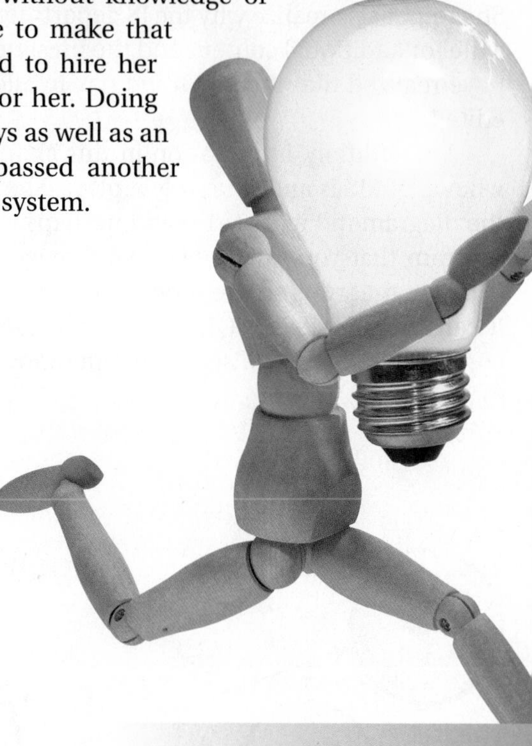

Active Review

Use this Active Review to verify that you understand the material in the chapter. You can read the entire chapter and then perform the tasks in this review, or you can read the material for just one question and perform the tasks in this review for that question before moving on to the next one.

Q1 What is content?

Describe what is meant by content. How has content changed with computers and access to the Internet?

Q2 How can content be organized?

What is a web content management system? How have content management systems evolved over time?

Q3 What is the purpose of a database?

Describe the purpose of a database. Explain when to use a spreadsheet and when to use a database.

Q4 What does a database contain?

Explain the hierarchy of data from bytes to tables. Show how a database stores the relationships among rows. Define *key* and *foreign key*. Define *metadata*, and explain how metadata makes databases more useful.

Q5 What is a DBMS, and what does it do?

Describe a database application system. Define *DBMS*. Name three prominent DBMS products. Describe the difference between a database and a DBMS. Explain the three major functions of a DBMS. What is SQL used for?

Q6 What is a database application?

Name and describe the components of a database application. Describe the circumstances that require a special logic for database applications. Describe the lost-update problem. Explain, in general terms, how this problem is prevented.

Q7 What is the difference between an enterprise and a personal DBMS?

Explain the function of an enterprise DBMS and describe its characteristics. Explain the function of a personal DBMS and describe its characteristics. Name the only surviving personal DBMS.

Key Terms and Concepts

Using Your Knowledge

1. Suppose you are a marketing assistant for a consumer electronics company and are in charge of setting up your company's booth at trade shows. Weeks before the shows, you meet with the marketing managers and determine what equipment they want to display. Then, you identify each of the components that need to be shipped and schedule a shipper to deliver them to the trade-show site. You then supervise convention personnel as they set up the booths and equipment. Once the show is over, you supervise the packing of the booth and all equipment as well as schedule its shipment back to your home office. Once the equipment arrives, you check it in to your warehouse to ensure that all pieces of the booth and all equipment are returned. If there are problems due to shipping damage or loss, you handle those problems. Your job is important; at a typical show, you are responsible for more than a quarter of a million dollars of equipment.
   a. You will need to track data about booth components, equipment, shippers, and shipments. List typical fields for each type of data.
   b. Could you use a spreadsheet to keep track of this data? What would be the advantages and disadvantages of doing so?
   c. Using your answer to question (a), give an example of two relationships that you need to track. Show the keys and foreign keys for each.
   d. Which of the following components of a database application are you likely to need: data entry forms, reports, queries, or application programs? Explain one use for each component you will need.
   e. Will your application be single-user or multiuser? Will you need a personal DBMS or an enterprise DBMS? If a personal DBMS, which product will you use?

2. Samantha Green owns and operates Twigs Tree Trimming Service. Recall from Chapter 3 that Samantha has a degree from a forestry program and recently opened her business in Winnipeg. Her business consists of many one-time operations (e.g., remove a tree or stump), as well as recurring services (e.g., trimming customers' trees every year or two). When business is slow, Samantha calls former clients to remind them of her services and of the need to trim their trees on a regular basis.
   a. Name and describe tables of data that Samantha will need to run her business. Indicate possible fields for each table.
   b. Could Samantha use a spreadsheet to keep track of this data? What would be the advantages and disadvantages of doing so?
   c. Using your answer to question (a), give an example of two relationships that Samantha needs to track. Show the keys and foreign keys for each.
   d. Which of the following components of a database application is Samantha likely to need: data entry forms, reports, queries, or application programs? Explain one use for each component she needs.
   e. Will this application be single-user or multiuser? Will she need a personal DBMS or an enterprise DBMS? If a personal DBMS, which product will she use?

3. FiredUp, Inc. is a small business owned by Curt and Julie Robards. Based in Brisbane, Australia, FiredUp manufactures and sells FiredNow, a lightweight camping stove. Recall from Chapter 3 that Curt used his previous experience as an aerospace engineer to invent a burning nozzle that enables the stove

to stay lit in very high winds. Using her industrial design training, Julie designed the stove so that it is small, lightweight, easy to set up, and very stable. Curt and Julie sell the stove directly to their customers over the Internet and via phone. The warranty on the stove covers five years of cost-free repair for stoves used for recreational purposes.

FiredUp wants to track every stove and the customer who purchased it. They want to know which customers own which stoves, in case they need to notify customers of safety problems or need to order a stove recall. Curt and Julie also want to keep track of any repairs they have performed.

a. Name and describe tables of data that FiredUp will need. Indicate possible fields for each table.
b. Could FiredUp use a spreadsheet to keep track of data? What would be the advantages and disadvantages of doing so?
c. Using your answer to (a), give an example of two relationships FiredUp needs to track. Show the keys and foreign keys for each.
d. Which of the following components of a database application is FiredUp likely to need: data entry forms, reports, queries, application programs? Explain one use for each needed component.
e. Will this application be single-user or multiuser? Will FiredUp need a personal DBMS or an enterprise DBMS? If a personal DBMS, which product will it use? If an enterprise DBMS, which product can it obtain licence-free?

Case Study 5

Behind the Race

For hundreds of thousands of athletes, competing in a marathon or triathlon is the culmination of dedicated training and endurance. Although largely invisible, a similar regime can exist for the organizers who must manage planning, donations, fundraising, custom websites, marketing, volunteer management, online registration, newsletters, and publication of results. While not directly related to the event itself, these activities can be individually and collectively overwhelming.

Originally established as a web portal providing regional grassroots sports information to recreational athletes, the founders of Active.com soon realized that each time one of the hundreds of autonomous athletic organizations planned an event, they were essentially re-inventing a wheel. The Active Network (www.active.com) was formed to leverage online technology and marketing solutions.

Now, with one contact, planning an event could be simplified through tried and tested solutions from an organization that specialized in providing tailored solutions for a better experience and exposure for participants. Rather than one-off or ad hoc solutions cobbled together by part-time administrators—who in many cases were doing things for the first time—all organizations regardless of their size could have access to state-of-the art systems.

It was a solution that had legs. By focusing on three areas, enhancing the technology to address customers' specific vertical market needs, enhancing the athletes' or participants' overall experience with good content and tools, and providing heightened exposure for its clients, the company has been able to work both sides of the business equation—driving revenue and reducing cost. The Active Network has grown to provide online technology and marketing solutions to thousands of business owners in over 80 sports and recreational markets that serve millions of participants worldwide. Additionally, the company has expanded its reach to offer these same services to other such verticals as parks and recreation departments, golf courses, schools and universities, business events, and camps.

The company currently has numerous media properties with Active.com being the most popular. Building upon its vision to enable and encourage every individual to visit one online community to learn about, share, register, and ultimately participate in any activity, The Active Network had become the largest searchable worldwide directory of sports and recreational activities. Providing access to tools such as community message boards and specialized moderators, and allowing members to post photographs and videos, The Active Network was a destination site for athletes and a trusted community among its members.

Source: The Active Network. Used with permission.

Questions

1. What problem does The Active Network solve for event organizers?
2. Does The Active Network have any other advantages other than economies of scale?
3. Are there are any network effects for Active.com? (*Hint:* What are the benefits to having a large number of events in one place?)
4. Would The Active Network be an advantage or a disadvantage if not used?
5. What kind of information would The Active Network have about its members? How would this be useful and to whom? What is the value of this information?

Visit MyMISLab at **www.pearsoned.ca/mymislab**. MyMISLab is a state-of-the-art, interactive, online solution that combines multimedia, tutorials, and quizzes. Use MyMISLab for *Experiencing MIS* to prepare for tests and exams, and go to class ready to learn!

What Do YOU Think?

Nobody Said I Shouldn't

"My name is Kelly, and I do systems support for our group. I configure the new computers, set up the network, make sure the servers are operating, and so forth. I also do all the database backups. I've always liked computers. After high school, I worked odd jobs to make some money, then I got an associate degree in information technology from our local community college.

"Anyway, as I said, I make backup copies of our databases. One weekend, I didn't have much going on, so I copied one of the database backups to a CD and took it home. I had taken a class on database processing as part of my associate degree, and we used SQL Server (our database management system) in my class. In fact, I suppose that's part of the reason I got the job. Anyway, it was easy to restore the database on my computer at home, and I did.

"Of course, as they'll tell you in your database class, one of the big advantages of database processing is that databases have metadata, or data that describe the content of the database. So, although I didn't know what tables were in our database, I did know how to access the SQL Server metadata. I just queried a table called sysTables to learn the names of our tables. From there it was easy to find out what columns each table had.

"I found tables with data about orders, customers, salespeople, and so forth, and just to amuse myself and to see how much of the query language SQL I could remember, I started playing around with the data. I was curious to know which order-entry clerk was the best, so I started querying each clerk's order data, the total number of orders, total order amounts, things like that. It was easy to do and fun.

"I know one of the order-entry clerks, Jason, pretty well, so I started looking at the data for his orders. I was just curious, and it was very simple SQL. I was just playing around with the data when I noticed something odd. All his biggest orders were with one company, Valley Appliances, and even stranger, every one of its orders had a huge discount. I thought, Well, maybe that's typical. Out of curiosity, I started looking at data for the other clerks, and very few of them had an order with Valley Appliances. But when they did, Valley didn't get a big discount. Then I looked at the rest of Jason's orders, and none of them had much in the way of discounts, either.

"The next Friday, a bunch of us went out for a beer after work. I happened to see Jason, so I asked him about Valley Appliances and made a joke about the discounts. He asked me what I meant, and then I told him that I'd been looking at the data for fun and that I saw this odd pattern. He laughed, said he 'just did his job,' and then changed the subject.

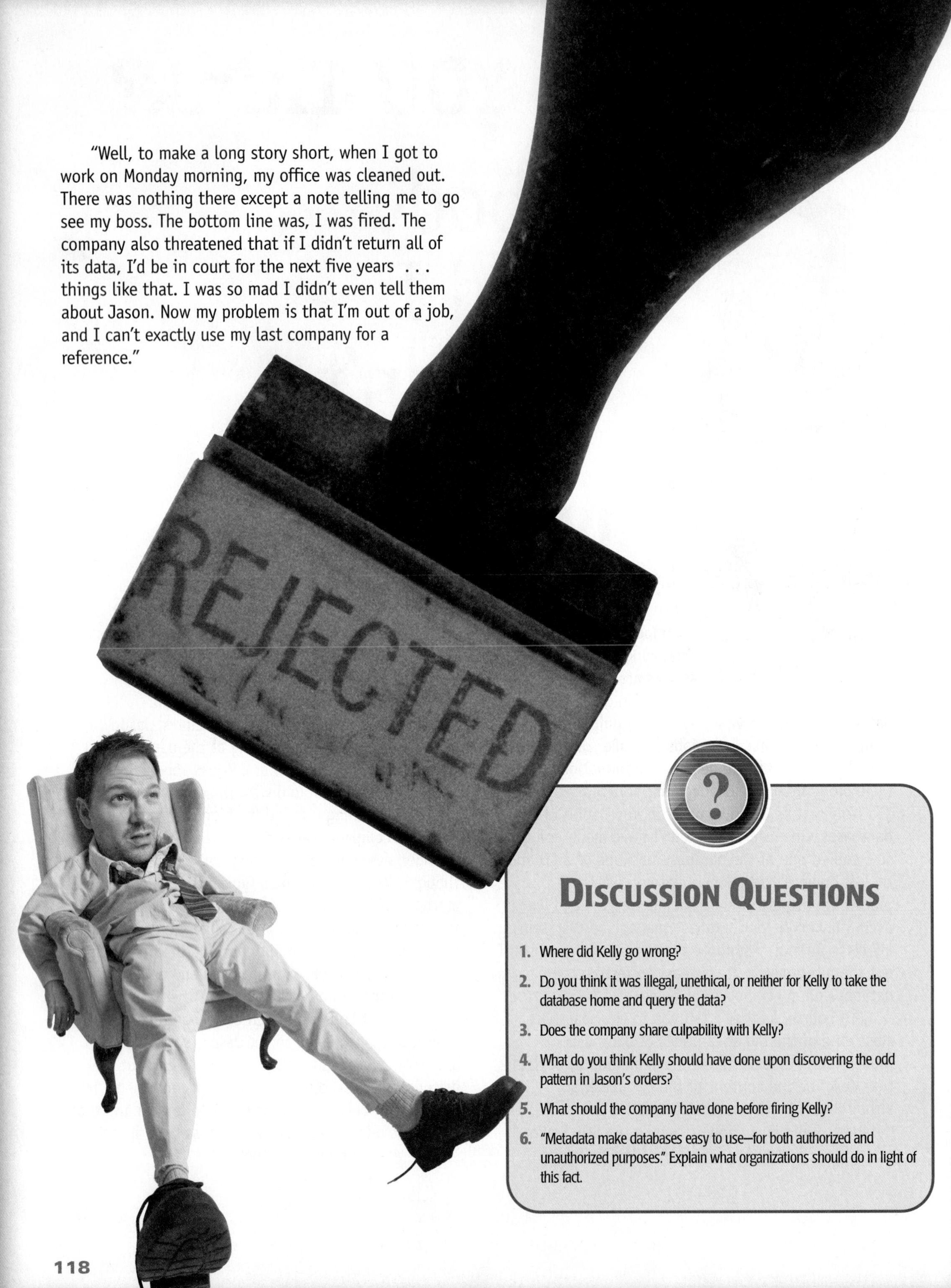

"Well, to make a long story short, when I got to work on Monday morning, my office was cleaned out. There was nothing there except a note telling me to go see my boss. The bottom line was, I was fired. The company also threatened that if I didn't return all of its data, I'd be in court for the next five years . . . things like that. I was so mad I didn't even tell them about Jason. Now my problem is that I'm out of a job, and I can't exactly use my last company for a reference."

Discussion Questions

1. Where did Kelly go wrong?
2. Do you think it was illegal, unethical, or neither for Kelly to take the database home and query the data?
3. Does the company share culpability with Kelly?
4. What do you think Kelly should have done upon discovering the odd pattern in Jason's orders?
5. What should the company have done before firing Kelly?
6. "Metadata make databases easy to use—for both authorized and unauthorized purposes." Explain what organizations should do in light of this fact.

Chapter Extension 5a

Database Design

In this chapter extension, you will learn about data modelling and how data models are transformed into database designs. You'll also learn the important role business professionals play in the development of a database application system.

Study Questions

- Q1 Who will volunteer?
- Q2 How are database application systems developed?
- Q3 What are the components of the entity-relationship data model?
- Q4 How is a data model transformed into a database design?
- Q5 What is the user's role?
- Q6 Who will volunteer? (continued)

Q1 Who Will Volunteer?

Suppose you are the manager of fundraising for a local public television station. Twice a year you conduct fund drives during which the station runs commercials that ask viewers to donate. These drives are important; they provide nearly 40 percent of the station's operating budget. One of your job functions is to find volunteers to staff the phones during these drives. You need 10 volunteers per night for six nights, or 60 people, twice per year. The volunteers' job is exhausting, and normally a volunteer will work only one night during a drive. Finding volunteers for each drive is a perpetual headache. Two months before a drive begins, you and your staff start calling potential volunteers. You first call volunteers from prior drives, using a roster that your administrative assistant prepares for each drive. Some volunteers have been helping for years; you'd like to know that information before you call them so that you can tell them how much you appreciate their continuing support. Unfortunately, the roster does not have that data.

Additionally, some volunteers are more effective than others. Some have a particular knack for increasing the callers' donations. Although those data are available, the information is not in a format you can use when calling for volunteers. You think you could better staff the fundraising drives if you had that missing information.

You know that you can use a computer database to keep better track of prior volunteers' service and performance, but you're not sure how to proceed. By the end of this chapter extension, when we return to this fundraising situation, you will know what to do.

Q2 How Are Database Application Systems Developed?

You learned in Chapter 5 that a database application system consists of a database, a DBMS, and one or more database applications. A database application, in turn, consists of forms, reports, queries, and possibly application programs.

Figure CE5a-1
Database Development Process

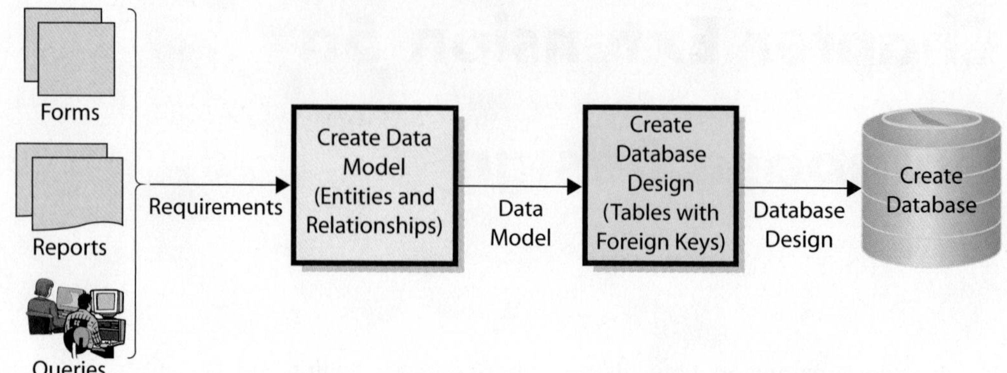

The question then becomes this: How are such systems developed? And, even more important to you, what is the user's role? We will address these questions in this chapter extension.

Figure CE5a-1 summarizes the database application system development process. First, the developers interview users and develop the requirements for the new system. During this process, the developers analyze existing forms, reports, queries, and other user activities. The requirements for the database are then summarized in something called a **data model,** which is a logical representation of the structure of the data. The data model contains a description of both the data and the relationships among the data. It is akin to a blueprint. Just as building architects create a blueprint before they start construction, so, too, do database developers create a data model before they start designing the database.

Once the users have validated and approved the data model, it is transformed into a database design. After that, the design is implemented in a database, and that database is then filled with user data.

You will learn much more about systems development in Chapter 11. We discuss data modelling here because users have a crucial role in the success of any database development: They must validate and approve the data model. Only the users know what should be in the database.

Consider, for example, a database of students that an adviser uses for his or her advisees. What should be in it? Students? Classes? Records of emails from students? Records of meetings with students? Majors? Student organizations? Even when we know what themes should be in the database, we must ask, How detailed should the records be? Should the database include campus addresses? Home addresses? Billing addresses?

In fact, there are many possibilities, and the database developers do not and cannot know what to include. They do know, however, that a database must include all the data necessary for the users to perform their jobs. Ideally, it contains that amount of data and no more. So, during database development, the developers must rely on the users to tell them what they need in the database. They will rely on the users to check the data model and to verify it for correctness, completeness, and appropriate level of detail. That verification will be your job. We begin with a discussion of the entity-relationship data model—the most common tool to use to construct data models.

Q3 What Are the Components of the Entity-Relationship Data Model?

The most popular technique for creating a data model is the **entity-relationship (E-R) data model.** With it, developers describe the content of a database by defining the things (*entities*) that will be stored in the database and the *relationships* among those entities. A second, less popular tool for data modelling is the **Unified Modelling Language (UML).** We will not describe that tool here. However, if you learn how to interpret E-R models, with a bit of study you will be able to understand UML models as well.

Entities

An **entity** is some thing that the users want to track. Examples of entities are *Order, Customer, Salesperson,* and *Item.* Some entities represent a physical object, such as *Item* or *Salesperson*; others represent a logical construct or transaction, such as *Order* or *Contract.* For reasons beyond this discussion, entity names are always singular. We use *Order,* not *Orders;Salesperson,* not *Salespersons.*

Entities have **attributes** that describe characteristics of the entity. Example attributes of *Order* are *OrderNumber, OrderDate, SubTotal, Tax, Total,* and so forth. Example attributes of *Salesperson* are *SalespersonName, Email, Phone,* and so forth.

Entities have an **identifier,** which is an attribute (or group of attributes) whose value is associated with one and only one entity instance. For example, *OrderNumber* is an identifier of *Order,* because only one *Order* instance has a given value of *OrderNumber.* For the same reason, *CustomerNumber* is an identifier of *Customer.* If each member of the sales staff has a unique name, then *SalespersonName* is an identifier of *Salesperson.*

Before we continue, consider that last sentence. Is the salesperson's name unique among the sales staff? Both now and in the future? Who decides the answer to such a question? Only the users know whether this is true; the database developers cannot know. This example underlines why it is important for you to be able to interpret data models, because only users like yourself will know for sure.

Figure CE5a-2 shows examples of entities for the *Student* database. Each entity is shown in a rectangle. The name of the entity is just above the rectangle,

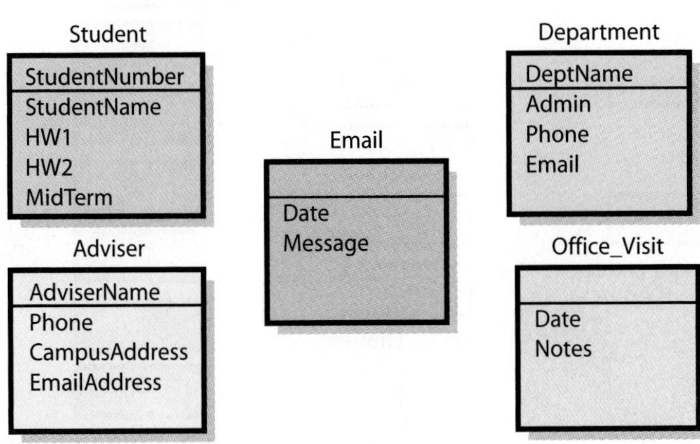

Figure CE5a-2
Student Data Model Entities

and the identifier is shown in a section at the top of the entity. Entity attributes are shown in the remainder of the rectangle. In Figure CE5a-2, the *Adviser* entity has an identifier called *AdviserName* and the attributes *Phone, CampusAddress,* and *EmailAddress.*

Observe that the entities *Email* and *Office_Visit* do not have an identifier. Unlike *Student* or *Adviser,* the users do not have an attribute that identifies a particular email. We could make one up. For example, we could say that the identifier of *Email* is *EmailNumber,* but if we do so we are not modelling how the users view their world. Instead, we are forcing something onto the users. Be aware of this possibility when you review data models about your business. Do not allow the database developers to create something that is not part of your business world.

Relationships

Entities have **relationships** to each other. An *Order,* for example, has a relationship to a *Customer* entity and also to a *Salesperson* entity. In the Student database, a *Student* has a relationship to an *Adviser,* and an *Adviser* has a relationship to a *Department.*

Figure CE5a-3 shows sample *Department, Adviser,* and *Student* entities and their relationships. For simplicity, this figure shows just the identifier of the entities and not the other attributes. For this sample data, *Accounting* has three professors, Jones, Wu, and Lopez, and *Finance* has two professors, Smith and Greene.

The relationship between *Advisers* and *Students* is a bit more complicated, because in this example an adviser is allowed to advise many students, and a student is allowed to have many advisers. Perhaps this happens because students can have multiple majors. In any case, note that Professor Jones advises students 100 and 400 and that student 100 is advised by both Professors Jones and Smith.

Diagrams like the one in Figure CE5a-3 are too cumbersome for use in database design discussions. Instead, database designers use diagrams called **entity-relationship (E-R) diagrams.** Figure CE5a-4 shows an E-R diagram for the data in Figure CE5a-3. In this figure, all the entities of one type are represented by a single rectangle. Thus, there are rectangles for the *Department, Adviser,* and *Student* entities. Attributes are shown as before in Figure CE5a-2.

Figure CE5a-3
Example of Department, Adviser, and Student Entities and Relationships

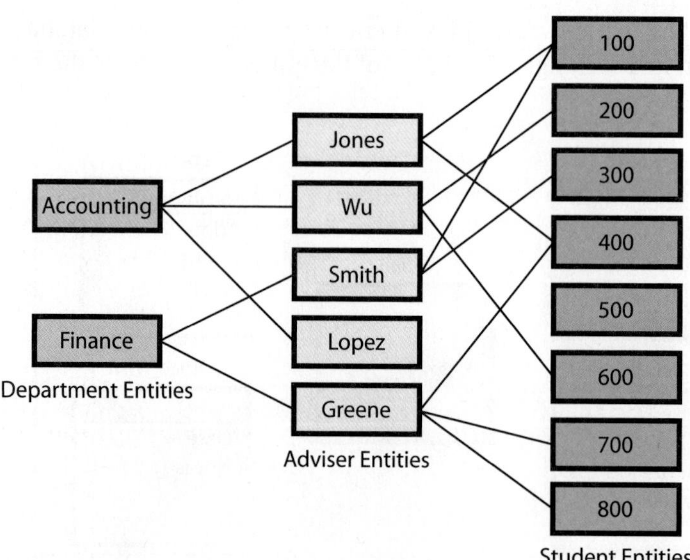

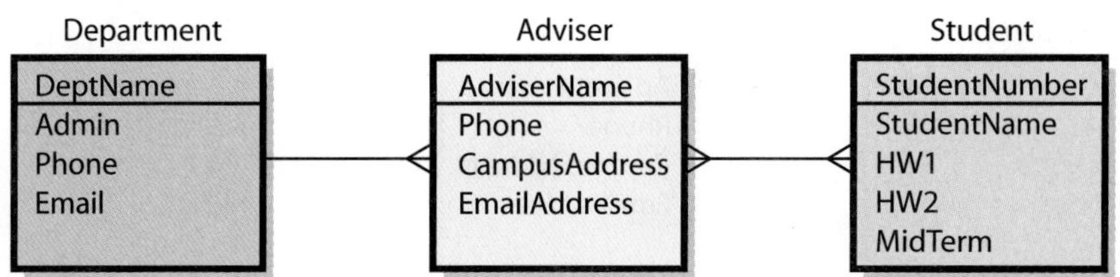

Figure CE5a-4
Example of Relationships—Version 1

Additionally, a line is used to represent a relationship between two entities. Notice the line between *Department* and *Adviser,* for example. The forked lines on the right side of that line signify that a department may have more than one adviser. The little lines, which are referred to as a **crow's foot,** are shorthand for the multiple lines between *Department* and *Adviser* in Figure CE5a-3. Relationships like this one are called **one-to-many (1:N) relationships** because one department can have many advisers.

Now examine the line between *Adviser* and *Student.* Here, a crow's foot appears at each end of the line. This notation signifies that an adviser can be related to many students and that a student can be related to many advisers, which is the situation in Figure CE5a-3. Relationships like this one are called **many-to-many (N:M) relationships**, because one adviser can have many students and one student can have many advisers.

Students sometimes find the notation N:M confusing. Interpret the *N* and *M* to mean that a variable number, greater than one, is allowed on each side of the relationship. Such a relationship is not written *N:N,* because that notation would imply that there are the same number of entities on each side of the relationship, which is not necessarily true. *N:M* means that more than one entity is allowed on each side of the relationship and that the number of entities on each side can be different.

Figure CE5a-4 is an example of an entity-relationship diagram. Unfortunately, there are several different styles of entity-relationship diagrams. This one is called, not surprisingly, a **crow's-foot diagram** version. You may learn other versions if you take a database management class.

Figure CE5a-5 shows the same entities with different assumptions. Here, advisers may advise in more than one department, but a student may have only one adviser, representing a policy that students may not have multiple majors.

Which, if either, of these versions is correct? Only the users know. These alternatives illustrate the kinds of questions you will need to answer when a database designer asks you to check a data model for correctness.

The crow's-foot notation shows the maximum number of entities that can be involved in a relationship. Accordingly, they are called the relationship's **maximum cardinality.** Common examples of maximum cardinality are 1:N, N:M, and 1:1 (not shown).

Another important question is, "What is the minimum number of entities required in the relationship?" Must an adviser have a student to advise, and must a student have an adviser? Constraints on minimum requirements are called **minimum cardinalities.**

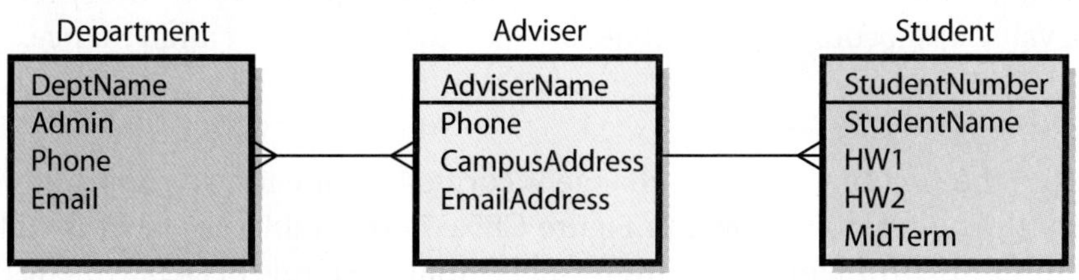

Figure CE5a-5
Example of Relationships—Version 2

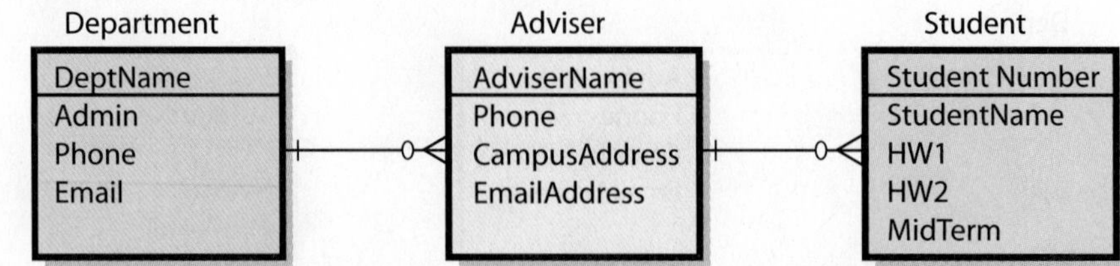

Figure CE5a-6
Example of Relationships Showing Minimum Cardinalities

Figure CE5a-6 presents a third version of this E-R diagram that shows both maximum and minimum cardinalities. The vertical bar on a line means that at least one entity of that type is required. The small oval means that the entity is optional; the relationship need not have an entity of that type.

Thus, in Figure CE5a-6, a department is not required to have a relationship to any adviser, but an adviser is required to belong to a department. Similarly, an adviser is not required to have a relationship to a student, but a student is required to have a relationship to an adviser. Note, also, that the maximum cardinalities in Figure CE5a-6 have been changed so that both are 1:N.

Is the model in Figure CE5a-6 a good one? It depends on the rules of the university. Again, only the users know for sure.

Q4 How Is a Data Model Transformed into a Database Design?

Database design is the process of converting a data model into tables, relationships, and data constraints. The database design team transforms entities into tables and expresses relationships by defining foreign keys. Database design is a complicated subject; as with data modelling, it occupies weeks in a database management class. In this section, however, we will introduce two important database design concepts: normalization and the representation of two kinds of relationships. The first concept is a foundation of database design, and the second will help you understand key considerations made during design.

Normalization

Normalization is the process of converting poorly structured tables into two or more well-structured tables. A table is such a simple construct that you may wonder how one could possibly be poorly structured. In truth, there are many ways that tables can be malformed—so many, in fact, that researchers have published hundreds of papers on this topic alone.

Consider the *Employee* table in Figure CE5a-7. It lists employee names, hire dates, email addresses, and the name and number of the department in which the employee works. This table seems innocent enough. But consider what happens when the Accounting department changes its name to Accounting and Finance. Because department names are duplicated in this table, every row that has a value of "Accounting" must be changed to "Accounting and Finance."

Data Integrity Problems

Suppose the Accounting name change is correctly made in two rows, but not in the third. The result is shown in Figure CE5a-7. This table has what is called a **data integrity problem:** Some rows indicate that the name of Department 100 is

Figure CE5a-7
A Poorly Designed Employee Table

Employee

Name	HireDate	Email	DeptNo	DeptName
Jones	Feb 1, 2002	Jones@ourcompany.com	100	Accounting
Smith	Dec 3, 2004	Smith@ourcompany.com	200	Marketing
Chau	March 7, 2004	Chau@ourcompany.com	100	Accounting
Greene	July 17, 2003	Greene@ourcompany.com	100	Accounting

a. Table before update

Employee

Name	HireDate	Email	DeptNo	DeptName
Jones	Feb 1, 2002	Jones@ourcompany.com	100	Accounting and Finance
Smith	Dec 3, 2004	Smith@ourcompany.com	200	Marketing
Chau	March 7, 2004	Chau@ourcompany.com	100	Accounting and Finance
Greene	July 17, 2003	Greene@ourcompany.com	100	Accounting

b. Table with incomplete update

Accounting and Finance, and another row indicates that the name of Department 100 is Accounting.

This problem is easy to spot in this small table. But consider a table in a large database that has more than 300 000 rows. Once a table that large develops serious data integrity problems, months of labour will be required to remove them.

Data integrity problems are serious. A table that has data integrity problems will produce incorrect and inconsistent information. Users will lose confidence in the information, and the system will develop a poor reputation. Information systems with poor reputations become heavy burdens to the organizations that use them.

Normalizing for Data Integrity

The data integrity problem can occur only if data are duplicated. Because of this, one easy way to eliminate the problem is to eliminate the duplicated data. We can do this by transforming the table in Figure CE5a-7 into two tables, as shown in Figure CE5a-8. Here, the name of the department is stored just once; therefore no data inconsistencies can occur.

Figure CE5a-8
Two Normalized Tables

Employee

Name	HireDate	Email	DeptNo
Jones	Feb 1, 2002	Jones@ourcompany.com	100
Smith	Dec 3, 2004	Smith@ourcompany.com	200
Chau	March 7, 2004	Chau@ourcompany.com	100
Greene	July 17, 2003	Greene@ourcompany.com	100

Department

DeptNo	DeptName
100	Accounting
200	Marketing
300	Information Systems

Of course, to produce an employee report that includes the department name, the two tables in Figure CE5a-8 will need to be joined back together. Because such joining of tables is common, DBMS products have been programmed to perform it efficiently, but it still requires work. From this example, you can see a trade-off in database design: Normalized tables eliminate data duplication, but they can be slower to process. Dealing with such trade-offs is an important consideration in database design.

The general goal of normalization is to construct tables such that every table has a *single* topic or theme. In good writing, every paragraph should have a single theme. This is true of databases as well; every table should have a single theme. The problem with the table in Figure CE5a-7 is that it has two independent themes: employees and departments. The way to correct the problem is to split the table into two tables, each with its own theme. In this case, we create an *Employee* table and a *Department* table, as shown in Figure CE5a-8.

As mentioned, there are dozens of ways that tables can be poorly formed. Database practitioners classify tables into various **normal forms** according to the kinds of problems they have. Transforming a table into a normal form to remove duplicated data and other problems is called *normalizing* the table.[3] Thus, when you hear a database designer say, "Those tables are not normalized," she does not mean that the tables have irregular, not-normal data. Instead, she means that the tables have a format that could cause data integrity problems.

Summary of Normalization

As a future user of databases, you do not need to know the details of normalization. Instead, understand the general principle that every normalized (well formed) table has one and only one theme. Further, tables that are not normalized are subject to data integrity problems.

Be aware, too, that normalization is just one criterion for evaluating database designs. Because normalized designs can be slower to process, database designers sometimes choose to accept non-normalized tables. The best design depends on users' requirements.

Representing Relationships

Figure CE5a-9 shows the steps involved in transforming a data model into a relational database design. First, the database designer creates a table for each entity. The identifier of the entity becomes the key of the table. Each attribute of the entity becomes a column of the table. Next, the resulting tables are normalized so that each table has a single theme. Once that has been done, the next step is to represent relationships among those tables.

For example, consider the E-R diagram in Figure CE5a-10(a). The *Adviser* entity has a 1:N relationship to the *Student* entity. To create the database design, we construct a table for *Adviser* and a second table for *Student*, as shown in

Figure CE5a-9
Transforming a Data Model into a Database Design

- Represent each entity with a table
  - Entity identifier becomes table key
  - Entity attributes become table columns
- Normalize tables as necessary
- Represent relationships
  - Use foreign keys
  - Add additional tables for N:M relationships

3. See Kroenke, D., *Database Processing*, 10th ed. (Upper Saddle River, NJ: Prentice Hall, 2006) for more information.

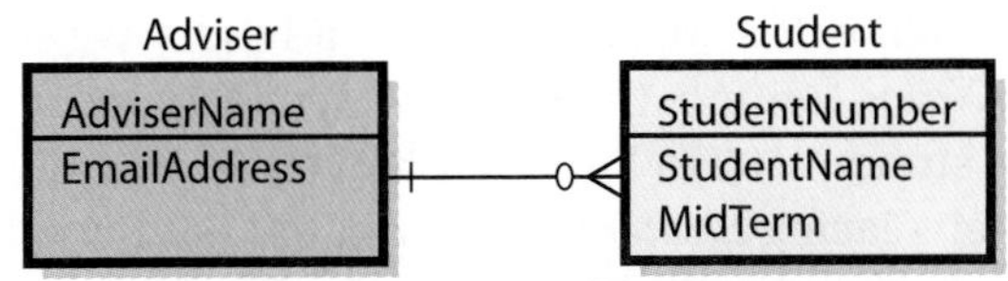

a. 1:N Relationship between Adviser and Student entities

Adviser Table—Key is AdviserName

AdviserName	EmailAddress
Jones	Jones@myuniv.edu
Choi	Choi@myuniv.edu
Jackson	Jackson@myuniv.edu

Student Table—Key is StudentNumber

StudentNumber	StudentName	MidTerm
100	Lisa	90
200	Jennie	85
300	Jason	82
400	Terry	95

b. Creating a table for each entity

Adviser Table—Key is AdviserName

AdviserName	Email
Jones	Jones@myuniv.edu
Choi	Choi@myuniv.edu
Jackson	Jackson@myuniv.edu

Student—Key is StudentNumber

Foreign Key Column Represents Relationship

StudentNumber	StudentName	MidTerm	AdviserName
100	Lisa	90	Jackson
200	Jennie	85	Jackson
300	Jason	82	Choi
400	Terry	95	Jackson

c. Using the AdviserName foreign key to represent the 1:N relationship

Figure CE5a-10
Representing a 1:N Relationship

Figure CE5a-10(b). The key of the *Adviser* table is *AdviserName*, and the key of the *Student* table is *StudentNumber*.

Further, the *EmailAddress* attribute of the *Adviser* entity becomes the *EmailAddress* column of the *Adviser* table, and the *StudentName* and *MidTerm* attributes of the *Student* entity become the *StudentName* and *MidTerm* columns of the *Student* table.

The next task is to represent the relationship. Because we are using the relational model, we know that we must add a foreign key to one of the two tables. The possibilities are: (1) place the foreign key *StudentNumber* in the *Adviser* table, or (2) place the foreign key *AdviserName* in the *Student* table.

The correct choice is to place *AdviserName* in the *Student* table, as shown in Figure CE5a-10(c). To determine a student's adviser, we just look into the *AdviserName* column of that student's row. To determine the adviser's students, we search the *AdviserName* column in the *Student* table to determine which rows have that adviser's name. If a student changes advisers, we simply change the value in the *AdviserName* column. Changing *Jackson* to *Jones* in the first row, for example, will assign student 100 to Professor Jones.

For this data model, placing *StudentNumber* in the *Adviser* table would be incorrect. If we were to do that, we could assign only one student to an adviser. There is no place to assign a second adviser.

This strategy for placing foreign keys will not work for all relationships, however. Consider the data model in Figure CE5a-11(a); here, there is an N:M relationship between advisers and students. An adviser may have many students, and a student may have multiple advisers (for multiple majors). The

Figure CE5a-11
Representing an N:M Relationship

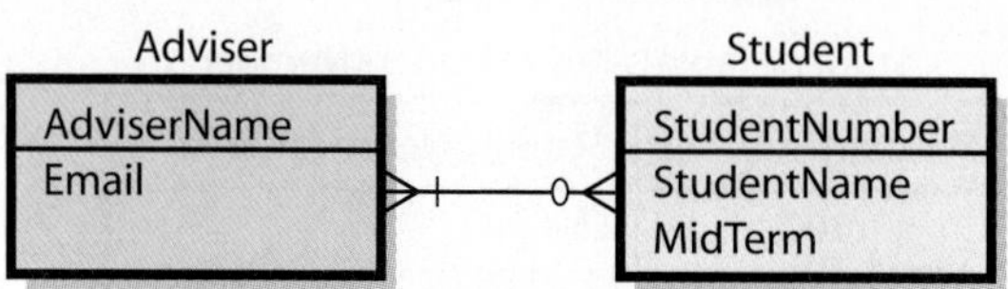

a. N:M Relationship between Adviser and Student

Adviser—Key is AdviserName

AdviserName	Email
Jones	Jones@myuniv.edu
Choi	Choi@myuniv.edu
Jackson	Jackson@myuniv.edu

Student—Key is StudentNumber

StudentNumber	StudentName	MidTerm	AdviserName
100	Lisa	90	Jackson
200	Jennie	85	Jackson
300	Jason	82	Choi
400	Terry	95	Jackson

No room to place second or third AdviserName

b. Incorrect representation of N:M relationship

Adviser—Key is AdviserName

AdviserName	Email
Jones	Jones@myuniv.edu
Choi	Choi@myuniv.edu
Jackson	Jackson@myuniv.edu

Student—Key is StudentNumber

StudentNumber	StudentName	MidTerm
100	Lisa	90
200	Jennie	85
300	Jason	82
400	Terry	95

Adviser_Student_Intersection

AdviserName	StudentNumber
Jackson	100
Jackson	200
Choi	300
Jackson	400
Choi	100
Jones	100

Student 100 has three advisers.

c. Adviser_Student_Intersection table represents the N:M relationship

strategy we used for the 1:N data model will not work here. To see why, examine Figure CE5a-11(b). If student 100 has more than one adviser, there is no place to record second or subsequent advisers.

It turns out that to represent an N:M relationship, we need to create a third table, as shown in Figure CE5a-11(c). The third table has two columns, *AdviserName* and *StudentNumber*. Each row of the table means that the given adviser advises the student with the given number.

As you can imagine, there is a great deal more to database design than we have presented here. Still, this section should give you an idea of the tasks that need to be accomplished to create a database. You should also realize that the database design is a direct consequence of decisions made in the data model. If the data model is wrong, the database design will be wrong as well.

Q5 What Is the User's Role?

As stated, a database is a model of how the users view their business world. This means that the users are the final judges as to what data the database should contain and how the records in that database should be related to one another.

The easiest time to change the database structure is during the data modelling stage. Changing a relationship from 1:N to N:M in a data model is simply a matter of changing the 1:N notation to N:M. However, once the database has been constructed, loaded with data, and with application forms, reports, queries, and application programs created, changing a 1:N relationship to N:M means weeks of work.

You can glean some idea of why this might be true by contrasting Figure CE5a-10(c) with Figure CE5a-11(c). Suppose that instead of having just a few rows, each table has thousands of rows; in that case, transforming the database from one format to the other involves considerable work. Even worse, however, is that application components will need to be changed as well. For example, if students have at most one adviser, then a single text box can be used to enter *AdviserName*. If students can have multiple advisers, then a multiple-row table will need to be used to enter *AdviserName*, and a program will need to be written to store the values of *AdviserName* into the *Adviser_Student_Intersection* table. There are dozens of other consequences as well, consequences that will translate into wasted labour and wasted expense.

The conclusion from this discussion is that user review of a data model is crucial. When a database is developed for your use, you must carefully review the data model. If you do not understand any aspect of it, you should ask for clarification until you do. The data model must accurately reflect your view of the business. If it does not, the database will be designed incorrectly, and the applications will be difficult to use, if not worthless. Do not proceed unless the data model is accurate.

As a corollary, when asked to review a data model, take that review seriously. Devote the time necessary to perform a thorough review. Any mistakes you miss will come back to haunt you, and by then the cost of correction may be very high with regard to both time and expense. This brief introduction to data modelling shows why databases can be more difficult to develop than spreadsheets. This difficulty causes some people to resist the idea of a database.

Q6 Who Will Volunteer? (continued)

Knowing what you know now, if you were the manager of fundraising at the TV station you would hire a consultant and expect the consultant to interview all the key users. From those interviews, the consultant would then construct a data model.

You now know that the structure of the database must reflect the way the users think about their activities. If the consultant did not take the time to interview you and your staff or did not construct a data model and ask you to review it, you would know that you are not receiving good service and would take corrective action.

Suppose you found a consultant who interviewed your staff for several hours and then constructed the data model shown in Figure CE5a-12. This data model has an entity for *Prospect*, an entity for *Employee*, and three additional entities for *Contact*, *Phone*, and *Work*. The *Contact* entity records contacts that you or other employees have made with the prospective volunteer. This record is necessary so that you know what has been said to whom. The *Phone* entity is used to record multiple phone numbers for each prospective volunteer, and the *Work* entity records work that the prospect has performed for the station.

After you reviewed and approved this data model, the consultant constructed the database design shown in Figure CE5a-13. In this design, table keys are underlined, foreign keys are shown in italics, and columns that are both table and foreign keys are underlined and italicized. Observe that the *Name* column is the table key of *Prospect*, and that it is both part of the table key and a foreign key in *Phone*, *Contact*, and *Work*.

The consultant did not like having the *Name* column used as a key or as part of a key in so many tables. Based on her interviews, she suspected that prospect names are fluid—and that sometimes the same prospect name is recorded in different ways (e.g., sometimes with a middle initial and sometimes without). If that were to happen, phone, contact, and work data could be misallocated to prospect names. Accordingly, the consultant added a new column—*ProspectID*—to the prospect table and created the design shown in Figure CE5a-14. Values of this ID will have no meaning to the users, but the ID will be used to ensure that each prospect obtains a unique record in the *Volunteer* database. Because this ID has no meaning to the users, the consultant will hide it on the forms and reports that users see.

Figure CE5a-12
Data Model for Volunteer Database

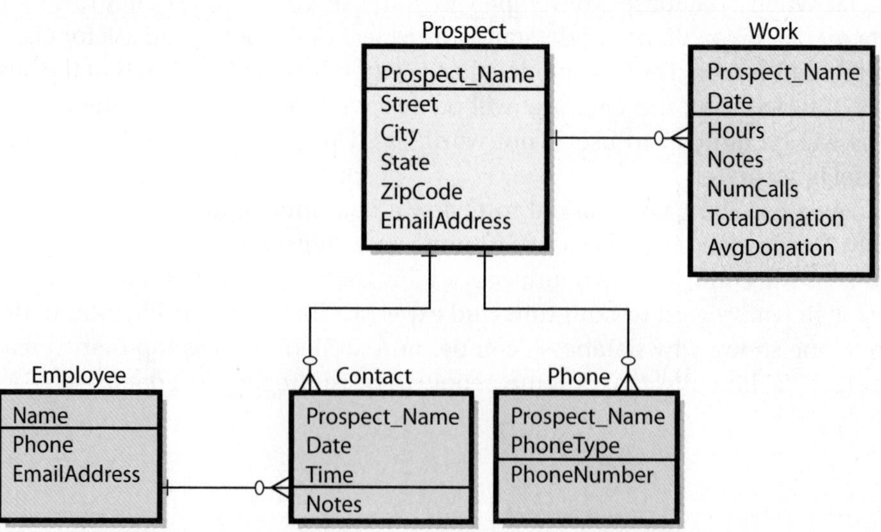

Prospect (<u>Name</u>, Street, City, State, Zip, EmailAddress)
Phone (<u>*Name*</u>, <u>PhoneType</u>, PhoneNumber)
Contact (<u>*Name*</u>, <u>Date</u>, <u>Time</u>, Notes, *EmployeeName*)
Work (<u>*Name*</u>, <u>Date</u>, Notes, NumCalls, TotalDonations)
Employee (<u>EmployeeName</u>, Phone, EmailAddress)

Note:
Underline means table key.
Italics means foreign key.
Underline and italics means both table and foreign key.

Figure CE5a-13
First Table Design for Volunteer Database

Prospect (<u>*ProspectID*</u>, Name, Street, City, State, Zip, EmailAddress)
Phone (<u>*ProspectID*</u>, <u>PhoneType</u>, PhoneNumber)
Contact (<u>*ProspectID*</u>, <u>Date</u>, Notes, *EmployeeName*)
Work (<u>*ProspectID*</u>, <u>Date</u>, Notes, NumCalls, TotalDonations)
Employee (<u>EmployeeName</u>, Phone, EmailAddress)

Note:
Underline means table key.
Italics means foreign key.
Underline and italics means both table and foreign key.

Figure CE5a-14
Second Table Design for Volunteer Database

There is one difference between the data model and the table designs. In the data model the *Work* entity has an attribute, *AvgDonation*, but there is no corresponding *AvgDonation* column in the *Work* table. The consultant decided that there was no need to store this value in the database because it could readily be computed on forms and reports using the values in the *NumCalls* and *TotalDonation* columns.

Once the tables had been designed, the consultant created a Microsoft Access database. She defined the tables in Access, created relationships among the tables, and constructed forms and reports. Figure CE5a-15 shows the primary data entry form used for the *Volunteer* database. The top portion of the form has contact data, including multiple phone numbers. It is important to know the type of the phone number so that you and your staff know if you're calling someone at work or another setting. The middle and bottom sections of this form have contact and prior work data. Observe that *AvgDonation* has been computed from the *NumCalls* and *Total Donation* columns.

You were quite pleased with this database application, and you're certain that it helped you improve the volunteer staffing at the station. Of course, over time, you thought of several new requirements, and you already have changes in mind for next year.

Figure CE5a-15
Volunteer Prospect Data-Entry Form

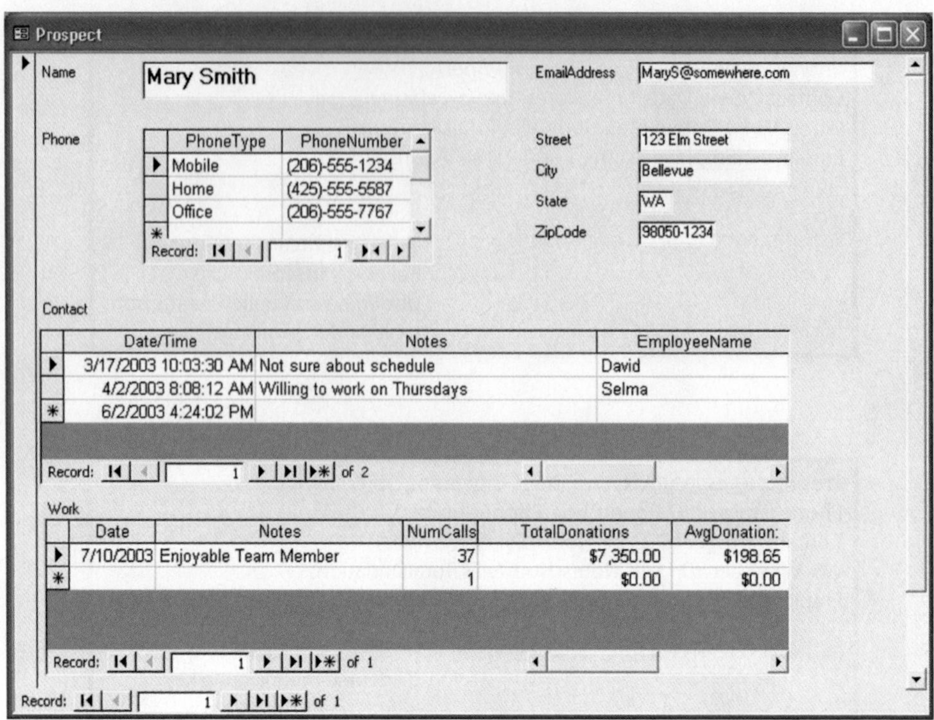

Active Review

Use this Active Review to verify that you understand the material in the chapter extension. You can read the entire extension and then perform the tasks in this review, or you can read the material for just one question and perform the tasks in this review for that question before moving on to the next one.

Q1 Who will volunteer?

Summarize the problem that the fundraising manager must solve. Explain how a database can help solve this problem. Describe the missing information. In your own words, what data must be available to construct the missing information?

Q2 How are database application systems developed?

Name and briefly describe the components of a database application system. Explain the difference between a database application system and a database application program. Using Figure CE5a-1 as a guide, describe the major steps in the process of developing a database application system. Explain what role is crucial for users and why that role is so important.

Q3 What are the components of the entity-relationship data model?

Define the terms *entity, attributes,* and *relationship.* Give an example of two entities (other than those in this book) that have a 1:N relationship. Give an example of two entities that have an N:M relationship. Explain the difference between maximum and minimum cardinality. Show two entities having a 1:N relationship in which one is required and one is optional.

Q4 How is a data model transformed into a database design?

Give an example of a data integrity problem. Describe, in general terms, the process of normalization. Explain how normalizing data prevents data integrity problems. Explain the disadvantage of normalized data. Using your examples from Question 3, show how 1:N relationships are expressed in relational database designs. Show how N:M relationships are expressed in relational database designs.

Q5 What is the users' role?

Describe the major role for users in the development of a database application system. Explain what is required to change a 1:N relationship to an N:M relationship during the data modelling stage. Explain what is required to make that same change after the database application system has been constructed. Describe how this knowledge impacts your behaviour when a database application system is being constructed for your use.

Q6 Who will volunteer? (continued)

Examine Figure CE5a-12. Describe the maximum and minimum cardinality for each relationship. Justify these cardinalities. Change the relationship between *Prospect* and *Phone* to N:M, and explain what this means. Change the relationship between *Prospect* and *Work* to 1:1, and explain what this means. Explain how each relationship is represented in the design in Figure CE5a-14. Show examples of both primary keys and foreign keys in this figure. In *Contact,* determine whether *EmployeeName* is part of a primary key or part of a foreign key. Explain what problem the consultant foresaw in the use of the *Name* attribute. Explain how that problem was avoided. The consultant added an attribute to the data model that was not part of the users' world. Explain why that attribute will not add unnecessary complication to the users' work experiences.

Key Terms and Concepts

Using Your Knowledge

1. Explain how you could use a spreadsheet to solve the volunteer problem at the television station. What data would you place on each column and row of your spreadsheet? Name each column and row of your spreadsheet. What advantages does a database have over a spreadsheet for this problem? Compare and contrast your spreadsheet solution to the database solution shown in the design in Figure CE5a-14 and the data entry form in Figure CE5a-15.

2. Suppose you're asked to build a database application for a sports league. Assume that your application is intended to keep track of teams and of equipment checked out to teams. Explain the steps that need to be taken to develop this application. Specify entities and their relationships. Build an E-R diagram. Ensure that your diagram shows both minimum and maximum cardinalities. Transform your E-R diagram into a relational design.

3. Suppose you're asked to build a database application for a bicycle rental shop. Assume that your database is intended to track customers, bicycles, and rentals. Explain the steps that need to be taken to develop this application. Specify entities and their relationships. Build an entity-relationship diagram. Ensure that your diagram shows both minimum and maximum cardinalities. Transform your E-R diagram into a relational design.

4. Assume you work at the television station and are asked to evaluate the data model in Figure CE5a-12. Suppose that you want to differentiate between prospects who have worked in the past and those who have never worked, but who are prospects for future work. Say that one of the data modellers tells you, "No problem. We'll know that because any *Prospect* entity that has no relationship to a *Work* entity is a prospect who has never worked." Restate the data modeller's response in your own words. Does this seem like a satisfactory solution? What if you want to keep Prospect data that pertains only to prospects who have worked? (No such attributes are shown in *Prospect* in Figure CE5a-12, but say there is an attribute such as *YearFirstVolunteered* or some other attribute that pertains to prospects who have worked in the past.) Show an alternative E-R diagram that would differentiate between prospects who have worked in the past and those who have not. Compare and contrast your alternative to the one shown in Figure CE5a-12.

5. Suppose you manage a department that is developing a database application. The IT professionals who are developing the system ask you to identify two employees to evaluate data models. What criteria would you use in selecting those employees? What instructions would you give them? Suppose one of the employees says to you, "I go to those meetings, but I just don't understand what they're talking about." How would you respond? Suppose that *you* go to one of those meetings and don't understand what they're talking about. What would you do? Describe a role for a prototype in this situation. How would you justify the request for a prototype?

Chapter Extension 5b

Using Microsoft Access

In this chapter extension, you will learn fundamental techniques for creating a database and a database application with Microsoft Access. The data model and database design in Chapter Extension 5a specified that the key of WORK is the combination (*ProspectID, Date*). Upon review, the users stated that prospects will sometimes work more than one time during the day. For scheduling and other purposes, the users want to record both the date and the hour that someone worked. Accordingly, the database designer added the *Hour* attribute and made it part of the key of WORK. The assumption in this design is that each row of WORK represents an hour's work. If a prospect works for consecutive hours, say from 7 to 9 p.m., then he or she would have two rows, one with an *Hour* value of 1900 and a second with an *Hour* value of 2000. Figure CE5b-1 further documents the attributes of the design. Sample data for this table are shown in Figure CE5b-2.

Study Questions

- **Q1** How do I create tables?
- **Q2** How do I create relationships?
- **Q3** How do I create a data entry form?
- **Q4** How can I create queries using the query design tool?
- **Q5** How do I create a report?

Q1 How Do I Create Tables?

Starting Access

Figure CE5b-3 shows the opening screen for Microsoft Access 2003. (If you use another version of Access, your screen will appear differently, but the essentials will be the same.) To create a new database, select Blank database under the New section in the pane on the right-hand side of the screen. It is also possible to create a new database from a template, but because we have done our own database design we need not consider that option. Other choices in this pane are beyond the scope of this extension.

When you select Blank database, Access asks you to provide a file name and location for your new database. Enter the name *Prospect1.mdb* and place it in some convenient directory. Press Enter and you will see the screen shown in Figure CE5b-4.

Figure CE5b-1
Attributes of the Database

Table	Attribute (Column)	Remarks	Data Type	Example Value
PROSPECT	ProspectID	An identifying number provided by Access when a row is created. The value has no meaning to the user.	AutoNumber	55
PROSPECT	Name	A prospect's name.	Text (50)	Emily Jones
PROSPECT	Street	Prospect's contact street address.	Text (50)	123 West Elm
PROSPECT	City	Prospect's contact city.	Text (40)	Miami
PROSPECT	State	Prospect's contact state.	Text (2)	FL
PROSPECT	Zip	Prospect's contact Zip code.	Text (10)	30210-4567 or 30210
PROSPECT	EmailAddress	Prospect's contact email address.	Text (65)	ExamplePerson@somewhere.com
WORK	ProspectID	Foreign key to PROSPECT. Value provided when relationship is created.	Number (Long Integer)	55
WORK	Date	The date of work.	Date	9/15/2007
WORK	Hour	The hour at which work is started.	Number (Integer)	0800 or 1900 (7 PM)
WORK	NumCalls	The number of calls taken.	Number (Integer)	25
WORK	TotalDonations	The total of donations generated.	Currency	$10,575
WORK	AvgDonations	The average donation.	Currency	To be computed in queries and reports

Example of PROSPECT Data

Prospect ID	Name	Street	City	State	Zip	EmailAddress
1	Carson Wu	123 Elm	Los Angeles	CA	98007	Carson@somewhere.com
2	Emily Jackson	2234 17th	Pasadena	CA	97005	JacksonE@elsewhere.com
3	Peter Lopez	331 Moses Drive	Fullerton	CA	97330	PeterL@ourcompany.com
4	Lynda Dennison	54 Strand	Manhattan Beach	CA	97881	Lynda@somewhere.com
5	Carter Fillmore III	Restricted	Brentwood	CA	98220	Carter@BigBucks.com
6	CJ Greene	77 Sunset Strip	Hollywood	CA	97330	CJ@HollywoodProducers.c
7	Jolisa Jackson	2234 17th	Pasadena	CA	97005	JacksonJ@elsewhere.com

Example of WORK Data

ProspectID	Date	Hour	NumCalls	TotalDonations
3	9/15/2006	1600	17	8755
3	9/15/2006	1700	28	11578
5	9/15/2006	1700	25	15588
5	9/20/2006	1800	37	29887
5	9/10/2007	1700	30	21440
5	9/10/2007	1800	39	37050
6	9/15/2006	1700	33	21445
6	9/16/2006	1700	27)	17558
6	9/10/2007	1700	31	22550
6	9/10/2007	1800	37	36700

Figure CE5b-2
Student Data Model Entities

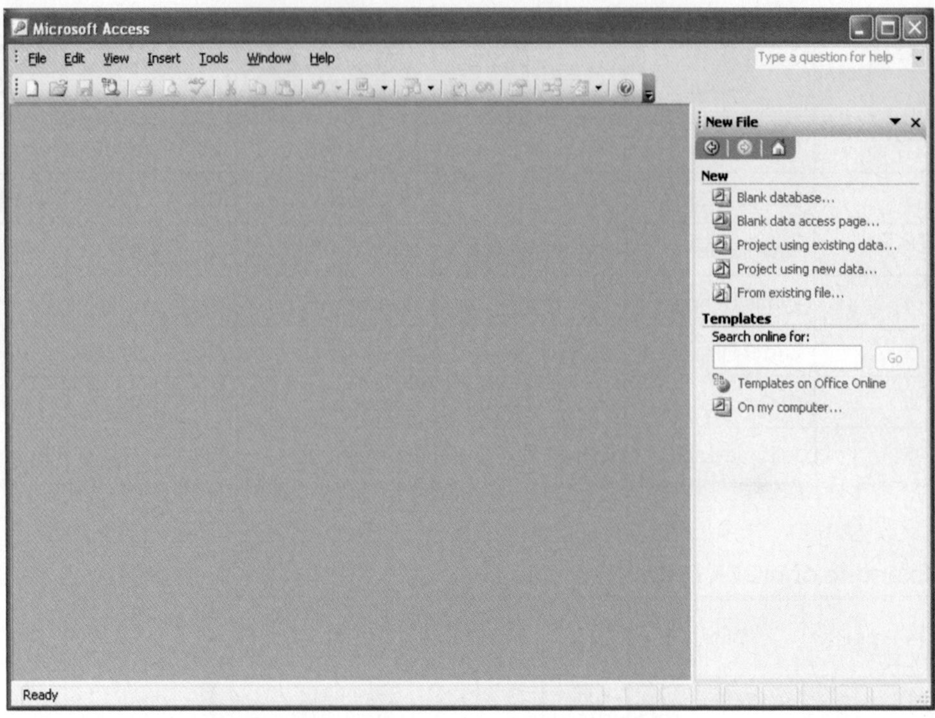

Figure CE5b-3
Opening Screen for Microsoft Access 2003

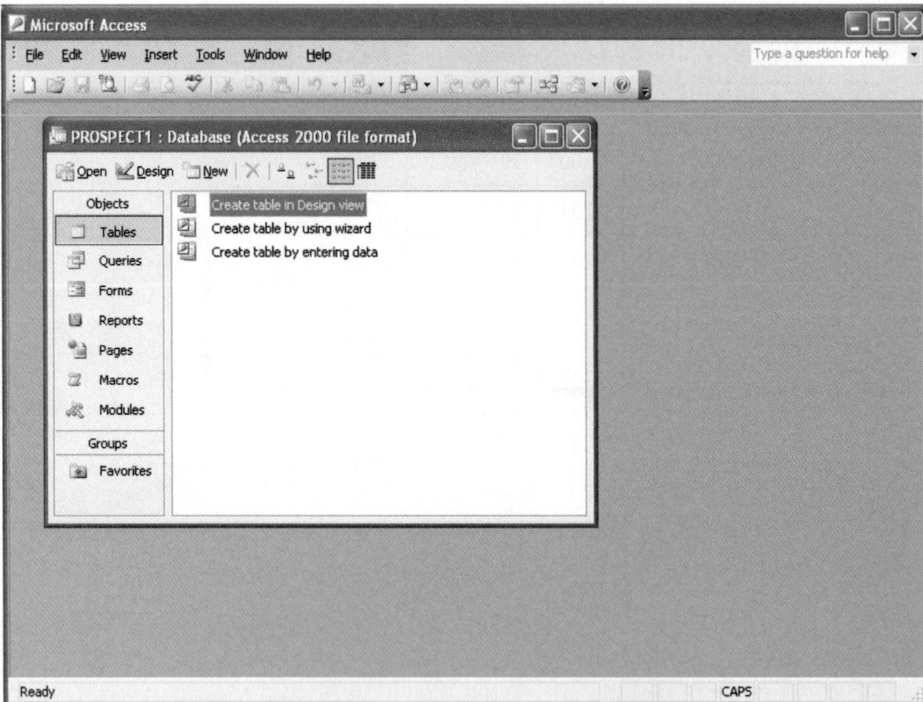

Figure CE5b-4
Naming the Database

Creating Tables

Because we have created our own database design, we can select Create table in Design view by double-clicking on that entry. When you do this, you will see the screen shown in Figure CE5b-5. This screen has two parts. In the upper part, we will enter the name of each attribute (called *Fields* by Access) and its *Data Type.*

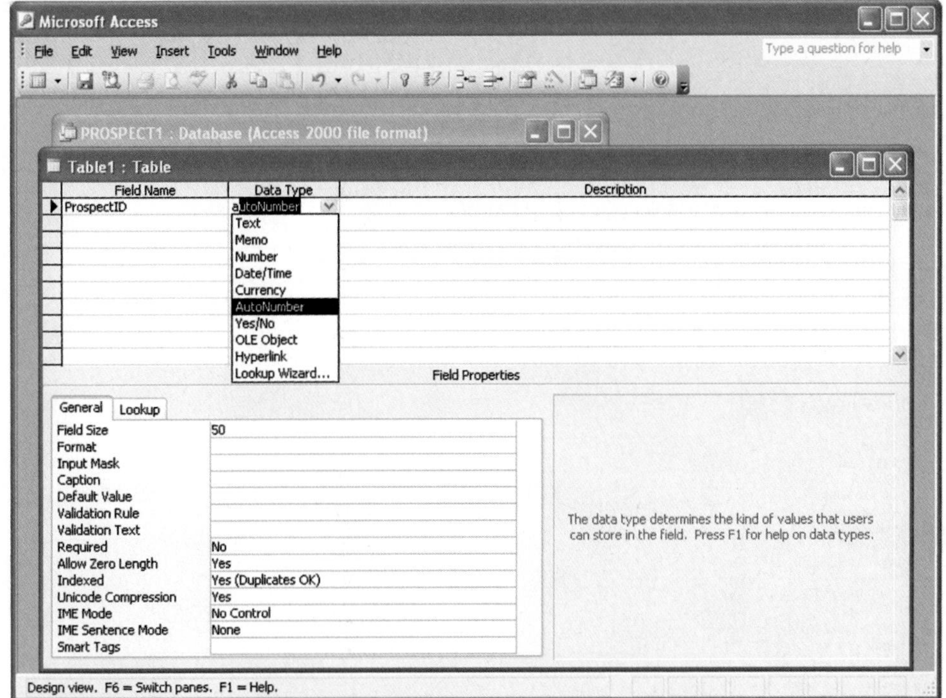

Figure CE5b-5
Creating Tables in Access, Step 1

We can optionally enter a Description of that field. The description is used for documentation; as you will see, Access displays any text you enter as help text on forms. In the bottom part of the screen, we set the properties of each field (or attribute, using our term). In Figure CE5b-5, the user has entered *ProspectID* and is selecting the Data Type *AutoNumber*.

To create the rest of the table, enter the Field Names and Data Types for our design. Figure CE5b-6 shows how to set the length of a Text Data Type. In this figure, the user has set City to Text and then has moved down into the bottom part

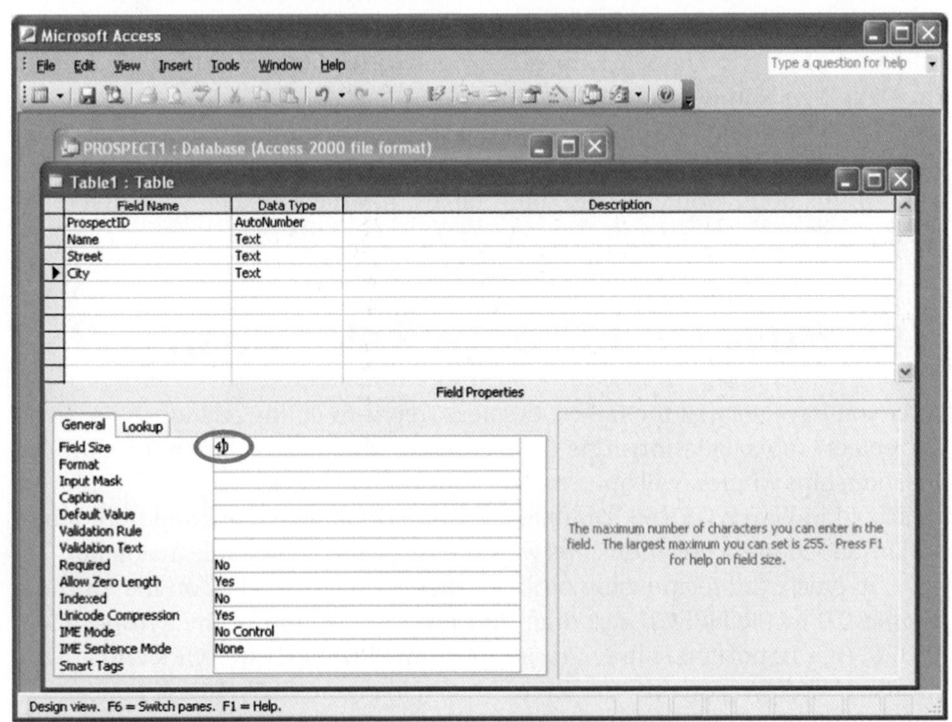

Figure CE5b-6
Creating Tables in Access, Step 2

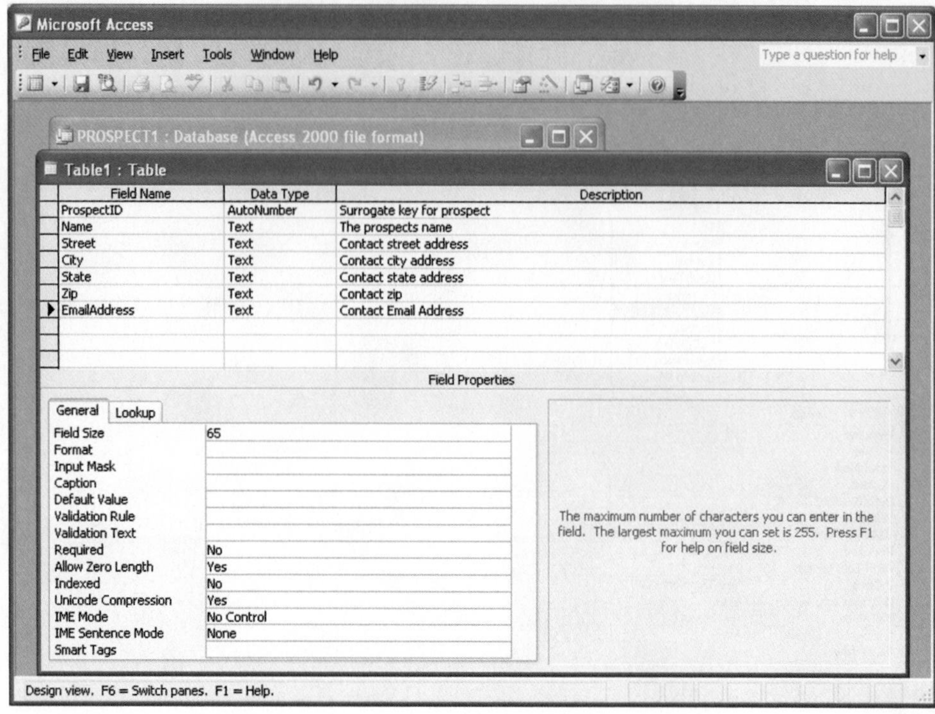

Figure CE5b-7
Complete Sample PROSPECT Table

of this form and entered 40 under Field Size. You will do the same thing to set the length of State and Zip. The complete table is shown in Figure CE5b-7.

Now we need to declare Prospect as the primary key of this table. To do so, highlight *ProspectID* by clicking on the square just to the left of it and then click on the Key icon (the yellow key a little to the right of the centre in the toolbar). At this point, the table definition is complete, and we can save the table. Do so by clicking the Save File icon. Name the table PROSPECT.

Follow similar steps to create the WORK table. The only difference is that you will need to create a key of the three columns (*ProspectID, Date, Hour*). To create that key, highlight all three rows by dragging the three squares to the left of the names of *ProspectID, Date,* and *Hour*. Then click the Key icon. The finished tables are shown in Figure CE5b-8. This figure also shows how the user created the Data Type Number (Integer) for the *NumCalls* field. This same technique was used to set the Data Type of *ProspectID* (in WORK) to Number (Long Integer) and that of Hour to Number (Integer).

At this point, you can close both tables. You have created your first database!

Q2 How Do I Create Relationships?

After you have created the tables, the next step is to define relationships. To do so, select Tools/Relationships . . . from the Access main menu. The Relationships window will open and the Show Table dialog box will be displayed, as shown in Figure CE5b-9. Double-click on both table names, and both tables will be added to the Relationships window. Close the Show Table dialog box.

To create the relationship between these two tables, click on the attribute *ProspectID* in PROSPECT and drag that attribute on top of the *ProspectID* in WORK. (It is important to drag *ProspectID* from PROSPECT to WORK and not the reverse.) When you do this, the screen shown in Figure CE5b-10 will appear.

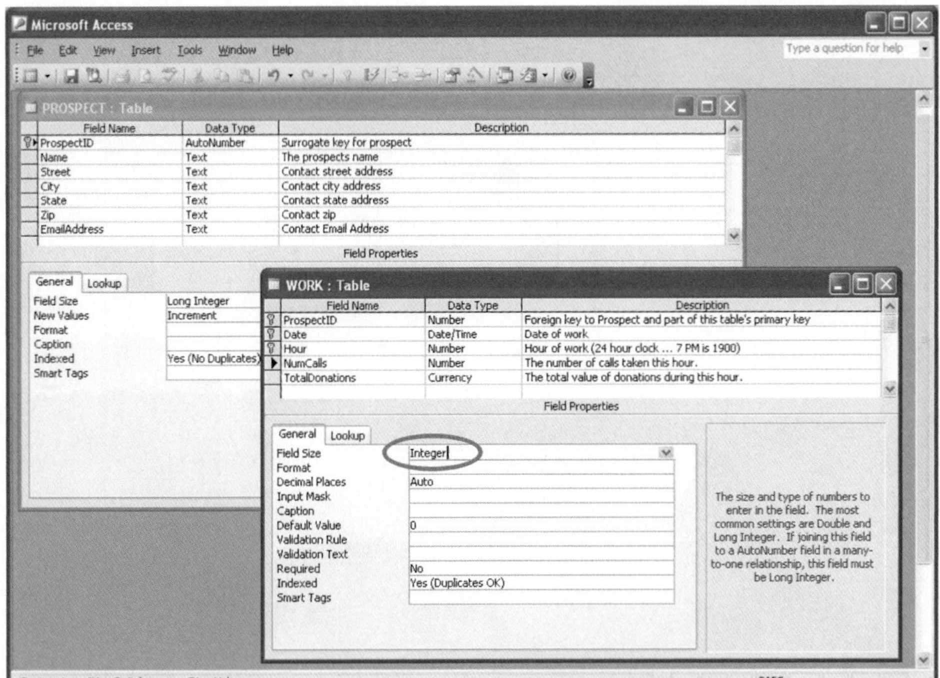

Figure CE5b-8
Finished PROSPECT and WORK Tables

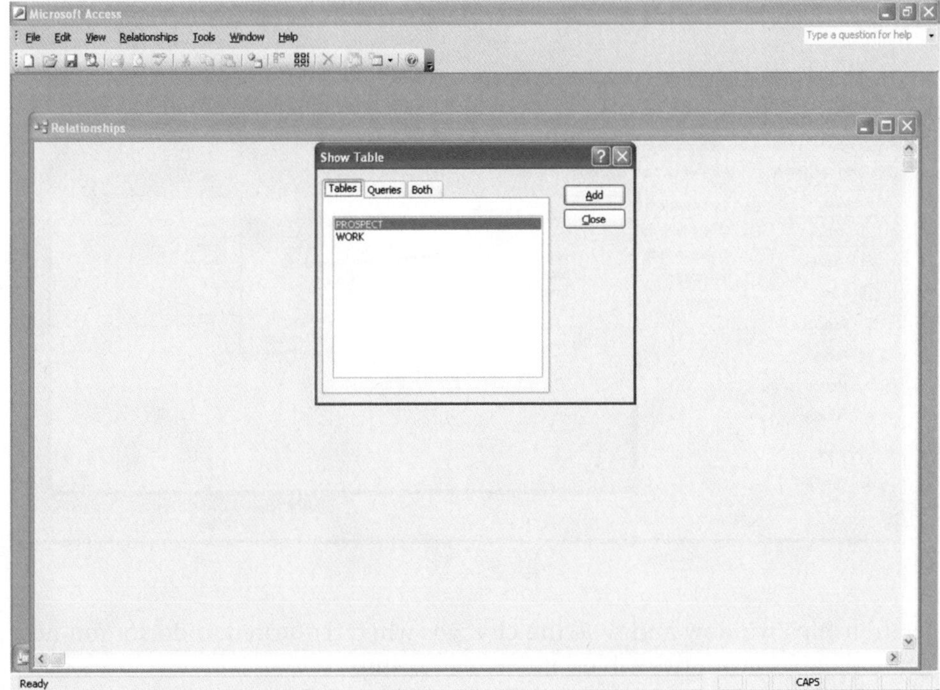

Figure CE5b-9
The "Show Table" Dialog Box in Access

In the dialog box, click Enforce Referential Integrity, click Cascade Update Related Fields, and click Cascade Delete Related Records. The specifics of these actions are beyond the scope of our discussion. Just understand that clicking these options will cause Access to make sure that *ProspectID* values in WORK also exist in PROSPECT. The completed relationship is shown in Figure CE5b-11. The notation *1. . . .* ∞ at the end of the relationship line means that one row of PROSPECT can be related to an unlimited number (*N*) rows in WORK. Close the

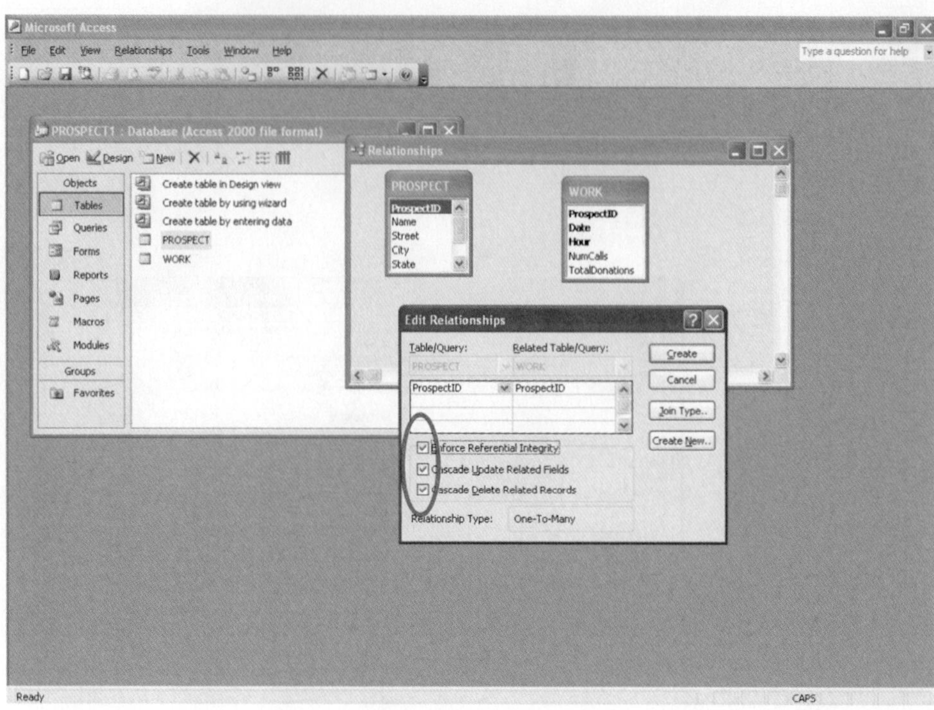

Figure CE5b-10
Creating a Relationship between Two Tables

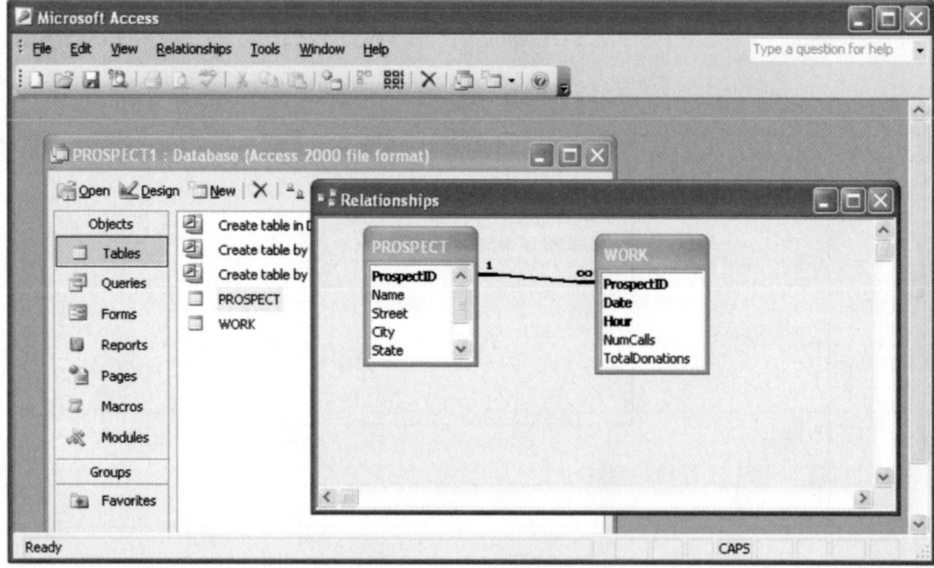

Figure CE5b-11
Completed Relationship between PROSPECT and WORK Tables

Relationships window and save the changes when requested to do so. You now have a database with two tables and a relationship.

The next step is to enter data. To enter data, double-click on the table name in the *Prospect1* Database window. The table will appear, and you can enter values into each cell. Enter the data in Figure CE5b-2 for both PROSPECT and WORK, and you will see a display like that in Figure CE5b-12. Examine the lower left-hand corner of this window. The text *The total value of donations during the hour* is the Description that was provided when you defined the *TotalDonations* column when the WORK table was created. (You can see this in the *TotalDonations* column in Figure CE5b-8.) Access displays this text because the focus is on the *TotalDonations* column in the active table window (WORK). Move your cursor from field to field and watch this text change.

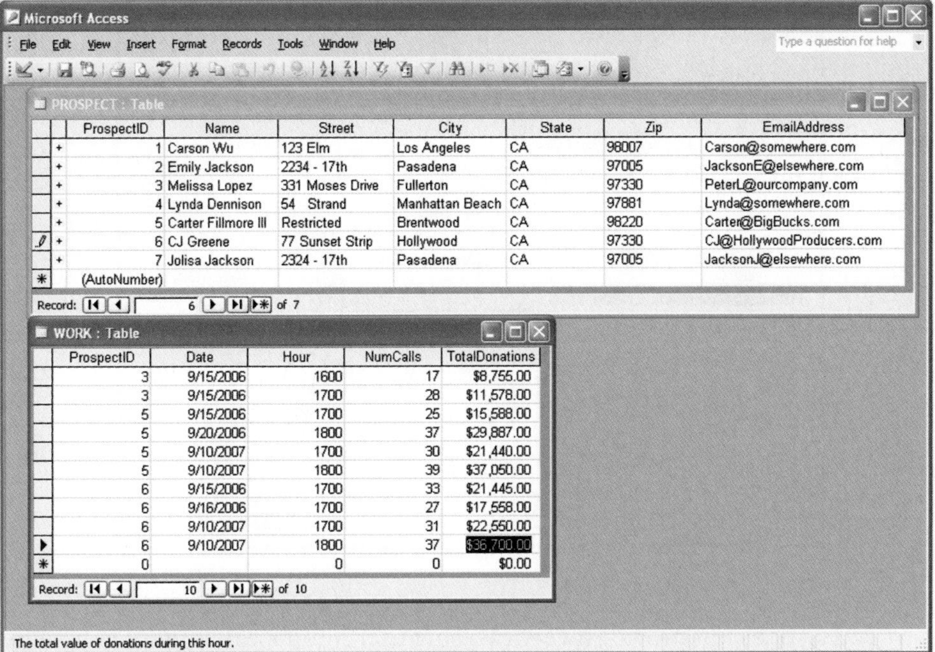

Figure CE5b-12
Tables with Data Entered

Q3 How Do I Create a Data Entry Form?

Access provides two alternatives for creating a data entry form. The first is to use the default table display as you did when you entered the data shown in Figure CE5b-12. In the PROSPECT table, notice the plus sign on the left. If you click on those plus signs, you will see the PROSPECT rows with their related WORK rows, as shown in Figure CE5b-13. This display, while convenient, is limited in its capability.

Microsoft Access - [PROSPECT : Table]

File Edit View Insert Format Records Tools Window Help

ProspectID	Name	Street	City	State	Zip	EmailAddress
7	Jolisa Jackson	2324 - 17th	Pasadena	CA	97005	JacksonJ@elsewhere.com

Date	Hour	NumCalls	TotalDonations
	0	0	$0.00

ProspectID	Name	Street	City	State	Zip	EmailAddress
6	CJ Greene	77 Sunset Strip	Hollywood	CA	97330	CJ@HollywoodProducers.com

Date	Hour	NumCalls	TotalDonations
9/15/2006	1700	33	$21,445.00
9/16/2006	1700	27	$17,558.00
9/10/2007	1700	31	$22,550.00
9/10/2007	1800	37	$36,700.00
	0	0	$0.00

ProspectID	Name	Street	City	State	Zip	EmailAddress
5	Carter Fillmore III	Restricted	Brentwood	CA	98220	Carter@BigBucks.com

Date	Hour	NumCalls	TotalDonations
9/15/2006	1700	25	$15,588.00
9/20/2006	1800	37	$29,887.00
9/10/2007	1700	30	$21,440.00
9/10/2007	1800	39	$37,050.00
	0	0	$0.00

ProspectID	Name	Street	City	State	Zip	EmailAddress
4	Lynda Dennison	54 Strand	Manhattan Beach	CA	97881	Lynda@somewhere.com

Date	Hour	NumCalls	TotalDonations
	0	0	$0.00

ProspectID	Name	Street	City	State	Zip	EmailAddress
3	Melissa Lopez	331 Moses Drive	Fullerton	CA	97330	PeterL@ourcompany.com

Date	Hour	NumCalls	TotalDonations
9/15/2006	1600	17	$8,755.00
9/15/2006	1700	28	$11,578.00
	0	0	$0.00

ProspectID	Name	Street	City	State	Zip	EmailAddress
2	Emily Jackson	2234 - 17th	Pasadena	CA	97005	JacksonE@elsewhere.com

Date	Hour	NumCalls	TotalDonations
	0	0	$0.00

ProspectID	Name	Street	City	State	Zip	EmailAddress
1	Carson Wu	123 Elm	Los Angeles	CA	98007	Carson@somewhere.com

Record: 1 of 1

Date of work

Figure CE5b-13
Default Table Display

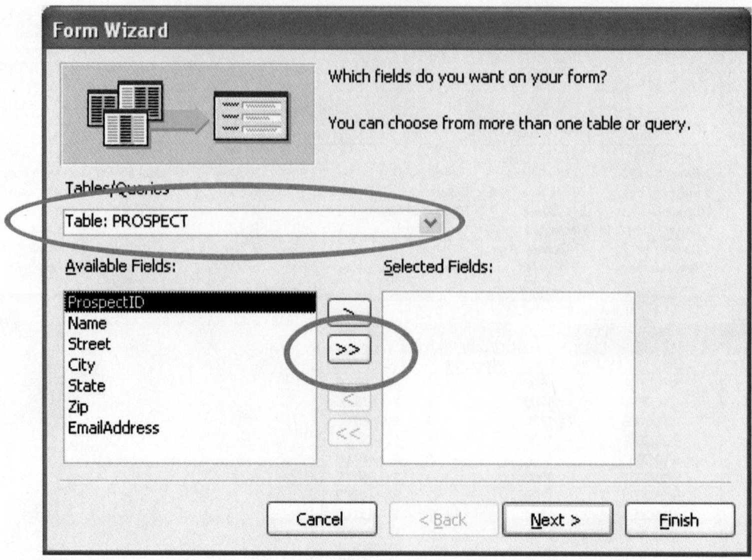

Figure CE5b-14
Selecting the First Table Using the Form Wizard

It also does not provide a very pleasing user interface. For more generality and better design, you can use the Access form generator. To start the form generator, click on Forms in the *Prospect1* Database window. Then double-click on Create form by using Form Wizard. As shown in Figure CE5b-14, ensure that the PROSPECT table is highlighted in the Tables/Queries combo box (shown in this figure by the top red oval), and then click the double chevron button (shown in this figure by the lower red oval). All the columns in the PROSPECT table should appear in the Selected Fields list box.

Next, go back to the Tables/Queries box and select the WORK table. Again, click on the double chevron button. Your screen should appear as shown in Figure CE5b-15. Click Finish. (We are skipping over numerous options that Access provides; those options are beyond the scope of this discussion.)

At this point, you should see the data entry form shown in Figure CE5b-16. Because you defined the relationship between PROSPECT and WORK, Access will automatically connect each row in PROSPECT with its matching rows in WORK. The first prospect, Jolisa Jackson, has not yet worked, and the form shows no WORK data for her. Click on the right arrow and you will see (in Figure CE5b-17) that CJ Greene, the next prospect, has numerous WORK rows related to him. You

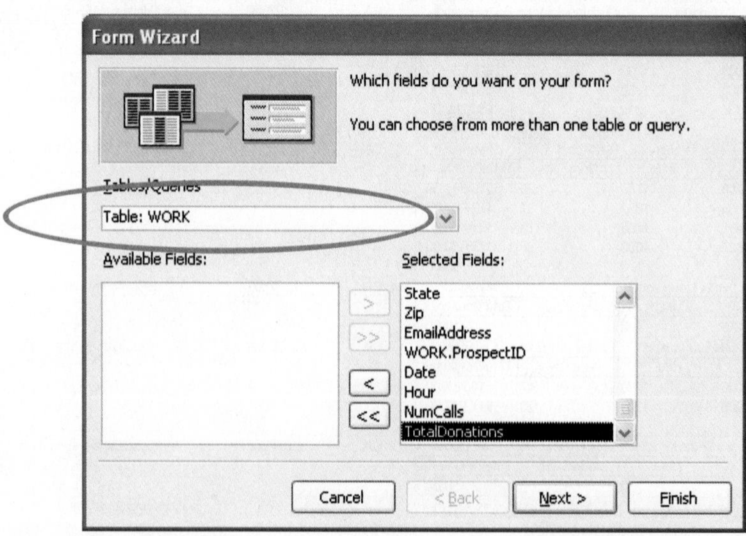

Figure CE5b-15
Selecting the Second Table Using the Form Wizard

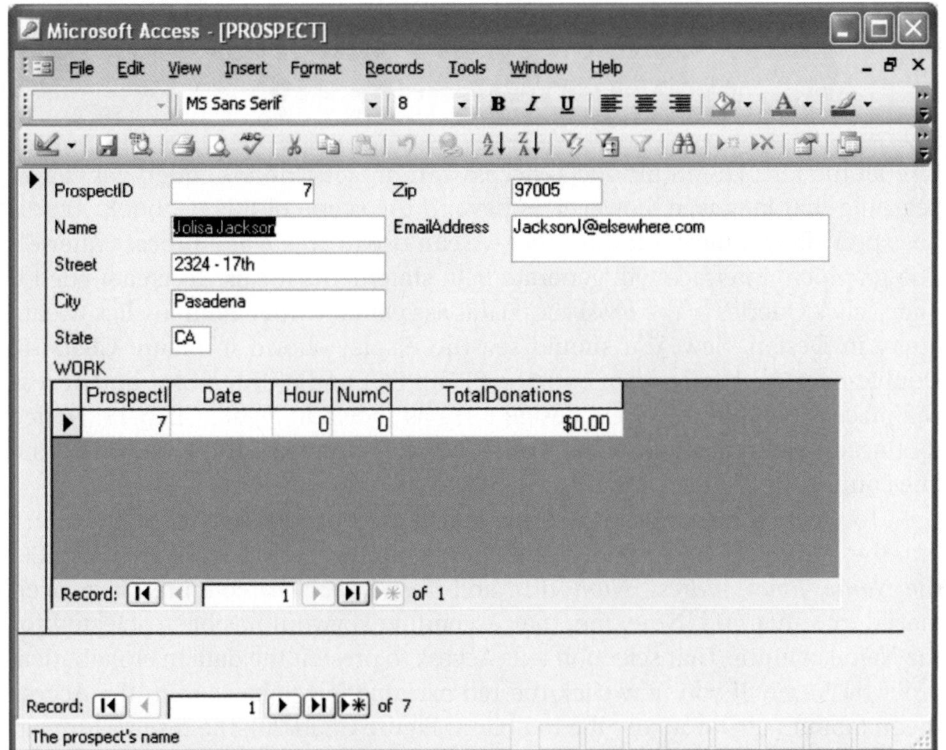

Figure CE5b-2
Data Entry Form, J. Jackson

can add, update, or delete any data in any of these forms. When you do so, Access will make the appropriate changes to the underlying tables.

Myriad options exist for customizing Access forms. You can learn about them if you take a database processing class after you complete this MIS class.

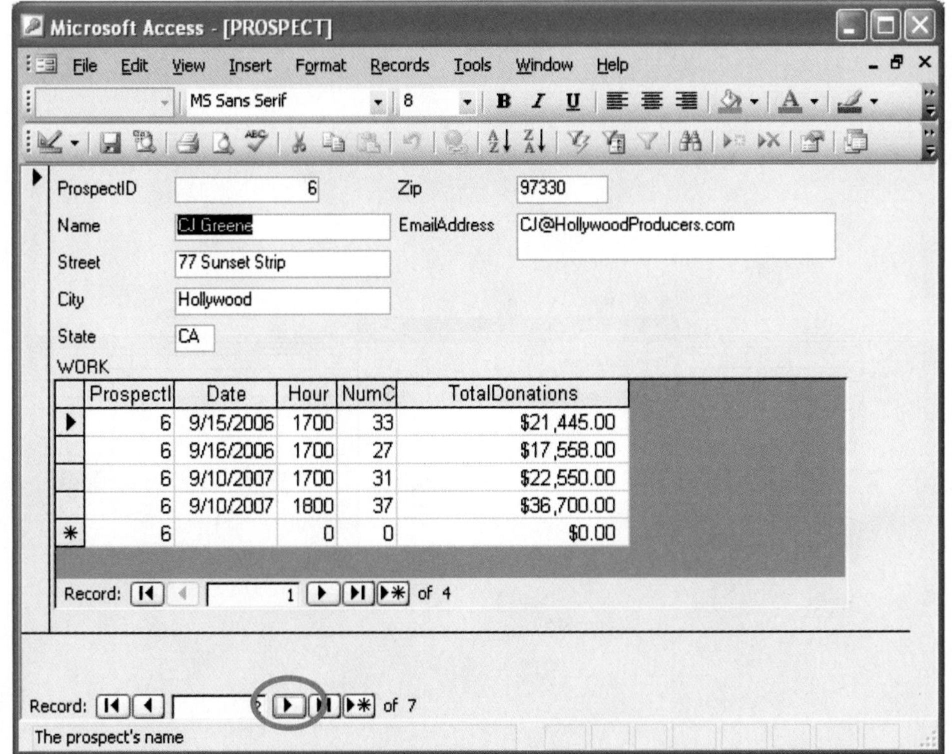

Figure CE5b-17
Data Entry Form, CJ Greene

Q4 How Can I Create Queries Using the Query Design Tool?

Like all modern DBMS products, Access can process the SQL query language. Learning that language, however, is beyond the scope of this textbook. Access does provide graphical interface that we can use to create and process queries. The graphical interface will generate SQL statements for us. To create such a query, click Queries in the *Prospect1* Database window. Then double-click Create query in Design View. You should see the display shown in Figure CE5b-18. Double-click on the names of both the PROSPECT and WORK tables, and Access will place them into the query design form as shown in Figure CE5b-19. Notice that Access remembers the relationship between the two tables (shown by the line connecting *ProspectID* in PROSPECT to the same attribute in WORK).

To create a query, drag columns out of the PROSPECT and WORK tables into the grid in the lower part of the query definition form. In Figure CE5b-20, the *Name, EmailAddress, NumCalls,* and *TotalDonations* columns have been placed into that grid. Note, too, that Ascending keyword has been selected for the Name column. That selection tells Access to present the data in alphabetical order by Name. If you now click the red exclamation point icon in the Access menu (about halfway across the toolbar in Figure CE5b-20), the result as shown in Figure CE5b-21 will appear. Notice that only PROSPECT rows having a match of *ProspectID* with *ProspectID* in WORK rows are shown. By default, for queries of two (or more) tables, Access (and SQL) show only rows that have value matches in both tables. Save the query under the name *NameAndDonationQuery.*

Queries have many useful purposes. For example, suppose we want to see the average dollar value of donation generated per hour of work. This query, which is just slightly beyond the scope of this chapter extension, can be readily created using either the Access graphical tool or SQL. The results of such a query are shown in Figure CE5b-22. This query processes the *NameAndDonationQuery*

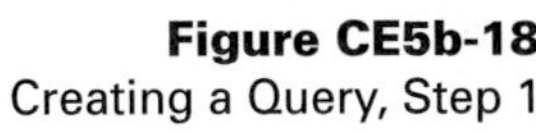
Figure CE5b-18
Creating a Query, Step 1

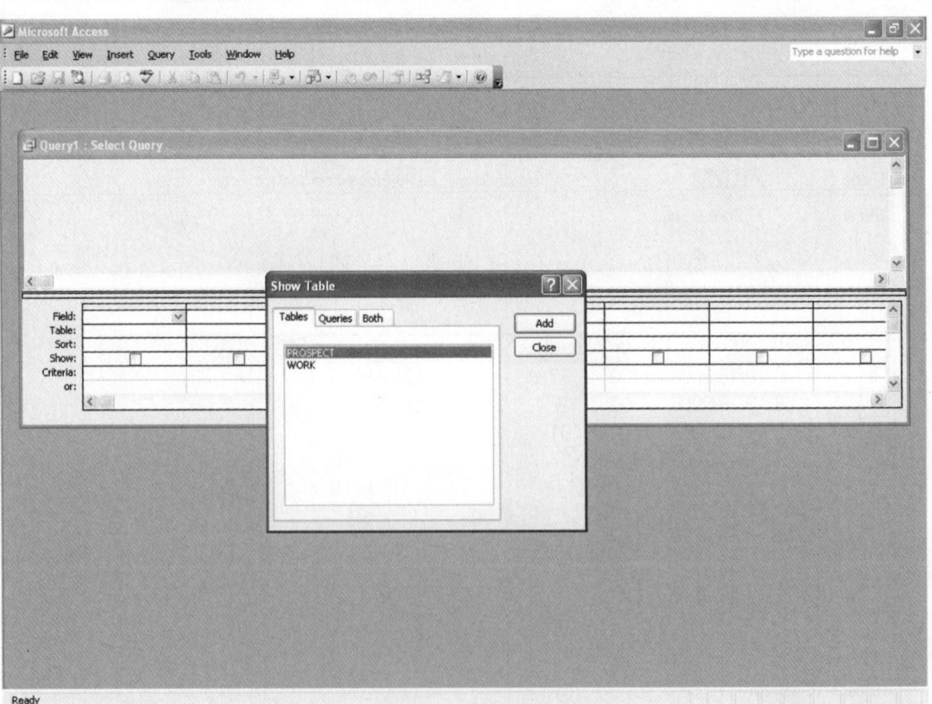

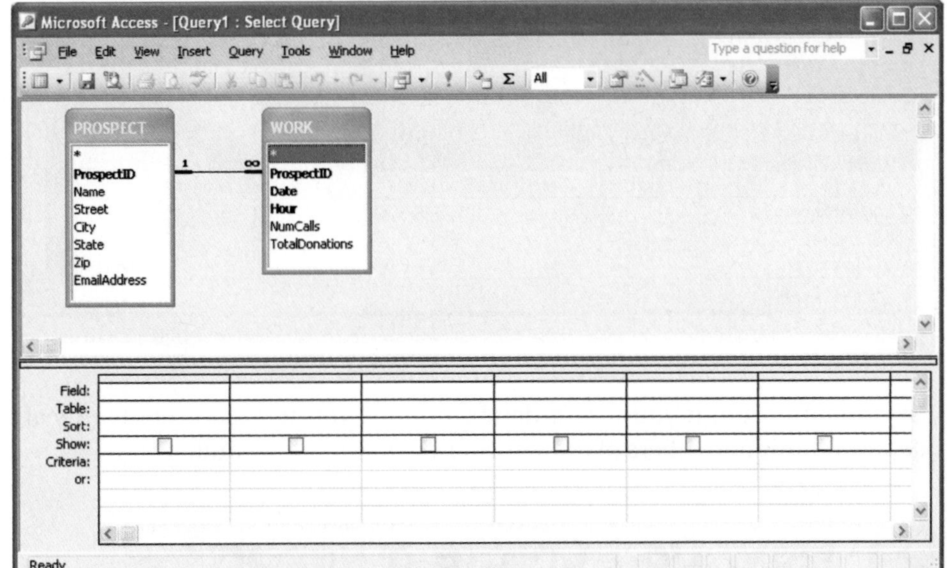

Figure CE5b-19
Creating a Query, Step 2

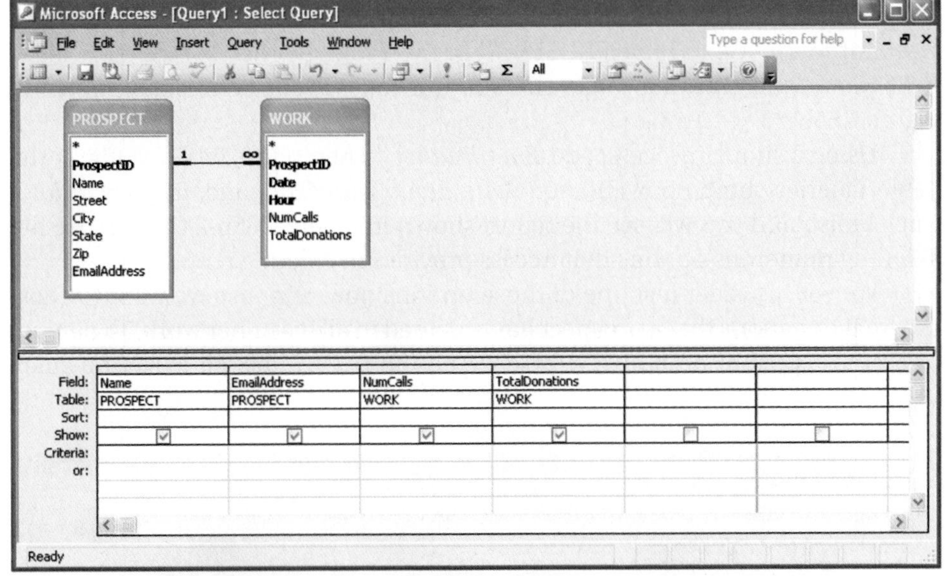

Figure CE5b-20
Creating a Query, Step 3

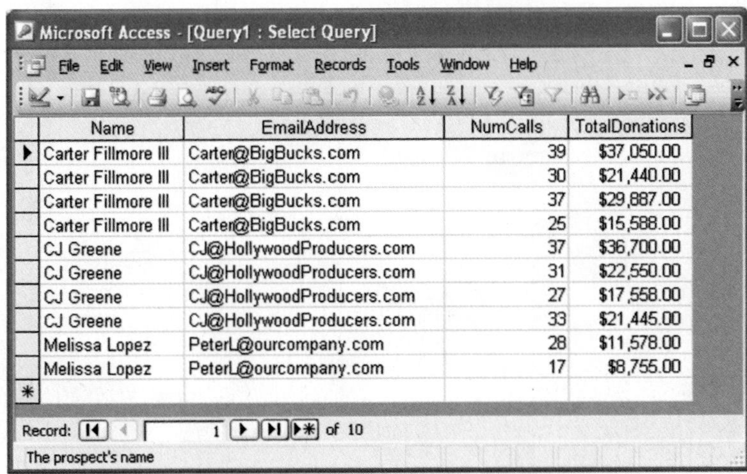

Name	EmailAddress	NumCalls	TotalDonations
Carter Fillmore III	Carter@BigBucks.com	39	$37,050.00
Carter Fillmore III	Carter@BigBucks.com	30	$21,440.00
Carter Fillmore III	Carter@BigBucks.com	37	$29,887.00
Carter Fillmore III	Carter@BigBucks.com	25	$15,588.00
CJ Greene	CJ@HollywoodProducers.com	37	$36,700.00
CJ Greene	CJ@HollywoodProducers.com	31	$22,550.00
CJ Greene	CJ@HollywoodProducers.com	27	$17,558.00
CJ Greene	CJ@HollywoodProducers.com	33	$21,445.00
Melissa Lopez	PeterL@ourcompany.com	28	$11,578.00
Melissa Lopez	PeterL@ourcompany.com	17	$8,755.00

Figure CE5b-21
Results of TotalDonations Query

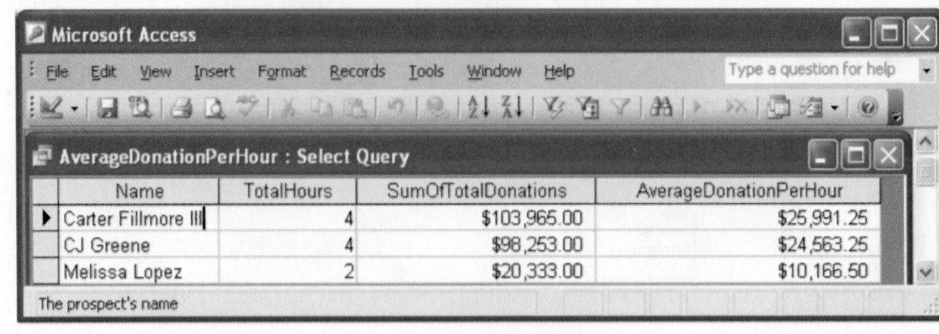

Name	TotalHours	SumOfTotalDonations	AverageDonationPerHour
Carter Fillmore III	4	$103,965.00	$25,991.25
CJ Greene	4	$98,253.00	$24,563.25
Melissa Lopez	2	$20,333.00	$10,166.50

Figure CE5b-22
Result of SQL Query

just created. Again, if you take a database class, you will learn how to create queries like this and others of even greater complexity (and utility).

Q5 How Do I Create a Report?

The process of creating a report is very similar to that for creating a form. From the *Prospect1* Database window, select Reports and then double-click Create report by using the Wizard. This time, however, we will be more specific in what we want to see. Click Table:PROSPECT in the Table/Queries combo box, highlight *Name,* and click the single chevron (>). You will see the display shown in Figure CE5b-23.

Using a similar process, add *EmailAddress.* Then select Table:WORK in the Table/Queries combo box and add *Date, Hour, NumCalls,* and *TotalDonations.* Click Finish and you will see the report shown in Figure CE5b-24. Again, we are skipping numerous options that Access provides in creating reports.

We will consider just one of those options now. Suppose we want to show the total donations that a prospect has obtained in all his or her work. To do that, open the report in design view by clicking the triangle pencil icon (the small

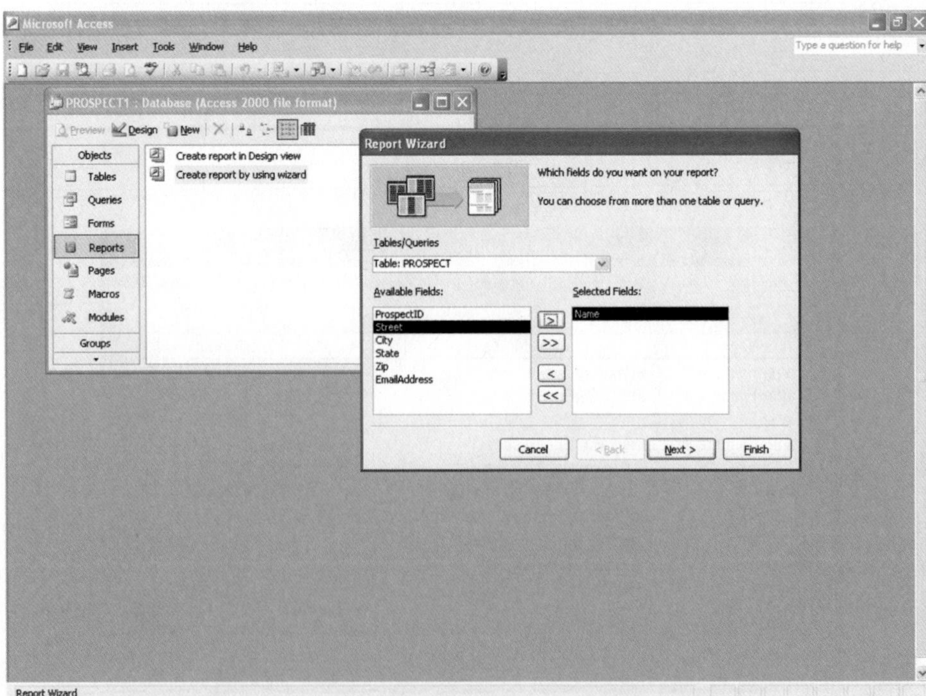

Figure CE5b-23
Selecting a Table to Show in a Report

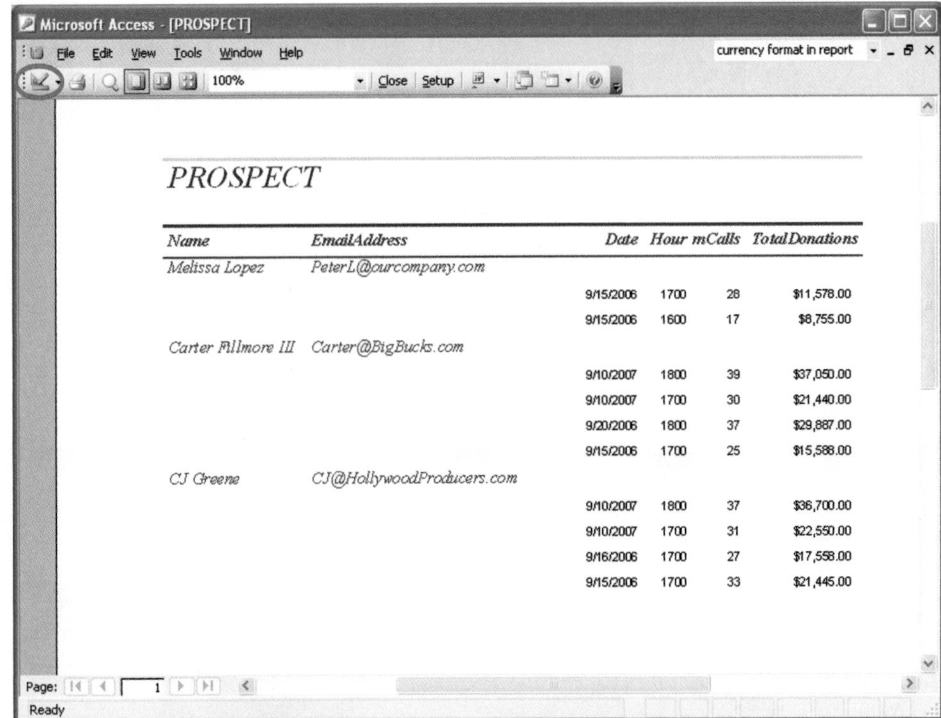

PROSPECT

Name	EmailAddress	Date	Hour	mCalls	TotalDonations
Melissa Lopez	PeterL@ourcompany.com				
		9/15/2006	1700	28	$11,578.00
		9/15/2006	1600	17	$8,755.00
Carter Fillmore III	Carter@BigBucks.com				
		9/10/2007	1800	39	$37,050.00
		9/10/2007	1700	30	$21,440.00
		9/20/2006	1800	37	$29,887.00
		9/15/2006	1700	25	$15,588.00
CJ Greene	CJ@HollywoodProducers.com				
		9/10/2007	1800	37	$36,700.00
		9/10/2007	1700	31	$22,550.00
		9/16/2006	1700	27	$17,558.00
		9/15/2006	1700	33	$21,445.00

Figure CE5b-24
Report on Total Donations, by Prospect

circle on the left in Figure CE5b-27) in the left-most position of the menu bar. Your report will appear as shown in Figure CE5b-25. From the View menu option, click on Sorting and Grouping. In the form that appears (Figure CE5b-26), the second element of Group Properties is Group Footer. Click on No, and change it to Yes as shown in Figure CE5b-26. Close this window.

Now click the textbox tool in the Toolbox (the small circle on the left in Figure CE5b-27) and drag and drop a toolbox under the rule labelled *ProspectID* footer. Your screen should appear as in Figure CE5b-27.

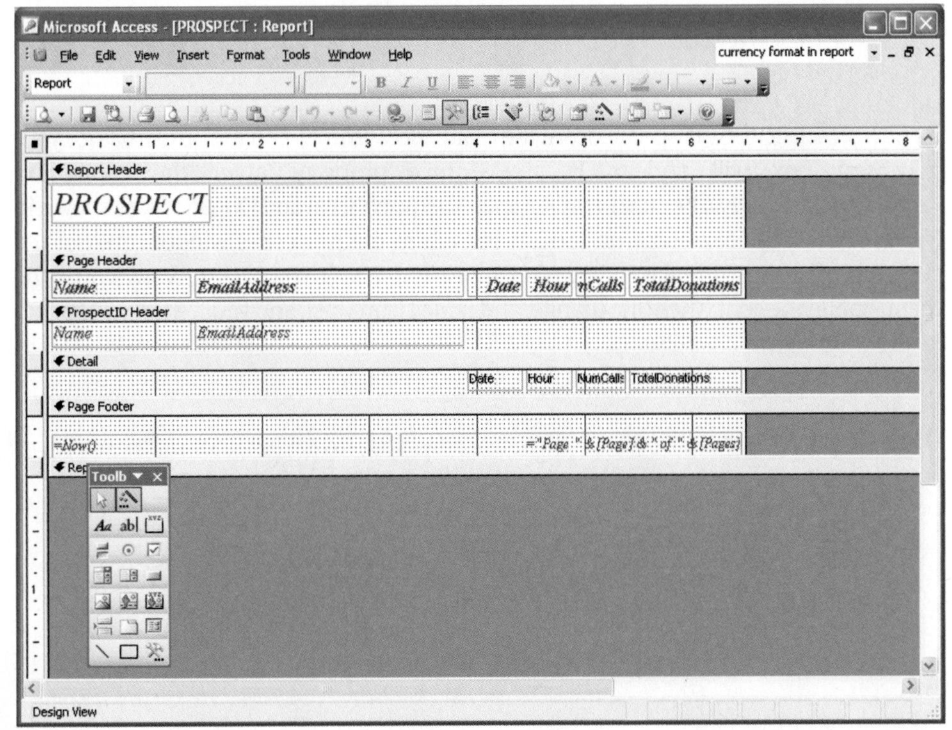

Figure CE5b-24
Showing Total Donations per Prospect, Step 1

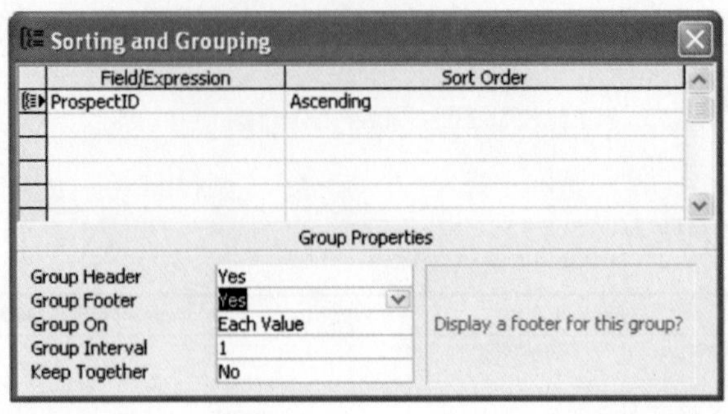

Figure CE5b-26
Showing Total Donations per Prospect, Step 2

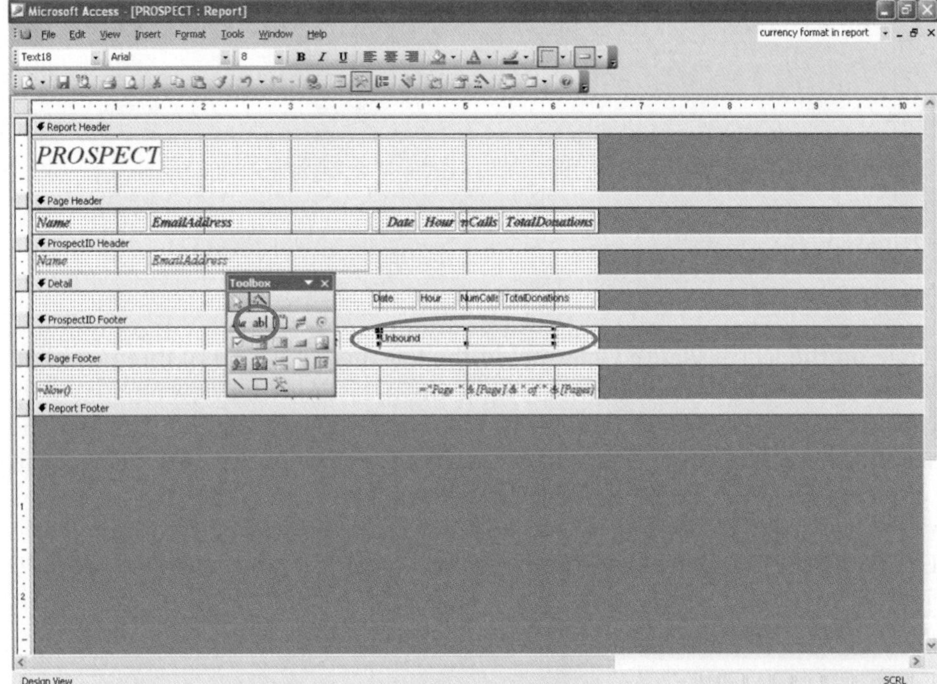

Figure CE5b-27
Showing Total Donations per Prospect, Step 3

Now select View/Properties from the main Access menu, and the properties for your new text box will appear. In the *Source* property, enter the expression *=sum(TotalDonations)*. Be sure to omit a space between Total and Donations, as shown in Figure CE5b-28(a). Now click on the Format tab in the properties window and set the Format property to Currency as shown in Figure CE5b-28(b). Now click the View icon in the menu bar (in the spot where the triangle and pencil icon was), and your report will appear as shown in Figure CE5b-29.

Figure CE5b-28
Showing Total Donations per Prospect, Step 4

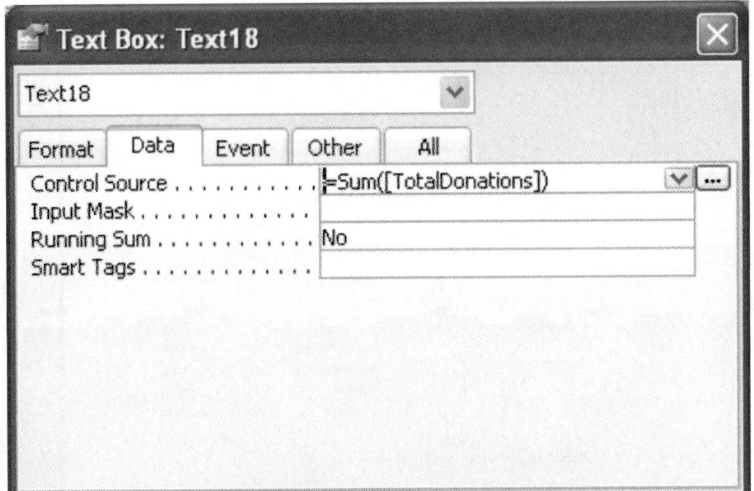

a. Set the Control Source to Sum the Donations

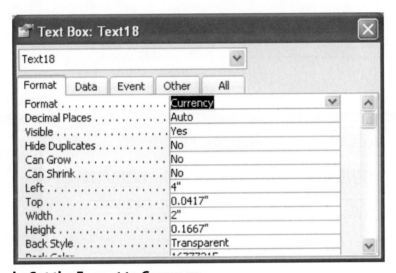

Text Box: Text18

Text18

Format | Data | Event | Other | All

Format	Currency
Decimal Places	Auto
Visible	Yes
Hide Duplicates	No
Can Grow	No
Can Shrink	No
Left	4"
Top	0.0417"
Width	2"
Height	0.1667"
Back Style	Transparent

b. Set the Format to Currency

The only thing left to do is to go back to the design window (click the triangle and pencil), change the label for the text box from Text18 to Career Donations, and align the new text box. The finished report is shown in Figure CE5b-30.

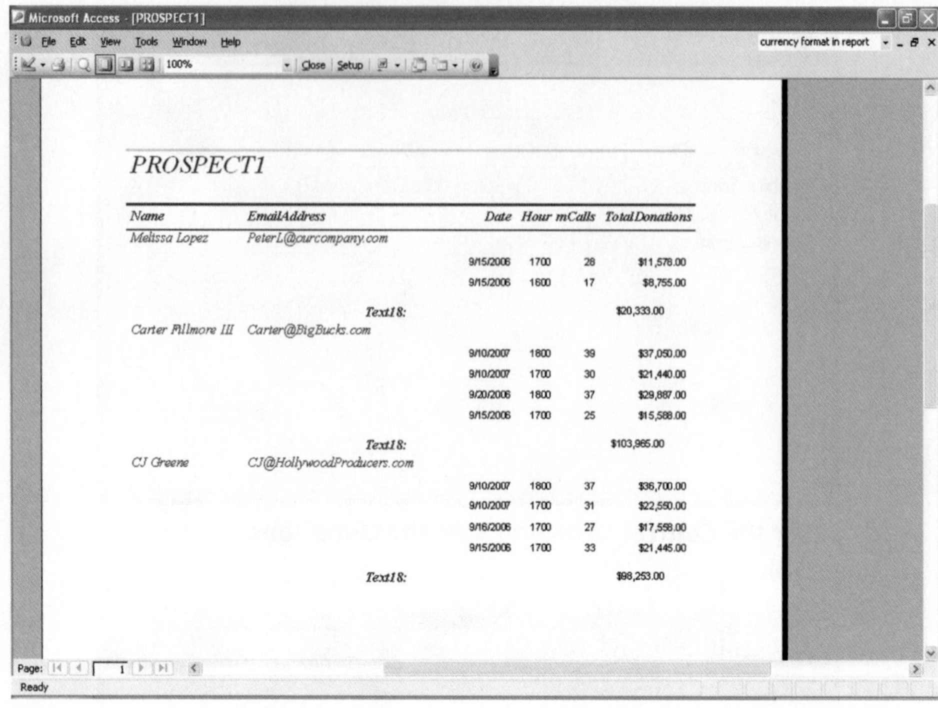

Figure CE5b-29
Reordered Report, Showing Total Donations History

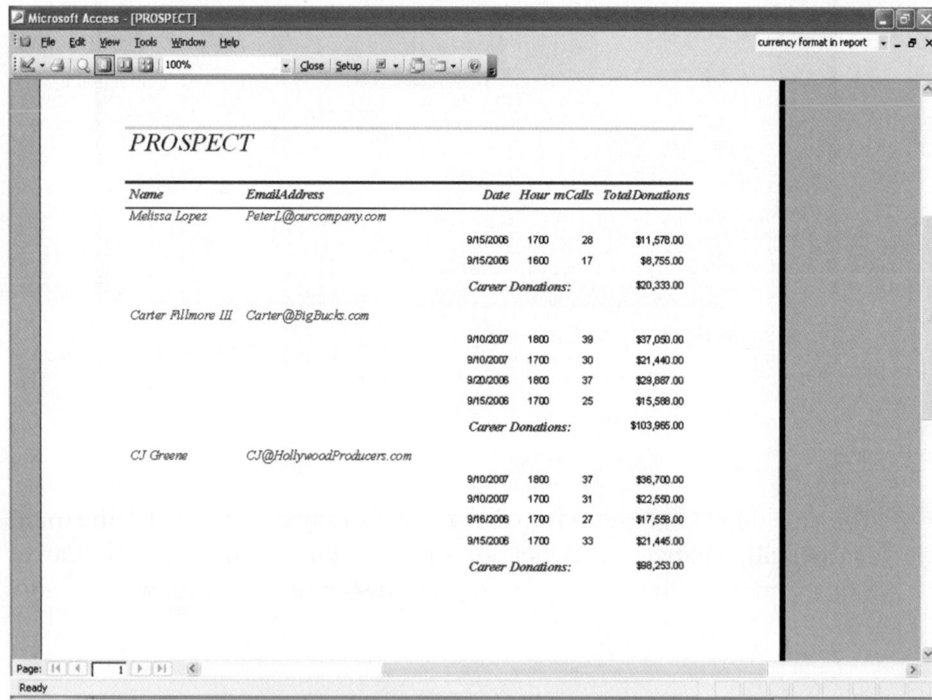

Figure CE5b-30
Finished Report

Active Review

Use this Active Review to verify that you understand the material in the chapter extension. You can read the entire extension and then perform the tasks in this review, or you can read the material for just one question and perform the tasks in this review for that question before moving on to the next one. For this active review, assume you are creating a database application having the following two tables:

CUSTOMER (<u>CustomerID</u>, Name, Email)
CONTACT (<u>CustomerID</u>, <u>Date</u>, Subject)

Q1 How do I create tables?

Open Access, and create a new database having a name of your choosing. Create the CUSTOMER and CONTACT tables. Assume the following data types:

Attribute (Field)	Data Type
CustomerID (in CUSTOMER)	AutoNumber
Name	Text (50)
Email	Text (75)
CustomerID (in CONTACT)	Number (Long Integer)
Date	Date
Subject	Text (200)

Add Description entries to the Field definitions you think are appropriate.

Q2 How do I create relationships?

Open the Relationships window and create a relationship from CUSTOMER to CONTACT using the *CustomerID* attribute. Click all the check boxes, as before. Enter sample data. Add at least five rows to CUSTOMER and at least seven rows to CONTACT. Ensure that some CUSTOMER rows have no matching CONTACT rows.

Q3 How do I create a data entry form?

Open the default data entry form for the CUSTOMER table. Click on the CUSTOMER rows to display the related CONTACT data. Use the Form Wizard to create a data entry form. Navigate through that form to see that CONTACT rows are correctly connected to CUSTOMER rows.

Q4 How can I create queries using the query design tool?

Create a query that displays *Name, Email, Date,* and *Subject.* Sort the results in alphabetical order by *Name.*

Q5 How do I create a report?

Use the Report Wizard to create a report that has *Name, Email, Date,* and *Subject.* View that report. Add a group total for each CUSTOMER that counts the number of contacts for each customer. Follow the procedure shown for creating career totals, except instead of entering the formula *=Sum(TotalDonations)*, enter the formula *=Count(*)*. Also, you need not set the Format property to Currency. The default Format property will be fine. Label your new text box correctly and position it for a pleasing display.

Using Your Knowledge

1. Perform all the tasks in the Active Review.

2. Answer question 2 at the end of Chapter Extension 5a. Implement your database design using Access. Create the tables and add sample data. Create a data entry form that shows teams and the equipment they have checked out. Verify that the form correctly processes new checkouts, changes to checkouts, and equipment returns. Create a report that shows each team, the items they have checked out, and the number of items they have checked out. [Use the *Count(*)* expression as explained in the Active Review.]

3. Answer question 3 at the end of Chapter Extension 5a. Implement an Access database for the CUSTOMER and RENTAL tables only. Create the tables and add sample data. Create a data entry form that shows customers and all of their rentals (assume customers rent bicycles more than once). Verify that the form correctly processes new rentals, changes to rentals, and rental returns. Create a report that shows each customer, the rentals they have made, and the total rental fee for all their rentals.

6 Networks and Communications Technology

This
could happen
to you

When Dee first proposed the idea of her blog, one of the first questions she was asked was, "Are you going to run it inside the Emerson network?" This question was crucial to the development of her blog, and she did not understand why. She wanted to say, "I don't know. What difference does it make?" but sensed that it would be unwise to reveal that much lack of knowledge.

In order to provide a competitive advantage, the information on Dee's blog needs to be kept private. She wants the sales reps to have easy access to the blog, but she wants to keep it from the competition. Many sales reps work from home and many travel extensively, using their computers from hotels. She knows that they can access the Internet from either home or hotel, but if she makes her blog publicly available on the Internet the competition could access it too.

An alternative is for Dee to require that the salespeople provide a user ID and password to access the blog. That, however, is just one more thing for them to remember to do, and, in the busy sales season, they are likely to forget their ID or password or leave it at home. Still, it could be done.

Emerson supports a private network that is protected from outside access by a firewall (discussed in this chapter). Employees can access that network from the Internet using a VPN (also discussed in this chapter). So, if Dee places the blog server within the Emerson network, it will be protected from unauthorized access and the salespeople can access it using the same password they use to access the VPN. Placing the blog within the network requires the permission and support of the internal IT department. As you will see, Dee could have used the knowledge from this chapter to enlist (or leverage) the support of that department.

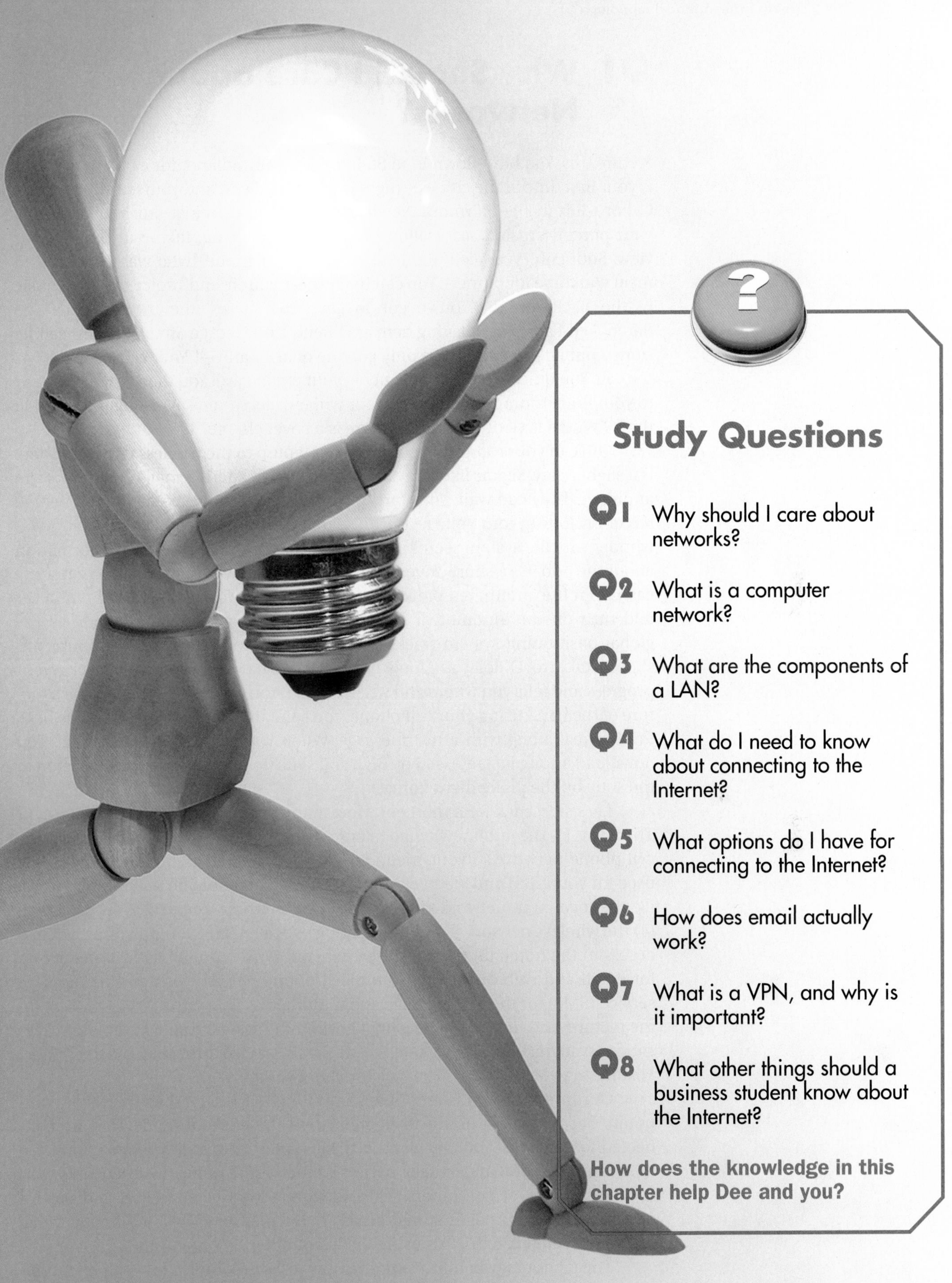

Study Questions

Q1 Why should I care about networks?

Q2 What is a computer network?

Q3 What are the components of a LAN?

Q4 What do I need to know about connecting to the Internet?

Q5 What options do I have for connecting to the Internet?

Q6 How does email actually work?

Q7 What is a VPN, and why is it important?

Q8 What other things should a business student know about the Internet?

How does the knowledge in this chapter help Dee and you?

Q1 Why Should I Care about Networks?

Picture this. You have flown in to St. John's, Newfoundland, for a business trip. It is your first time in the city. The night is young and you find yourself sitting in the Cabot Club in the Fairmont Newfoundland. You have just finished savouring your porcini-crusted sea scallops and you are relaxing, taking in the harbour view. Suddenly, your cell phone rings. It is your friend (who was supposed to meet you there for dinner). You can barely hear your friend's voice over the music in the background. "You've got to get down here," the friend says. "The Barenaked Ladies are playing here at O'Reilly's on George Street . . . I'm calling from a public phone . . . I've only got one quarter and—" Your cell phone drops the call. You quickly pay your bill using your credit card. You then make your way to your hotel room. You open the door with an electronic key. Along the way you think "Where is George Street? Is there is a cover charge?"

Once in your room, you connect your laptop to the wireless network. There is a slight delay. Seems like forever. You find you've had 15 emails while you were at dinner. They can wait. You start up your browser and type "O'Reilly's George Street St. John's" into your favourite search engine. A second rolls by and you wonder why the system seems so slow. The search comes back with information about the pub. It's a short drive. In the lobby you use your debit card to get some cash from the automated banking machine (ABM). You get into your rental car and turn on the automotive navigation system. You wait impatiently as the global positioning system tracks your exact location and plans the route you should take to O'Reilly's. Along the way, the navigation system tracks your progress and tells you where and when to turn. You get to the pub and take a picture of the band using your cell phone. You send the picture to your friends back in Montreal along with a text message. When you get back to your hotel, you download a song just released by BNL and sync up your iPod so you can listen to the song on the plane flight home.

Let's step back for a moment. How many networks did you use that night? There was (1) the public switched telephone network (PSTN), which is tied to the cell phone network so your friend could reach you; (2) the financial networks used for your ABM and credit card transactions (this could be a chapter in itself); (3) the local area network (LAN) handling electronic key access in the hotel; (4) the wireless network (802.11) operating over a LAN (802.3) providing wireless access in the hotel; (5) the wide area network (WAN) providing Internet access for email and web browsing; (6) the cell phone network using short message service (SMS) for the text message and multimedia messaging service (MMS) for the picture; and finally, (7) the global positioning system in the automated navigation system, which is a satellite network service provided by the Global Positioning System (GPS). That is a lot of networks.

Our brief history of electronic computing in Chapter 4 showed that computers become more useful to people when the computing devices are connected to networks. You will learn in this chapter that when you are connected to the Internet, you are actually part of a functioning network of networks containing millions of computers. This network allows you to send and receive email, browse web pages stored across the globe, download audio and video files, and even talk to friends using the telephone.

The technology behind computer networks is complex and can be intimidating to those who are unfamiliar with the terminology. And a large number of electronic networks exist, so it can get overwhelming. We will focus on only a few electronic networks that are related to computers. The goal of this chapter is not to make you into a networking guru. Instead, the goal is to improve your understanding of basic terminology in computer networks. Knowing these terms and understanding how networks function will help make you a more informed user of network technology and help you realize the potential and limitations of computer networks.

WHAT IS THE GLOBAL POSITIONING SYSTEM (GPS)?

The **Global Positioning System (GPS)** uses a collection of dozens of satellites orbiting the earth that transmit precise microwave signals. A GPS receiver, perhaps one you have in your car, can calculate its position by measuring the distance between itself and several of the satellites. Believe it or not, with microwave signals from at least three satellites, you can compute a GPS receiver's position. The GPS can even calculate the direction and speed of a GPS receiver. Combining the GPS with a map database enables the development of automobile navigation systems (ANS). These ANS sell for a few hundred dollars and help guide car drivers from point A to point B in real time.

Q2 What Is a Computer Network?

A computer **network** is a collection of computers that communicate with one another over transmission media. As shown in Figure 6-1, the three basic types of networks are local area networks, wide area networks, and internets.

A **local area network (LAN)** connects computers that reside in a single geographic location on the premises of the company that operates the LAN. The number of connected computers can range from two to several hundred. The distinguishing characteristic of a LAN is *a single location.* **Wide area networks (WANs)** connect computers at different geographic locations.

The single versus multiple-site distinction is important. With a LAN, an organization can place communications lines wherever it wants, because all lines reside on its premises. The same is not true for a WAN. A company with offices in Vancouver and Toronto cannot run a wire to connect computers in the two cities. Instead, the company must contract with a communications vendor that is licensed by the government and already has lines or has the authority to run new lines between the two cities.

An **internet** is a network of networks. Internets connect LANs, WANs, and other internets. The most famous internet is "**the Internet**" (with an upper-case letter *I*), the collection of networks that you use when you send email or access a

Type	Characteristic
Local Area Network (LAN)	Computers connected at a single physical site
Wide Area Network (WAN)	Computers connected between two or more separated sites
The Internet and internets	Networks of networks

Figure 6-1
Major Network Types

website. In addition to the Internet, private networks of networks, called internets, also exist.

The networks that comprise an internet use a large variety of communication methods and conventions, and data must flow seamlessly across them. To provide seamless flow, an elaborate scheme called a *layered protocol* is used. A **protocol** is a set of rules that two communicating devices follow. There are many different protocols; some are used for LANs, some are used for WANs, some are used for internets and the Internet, and some are used for all of these. The important point is that for two devices to communicate, they must both use the same protocol.

Q3 What Are the Components of a LAN?

A local area network (LAN) is a group of computers connected together on a single company site. Usually the computers are located within a kilometre or so of each other, although longer distances are possible. The key distinction, however, is that all the computers are located on property controlled by the company that operates the LAN. This means that the company can run cables wherever needed to connect the computers.

Consider the LAN in Figure 6-2. Here, five computers and two printers connect via a **switch**, which is a special-purpose computer that receives and transmits messages on the LAN. In Figure 6-2, when Computer 1 accesses Printer 1, it does so by sending the print job to the switch, which then redirects that data to Printer 1.

Each device on a LAN (computer, printer, etc.) has a hardware component called a **network interface card (NIC)** that connects the device's circuitry to the network cable. The NIC works with programs in each device to implement the protocols necessary for communication. On older machines, the NIC is a card that fits into an expansion slot. Newer machines have an **onboard NIC**, which is a NIC built into the computer.

Figure 6-3 shows a typical NIC device. Each NIC has a unique identifier, which is called the **MAC (media access control) address**. The computers, printers, switches, and other devices on a LAN are connected using one of two media.

Figure 6-2
Local Area Network (LAN)

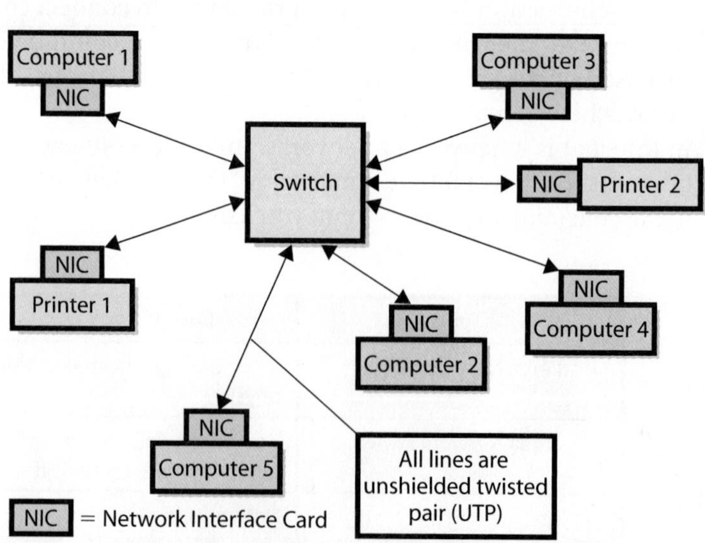

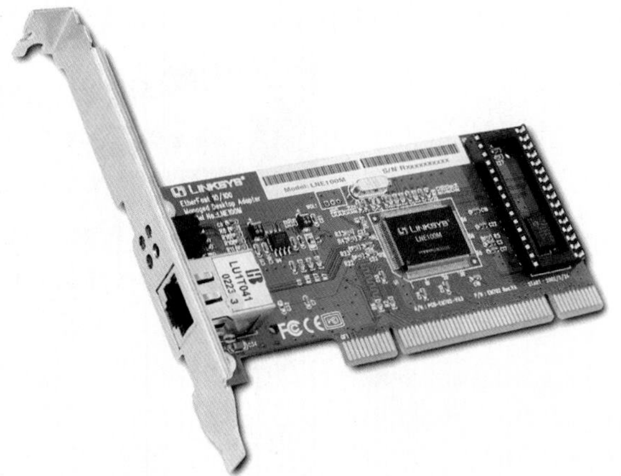

Figure 6-3
Network Interface Card (NIC)

Most connections are made using **unshielded twisted pair (UTP) cable**. Figure 6-4 shows a section of UTP cable that contains four pairs of twisted wire. A device called an RJ-45 connector is used to connect the UTP cable into NIC devices on the LAN. (By the way, wires are twisted for reasons beyond aesthetics and style. Twisting the wires substantially reduces the cross-wire signal interference that occurs when wires run parallel for long distances.)

Some LANs, usually those larger than the one in Figure 6-2, use more than one switch. Typically, in a building with several floors, a switch is placed on each floor, and the computers on that floor are connected to the switch with UTP cable. The switches on each floor are connected by a main switch, which is often located in the basement.

The connections between switches can use UTP cable, but if they carry a lot of traffic or are far apart, UTP cable may be replaced by **optical fibre cables**. The signals on such cables are light rays, and they are reflected inside the glass core of the optical fibre cable. The core is surrounded by a *cladding* to contain the light signals, and the cladding, in turn, is wrapped with an outer layer to protect it. Optical fibre cable uses special connectors called ST and SC connectors, which are shown as the blue plugs in Figure 6-5. The meaning of the abbreviations ST and SC are unimportant; they are just the two most common optical connectors.

The IEEE 802.3, or Ethernet, Protocol

For a LAN to work, all devices on the LAN must use the same protocol. The Institute for Electrical and Electronics Engineers (IEEE, pronounced "I triple E") sponsors committees that create and publish protocols and other standards. The committee that addresses LAN standards is called the *IEEE 802 Committee*. Thus, IEEE LAN protocols always start with the numbers 802.

Today, the world's most popular protocol for LANs is the **IEEE 802.3 protocol**. This protocol standard, also called **Ethernet**, specifies hardware characteristics, such as which wire carries which signals. It also describes how messages are to be packaged and processed for transmission over the LAN.

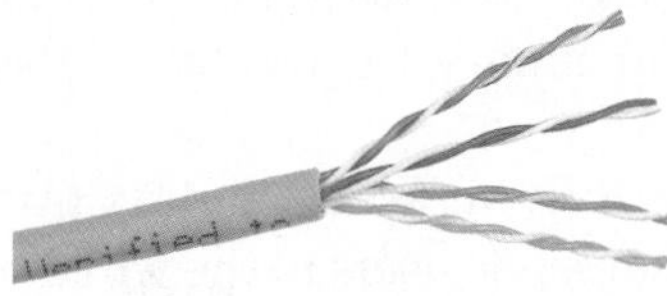

Figure 6-4
Unshielded Twisted Pair (UTP) Cable

Figure 6-5
Optical Fibre Cable

Most personal computers today are equipped with an onboard NIC that supports what is called **10/100/1000 Ethernet**. These products conform to the 802.3 specification and allow for transmission at a rate of 10, 100, or 1000 Mbps (megabits per second). Switches detect the speed that a given device can handle and communicate with it at that speed. If you check computer listings at Dell, Hewlett-Packard, Toshiba, and other manufacturers, you will see PCs advertised as having 10/100/1000 Ethernet.

By the way, the abbreviations used for communication speeds differ from those used for computer memory. For communications equipment, *k* stands for 1000, not 1024 as it does for memory. Similarly, *M* stands for 1 000 000, not 1 024 × 1024; *G* stands for 1 000 000 000, not 1024 × 1024 × 1024. Thus, 100 Mbps is 100 000 000 bits per second. Also note that communications speeds are expressed in *bits,* whereas memory sizes are expressed in *bytes.*

Wireless LANs

A Wireless LAN is a computer network that allows users to connect to a network without the need for a network cable. Figure 6-6 shows a LAN in which two of the computers and one printer have wireless connections. A laptop or personal digital assistant (PDA) equipped with a **wireless NIC (WNIC)** card lets a user move around and stay connected to their network without needing to "plug in" with a cable. For laptop computers, such devices can be cards that slide into an expansion slot, or they can be built-in, onboard devices. The most popular wireless LAN today is called an 802.11g network, which allows for transfer speeds up to 54Mbps. The 802.11n standard, due for release in September 2008, will allow speeds of up to 248 Mbps. Other names for wireless LANs are "802.11" and "Wi-Fi."

Wireless LANs require one or more **access points (AP)** that the wireless devices connect to. The AP then connects users to the wired network. The cover-

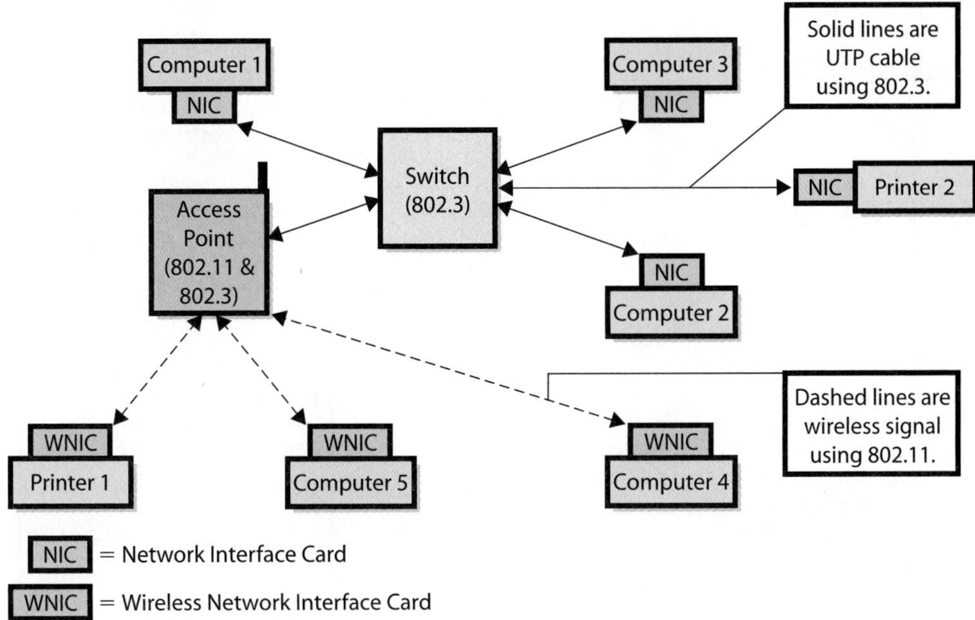

Figure 6-6
Local Area Network with Wireless

age of a wireless access point can be up to 45 metres indoors and 90 metres outdoors. Observe that the LAN in Figure 6-6 uses both the 802.3 and 802.11 protocols. The WNICs operate according to the 802.11 protocol and connect to an access point (AP). The NICs operate according to the 802.3 protocol and connect directly to the switch, which also operates on the 802.3 standard. The AP must be able to process messages according to both the 802.3 and 802.11 standards, because it sends and receives wireless traffic using the 802.11 protocol and then communicates with the switch using the 802.3 protocol. Characteristics of LANs are summarized in the top part of Figure 6-7.

Knowledge of local area networks and wireless technology enabled one student to start a successful and profitable business while still in college. Read *Case Study 6* at the end of this chapter to see how.

Q4 What Do I Need to Know about Connecting to the Internet?

The Internet is a wide area network (WAN). A WAN connects computers located at physically separated sites. A company with offices in Regina and Toronto, for example, must use a WAN to connect its computers together because the sites are physically separated. Today, the company would use the Internet to make this connection.

An important component in any WAN is a **router.** Routers are special-purpose computers that implement the protocol for WANs. When you connect your personal computer to the Internet, you are working with a router to use the Internet. The router normally connects your computer to computers owned and operated by your **Internet service provider (ISP).**

An ISP has three important functions. First, it provides your computer, or router, with a legitimate Internet address (see the discussion of IP address below). Second, it serves as your gateway to the Internet. The ISP receives the communications from your router and passes them on to the Internet. The ISP also receives communications from the Internet and passes them back to your

Type	Topology	Transmission Line	Transmission Speed	Equipment Used	Protocol Commonly Used	Remarks
Local Area Network	Local area network	UTP or optical fibre	10 100, or 1000 Mbps	Switch NIC UTP or optical	IEEE 802.3 (Ethernet)	Switches connect devices, multiple switches on all but small LANs.
	Local area network with wireless	UTP or optical for non-wireless connections	Up to 54 Mbps	Wireless access point Wireless NIC	IEEE 802.11g	Access point transforms wired LAN (802.3) to wireless LAN (802.11).
Wide Area Network	Dial-up modem to Internet service provider (ISP)	Regular telephone	Up to 55 kbps	Modem Telephone line	Modulation standards (V.32, V90, V92), PPP	Modulation required for first part of telephone line. Computer use blocks telephone use.
	DSL modem to ISP	DSL telephone	Personal: Upstream to 256 kbps, down-stream to 768 kbps Business: to 1.544 Mbps	DSL modem DSL-capable telephone line	DSL	Can have computer and phone use simultaneously. Always connected.
	Cable modem to ISP	Cable TV lines to optical cable	Upstream to 256 kbps Downstream 300–600 kbps (10 Mbps in theory)	Cable modem Cable TV cable	Cable	Capacity is shared with other sites; performance varies depending on others' use.
	Point to point lines	Network of leased lines	T1–1.5 Mbps T3– 44.7 Mbps OC48–2.5 Gbps OC768–40 Gbps	Access devices Optical cable Satellite	PPP	Span geographically distributed sites using lines provided by licensed communications vendors. Expensive to set up and manage.
	PSDN	Lease usage of private network	56 Kbps–40 Mbps+	Leased line to PSDN POP	Frame-relay ATM 10 Gbps and 40 Gbps Ethernet	Lease time on a public switched data network–operated by independent party. Ineffective for intercompany communication.
	Virtual private network (VPN)	Use the Internet to provide private network	Varies with speed of connection to Internet	VPN client software VPN server hardware and software	PPTP IPSec	Secure, private connection provides a tunnel through the Internet. Can support inter-company communication.

Figure 6-7
Summary of LANs and WANs

router and then on to you. Finally, ISPs help pay for the Internet. They collect money from their customers and pay access fees and other charges on your behalf.

It is important to note that the web and the Internet are not the same thing. The web, which is a subset of the Internet, consists of sites and users that process the **hypertext transfer protocol (HTTP)**. Programs that implement the HTTP protocol are called **browsers.** Two common browsers are Mozilla Firefox and Microsoft Internet Explorer. When you type the address www.rim.com into your browser, notice that your browser adds the notation http:// (try this, if you've never noticed that it happens). By filling in these characters, your browser is indicating that it will use HTTP to communicate with the Research In Motion website.

The Internet, on the other hand, is the communications structure that supports all application-layer protocols, including HTTP, simple mail transfer protocol (SMTP), and file transfer protocol (FTP). When you send email you generally use SMTP. When you view web pages you use HTTP, and when you transfer files between computers on the Internet you generally use FTP. These are all part of the Internet.

Names and Addresses

There are some rules for how sites are named on the Internet. The last letters in any domain name are referred to as the top-level domain (TLD). For example, in the domain name www.canada.ca, the TLD is .ca. This indicates that the site is a Canadian site. Other TLDs include .com, .org, and .biz. If you want to register a domain name, the first step is to determine the appropriate TLD. You can then visit the website for the Internet Corporation for Assigned Names and Numbers (ICANN) at icann.org and determine which agencies ICANN has licensed to register domains for that TLD. You then follow the registration process as required by one of those agencies. If the domain name you want is already in use, your registration will be disallowed.

The letters "www.canada.ca" are an example of a **uniform resource locator (URL).** The URL is an address on the Internet that is stated in a way humans can remember. But this is not the actual address on the network. In every electronic network, each machine has a numbered address. For the Internet, the address is given by four numbers each separated by a period. This is called the IP address (we'll talk about IP later). An IP address is a logical address (meaning it is assigned through software) and not a physical address (like a MAC on a NIC). For example, the site www.canada.ca is actually located at the following IP address: 198.103.238.30. If you type this number into your web browser, you will go to the same site as if you typed www.canada.ca. (Try it—it works!)

Obtaining an IP Address

In practice, two kinds of **IP addresses** exist. Public IP addresses are used on the Internet. Such IP addresses are assigned to ISPs and major institutions in blocks by ICANN. Each IP address is unique across all computers on the Internet. In contrast, private IP addresses are used within private networks and internets. They are controlled only by the company that operates the private network or internet.

Today, in most cases, when you plug your computer in to a local area network (or sign on to a wireless network), a program in your operating system will search the network for a DHCP server. This is a computer or router that hosts a program called Dynamic Host Configuration Protocol (DHCP). When the program finds such a device, your computer will request a temporary IP address from the DHCP server. That IP address is loaned to you while you are connected to the LAN. When you disconnect, that IP address becomes available again, and the DHCP server will reuse it when needed.

Finding Domain Names

Once you have an IP address, you can access the network. You might, for example, open a browser and type "www.canada.ca." We learned earlier that when we type "www.canada.ca" the computer actually calls up the IP address "198.103.238.30." The question is, "How does the computer figure out the IP address when we type in only the URL?" This service is provided by the **Domain Name System (DNS)**. The purpose of DNS is to convert human-friendly URLs into computer-friendly IP addresses. You can think of it as a giant index that links the human names for sites with the IP addresses.

The process of converting a domain name into a public IP address is called *domain name resolution*. In the very early days of the Internet, a human being was in charge of keeping the domain name index up to date. That didn't last for long. Way too much work.

Domain name resolution is now done by computers called *domain name resolvers*. The resolvers reside at ISPs, academic institutions, large companies, and government organizations. The resolvers keep track of domain name requests and store locations for future use. When a resolver cannot find a domain name, it searches for the IP address at a resolver at a higher level in the network. While the highest-level resolvers are always up to date, it can take some time for lower-level resolvers to acquire accurate information. This is why it sometimes takes time for domain name changes to work through the DNS.

Q5 What Options Do I Have for Connecting to the Internet?

The extension for this chapter reinforces the ideas in this section and provides more detail about how small office and home office (SOHO) networks can be set up. Home and small-business computers are commonly connected to an ISP in one of three ways: using a regular telephone line, using a special telephone line called a DSL line, or using a cable TV line. All three of these alternatives require that the digital data in the computer be converted to an **analog,** or wavy, signal before being sent. When receiving data, the analog signal must be converted to digital before the computer can read it. A device called a modulator/demodulator, or **modem**, performs these conversions. Figure 6-8 shows one way of converting the digital byte 01000001 to an analog signal. Different modems use different protocols and speeds. When two devices connected by modems use the same protocols but different speeds, the slower speed is the one at which they operate. As shown in Figure 6-9, once the modem converts your computer's digital data to analog, that analog signal is then sent over the telephone line or TV cable.

Figure 6-8
Analog versus Digital Signals

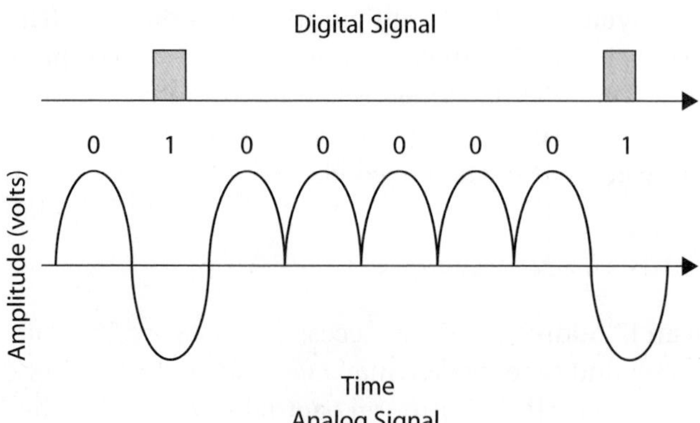

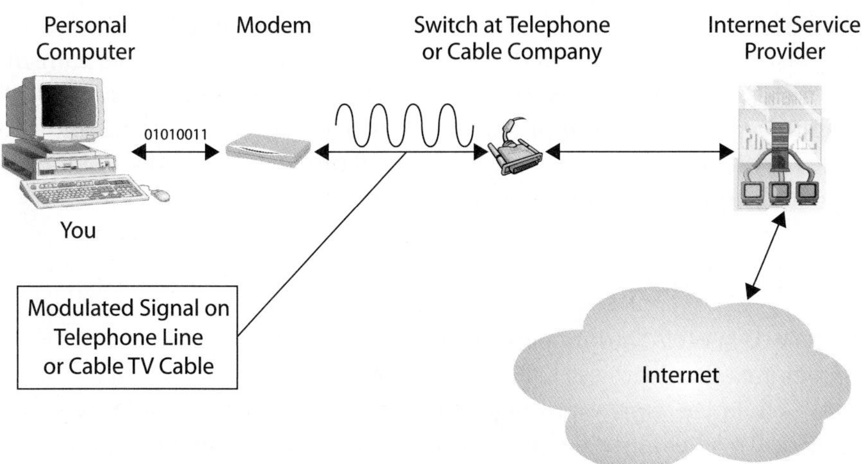

Figure 6-9
Personal Computer (PC) Internet Access

A **dial-up modem** performs the conversion between analog and digital in such a way that the signal can be carried on a regular telephone line. As the name implies, you dial the phone number for your ISP and connect. The maximum transmission speed for a switch is 56 kbps. You cannot use the telephone to make calls while you are using a dial-up modem because the dial-up modem signal interferes with voice telephone service. The dial-up modem was once a common way of connecting, but its popularity is decreasing as faster and more convenient transmission methods become available.

A **DSL (digital subscriber line) modem** is the second modem type. DSL modems operate on the same lines as voice telephones and dial-up modems, but they operate so that their signals do not interfere with voice telephone service. Because DSL signals do not interfere with telephone signals, DSL data transmission and telephone conversations can occur simultaneously. DSL modems provide much faster data transmission speeds than dial-up modems. Additionally, DSL modems always maintain a connection, so there is no need to dial in; the Internet connection is available immediately.

There are gradations of DSL service and speed. Most home DSL lines can download data at speeds ranging from 256 kbps to 768 kbps and can upload data at slower speeds—for example, 256 kbps. DSL lines that have different upload and download speeds are called **asymmetric digital subscriber lines (ADSL).** Most homes and small businesses can use ADSL because they receive more data than they transmit and hence do not need to transmit as fast as they receive. Some users and larger businesses, however, need DSL lines that have the same receiving and transmitting speeds. They also need performance-level guarantees. **Symmetrical digital subscriber lines (SDSL)** meet this need by offering the same fast speed in both directions. As much as 1.544 Mbps can be guaranteed.

A **cable modem** is the third modem type. Cable modems provide high-speed data transmission using cable television lines. The cable company installs a fast, high-capacity optical fibre cable to a distribution centre in each neighbourhood it serves. At the distribution centre, the optical fibre cable connects to regular cable-television cables that run to subscribers' homes or businesses. Cable modems modulate in such a way that their signals do not interfere with TV signals. Like DSL lines, they are always on.

Because up to 500 user sites can share the distribution centre, performance varies depending on how many other users are sending and receiving data. At the maximum, users can download data up to 10 Mbps and can upload data at 256 kbps. Typically, performance is much lower than this. In most cases, the speed of cable modems and DSL modems is about the same.

You will sometimes hear the terms **narrowband** and **broadband** with regard to communications speeds. Narrowband lines typically have transmission speeds less than 56 kbps. Broadband lines have speeds in excess of 256 kbps. Thus, a dial-up modem provides narrowband access, and DSL and cable modems provide broadband access. Figure 6-10 provides a summary of the lines and speeds used to connect to various networks.

What about Wireless WAN?

A wireless WAN (WWAN) differs from a wireless LAN in two ways. A WWAN covers a larger area than wireless LANs, and WWANs use cellular networks to transfer data. Cellular networks coverage is generally offered on a nationwide level and provided by a wireless service carrier for a monthly usage fee, much like a cell phone subscription. For someone travelling across the country, access to a WWAN would allow access to the Internet from anywhere a cellular telephone receives a signal.

How does it work? Just like a cell phone. A portable computer with a wireless WAN modem connects to a base station on the wireless networks via radio waves. The radio tower then carries the signal to a mobile switching centre, where the data are passed on to the appropriate network. The wireless service provider then provides the connection to the Internet, and that's it, you are connected. Since wireless WANs use existing cellular telephone networks, it is possible to make voice calls over a wireless WAN. Some cellular telephones and all wireless WAN cards have the ability to make voice calls as well as pass data traffic on wireless WAN networks.

Should I Use a Firewall?

A **firewall** is a computing device that prevents unauthorized network access. A firewall can be a special-purpose computer, or it can be a program on a general-purpose computer or on a router. To understand how firewalls work, you need to understand the idea of ports.

A **port** is a number used to uniquely identify a transaction over a network. The port number specifies the service provided. For example, a person could have a network server running web service (HTTP), mail service (SMTP), and file

Figure 6-10
Transmission Line Types, Uses, and Speeds

Line Type	Use	Maximum Speed
Telephone line (twisted pair copper lines)	Dial-up modem	56 kbps
	DSL modem	1.544 Mbps
	WAN—T1—using a pair of telephone lines	1.544 Mbps
Coaxial cable	Cable modem	Upstream to 256 kbps Downstream to 10 Mbps (usually much less, however)
Unshielded twisted pair (UTP)	LAN	100 Mbps
Optical fibre cable	LAN and WAN—T3, OC-768, etc.	40 Gbps or more
Satellite	WAN—OC-768, etc.	40 Gbps or more

transfer (FTP). When another computer connects to the server it needs to indicate the correct IP address for the server as well as what service it wants to communicate with. The port number identifies that service. For example, the default port number for HTTP is 80. If a packet requests the host "www.canada.ca" and port 80, then the data in the packet is transferred to the HTTP web server. The default for SMTP is 25. If the packet requests port 25, the data are transferred to the SMTP mail server. Port numbers can be used to create firewalls. An **intranet** can be thought of as a private version of the Internet that is only available to employees within the organization who are behind the firewall. For example, if you don't want anyone outside of your intranet to access your web server, you could set up a firewall that would prohibit packets destined to port 80 (the port assigned to your HTTP server) from passing through your routers. A firewall also often has an **access control list (ACL),** which keeps track of which IP addresses are to be allowed and which are to be prohibited. As a future manager, if you have particular sites with which you do not want your employees to communicate, you can ask your IS department to enforce that limit via the ACL in one or more routers.

Most likely, your IS organization will have a procedure for making such requests. **Packet-filtering firewalls** are the simplest type of firewall. A packet-filtering firewall examines each part of a message and determines whether to let that part pass. To make this decision, it examines the source address, the destination address(es), and other data. Packet-filtering firewalls can prohibit outsiders from starting a session with any user behind the firewall. They can disallow traffic from particular sites, such as known hacker addresses. They can also prohibit traffic from legitimate but unwanted addresses, such as competitors' computers. Firewalls can filter outbound traffic as well. They can keep employees from accessing specific sites, such as competitors' sites, sites with pornographic material, or popular news sites. Other firewalls filter on a more sophisticated basis. If you take a data communications class, you will learn about them. For now, just understand that firewalls help protect organizational computers from unauthorized network access.

Many ISPs provide firewalls for their customers. By nature, these firewalls are generic and have the ability to limit access to ports and IP addresses. Large organizations supplement such generic firewalls with their own. Most home routers include firewalls, and Windows XP and Vista have a built-in firewall as well. Third parties also license firewall products. The bottom line is that no computer should connect to the Internet without firewall protection. It is a minimum standard for access to the Internet. You will learn more about firewalls and security issues in Chapter 12.

Q6 How Does Email Actually Work?

We now have just about enough information to talk about the technological miracle that occurs when you send an email. As an example, let's say you are sending a message from your hotel room in Niagara Falls to a friend who works in Ottawa for Service Canada. The email begins with an address for your friend (for example, nobody@canada.ca). We noted earlier that communication protocols coordinate activity between the computer sending the message and the computer receiving the message. There is quite a bit of complicated work to do when sending an email message. To handle the complexity, communication protocols are broken down into levels or layers.

Network Layers

The Internet Engineering Task Force (IETF) developed a four-layer scheme called the **Transmission Control Program/Internet Protocol (TCP/IP)** architecture. Other schemes exist, and the four-layer model has been expanded to five layers. To simplify, we will discuss the original four-layer scheme.

Figure 6-11 shows the four layers. As shown in the right-most column, the bottom layer, Layer 1, is used to transmit data within a single network. The next two layers are used for data transmission across an internet (a network of networks, including the Internet). The top layer, Layer 4, provides protocols that help different applications interact with each other and the person using the computer.

Step 1: Getting Internet Access and Pressing "Send/Receive"

Consider Figure 6-12, which shows the LAN operated by your hotel in Niagara Falls. You occupy a suite and you plug your computer into the network as Computer C3. When you do so, a program in your operating system will search the LAN at the hotel for a DHCP server; you are operating at Layer 1 on the LAN. The router labelled RH is such a server. Your computer asks RH for an IP address, and RH assigns one.

Your email program operates at Layer 4. It generates and receives email and attachments according to one of the standard email protocols, most likely a protocol called simple mail transfer protocol (SMTP). Let's say you have created an email message to a friend and have attached a picture of yourself on the *Maid of the Mist.* When you press "Send/Receive," you start the process described in detail in the steps that follow on the next page.

Figure 6-11
IETF Network Levels

Layer	Name	Specific Function	Broad Function
4	Application Layer	Data are passed between programs (such as email application, web browser, and file transfer programs) and the transport layer	Programs for Mail, Web Browsing, File Transfer
3	Transport Layer	This layer deals with opening connections and maintaining them. Uses the Transmission Control Program (TCP). TCP works to ensure packets are received with correct content.	Transmission across an internet (TCP/IP)
2	Internet Layer	This layer works with IP addresses. There are many ways to navigate packets from one IP address to another. The Internet layer standards also control packet organization and timing constraints.	
1	Network Access Layer	This layer describes the equipment that is used for communications (UTP, fibre-optic) the signalling used (analog, digital), and the protocols that will be used to communicate between machines.	Transmission within a single network (Local Area Network)

Step 2: Break Apart Message and Get Ready for Transport

The next step is to get ready to transport the message. This is the job of the Transmission Control Program (TCP) that operates at Layer 3. TCP performs many important tasks. The most important job TCP does is to examine the email (and any attached files) you are sending and break apart large messages (like an attached photograph) into pieces called *segments*. When it does this, TCP also places identifying data at the front of each segment so that the segments can be correctly ordered, content of the segment can be validated, and segments do not get lost. TCP also works to translate segments between operating systems. If you send an email from an Apple computer to a person working on a PC, TCP will help format the message correctly so that your friend using a PC will be able to see the segments in the correct format.

Step 3: Send and Receive Packets

TCP interacts with protocols that operate at Layer 2. The Layer-2 protocol is the Internet Protocol (IP). The chief purpose of IP is to route messages across an internet. In the case of your email, the IP program on your computer does not know how to reach your friend's mail server, but it does know how to start. Namely, it knows to send all the pieces or segments of your email to a device on the network called a router.

To send a segment to the router, the IP layer program first packages each segment into a *packet*. The Internet Protocol places IP data at the front of the packet, which is in front of the TCP segment data. Adding the IP information to the segment is like wrapping an envelope that already contains a letter inside another envelope, and then placing additional To/From data on the outer envelope.

The router examines the destination of each packet, one at a time, and uses the rules defined in the Internet Protocol to decide where to send each packet. The router does not know how to get the messages all the way to their destination, but it knows how to get them started. The router bounces the packet to another router. When the packet arrives, it "asks" the new router *"Are you my destination?"* If not, the receiving router bounces the packet to yet another router.

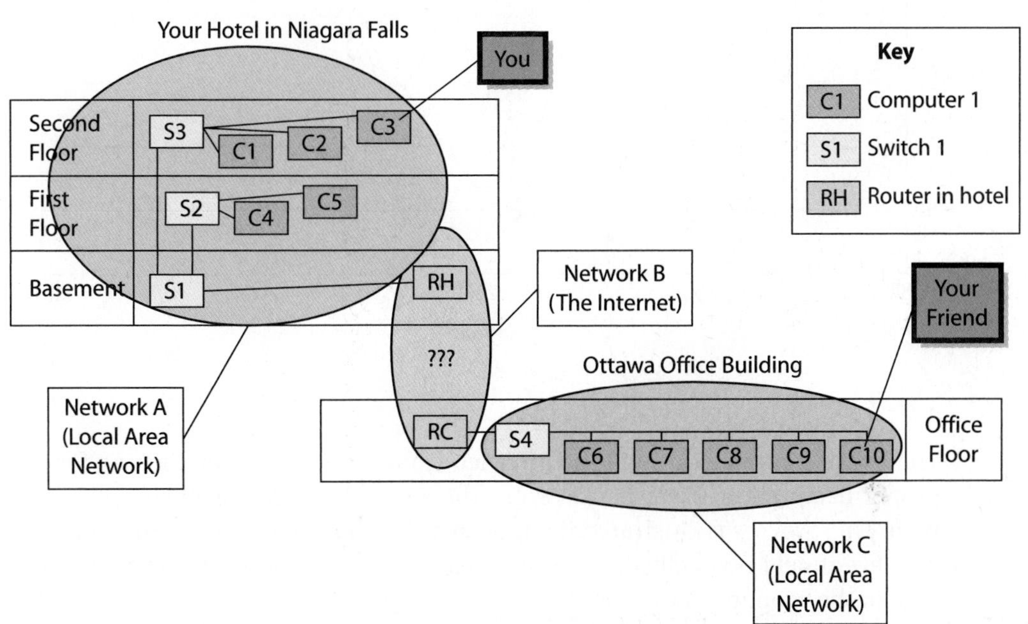

Figure 6-12
Example Networks

WHY DOES THE INTERNET USE PACKETS?

The basis for today's Internet was developed in a project completed in 1969 for the U.S. Department of Defense as part of the **Advanced Research Projects Agency Network (ARPANET).** The ARPANET was the world's first operational packet switching network. The ARPANET provided access to many research investigators who were geographically separated from the small number of large, powerful research computers available at the time.

In a **packet-switching network,** messages are first disassembled into small packets, then sent through the network and reassembled at the destination. The reason for this is twofold. First, communication lines could be shared by many computers at the same time. In packet switching there is no need to reserve the line to send messages. The second reason was that each packet could be routed independently of other packets. This might be important for the military. If one of the computers in the network was not working well (for example, if it had been damaged in some way), the packets in a packet switching network could independently find their own way to the destination.

These two features of packet switching made the Internet both efficient and resilient and helped support the dramatic growth of the Internet since 1993, as shown on the graph in Figure 6-13.

Figure 6-13
Internet Hosts, 1992–2008

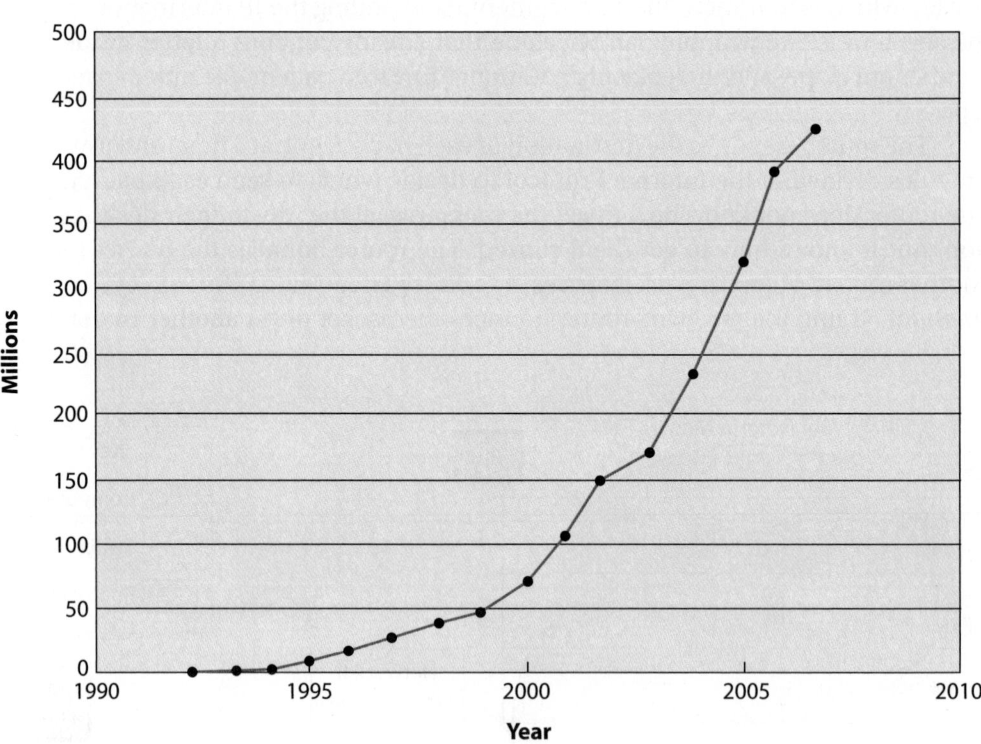

The packets bounce through the Internet, from router to router, looking for the proper destination. Each packet from the same message can take a different path. This process is illustrated in Figure 6-14. Dozens of routers on the Internet may eventually be involved in sending each packet associated with your message to the proper destination.

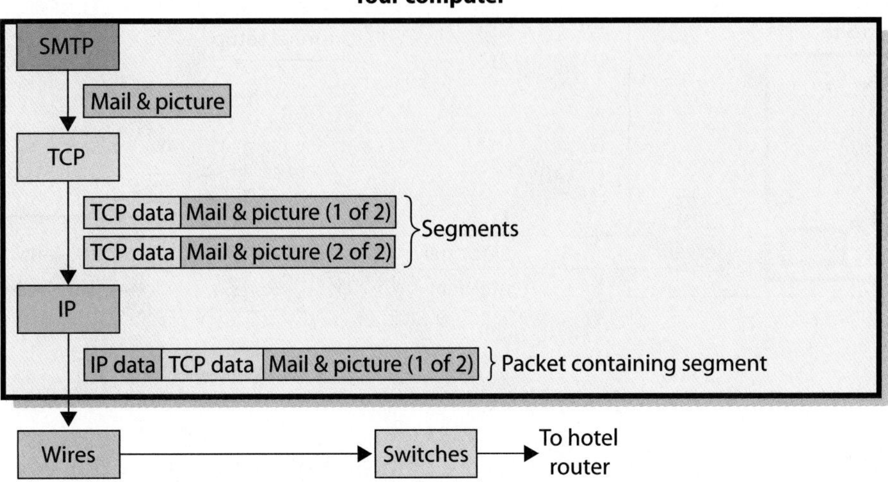

Figure 6-14
TCP/IP on Your Computer

Step 4: Reassemble Packets and Display Message

Once the email packets arrive at the correct destination router, they are sent off to a mail server. TCP waits for all the packets to arrive and then unpacks the packets back into segments. TCP also works to make sure the content of the message is correct by validating the content and checking to make sure all segments were received. If all the segments are not received, TCP will resend the missing segment (using the same process). It then assembles the segments in sequential order as indicated by the data that the TCP originally provided with each segment. The email message now rests on the mail server in Ottawa waiting for your friend to open her email program and receive and read the email.

What is truly amazing about this process is that it happens millions of times per second all across the world, 24 hours a day, seven days a week in a network that includes hundreds of millions of computers. Instead of wondering why we have to wait a few seconds to receive an email, with all those packets bouncing around we should be marvelling that we receive any email at all!

Q7 What Is a VPN, and Why Is It Important?

The **virtual private network (VPN)** is the fourth WAN alternative shown in Figure 6-7 (page 164). A VPN uses the Internet or a private internet to create the appearance of private point-to-point connections. In the IT world, the term *virtual* means something that appears to exist but does not in fact exist. Here, a VPN uses the public Internet to create the appearance of a private connection.

A Typical VPN

Figure 6-15 shows one way to create a VPN to connect a remote computer, perhaps an employee working at a hotel in Miami, to a LAN at the Chicago site. The remote user is the VPN client. That client first establishes a connection to the Internet. The connection can be obtained by accessing either a local ISP, as shown in the figure, or a direct Internet connection that some hotels provide.

In either case, once the Internet connection is made, VPN software on the remote user's computer establishes a connection with the VPN server in Chicago.

Figure 6-15 Remote Access Using VPN: Actual Connections

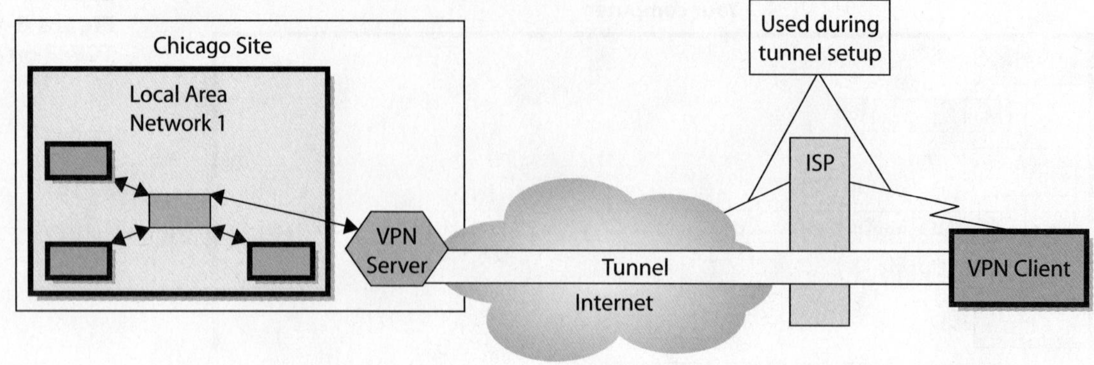

The VPN client and VPN server then have a point-to-point connection. That connection, called a **tunnel**, is a virtual, private pathway over a public or shared network from the VPN client to the VPN server. Figure 6-16 illustrates the connection as it appears to the remote user.

VPN communications are secure, even though they are transmitted over the public Internet. To ensure security, VPN client software *encrypts,* or codes, the original message so that its contents are hidden. Then the VPN client appends the Internet address of the VPN server to the message and sends that package over the Internet to the VPN server. When the VPN server receives the message, it strips its address off the front of the message, *decrypts* the coded message, and sends the plain text message to the original address on the LAN. In this way, secure private messages are delivered over the public Internet.

VPNs offer the benefit of point-to-point leased lines, and they enable remote access, both by employees and by any others who have been registered with the VPN server. For example, if customers or vendors are registered with the VPN server, they can use the VPN from their own sites. Figure 6-17 shows three tunnels: One supports a point-to-point connection between the Atlanta and Chicago sites, and the other two support remote connections.

In this chapter, you've learned (a lot, we hope) about computer networks. Read the Exercise at the end of this chapter for insights into the importance of your *human* networks as well.

Figure 6-16 Remote Access Using VPN: Apparent Connections

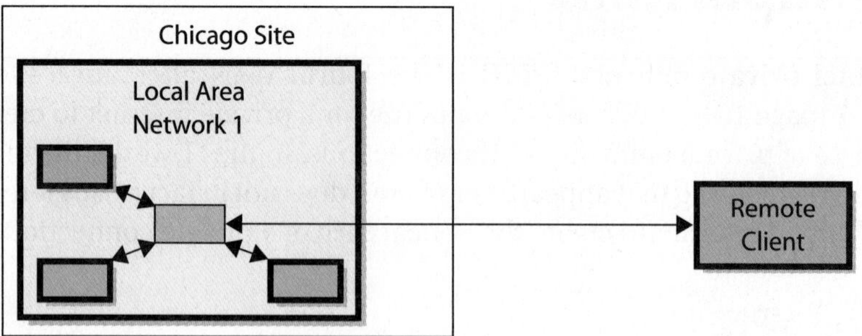

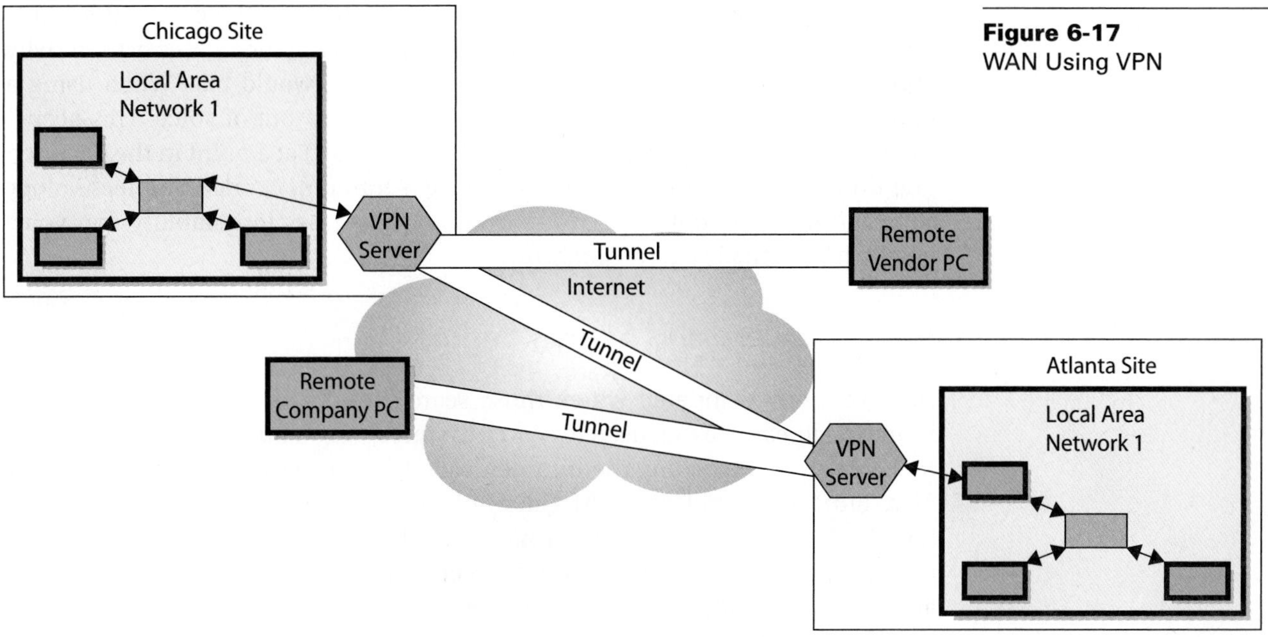

Figure 6-17
WAN Using VPN

Q8 What Other Things Should a Business Student Know about the Internet?

The Internet continues to expand, and as the network expands the amount of interesting things on the net expands exponentially. It would be impossible to list all the things a business student might want to know about the Internet. We have chosen two more issues to talk about. The first is Voice over Internet Protocol (VoIP), and the second is the technology behind search engines such as Google and Yahoo!.

Voice over Internet Protocol

Have you ever talked to someone using Skype™? If you have, you were using a **Voice over Internet Protocol (VoIP)** to send packets containing your conversation across the Internet. Commercial VoIP services using broadband have been available since 2004 in Canada. VoIP that is linked to traditional public switched telephone networks, PSTN, may have a cost that's borne by the VoIP user; however, VoIP to VoIP phone calls are sometimes free.

VoIP has advantages and disadvantages when compared to traditional phone services. One of the main advantages of VoIP, through Skype for example, is that the call can be made for free (well, not quite—you are still paying your ISP for your Internet connection). Commercial VoIP providers charge a monthly fee for broadband VoIP service but do not limit the amount of international calling. Another advantage is the ability to route incoming calls to your VoIP phone regardless of where you are connected. If you travel, or even if you move around your office, your calls can be routed to you. VoIP also has the ability to move more than one telephone call down the same connection, so it can be a way to add an extra telephone line to a small office.

One of the disadvantages of VoIP is the reliability of the connection. Now that we understand how email works (see Q6 in this chapter), it is easy to see why VoIP packets might not assemble as quickly as we would like. When using a phone using VoIP, you may notice a momentary drop-out of voice. This occurs when one or more IP packets are delayed (or even lost) at a point in the network. The dropouts occur more frequently in high-traffic networks. The technology surrounding VoIP continues to improve, and increases in reliability and voice quality have already been recognized.

Web Crawlers and Search Engines

Have you ever wondered where those search results on the web come from? Search engines are a tool used to search for information on the Internet. The first tool created for searching the Internet, called Archie, was developed in 1990 by Alan Emtage, a student at McGill University in Montreal. Archie stood for "archive" without the "v." The program created a searchable database of filenames by downloading and storing directory listings of files located on public anonymous FTP sites. Search engines have grown tremendously since that time, but the technology behind them remains similar.

Web search engines require two things: a way to collect URLs, and a method for storing/accessing the URLs so that the URLs can be searched. Finding URLs is usually the job of a *web crawler*. A **web crawler** (sometimes referred to as a *web spider*) is a software program that browses the web in a very methodical way. The crawler starts with a list of "seed" URLs. The crawler visits the URLs and identifies, for example, hyperlinks in the page. Some crawlers harvest specific things like email addresses, which can then be used for spam. If you have your email address listed on web pages, one of these web crawlers may find it. This is why you will see some people list their email addresses on a web page as "nobody at Canada dot ca" (as opposed to nobody@canada.ca, which is easy for a web crawler to harvest). Other crawlers might collect not only hyperlinks and email but also full text and images. Crawlers are even used to maintain corporate websites. The crawlers can make sure links are still active and validate HTML code on the site. The list of URLs created by the crawler can be referred to as the *crawl frontier*.

URLs from the frontier are just the start for a search engine. Once a URL is identified, it is necessary to organize the information retrieved. This process is called *search engine indexing*. It is accomplished by different programs that are organized by a set of rules. These programs work to create indexes for the results from the web crawling. These indexes provide the ability to make fast searches from a vast amount of information. The specifics of search engine technology are important business secrets, and search engine companies do not normally publish information about the techniques they use to crawl through and index the web.

Two important considerations in understanding search engines are the breadth of coverage (what percentage of the web is covered by search engines) and the ordering of the results from a search. There are no official numbers on the breadth of coverage of search engines, but a study by Lawrence and Giles (1999)[1] showed that search engines do not index sites equally, that they may not index new pages for months, and that no engine indexes more than about 16 percent of the web. While these numbers have likely changed, it is important to

[1] Lawrence, S., and C. L. Giles, "Accessibility of Information on the Web," *Nature* 400, no. 6740 (1999): 107–109.

recognize that if a page is on the web it does not mean the page has been indexed by, and is accessible through, search engines.

This brings us to our final point. How does a search engine choose to display results from a search? Commonly used search engines focus on indexing full-text documents; however, there are other searchable media types such as graphics, audio, and video. When a person enters a query into a search engine, the engine first examines its index. It then provides a listing of the "best" web pages that match the query. The match depends on the criteria used. Search engines differ in how they assign relevance. There can be millions of web pages that are somewhat relevant, and the same search on two different search engines may provide different results.

"Never Miss Your Bus"

Students John Boxall and Igor Faletski have not added up how many hours they spent waiting for the bus, nor counted the number of buses they missed, but during their four years at Simon Fraser University's Burnaby campus they spent a lot of time commuting. They knew there had to be a better way. The problem was that in order to know when a bus was coming you had to know the location of every bus stop and either have a copy of every bus schedule or be connected to the Internet—neither of which was very practical.

Not content to simply complain, John and Igor decided to take matters into their own hands. Although they realized that they could quickly assemble a java-based application that would enable them to browse the transit website, they also knew that the number of students with a compatible unlocked handset and a low-cost data plan was below 1 percent. Instead, they realized that text messaging covered the majority of cell phone users and did not require any special configuration. More importantly, the population that sent the most number of text messages, teenagers and young adults, was also one of the biggest users of public transit.

Connecting with Translink, the Greater Vancouver Transportation Authority's website, and using each bus stop's unique 5-digit numerical ID, they built a system they call MyBus. Using the university's existing access to a text messaging application programming interface (API), MyBus parses text messages, retrieves bus information, and sends the results back in a properly formatted text message. Of course this requires that you first know the bus stop number, but even this was solved through the use of aliases created for the most popular stops and posted on their website.

The system worked well. With minimal advertising it received more than 200 requests during the first three-week trial, and some students began to use it on a regular basis. MyBus received coverage in the local media and John and Igor were soon invited to present it to the transit authority, which had been developing its own version.

Keeping in mind Alfred Sloan's admonishment that there is no resting place for competition, Igor and John are continuing to refine, improve, and extend the system. Working with Peter McLachlan, a Ph.D. student at the University of British Columbia, they have just developed a Facebook version of the application, and with input from a few faculty members and advisers they have formed a corporation to commercialize the technology.

Questions

1. What problem does MyBus solve?
2. How important was access to the Translink website and the text messaging API?
3. Does this system cooperate or compete with Translink?
4. What technological changes could affect John and Igor's efforts to commercialize MyBus?
5. What advice would you give John and Igor?

It is important to recognize that search engines are normally operated by private companies that make money primarily on advertising revenue. Certain search engines may therefore employ the practice of allowing advertisers to pay to have their listings ranked higher in search results. Search engines that do not accept money for their results have to make their money through advertising. These engines might place related ads alongside the regular search engine results or might provide increased information for companies (like a picture or map) when displaying the results. Every time someone clicks on one of the ads, the search engine company makes a little bit of money (a few cents). With millions of users every day, it can be a pretty good business.

As an example of potential value, Google's initial public offering (IPO) on August 19, 2004, raised $1.67 billion. Pretty good for a business started only six years earlier—and another good reason why you should care about computer networks. *MIS in Use 6* outlines how some students have found business opportunities using networks. But while computer networks are important, human networks are even more important. Take some time to read the Exercise "Human Networks Matter More" at the end of this chapter to gain insight into the importance of the human network you are building.

How does the knowledge in this chapter help Dee and you?

The knowledge in this and the prior two chapters enables Dee to understand a diagram of the IS that supports her blog, like the one shown in Figure 6-18. On the left are two types of client computers: Dee's and the computers used by the salespeople. Both types are thin clients: Dee uses a page provided by Movable Type that enables her to create blog entries, and the salespeople use pages of blog content that are also served by Movable Type.

The client computers contain VPN client software. That software interacts with the VPN server via the Internet. By using the VPN, both Dee and the salespeople have a secure, private connection over the Internet. On the server side, a firewall stops any traffic that is not addressed to the VPN server; only snoopers or viruses would attempt to access this network without using the VPN. Once authenticated by user ID and password, the VPN server will allow access to the servers within the network, including the blog server.

The salespeople already know how to access the VPN, so Dee wants them to use this system. Because of the short time frame, however, the Emerson IT department says that it is unable to schedule the resources necessary to set up the blog server. Dee's consultant Don has the time and skill to set up that server, but the Emerson IT department will not allow an outside person to access their network. Once inside, anyone with technical skills and a desire to cause mischief could easily do so.

Dee is at an impasse. She understands why Emerson doesn't want a stranger installing programs on her computer. Meanwhile, her boss is asking her daily whether her blog will be ready for the national sales meeting.

In desperation, she calls Don, who suggests the following compromise: If Emerson will make an unprotected, test server available to him, one that is outside its network, he can set up all the blog software exactly as it will need to exist

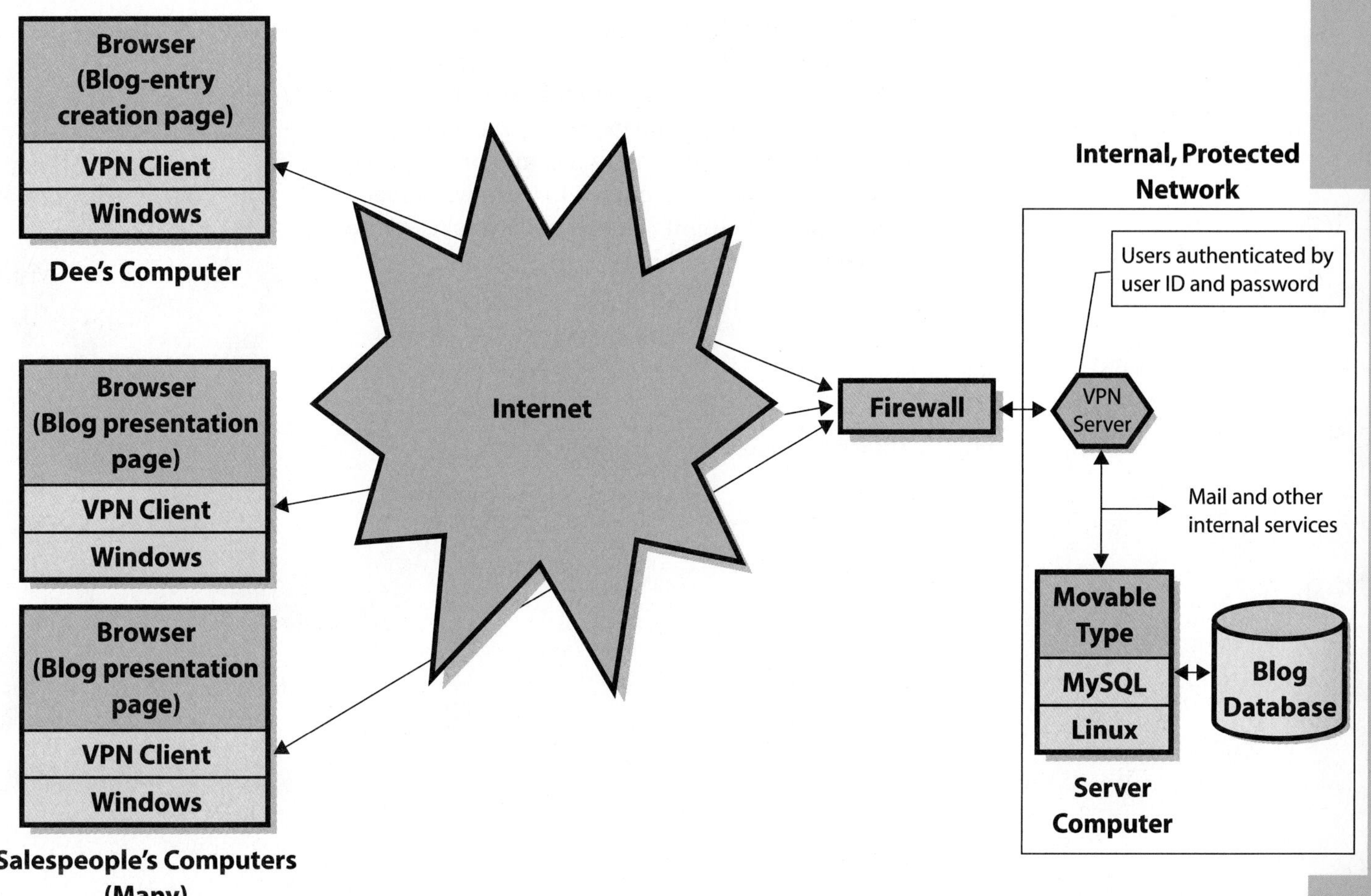

Figure 6-18
Using a Firewall and the VPN for Dee's Blog

on the operational server. He, Dee, and the IT department can test that server. Once it's working, he can write instructions for the IT personnel to copy the test-server software onto a server within the network, and the production blog will be up and running.

This is not a perfect solution. It does require some internal IT department labour. Also, were Don a criminal, it would be possible for him to include a virus in his code. To avoid this possibility, Don creates the instructions so that the IT department will be installing only public software from known sources; they can obtain Movable Type from its vendor, MySQL from its vendor, and Linux from its vendor. Then they copy the blog database from the test server. In this way, the IT department will be installing software from known sources, and none of Don's code will ever reside on any production server.

Ultimately, this is exactly what happened. However, it wasn't easy for Dee. She had to get an email from her boss's boss to a high-level IT manager in order to get the approval. Also, she used the knowledge she'd gained from Don and her negotiating skills to force the IT department's hand. She threatened that if they didn't cooperate, she would set up her own system of user IDs and passwords and place her blog on a public server on which she would rent time. She hoped it would not come to that, but she knew that the IT department knew that such a duplicate set of user IDs and passwords would confuse the salespeople. Ultimately, it would be the IT department who would have to straighten out the mess. She wanted them to view her proposal as the lesser of two evils. That's not exactly fair play, as we learn when we view this situation from the IT department's perspective in Chapter 10, but it worked for Dee in this instance.

You are the ultimate beneficiary of this story, however. Dee had to pay in blood, sweat, tears, lost sleep, and money to learn what she needed to know. All you had to do was read three chapters.

Active Review

Use this Active Review to verify that you understand the material in the chapter. You can read the entire chapter and then perform the tasks in this review, or you can read the material for just one question and perform the tasks in this review for that question before moving on to the next one.

Q1 Why should I care about networks?

Think about and identify all the computer networks you have used today. Did you buy gas? Check email? Take out money? Use your cell phone? Consider how your day might have changed if you didn't have access to these networks.

Q2 What is a computer network?

Define *computer network*. Explain the differences among LANs, WANs, internets, and the Internet. Describe the purpose of a protocol.

Q3 What are the components of a LAN?

Explain the key distinction of a LAN. Describe the purpose of each of the components in Figure 6-2. Define MAC and UTP. Describe the placement of switches on a building with many floors. Explain when optical fibre cables are used for a LAN. Explain Ethernet. Describe the purpose of each of the wireless components in Figure 6-6.

Q4 What do I need to know about connecting to the Internet?

Explain what a router does. Explain what an IP address is and what the difference is between a public and private IP address. Describe the purpose of DHCP and how it helps you get connected to the Internet. Explain what a domain name is and what DNS does.

Q5 What options do I have for connecting to the Internet?

Describe what a modem does. What is the difference between a dial-up modem and DSL? How do DSL and cable modems differ? How does a wireless WAN work? What is a firewall and how does it work? Why should any computer connected to the Internet have a firewall?

Q6 How does email actually work?

Can you describe the process of sending an email? What are network layers and why are they necessary? What is a packet? What is TCP/IP? What was the first packet switching network?

Q7 What is a VPN, and why is it important?

Describe the problem that a VPN solves. Use Figure 6-15 to explain one way that a VPN is set up and used. Define *tunnel*. Describe how encryption is used in a VPN. Explain why a Windows user need not license nor install other software to use a VPN.

Q8 What other things should a business student know about the Internet?

What is VoIP? What are the advantages and disadvantages of VoIP when compared to traditional phone service? What is a web crawler and how is it related to the crawl frontier? What is a search engine and why is search engine indexing important? How do search engine companies make money?

Key Terms and Concepts

Access control list (ACL) 169
Access point (AP) 162
Analog signal 166
Advanced Research Projects Agency Network (ARPANET) 172
Asymmetric digital subscriber line (ADSL) 167
Broadband 168
Browser 164
Cable modem 167
Dial-up modem 167
Domain Name System(DNS) 166
DSL (digital subscriber line) modem 167
Ethernet 161
Firewall 168
Global Positioning System (GPS) 159
hypertext transfer protocol (HTTP) 164
IEEE 802.3 protocol 161
Internet 159
Internet service provider (ISP) 163
intranet 169
IP address 165
Local area network (LAN) 159
MAC (access control) address 160
Modem 166
Narrowband 168
Network 159
Network interface card (NIC) 160
Onboard NIC 160
Optical fibre cable 161
Packet-filtering firewall 169
Packet switching network 172
Port 168
Protocol 160
Router 163
Switch 160
Symmetrical digital subscriber line (SDSL) 167
10/100/1000 Ethernet 162
Transmission Control Program/Internet Protocol (TCP/IP) 170
Tunnel 174
Uniform resource locator (URL) 165
Unshielded twisted pair (UTP) cable 161
Virtual private network (VPN) 173
Voice over Internet protocol (VoIP) 175
Web crawler 176
Wide area network (WAN) 159
Wireless NIC (WNIC) 162

Using Your Knowledge

1. Suppose you manage a group of seven employees in a small business. Each of your employees wants to be connected to the Internet. Consider two alternatives:
   - Alternative A: Each employee has a modem and connects individually to the Internet.
   - Alternative B: The employees' computers are connected using a LAN and the network uses a single modem to connect.

   a. Sketch the equipment and lines required for each alternative.
   b. Explain the actions you need to take to create each alternative.
   c. Compare the alternatives using the criteria in Figure 6-7.
   d. Which of these two alternatives do you recommend?

2. You have decided to start up a web-based business. You are considering what you need to make it happen.
   a. Explain the steps you would take in assigning a domain name for your website.
   b. Use the web to find the options available for ISPs to host your website. Find at least three different options and explore the differences between them. Explain why choosing a reliable ISP is important to your site.
   c. You have also decided to set up a small office network for your company. Provide an example setup for your company that includes everything you need to connect to the Internet.

d. Create an estimate for how much it would cost you to start up your business (including computer equipment, domain registration, ISP charges, software). Did you consider web designer charges? Explain why or why not.

3. You have decided to set up a web-based business. You have investigated the costs, chosen an ISP, and are ready to get working on your site. You've heard that a quick way to get your site up and running is to use a website template. Some examples are provided at www.templatemonster.com or www.websitetemplates.com.
   a. Choose an example web business and look for a template that you think fits your business.
   b. Describe the changes you would have to make to the template to fit your business.
   c. Determine the cost of the template and estimate the cost for the work needed to modify the template to fit your business.
   d. Discuss the advantages and disadvantages of using a template for your website.

Case Study 6

Larry Jones (Student) Network Services

In 2003, Larry Jones was starting his first year at a large university. (This case is real; however, to protect privacy, the student and university names are fictional.) Larry had always been interested in technology and as a high school student had won a scholarship from Cisco Corporation (a maker of communications hardware). As part of his scholarship, Larry had attended several Cisco training classes on setting up LANs, switches, and other devices.

Larry pledged a fraternity at school, and when the fraternity leadership learned of his expertise, they asked him to set up a LAN with an Internet connection for the fraternity house. It was a simple job for Larry, and his fraternity brothers were quite satisfied with his solution. He did it for free, as a volunteer, and appreciated the introductions the project gave him to senior leaders of the fraternity. The project enabled him to build his network of personal contacts.

Over the summer of 2003, however, it dawned on Larry that his fraternity wasn't the only one on campus that had the need for a LAN with access to the Internet. Accordingly, that summer he developed marketing materials describing the need and the services he could provide. That fall he called on fraternities and sororities and made presentations of his skills and of the network he had built for the fraternity. Within a year, he had a dozen or so fraternities and sororities as customers.

Larry quickly realized that he couldn't just set up a LAN and Internet connection, charge his fee, and walk away. His customers had continuing needs that required him to return to resolve problems, add new computers, add printer servers, and so forth. At first, he provided such support as part of his installation package price. He soon learned that he could charge a support fee for regular support, and even add extra charges for support beyond normal wear and tear. By the end of 2004, the support fees were meeting all of Larry's college expenses, and then some.

Small office, home office (SOHO) networks are increasing in popularity. Today, many homes have multiple computers, and although they have a need to share resources like printers, the major drive for networking home computers is to share an Internet connection. Each home user must have Internet access, but no one wants (or needs) to pay for a separate connection for each. See Chapter Extension 6A for more information.

The situation is likely to become more complex in the future as computer networks are used for entertainment as well as for information. We can see the start of that movement in Internet games, but those games require little networking compared to what will be needed when TV, radio, movies, and music are downloaded over the Internet. At that point, every computing device in the home will need to be networked.

Questions

1. Consider the first fraternity house that Larry equipped. Explain how a LAN could be used to connect all the computers in the house. Would you recommend an Ethernet LAN, an 802.11 LAN, or a combination? Justify your answer.
2. This chapter did not provide enough information for you to determine how many switches the fraternity house might need. However, in general terms, describe how the fraternity could use a multiple-switch system.
3. Considering the connection to the Internet, would you recommend that the fraternity house use a dial-up, a DSL, or a cable modem? Although you can rule out at least one of these alternatives with the knowledge you already have, what additional information do you need in order to make a specific recommendation?
4. Should Larry develop a standard package solution for each of his customers? What advantages accrue from a standard solution? What are the disadvantages?

5. Do you perceive an opportunity at your campus for a service like Larry's? If you do not have fraternities and sororities, are there apartments and condos for which you could provide such services?
6. Using Larry Jones's experience as a guide, what opportunities will exist for small, local consulting companies for setting up SOHO networks?
7. Few home entertainment consumers will want to learn the technical details of network setup. In response, vendors will attempt to ease the setup of home entertainment networks by hiding the technology. Ultimately, they will be successful, but in the near-term, customer support will be a burden to them. Although some of that support can be outsourced and sent overseas, the installation and setup of equipment must be done locally. Describe business opportunities that exist for you to provide customer support for vendors.
8. Are there local retailers selling home entertainment equipment that might be interested in a home network setup service? If so, describe their needs and the services you could provide.

Visit MyMISLab at **www.pearsoned.ca/mymislab**. MyMISLab is a state-of-the-art, interactive, online solution that combines multimedia, tutorials, and quizzes. Use MyMISLab for *Experiencing MIS* to prepare for tests and exams, and go to class ready to learn!

What Do YOU Think?

Human Networks Matter More

Six Degrees of Separation is a play by John Guare that was made into a movie starring Stockard Channing and Donald Sutherland. The title is related to the idea, originated by the Hungarian writer Frigyes Karinthy, that everyone on earth is connected to everyone else by five (Karinthy) or six (Guare) people.[2*] For example, according to the theory, you are connected to, say, Eminem by no more than five or six people, because you know someone who knows someone, who knows someone . . . and so on. By the same theory, you are also connected to a Siberian seal hunter. Today, in fact, with the Internet, the number may be closer to three people than to five or six, but in any case, the theory points out the importance of human networks.

Suppose you want to meet your university's president. The president has a secretary who acts as a gatekeeper. If you walk up to that secretary and say, "I'd like a half-hour with President Jones," you're likely to be palmed off to some other university administrator. What else can you do?

If you are connected to everyone on the planet by no more than six degrees, then surely you're connected to your president in fewer steps. Perhaps you play on the tennis team, and you know that the president plays tennis. In that case, it's likely that the tennis coach knows the president. So arrange a tennis match with your coach and the president. Voilà! You have your meeting. It may even be better to have the meeting on the tennis court than in the president's office.

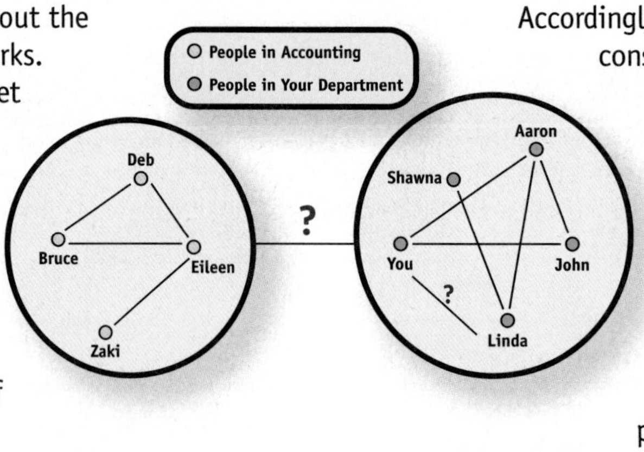

People in Accounting
People in Your Department
Deb
Bruce
Eileen
Zaki
?
Aaron
Shawna
You
John
Linda
?

The problem with the six-degree theory, as Stockard Channing said so eloquently, is that even though those six people do exist, we don't know who they are. Even worse, we often don't know who the person is with whom we want to connect. For example, there is someone right now who knows someone who has a job for which you are perfectly suited. Unfortunately, you don't know the name of that person.

It doesn't stop when you get your job, either. When you have a problem at work, like setting up a blog within the corporate network, there is someone who knows exactly how to help you. You, however, don't know who that is.

Accordingly, most successful professionals consistently build personal human networks. They keep building them because they know that somewhere there is someone whom they need to know or will need to know. They meet people in professional and social situations, collect and pass out cards, and engage in pleasant conversation (all part of a social protocol) to expand their networks.

You can apply some of the ideas about computer networks to make this process more efficient. Consider it as a type of network diagram. Assume that each line represents a relationship between two people. Notice that the people in your department tend to know each other, and that the people in the accounting department also tend to know each other. That's typical.

Now suppose you are at the weekly employee after-hours party and you have an opportunity to introduce yourself either to Linda or Eileen. Setting aside personal considerations and thinking just about network building, which person should you meet?

If you introduce yourself to Linda, you shorten your pathway to her from two steps to one and your pathway to Shawna from three to two. You do not open up any new channels because you already have them to the people on your floor.

However, if you introduce yourself to Eileen, you open up an entirely new network of acquaintances. So, considering just network building, you use your time better by meeting Eileen and other people who are not part of your current circle. It opens up many more possibilities.

The connection from you to Eileen is called a *weak tie* in social network theory,** and such links are crucial in connecting you to everyone in six degrees. *In general, the people you know the least contribute the most to your network.*

This concept is simple, but you'd be surprised by how few people pay attention to it. At most company events, everyone talks with the people they know—and if the purpose of the function is to have fun, then that behaviour makes sense. In truth, however, no business social function exists for having fun, regardless of what people say. Business functions exist for business reasons, and you can use them to create and expand networks. Given that time is always limited, you may as well use such functions efficiently.

* See "The Third Link" in Albert Laszlo Barabasi's book *Linked* (New York: Perseus Publishing, 2002) for background on this theory.

** See Terry Granovetter, "The Strength of Weak Ties," *American Journal of Sociology*, May 1973.

Discussion Questions

1. Determine the shortest path from you to your university's president. How many links does it have?
2. Give an example of a network to which you belong and sketch a diagram of who knows whom for six or so members of that group.
3. Recall a recent social situation and identify two people, one of whom could have played the role of Linda (someone in your group whom you do not know) and one of whom could have played the role of Eileen (someone in a different group whom you do not know). How could you have introduced yourself to either person?
4. Does it seem too contrived and calculating to think about your social relationships in this way? Even if you don't approach relationships like this, are you surprised to think that others do? Under what circumstances does this kind of analysis seem appropriate, and when does it seem inappropriate? Are you using people?
5. Consider the phrase "It's not what you know, it's whom you know that matters." Relate this phrase to a network diagram. Under what circumstances is this likely to be true? When is it false? When is it ethical?
6. Describe how you can apply the principle "The people you know the least contribute the most to your network" to the process of a job search. Are you abusing your relationships for personal advancement?

Chapter Extension 6a

Small Office, Home Office (SOHO) Networks

Q1 What Are the Components of a SOHO LAN?

Study Questions

- **Q1** What are the components of a SOHO LAN?
- **Q2** How do I access programs in the device access router?
- **Q3** How does a SOHO network use DHCP?
- **Q4** What security options do I have?
- **Q5** How do I set up a SOHO network?

Figure CE6a-1 shows a portion of a LAN and Internet hardware used by a **small office, home office (SOHO)** company. The messy set of wires, devices, and office paraphernalia illustrates the need for many of the concepts in Chapter 6. The small, flat black box is a DSL modem that is connected to a telephone line. The DSL modem also connects to the silver upright box with the small dark grey antenna. That silver box is a **device access router.** Amazingly, that little box contains an Ethernet LAN switch, an 802.11g wireless access point, a router, and a special-purpose computer with programs loaded in firmware. Those firmware programs act as a DHCP server and perform network address translation (NAT). Those firmware programs also set up wireless security and perform administrative tasks.

Note the several UTP cables that connect the device access router to computers and other devices on the LAN. The printer (behind the tape dispenser) has a small black box with a grey UTP cable and a small black power line going into it. The black box is a NIC that connects the printer to the LAN via the device access

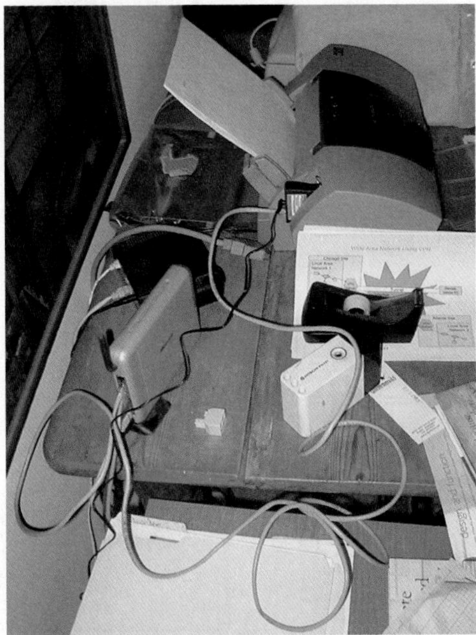

Figure CE6a-1
A SOHO Network

router. This NIC is called a **printer server,** and it, too, contains a special-purpose computer with firmware programs. These programs can be used to set up and administer the printer server and printer. By using the printer server, it is unnecessary to connect the printer to any computer. Any of the users on the LAN can use the printer without turning on a computer to serve the printer. Figure CE6a-2 shows a schematic of the contents of the device access router in the context of a typical SOHO LAN.

Q2 How Do I Access Programs in the Device Access Router?

The router in the device access router has two IP addresses. One is a private IP address that is used only within the LAN. Any computer or printer server on the LAN that wishes to send traffic to the router will use the private IP address. The device access router also has a second, public IP address that is provided by the ISP. That address is valid on the public Internet, worldwide. Any outside computer or server that wishes to send traffic to any device on this LAN will use the router's public IP address to do so.

The manufacturer of the device access router assigns the local IP address to the router. That IP address is always stated in the device's documentation. If you cannot locate that documentation, you can Google the brand name and model of your device, and you will most likely be able to find a copy of it. (Of course, if you're setting up your network, you won't have access to the Internet yet. Go next door and ask to borrow your neighbour's Internet connection.)

The internal IP address for the device access router in Figure CE6a-1 is 192.168.2.1. To contact that router, the network administrator used a browser on a computer on the LAN and keyed http://192.168.2.1 in the address field. The router responded with a page that looks like that in Figure CE6a-3. We have not

Figure CE6a-2
Components of a SOHO LAN

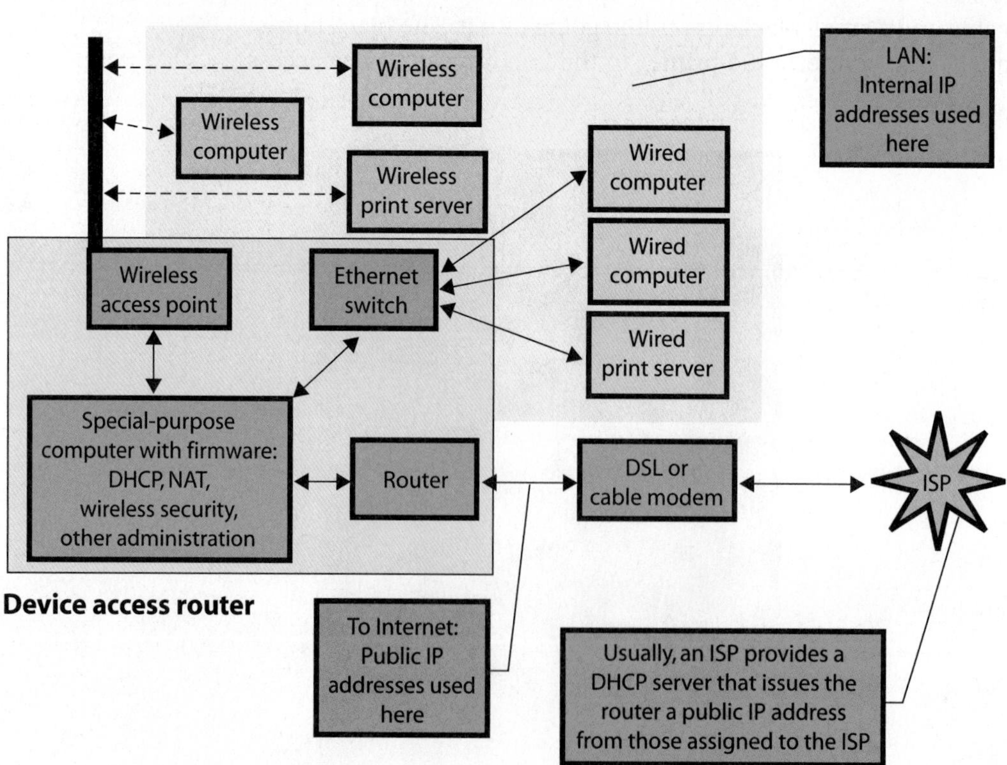

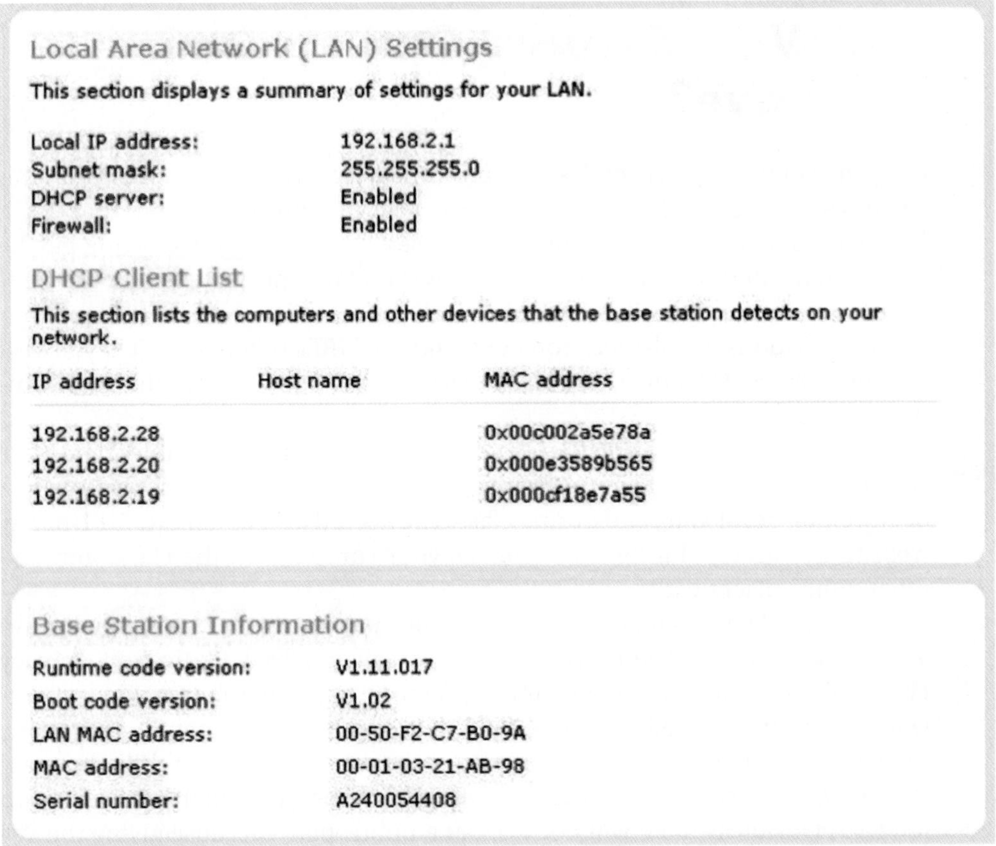

Local Area Network (LAN) Settings

This section displays a summary of settings for your LAN.

Local IP address:	192.168.2.1
Subnet mask:	255.255.255.0
DHCP server:	Enabled
Firewall:	Enabled

DHCP Client List

This section lists the computers and other devices that the base station detects on your network.

IP address	Host name	MAC address
192.168.2.28		0x00c002a5e78a
192.168.2.20		0x000e3589b565
192.168.2.19		0x000cf18e7a55

Base Station Information

Runtime code version:	V1.11.017
Boot code version:	V1.02
LAN MAC address:	00-50-F2-C7-B0-9A
MAC address:	00-01-03-21-AB-98
Serial number:	A240054408

Figure CE6a-3
Router Response Page

discussed *subnet masks* in this text. Other than that, however, you should be able to understand this figure based on the knowledge you gained in this chapter.

Q3 How Does a SOHO Network Use DHCP?

The device access router provides a DHCP server. When a computer, printer server, or other device wishes to sign on to the network, it contacts the device access router and obtains an internal IP address from it. The DHCP client list in Figure CE6a-3 shows the three computers or other devices that asked for an IP address. This list shows the addresses assigned by the device access router, as well as the MAC address of each device. If another device signs on to the LAN, the device access router will issue it an internal IP address and add its MAC address to the list.

The last part of Figure CE6a-3 shows data about the base station itself. The LAN MAC address is the MAC address of the Ethernet switch in the device. The MAC address is the MAC address of the router.

A similar scheme is used whenever you sign on to a LAN at your university or at your favourite coffee shop. Your computer will search the neighbourhood for a wireless connection (really a wireless access point within a device access router). When it finds one, it will ask for an Internal IP address. The DHCP server in the device access router will issue one. When you sign off, that IP address goes back into the unused set of IP addresses to be reused by another student or customer.

Q4 What Security Options Do I Have?

If you are connecting via wireless to a network at a public place such as your university or a coffee shop, you have no security protection on that LAN. Understand that any unprotected text you send over a wireless network can be easily intercepted by anyone nearby. Unless you take special precautions—precautions that are rare and seldom taken—all your email is unprotected text. Your IM conversations are also unprotected, and the URLs of any websites you visit are unprotected. Of course, any text you send using *https* is encrypted and comparatively safe.

Intercepting wireless traffic is quite easy. Using readily available shareware, your professor or any of your classmates could readily obtain and read the text of any email or IM you send during class. They could also obtain the URL of any website you access during class. So, use your computer in the classroom and other public places with care!

The good news is that if you're setting up your own SOHO LAN, you do have a number of security options. The first is called **Wired Equivalent Privacy (WEP).** The goal of WEP is to provide the same level of security over wireless networks as exists on wired networks. WEP requires that each computer accessing the LAN enter a lengthy key (a long string consisting of digits and the letters *A* through *F*). That string is a symmetric key used to encrypt data transmissions on the LAN. Obviously, WEP will not work at a public place because giving the key to every customer who wants to use the LAN would invalidate security.

Unfortunately, WEP was rushed to market before it was sufficiently tested, and it has serious flaws. In response, the IEEE 802.11 committee developed improved wireless standards known as **Wi-Fi Protected Access (WPA),** and a newer, better version called **WPA2.** Only newer wireless devices can use these techniques.

Another security option for SOHO LANs is **MAC address filtering.** This option will not protect data transmissions from being intercepted, but it will prevent unauthorized users from accessing the device access router and the LAN. To set up MAC address filtering, you first need to obtain the MAC address of every computer and device that you want to allow to sign on to your network. You can obtain the MAC address of NIC devices in a variety of ways. On Windows computers, you can go to the Start menu, select Run, type in the letters **Cmd,** and click OK. You will see a flashing underscore in a black window. Type the letters **Ipconfig** (all one word) and press Enter. Windows will respond with the MAC addresses for all NIC devices on your computer. Select the MAC address that corresponds to the wireless device on that computer. Note, too, that if you employ MAC address filtering you will need to enter the MAC addresses of all devices on the LAN—and not just the wireless devices.

Once you have the list of MAC addresses, connect to your device access router from your browser using its internal IP address as described. Then find and select the Wireless Security menu on the device's page, and find the entry for MAC Address Filtering. The particular format of the screen varies depending on the product, but it will appear as something like what's shown in Figure CE6a-4. Enter the MAC addresses for all your devices. Be sure to enter at least one of them correctly, because once you've saved those addresses, if none is correct, you will be locked out of your own LAN!

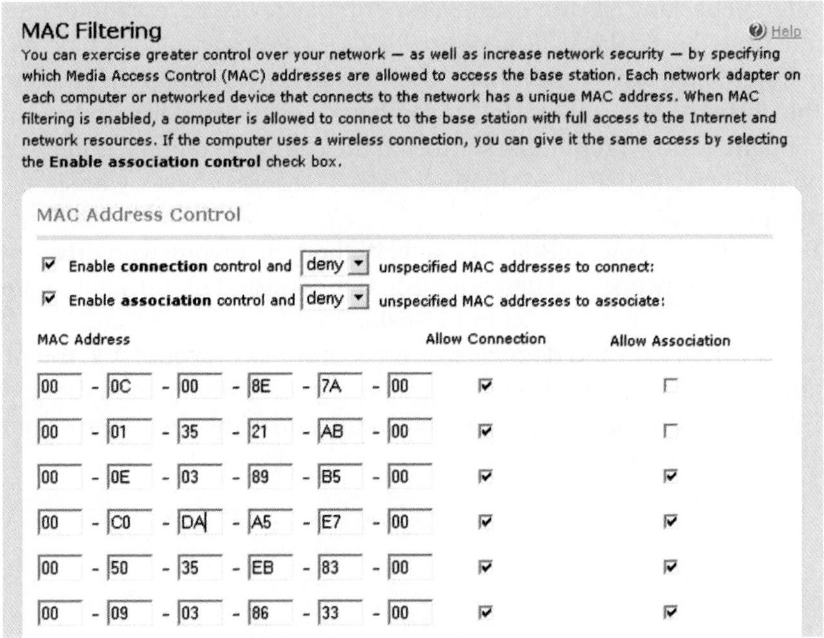

MAC Filtering

Help

You can exercise greater control over your network — as well as increase network security — by specifying which Media Access Control (MAC) addresses are allowed to access the base station. Each network adapter on each computer or networked device that connects to the network has a unique MAC address. When MAC filtering is enabled, a computer is allowed to connect to the base station with full access to the Internet and network resources. If the computer uses a wireless connection, you can give it the same access by selecting the **Enable association control** check box.

MAC Address Control

☑ Enable **connection** control and deny unspecified MAC addresses to connect:

☑ Enable **association** control and deny unspecified MAC addresses to associate:

MAC Address	Allow Connection	Allow Association
00 - 0C - 00 - 8E - 7A - 00	☑	☐
00 - 01 - 35 - 21 - AB - 00	☑	☐
00 - 0E - 03 - 89 - B5 - 00	☑	☑
00 - C0 - DA - A5 - E7 - 00	☑	☑
00 - 50 - 35 - EB - 83 - 00	☑	☑
00 - 09 - 03 - 86 - 33 - 00	☑	☑

Figure CE6a-4
MAC Address Filtering

Q5 How Do I Set Up a SOHO Network?

Given the knowledge you gained in Chapter 6 and Chapter Extension 6a, it should be easy for you to set up a SOHO network. Before doing anything, however, first read the instructions that come with your device access router. It will have specific instructions for tasks to perform and the order in which they should be performed. If you follow those instructions in the proper order, setting up the SOHO LAN should not be difficult.

Most likely, the instructions will call for you to set up cabling correctly before turning on any devices. The reason for this is that your computer and other devices will attempt to obtain IP addresses or take other actions when they are turned on. If the cabling is not present, those attempts will fail, and the devices will go into indeterminate states.

In most cases (not all—see your device access router documentation), you will work upstream from the modem to your computer. If so, you will first turn on the modem and then turn on the device access router. In almost every case, the device access router will communicate via the modem to the ISP in an attempt to contact a DHCP server. If that attempt succeeds, then the modem has a connection to the Internet. At the same time, the Ethernet switch and the wireless access point become live. At that point, turn on your computers and other devices, and they will contact the device access router for an IP address for use within the LAN.

If you have problems, they are most likely in the cabling. Ensure that you have connected all wires to the proper sockets. If you're using a DSL line, you may have a splitter—one side of which is for your phone and the other is for the modem. Make sure the lines are connected to the correct sockets. On the device access router, a particular socket is designated for the line from the modem. Ensure that the line is connected to the proper socket. Also, make sure that all the cable connections are fully inserted into their sockets; you will normally hear a click when the connector seats correctly.

After rechecking all your cabling, turn off the device access router and wait a minute or so. This delay will cause the ISP's DHCP server to terminate its prior connection (if any) with your router. After that delay, power up the modem and then the device access router. Unless you have a defective device (very unlikely if you bought it from a reputable source), if the cabling is correct, and if you follow the instructions that accompany the device access router, you should not have any problems.

Be sure to use MAC address filtering. Without it, anyone who drives by can sign on to your network, and depending on their skill and intent, cause potential harm. At the least, they'll be able to freeload on your ISP connection. At the worst, they can invade and damage files on computers on your LAN. You may or may not want to use WEP or WPA. If you do not, then understand that all your email, IMs, and URLs are readily readable by anyone within receiving distance of your wireless network.

Good luck!

Active ? Review

Use this Active Review to verify that you understand the material in the chapter extension. You can read the entire extension and then perform the tasks in this review, or you can read the material for just one question and perform the tasks in this review for that question before moving on to the next one.

Q1 What are the components of a SOHO LAN?

List the components of a SOHO LAN. List the components of a device access router, and describe the function of each. Explain the purpose and advantage of a printer server.

Q2 How do I access programs in the device access router?

Explain why the device access router has two IP addresses, and explain the role of each. Describe how you can access programs on the device access router. Assume that the internal IP address of your device access router is 192.168.2.8.

Q3 How does a SOHO network use DHCP?

Explain what happens when a computer, printer server, or other LAN device attempts to sign on to a SOHO network like the network described here. Explain the entries in Figure CE6a-3. Ignore subnet mask.

Q4 What security options do I have?

Describe the security protection you have when signing on using a wireless connection at your university or in a public coffee shop. Describe the traffic you send that is protected by encryption. Describe the traffic that is not protected. Explain your privacy vulnerability when using a wireless network in class. Explain the purpose of WEP, and describe why it cannot be used for a public network. Explain the problem with WEP. Explain the purposes and limitations of WPA and WPA2. Explain MAC address filtering. Describe one way to obtain the MAC address of NIC devices on your computer. Describe the process of setting up MAC address filtering. Describe the process for enabling MAC address filtering.

Q5 How do I set up a SOHO network?

Describe the first step in setting up a SOHO network. Describe why it is usually important to set up cabling before powering up any devices. Describe the order of powering devices that is most commonly used. Explain the most common source of problems in setting up a SOHO LAN. Explain why it is important to wait a minute or so before restarting your device access router.

Key Terms and Concepts

Using Your Knowledge

1. Suppose that you're a consultant and that you share an office suite with two other consultants. The suite has three offices, a small lobby, and a utility room. All five rooms are on the same level and within close proximity to one another. Assume that each of you has a laptop computer and that the three of you want to share a fast, black-and-white laser printer and a slower, full-colour printer. Describe a SOHO LAN that would meet your needs. Assume you have no Internet cabling and no authority to install any in your building. What devices would each computer or printer require? What other device is necessary?

2. Describe security alternatives that are available to the SOHO LAN in your answer to question 1. Explain the advantages and disadvantages of each. Which alternatives would you recommend?

3. Assume that one of the consultants for the LAN in question 1 runs Windows, and that when he clicked on the small LAN icon at the bottom of his computer screen, the following screen appeared:

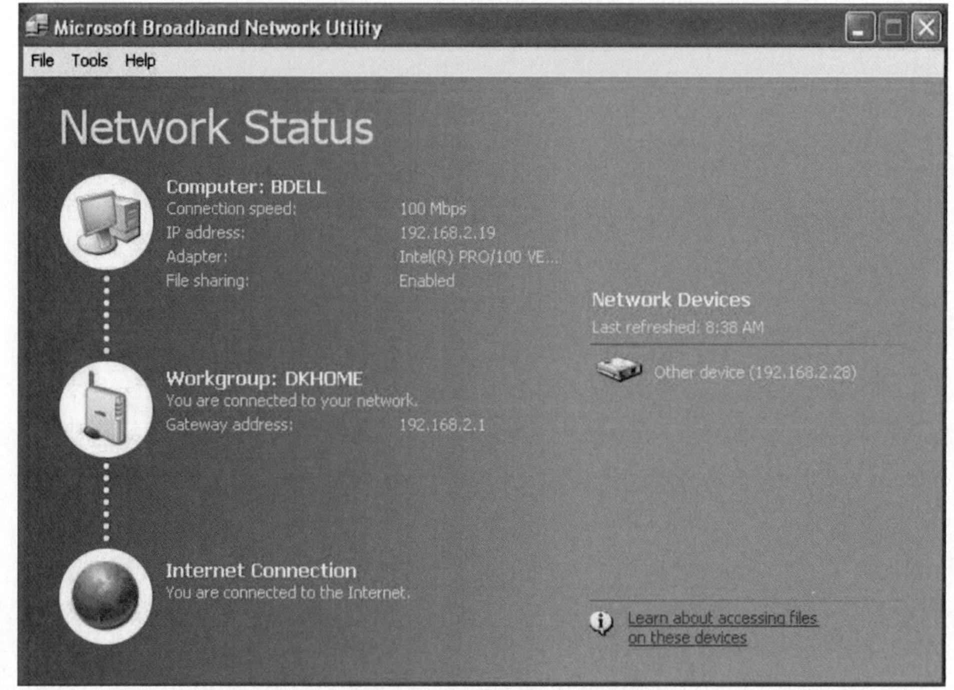

Figure CE6a-5
MS Windows Screen Shot

Source: Microsoft product screen shot reprinted with permission from Microsoft Corporation.

a. Are the IP addresses in the screen private or public IP addresses?
b. What computer is located at IP address 192.168.2.19?
c. What device is located at IP address 192.168.2.1?
d. What will happen if the user enters *http://192.168.2.1* into her browser?

4. The user did not know what device was located at IP address 192.168.2.28, so she typed *http://192.168.2.28* into her browser and the following screen appeared:

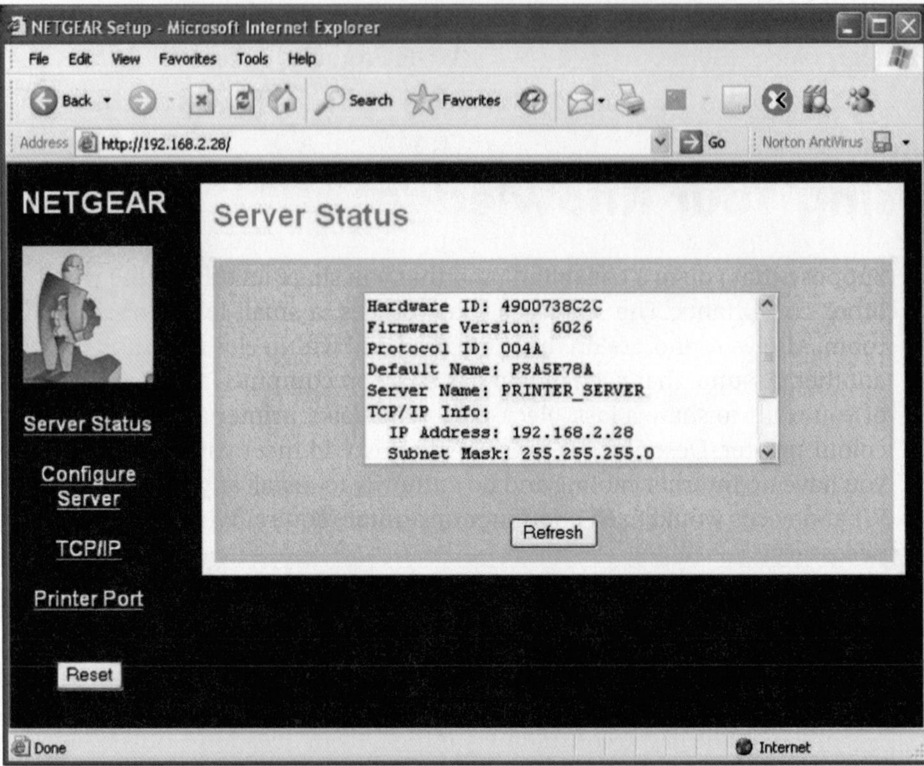

Figure CE6a-6
Netgear Server Status

Source: Used with permission of NETGEAR, Inc.

a. What type of device has been assigned to this IP address?
b. Which device created this display?
c. What seems to be the purpose of this display?

5. The user then entered *http://192.168.2.1* into her browser and received back several pages of screens. One of them appeared as follows:

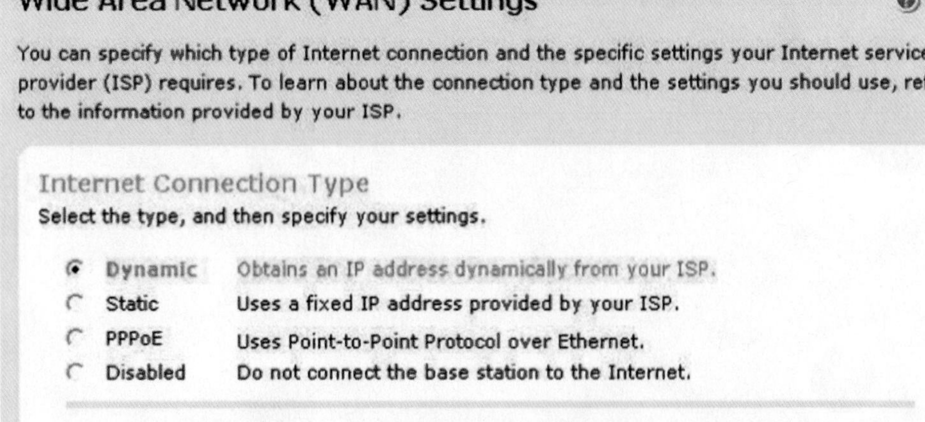

Figure CE6a-7
WAN Settings

a. Do the data in this display pertain to the Ethernet switch or the router?
b. This screen allows the base station to use DHCP to obtain its public IP address from the ISP. What benefits accrue to the ISP of using DHCP?

c. When would the network administrator *not* use DHCP to connect to the ISP?
d. Under what circumstances would someone use a device access router and not connect it to the Internet?

PART 3

IS and Competitive Advantage

This could happen to you

Dorset-Stratford Interiors (DSI) is a partnership located near Calgary, Alberta. It leases facilities on the site of a former airbase. Facilities include a large hangar capable of handling three aircraft at a time, as well as a machine shop, production facility, and office and inventory space. Eleanor Dorset, one of the partners in DSI,[1] describes the origins of the partnership as follows:

"I came into this business through the back door. I was designing interiors for well-to-do clients here in Alberta, and one of them asked me to design the interior of his airplane. I really enjoyed it and saw that I have an ability to express clients' needs within the space and safety constraints of an airplane. It helps that I've been crazy about aviation all my life.

"John Stratford was running a Boeing 737 aircraft refitting and maintenance company when I met him. In fact, we chose his company for the build-out of the design for my original client. John has the same passion for quality that I have, and he also knows how to manage projects and costs. After we finished that first project, John asked me to provide design services for one of his customers, and DSI was born. I handle the front-end sales and manage the design department; John runs operations and all of the back-office. He also manages customer service and support.

"We specialize in Boeing 737 interiors for individuals, corporations, and governments. Most often, we design and construct what are called *head-of-state* interiors. The projects vary, but usually they include a main cabin with 20 or

[1] This case is based on a real company, and the problems, situations, and systems described are real. DSI, however, is fictitious. The actual company declined to allow us to publish its name or other identifying data. Company executives decided not to reveal the information about their competitive strategy and the means they use to accomplish that strategy. The actual company, like DSI, provides custom, high-end, high-quality products. It does so, however, to a segment of a different industry.

fewer seats, a deluxe galley, some type of office suite, and a bedroom. Everything is first-rate: the fit and finish of our woodwork, the quality of our fabrics, the overall design tailored to the needs of the customer. And, of course, we pay careful attention to the safety systems of the aircraft.

"There are some variances among interiors. Corporations often want more seating and hold back on the more exotic options. For individuals, the sky is literally the limit when it comes to luxury accommodations. Interiors for government aircraft vary; some are spartan, while others are elaborate.

"We build to the client's needs, and we believe we provide the very highest quality. If you want the lowest possible price, you should go to an offshore vendor. Its labour will be cheaper, and the company doesn't have our notions of quality. It can do a fine job of crafting a safe interior, but the look and feel will be another quality altogether.

"I don't mean to say we don't care about costs; we do. We want to give our customers the best possible value. So we constantly ask, 'Where can we save?' Everyone pays more or less the same for materials, so DSI is not going to gain an advantage there. The savings have to be in labour. And, in fact, we're constructing interiors for 25 percent less today than when we started. Part of this is due to our specialization on the 737. But most of our labour savings occur because every employee focuses on productivity.

"Three factors account for our high productivity: equipment, processes, and information systems. We use modern manufacturing equipment, computer-guided cutting and milling, specialty welding machines, and so forth. We also carefully design our work processes to make our workers as efficient as we can. For example, we station consumable tool parts like sandpaper as close to workers as possible. Also, for any type of assembly, all the necessary parts and materials are delivered in carts or buckets right to the line. Everything is carefully labelled.

"One of our advantages is that we were able to design new processes as we grew. One of our competitors, which has been in this business since World War II, is hampered by decades-old work processes. It hasn't been able to tear itself away from how something's always been done in order to improve its operations.

"On the other hand, we don't move want to move forward so fast that no one can keep up. If you change too fast, chaos and resistance result. One of our young employees, fresh out of school, wanted to change too many things too fast, and finally, we had to let him go. It's got to be evolution, not revolution.

"The third factor in our productivity is use of information systems. But we need systems that provide real, tangible benefits—and that do so *now*. We're not interested in something just because it's new or is supposed to be great. We're a small builder in a very competitive industry. We can't afford expensive experiments that don't work out."

The employee count at DSI varies from 100 to 200 people, depending on the work in progress. A typical project costs between \$5 million and \$10 million. Project duration from contract signing to rollout is about six months. As a privately held partnership, DSI does not release financial data, but we can estimate its revenue. Because the company can work on at most three projects at one time and because each project lasts about six months, DSI could complete six projects a year. If each project costs from \$5 million to \$10 million, DSI's total revenue runs \$30 million to \$60 million a year. Because planning and design do not occupy hangar space, the company actually does more than six projects; in a good year, its revenue would be closer to \$60 million.

Ms. Dorset knows that the key goal for DSI's competitive advantage is labour productivity, and she understands how IS contributes to that key goal. You may find yourself in the same position at some point in your career. Your key competitive factor may not be labour productivity, but the success of some other competitive factor may be related to the use of IS.

7 Information Systems for Competitive Advantage

This
could happen
to you

In the part-opening pages, Eleanor Dorset stated DSI's competitive strategy: quality differentiation within the 737 high-end refurbishing market. However, many of DSI's customers require competitive bidding. Therefore, the company needs to be cost-conscious. In terms of its value chain, it must ensure that every activity creates demonstrable value that justifies additional costs.

Suppose you have been hired as a summer intern at DSI. You're one of three interns, and when Ms. Dorset hired you she made it clear that only one of the three of you has a chance at a full-time job. You very much want to be the intern selected for the full-time job.

You're working late one night on a task to support a bid proposal, and your direct supervisor, for whom you've worked very hard, stops by your cubicle.

"Thanks for helping us get out this proposal. If you keep working like this, I'm going to want to offer you a job when you finish school. . . . But there's a problem. Few people know this, but one of the other interns is John Stratford's niece. Don't spread it around, but I wanted you to know that she's got the inside track."

Needless to say, this news is depressing. "Is there no chance, then?" you ask.

"Well, if it's a tie between the two of you in his mind, he'll probably pick her. But John's a good businessman, and if you can show that you're someone DSI just *has* to have on staff, then either he'll pick you, or he and Eleanor will create a job for you. But you've got to show them you're superior."

"How?" you ask.

"Well, I'm not sure. Part of showing that you're superior is for you to figure out something on your own. But here's a thought: Almost everything John does is aimed at making labour more productive. So think along the lines of making our labour more productive. It doesn't necessarily have to be something that he decides to do . . . just some good idea that shows you know what drives our business and that you're thinking of innovative ideas to help."

Because this is an MIS class and because Ms. Dorset says the company uses information systems to gain labour productivity, we'll focus on innovative information systems for you to propose. Read this chapter with this task in mind because . . . this could happen to you.

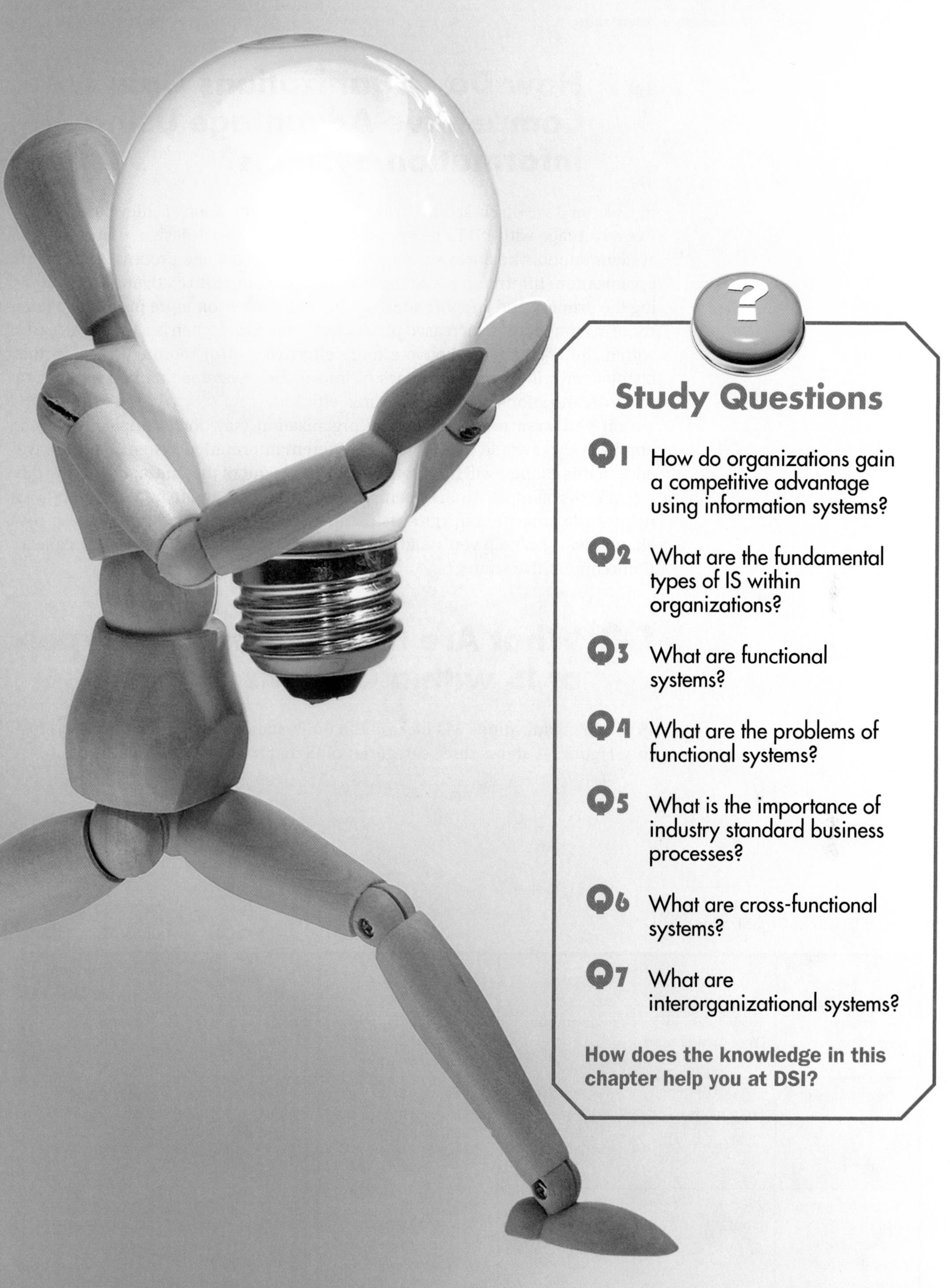

Study Questions

Q1 How do organizations gain a competitive advantage using information systems?

Q2 What are the fundamental types of IS within organizations?

Q3 What are functional systems?

Q4 What are the problems of functional systems?

Q5 What is the importance of industry standard business processes?

Q6 What are cross-functional systems?

Q7 What are interorganizational systems?

How does the knowledge in this chapter help you at DSI?

Q1 How Do Organizations Gain a Competitive Advantage Using Information Systems?

In Chapter 3 we discussed the ways in which organizations achieve a competitive advantage with IS. To recap, we would say that well-designed information systems support business strategy by supporting business processes within an organization. Information systems can impact competitive advantage by making the primary and support activities in an organization more productive than those of competitors. Increased productivity is realized when business processes within the organization become more effective and/or more efficient. In this chapter, we will discuss the types of information systems that can be used to make organizations more effective and efficient.

If you were to walk into any organization (say, for example, your first employer), you would find a maze of different information systems. The knowledge in this chapter will help you to make sense out of that maze, to identify different kinds of information systems and what they do, and to understand how IS helps an organization achieve its competitive strategy. The knowledge in this chapter will also help you avoid creating an IS that is unrelated to the organization's competitive strategy.

Q2 What Are the Fundamental Types of IS within Organizations?

IS within organizations will be easier to understand if we begin with a short history. Figure 7-1 shows three categories of IS that have evolved over time.

Figure 7-1
History of IS within Organizations

Name	Era	Scope	Perspective	Example	Technology Symbols
Calculation systems	1950–1980 (Your grandfather)	Single purpose	Eliminate tedious human calculations. "Just make it work!"	Payroll General ledger Inventory	Mainframe Punch card
Functional systems	1975–20?? (Your mother)	Business function	Use computer to improve operation and management of individual departments.	Human resources Financial reporting Order entry Manufacturing (MRP and MRP II)	Mainframe Stand-alone PCs Networks and LANs
Integrated systems (also cross-functional or process-based systems)	2000— (You)	Business process	Develop IS to integrate separate departments into organization-wide business processes.	Customer relationship management (CRM) Enterprise resource planning (ERP)	Networked PCs Client-servers The Internet Intranets

Calculation Systems

The very first information systems, **calculation systems**, seem antiquated today, but they were in use not very long ago. The purpose of those early systems was to relieve workers of tedious, repetitive calculations. The first systems computed payroll and wrote paycheques; they applied debits and credits to the general ledger and balanced the company's accounting records. They also kept track of inventory quantities—that is, quantities that were verified by physical item counts about once a quarter. As calculating machines, they were more accurate than humans—as long as the systems actually worked. (Computer failure rates were high.) Those systems were labour-saving devices, but in truth they produced little information. None of them survive today, and we will not consider them further.

Functional Systems

The **functional systems** of the second era facilitated the work of a single department or function. They grew as a natural expansion of the capabilities of the systems of the first era. For example, payroll expanded to become human resources, general ledger became financial reporting, and inventory was merged into operations or manufacturing. The changes were more than just in name. In each functional area, companies added features and capabilities to information systems to support more functional-area activity.

The problem with functional applications is their isolation. In fact, functional applications are sometimes called **islands of automation** because they work independently of one another. Unfortunately, independent, isolated systems cannot produce the productivity and efficiency necessary for many businesses. Purchasing influences inventory, which influences production, which influences customer satisfaction, which influences future sales. Decisions that are appropriate when considering only a single function like purchasing may create inefficiencies when the entire process is considered.

Integrated, Cross-Functional Systems

The isolation problems of functional systems led to the third era of information systems. In this era, systems were designed not to facilitate the work of a single department or function, but rather to integrate the activities in an entire business process. Because those activities cross departmental boundaries, such systems are sometimes called **cross-departmental** or **cross-functional systems**. Because they support complete business processes, they are sometimes also called **process-based systems**.

Unfortunately, the transition from functional systems to integrated systems is difficult. Integrated processing requires many departments to coordinate their activities. There is no clear line of authority, peer competition can be fierce, and interdepartmental rivalries can subvert the development of the new system.

As cross-functional systems have become more sophisticated, some information systems have begun to cross not only functional boundaries but also organizational boundaries. These systems that are used by two or more related companies are referred to as **interorganizational systems.** The most common include e-commerce and supply chain management systems. We will talk about these systems in more detail later in the chapter.

Most organizations today have a mixture of functional and integrated systems. To successfully compete internationally, however, organizations must eventually achieve the efficiencies of integrated, cross-departmental, process-based systems. Thus, during your career, you can expect to see an increasing number of integrated systems and fewer functional systems. In fact, you will likely be one of the business leaders asked to implement new integrated systems.

By the way, do not assume that the systems and processes discussed in the remainder of the chapter apply only to commercial, profit-making organizations. Not-for-profit and government organizations have most of these same processes, but with a different orientation. Your province's Ministry of Labour, for example, has both employees and customers. Information systems for not-for-profit and for government organizations are oriented toward quality of service and efficiency rather than toward profit, but those systems still exist.

Q3 What Are Functional Systems?

We can use Porter's value chain model (introduced in Chapter 3) to explain the scope and purposes of different types of information systems within the organization. For our purposes, the value chain model will be more useful if we redraw it as shown in Figure 7-2. The value chain starts with marketing and sales activities. Sales and order activities are followed by in-bound logistics, operations and manufacturing, out-bound logistics, and, finally, service and support.

The primary activities are facilitated by human resources, accounting and infrastructure, procurement, and technology activities. As we have redrawn the value chain in Figure 7-2, the primary activities occur in the order shown: They are supported first by the humans that perform work in the primary activities, and the human resources with primary activities are supported, in turn, by accounting and other infrastructure.

Figure 7-3 shows five functional systems and their relationship to the value chain. As you would expect, each functional system is closely allied with the activities it supports, and there is little cross-over among activities. To help you understand these systems, we will briefly survey them next. Figure 7-4 lists principal functional systems used in five value chain activities.

Marketing and Sales Systems

Product management is the primary functional system for marketing. Product managers use such systems to help assess how well their product-marketing efforts are working. In such a system, sales data are summarized by product,

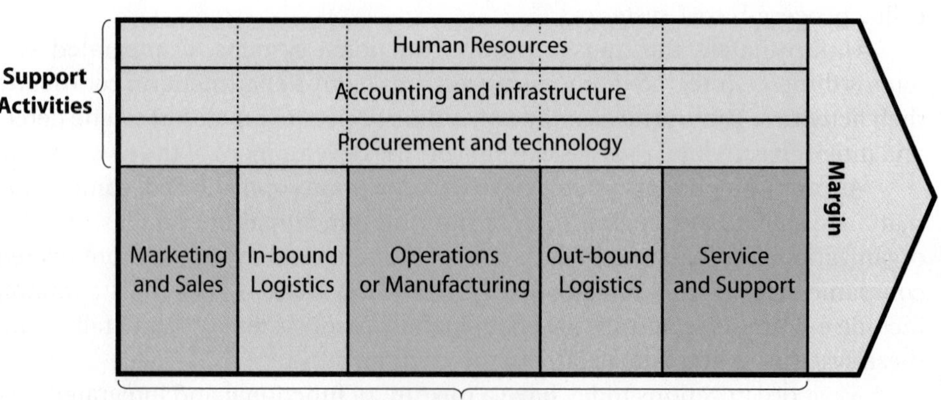

Figure 7-2
Reorganized Porter Value Chain Model

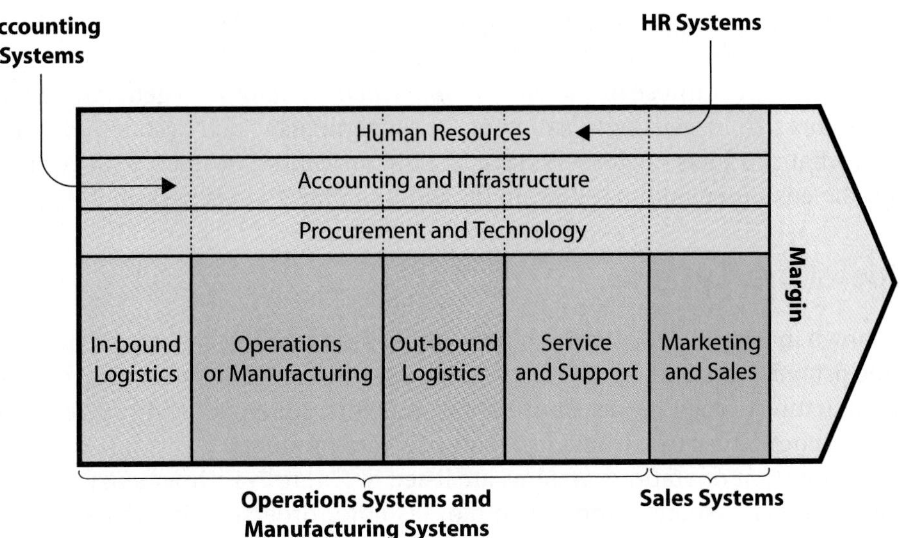

Figure 7-3
Reorganized Porter Value Chain Model and Its Relationship to Functional Systems

product category, and business line. Sales to date are compared to forecasts, sales in past periods, and other expectations. If the data are current enough, adjustments can be made in advertising and promotion programs by moving dollars from, say, overperforming products to underperforming products.

Other sales examples, as listed in Figure 7-4, include lead tracking, sales forecasting, customer management, and customer service (shown on the far right in Figure 7-4). *Lead tracking* records prospects and keeps track of sales contacts with potential customers. *Sales forecasting* is vital not only for planning

Function	Example Information Systems
Marketing and sales	Product management Lead tracking Sales forecasting Customer management
Operations	Order entry Order management Inventory management Customer service
Manufacturing	Inventory Planning Scheduling Manufacturing operations
Human resources	Payroll and compensation Recruiting Assessment Development and training Human resources planning
Accounting and finance	General ledger Financial reporting Accounts receivable Accounts payable Cost accounting Budgeting Cash management Treasury management

Figure 7-4
Typical Functional Systems

production or managing inventories, but also for financial reporting by publicly held companies.

The major purpose of *customer management* systems is to generate follow-up business from existing customers. Salespeople use such systems to determine what products customers have already purchased, to record all contacts with the customer, and to follow up for additional revenue generation.

Operations Systems

As shown in Figure 7-3, both operations and manufacturing systems support the same primary activities in the value chain. **Operations systems** are used by non-manufacturers, such as distributors and retailers. Manufacturing systems are used by companies that transform materials into products.

Important operations systems are listed in Figure 7-4. *Order entry* can take place in-house, where company employees enter orders, or it can be done at web-based, e-commerce sites such as retailer Amazon.ca. *Order management* systems track orders through the fulfillment process, handling back orders and order changes as well as providing order status.

Inventory management systems analyze sales activity and generate product orders as required. Inventory management is a balancing act between the cost of carrying excessive inventory and the cost of lost orders due to product outage. Modern inventory management seeks to minimize the investment in inventory.

Customer service is a fourth operations function. Such systems provide information about the status of orders and are also used to process complaints, to respond to product or service issues, and to receive returned goods.

Manufacturing Systems

Manufacturing information systems support the transformation of materials into products. They process data about inventories for raw materials, work-in-process, and finished goods. They also concern production planning. The case study at the end of this chapter ("Moving Like a Deere") shows how manufacturing systems can provide opportunities for innovation.

Most manufacturers typically choose one of two manufacturing philosophies: With **push production planning**, the organization creates a production plan or schedule and pushes goods through manufacturing and sales. "We're going to produce 500 widgets: Make them and sell them." **Pull production planning** responds to customer demand. As the company sells goods, its finished goods inventories fall, and the reduction in inventory triggers the production of more goods. Whichever philosophy a manufacturer uses, it will choose a *planning system* to match.

Organizations that produce custom, "one-off," expensive products fall outside of the push/pull categories. When aircraft detailer DSI sells a $10-million interior, it plans its activities to build that particular interior. Such manufacturers differ from those that produce, say, tennis shoes, where production is either pushed or pulled through the manufacturer.

Manufacturing scheduling and operations are additional functional systems. A tennis shoe manufacturer that needs to produce 15 types of shoes in various sizes and in various colours has many choices about how to produce those shoes. Some methods require less setup and less idle time for workers or machines and are, therefore, cheaper. *Scheduling systems* help organizations determine the optimal methods. *Manufacturing operations systems* control manufacturing plants and machines. A production line of robots, for example, is controlled by a manufacturing operations system.

Human Resources Systems

Functional systems for human resources (HR) include *payroll* and *related compensation systems,* such as sick leave and vacation-time accounting. Other HR functions systems include those used for *recruiting* personnel as well as for *assessing* employee performance.

In organizations with formal development and training programs, such as large corporations, government agencies, and military organizations, functional systems are used to categorize the skills of employees, their training requirements, and the training they have had. Such systems feed *HR planning systems* to ensure that sufficient numbers of workers with appropriate skills will be available to fill needed job requirements. Imagine an organization of 5000, and you will see the need for such systems.

RFID

Today, both operations and manufacturing activities are beginning to use an important technology called **radio-frequency identification (RFID) tags**. Major retailers such as Wal-Mart have specified that their suppliers must place RFID tags on all products they supply. An RFID is a computer chip that transmits data about the container, product, or equipment to which it is attached. RFID data include not just product numbers, but also data about where the product was made, the product's components, special handling requirements, and, for perishable products, when the contents will expire. RFID tags can record and transmit custom, application-specific data as well. Sensors connected to inventory and other functional systems receive RFID signals and automatically record the arrival, departure, or movement of the item. Many innovative applications of RFIDs are being developed today, even as you read this paragraph.

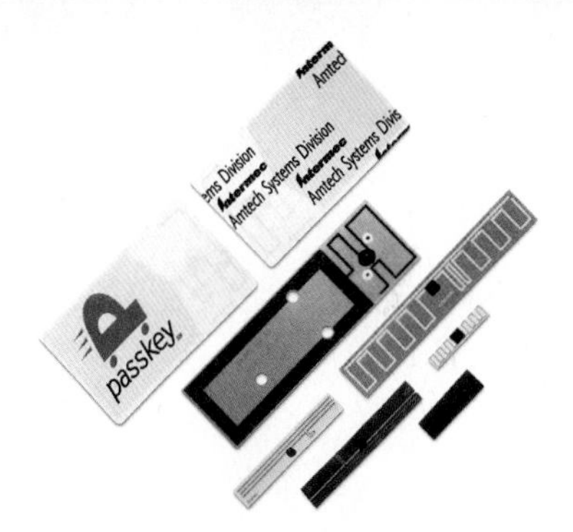

Radio-Frequency Identification Tags (RFIDs)

Accounting and Finance Systems

Accounting functional systems support all of the organization's accounting activities. Such systems were some of the earliest calculation systems, and they have retained their importance as functional systems have evolved. Examples are *general ledger, financial reporting, accounts receivable,* and *accounts payable systems.* Other important accounting systems include *cost accounting, budgeting, cash management,* and management of the organization's stocks and bonds, borrowings, and capital investments via *treasury management.*

Over the years, one of the key improvements in accounting systems has been a reduction in time required to provide results. Nothing is more aggravating to a manager than to find out—six weeks after the quarter has closed—that his or her department was over budget. Managers need to know the relationship of expenses accrued, encumbered, and budgeted as close to real time as they can. Similarly, management would like to close the books as close to the end of an accounting period as possible. In the history of computing, accounting systems have reduced the time required to produce results from months to weeks or even to days. Many systems can now provide near–real time accounting information.

One important consideration in accounting systems is the impact on organizations of legislation such as the Sarbanes-Oxley Act in the U.S. and Bill 198 or the Budget Measures Act in Canada. This legislation was enacted to prevent corporate frauds like those perpetrated by directors at Enron and WorldCom. The legislation requires management to create internal controls to provide more reliable financial statements and protect the organization's assets. We will cover this in more detail when considering governance in Chapter 9.

Q4 What Are the Problems of Functional Systems?

Functional systems provide tremendous benefits to the departments that use them, but as stated earlier, their benefits are limited because they operate in isolation. In particular, functional systems have the problems listed in Figure 7-5. First, with isolated systems, data are duplicated because each application has its own database. For example, customer data may be duplicated and possibly inconsistent when accounting and sales/marketing applications are separated. The principal problem of duplicated data is a potential lack of data integrity. Changes to product data made in one system may take days or weeks to reach the other systems. During that period, inconsistent data will cause inconsistent application results.

Additionally, when systems are isolated business processes are disjointed. There is no easy way for the sales/marketing system to integrate activity with the accounting system, for example. Just sending the data from one system to the other can be problematic.

Consider the simple example in Figure 7-6. Suppose the order entry and inventory systems define a product number as three characters, a dash, and four numeric digits. Yet, suppose the manufacturing system in the same company defines a product as four digits followed by characters. Every time parts data are

Figure 7-5
Major Problems of Isolated Functional Systems

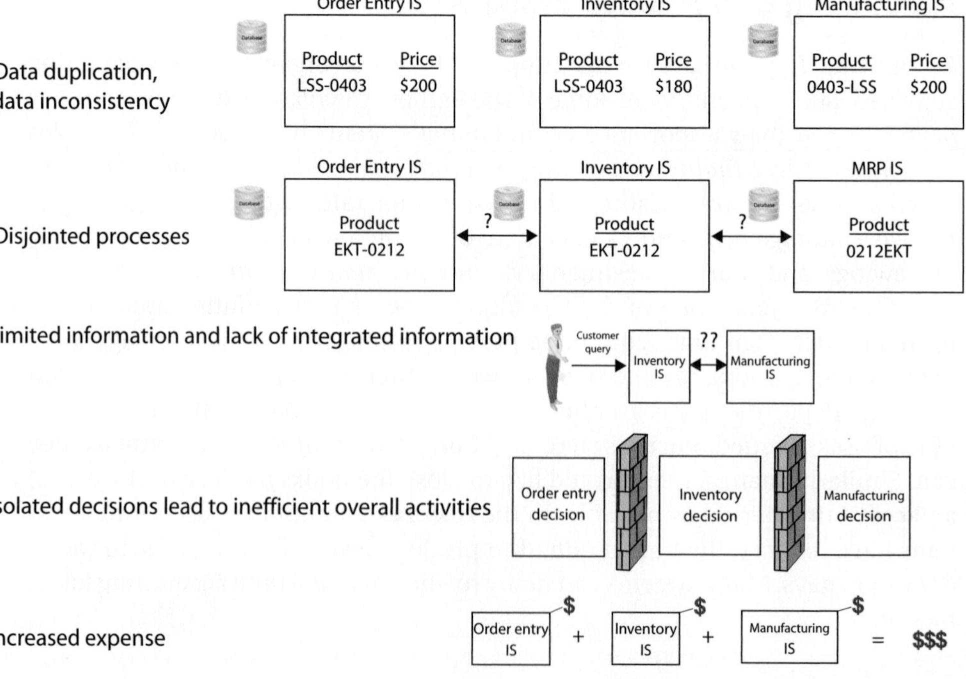

- Order Entry System Product Number:
  Format: ccc–nnnn
  Example: COMP–3344
- Manufacturing System Product Number:
  Format: nnnnccc
  Example: 3344COMP

Figure 7-6
Example of System Integration Problem

exported from order entry and imported into manufacturing (or the reverse), the data must be converted from one scheme to the other. Multiply this conversion process by several hundred data items, and possibly dozens of other systems, and you can see why processing is disjointed across functional applications.

A consequence of such disjointed systems is the lack of integrated enterprise information. When a customer inquires about an order, several systems may need to be queried. For example, some order information is in the order entry system, some is in the finished-goods inventory system, and some is in the manufacturing system. Obtaining a consolidated statement about the customer's order will require processing each of these systems, with possibly inconsistent data.

A fourth consequence of isolated systems is inefficiency. When using isolated functional systems, a department can make decisions based only on the isolated data that it has. So, for example, raw materials inventory systems will make inventory replenishment decisions based only on costs and benefits in that single inventory. However, it might be that the overall efficiency of the sales, order entry, and manufacturing activities, considered together across the enterprise, will be improved by carrying a less than optimal number of products in raw materials inventory.

Finally, isolated functional systems can result in increased cost for the organization. Duplicated data, disjointed systems, limited information, and inefficiencies all mean higher costs.

Organizations recognized the problems of isolated systems back in the 1980s, and business consultants began searching for ways to build more integrated systems. We consider those systems next.

Q5 What Is the Importance of Industry Standard Processes?

As computer networks became prevalent in the 1990s, systems developers realized that networks provided a means to do more than simply automate functional applications. As technologists pondered the question, "What, exactly, do networks enable?" systems developers began to wonder how they could develop information systems that would integrate several, or many, different areas in an entire value chain. This thinking became the foundation of a movement called **business process design,** or sometimes *business process redesign.* The central idea is that organizations should not automate or improve existing functional systems. Rather, they should create new, more efficient business processes that integrate the activities of all departments involved in a value chain.

Thus, in the early 1990s some organizations began to design new cross-departmental business processes. The goal was to take advantage of as many activity linkages as possible. For example, a cross-departmental customer management process integrates all interactions with the customer, from prospect through initial order through repeat orders, including customer support, credit, and accounts receivable.

Challenges of Business Process Design

Unfortunately, process design projects are expensive and difficult. Highly trained systems analysts interview key personnel from many departments and document the existing system as well as one or more system alternatives. Managers review the results of the analysts' activity, usually many times, and attempt to develop new, improved processes. Then new information systems are developed to implement those new business processes. All of this takes time, and meanwhile the underlying processes are changing, which means the process design may need to be redesigned before the project is completed.

Once these difficulties have been overcome and the new integrated systems designed, an even greater challenge arises: Employees resist change. People do not want to work in new ways, they do not want to see their department reorganized or abolished, and they do not want to work for someone new. Even if the system can be implemented over this resistance, some people will continue to resist. All these difficulties translate into labour hours, which translate into costs. Thus, business process design is very expensive.

Even worse, the ultimate outcome is uncertain. An organization that embarks on a business process design project does not know ahead of time how effective the ultimate outcome will be.

Some businesses have been successful in their process design activities, but many others have failed. In some cases, millions of dollars were spent on projects that were ultimately abandoned. The idea of designing business processes for greater integration was floundering when it received a boost from an unexpected source: integrated application vendors.

Benefits of Industry Standard Processes

Many early business process design projects failed because they were tailor-made. They were custom-fit to a particular organization, and so just one company bore the cost of the design effort. In the mid-1990s, a number of successful software vendors began to market premade integrated applications, with built-in processes. Such processes saved hundreds of hours of design work.

When an organization acquires, say, a business application from companies like Oracle or SAP, the processes for using the software are built-in or **industry standard processes**. In most cases, the organization must conform its activities to those processes. If the software is designed well, the industry standard process will effectively integrate activities across departments. These pre-built processes can save the organization the substantial, sometimes staggering, costs of designing new processes itself.

Figure 7-7 shows an example of an industry standard process in a software product called **SAP R/3**, a product licensed by SAP (www.sap.com). When an organization licenses this product, SAP provides hundreds of diagrams just like this one. These diagrams show the business processes that must be created in order to effectively use the software.

This diagram shows the flow and logic of one set of processes. In the top lines, if the purchase requisition does not exist and if the request for quotation (RFQ) is to be created, then the purchasing department creates an RFQ and sends it to potential vendors. You can read through the rest of this sample diagram to obtain the gist of this process snippet.

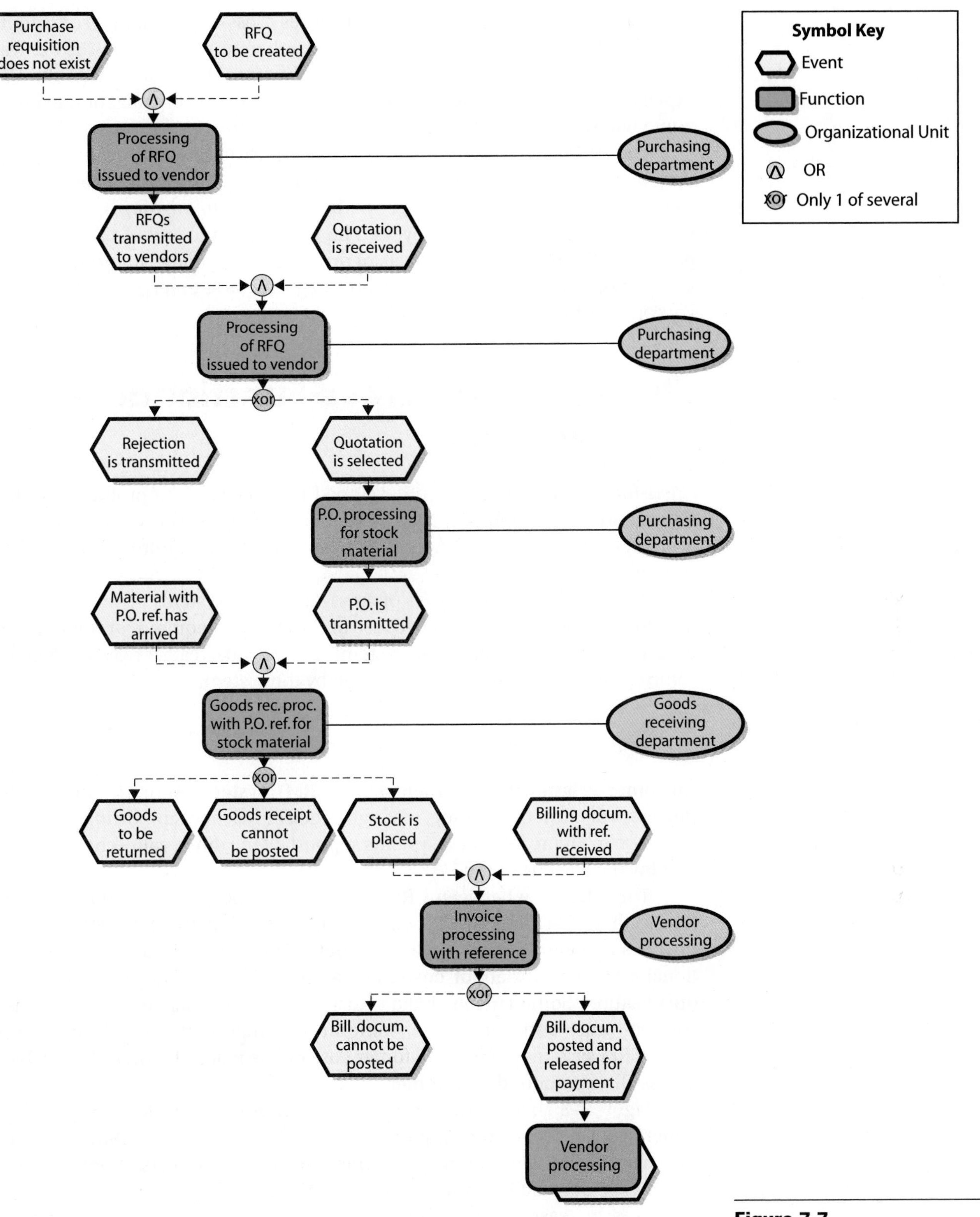

Figure 7-7
Example of SAP R/3 Ordering Process

Source: Thomas A. Curran, Andrew Ladd, Dennis Ladd, *SAP R/3 Reporting and e-Business Intelligence,* 1st ed., © 2000. Reprinted by permission of Pearson Education, Inc., Upper Saddle River, NJ.

To some, when an organization licenses cross-departmental software the primary benefit is not the software but the inherent processes in the software. Licensing an integrated application not only saves the organization the time, expense, and agony of process design; it also enables the organization to benefit immediately from tried and tested cross-departmental processes.

Of course, there is a disadvantage. The industry standard processes may be very different from existing processes and thus require the organization to change substantially. Such change will be disruptive to ongoing operations and very disturbing to many employees. The Exercise at the end of this chapter on pages 230–231 discusses the effects of organizational change in more detail.

Two cross-functional application categories have emerged: CRM and ERP. We consider these categories next.

Q6 What Are Cross-Functional Systems?

Cross-functional systems were developed to overcome the problems of functional systems. Two types of cross-functional systems are important today: customer relationship management (CRM) and enterprise resource planning (ERP) systems.

As you will see, these types of cross-functional systems provide numerous benefits for organizations. Yet because of the changes required for organization-wide process integration, these systems also at times cause resistance among some employees whose jobs are affected by the system.

Customer Relationship Management (CRM)

Customer relationship management (CRM) systems support the business processes of attracting, selling, managing, delivering, and supporting customers. As shown in Figure 7-7, CRM systems support all the direct value chain activities that involve the customer.

The difference between CRM systems and traditional functional applications is that CRM addresses all activities and events that touch the customer and provides a single repository for data about all customer interactions. With functional systems, data about customers are sprinkled in databases all over the organization. Some customer data exist in customer management databases, some in order entry databases, some in customer service databases, and so forth. CRM systems store all customer data in one place and make it possible to access all data about the customer.

Figure 7-8 shows four phases of the **customer life cycle**: marketing, customer acquisition, relationship management, and loss/churn. Marketing sends messages to the target market to attract customer prospects. When prospects order, they become customers who need to be supported. Additionally, resell processes increase the value of existing customers. Inevitably, over time the organization loses customers. When this occurs, win-back processes categorize customers according to value and attempt to win back high-value customers.

The organizational website is an increasingly important solicitation tool. Web addresses are easy to promote (and remember), and once a target prospect is on the site, product descriptions, use cases, success stories, and other solicitation materials can be provided easily. Further, the cost of distributing these materials via the web is substantially less than the cost of creating and distribut-

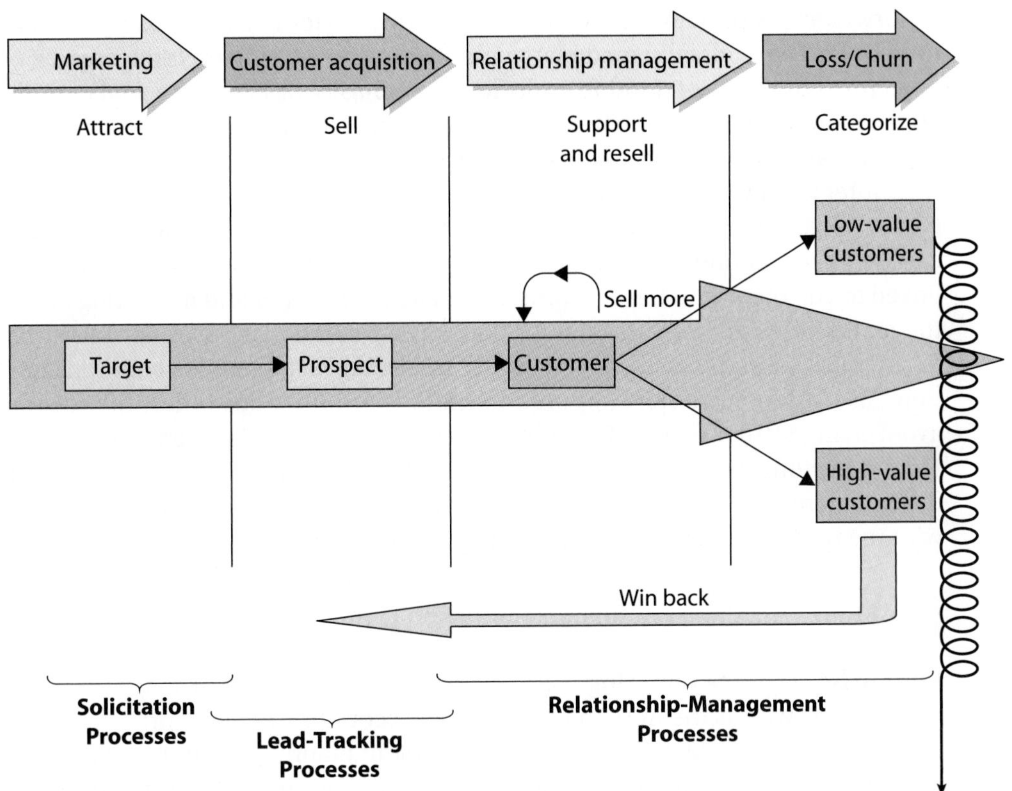

Figure 7-8
The Customer Life Cycle

Source: Douglas MacLachlan, University of Washington.

ing printed materials. Many websites require customer name and contact information before releasing high-value promotional materials. That contact information then feeds lead-tracking applications.

The purpose of relationship management applications is to maximize the value of the existing customer base. As Figure 7-9 shows, two types of applications are used. Sales management applications support sales to existing customers. They have features to prioritize customers according to their purchase

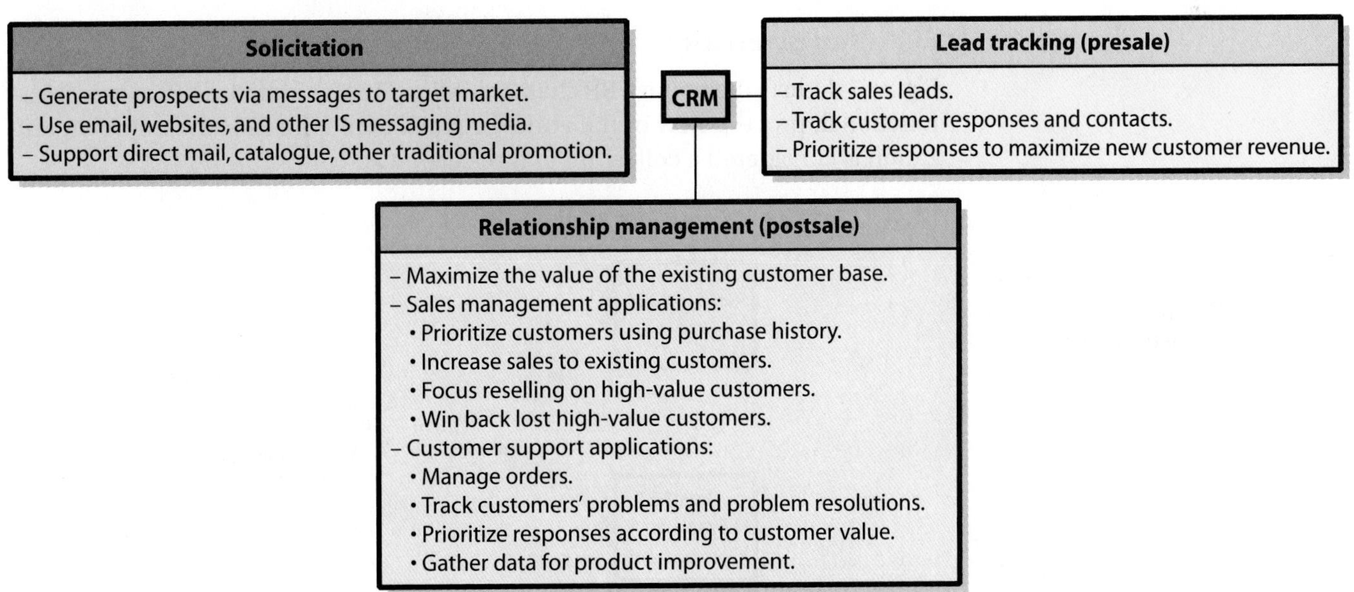

Figure 7-9
CRM Components

history. Salespeople can increase sales to existing customers by focusing on customers who have already made large purchases, by focusing on large organizations that have the potential to make large purchases, or both. The goal of such applications is to ensure that sales management has sufficient information to prioritize and allocate sales time and effort.

Integrated CRM applications store data in a single database, as shown in Figure 7-10. Because all customer data reside in one location, CRM processes can be linked to one another. For example, customer service activities can be linked to customer purchase records. In this way, both sales and marketing know the status of customer satisfaction, both on an individual customer basis for future sales calls and also collectively for analyzing customers' overall satisfaction. Also, many customer support applications prioritize customers in order to avoid giving $10 000 worth of support to a customer with a lifetime value of $500. Finally, customer support has an important linkage to product marketing and development; it knows more than any other group what customers are doing with the product and what problems they are having with it.

Enterprise Resource Planning (ERP)

Enterprise resource planning (ERP) systems support all the primary business processes as well as the human resource and accounting support processes.

ERP is an outgrowth of material requirement planning MRP II, and the primary ERP users are manufacturing companies. The first and most successful vendor of ERP software is SAP (SAP AG Corp., headquartered in Germany). More than 12 million people use SAP in over 100 000 SAP installations worldwide.[2]

Thus far, ERP represents the ultimate in cross-departmental process systems. ERP integrates sales, order, inventory, manufacturing, and customer service activities. ERP systems provide software, predesigned databases, procedures, and job descriptions for organization-wide process integration.

Before continuing, be aware that some companies misapply the term *ERP* to their systems. It is a hot topic, and there is no truth-in-ERP-advertising group to ensure that all the vendors that claim ERP capability have anything remotely similar to what we describe here. Again, let the buyer beware.

ERP Characteristics

Figure 7-11 lists the major ERP characteristics. First, as stated, ERP takes a cross-functional, process view of the entire organization. With ERP, the entire organization is considered a collection of interrelated activities.

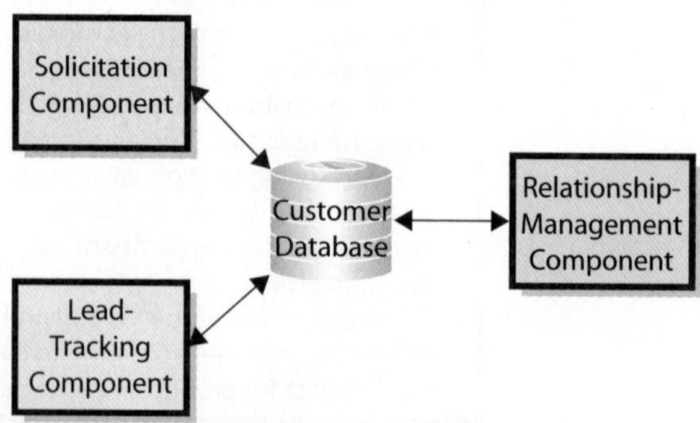

Figure 7-10
CRM Centred on Integrated Customer Database

2. Sap.com/company (accessed November 2007).

- Provides cross-functional, process view of organization

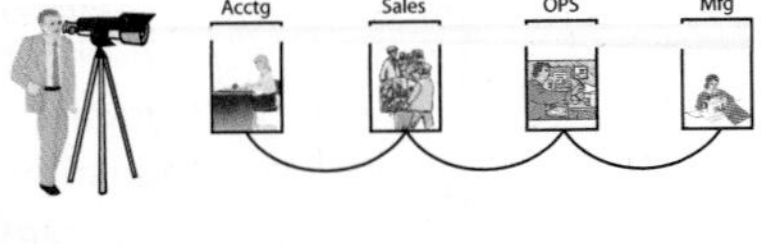

- Has a formal approach based on formal business models

- Maintains data in centralized database

Data → Data → ← Data ← Data

- Offers large benefits but is difficult, fraught with challenges, and can be slow to implement

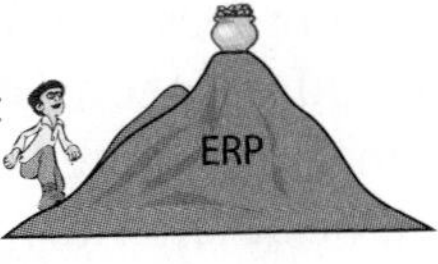

- Often VERY expensive

$ $ $ Separate functional applications — $ ERP

Figure 7-11
Characteristics of ERP

Second, true ERP is a formal approach that is based on documented, tested business models. ERP applications include a comprehensive set of inherent processes for all organizational activities. SAP defines this set as the **process blueprint** and documents each process with diagrams that use a set of standardized symbols.

Because ERP is based on formally defined procedures, organizations must adapt their processing to the ERP blueprint. If they do not, the system cannot operate effectively, or even correctly. In some cases, it is possible to adapt ERP software to procedures that are different from the blueprint, but such adaptation is expensive and often problematic. See the exercise at the end of this chapter ("Available Only in Vanilla") for a larger discussion of this issue.

As stated, with isolated systems each application has its own database. This separation makes it difficult for authorized users to readily obtain all the pertinent information about customers, products, and so forth. With ERP systems, organizational data are processed in a centralized database. Such centralization makes it easy for authorized users to obtain needed information from a single source.

Once an organization has implemented an ERP system, it can achieve large benefits. However, as shown in Figure 7-11, the process of moving from separated, functional applications to an ERP system is difficult, fraught with challenges, and can be slow. In particular, changing organizational procedures has proved to be a great challenge for many organizations, and in some cases was even a pitfall that prevented successful ERP implementation. Finally, the switch to an ERP system is very costly—not only because of the need for new hardware and software, but also due to the costs of developing new procedures, training employees, converting data, and other developmental expenses.

Benefits of ERP

Figure 7-12 summarizes the major benefits of ERP. First, the processes in the business blueprint have been tried and tested over hundreds of organizations. The processes are effective and often very efficient. Organizations that convert to ERP do not need to reinvent business processes. Rather, they gain the benefit of processes that have already been proved successful.

Figure 7-12
Potential Benefits of ERP

- Efficient business processes
- Inventory reduction
- Lead-time reduction
- Improved customer service
- Greater, real-time insight into organization
- Higher profitability

By taking an organization-wide view, many organizations find they can reduce their inventory, sometimes dramatically. With better planning, it is not necessary to maintain large buffer stocks. Additionally, items remain in inventory for shorter periods of time, sometimes no longer than a few hours or a day.

As discussed earlier, data inconsistency problems are not an issue because all ERP data are stored in an integrated database. Further, because all data about a customer, order, part, or other entity reside in one place, the data are readily accessible. This means that organizations can provide better information about orders, products, and customer status to their customers. All of this results in not only better, but also less costly customer service. Integrated databases also make company-wide data readily accessible and result in greater, real-time visibility, thus allowing a peek into the status of the organization.

Finally, ERP-based organizations often find that they can produce and sell the same products at lower costs due to smaller inventories, reduced lead times, and cheaper customer support. The bottom-line result is higher profitability. The trick, however, is getting there. Despite the clear benefits of inherent processes and ERP, there may be an unintended consequence.

For example, it is reasonable to ask what the competitive advantage of ERP systems are if all competitors use the same "industry standard" processes. While each firm might become more productive, the competitive advantage of ERP systems erodes as more and more competitors implement the ERP products. This statement suggests that all companies within an industry that install ERP will receive the same benefits. We learned in Chapter 3 that this is not the case, however. Software and hardware do not necessarily provide a sustained advantage. It is the combination of people, procedures, hardware, software, and data that creates sustainable advantage. Installing ERP therefore creates an initial hurdle for competitors. Learning to effectively use the information provided by the ERP will be the source of advantage to those companies that are best able to use the system.

Q7 What Are Interorganizational Systems?

Many types of information systems cross organizations. The most common type involves selling and purchasing, and we will consider that type in this section. In addition to selling and purchasing, however, other interorganizational systems, such as cheque clearing or credit card processing, integrate multiple-company operations. We will not attempt to discuss every type of interorganizational IS here. Instead, we will use the example of selling and purchasing to discuss and illustrate basic ideas and concepts.

Consider Dell Computer. Dell structures its website so that almost anyone can configure and order a computer online, with no human assistance from Dell. The site guides home users, novice business users, and expert users into different parts of the site that provide different experiences. Dell offers home users packages with easy-to-understand options. Experts—who are more likely to be buying, say, high-performance server computers—can choose base computers and select from a complex array of options and choices. Dell's site gives extensive support with definitions and explanations, all online. In this way Dell nearly automates ordering, and thus dramatically reduces the cost of processing an order. This system is consistent with Dell's competitive strategy, which is to provide the lowest-cost computers across the computer industry. Go to www.dell.com and investigate the ordering experience it provides. As well, look for ways Dell has structured its site to reduce the cost of processing an order.

Types of Interorganizational Systems

Applications of interorganizational systems continue to grow. We will provide a brief overview of two of these categories:

1. E-commerce
2. Supply chain management

As you read about these systems, it is important to keep in mind how they provide a competitive advantage to both parties involved in the transaction. You will discover that it's often quite easy to find benefits for one of the organizations but often difficult to find benefits for both. This disparity is often what makes interorganizational systems difficult to implement.

E-Commerce

E-commerce is the buying and selling of goods and services over public and private computer networks. Notice that this definition restricts e-commerce to buying and selling transactions. Checking the weather at yahoo.ca is not e-commerce, but buying a weather service subscription that is paid for and delivered over the Internet is. E-commerce is an interorganizational system because it links parties that buy goods and services with parties that sell goods and services.

Figure 7-13 lists the different categories of e-commerce companies. **Merchant companies** are defined as those that take title to the goods they sell. They buy goods and resell them. **Nonmerchant companies** are those that arrange for the purchase and sale of goods without ever owning or taking title to those goods. Regarding services, merchant companies sell services that they provide; nonmerchant companies sell services provided by others. We will consider merchants and nonmerchants separately in the following sections.

E-Commerce Merchant Companies

There are three main types of merchant companies: those that sell directly to consumers, those that sell to companies, and those that sell to government. Each uses slightly different information systems in the course of doing business.

Merchant companies	Nonmerchant companies
- Business-to-consumer (B2C) - Business-to-business (B2B) - Business-to-government (B2G)	- Auctions - Clearinghouses - Exchanges

Figure 7-13
E-Commerce Categories

Business-to-consumer (B2C) e-commerce concerns sales between a supplier and a retail customer (the consumer). A typical information system for B2C provides a web-based application or **web storefront** by which customers enter and manage their orders. Chapters Indigo (www.chapters.indigo.ca) is an example of a Canadian company that uses B2C information systems.

The term **business-to-business (B2B)** e-commerce refers to sales between companies. As Figure 7-14 shows, raw materials suppliers use B2B systems to sell to manufacturers, manufacturers use B2B systems to sell to distributors, and distributors use B2B systems to sell to retailers. Grand and Toy (www.grandandtoy.com) is an example of a company that sells B2B.

Business-to-government (B2G) refers to sales between companies and governmental organizations. As Figure 7-14 shows, a manufacturer that uses an e-commerce site to sell computer hardware to a government ministry is engaging in B2G commerce. Suppliers, distributors, and retailers can sell to the government as well.

B2C applications first captured the attention of mail-order and related businesses. However, companies in all sectors of the economy soon realized the enormous potential of B2B and B2G. The number of companies engaged in B2B and B2G commerce now far exceeds those engaging in B2C commerce.

Furthermore, today's B2B and B2G applications implement just a small portion of their potential capability. Their full utilization is some years away. Although most experts agree that these applications involve some sort of integration of CRM and supplier relationship management (SRM) systems, the nature of that integration is not well understood and is still being developed. Consequently, you can expect further progress and development in B2B and B2G applications during your career.

Nonmerchant E-Commerce

The most common nonmerchant e-commerce companies are auctions (like eBay) and clearinghouses. **E-commerce auctions** match buyers and sellers by using an e-commerce version of a standard auction. This e-commerce application enables the auction company to offer goods for sale and to support a competitive-bidding process. The best-known auction company is eBay, but many other auction companies exist; many serve particular industries.

Clearinghouses provide goods and services at a stated price and they arrange for the delivery of the goods, but they never take title. One division of Amazon.ca, for example, operates as a nonmerchant clearinghouse and sells books owned by others. As a clearinghouse, Amazon.ca matches the seller and the buyer and then takes payment from the buyer and transfers the payment to the seller, minus a commission.

Other examples of clearinghouse businesses are **electronic exchanges** that match buyers and sellers; the business process is similar to that of a stock exchange. Sellers offer goods at a given price through the electronic exchange,

Figure 7-14
Example of Use of B2B, B2G, and B2C

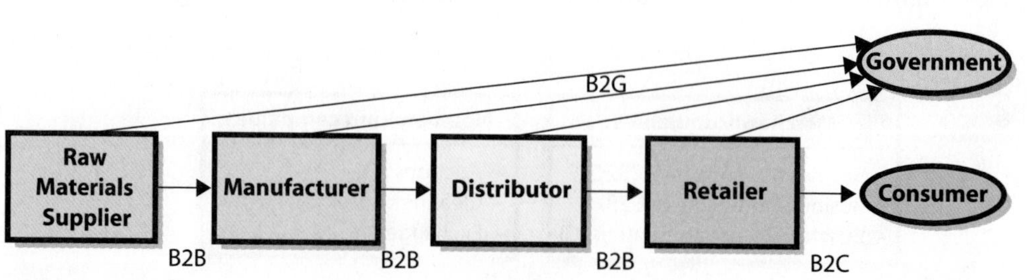

and buyers make offers to purchase over the same exchange. Price matches result in transactions from which the exchange takes a commission. Priceline.com is an example of an exchange used by consumers.

Benefits of E-Commerce

The debate continues among business observers as to whether e-commerce is something new or if it is just a technology extension to existing business practice. During the dot-com heyday in 1999–2000, some claimed that e-commerce was ushering in a new era and a "new economy." Although experts differ as to whether a "new economy" was created, all agree that e-commerce does lead to greater market efficiency.

For one, e-commerce leads to **disintermediation**, which is the elimination of middle layers in the supply chain. You can buy a flat-screen LCD HDTV from a typical electronics store or you can use e-commerce to buy it from the manufacturer. If you take the latter route, you eliminate the distributor, the retailer, and possibly more. The product is shipped directly from the manufacturer's finished goods inventory to you. You eliminate the distributor's and retailer's inventory carrying costs, and you eliminate shipping overhead and handling activity. Because the distributor and associated inventories have become unnecessary waste, disintermediation increases market efficiency.

E-commerce also improves the flow of price information. As a consumer, you can go to any number of websites that offer product price comparisons. You can search for the HDTV you want and sort the results by price and vendor reputation. You can find vendors that omit or reduce shipping charges. The improved distribution of information about price and terms enables you to pay the lowest possible cost and serves ultimately to remove inefficient vendors. The market as a whole becomes more efficient.

From the seller's side, e-commerce produces information about **price elasticity** that has not been available before. Price elasticity measures the amount that demand rises or falls with changes in price. Using an auction, a company can learn not just what the top price for an item is, but also the second, third, and other prices from the losing bids. In this way, the company can determine the shape of the price elasticity curve.

Similarly, e-commerce companies can learn price elasticity directly from experiments on customers. For example, in one experiment, Amazon.com created three groups of similar books. It raised the price of one group 10 percent, lowered the price of the second group 10 percent, and left the price of the third group unchanged. Customers provided feedback to these changes by deciding whether to buy books at the offered prices. Amazon.com measured the total revenue (quantity times price) of each group and took the action (raise, lower, or maintain prices) on all books that maximized revenue. Amazon.com repeated the process until it reached the point at which the indicated action was to maintain current prices.

Managing prices by direct interaction with the customer yields better information than managing prices by watching competitors' pricing. By experimenting with customers, companies learn how customers have internalized competitors' pricing, advertising, and messaging. It might be that customers do not know about a competitor's lower prices, in which case there is no need for a price reduction. Or, it may be that the competitor is using a price that, if lowered, would increase demand sufficiently to increase total revenue. Figure 7-15 summarizes e-commerce market consequences.

Figure 7-15
E-Commerce Market Consequences

Greater market efficiency	Knowledge of price elasticity
- Disintermediation - Increased information on price and terms	- Losing-bidder auction prices - Price experimentation - More accurate information obtained directly from customer

Issues with E-Commerce

Although there are tremendous advantages and opportunities for many organizations to engage in e-commerce, the economics of some industries may disfavour e-commerce activity. Companies need to consider the following economic factors:

- Channel conflict
- Price conflict
- Logistics expense
- Customer service expense

Figure 7-14 shows a manufacturer selling directly to a government agency. Before engaging in such e-commerce, the manufacturer must consider each of the economic factors just listed. First, what *channel conflict* will develop? Suppose the manufacturer is a computer maker that is selling directly, B2G, to a government agency. When the manufacturer begins to sell goods B2G that employees of the agency previously purchased from a retailer down the street, that retailer will resent the competition and may drop the manufacturer. If the value of the lost sales is greater than the value of the B2G sales, e-commerce is not a good solution, at least not on that basis.

Furthermore, when a business engages in e-commerce it may also cause *price conflict* with its traditional channels. Because of disintermediation, the manufacturer may be able to offer a lower price and still make a profit. However, as soon as the manufacturer offers the lower price, existing channels will object. Even if the manufacturer and the retailer are not competing for the same customers, the retailer still will not want a lower price to be readily known via the web.

Also, the existing distribution and retailing partners do provide value; they are not just a cost. Without them, the manufacturer will have the increased *logistic expense* of entering and processing orders in small quantities. If the expense of processing a 1-unit order is the same as that for processing a 12-unit order (which it might be), the average logistic expense per item will be much higher for goods sold via e-commerce.

Similarly, *customer service expenses* are likely to increase for manufacturers that use e-commerce to sell directly to consumers. The manufacturer will be required to provide service to less-sophisticated users and on a one-by-one basis. For example, instead of explaining to a single sales professional that the recent shipment of 100 Gizmo 3.0s requires a new bracket, the manufacturer will need to explain that 100 times to less knowledgeable, frustrated customers. Such service requires more training and more expense.

All four economic factors are important for organizations to consider when they contemplate e-commerce sales.

Supply Chain Management

A **supply chain** is a network of organizations and facilities that transforms raw materials into products delivered to customers. Figure 7-16 shows a generic supply chain. Customers order from retailers, who in turn order from distributors, who in turn order from manufacturers, who in turn order from suppliers. In addition to the organizations shown here, the supply chain includes transportation companies, warehouses, inventories, and some means for transmitting messages and information among the organizations involved.

Because of disintermediation, not every supply chain has all these organizations. Dell, for example, sells directly to the customer. Both the distributor and retailer organizations are omitted from its supply chain. In other supply chains, manufacturers sell directly to retailers and omit the distribution level.

The term *chain* is misleading. *Chain* implies that each organization is connected to just one company up (toward the supplier) and down (toward the customer) the chain. That is not the case. Instead, at each level, an organization can work with many organizations both up and down the supply chain. Thus, a supply chain is a network.

To understand the operation of a supply chain, consider Figure 7-17. Suppose you decide to take up cross-country skiing. You go to REI.com (a company that sells outdoor sporting equipment and supplies) and purchase skis, bindings, boots, and poles. To fill your order, REI removes those items from its inventory of goods.

Those goods have been purchased, in turn, from distributors. According to Figure 7-17, REI purchases the skis, bindings, and poles from one distributor and boots from a second. The distributors in turn purchase the required items from the manufacturers, which in turn buy raw materials from their suppliers.

The only source of revenue in a supply chain is the customer. In the REI example, you spend your money on the ski equipment. From that point all the way back up the supply chain to the raw material suppliers there is no further injection of cash. The money you spend on the ski equipment is passed back up the supply chain as payments for goods or raw materials. Again, the customer is the only source of revenue.

Four major factors, or *drivers,* affect supply chain performance: facilities, inventory, transportation, and information.[3] We will focus our attention on the fourth factor, information. (You can learn in detail about the first three factors in operations management classes.)

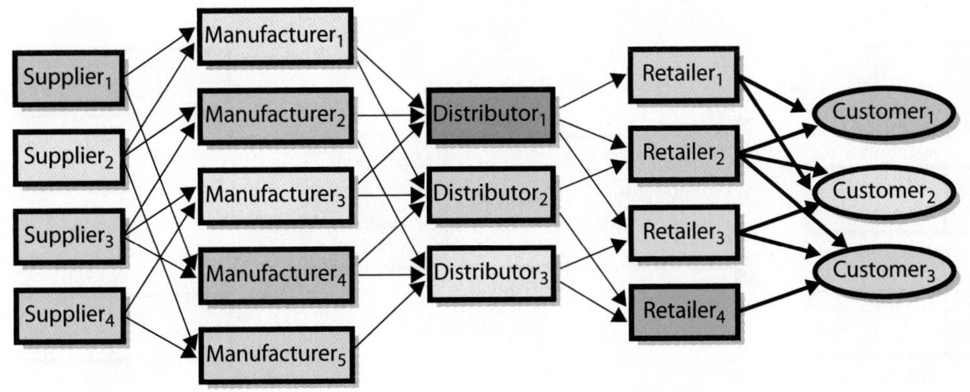

Figure 7-16
Supply Chain Relationships

3. Chopra, S., and P. Meindl, *Supply Chain Management* (Upper Saddle River, NJ: Prentice Hall, 2004), pp. 51–53.

Figure 7-17
Supply Chain Example

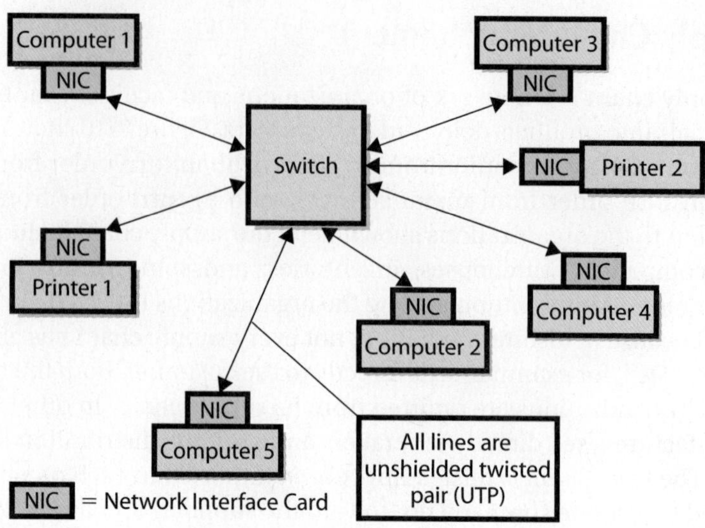

Information influences supply chain performance by affecting the ways that organizations in the supply chain request, respond, and inform one another. There are three factors of information: purpose, availability, and means. The *purpose* of the information can be transactional, such as orders and order returns, or it can be informational, such as the sharing of inventory and customer order data. *Availability* refers to the ways in which organizations share their information; that is, which organizations have access to which information and when. Finally, *means* refers to the methods by which the information is transmitted.

Supplier Relationship Management

Figure 7-18 shows the three fundamental information systems involved in **supply chain management:** supplier relationship management (SRM), inventory, and customer relationship management (CRM). We have discussed all these applications except SRM. We discuss it here.

Supplier relationship management (SRM) is a business process for managing all contacts between an organization and its suppliers. The term *supplier* in *supplier relationship management* is broader than the use of the term *supplier* in Figures 7-17 and 7-18. In those figures, the term refers to the supplier of raw materials and assemblies to a manufacturer. *Supplier* in SRM is used generically:

Figure 7-18
B2B in One Section of the Supply Chain

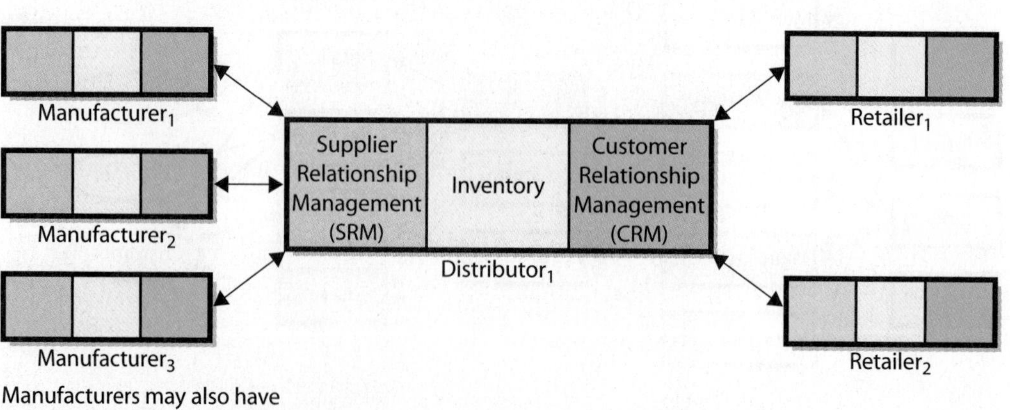

It refers to *any organization* that sells something to the organization that has the SRM application. Thus, in this generic sense, a manufacturer is a supplier to a distributor.

SRM is an integrated system in the same sense of CRM and ERP. With regard to Porter's model, an SRM supports both the in-bound logistics primary activity and the procurement support activity. Considering business processes, SRM applications support three basic processes: source, purchase, and settle, as summarized in Figure 7-19.

Considering sourcing, the organization needs to find possible vendors of needed supplies, materials, or services; to assess the vendors that it does find; to negotiate terms and conditions; and to formalize those terms and conditions in a procurement contract. SRM software is especially relevant to finding and assessing vendors. Some SRM applications have features to search for product sources and to find evaluations of vendors and products. You see something akin to this functionality when you search for electronics products on a site such as CNET.com. There, you can readily determine which vendors provide which products, and you can also obtain evaluations of products and vendors. Similar capabilities are built into SRM packages.

Once the company has identified vendors and has procurement contracts in place, the next stage is to procure the goods. The SRM application requests information, quotations, and proposals from would-be suppliers. The company can then use the SRM to manage the approval workflow in order to approve the purchase and issue the order.

The third major SRM activity is to settle. Here, the accounting department reconciles the receipt of the goods or services against the purchase documents and schedules the vendor payment. The payment portion of the SRM typically connects to the cash management subsystem in the financial management application.

Information systems have had an exceedingly positive impact on supply chain performance. CRM, SRM, and less-integrated functional systems such as e-commerce sales systems have dramatically reduced the costs of buying and selling. Sourcing, buying, and settling have all become faster, easier, more effective, and less costly.

Furthermore, the presence of information systems has expanded **supply chain speed,** which is the dollar value of goods exchanged in a given period of time. Without information systems, Amazon.com would not have been able to process an average of 41 items per second for 24 hours on December 14, 2005. And, without information systems, it would not have been able to deliver 99 percent of those items on time.

As shown in Figure 7-20, a third factor is that information systems have enabled both suppliers and customers to reduce the size of their inventories and thus reduce their inventory costs. This reduction is possible because the speed and efficiency provided by information systems enables processing of small orders, quickly.

Figure 7-19
Summary of SRM Processes

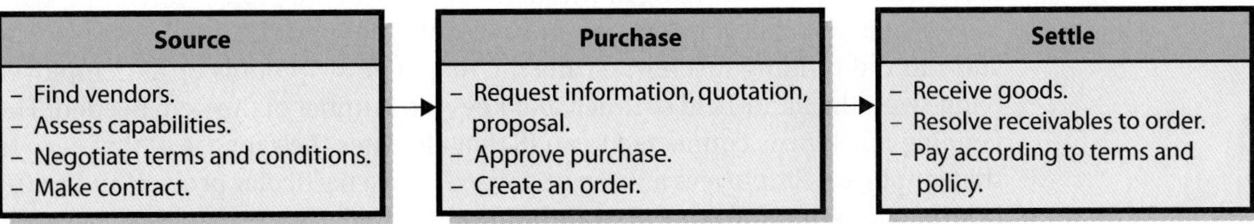

Figure 7-20
Benefits of Information Systems on Supply Chain Performance

- Reduce costs of buying and selling.
- Increase supply chain speed.
- Reduce size and cost of inventories.
- Improve delivery scheduling—enable JIT.

Information systems also improve delivery scheduling. Using information systems, suppliers can deliver materials and components at the time and in the sequence needed. Such delivery enables just-in-time inventory, and it allows manufacturers to reduce raw materials inventory size as well as the handling of raw materials.

How does the knowledge in this chapter help you at DSI?

In this chapter we have discussed how information systems enable companies to create competitive advantage. *Case Study 7* shows a further example of how technology can provide competitive advantage for a company. You can use the knowledge you've gained in this chapter to help not only the company you work for but also you.

We started out this chapter suggesting that you need to close the gap on the niece who has the inside track for the job at DSI. You know that DSI's competitive strategy is to differentiate on quality, subject on some projects to a competitive-bidding process. Theoretically, you could propose a system that increases quality and labour costs, as long as the value generated by the increased quality is sufficiently greater than the marginal cost. But doing so increases the sales challenges of explaining why the additional costs are a worthy investment for the customer. It is unlikely that DSI wants to increase its sales challenges, no matter how great your idea is, so you decide not to pursue that theoretical possibility.

Instead, you decide to focus directly on what your boss recommended: increase labour productivity and, therefore, reduce labour costs. Assume DSI does not use ERP. You know ERP could save labour costs, but developing a new ERP system will impact many departments and mean substantial disruption of existing operations. As a summer intern, you're certain you do not have the credibility necessary to obtain serious consideration of a system with such high transition costs.

You begin looking for examples of how DSI currently saves labour. One way is by using recycled vending machines, like the one in Figure 7-21. Rather than candy bars and potato chips, this machine vends consumable tools, such as sandpaper, burnishing wheels, and drill bits. These vending machines are located throughout the hangar, within a few steps of the production lines.

When a worker needs a new consumable tool part, he or she walks a few steps to the vending machine, scans the magnetic strip of his or her employee badge with the hand-held scanner, and keys the number of the item needed. The vending machine is connected to an IS that allocates the expense of that item to that employee. Employees are always logged in to a particular project, and so the cost of the item is allocated to the project as well. These machines save the

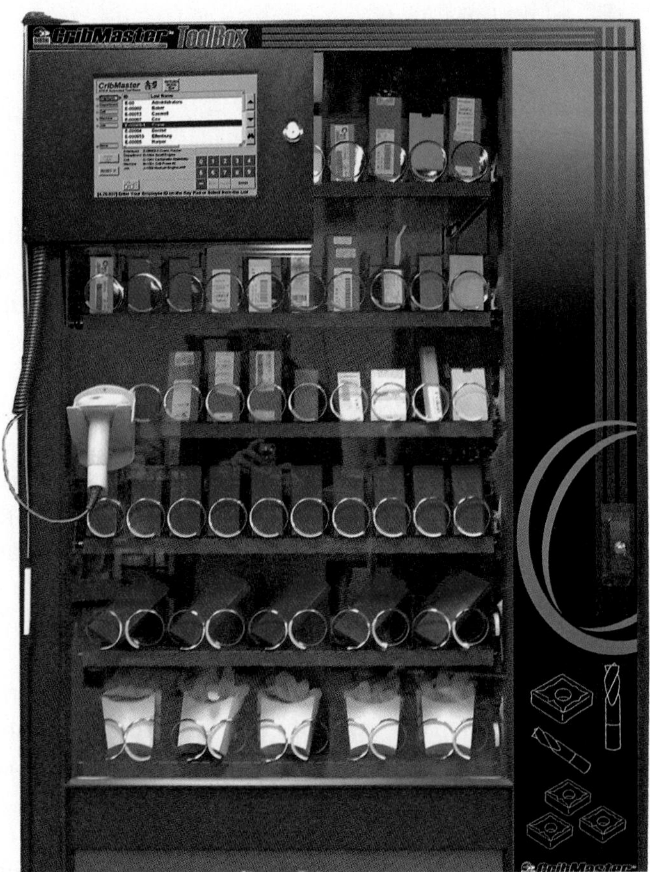

Figure 7-21
Vending Machines That Hold Consumable Tools Reduce Wasted Labour

labour time of having the welder walk to a centralized tool crib and possibly stand in line, chatting with other workers, before obtaining that same item.

What other systems might increase labour productivity? On your way to your lunch break, you've noticed that DSI maintains a shop where it repairs tools. A broken tool means that whoever was using that tool has lost time. And, if there is no replacement for the broken tool, work may need to be delayed or rescheduled until the tool is fixed or repaired.

You wonder what data are kept about tool repairs. The repair shop has two or three computer monitors, so workers in the tool shop must enter something about the repairs. Perhaps there is a way to process the repair data to determine how much time is lost when a tool is in repair. If it is a substantial amount of time, maybe the data could be analyzed and a system developed that would recommend the acquisition of backups for frequently breaking tools. You decide to think more about this possibility.

You have also noticed that DSI operates a tool crib from which workers check out portable tools, such as impact hammers, sanders, and grinders. From time to time, you see a line in front of that tool crib. Workers standing in that line represent lost labour time. You haven't seen any evidence that DSI is using RFID. You begin to wonder if it would be possible to propose a "virtual tool crib." Each item of equipment would have its own RFID chip, and that chip could be used to record and report who has the tool checked out and where it is currently located. You think that idea has potential promise and decide to consider it as well.

Active Review

Use this Active Review to verify that you understand the material in the chapter. You can read the entire chapter and then perform the tasks in this review, or you can read the material for just one question and perform the tasks in this review for that question before moving on to the next one.

Q1 How do organizations gain a competitive advantage using information systems?

Define *competitive strategy*. Explain the relationship between competitive strategy, value chains, business processes, and information systems.

Q2 What are the fundamental types of IS within organizations?

Using Figure 7-1, explain the three types of IS. Give an example of each. Describe how each type overcomes problems in the earlier type. Explain which of these systems you are likely to encounter in your career. Describe a problem that is likely to concern you.

Q3 What are functional systems?

Name five categories of functional systems. Explain the general purpose of each. Explain the differences among manufacturing operations, scheduling, inventory, and planning systems. Explain the role of RFID tags.

Q4 What are the problems of functional systems?

Name five problems of functional systems and describe each. Give an example of a data integration problem. Describe the consequences of a lack of data integration.

Q5 What is the importance of industry standard processes?

Describe what is meant by the term "industry standard best practices." What are the advantages of standard processes? What are the disadvantages? Can an organization develop competitive advantage with industry standard practices?

Q6 What are cross-functional systems?

Name two types of cross-functional systems. How do these systems address the problems that arise from functional systems?

Q7 What are interorganizational systems?

Provide two examples of interorganizational systems. Explain why there can be conflict between companies using interorganizational systems. Explain how these systems provide a competitive advantage for firms.

Key Terms and Concepts

Accounting functional systems 207
Business process design 209
Business-to-business (B2B) 218
Business-to-consumer (B2C) 218
Business-to-government (B2G) 218
Calculation system 203
Clearinghouse 218
Cross-departmental system 203
Cross-functional system 203
Customer life cycle 212
Customer relationship management (CRM) system 212
Disintermediation 219
E-commerce 217
E-commerce auction 218
Electronic exchange 218
Enterprise resource planning (ERP) system 214
Functional system 203
Industry standard processes 210
Interorganizational system 203
Islands of automation 203
Manufacturing information systems 206
Merchant companies 217
Nonmerchant companies 217
Operations systems 206
Price elasticity 219
Process blueprint 215

Using Your Knowledge

1. Choose one of the following basic business processes: inventory management, operations, manufacturing, HR management, or accounting/ financial management. Use the Internet to identify three vendors that license a product to support that process. Compare offerings from the three vendors as follows.
   a. Determine differences in terminology, especially differences in the ways vendors use the same terms.
   b. Compare the features and functions of each product offering.
   c. For each vendor, specify the characteristics of a company for which that vendor's offering would be ideal.

2. As an intern at DSI, do you agree with the conclusions reached? Do you agree with the statement of competitive advantage? Do you agree with the decision not to explore a system that adds both value and cost? Do you agree not to propose an ERP system? Do you agree with the decision to explore the tool repair data and the possible virtual tool crib? For each of these questions, explain why or why not.

3. Examine the list of problems of functional systems in Figure 7-5. Assuming that DSI uses only functional systems, give an example of each one of these problems. You don't have all the data necessary to know whether or not DSI has those problems, but describe problems that are plausible. State your assumptions when necessary.

4. Consider the possibility of processing the tool repair data to determine possible wasted labour costs. Does the fact that a tool is in the repair shop necessarily indicate that labour was lost? How could you find out if that was the case? Acquiring backup tools could be expensive. How would you go about justifying the additional expense? What economic argument would you make to justify the purchase of the backups? How do the cost of the tool and the frequency of the failure impact the decision to buy a backup? Does the length of time to repair a tool impact this decision? How could a system of priorities for tool repair also save labour hours?

5. Investigate the possibility of a virtual tool crib. Assume each tool has an RFID. (Google RFID to learn more if you need to.) Assume that each production facility has racks on which tools can be placed when not in use. Assume that tools reside in only one of those racks; there is no centralized tool crib or other repository. Describe the nature of an IS for tracking tools. Could that system prevent tool theft? If so, how? How would an employee obtain a tool when needed? How would the IS help employees learn the location of tools? On balance, does this seem like a workable idea? Or is it just some high-tech option that would create confusion?

6. Distance learning is an application of interorganizational information systems. Although it may seem odd to label students as organizations, they are customers in the same sense that consumers are customers in B2C e-commerce systems.
   a. Draw a process diagram of a regular, non–distance learning class. Label the activities and the flows among the activities.
   b. Draw a second process diagram of a distance-learning class. In what ways are the two diagrams similar? In what ways are they different?
   c. What is the competitive strategy of your university? How do distance-learning classes contribute to that competitive strategy?
   d. Assuming that no face-to-face meeting is required to successfully teach a distance-learning class, neither students nor professors need live near campus. In fact, they don't even need to reside on the same continent. What opportunities does that fact present to your university? What new educational products might your university develop?
   e. Considering your answer to (d), what opportunities does distance learning provide your professor? Is there any reason a professor should not teach for more than one university? Do you think there is a realistic opportunity for a group of professors from different universities to band together to form a virtual college? What competitive advantage might they accrue by doing so?

Case Study 7

Moving Like a Deere: Deere's Innovative Revolution

Looking at cotton growing on a farm, one could be forgiven for thinking that, other than fertilizer, pesticides, and the practical deployment of the modern cotton picker in the 1950s, the picture is timeless. However, at Deere & Company, or John Deere, (www.deere.com) a second revolution is brewing, and this one is definitely adding cutting-edge technology to an old-economy business.

Founded in 1837 as a one-man blacksmith operation, John Deere is now a $22.1-billion corporation that employs more than 47 000 people worldwide and is one of the oldest publicly traded industrial companies in the United States. But rather than the brutality and razor-thin margins that usually accompany price competition, market leader John Deere has staked out a bold differentiation strategy that incorporates technology to compete on innovation.

John Deere's machines still pluck cotton fibres with hundreds of finger-like spindles and then vacuum the cotton into a huge bin, but this is where the similarities with its old machines end. The company has used advanced computer-aided design (CAD) to reshape the intake ducts, allowing the cotton to travel 20 percent faster and reducing horsepower requirements by 5 percent, thus saving fuel consumption while maintaining speed. Inside the new cotton pickers is the computing power of eight personal computers and a communications system that beams wireless information to a base station, which can automatically monitor and signal when service is needed. At the same time, microwave sensors and Global Positioning System (GPS) technology allow the farmer to map the fields' exact yield while harvesting the cotton. And by overlaying this information with other enabled systems, fertilizer, pesticides, and water can be applied with precision rather than indiscriminately distributed across the entire field. Finally, in an industry first, John Deere's latest generation of picker spools the cotton into cylindrical bales that are wrapped and gently placed on the field without the machine having to stop every 10 to 15 minutes.

While prices for the new technology have still to be set, the two-storey harvester replaces four to six pieces of support equipment and enables a sole operator to harvest non-stop until the 1100-litre fuel tank is sucked dry.

Questions

1. What are the advantages of this technology?
2. How does this technology allow John Deere to compete against lower-cost manufacturers and producers?
3. Are there any other advantages to using this technology? What adaptation and extensions would increase the advantage? (*Hint:* Radio-frequency tags can be inserted into each bundle to track harvesting information and pinpoint where the cotton came from, identifying for example if the cotton qualifies as organic.)

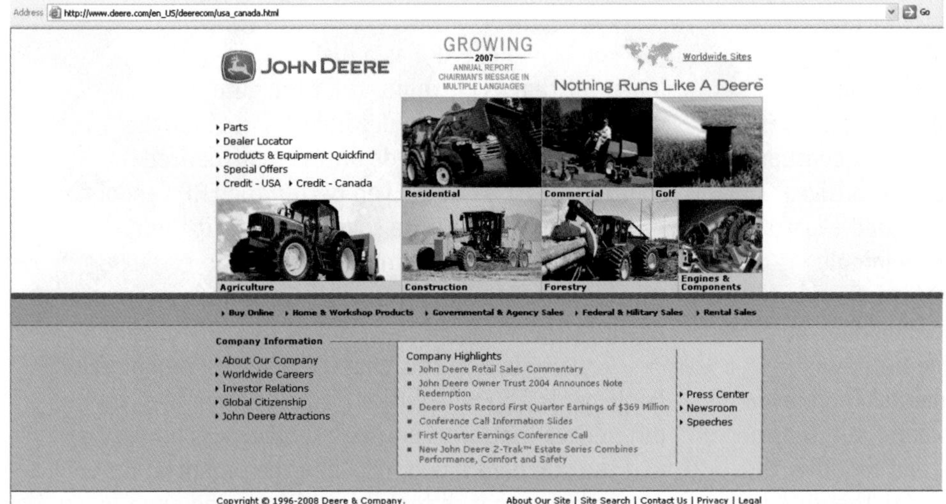

Figure 7-22
www.deere.com

Visit MyMISLab at **www.pearsoned.ca/mymislab**. MyMISLab is a state-of-the-art, interactive, online solution that combines multimedia, tutorials, and quizzes. Use MyMISLab for *Experiencing MIS* to prepare for tests and exams, and go to class ready to learn!

What Do YOU Think?

Available Only in Vanilla?

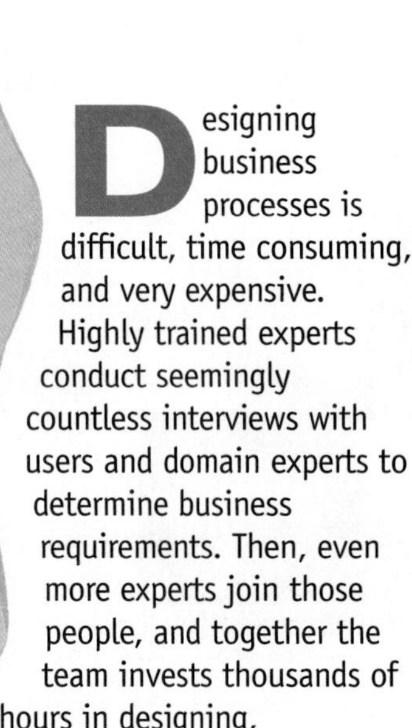

Designing business processes is difficult, time consuming, and very expensive. Highly trained experts conduct seemingly countless interviews with users and domain experts to determine business requirements. Then, even more experts join those people, and together the team invests thousands of hours in designing, developing, and implementing effective business processes that meet those requirements. All this amounts to a very high-risk activity that is prone to failure. And it must be done before IS development can even begin.

ERP vendors, such as SAP, have invested millions of labour hours into the business blueprints that underlie their ERP solutions. These blueprints consist of hundreds or thousands of different business processes. Examples include processes for hiring employees, processes for acquiring fixed assets, processes for acquiring consumable goods, and processes for custom "one-off" (a unique product with a unique design) manufacturing, to name just a few. Additionally, since ERP vendors implement their business processes in hundreds of organizations, they are forced to customize their standard blueprint for use in particular industries.

For example, SAP has a distribution-business blueprint that is customized for the auto parts industry, for the electronics industry, and for the aircraft industry. Hundreds of other customized solutions exist as well. Even better, the ERP vendors have developed software solutions that fit their business-process blueprints. In theory, no software development is required at all if the organization can adapt to the standard blueprint of the ERP vendor.

As described in this chapter, when an organization implements an ERP solution, it first determines any differences that exist between its business processes and the standard blueprint. Then the organization must remove that difference, which can be done in one of two ways: It can change business processes to fit the standard blueprint, or the ERP vendor or a consultant can modify the standard blueprint (and software solution that matches the blueprint) to fit the unique requirements. In practice, such variations from the standard blueprint are rare. They're difficult and expensive to implement, and they require the using organization to maintain the variations from the standard as new versions of the ERP software are developed.

Consequently, most organizations choose to modify their processes to meet the blueprint rather than the other way around. This is often referred to as installing the software *vanilla* (the basic software with no custom features). Although such process changes are also difficult to implement, once the organization has converted to the standard blueprint it no longer needs to support a "variation." So from a standpoint of cost, effort, risk, and avoidance of future problems,

there is a huge incentive for organizations to adapt to the standard ERP blueprint. Initially, SAP was the only true ERP vendor, but other companies have since developed and acquired ERP solutions as well. And given the competitive pressure across the software industry, these products are beginning to have the same sets of features and functions. ERP solutions are becoming a commodity.

All this is fine as far as it goes, but it introduces a nagging question: If, over time, every organization tends to implement the standard ERP blueprint, and if, over time, every software company develops essentially the same ERP features and functions, then won't every business come to look just like every other business? How will organizations gain a competitive advantage if they all use the same business processes?

If every auto parts distributor uses the same business processes, based on the same software, are they not all clones of one another? How will a company distinguish itself? How will innovation occur? Even if one parts distributor does successfully innovate a business process that gives it a competitive advantage, will the ERP vendors be conduits to transfer that innovation to competitors? Does the use of "commoditized" standard blueprints mean that no company can sustain a competitive advantage?

Discussion Questions

1. In your own words, explain why an organization might choose to change its processes to fit the standard blueprint. What advantages does it accrue by doing so?
2. Explain how competitive pressure among software vendors will cause the ERP solutions to become commodities. What does this mean to the ERP software industry?
3. If two businesses use exactly the same processes and exactly the same software, can they be different in any way at all? Explain why or why not.
4. Explain the statement that an ERP software vendor can be a conduit to transfer innovation. What are the consequences to the innovating company? To the software company? To the industry? To the economy?
5. Such standardization might be possible in theory, but since worldwide there are so many different business models, cultures, people, values, and competitive pressures, can any two businesses ever be exactly alike?

8 Decision Making and Business Intelligence

This could happen to you

You're getting depressed. You've got to find a way to distinguish yourself, and while you've thought of two interesting possible systems for increasing labour productivity, you're not sure any of them is outstanding. What to do?

You might take another tack. Chapter 7 discussed the ways information systems support the development of competitive advantage. What about considering ways in which information systems improve decision making?

Of course, business processes and decision making are closely related. Every business process involves decision making, and every business decision occurs in the context of a business process. The distinction is one of perspective. From the process perspective, we consider how information systems facilitate competitive strategy by adding value to or reducing the costs of processes. From the decision-making perspective, we consider how information systems add value or reduce costs by improving the quality of human decisions.

Consider your situation at DSI. You want to propose a system that increases labour productivity. You've thought about systems that facilitate processes. Is there an information system that improves decision making?

For example, last week DSI learned that one of its suppliers was incapacitated by an ice storm. The supplier expects to be back in business soon, but there is no way it can produce components for DSI's current projects on time. DSI had to select a different vendor, and fast. Is there a way to build an IS to select a supplier based on past supplier performance?

That's a possibility you need to consider. But what would you recommend? A reporting system? A data-mining system? A knowledge management system? An expert system? In responding to this task, how would you describe the alternative you recommend? The knowledge you gain from this chapter will help.

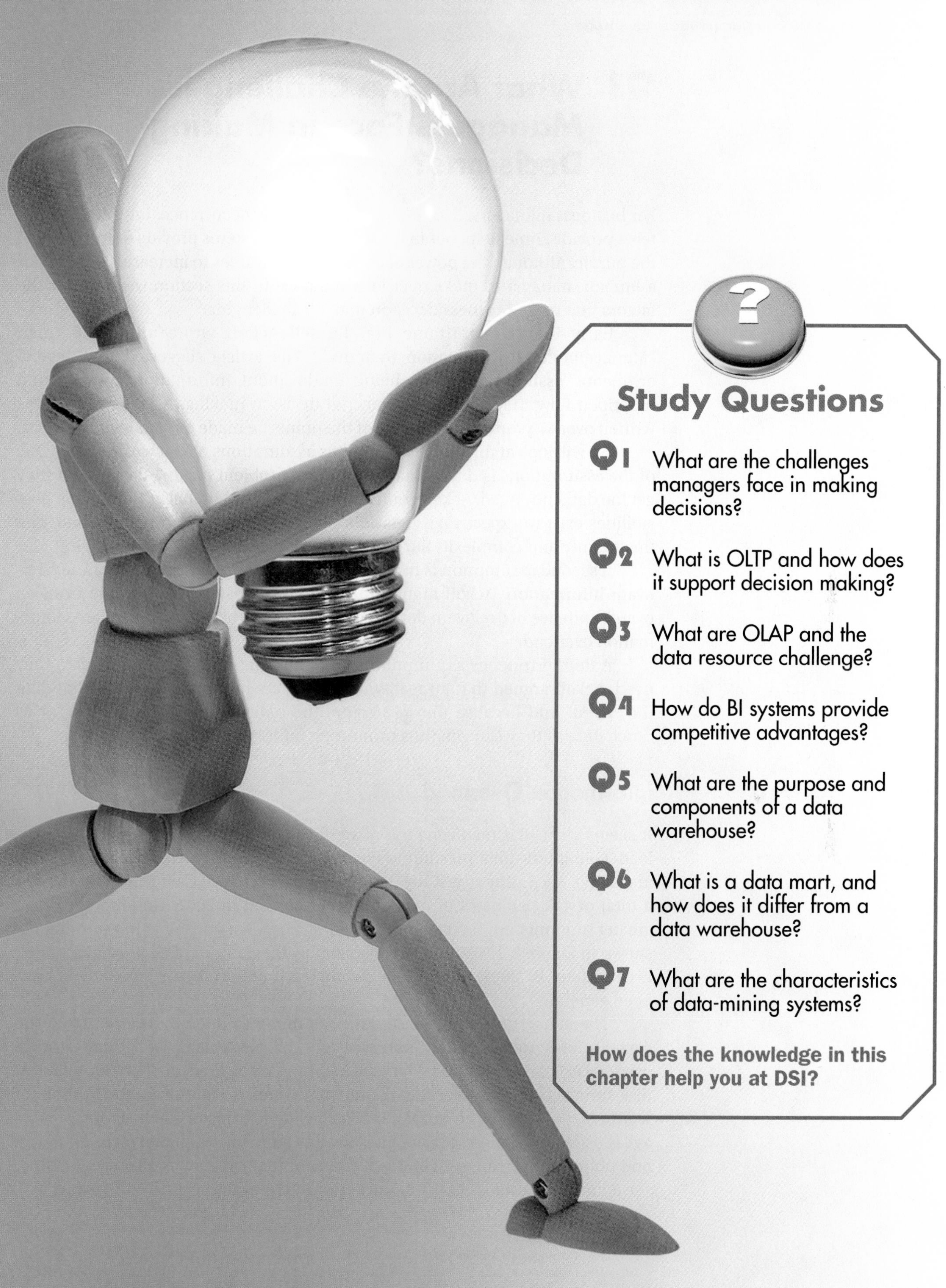

Study Questions

Q1 What are the challenges managers face in making decisions?

Q2 What is OLTP and how does it support decision making?

Q3 What are OLAP and the data resource challenge?

Q4 How do BI systems provide competitive advantages?

Q5 What are the purpose and components of a data warehouse?

Q6 What is a data mart, and how does it differ from a data warehouse?

Q7 What are the characteristics of data-mining systems?

How does the knowledge in this chapter help you at DSI?

Q1 What Are the Challenges Managers Face in Making Decisions?

For business managers, decision making is a daily occurrence. Information systems provide some help, but in most cases these systems provide only a piece of the puzzle. Although the power of computers continues to increase, the need for a human manager to make decisions remains. In this section we consider the factors that make business decision making challenging.

Early in the mainframe era, Russell Ackoff wrote an article titled "Management Misinformation Systems."[1] The article suggested that several erroneous assumptions were being made about information systems and described how they affected managerial decision making. Ackoff's article was written over 40 years ago, but some of the points he made remain relevant today.

We will look at three of the erroneous assumptions Ackoff wrote about. One of the assumptions is that managers have no problem making decisions if they get the data they need. Ackoff countered that, for most managers, too many possibilities exist to expect their decisions to improve even with perfect data. The uncertainty and complexity surrounding decisions make them challenging.

A second assumption is that decisions are poor because managers lack relevant information. Ackoff argued that managers instead suffer more from an overabundance of irrelevant data. Today we refer to this overabundance as information overload.

A third erroneous assumption is that managers are aware of the data they need. Ackoff argued that, in reality, managers are often not sure just what data they need. And because they're unsure, the natural tendency is to ask for as much data as they can get, thus promoting information overload.

Information Overload

It seems clear that managers today are facing some level of information overload. One interesting question to consider is just how much of an overload we are facing. According to a study done at the University of California at Berkeley,[2] a total of 403 petabytes of new data were created in 2002. Undoubtedly even greater amounts are being generated today, but just consider that number. As shown in Figure 8-1, 403 **petabytes** is roughly the amount of all printed material ever written. By 2007, nearly 2500 petabytes, or 2.5 **exabytes**, of data will have been generated.

The generation of all these data has much to do with Moore's Law. The capacity of storage devices increases as their costs decrease. Today, storage capacity is nearly unlimited. Figure 8-2 shows that by the end of 2003 total hard-disk storage capacity exceeded 41 exabytes, which is eight times the number of words ever spoken by all human beings throughout history. Not all of that storage is used for business. Much of it is used to store music, digital pictures, video, and phone conversations. However, much of that capacity is also used to store the data from business information systems. For example, in 2004 Verizon's SQL

[1] Ackoff, R., "Management Misinformation Systems," *Management Science* 14, no. 4 (December 1967): B147–156.

[2] "How Much Information, 2003," sims.berkeley.edu/research/projects/how-much-info-2003 (accessed September 2007).

Kilobyte (KB)	*1000 bytes OR 10^3 bytes* 2 Kilobytes: A typewritten page 100 Kilobytes: A low-resolution photograph
Megabyte (MB)	*1 000 000 bytes OR 10^6 bytes* 1 Megabyte: A small novel OR a 3.5-inch floppy disk 2 Megabytes: A high-resolution photograph 5 Megabytes: The complete works of Shakespeare 10 Megabytes: A minute of high-fidelity sound 100 Megabytes: One meter of shelved books 500 Megabytes: A CD-ROM
Gigabyte (GB)	*1 000 000 000 bytes OR 10^9 bytes* 1 Gigabyte: A pickup truck filled with books 20 Gigabytes: A good collection of the works of Beethoven 100 Gigabytes: A library floor of academic journals
Terabyte (TB)	*1 000 000 000 000 bytes OR 10^{12} bytes* 1 Terabyte: 50 000 trees made into paper and printed 2 Terabytes: An academic research library 10 Terabytes: The print collections of the U.S. Library of Congress 400 Terabytes: National Climactic Data Center (NOAA) database
Petabyte (PB)	*1 000 000 000 000 000 bytes OR 10^{15} bytes* 1 Petabyte: Three years of EOS data (2001) 2 Petabytes: All U.S. academic research libraries 20 Petabytes: Production of hard-disk drives in 1995 200 Petabytes: All printed material
Exabyte (EB)	*1 000 000 000 000 000 000 bytes OR 10^{18} bytes* 2 Exabytes: Total volume of information generated in 1999 5 Exabytes: All words ever spoken by human beings

Figure 8-1
How Big Is an Exabyte?

Source: sims.berkeley.edu/research/projects/how-much-info/datapowers.html (accessed May 2005). Used with the permission of Peter Lyman and Hal R. Varian, University of California at Berkeley.

Server database contained more than 15 terabytes of data. If that amount of data were published in books, a bookshelf 725 kilometres long would be required to hold it.

Why does this exponential growth in data matter to us? First, understand that it occurs inside organizations just as much as outside of them. Every time DSI builds another airplane interior, its information systems generate megabytes of data about designs, bills of materials, supplier performance, production costs, employee productivity, customer payment patterns, market and product trends, and so forth.

Buried in all these data is information that, if found and made available to the right people at the right time, can improve the decisions DSI makes. For example, when negotiating with a prior customer, how flexible does Ms. Dorset want to be when negotiating price? The decision to reduce price must be based, in part, on past experience with that customer. How stable were that customer's requirements? How many change-orders did that customer require? How quickly did the customer pay? How much service and support has the customer needed?

The challenge for managers in a world overloaded with information is to find the appropriate data and incorporate them into their decision processes. Information systems can both help and hinder this process.

Figure 8-2
Hard-Disk Storage Capacity

Source: sims.berkeley.edu/research/projects/how-much-info/datapowers.html (accessed May 2005). Used with the permission of Peter Lyman and Hal R. Varian, University of California at Berkeley.

Year	Disks Sold (Thousands)	Storage Capacity (Petabytes)
1992	42 000	
1995	89 054	104.8
1996	105 686	183.9
1997	129 281	343.63
1998	143 649	724.36
1999	165 857	1394.60
2000	200 000 (IDEMA)	4630.5
2001	196 000 (Gartner)	7279.14
2002	213 000 (Gartner projection)	10 849.56
2003	235 000	15 892.24
TOTAL	**1 519 527 (1.5 billion drives)**	**41 402.73 (41 exabytes)**

Data Quality

A final challenge in decision making is the quality of the data. Up to this point we have assumed that the data stored in systems are clean and accurate. But this is the exception rather than the rule in most systems. It's hard enough to make decisions when you have good data. But what if the data are of low quality? How would this affect your decisions?

Data from operational systems can be processed to create basic reports without any problems. If we want to know, for example, current sales and how those sales relate to sales projections, we simply process data in the order-entry database.

However, raw operational data are seldom suitable for more sophisticated reporting or data mining. Figure 8-3 lists the major problem categories. First, although data that are critical for successful operations must be complete and accurate, data that are only marginally necessary do not need to be. For example, some systems gather demographic data in the ordering process. But because such data are not needed to fill, ship, and bill orders, their quality suffers.

Problematic data are termed **dirty data**. Examples are values of *B* for customer gender and of *213* for customer age. Other examples are a value of *999-999-9999* for a phone number, a part colour of *gren,* and an email address of WhyMe@GuessWhoIAM.org. All these values can be problematic for data-mining purposes.

Missing values are a second problem. A non-for-profit organization can process a donation without knowing the donor's gender or age, but a data-mining application will suffer if many such values are missing.

Figure 8-3
Problems of Using Operational Data for BI Systems

- Dirty data
- Missing values
- Inconsistent data
- Data not integrated
- Wrong granularity
  - Too fine
  - Not fine enough
- Too much data
  - Too many attributes
  - Too many data points

Inconsistent data, the third problem shown in Figure 8-3, are particularly common in data that have been gathered over time. When an area code changes, for example, the phone number for a given customer before the change will not match the customer's number after the change. Likewise, part codes can change, as can sales territories. Before such data can be used, they must be recoded for consistency over the period of the study.

Data can also be too fine or too coarse. Data **granularity** refers to the degree of summarization or detail. Coarse data are highly summarized; fine data express precise details. For example, suppose we want to analyze the placement of graphics and controls on an order-entry web page. It is possible to capture the customers' clicking behaviour in what is termed **clickstream data**. Those data are very fine, however, including everything the customer does at the website. In the middle of the order stream are data for clicks on the news, email, instant chat, and a weather check. Although all those data are needed for a study of consumer computer behaviour, such data will be overwhelming if all we want to know is how customers respond to ad locations. Because the data are too fine, the data analysts must throw away millions and millions of clicks.

Generally, it is better to have too fine a granularity than too coarse. If the granularity is too fine, the data can be made coarser by summing and combining. Only analysts' labour and computer processing are required. If the granularity is too coarse, however, there is no way to separate the data into constituent parts.

This section has suggested that a number of factors, including complexity, uncertainty, information overload, and data quality, make management decision making challenging. Information has the potential to meet some of these challenges. In this chapter we outline categories of systems that support the decision-making process.

Q2 What Is OLTP and How Does It Support Decision Making?

In Chapter 7 we noted that functional information systems are used to capture details about business transactions and then create updated information by processing these transaction details. There are many types of business transactions. Purchasing a product or service, receiving a shipment from a supplier, creating a purchase order for a new printer, making a customer service call, and returning defective items to a store are all examples of transactions. Information systems are a critical component for capturing and processing the details about these transactions because they are very efficient and accurate.

Using computers to capture information electronically is often referred to as being "online." When a bank's customer service representative accepts your deposit, he or she enters the transaction online so that he or she does not have to write down information on paper and then copy it into the system at a later time. Most web-based applications are examples of online systems.

If you are collecting data electronically and processing the transactions online, then you are using an **online transaction processing (OLTP)** system. There are two basic ways that transactions can be processed. If transactions are entered and processed immediately upon entry, then the system is operating in "real time." It's called real time because there is little or no delay in updating the systems with new data.

The other option in processing is to wait for many transactions to pile up before you process them. For example, at a gas station you might collect all the transactions that occurred during the day and then send them at the end of the day to the central office for processing. This is an example of "batch" processing, because the system waits until it has a batch of transactions before the data are processed and the information is updated.

The choice of whether to use real-time or batch processing depends on the nature of the transactions, the cost of the system, and the needs of the organization. Real-time systems tend to be more complex and to cost more to implement. However, real-time systems provide the most up-to-date information, and that's often important. For example, a company selling tickets to a concert event over the phone would find it difficult to use a batch processing system. Why? The most important thing is to make sure you don't sell more than one ticket for the same seat. A real-time system will ensure that only one ticket is sold per seat because the system is updated after each transaction. A batch system, on the other hand, might register two tickets for one seat if the sales occur within a single batch.

OLTP systems are the backbone of all functional, cross-functional, and interorganizational systems in an organization. They are designed to efficiently enter, process, and store data. OLTP systems combine large databases with efficient input devices such as grocery store scanners, automated cash registers, and debit and credit card readers to process transactions quickly and accurately. Large OLTP systems such as airline reservation systems and banking systems are capable of reliably processing thousands of transaction per second over a long period of time. Whether big or small, OLTP systems support decision making by providing the raw information about transactions and status for an organization.

Q3 What Are OLAP and the Data Resource Challenge?

Using OLTP to collect data is important. We have all heard that information is a competitive weapon and can be a source of competitive advantage for the firm. It is important to realize that the competitive advantage of information is realized when organizations *use* the data they have collected to help make better decisions.

Not all organizations use their data effectively. For example, Thomas Davenport[3] noted that a major grocery chain used less than 2 percent of the scanner data it had collected over the years. So, while data may be collected in OLTP, the data may not be used to improve decision making. We refer to this as the **data resource challenge.**

The quickest way to explain the challenge is to consider whether a company views its data as an asset. An asset can be defined as a resource from which future economic benefits may be obtained. When you think about it closely, data is a particularly good asset. It doesn't take up much space, it is easy to store, it does not depreciate in the same way physical assets depreciate, yet it can provide input for improved decision making.

[3] Davenport, T. H., et al., "Data to Knowledge to Results: Building an Analytic Capability," *California Management Review* 43, no. 2 (2001): 117–138.

But here is the challenge. If data is an asset, like money and real estate, who in the company is in charge of managing the data? What are the generally accepted accounting principles associated with valuing data as an asset? Where does data show up on a balance sheet? Who is in charge of extracting as much value as they can out of the data? You will find that most companies have a hard time answering these questions. What this means is that although we like to think of data as an asset, we are not really treating it as an important resource.

Systems that focus on making OLTP-collected data useful for decision making are often referred to as **decision support systems (DSS),** or more generally as **online analytic processing (OLAP)** systems. OLAP provides the ability to sum, count, average, and perform other simple arithmetic operations on groups of data. The remarkable characteristic of OLAP reports is that their format is dynamic. The viewer of the report can change the report's structure—hence the term *online.*

An OLAP report has measures, or facts, and dimensions. A measure is the data item of interest. It's the item that is to be summed or averaged or otherwise processed in the OLAP report. Total sales, average sales, and average cost are examples of measures. A dimension is a characteristic of a measure. Purchase date, customer type, customer location, and sales region are all examples of dimensions.

Figure 8-4 shows a typical OLAP report for a grocery chain. Here, the measure is Store Sales Net, and the dimensions are Product Family and Store Type. This report shows how net store sales vary by product family and store type. Stores of type Supermarket, for example, sold a net of $36 189.40, in nonconsumable goods.

The presentation of a measure with associated dimensions like that in Figure 8-4 is often called an OLAP cube, or sometimes simply a cube. The reason for this term is that some products show these displays using three axes, like a cube in geometry. The origin of the term is unimportant here, however. Just know that an OLAP cube and an OLAP report are the same thing.

The OLAP report in Figure 8-4 was generated by SQL Server Analysis Services and is displayed in an Excel pivot table. The data were taken from a sample instructional database, called FoodMart, that is provided with SQL Server. It is possible to display OLAP cubes in many ways other than Excel. Some third-party vendors provide more extensive graphical displays. For more information about such products, check for OLAP vendors and products at the Data Warehousing Review at www.dwreview.com/OLAP. Note, too, that OLAP reports can be delivered just like any of the other reports described for report management systems.

As stated earlier, the distinguishing characteristic of an OLAP report is that the user can alter the format of the report. Figure 8-5 shows such an alteration. Here, the user added another dimension, store country and state, to the horizontal display. Product-family sales are now broken out by the location of the stores.

Figure 8-4
OLAP Product Family by Store Type

	A	B	C	D	E	F	G
1							
2							
3	Store Sales Net	Store Type					
4	Product Family	Deluxe Supermarket	Gourmet Supermarket	Mid-Size Grocery	Small Grocery	Supermarket	Grand Total
5	Drink	$8119.05	$2392.83	$1409.50	$685.89	$16 751.71	$29 358.98
6	Food	$70 276.11	$20 026.18	$10 392.19	$6109.72	$138 960.67	$245 764.87
7	Nonconsumable	$18 884.24	$5064.79	$2813.73	$1534.90	$36 189.40	$64 487.05
8	Grand Total	$97 279.40	$27 483.80	$14 615.42	$8330.51	$191 901.77	$339 610.90

	A	B	C	D	E	F	G	H	I
1									
2									
3	Store Sales Net			Store Type					
4	Product Family	Store	Store State	Deluxe Supermarket	Gourmet Supermarket	Mid-Size Grocery	Small Grocery	Supermarket	Grand Total
5	Drink	USA	CA		$2392.83		$227.38	$5920.76	$8540.97
6			OR	$4438.49				$2862.45	$7300.94
7			WA	$3680.56		$1409.50	$458.51	$7968.50	$13 517.07
8		USA Total		$8119.05	$2392.83	$1409.50	$685.89	$16 751.71	$29 358.98
9	Drink Total			$8119.05	$2392.83	$1409.50	$685.89	$16 751.71	$29 358.98
10	Food	USA	CA		$20 026.18		$1960.53	$47 226.11	$69 212.82
11			OR	$37778.35				$23 818.87	$61 597.22
12			WA	$32 497.76		$10 392.19	$4149.19	$67 915.69	$114 954.83
13		USA Total		$70 276.11	$20 026.18	$10 392.19	$6109.72	$138 960.67	$245 764.87
14	Food Total			$70 276.11	$20 026.18	$10 392.19	$6109.72	$138 960.67	$245 764.87
15	Nonconsumable	USA	CA		$5064.79		$474.35	$12 344.49	$17 883.63
16			OR	$10 177.89				$6428.53	$16 606.41
17			WA	$8706.36		$2813.73	$1060.54	$17 416.38	$29 997.01
18		USA Total		$18 884.24	$5064.79	$2813.73	$1534.90	$36 189.40	$64 487.05
19	Nonconsumable Total			$18 884.24	$5064.79	$2813.73	$1534.90	$36 189.40	$64 487.05
20	Grand Total			$97 279.40	$27 483.80	$14 615.42	$8330.51	$191 901.77	$339 610.90

Figure 8-5
OLAP Product Family and Store Location by Store Type

Observe that the sample data include only stores in the United States and only in the western states of California, Oregon, and Washington. With an OLAP report, it is possible to **"drill down"** into the data. This term means to further divide the data into more detail.

In Figure 8-6, for example, the user has drilled down into the stores located in California; the OLAP report now shows sales data for the four cities in California that have stores.

Notice another difference between Figures 8-5 and 8-6. The user has not only drilled down, but has also changed the order of the dimensions. Figure 8-5 shows Product Family and then store location within Product Family. Figure 8-6 shows store location and then Product Family within store location.

Both displays are valid and useful, depending on the user's perspective. A product manager might like to see product families first and then store location data. A sales manager might like to see store locations first and then product data. OLAP reports provide both perspectives, and the user can switch between them while viewing the report. Unfortunately, all this flexibility comes at a cost. If the database is large, doing the necessary calculating, grouping, and sorting for such dynamic displays will require substantial computing power. Although standard, commercial DBMS products do have the features and functions required to create OLAP reports, they are not designed for such work. They are designed instead to provide rapid response to transaction processing applications such as order entry or manufacturing operations. Accordingly, special-purpose products called OLAP servers have been developed to perform OLAP analysis.

OLAP tools have become the primary tools used in the area of business intelligence (BI). *MIS in Use 8,* "Decisions on Ice," provides an example of how BI can be used to support decisions in pro hockey. We will learn more about BI in the section below.

Q4 How Do BI Systems Provide Competitive Advantages?

A **business intelligence (BI) system** is a system that provides information for improving decision making. BI systems vary in their characteristics and capabilities and in the way they foster competitive advantage.

Figure 8-7 summarizes the characteristics and competitive advantages of four categories of business intelligence systems. **Reporting systems** integrate data from multiple sources and process those data by sorting, grouping, summing, averaging, and comparing. Such systems format the results into reports and deliver those reports to users. Reporting systems improve decision making by providing the right information to the right user at the right time.

Data-mining systems process data using sophisticated statistical techniques like regression analysis and decision tree analysis. Data-mining systems might find patterns and relationships that cannot be found by simpler reporting operations like sorting, grouping, and averaging. Data-mining systems improve decision making by using the discovered patterns and relationships to *anticipate* events or to *predict* future outcomes. An example of a data-mining system is one that predicts the likelihood that a prospect will donate to a cause or political campaign based on the prospect's characteristics, such as age, sex, and home postal code. **Market-basket analysis** is another data-mining system, which computes correlations of items on past orders to determine items that are frequently

	A	B	C	D	E	F	G	H	I	J
1										
2										
3	Store Sales Net				Store Type					
4	Store Country	Store Sta	Store City	Product Family	Deluxe Super	Gourmet Supermarket	Mid-Size Grocery	Small Grocery	Supermarket	Grand Total
5	USA	CA	Beverly Hills	Drink		$2392.83				$2392.83
6				Food		$20 026.18				$20 026.18
7				Nonconsumable		$5064.79				$5064.79
8			Beverly Hills Total			$27 483.80				$27 483.80
9			Los Angeles	Drink					$2870.33	$2870.33
10				Food					$23 598.28	$23 598.28
11				Nonconsumable					$6305.14	$6305.14
12			Los Angeles Total						$32 773.74	$32 773.74
13			San Diego	Drink					$3050.43	$3050.43
14				Food					$23 627.83	$23 627.83
15				Nonconsumable					$6039.34	$6039.34
16			San Diego Total						$32 717.61	$32 717.61
17			San Francisco	Drink				$227.38		$227.38
18				Food				$1960.53		$1960.53
19				Nonconsumable				$474.35		$474.35
20			San Francisco Total					$2662.26		$2662.26
21		CA Total				$27 483.80		$2662.26	$65 491.35	$95 637.41
22		OR		Drink	$4438.49				$2862.45	$7300.94
23				Food	$37 778.35				$23 818.87	$61 597.22
24				Nonconsumable	$10 177.89				$6428.53	$16 606.41
25		OR Total			$52 394.72				$33 109.85	$85 504.57
26		WA		Drink	$3 680.56		$1409.50	$458.51	$7968.50	$13 517.07
27				Food	$32 497.76		$10 392.19	$4149.19	$67 915.69	$114 954.83
28				Nonconsumable	$8706.36		$2813.73	$1060.54	$17 416.38	$29 997.01
29		WA Total			$44 884.68		$14 615.42	$5668.24	$93 300.57	$158 468.91
30	USA Total				$97 279.40	$27 483.80	$14 615.42	$8330.51	$191 901.77	$339 610.90
31	Grand Total				$97 279.40	$27 483.80	$14 615.42	$8330.51	$191 901.77	$339 610.90

Figure 8-5
OLAP Product Family and Store Location by Store Type

Decisions on Ice: Pro Hockey Goes Hi Tech

"When I first started working for an NHL team, there wasn't a lot of technology being used," noted Frank Provenzano, assistant general manager for the Dallas Stars. "Most scouts used small paper books to keep track of players and record scouting reports. The books were convenient to use on the road and most scouts weren't used to computers. So there wasn't a lot of call for laptops or electronic data initially." But things have changed. "The stakes are high in pro hockey. My job is about negotiation and making good decisions. The collective bargaining agreement has become complex, and that has meant more analysis has to be done on player performance and player salaries. These are million-dollar decisions we make, and they can affect the team for several years in the future. We spend over a million dollars on our pro and amateur player scouting a year. Understanding the data is a critical part of my job."

Frank has worked with several teams, including the Vancouver Canucks, Washington Capitals, and Dallas Stars. "It took several years to take hold, but now things have changed. Most scouts use laptops, and data is in electronic form. Every team has their own way of entering the data. The real differences come from how the systems allow you to use the data to make better decisions."

Questions

1. What benefits would a professional hockey team gain by switching its data collection from paper books to electronic format? Do you think electronic data would really help a team make better decisions?
2. A scouting staff usually travels the world to collect scouting reports. Do you see any issues that might occur when new players are added to the system? How would this affect decision making?
3. The real power of data comes when you're able to link different sets of data. Assume that a team stores its scouting reports separately from information about player salary, which is separate from performance data (how many games, goals, assists, or penalty minutes a player has). What kind of reports do you think can emerge when you combine these data and collect them historically?

purchased together. We will discuss data mining in more detail at the end of this chapter.

Knowledge-management (KM) systems create value from intellectual capital by collecting and sharing human knowledge of products, product uses, best practices, and other critical knowledge with employees, managers, customers, suppliers, and others who need it. Knowledge management is a process supported by the five components of an information system. By sharing knowledge, KM systems foster innovation, improve customer service, increase organizational responsiveness by getting products and services to market faster, and reduce costs.

Expert systems are the fourth category of BI system shown in Figure 8-7. Expert systems encapsulate the knowledge of human experts in the form of *If/Then* rules. In a medical diagnosis system, for example, an expert system might have a rule such as:

If Patient_Temperature > 103, *Then* Initiate High_Fever_Procedure

Figure 8-7
Characteristics and Competitive Advantage of BI Systems

Business Intelligence System	Characteristics	Competitive Advantage
Reporting Systems	Integrate and process data by sorting, grouping, summing, and formatting. Produce, administer, and deliver reports.	Improve decisions by providing relevant, accurate, and timely information to the right person.
Data-Mining Systems	Use sophisticated statistical techniques to find patterns and relationships.	Improve decisions by discovering patterns and relationships in data to predict future outcomes.
Knowledge Management Systems	Share knowledge of products, product uses, best practices, etc., among employees, managers, customers, and others.	Improve decisions by publishing employee and others' knowledge. Create value from existing intellectual capital. Foster innovation, improve customer service, increase organizational responsiveness, and reduce costs.
Expert Systems	Encode human knowledge in the form of If/Then rules and process those rules to make a diagnosis or recommendation.	Improve decision making by non-experts by encoding, saving, and processing expert knowledge.

Operational expert systems can have hundreds or even thousands of such rules. While few expert systems have demonstrated a capability equivalent to a human expert, some are good enough to considerably improve the diagnosis and decision making of non-experts.

As with all information systems, it is important to distinguish between business intelligence tools and business intelligence systems. Business Objects licenses the reporting tool Crystal Reports. SPSS licenses the data-mining suite Clementine, and Microsoft offers SharePoint Server as, in part, a knowledge-management system. All these products are, however, just software. They represent only one of the five components.

To gain the promise of improved decision making, organizations must incorporate data-mining products into complete information systems. A reporting tool can generate a report showing that a customer has cancelled an important order. It takes a reporting *system,* however, to alert the customer's salesperson to this unwanted news in time for the salesperson to attempt to reverse the decision. Similarly, a data-mining tool can create an equation that computes the probability that a customer will default on a loan. A data-mining *system,* however, uses that equation to enable banking personnel to approve or reject a loan on the spot.

Q5 What Are the Purpose and Components of a Data Warehouse?

The purpose of a **data warehouse** is to extract and clean data from operational systems and other sources, and to store and catalogue that data for processing by BI tools. Figure 8-8 shows the basic components of a data warehouse.

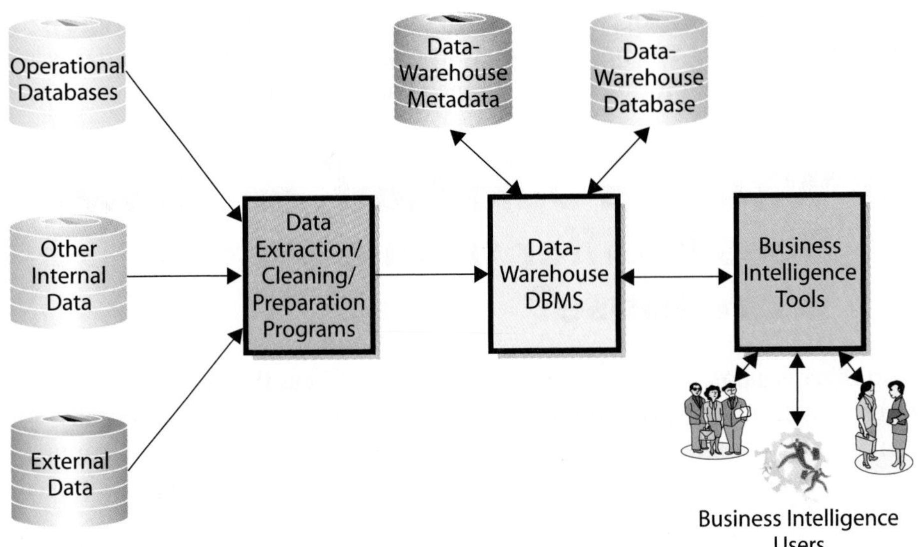

Figure 8-8
Components of a Data Warehouse

Programs read operational data and extract, clean, and prepare that data for BI processing. The prepared data are stored in a data-warehouse database using a data-warehouse DBMS, which can be different from the organization's operational DBMS. For example, an organization might use Oracle for its operational processing, but use SQL Server for its data warehouse. Other organizations use SQL Server for operational processing, but use a DBMS from statistical package vendors, such as SAS or SPSS, in the data warehouse.

Data warehouses include data that are purchased from outside sources. A typical example is customer credit data. Figure 8-9 lists some of the consumer data that can be purchased from commercial vendors today. An amazing (and, from a privacy standpoint, frightening) amount of data is available.

Metadata is data about data. For example, a database might store not only data but also data about the source of the data, the format of the data, and other facts about the data. This type of data is stored as metadata in the data warehouse. The DBMS that runs the data warehouse can be used to extract information, and provides data to business intelligence tools such as data-mining programs.

By the way, do not interpret the term *warehouse* literally. It's a warehouse only in the sense that it's a facility for storing data for use by others. It is *not* a large building with shelves and forklifts buzzing through aisles loaded with pallets. Physically, a data warehouse consists of a few fast computers with very large storage devices. The data warehouse is usually staffed by a small department consisting of both technical personnel and business analysts. The technical

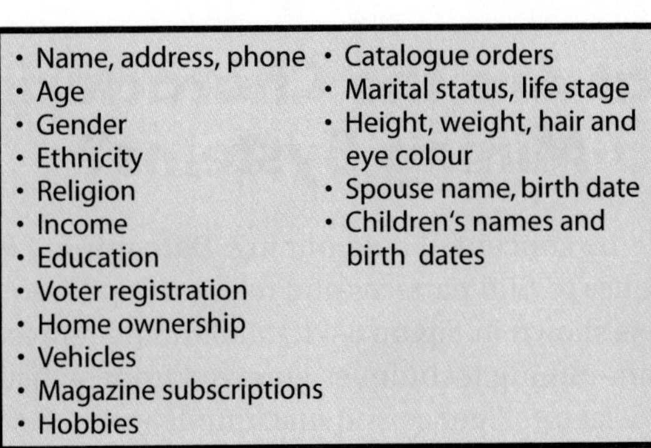

Figure 8-9
Consumer Data Available for Purchase from Data Vendors

personnel work to develop the best ways of storing and cataloguing the data warehouse's contents. The business analysts work to ensure that the contents are relevant and sufficient for the business needs of BI system users.

Q6 What Is a Data Mart, and How Does It Differ from a Data Warehouse?

A **data mart** is a data collection that is created to address the needs of a particular business function, problem, or opportunity. An e-commerce company, for example, might create a data mart storing clickstream data that are presampled and summarized in such a way as to enable the analysis of web page design features.

That same company might have a second data mart for market-basket analysis. This second data mart would contain records of past sales data organized to facilitate the computation of item–purchase correlations. A third data mart could contain inventory data and be organized to support a BI system used to plan the layout of inventory.

So how is a data warehouse different from a data mart? In a way, you can think of a *data warehouse* as a distributor in a supply chain. The data warehouse takes data from the data manufacturers (operational systems and purchased data), cleans and processes the data, and locates the data on its shelves, so to speak—that is, on the disks of the data warehouse computers. The people who work with a data warehouse are experts at data management, data cleaning, data transformation, and the like. However, they are not usually experts in a given business function.

As stated, a *data mart* is a data collection, smaller than the data warehouse, that addresses a particular component or functional area of the business. If the data warehouse is the distributor in a supply chain, then a data mart is like a retail store in a supply chain. Users in the data mart obtain data from the data warehouse that pertain to a particular business function. Such users do not have the data management expertise that data warehouse employees have, but they are knowledgeable analysts for a given business function. Figure 8-10 illustrates these relationships.

As you can imagine, it is expensive to create, staff, and operate data warehouses and data marts. Only large organizations with deep pockets can afford to operate a system like that shown in Figure 8-10. Smaller organizations operate subsets of this system; they may have just a simple data mart for analyzing promotion data, for example.

Q7 What Are the Characteristics of Data-Mining Systems?

We now return to the concept of data mining. **Data mining** is the application of statistical techniques to find patterns and relationships among data and to classify and predict. As shown in Figure 8-11, data mining represents a convergence of disciplines. Data-mining techniques emerged from statistics and mathematics and from artificial intelligence and machine-learning fields in computer science. As a result, data-mining terminology is an odd blend of terms from these

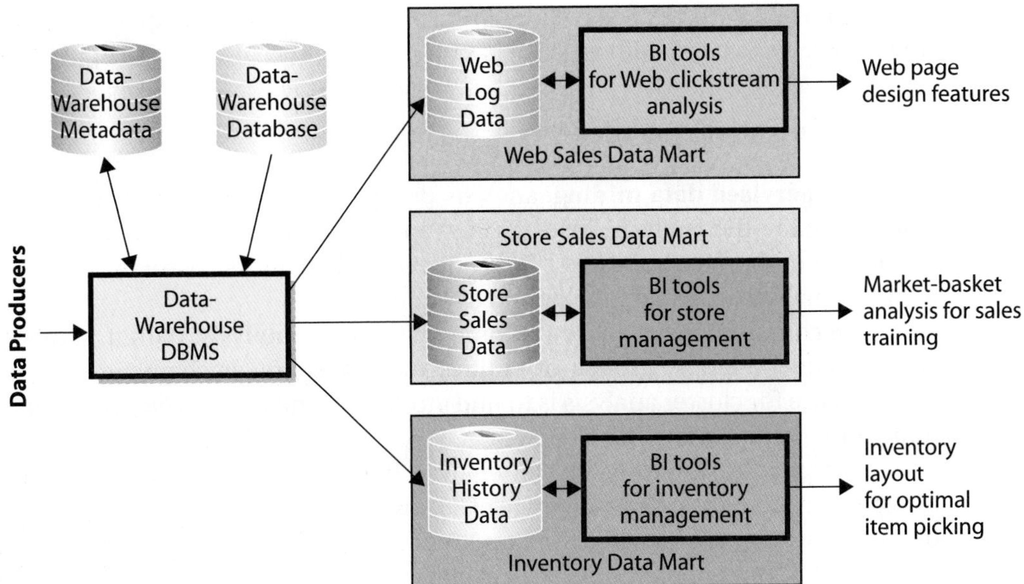

Figure 8-10
Data Mart Examples

different disciplines. Sometimes people use the term *knowledge discovery in databases* (*KDD*) as a synonym for *data mining*.

Data-mining techniques take advantage of developments in data management for processing the enormous databases that have emerged in the last 10 years. Of course, these data would not have been generated were it not for fast and cheap computers—and without such computers, the new techniques would be impossible to compute.

Most data-mining techniques are sophisticated, and many are difficult to use as well. Such techniques are valuable to organizations, however, and some business professionals, especially those in finance and marketing, have become expert in their use. Today, in fact, there are many interesting and rewarding careers for business professionals who are knowledgeable about data-mining techniques. It is important to recognize that data mining has limitations, which we discuss in the Exercise "Data Mining in the Real World" provided at the end of this chapter.

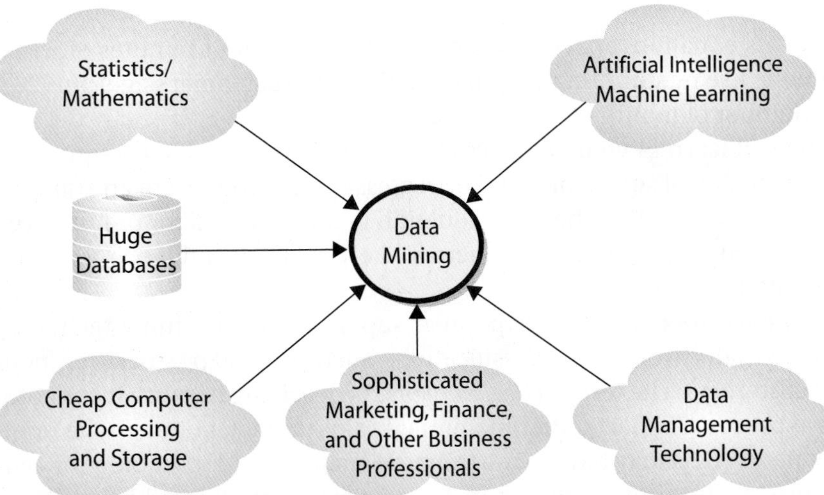

Figure 8-11
Convergence Disciplines for Data Mining

Data-mining techniques fall into two broad categories: unsupervised and supervised. We explain both types below.

Unsupervised Data Mining

With **unsupervised data mining**, analysts do not create a model or hypothesis before running the analysis. Instead, they apply the data-mining technique to the data and observe the results. With this method, analysts create hypotheses after the analysis to explain the patterns found.

One common unsupervised technique is **cluster analysis**. With it, statistical techniques identify groups of entities that have similar characteristics. A common use for cluster analysis is to find groups of similar customers from customer order and demographic data.

For example, suppose a cluster analysis finds two very different customer groups: One group has an average age of 33, owns at least one laptop and at least one PDA, drives an expensive SUV, and tends to buy expensive children's play equipment. The second group has an average age of 64, owns vacation property, plays golf, and buys expensive wines. Suppose the analysis also finds that both groups buy designer children's clothing.

These findings are obtained solely by data analysis. There is no prior model about the patterns and relationships that exist. It is up to the analyst to form hypotheses, after the fact, to explain why two such different groups are both buying designer children's clothes.

Supervised Data Mining

With **supervised data mining**, data miners develop a model prior to the analysis and apply statistical techniques to data to estimate parameters of the model. For example, suppose marketing experts in a communications company believe that cell phone usage on weekends is determined by the age of the customer and the number of months the customer has had the cell phone account. A data-mining analyst would then run an analysis that estimates the impact of customer and account age. One such analysis, which measures the impact of a set of variables on another variable, is called a **regression analysis**. A sample result for the cell phone example is:

```
CellPhoneWeekendMinutes =
12 + (17.5 * CustomerAge) + (23.7 * NumberMonthsOfAccount)
```

Using this equation, analysts can predict the number of minutes of weekend cell phone use by summing 12, plus 17.5 times the customer's age, plus 23.7 times the number of months of the account.

As you will learn in your statistics classes, considerable skill is required to interpret the quality of such a model. The regression tool will create an equation such as the one shown. Whether that equation is a good predictor of future cell phone usage depends on statistical factors like t values, confidence intervals, and related statistical techniques.

Neural networks are another popular supervised data-mining technique used to predict values and make classifications, such as "good prospect" or "poor prospect" customers. The term *neural networks* is deceiving because it connotes a biological process similar to that in animal brains. In fact, although the original *idea* of neural nets may have come from the anatomy and physiology of neurons, a neural net is nothing more than a complicated set of possibly nonlinear equations. Explaining the techniques used for neural networks is beyond the scope of this text. If you want to learn more, search KDnuggets.com for the term "neural network."

How does the knowledge in this chapter help you at DSI?

You're still seeking an IS that will provide higher labour productivity for DSI. Your most recent idea has been to focus on a system that would analyze past supplier performance in order to help DSI select suppliers. Using the knowledge in this chapter, you can describe four categories of possible information systems and describe, at least at a high level, the advantages and disadvantages of each.

A reporting system would process the data about past suppliers, the products they've supplied, and the timeliness of component delivery. If quality data are kept in the manufacturing systems, the reporting system can process those data to rank supplier quality.

A data-mining system would search for patterns and relationships for predicting future events. You could use such a system to predict the likelihood of a delivery delay or of a quality problem. Knowledge-management systems enable humans to share their knowledge, and you might be able to construct one that would enable buyers and manufacturing managers to rank suppliers or to share their experiences working with suppliers.

Finally, you could conceivably build an expert system containing rules for selecting a supplier, given a component or part need. Anticipating questions Mr. Stratford might ask, you probably should also describe the advantages and disadvantages of each.

In addition to these systems, you might also consider a data warehouse or data mart. DSI is probably too small for a data warehouse, but it might make sense for it to gather in-bound logistics and manufacturing data into some type of data mart. Doing so would facilitate not only the selection of suppliers, but also the process of creating a bid.

Once you have all this analysis, what should you do with it? Which of the systems you've investigated should you recommend for use at DSI? For answers to these questions, and to continue the story, you'll have to read Chapter 11. Meanwhile, answer the questions in the exercises that follow—answer them well, because . . . this could happen to you.

Active Review

Use this Active Review to verify that you understand the material in the chapter. You can read the entire chapter and then perform the tasks in this review, or you can read the material for just one question and perform the tasks in this review for that question before moving on to the next one.

Q1 What are the challenges managers face in making decisions?

Describe the factors, including information overload, uncertainty, and poor data quality, that make management decision making challenging. Explain how information systems have the potential to meet some of these challenges.

Q2 What is OLTP and how does it support decision making?

Explain why information systems are a critical component for capturing details about transactions. Explain how online transaction processing (OLTP) can be used to support decision making.

Q3 What are OLAP and the data resource challenge?

Explain what is meant by the term OLAP. What is the data resource challenge? Do you believe that information is a company asset? What does this have to do with viewing data as an asset?

Q4 How do BI systems provide competitive advantages?

Define *business intelligence systems.* Name four categories of BI systems, and describe the basic characteristics of each. Explain how systems in each category contribute to competitive advantage.

Q5 What are the purpose and components of a data warehouse?

State the purpose of a data warehouse. Explain the role of each component in Figure 8-8. Of the many different types of data that can be purchased, name five that you think are the most concerning from a privacy standpoint. State reasons why some businesses might want to purchase this data. Explain why the term *warehouse* is misleading.

Q6 What is a data mart, and how does it differ from a data warehouse?

Define *data mart,* and give an example of one not described in this chapter. Explain how data warehouses and data marts are like components of a supply chain. Under what conditions does an organization staff a data warehouse with several data marts?

Q7 What are the characteristics of data-mining systems?

State the purpose of data-mining systems. Explain how data mining emerged from the convergence of different disciplines. Describe the impact this history had on data-mining terminology. Explain the characteristics and uses of unsupervised data mining. Explain the characteristics and uses of supervised data mining. Explain why the term *neural network* is a misnomer.

Key Terms and Concepts

Business intelligence (BI) system 243
Clickstream data 237
Cluster analysis 248
Data marts 246
Data mining 246
Data resource challenge 238
Data warehouses 244
Data-mining system 243
Decision support systems (DSS) 239
Dirty data 236
Drill down 241
Exabyte 234
Expert systems 244
Granularity 237
Knowledge-management (KM) system 244
Market-basket analysis 244
Neural network 248
Onlineanalytic processing (OLAP) 239
Onlinetransactionprocessing (OLTP) 237

Petabyte 234
Regression analysis 248
Reporting systems 243
Supervised data mining 248
Unsupervised data mining 248

Using Your Knowledge

1. The data in Figure 8-2 are as of 2003. Using the trend of the years from 2000 to 2003, estimate the storage capacity sold during 2007. Search the web for an estimate of the same number. Compare your estimate to the size of all printed material (shown in Figure 8-1). Do you agree with the statement, "Today, disk storage is essentially free"? Describe two business opportunities that this trend creates. How does a site like YouTube benefit from this trend?

2. How does the data storage trend impact your university? What types of data are growing the fastest? Of the fast-growing data, what amount is generated by students? What amount is generated by classroom activities? What amount is generated by administration? What amount is generated by research?

3. OLTP systems are focused on providing three things: (1) efficient data input, (2) reliability, and (3) effective processing of a single transaction at a time. Use the knowledge you have gained to contrast these OLTP design principles with the design of OLAP systems. Do you see why the two types of systems require different designs?

4. Suppose you work for the university and have access to student, class, professor, department, and grade data. Suppose you want to determine whether grade inflation exists, and if so, where it seems to be the greatest. Describe a reporting system that would produce evidence of grade inflation. How would you structure the reports to determine where it is the greatest?

5. Suppose you work for the university and have access to student, class, professor, department, and grade data. Assume the student data include students' home address, high school, and prior postsecondary performance (if any). Describe an unsupervised data-mining technique that could be used to predict which applicants are likely to succeed academically. Is it responsible or irresponsible to use an unsupervised technique for such a problem?

6. Same as question 5, but describe a supervised data-mining technique that could be used to predict the success of applicants. Is using a supervised technique more justifiable than using an unsupervised technique? Explain your answer.

7. Explain how a set of If/Then rules could be used to select a supplier. Give an example of five rules that would be pertinent to this problem. Given the nature of DSI's product, and the size and culture of the organization, do you think it's likely that DSI would embrace an expert system? Consider Ms. Dorset's commentary at the start of Part 3 (page 198) as you formulate your answer.

8. Do you think a data warehouse is appropriate for DSI? Why or why not? Figure 8-10 implies that data marts require the existence of a data warehouse, but this is not always true. DSI could construct a data mart containing in-bound logistic and manufacturing data without a data warehouse. In this case, the data mart would need to clean and prep its own operational data. Given DSI's product and the nature of its business, what value might such a data mart provide? List seven decisions that such a data mart might support. Describe the BI system that would support each decision. Explain how such BI systems contribute to DSI's competitive strategy.

9. Summarize the four systems proposed for use at DSI. Compare and contrast the features and functions of each. Rate these systems on their ability to increase labour productivity. Which system would you choose to propose for DSI to use? Write a short (no more than one page) description of the alternatives, your analysis, and the rationale for your recommendation. Do you think your analysis demonstrates innovative thinking on ways to facilitate DSI's competitive strategy?

Case Study 8

Building Data for Decision Making at Home Depot

Home Depot is a major retail chain specializing in the sale of construction, home repair, and maintenance products. The company has more than 2000 retail stores in North America, from which it generated $81.5 billion in sales in 2005. Home Depot carries more than 40 000 products in its stores and employs 355 000 people worldwide.

Suppose you are a buyer for the clothes washer and dryer product line at Home Depot. You work with seven different brands and numerous models within each brand. One of your goals is to turn your inventory as many times a year as you can, and to do so you want to identify poorly selling models (and even brands) as quickly as you can. This identification is not as easy as you might think, because competition is intense among washer and dryer manufacturers and a new model can quickly capture a substantial portion of another model's market share. Thus, a big seller this year can be "a dog" (a poor seller) next year.

Another problem is that while some sales trends are national, others pertain to specific regions. A strong seller on the East Coast may not sell as well on the West Coast. In other words, a brand can be a big seller in one region and a dog in another.

In answering the following questions, assume you have total sales data for each brand and model, for each store, for each month. Assume also that you know the store's city and province.

Questions

1. Explain how reporting systems could be helpful to you.
2. Show the structure of one or two reports you could use to identify poorly selling models. How would you structure the reports to identify different sales trends in different regions?
3. For one of your reports in question 2, write a description of your requirements suitable for giving to an IT professional. Be as complete and thorough as you can in describing your needs.

4. Explain how data-mining systems could be helpful to you.
5. How could cluster analysis help you identify poorly selling brands? How could cluster analysis help you determine differences in sales for different geographic regions? Is the unsupervised nature of cluster analysis an advantage or a disadvantage for you?
6. How could regression analysis help you determine poorly selling brands?
7. Do you believe there is an application for a KM system for identifying poorly selling brands? Why or why not?
8. Do you believe there is an application for an expert system for identifying poorly selling brands? Why or why not?

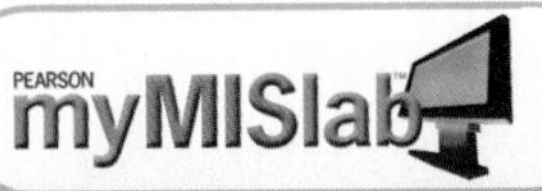

Visit MyMISLab at **www.pearsoned.ca/mymislab**. MyMISLab is a state-of-the-art, interactive, online solution that combines multimedia, tutorials, and quizzes. Use MyMISLab for *Experiencing MIS* to prepare for tests and exams, and go to class ready to learn!

What Do YOU Think?

Data Mining in the Real World

"I'm not really a contrarian about data mining. I believe in it. After all, it's my career. But data mining in the real world is a lot different from the way it's described in textbooks.

"There are many reasons it's different. One is that the data are always dirty, with missing values, values way out of the range of possibility, and time values that make no sense. Here's an example: Somebody sets the server system clock incorrectly and runs the server for a while with the wrong time. When they notice the mistake, they set the clock to the correct time. But all the transactions that were running during that interval have an ending time before the starting time. When we run the data analysis and compute elapsed time, the results are negative for those transactions.

"Missing values are a similar problem. Consider the records of just 10 purchases. Suppose that two of the records are missing the customer number and one is missing the year part of the transaction date. So you throw out three records, which is 30 percent of the data. You then notice that two more records have dirty data, and so you throw them out, too. Now you've lost half your data.

"Another problem is that you know the least when you start the study. So you work for a few months and learn that if you had another variable, say the customer's postal code, or age, or something else, you could do a much better analysis. But those other data just aren't available. Or, maybe they are available, but to get the data you have to reprocess millions of transactions, and you don't have the time or budget to do that.

"Overfitting is another problem, a huge one. I can build a model to fit any set of data you have. Give me 100 data points, and in a few minutes I can give you 100 different equations that will predict those 100 data points. With neural networks, you can create a model of any level of complexity you want, except that none of those equations will predict new cases with any accuracy at all. When using neural nets, you have to be very careful not to overfit the data.

"Then, too, data mining is about probabilities, not certainty. Bad luck happens. Say I build a model that predicts the probability that a customer will make a purchase. Using the model on new-customer data, I find three customers who have a .7 probability of buying something. That's a good number, well over a 50–50 chance, but it's still possible that none of them will buy. In fact, the probability that none of them will buy is $.3 \times .3 \times .3$, or .027, which is 2.7 percent.

"Now suppose I give the names of the three customers to a salesperson who calls on them, and sure enough, we have a stream of bad luck and none of them buys. This bad result doesn't mean the model is wrong. But what does the salesperson think? He thinks the model is worthless and that he can do better on his own. He tells his manager, who tells her associate, who tells the northeast region, and sure enough, the model has a bad reputation all across the company.

"Another problem is seasonality. Say all your training data are from the summer. Will your model be valid for the winter? Maybe, but maybe not. You might even know that it won't be valid for predicting winter sales, but if you don't have winter data, what do you do?

"When you start a data-mining project, you never know how it will turn out. I worked on one project for six months, and when we finished, I didn't think our model was any good. We had too many problems with data: wrong, dirty, and missing. There was no way we could know ahead of time that it would happen, but it did.

"When the time came to present the results to senior management, what could we do? How could we say we took six months of our time and substantial computer resources to create a bad model? We had a model, but I just didn't think it would make accurate predictions. I was a junior member of the team, and it wasn't for me to decide. I kept my mouth shut, but I never felt good about it."

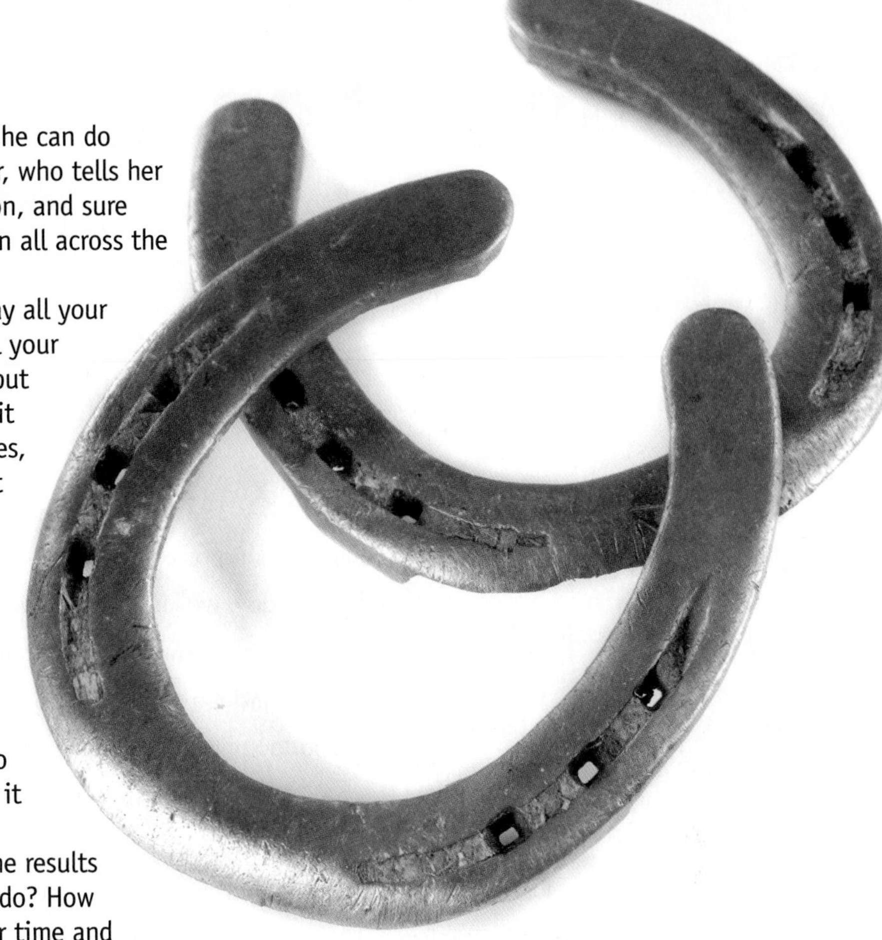

Discussion Questions

1. Did this employee have an ethical responsibility to speak up regarding his belief about the quality of the data-mining model? Why or why not?
2. If you were this employee, what would you have done?
3. The case doesn't indicate how the data-mining model was to be used. Suppose it was to be used at a hospital emergency room to predict the criticality of emergency cases. In this case, would you change your answers to questions 1 and 2? Why or why not?
4. Suppose the data-mining model was to be used to predict the likelihood of sales prospects responding to a promotional postal mailing. Say the cost of the mailing is $10 000 and will be paid by a marketing department having an annual budget of $25 million. Do your answers to questions 1 and 2 change for this situation? Why or why not?
5. If your answers are different for questions 3 and 4, explain why. If they are not different, explain why not.
6. Suppose you were this employee and you spoke to your direct boss about your misgivings. Your boss said, "Forget about it, junior." How would you respond?
7. Suppose your boss told you to forget about it, but in a meeting with your boss and your boss's boss, the senior manager asks what you think of the predictive ability of this model. How do you respond?

9 Information Systems Strategy, Governance, and Ethics

This
could happen
to you

You're working as an intern at DSI, and you're competing for a full-time job. One day, walking back to your desk to eat your sack lunch, you walk past a window overlooking the parking lot and see Mr. Stratford, his sister, and the niece-intern against whom you are competing. They are chatting together as they get into Mr. Stratford's car.

"Aaah," you silently scream to yourself, "they're probably going for lunch."

You've lost your appetite for the tuna sandwich in your brown bag, and you decide to focus even harder on an innovative IS to increase labour productivity.

DSI designs and builds Boeing 737 interiors. It specializes in high-quality, head-of-state-calibre fit and finish. The company does not make aluminum, nor does it cut and bend aluminum into needed shapes. Further, it doesn't manufacture fabrics, carpets, furniture, air filtration systems, or other components. Instead, DSI relies on other companies for those products.

Thus, DSI relies on an efficient supply chain to obtain needed components and materials. It follows, then, that the DSI business processes and the information systems that support those supply chain processes would be of the highest strategic importance in the organization. Is there some way to use cross-organizational information systems to gain labour productivity? You developed two interesting possibilities for new systems within the firm in Chapter 7. Those ideas were okay, maybe even good enough to propose, but is there some better system that might be more strategic?

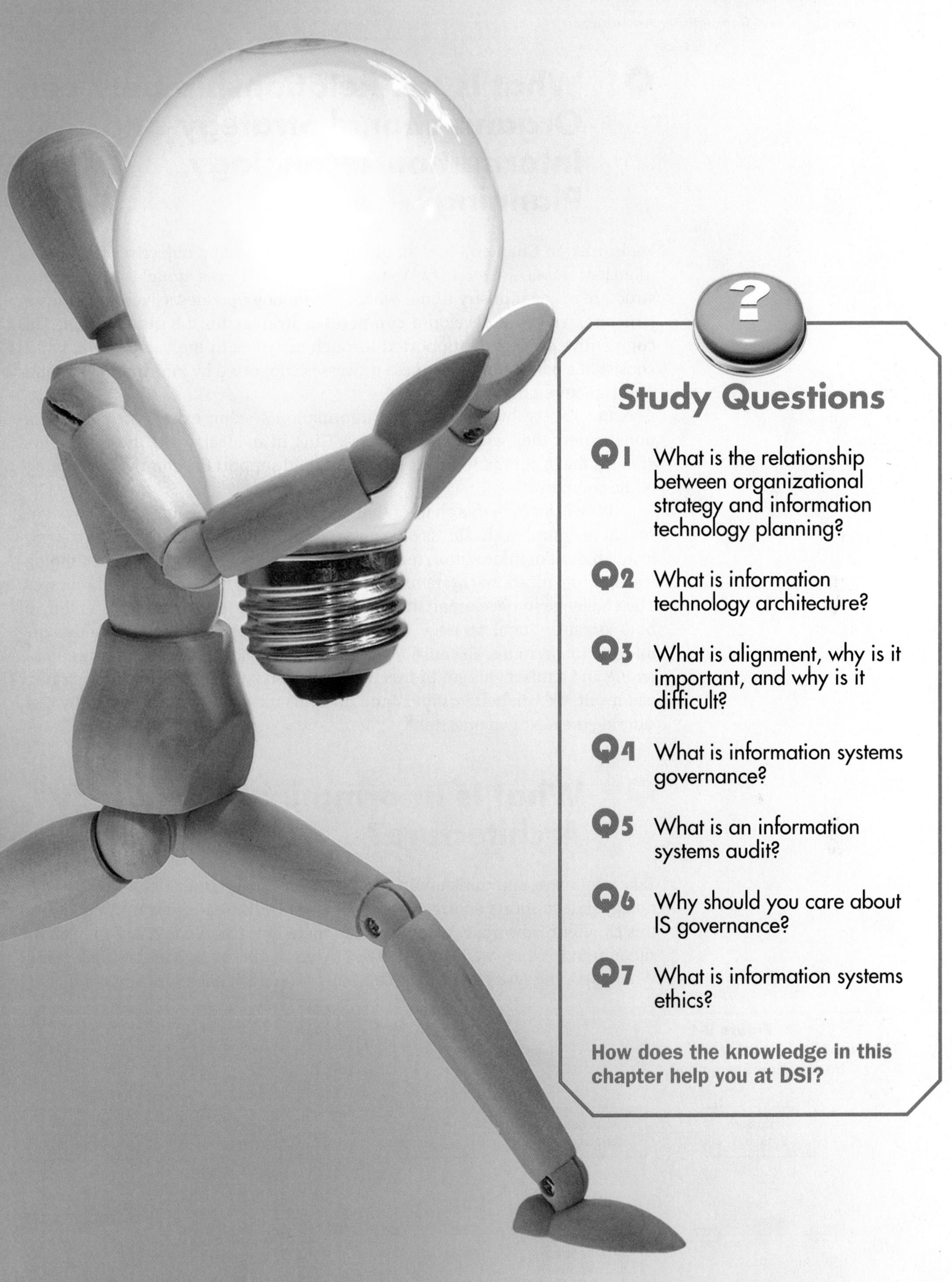

Study Questions

Q1 What is the relationship between organizational strategy and information technology planning?

Q2 What is information technology architecture?

Q3 What is alignment, why is it important, and why is it difficult?

Q4 What is information systems governance?

Q5 What is an information systems audit?

Q6 Why should you care about IS governance?

Q7 What is information systems ethics?

How does the knowledge in this chapter help you at DSI?

Q1 What Is the Relationship between Organizational Strategy and Information Technology Planning?

We learned in Chapter 3 that an organization's goals and objectives help determine its competitive strategy. We used Porter's five forces model to consider the structure of the industry under which a company operates. Given the industry structure, we could develop a **competitive strategy** for the organization. This competitive strategy is supported through activities in the value chain, which consist of a collection of business processes supported by information systems. This is pictured in Figure 9-1.

In Chapter 2 we learned that information systems exist to help organizations achieve their goals and objectives. Thus, in an ideal world, the information systems that a company chooses to use should support the competitive strategy of the company.

We will learn in this chapter that effectively managing information systems so that they support business objectives is a difficult process. It requires a significant amount of information technology planning that includes how technological and organizational systems should be acquired, maintained, and renewed. The challenge in developing these plans is that it requires an understanding of both organizational strategy and the technological architecture underlying information systems. Because it's challenging, organizations sometimes get it wrong and a misalignment between information systems and business strategy can result. We will better understand how this misalignment can occur by considering the next two questions.

Q2 What Is Information Technology Architecture?

Take a moment and think about what is involved with understanding the technology that supports an organization such as DSI (used in our introduction to this chapter). How many computers are there in the company? Are they all the same brand? When were they bought? What operating system are they using? What operating systems does the company support? What applications are being

Figure 9-1
Organizational Strategy and Information Systems

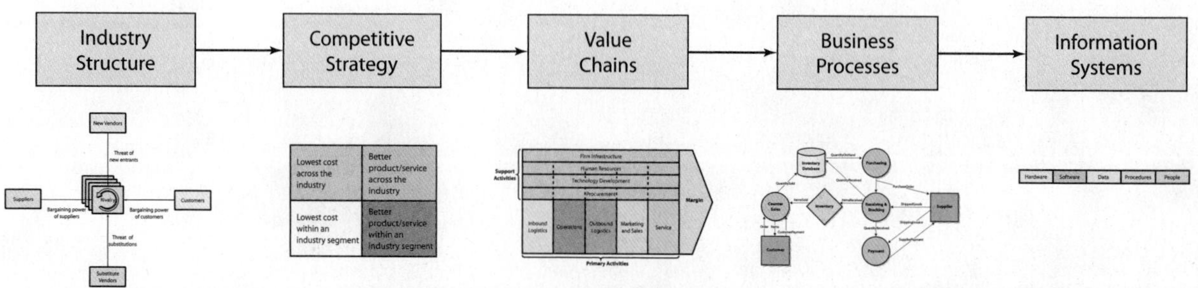

run by the company? What software is installed legally on desktops? Who purchased the software? What company is supporting the software if there are bugs or other problems? What networks are the computers connected to? Is the company limiting Internet addresses to and from computers within the company? If so, who is monitoring it? What email package is the company using? What is the company's policy regarding spam? What are the privacy and security policies the company uses? When is the company upgrading machines, software licences, network protocols? Does the company support wireless access? If so, what levels of access and where? The questions can go on, and on, and on. . . .

An **IT architecture** is like a plan for a city that lays out the street network, the water system, and the power grids. It is the basic framework for all the computers, systems, and information management that support organizational services. The complexity in a company's information systems continues to increase rapidly. In response, some organizations have created a new job description, the **enterprise architect,** to describe people who do this work. One example of an organization supporting enterprise architects is at www.ewita.com.

The job of the enterprise architect is to create a blueprint of an organization's information systems and the management of these systems. The blueprint should provide an overview that helps people in the organization better understand current investments in technology and plan for changes. In developing the architecture, the enterprise architect usually considers organizational objectives, business processes, databases, information flows, operating systems, applications and software, and supporting technology.

So what does an IT architecture look like?[1] The first thing to note is that there are few standards, because companies and systems are so diverse that it's hard to develop a standard. An architecture is usually a long document with many sections that includes some pretty complicated diagrams (see footnote) as well as management policies (such as privacy, sourcing, and security) and discussion of future changes to the architecture.

Since the development of an IT architecture is complex, it's often helpful to use a method that organizes the development. One of the most popular methods remains the **Zachman framework,** conceived by John Zachman at IBM in the 1980s. The framework divides systems into two dimensions: one is based on six reasons for communication (what—data, how—function, where—network, who—people, when—time, why—motivation), and the other is based on stakeholder groups (Planner, Owner, Designer, Builder, Implementer, and Worker). The intersection of these two dimensions helps provide a relatively holistic view of the enterprise. An example from the Zachman Institute of Framework Advancement (www.zifa.com) is provided in Figure 9-2.

While it may sound boring to some people, the development of an enterprise architecture is a significant undertaking that is often of strategic importance to the organization. It is not uncommon for enterprise architecture projects in large firms to involve dozens of people and to last for several years.

Defining the architecture is the first step in understanding how information systems support business objectives. As a future employee, you should carefully consider getting involved in discussions about enterprise architecture. They are a great opportunity to better understand how the company currently works and how the company will have to change in order to work even more effectively.

1. A number of graphic models of enterprise architectures can be viewed on the web. Examples include an enterprise modelling process (www.enterpriseunifiedprocess.com/essays/enterpriseArchitecture.html); an enterprise model for a laboratory (www.lbl.gov/CIO/Architecture); and an architecture developed using the Zachman method (www.zifa.com).

Figure 9-2 A Framework of Enterprise Architecture

Layer	What? Data	How Function?	Where? Network	Who? People	When? Time	Why? Motivation
Planner	List of important things for business	List of business processes	List of where enterprise operates	List of business functional units	List of business events and cycle	List of business Goals and Strategies
Owner	Entity Relationship Model					
Builder	Normalized Data Model					
Implementer	Relational Data Model					
Worker	Input Screens					

Moving down provides higher levels of detail

Moving across shows different perspectives on systems

This knowledge is often very valuable regardless of where you work, so try not to run too fast when you hear the architects coming your way.

Q3 What Is Alignment, Why Is It Important, and Why Is It Difficult?

The process of matching organizational objectives with IT architecture is often referred to as **alignment,** but the term has been somewhat difficult to define. MIS researchers have suggested that alignment should be viewed as an ongoing process—meaning that fitting IT architecture to business objectives is a challenge that continually evolves. The alignment process works to take advantage of IT capabilities as they develop while at the same time maintaining a balance between business objectives and IT architecture. What is important to recognize is that what works for one organization as a balance may not work for another, since alignment depends on business goals, the organizational context, and the state of IT architecture in an organization.

Matching investments in information technology with organizational strategy is not as straightforward as it may seem. Take the example of Wal-Mart, the largest retailer in the world. Customers know that when they shop at Wal-Mart they are getting the goods they buy at low prices. Wal-Mart has been very successful in maintaining a competitive strategy based on being a low-price retailer, which means maintaining lower costs than industry average. So, if Wal-Mart is focused on maintaining low cost, one might think that aligning information technology objectives with this strategy would see Wal-Mart spending less on information technology than the industry average.

In fact, just the opposite is true. Wal-Mart spends more than the industry average on information technology. Why? Because over several decades Wal-Mart has developed a sophisticated network of information technology applications that allows the company to collect and share vast amounts of enterprise information throughout the organization. Access to these data allows Wal-Mart employees and suppliers to make more effective decisions and to operate more efficiently. Wal-Mart is very much a high-technology company that has found success as a low-cost retailer.

It is clear that supporting business objectives with appropriate IT investments remains a critical part of IT management. For example, Chan, Sabherwal, and Thatcher (2006)[2] considered both the factors affecting alignment and the impact of alignment on perceived business performance. Results showed improvements in perceived performance when technology was aligned with some strategy objectives.

So if alignment is recognized as important, what makes it so difficult? Canadian researchers Reich and Benbasat (1996)[3] first measured alignment as the degree to which the IT department's missions, objectives, and plans overlapped with the overall business missions, objectives, and plans. In a later paper, Reich and Benbasat (2000)[4] recognized the importance of the social dimension of alignment. Effective alignment occurred in organizations that had developed a climate supporting the sharing of domain knowledge and common business practices. The importance of the social dimension was confirmed in a recent summary article.[5]

Communication between business and IT executives is the most important indicator of alignment. Successful companies find ways to help share knowledge and frustrations between the IT department and the business functions. This shared knowledge can become a source of competitive advantage for firms because the firms are better able to align their IT investments with the overall business objectives.

Alignment remains a difficult issue for many firms, but one that can help provide competitive advantage for those firms willing to make the investment in developing communication and sharing knowledge.

Q4 What Is Information Systems Governance?

Governance has become a popular word in the field of information systems. The term suggests that some committee or political party has the ability to decide on expectations for performance, to authorize appropriate resources and power to meet expectations, and perhaps eventually to verify whether expectations have been met. In publicly traded organizations, one purpose of governance is to ensure, on behalf of the firm's shareholders, that an organization produces good results while working to avoid bad results.

For business organizations, governance is often designed to work toward the development of consistent, cohesive management policies and verifiable internal processes. Managing at a corporate level often involves establishing the way in which boards oversee a corporation, and establishing the rules that apply to issues such as sourcing, privacy, security, and internal investments. The goal

2. Chan, Y., R. Sabherwal, and J. B. Thatcher, "Antecedents and Outcomes of Strategic IS Alignment: An Empirical Investigation," *IEEE Transactions on Engineering Management* 53, no. 1 (February 2006): 27–47.
3. Reich, B. H., and I. Benbasat, "Measuring the Linkage between Business and Information Technology Objectives," *MIS Quarterly* 20, no. 1 (March 1996): 55–81.
4. Reich, B. H., and I. Benbasat, "Factors That Influence the Social Dimension of Alignment between Business and Information Technology Objectives," *MIS Quarterly* 24, no. 1 (March 2000): 81–111.
5. Chan, Y. E. and Reich, B. H., "IT Alignment: What Have We Learned?" *Journal of Information Technology*, 4, 22, 2007: 297–315.

of IS governance is to improve the benefits of an organization's IT investment over time. Reporting structures and review processes can be established and can work over a period of time to improve quality, reduce service costs and delivery time, reduce IT risks, and better support business processes, as shown in Figure 9-3.

Information systems governance is a piece of organizational governance that is associated with information technology architecture. The increasing interest in information systems governance is likely a result of laws such as the **Sarbanes-Oxley (SOX) Act** in the U.S. and **Bill 198,** commonly known as the **Budget Measures Act,** in Canada. The laws act to force companies to comply with standards for collecting, reporting, and disclosing information.

The Sarbanes-Oxley Act and the Budget Measures Act

In recent years, legislation known as the Sarbanes-Oxley Act in the U.S. and the Budget Measures Act (or Bill 198) in Canada has impacted many information systems, particularly accounting information systems. The Sarbanes-Oxley Act of 2002 is a revision of the Exchange Act of 1934 that governs the reporting requirements of publicly held companies. Sarbanes-Oxley was enacted to prevent corporate frauds like those perpetrated by WorldCom, Enron, and others. Canada quickly introduced similar legislation in the form of Bill 198, commonly known as the Budget Measures Act. Its regulations increase the level of responsibility and accountability of executive management of publicly held Canadian companies in a fashion similar to that described in the SOX Act.

Both pieces of legislation require management to create internal controls sufficient to produce reliable financial statements and to protect the organization's assets. Management is further required to issue a statement indicating it has done so. The organization's external auditor must also issue an opinion on the quality of the internal controls and the credibility of management's statement. Bill 198 and SOX expose both management and the external auditor to financial and potential criminal liability if subsequent events show that internal controls were defective.

An example of an internal control is separation of duties and authorities. In an accounts payable system, for example, three separate individuals are required: one to authorize the expense, one to issue the cheque, and a third to

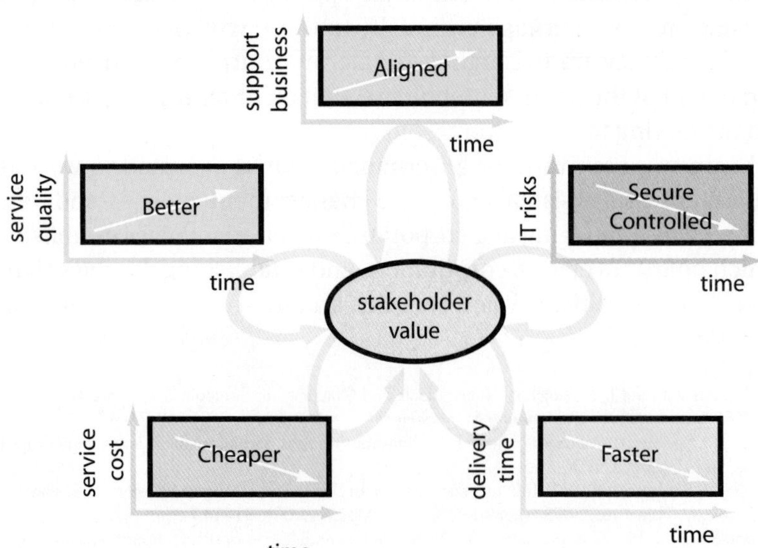

Figure 9-3
Creating Benefits from IT Governance

account for the transaction. No one person should perform two or more of these actions. You will learn about other such controls in your accounting classes.

If management is relying on computer-based accounting information systems for the preparation of financial statements—and all large organizations do—then those computer-based systems must have appropriate controls, and management must assert that those controls are reliable. This places a greater burden on the development and use of IS than was prevalent prior to these acts.

Additionally, IS can produce valuable assets that are subject to liability. For example, the database of an order-processing information system that stores customer identities and credit card data represents an organizational asset. If the design of the IS ineffectively prevents unauthorized persons from accessing that data, then a contingent (possible) liability exists. Without effective controls, someone could steal a customer's name and credit card data and damage the customer. The customer could then sue the organization, and likely prevail. Even if no one has yet sued, management is required both to report the liability in its financial statements and to take action to remedy the situation by eliminating the contingent liability.

Summary

A consistent message surrounding IS governance is that the IT function can no longer appear as a black box to the organization or to external stakeholders. In previous years, corporate boards have tended to leave key IT decisions to IT professionals. This often occurred because board members lacked expertise in the IT area. IS governance in the future will require that all stakeholders, including corporate board members, have input into important IS decisions. This may be a silver lining for some IT departments. They may no longer be blamed exclusively for poor decisions, and users will have fewer grounds to complain that systems did not perform as forecasted.

Q5 What Is an Information Systems Audit?

A financial audit can be defined as an examination and verification of a company's financial and accounting records and supporting documents by an accredited professional. In Canada, that could be a chartered accountant (CA), a certified management accountant (CMA), or a certified general account (CGA). A financial audit is closely related to the processes involved in financial governance of an organization.

The concept of an **information systems audit** is analogous to a financial audit. However, instead of financial and accounting records, the focus is placed on information resources that are used to collect, store, process, and retrieve information. Standards for information systems audits were first developed in the early 1970s and have been evolving with changes in technology. The recent increase in attention on IS governance has meant a greater focus on the IS audit and the establishment of methods for examining and verifying organizations' IS policies and procedures.

Many firms offer IS audit services. The **Information Systems Audit and Control Association (ISACA;** www.isaca.org) is an organization that was formed in 1969 by a group of individuals in charge of auditing controls for newly developed computer systems. The group has grown to more than 65 000 members in

2008 and has become a key organization in developing knowledge and standards relating to IT audit and IT governance. The **Certified Information Systems Auditor (CISA)** certification is recognized globally and has been earned by more than 50 000 professionals. Members have job titles like IS auditor, consultant, IS security professional, regulator, chief information officer, and internal auditor.[6]

In Canada, the Canadian Institute of Chartered Accountants (CICA) announced an agreement in 2007 with ISACA that recognizes the Certified Information Systems Auditor (CISA) designation developed by ISACA as the only designation that leads to recognition as a CA-designated specialist in information systems audit, control, and security. One of the developments provided by ISACA along with the IT Governance Institute (ITGI) is the **Control Objectives for Information and Related Technology (COBIT).** COBIT is a framework of best practices designed for IT management. The framework provides board members, managers, auditors, and IT users with a set of generally accepted measures, indicators, processes, and best practices to assist them in getting the best from their organizational IT investments.

The latest edition, COBIT 4,[7] was released in December 2005 and provides a set of tools and guidelines for establishing IT management practices. The COBIT control framework establishes links between strategic objectives and business requirements, organizes IT activities into a generally accepted process model, identifies the major IT resources in the organization, and defines the management control objectives to be considered. In establishing these foundations, COBIT can help link business goals to IT goals, providing metrics and maturity models to measure their achievement and identifying the associated responsibilities of business and IT process owners.

The simple translation is that COBIT provides a process through which alignment between IT and business objectives is developed. As noted earlier, processes such as COBIT alone are not likely to guarantee alignment; researchers have found that the ability to communicate and share knowledge across organizational boundaries remains an important determinant for successful alignment. IT auditing frameworks such as COBIT do, however, enable the organization to move in the right direction.

Q6 Why Should You Care about IS Governance?

Our discussion of IS governance and IS audit has shown the growing importance of information systems issues and operations across all business functions. The increased need to report and disclose IS operational information will require employees at all levels of an organization to become more familiar with the issues facing information technology management. While this familiarity comes at a cost, the increased exposure to IT issues should improve the ability of organizations to use information technology more effectively and efficiently. An argument can be made that the result of increased reporting compliance should be improved alignment between organizational strategy and business objectives. Since compliance issues will remain for the foreseeable future, business students across all functions will gain from increased knowledge of IT issues.

6. For those students interested, ISACA offers an inexpensive ($25 annual fee) student membership. You can find more details at the ISACA site (www.isaca.org) under the heading "Students and Educators."

7. For those interested in understanding more about COBIT, an executive summary of COBIT can be found at the ISACA site (www.isaca.org).

Case Study 9 at the end of this chapter, "Governance at Pacific Blue Cross," provides a glimpse of the importance of IS governance. If you're not yet convinced that you, as a general business major, need the knowledge of this MIS class, the advent of legislation such as the Sarbanes-Oxley Act and Bill 198 should convince you. As a senior manager, you will be required to make assertions about the controls on your IS that will expose you to both financial and criminal penalties. When that day arrives, it will be well worth knowing the fundamentals of IS. For a more critical review of the Sarbanes-Oxley Act, see *MIS in Use 9*.

Q7 What Is Information Systems Ethics?

In Part 3 of this book, we have discussed how organizations can gain a competitive advantage by achieving corporate objectives with the effective use of information technology. We understand that functional, cross-functional, and interorganizational systems help realize advantages by more efficiently or effectively handling business processes. We learned in Chapter 8 that the information we collect with our systems can be used to improve decision making and ultimately business performance. In Chapter 9, we have shown that aligning organizational objectives with information systems architecture provides further advantages by enabling organizations to more consistently realize these objectives.

It may seem as though there are few limits to the use of information technology and information systems in developing competitive advantage. But there are limits. For example, it may be against the law—and illegal behaviour would have legal consequences. Other important limits for future business students to recognize are those placed by ethical behaviour. Actions may not be illegal, but they may be unethical. It is important to understand the difference. The Exercises provided at the end of Chapters 2, 3, and 5 help to make this difference clear.

In previous chapters, some of our What Do YOU Think? exercises have focused on specific ethical issues. These exercises help you to establish the ethical boundaries that are comfortable for you. In this section, we address the issue of **information systems ethics** more generally.

It is important to note that information systems ethics is not about hardware or software, but rather the people involved with the system. Computers do not threaten our privacy; it is the people who will use our private information that create threats. Computers are great at manipulating logic, but a machine does not understand what it's doing. Machines are not people, so they have no sense of decency, nor have they established character, which is an important part of being human.

Advances in information technology bring new opportunities for individuals and organizations as well as new risks. As humans, we can choose to take advantage of technological innovation; however, we should be sensitive to the possibility of abusing these advances. Our concern should be placed on the people whose lives we can affect by our actions, and not on the computers that complete the actions.

Sarbanes-Oxley: Boon or Bane?

In 2002, in response to the corporate crimes committed by Enron, WorldCom, and others, the U.S. Congress passed the Sarbanes-Oxley Act. Its goal was to strengthen and upgrade financial reporting, and thus maintain and improve trust in public companies' financial reports. Such trust is crucial; without it, the investment community and the entire U.S. economy would come to a standstill.

CIO Magazine publishes articles of interest and importance to chief information officers (CIOs, discussed in Chapter 10). If you search for topics on Sarbanes-Oxley at www.CIO.com, you'll find a revealing sequence of articles. Initial articles reported confusion and concern among CIOs. Then articles appeared that explained how to comply.

Most recently, *CIO Magazine*'s editor, Gary Beach, published an editorial entitled "Repeal Sarbanes-Oxley." What happened? Surely no one is opposed to accurate financial reporting. According to Mr. Beach, " . . . while foreign companies are free to grab market share, U.S. executives are instead grabbing their Sarbanes-Oxley manuals" to learn how to comply with the act.[1]

According to a poll conducted by *CIO Magazine*, large companies expect to divert more than 15 percent of their IS budgets to Sarbanes-Oxley compliance. That represents a huge investment, but given the importance of a favourable audit report, it's an expense that organizations view as mandatory, whether or not it's sensible.

[1]Gary Beach, "Repeal Sarbanes-Oxley," *CIO*, April 1, 2005, *www.CIO.com* (accessed August 2006).

Part of the problem is that, even in 2008, no one knows exactly what's necessary in order to comply with Sarbanes-Oxley. The act requires external auditors to become even more independent than they had been in the past, and thus many will not issue opinions on the specific controls IS needs. The attitude seems to be, "Show us what you have, and we'll tell you if it's enough." IT managers are understandably frustrated. Further, the wording of the act is so vague that, to protect themselves, auditors have taken the broadest possible interpretation. Consider, for example, Section 409, which requires disclosure of significant financial events within 48 hours. What characterizes an event as significant? If a customer cancels a large order, is that significant? If so, how large must an order be before it's considered large? If a supplier is devastated by a hurricane, is that significant? "How," many CIOs ask, "can we determine from our information systems that a significant event has occurred? And within 48 hours? Are we supposed to reprogram our applications to include alerts on all such events? What other events should we look for? And who's paying for all this?"

One thing is certain—the Sarbanes-Oxley Act will provide full employment for internal auditors in general and for IT auditors in particular. Organizations will have to sponsor a flurry of activity, however uneconomic, to show that they are doing something to comply. No company can afford to ignore the act.

Senators Sarbanes and Oxley are both attorneys, neither of whom has ever worked in a publicly traded company. In light of the financial disasters at Enron and WorldCom, their law was highly praised by the public. But is it worth its cost?

Questions

1. In your opinion, will millions, perhaps billions of dollars be wasted in unnecessary compliance with Sarbanes-Oxley and the Budget Measures Act?
2. In the long run, will these acts hamper North American corporations that must compete internationally against corporations that are not burdened by them? Will they ultimately work to reduce investor choices?
3. Given the requirements of the Sarbanes-Oxley Act, do you believe that a privately owned company like DSI would have incentives to choose to become a public company?

Information systems ethics is not about detailing appropriate rules for our behaviour. The legal system develops rules of law and their enforcement. If we could put ethics into rule-based behaviour, then computers could control ethics. Instead, information systems ethics is about understanding our own behaviour—the way we think and act in situations where our choices affect others. We face a choice in ethical situations. These choices can be guided by principles. There are many examples of ethical principles: the United Nations Declaration of Human Rights, Canada's Charter of Rights and Freedoms, and the Association of Computing Machinery's code of ethics (www.acm.org/about/code-of-ethics) are three examples of sets of principles.

It is not our intention in this chapter to establish any set of principles for ethical behaviour relating to information systems. Our intention is rather to raise your awareness of the need to understand your own principles related to your use of information systems. When your actions can cause harm to others, you need to be aware of the harm you might cause and understand the principles you are working under in making your choice.

Whistleblowers have shown us that it is no longer acceptable to "do what your boss says" or "do what the system tells you" when it comes to ethical situations. It is up to you to establish the boundaries you are comfortable working within. Understanding your own personal principles is an important part of establishing your ethical behaviour. We invite you to test your principles using the What Do YOU Think? exercises provided at the end of Chapters 2, 3, 5, and 10.

How does the knowledge in this chapter help you at DSI?

We left you at the start of this chapter agonizing over your tuna sandwich and pondering information systems to increase labour productivity. Now, after considering the company's supply chain, you have come up with an interesting idea.

You've noticed that there is considerable moving of components in inventory. This movement costs time and can damage parts as they are being moved. Less movement would save the company a significant amount of money. But how can you reduce the amount of movement of inventory?

DSI receives components in the order in which the manufacturers and fabricators happen to produce and deliver them. For example, a large bulkhead that will be used late in the project might arrive early and need to be moved again and again in inventory as other components arrive. A possibility occurs to you. Why not use RFID tags to record the construction phase in which a component will be used? DSI could build an IS that would read the RFID tag as the component arrives and allocate that component to a location in the raw materials inventory that would minimize the subsequent moving of components. Such a system would not only save the labour of the movement, but also reduce the likelihood that components will be damaged while in inventory.

As you take the remains of your tuna sandwich to the trash, you glance out the window and notice that the car is still not back. You like the ideas you have so far, but you wonder if they are enough. Is there something more interesting than what you've got so far? Think about it . . . because this could happen to you!

It's important for business students to realize how information systems provide a competitive advantage. It's even more important for business students to realize what their unique competitive advantage is. We encourage you to explore your own personal competitive advantage by completing the Exercise at the end of this chapter (pages 272–273).

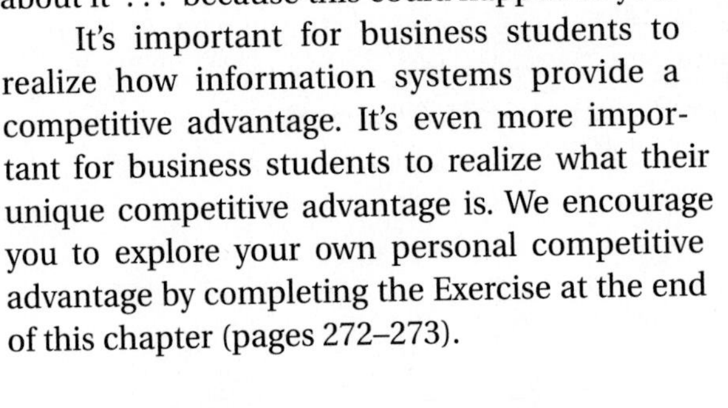

Active Review

Use this Active Review to verify that you understand the material in the chapter. You can read the entire chapter and then perform the tasks in this review, or you can read the material for just one question and perform the tasks in this review for that question before moving on to the next one.

Q1 What is the relationship between organizational strategy and information technology planning?

Explain how corporate strategy is linked to information system objectives. Can you explain why it is difficult to effectively manage information systems so that they support an organization's strategic objectives?

Q2 What is information technology architecture?

Why do organizations need an IT architecture? What is an enterprise architect? What does an IT architectural document look like? How can a method such as the Zachman framework support the development of an IT architecture?

Q3 What is alignment, why is it important, and why is it difficult?

Why do organizations have a difficult time aligning IT planning and organizational objectives? In what ways can you measure alignment? What factors make for improved alignment? When should organizations care about alignment and what can they do to improve it?

Q4 What is information systems governance?

What is governance? Why do organizations need governance? How does IT governance differ from financial governance? Why has IT governance increased in prominence only recently?

Q5 What is an information systems audit?

Why do companies need auditors? What do information systems auditors do? What organization supports information systems auditors? What is the designation for an IS auditor in Canada? What is the relationship between IS audit and IS governance?

Q6 Why should you care about IS governance?

Do you believe that IS governance is an issue that will affect many business people? Justify your answer.

Q7 What is information systems ethics?

Do you believe ethics is an important consideration in information systems? Can computers act unethically? What is the difference between illegal and unethical behaviour? Why is it important to understand your ethical behaviour?

Key Terms and Concepts

Alignment 260
Budget Measures Act 262
Bill 198 262
Certified Information Systems Auditor (CISA) 264
Competitive strategy 258
Control Objectives for Information and Related Technology (COBIT) 264
Enterprise architect 259
Governance 261
Information systems audit 263
Information Systems Audit and Control Association (ISACA) 263
Information systems ethics 265
IT architecture 259
Sarbanes-Oxley (SOX) Act 262
Zachman framework 259

Using Your Knowledge

1. Figure 9-1 shows the linkage between industry structure, competitive strategy, value chains, business processes, and information systems. The figure shows a logical progression, but we learned in the chapter that misalignment between strategy and information systems often occurs. In your opinion, where do things go wrong? How do organizations get out of alignment?

2. Do some research on the IT architecture at your university or college. Is there an IT architecture available on the web for your school? Is there an enterprise architect position? What IT architectural issues can you see developing in your university or college? Take a look at one of these issues and discuss how you would manage it.
3. Consider two car repair shops. Repair shop A is newly renovated and has a bright, clean reception/office area at the front of the shop and standard company overalls for all employees. Repair Shop A has just invested in a new computer application that integrates its parts ordering, repair, and service cost estimate and accounting. Next door, Repair Shop B has a small, dimly lit office at the rear of the shop crammed with notes and papers. The office looks as though it was last painted in the early 1960s. Repair Shop B has no computer and still runs on a paper-based system. When you ask the owners of the two repair shops, they both note that their company's strategic objectives are well aligned with their information technology planning and that each shop maintains a competitive advantage. How can this be true?
4. The goal of IS governance is to improve the benefits of an organization's IT investment over time. However, people who do governance usually do not work for a company but rather sit on a "board" that oversees the company's operations. What mechanisms can the people who sit on boards use to improve the benefits a company realizes from its IT investments? Use the web or other resources to provide some specific examples of techniques used by boards to improve the IT performance in a firm.
5. Explain how IS governance and IS audit are related. Can a firm complete an IS audit without having IS governance in place? Can IS governance exist without an IS audit?
6. The Zachman framework is explained in more detail at this site (www.zifa.com). Use this information and the Zachman framework to develop a diagram of your personal IT architecture. Remember to include all the technical support you would use (including resources and school as well as mobile devices).
7. COBIT is just one method for developing a document to support IT governance. List some reasons why companies would choose not to use COBIT for an information systems audit. Search the web for at least one other method, and develop a comparison between this method and COBIT. What are the benefits of using the new method? Can you suggest ways for improving COBIT?

Case Study 9

Governance at Pacific Blue Cross

The data on information systems projects almost speaks for itself. Although better than its 1994 survey results, the 2004 Standish Group (www.standishgroup.com) survey on information technology projects found that only 34 percent of these projects could be considered a success (on time, on budget, and delivering the desired benefits), 51 percent were "challenged" (delivered late, exceeded their budget, or lacked critical features and requirements), and a full 15 percent were out-and-out failures.

For Dr. Catherine Boivie, a large part of the solution begins with governance. Before joining Pacific Blue Cross (PBC)—British Columbia's leading provider of extended health and dental benefits—as chief information officer and senior vice-president, her impression of information technology projects was that while all of them were important to some aspect of the business, most information technology departments were kept busy constantly putting out fires.

Governance, says Dr. Boivie, simply deals with who makes which decisions and does not have to be complex; it consists of four iterative steps. First, identify the areas that require formal decision-making processes. Second, document how decisions are currently made, the people involved, and their role (that is, do they recommend, approve, or concur with the decision, or do they provide input or need to be notified). Third, use this information as input to a discussion of how decision processes could be improved. Fourth, develop a plan for implementing the new decision processes—including communication and buy-in with all affected parties.

Building on these ideas, Dr. Boivie's first action at PBC was to make certain that her two foundational principles—that technology has no value by itself, and that the technology management department must switch its focus from operations to business enablement—were shared by the chief executive officer. Once this was done and working through the governance stages, PBC implemented a process to ensure that all projects under consideration were evaluated using the same mechanism and criteria. Using a Balanced Scorecard approach, the strategic alignment, architecture, business process impact, direct payback, and risk of each project were measured against qualitative and quantitative perspectives and infrastructure, clients, people, and community-related goals.

The project approval process consists of five stages, or gates. The first stage, sometimes called the "Thumbs Up/Down" gate, requires sponsorship by a vice-president who presents the idea to the executive committee. If approved, the project proceeds to gate two, which requires a business case outlining the costs and benefits. Gates three and four are similar, but with minimum floors of $500 000 or $1 000 000 are considered very complex. Gate five is the post-implementation review, which verifies and validates the costs and attainment of the benefits previously described in the business case.

Ongoing project reports are provided to the executive committee and board of directors using an aptly named "Traffic-Light Report." This report visually identifies, with red, yellow, or green symbols, whether a project is on time, on budget, and on scope.

While Dr. Boivie does plan further enhancements, so far the process seems to be working. Business leaders have welcomed the new ideas and noted that it gives them enhanced visibility, a much better view of all projects, and greater control and accountability.

Questions

1. What are the various roles of decision participants at PBC?
2. How important is communication and buy-in to implementation of the new system?
3. Can you think of reasons why an organization would resist governance processes?
4. What challenges may exist in the system?
5. Are the foundational principles valid or reasonable? Why did Dr. Boivie make sure these were shared by the CEO?

Visit MyMISLab at **www.pearsoned.ca/mymislab**. MyMISLab is a state-of-the-art, interactive, online solution that combines multimedia, tutorials, and quizzes. Use MyMISLab for *Experiencing MIS* to prepare for tests and exams, and go to class ready to learn!

What Do YOU Think?

Your Personal Competitive Advantage

Consider the following possibility: You work hard, earning your degree in business, and you graduate only to discover that you cannot find a job in your area of study. You look for six weeks or so, but then you run out of money. In desperation, you take a job waiting tables at a local restaurant. Two years go by, the economy picks up, and the jobs you'd been looking for become available. Unfortunately, your degree is now two years old and you're competing with students who have just graduated with fresh degrees (and fresh knowledge). Two years of waiting tables, great as you are at it, does not appear to be good experience for the job you want. You're stuck in a nightmare—one that will be hard to get out of, and one that you cannot allow to happen.

Consider the elements of competitive advantage as they apply to you personally. As an employee, the skills and abilities you offer are your personal product. Examine the first three items in the list in Figure 3-7, and ask yourself, "How can I use my time in school—and in this MIS class, in particular—to create new skills, to enhance those I already have, and to differentiate my skills from the competition?" (By the way, you will enter a national/international market. Your competition is not just the students in your class; it's also students in classes in New York, British Columbia, China, Florida, Finland, and every place else they're teaching MIS today.)

Suppose you are interested in a sales job. Perhaps, like Dee (featured in previous chapter vignettes in this book), you want to sell in the pharmaceuticals industry. What skills can you learn from your MIS class that will make you more competitive as a future salesperson? Ask yourself, "How does the pharmaceuticals industry use MIS to gain competitive advantage?" Get on the Internet and find examples of the use of information systems in the pharmaceuticals industry. How does Parke-Davis, for example, use a customer information system to sell to doctors? How can your knowledge of such systems differentiate you from your competition for a job there? How does Parke-Davis use a knowledge management system? How does the firm keep track of drugs that have an adverse effect on each other?

What about buyers and suppliers? How can you interpret those elements in terms of your personal competitive advantage? Well, to lock in a job, you first need to have a working relationship. So do you have a co-op or internship? If not, can you get one? And once you have a co-op or internship, how can you use your knowledge of MIS to lock in your job so that you get a job offer? Does the company you're interning for have a CRM system (or any other information system that's important to the company)? If users are happy with the system, what characteristics make it worthwhile? Can you lock in a job by becoming an expert user of this system? Becoming an expert user will also raise barriers to entry for others who might be competing for the job. As well, can you suggest ways to improve the system, thus using your knowledge of the company and the system to lock in an extension of your job?

Human resources personnel say that networking is one of the most effective ways of finding a job. How can you use this class to establish alliances with other students? Does your class have a website? Is there an email list server for the students in your class? How can you use those facilities to develop job-seeking alliances with other students? Who in your class already has a job or an internship? Can any of those people provide hints or opportunities for finding a job?

Don't restrict your job search to your local area. Are there regions of your country where jobs are more plentiful? How can you find out about student organizations in those regions? Search the web for MIS classes in other cities, and make contact with students there. Find out what the hot opportunities are in other cities.

Finally, as you study MIS, think about how the knowledge you gain can help you save costs for your employers. Even more, see if you can build a case that an employer would actually save money by hiring you. The line of reasoning might be that, because of your knowledge of IS, you'll be able to facilitate cost savings that more than compensate for your salary.

In truth, few of the ideas you generate for a potential employer will be feasible or pragmatically useful. The fact that you're thinking creatively, however, will indicate to a potential employer that you have initiative and are grappling with the problems that real businesses have. As this course draws to a close, keep thinking about competitive advantage and strive to understand how the topics you study can help you accomplish, personally, one or more of the objectives you've set out for yourself.

Discussion Questions

1. Summarize the efforts you have taken thus far to build an employment record that will lead to job offers after graduation.
2. Describe one way in which you have a competitive advantage over your classmates. If you do not have such competitive advantage, describe actions you can take to obtain one.
3. In order to build your network, you can use your status as a student to approach business professionals. Namely, you can contact them for help with an assignment or for career guidance. For example, suppose you want to work in banking and you know that your local bank has a customer information system. You could call the bank manager and ask him or her how that system creates a competitive advantage for the bank. You also could ask to interview other employees. Describe two specific ways in which you can use your status as a student to build your network in this way.
4. Describe two ways you can use student alliances to obtain a job. How can you use information systems to build, maintain, and operate such alliances?

PART 4

Information Systems Management

This could happen to you

Emerson Pharmaceuticals (where Dee is creating her blog) and DSI (where you are an intern hoping to be hired on full time) are very different companies. Emerson is a multinational organization with a billion dollars in sales per year and with facilities, offices, and personnel throughout the world. Emerson Canada (its Canadian division) has 450 salespeople, plus thousands of other employees in labs, production facilities, and headquarters. DSI is a company with a single facility and an estimated $50 million in sales (as a private company, it does not release financial data). The total number of DSI employees is about half the number of sales people at Emerson.

Both Emerson and DSI use information systems, but they manage them very differently. Emerson Canada has more than 200 employees in its IT department, and it outsources several important functions to other vendors as well (we will learn more about outsourcing in Chapter 11). DSI has one employee in its "IT department" (and the day I interviewed him, I found him sitting on the floor repairing a computer).

In Part 4, we will consider how both companies develop information systems, how they manage their IT and IS resources, and how they protect their systems with security. Not surprisingly, the two companies take very different approaches to all three of these topics.

10 Understanding the IS Department: Operations and Projects

This
could happen
to you

Dee Clark created a blog for communicating to her sales force, and she wanted to restrict access to that blog to authorized Emerson personnel. The easiest way to protect her blog from outside eyes was to put it inside the corporate network, where the salespeople could access it using Emerson's VPN.

Of course, to place the blog software on an Emerson server, Dee needed the permission and help of the IT department. Dee didn't understand the IT department's mission and was surprised when she met substantial resistance. Her response was to use her manager's manager to bludgeon the IT department into submission. In the process, her management chain exposed Emerson to a large security risk: given his knowledge and experience, once Dee's consultant Don Gray was inside the system he could have played havoc with their internal information systems. Dee should have known about that risk. Even if she didn't know, her boss's boss ought to have known about it.

Dee's problems were compounded because she did not understand the IT department's responsibilities, nor did she know their problems and concerns. Consequently, she didn't know how to talk with them. Empathy was not Dee's strength, and with no knowledge of the responsibilities of the IT department she was unable to practise empathetic thinking when she made her request. Had she approached the IT department with knowledge of its concerns, she would have had a more supportive response and could have avoided exposing Emerson to such risk. This chapter will explain the organization and operation of typical IT departments. If you find yourself in the position Dee was, you will have the knowledge to interact with IT personnel in a more professional and effective way.

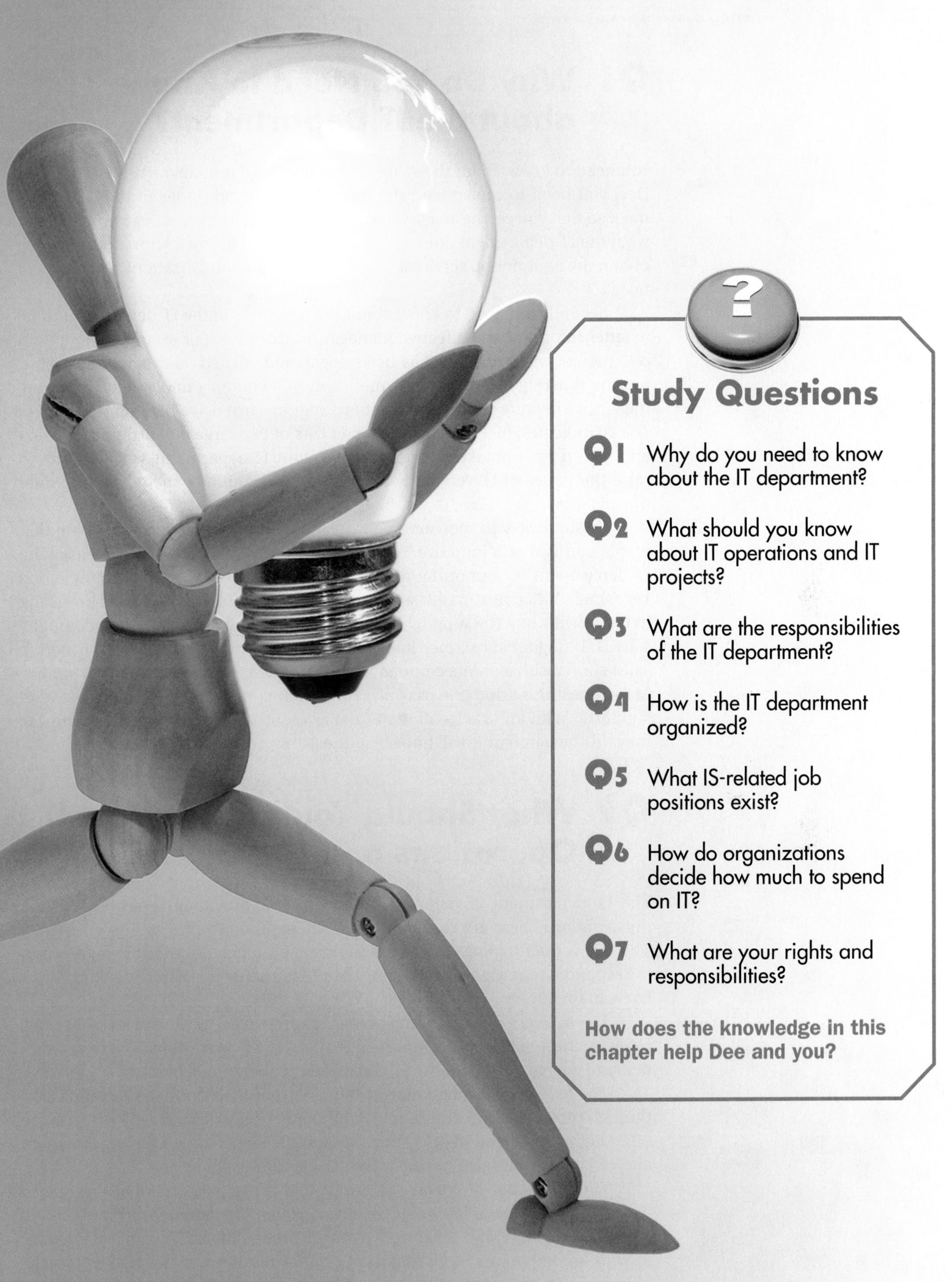

Study Questions

Q1 Why do you need to know about the IT department?

Q2 What should you know about IT operations and IT projects?

Q3 What are the responsibilities of the IT department?

Q4 How is the IT department organized?

Q5 What IS-related job positions exist?

Q6 How do organizations decide how much to spend on IT?

Q7 What are your rights and responsibilities?

How does the knowledge in this chapter help Dee and you?

Q1 Why Do You Need to Know about the IT Department?

You need to know about the IT department for two principal reasons. First, like Dee, you need to understand the responsibilities and duties of the IT department so that you can be an effective consumer of its resources. If you understand what the IT department does and how it is organized, you'll know better how to obtain the equipment, services, or systems you (and organizations you manage) need.

Second, you need to know about the functions of the IT department to be a better informed and effective manager or executive. For example, more than one merger or acquisition has been negotiated, signed, and planned without anyone thinking of the IT departments. As you can now understand, marrying the IT architecture of two organizations requires extensive planning. As *MIS in Use 10* indicates, just merging the email lists of two large organizations is a sizable task. If you understand the functions of the IT department, you will know to raise the issues of IT very early in any plan to acquire or merge with another organization.

Or suppose you sponsor a new business initiative, or work on a team that is sponsoring a new initiative. You need to know to think about the needs of the IT department in supporting that new initiative. Dee's blog is an example of a very small initiative. Instead, suppose you're working on a team to set up selling in teams with, say, the supplier of a companion product. Perhaps your company sells DSL (digital subscriber line) modems, and you're thinking of partnering sales efforts with a phone company that leases DSL lines to business customers. Many questions arise, one of which is, "Which company will provide customer support?" With knowledge of the IT department's functions, you'll know to ask how this new initiative will impact your existing customer support systems.

Q2 What Should You Know about IT Operations and IT Projects?

The IT department is generally responsible for providing IT services to the organization. There are two basic activities required to provide these services. The first is maintaining the current information technology infrastructure, and the second is renewing and adapting the infrastructure to keep IT working effectively in the future.

The delivery of service, maintenance, protection, and management of IT infrastructure is often accomplished as part of **IT operations.** These services demand a large portion of the IT department's operational budget.

The renewal and adaptation of IT infrastructure is normally accomplished through projects. **IT projects** come in all shapes and sizes. Large IT projects are often high-profile and high-cost changes to the status quo of the organization, and can often be funded outside of the IT operations budget.

The distinction between operations and projects is an important one to understand for several reasons. One reason is that operational work and project work tend to attract two different types of IT professionals. IT people who prefer to work in operations often seek to specialize more deeply in particular technologies. Networking specialists, operating systems specialists, database admin-

Cingular Wireless CIO Plans for Successes

SBC Communications and BellSouth merged in 2000 to form Cingular Wireless. In 2004, Cingular purchased AT&T Wireless, creating the largest U.S. wireless carrier, with more than 49 million customers and revenues in excess of $15.4 billion. A key player in the success of the activities was F. Thaddeus Arroyo, Cingular's CIO.

The CIO's first major challenge was blending the 1400 different information systems and 60 separate call centres that existed when Cingular was born. For example, there were 11 different and separated billing systems. Since then, Cingular has consolidated those 11 systems into one and has replaced the 60 call centres with 20 new ones.

Cross-functional teams composed of both users and IT personnel played key roles in the consolidation. According to Arroyo, the IT professionals did not choose the computer systems for the users, but instead consulted with the cross-functional teams to make decisions. Of course, business didn't stop during this integration; in fact, the wireless industry was expanding tremendously. Arroyo says, "During the growth period, we were rushing to keep the shelves stocked. . . . It exasperated the complex infrastructure we had to support."

To add complexity, in 2003, while the integration projects were underway, the U.S. Federal Communications Commission (FCC) created new regulations requiring the top 100 wireless companies to allow customers to keep their phone numbers when they changed carriers. The new regulation required Cingular to make major modifications to its billing and customer service applications—and to do so on short notice.

Even before the dust settled on that project, Cingular bought AT&T Wireless. Arroyo, as CIO, participated in months of merger preplanning involving more than 100 different and complex projects. For example, according to Arroyo, "The day after the deal was closed, over 70 000 employees were merged into one email directory. Also, we had to merge our corporate intranets within 24 hours of closing." The company needed to accomplish dozens of other, similar projects as well.

In light of his accomplishments, Arroyo has earned numerous industry awards. In 2004, the magazine *Business 2.0* selected him as a member of its "Dream Team." His keys to success in managing all these programs are to build strong teams, to work hard, and to "plan, plan, plan."

Sources: www.cingular.com/download/business_solutions_cio.pdf (accessed March 2005); Bruce E. Phillips, "Thaddeus Arroyo, Chief Information Officer, Cingular Wireless," January 13, 2005, www.hispanicengineer.com (accessed July 2005).

Questions

1. Discuss some of the difficulties associated with integrating information systems from different companies. Make use of the model of information systems we introduced in Chapter 1 that includes hardware, software, data, procedures, and people.
2. What characteristics do you think a successful CIO requires? Do you think technical skills are more important than non-technical (business and people) skills? Do you think a CIO needs to know about the technical side of systems?
3. How can a company be successful trying to complete so many projects? As a future employee, what are the skills you think Cingular would be looking for in its employees?

istrators, and hardware specialists are examples of these types of positions. Their jobs are to continually seek ways to improve the efficiency and security of the entire production system. Stability, predictability, accountability, reliability, and security are the key words in IT operations.

Other people in the IT department are responsible for changing the production system rather than maintaining it. These professionals work in IT projects. Because projects are temporary and often change existing infrastructure, projects generally require broad skills and challenge project team members to learn new technologies. Since several projects often operate at the same time, project team members may work on several projects simultaneously. This makes for an exciting (and, some would argue, hectic and chaotic) workday for many project team members. Since large IT projects are often funded outside of the IT department, IT projects often provide more opportunities for contact with project stakeholders (such as users, managers, and sponsors) in other departments.

Beyond the people involved, there are also differences in the core practices that IT professionals in IT operations and IT projects recognize. Within IT operations, the **Information Technology Infrastructure Library (ITIL)** is a well-recognized collection of books providing a framework of best-practice approaches to IT operations. ITIL offers a large set of management procedures that are designed to support businesses in achieving value from IT operations. Developed during the 1980s, ITIL has gone through several refreshes; core books from the latest refresh (ITIL v3) were published in June 2007. As business students, it is not important for you to know the details of ITIL. What is important is that you recognize that a well-developed set of best practices that can support IT operations has been established.

Within IT projects, the **project management body of knowledge (PMBOK),** developed by the project management institute (www.pmi.org), provides project managers, sponsors, and team leaders with a large array of accepted project management techniques and practices. The PMI offers a certification called the project management professional (PMP) that now has approximately 250 000 members.

It is important to note that while operations and IT projects are separate fields, they naturally rely on each other for success. Projects eventually end and must be maintained, and infrastructure eventually gets old and must be replaced. So there is always a natural balance between projects and operations within any IT department. This balance is shown in Figure 10-1.

Figure 10-1
What the IT Department Does

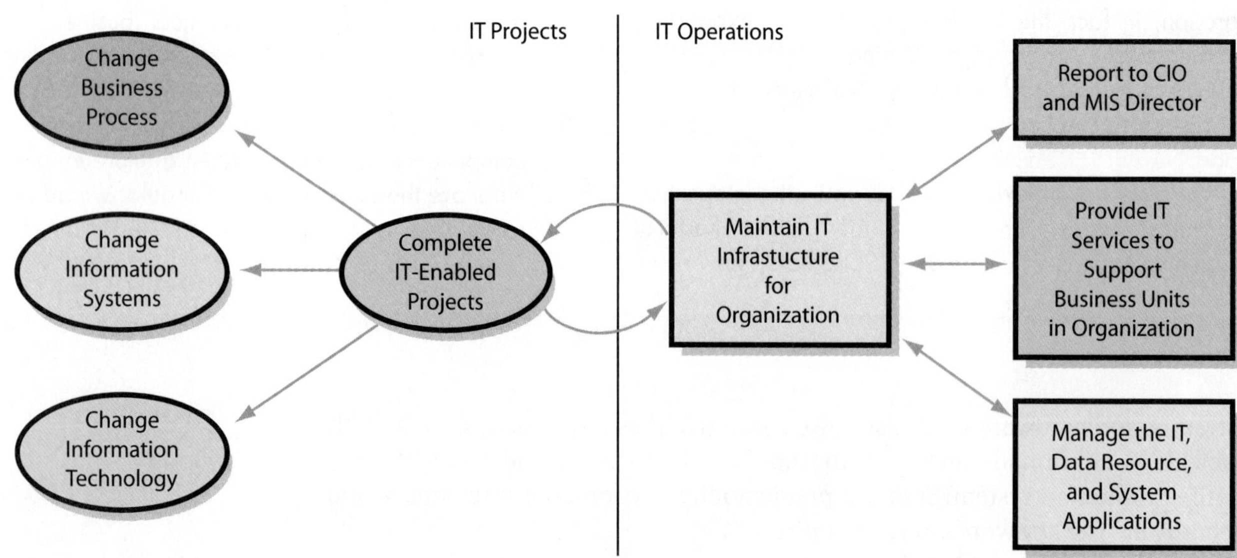

What about the Web?

In Chapter 6 we discussed how the web has become an important avenue for delivering IT services to both internal employees and external customers. Large and small IT departments use the web as a first step in many internal service requests. For example, when a new employee joins a company, many IT services need to be provided. The new employee will require a computer, which needs to be set up with software the company uses. The employee will need network access, which requires an ID and password, and also an email account. The employee may travel with a laptop computer, which requires a VPN connection provided by the IT department. The IT department also determines where the employee can print documents, and sometimes provides an access card so that the employee can get into the building. Where can all these services be accessed?

In many companies, the IT department has developed an intranet website with frequently asked questions (FAQs), web-based forms for requesting services, and some web-based applications that help support tasks such as adding a new employee. Your college or university likely has a site like this. The people working at the IT help desk, which is normally the front line of IT department services, often rely heavily on the intranet site to help support customer issues and requests.

Support for external customers, such as FAQs, customer support information, and company director and contact information, is likely to be available on the company's Internet site. The IT department is normally responsible for maintaining information about IT services on the company site. In addition, the IT department supports the company website itself, making sure the servers and applications that provide the website are up and running. The web therefore plays an increasingly important role in the delivery of IT services in many organizations.

Q3 What Are the Responsibilities of the IT Department?

Our previous discussion has suggested that two basic functions for the IT department exist:

1. Managing the information technology infrastructure to provide IT services, which requires
   a. Managing and protecting the information technology
   b. Managing and protecting the data resource
   c. Managing and protecting the system applications
2. Developing and adapting information systems and IT infrastructure.

These functions are discussed briefly below.

Managing the Information Technology Infrastructure

Information systems exist to further the organization's competitive strategy. IT departments therefore exist to facilitate business processes and improve decision making within the organization. The IT department supports these processes with IT services. The IT department has the responsibility of aligning its activities and services with the primary goals and objectives of the organization. As new technology emerges, the IT department is responsible for assessing that technology and determining if it can be used to advance the organization's goals. Furthermore, as the business changes, the IT department is responsible for adapting infrastructure and systems to the new business goals.

The responsibility for managing the information technology infrastructure and the services it provides is held in large organizations by the chief information officer (CIO) and the MIS director, as shown in Figure 10-1. To accomplish this, these managers often consider separately the impact on information technology (hardware, software, and networks), the data resource, and the system applications.

Managing and Protecting the Information Technology

IT infrastructure is not like the building's plumbing or wiring. You cannot install a network or a server and then forget it. IT infrastructure must be operated and maintained. Networks and servers need to be powered on, and they need to be monitored. From time to time, they need to be adjusted or **tuned** to changes in the workload. Components fail, and when they do the IT department is called upon to repair the problem.

To understand the importance of this function, consider what happens when a network fails. Users cannot connect to their local servers; they cannot run the information systems they need to perform their jobs. Users cannot connect with the Internet or send or receive email. Users may not even be able to reach their contact lists to find phone numbers to make telephone calls to explain why they are not responding. Truly, the business stops. And if (as with Emerson) information systems have been distributed to customers or suppliers, personnel in other businesses are impacted as well.

Because of the high cost and serious disruption of system outages, information systems personnel are particularly sensitive to possible threats to information technology. The Emerson IT personnel had every right to object to Dee's allowing a consultant to access their network. And, had the consultant done something to disrupt the network, the IT department would be accountable. Most of the company would judge the problem to have been an IT failure, even though Dee and her bosses were the true source of the problem.

Managing and Protecting the Data Resource

The IT department is also responsible for protecting data from threats. We will discuss threats and the safeguards against them in Chapter 12. For now, just understand that threats to data arise from three sources: human error and mistakes, malicious human activity, and natural events and disasters.

The IT department helps the organization manage risk. The department needs to identify potential threats, estimate both financial and other risks, and specify appropriate safeguards. Nothing is free, including safeguards, and indeed some safeguards are very expensive. The IT department in a large organization works with business units to determine what safeguards to implement—or, stated differently, what level of risk to assume.

Managing and Protecting the System Applications

Hardware and data are not the only assets the IT department is responsible for. The system applications, such as ERP, CRM, SCM, and many other functional and cross-functional applications, are also supported by the IT department. If the IT department has built an application, then it is involved in supporting the system. When an organization buys an application, for example an ERP from SAP, the IT department is not responsible for fixing bugs. That is SAP's job, and it's covered under a maintenance agreement that the organization signs with SAP. However, the IT department is often responsible for managing the system upgrades and for performing basic system maintenance relating to the system. The IT department may also monitor the installation of these systems to make sure proper licensing of the products has been provided.

Renewing the IT Infrastructure

The previous sections have described the responsibilities for IT operations within an IT department. The IT department is also charged with the responsibility to create, develop, and adapt the IT infrastructure to enable business projects to be completed.

This might include developing or modifying new system applications or adapting infrastructure—computer networks, servers, data centres, data warehouses, data marts, and other IT resources—to changes in business systems. The IT department is also charged with creating systems infrastructures, such as email systems, VPNs, instant messaging, blogs, net meetings, and any other IT-based infrastructure the company needs.

In most organizations, user departments pay for computers and related equipment out of their own budgets. However, because the IT department is responsible for maintaining that equipment and for connecting it to the organizational networks, the IT department will specify standard computer systems and configurations that it will support. The IT department is responsible for defining those specifications. Projects that go beyond this scope are usually funded through budgets provided by business functions outside of IT. Have another look at Figure 10-1 to develop your understanding about what a large IT department is responsible for in an organization.

Q4 How Is the IT Department Organized?

Figure 10-2 shows typical top-level reporting relationships. As you will learn in your management classes, organizational structure varies depending on the organization's size, culture, competitive environment, industry, and other factors. Larger organizations with independent divisions will have a group of senior executives like those shown here for each division. Smaller companies may combine some of these departments. Consider the structure in Figure 10-2 as a typical example.

The title of the principal manager of the IT department varies from organization to organization. A common title is **chief information officer (CIO)**. Other common titles are vice-president of information services, director of information services, and, less commonly, director of computer services.

In Figure 10-2, the CIO, like other senior executives, reports to the chief executive officer (CEO), though sometimes these executives report to the chief operating officer (COO), who in turn reports to the CEO. In some companies, the CIO reports to the chief financial officer (CFO). That reporting arrangement may make sense if the primary information systems support accounting and finance activities. In organizations such as manufacturers that operate significant nonaccounting information systems, the arrangement shown in Figure 10-2 is more common and effective.

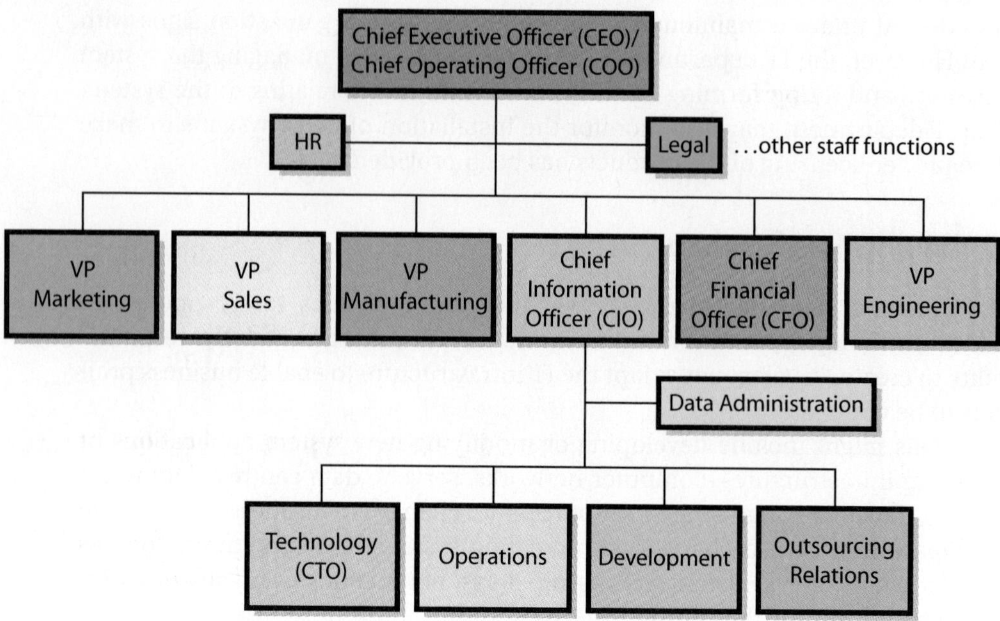

Figure 10-2
Typical Senior-Level Reporting Relationships

The structure of the IT department also varies among organizations. Figure 10-2 shows a typical IT department with four groups and a data administration staff function.

Most IT departments include a technology office that investigates new information systems technologies and determines how the organization can benefit from them. For example, today many organizations are investigating web services technology and planning how they can best use that technology to accomplish their goals and objectives. An individual called the **chief technology officer (CTO)** often heads the *technology* group. The CTO sorts through new ideas and products to identify those that are most relevant to the organization. The CTO's job requires deep knowledge of information technology and the ability to envision how new IT will affect the organization over time.

The next group in Figure 10-2, *operations,* manages the computing infrastructure, including individual computers, computer centres, networks, and communications media. This group includes system and network administrators. As you will learn, an important function for this group is to monitor user experience and respond to user problems.

The third group in the IT department in Figure 10-2 is *development.* This group manages projects that acquire new information systems as well as maintain existing information systems. (In Chapter 11 we will learn that, in the context of information systems, maintenance means either removing problems or adapting existing information systems to support new features and functions.)

The size and structure of the development group depends on whether programs are developed in-house. If not, this department will be staffed primarily by **business analysts** and/or **systems analysts** who work with users, operations, and vendors to acquire and install licensed software and to set up the system components around that software. Business analysts are normally involved in developing the business case for a newly proposed system and developing the requirements for the system. System analysts are normally involved in designing and implementing the new system. If the organization develops programs in-house, then this department will also include programmers, project managers, test engineers, technical writers, and other development personnel.

The last IT department group in Figure 10-2 is *outsourcing relations.* This group exists in organizations that have negotiated outsourcing agreements with other companies to provide equipment, applications, or other services. These relationships require constant attention, so this department monitors service levels and focuses on developing good relations with outsourcing vendors. You will learn more about outsourcing in Chapter 11.

Figure 10-2 also includes a *data administration* staff function. The purpose of this group is to protect data and information assets by establishing data standards and data management practices and policies.

There are many variations on the structure of the IT department shown in Figure 10-2. In larger organizations, the operations group may itself consist of several different departments. Sometimes there is a separate group for data warehousing and data marts.

As you examine Figure 10-2, keep the distinction between IS and IT in mind. Information systems (IS) exist to help the organization achieve its goals and objectives. Information systems have the five components we have discussed throughout this text. Information technology (IT) is just technology. It concerns the products, techniques, procedures, and designs of computer-based technology. IT must be placed into the structure of an IS before an organization can use it.

What about the Web?

The web has had a significant impact on the organization of IT departments within many organizations. In the early years of the web, the responsibility for technology supporting the web, as well as for the content and design of the company website, was in the hands of the IT department personnel. But once companies recognized the impact the web could have on the company brand and on its customers, control of the content and look and feel of the website was moved toward the marketing department while IT maintained the technical responsibilities.

Of course, creating well-designed company web pages requires knowledge of branding and marketing. But it also requires knowledge of things such as TCP/IP networks, HTML, XML (eXtensible Markup Language), content management systems, and web design applications such as Adobe Flash™. Recognition of the importance of website design created a whole new set of jobs relating to website design. These jobs combine traditional business skills (like branding and marketing) with technical skills.

Many companies have faced a difficult time attracting and retaining employees who have the combination of web design skill and business skill necessary to create excellent websites. (Perhaps this is a competitive advantage you could employ when you graduate. It's certainly a good reason to include some IS courses, or even an IS major, in your marketing degree.)

As a result, a whole new industry, the web design consulting industry, was born. There are many, many small and large web design firms. One large Canadian firm is Blast Radius (www.blastradius.com). Created in 1997, the company has grown to over 350 employees and serves international clients such as Nike, BMW, Nintendo, and Virgin.

One important thing you should learn in this chapter is that, because there are a lot of skills involved, it takes a lot of people to make a great website. For example, a web design project of any size will require the following people:

- Project manager: Responsible for interacting with the client and moving the project successfully toward completion
- Lead designer/analyst: Responsible for understanding client needs and developing the overall look and feel of the site and all the design elements (colours, navigation, graphics, buttons, animation, etc.)
- Developer: Responsible for taking the design and creating the functioning site. Usually specializes in static content (that is, content that does not automatically update)
- Technical architect: Responsible for making decisions about technical issues related to the site, including server/browser support, database integration, administrator access, and any scripting issues

There is a misperception among many business people that putting things on the web is relatively easy. Actually, it's harder than most people think, if you want to do it right. While it might be easy to get a site onto the web, getting a site that's properly designed, easy to maintain, and provides an enjoyable customer experience is work for professionals. The fact that customers view company websites has meant that almost all the applications that used to be internal to companies are now required to be seen by customers. This has made the job of the IT department both more important and more challenging. It has also changed the skill set of many IT workers; more attention has to be paid to design. This creates both change and opportunities for employees who can combine the right types of business design and technical skills.

Q5 What IS-Related Job Positions Exist?

The IS industry has a wide range of interesting and well-paying jobs. Many students enter the MIS class thinking that the IS industry consists only of programmers and computer technicians who have great technical skills. If you reflect on the five components of an information system, you can understand why this cannot be true. The data, procedure, and people components of an information system require professionals with highly developed interpersonal communication skills. The truth is that most jobs in the IS industry require a mix of interpersonal and technical skills. The most effective MIS personnel are often people who are thoughtful communicators with basic technology skills; people who can bridge the knowledge gap between computer technicians and business system users.

Figure 10-3 summarizes the major job positions in the IS industry. With the exception of computer technician and possibly QA test engineer, all these positions require a four-year degree. Furthermore, with the exception of programmer and QA test engineer, all these positions require business knowledge. In most cases, successful professionals have a degree in business. Note, too, that most positions require good verbal and written communication skills. Business, including information systems, is a social activity.

Many of the positions in Figure 10-3 have a wide salary range. Lower salaries are for professionals with limited experience, or for those who work in smaller companies or on small projects. The larger salaries are for those with deep knowledge and experience who work for large companies on large projects. Do not expect to begin your career at the high end of these ranges.

Title	Responsibilities	Knowledge, Skill, and Characteristics Requirements	2006 Cdn. Salary Range ($CDN)
Computer technician	Install software, repair computer equipment and networks	Associate degree, diagnostic skills.	$30 000–$60 000
Quality Assurance (QA) test engineer	Develop test plans, design and write automated test scripts, perform testing.	Logical thinking, basic programming, superb organizational skills, detailed.	$40 000–$75 000
User support representative	Help users solve problems, provide training.	Communications and people skills. Product knowledge. Patience.	$35 000–$60 000
Technical writer	Write program documentation, help-text, procedures, job descriptions, training materials.	Quick learner, clear writing skills, high verbal communications skills.	$35 000–$60 000
Programmer/ Developer	Design and write computer programs.	Logical thinking and development, skills, programming.	$45 000–$110 000
Website Designer	Work with clients to develop designs for websites, work with developers to finalize designs	Excellent interpersonal skills, design skills, detail oriented, good technical skills, flexible business/marketing skills.	$45 000–$110 000
Network administrator	Monitor, maintain, fix, and tune computer networks.	Diagnostic skills, in-depth knowledge of communications technologies and products.	$65 000–$120 000+
Database administrator	Manage and protect database (see Chapter 12).	Diplomatic skills, database technology knowledge.	$65 000–$120 000
System analyst, Business analyst	Work with users to determine system requirements, design procedure	Strong interpersonal and communications skills. Business and technology knowledge.	$50 000–$110 000
Consultant	Wide range of activities: programming, testing, database design, communications and networks, project management, strategic planning.	Quick learner, entrepreneurial attitude, communications and people skills. Respond well to pressure. Particular knowledge depends on work.	From $35 per hour for a contract tester to more than $400 per hour for strategic consulting to executive group.
Salesperson	Sell software, network, communications, and consulting services.	Quick learner, knowledge of product, superb professional sales skills.	$65 000–$200 000+
Project manager (PM)	Initiate, plan, manage, monitor, and close down projects.	Management and people skills, technology knowledge. Highly organized.	$75 000–$150 000
Enterprise Architect (EA)	Manage and document the technological infrastructure of the firm.	Diplomatic skills, database technology knowledge, strategic planning.	$100 000–$200 000
Chief technology officer (CTO)	Advise CIO, executive group, and project managers on emerging technologies.	Quick learner, good communications skills, deep knowledge of IT.	$100 000–$250 000+
Chief information officer (CIO)	Manage IT department, communicate with executive staff on IT- and IS-related matters. Member of the executive group.	Superb management skills, deep knowledge of business, and good business judgment. Good communicator. Balanced and unflappable.	$150 000–$300 000, plus executive benefits and privileges

Figure 10-3
Job Positions in the Information Systems Industry

In the nearly 80 years of combined experience among the authors of this book, we have worked as systems analysts, programmers, small- and large-scale project managers, consultants, and chief technology officers (CTOs). It has been great fun, and the industry becomes more and more interesting each year. Give these IT careers some thought while you're in school. Keep in mind that the changing nature of technology—and of business generally—will demand that you incorporate technology into the way you work.

JUMPING ABOARD THE BULLDOZER

A recent popular theme in the media is how overseas outsourcing is destroying the North American labour market. The "jobless recovery" is how it's headlined. However, a closer look reveals that overseas outsourcing is not the culprit. The culprit—if culprit is the right word—is productivity. Because of information technology, Moore's Law, and all the information systems that you've learned about in this book, worker productivity continues to increase, and it is possible to have an economic recovery without a binge of new hiring.

So what do you do? How do you respond to the dynamics of shifting work and job movements? As you have learned, MIS is the development and use of information systems that enable organizations to achieve their goals and objectives. When you work with information systems, you are not a professional in a particular system of technology; rather, you are a developer or user of a system that helps your organization achieve its goals and objectives.

From this perspective, the technology you learned in this class can help you start your career. If IS-based productivity is the bulldozer that is mowing down traditional jobs, then use what you have learned here to jump aboard that bulldozer. Not as a technologist, but as a business professional who can determine how best to use that bulldozer to enhance your career. Your long-term success depends not on your knowledge of specific technologies, but rather on your ability to think, to solve problems, and to use technology and information systems to help your organization achieve its goals and objectives.

By the way, for all but the most technical positions, knowledge of a business specialty can really add to your marketability. Notice that the high-paying jobs near the end of the figure all require communication, leadership, and business skills. If you have the time, a dual major can be an excellent choice that can open up opportunities for you. Popular and successful dual majors include accounting and information systems, marketing and information systems, and management strategy and information systems.

Q6 How Do Organizations Decide How Much to Spend on IT?

Information systems and information technology are expensive. Consequently, organizations need to address the investment in IS and IT in the same way that they address investments in plant, inventories, or any other substantial project.

Typically, decisions to invest in any business project involve an analysis of the costs and benefits.

All such techniques require estimates of the costs and benefits of the project. However, to compare costs to benefits, both the costs and benefits need to be expressed in dollars, or other currency. Estimating dollar costs of IS or IT projects isn't more difficult than estimating them for other projects. The difficulty arises when attempting to place a dollar value on benefits.

For example, what is the dollar value of an email system? Employees require access to email in order to do any work. Asking the dollar value of the email system is like asking the dollar value of the restroom. How can you compute it?

Other value computations are difficult, but possible. For example, if a customer support system reduces the likelihood of losing a customer, then the value of that system can be computed by multiplying the probability of loss times the lifetime value of that customer. Or, if an information system enables customer support representatives to service customers 10 percent faster, then the dollar value of that system is 10 percent of the anticipated customer support costs.

Most IS and IT investment analyses divide benefits into tangible and intangible. **Tangible benefits** are those for which a dollar value can be computed. Reducing customer support costs by 10 percent is a tangible benefit. **Intangible benefits** are those for which it is impossible to compute a dollar value. The benefits of the email system are intangible.

One common method for justifying IS and IT projects is to compute the costs and tangible benefits of the system and to perform a financial analysis. If the project can be justified on tangible benefits alone, then a favourable decision is made. If it cannot be justified on the basis of tangible benefits, then the intangible benefits are considered, and a subjective decision is made as to whether the intangibles are sufficiently valuable to overcome any missing tangible benefits that would be required.

Q7 What Are Your Rights and Responsibilities?

We conclude this chapter with a summary of your rights and responsibilities with regard to the IT department. The items in Figure 10-4 list what you are entitled to receive and indicate what you are expected to contribute.

Your Rights

You have a right to have the computing resources you need to perform your work as proficiently as you want. You have a right to the computer hardware and programs you need. If you process huge files for data-mining applications, you have a right to the huge disks and the fast processor you need. However, if you merely receive email and consult the corporate web portal, then your right is for more modest requirements (leaving the more powerful resources for those in the organization who need them).

You have a right to reliable network and Internet services. Reliable means that you can process without problems almost all the time. It means that you never go to work wondering, "Will the network be available today?" Network problems should be a rare occurrence.

You have a right to:
- Computer hardware and programs that allow you to perform your job proficiently
- Reliable network and Internet connections
- A secure computing environment
- Protection from viruses, worms, and other threats
- Contribute to requirements for new system features and functions
- Reliable systems development and maintenance
- Prompt attention to problems, concerns, and complaints
- Properly prioritized problem fixes and resolutions
- Effective training

You have a responsibility to:
- Learn basic computer skills
- Learn standard techniques and procedures for the applications you use
- Follow security and backup procedures
- Protect your password(s)
- Use computer resources according to your employer's computer-use policy
- Make no unauthorized hardware modifications
- Install only authorized programs
- Apply software patches and fixes when directed to do so
- When asked, devote the time required to respond carefully and completely to requests for requirements for new system features and functions
- Avoid reporting trivial problems

Figure 10-4
User Information Systems Rights and Responsibilities

You also have a right to a secure computing environment. The organization should protect your computer and its files, and you should not normally even need to think about security. From time to time the organization may ask you to take particular actions to protect your computer and files, and you should take those actions. But such requests should be rare and related to specific outside threats.

You have a right to participate in requirements meetings for new applications you will use and for major changes to applications you currently use. You may choose to delegate this right to others, or your department may delegate that right for you, but if so, you have a right to contribute your thoughts through that delegate.

You have a right to reliable systems development and maintenance. Although schedule slippages of a month or two are common in many development projects, you should not have to endure schedule slippages of six months or more. Such slippages are evidence of incompetent systems development.

Additionally, you have a right to receive prompt attention to your problems, concerns, and complaints about information services. You have a right to have a means to report problems, and you have a right to know that your problem has been received and at least registered with the IT department. You have a right to have your problem resolved, consistent with established priorities. This means that an annoying problem that nonetheless allows you to conduct your work will be prioritized below another's problem that interferes with his or her ability to do the job.

Finally, you have a right to effective training. It should be training that you can understand and that enables you to use systems to perform your particular job. The organization should provide training in a format and on a schedule that is convenient to you.

Your Responsibilities

You also have responsibilities toward the IT department and your organization. Specifically, you have a responsibility to learn basic computer skills and to learn the basic techniques and procedures for the applications you use. You should not expect hand-holding for basic operations. Nor should you expect to receive repetitive training and support for the same issue.

You have a responsibility to follow security and backup procedures. This is especially important because actions you fail to take may cause problems for your fellow employees and your organization as well as for you. In particular, you are responsible for protecting your password(s). In Chapter 12 you will learn that this is important not only to protect your computer, but, because of intersystem authentication, also to protect your organization's networks and databases.

You have a responsibility for using your computer resources in a manner that is consistent with your employer's policy. Many employers allow limited email for critical family matters while at work, but discourage frequent and long casual email. You have a responsibility to know your employer's policy and to follow it. See the Exercise "Using the Corporate Computer" at the end of this chapter for additional discussions on computer-use policy.

You also have a responsibility to make no unauthorized hardware modifications to your computer and to install only authorized programs. One reason for this policy is that your IT department constructs automated maintenance programs for upgrading your computer. Unauthorized hardware and programs may interfere with these programs. Additionally, the installation of unauthorized hardware or programs can cause problems that the IT department will have to fix.

You have a responsibility to install computer patches and fixes when asked to do so. This is particularly important for patches that concern security and backup and recovery. When asked for your input on requirements for new and adapted systems, you have a responsibility to take the time necessary to provide thoughtful and complete responses. If you do not have that time, you should delegate your input to someone else.

Finally, you have a responsibility to treat information systems professionals professionally. Everyone works for the same company, everyone wants to succeed, and professionalism and courtesy will go a long way on all sides. One form of professional behaviour is to learn basic skills so that you avoid reporting trivial problems.

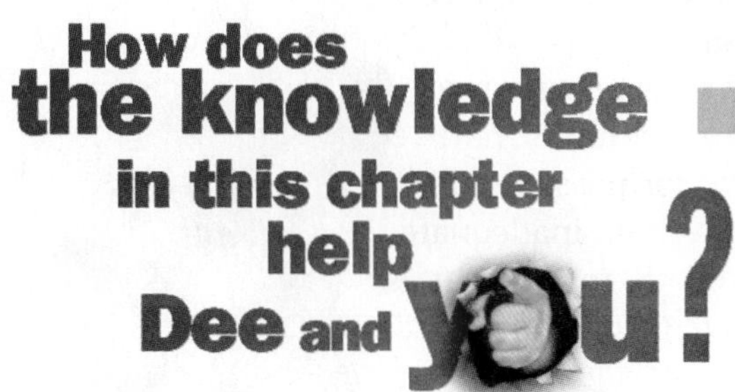

We have already discussed how you, in Dee's position, could use the knowledge in this chapter. By understanding the need for the IT department to protect the network infrastructure, you would be sensitive to the problem of allowing non-employees to work within the network. You might suggest alternatives, such as having your consultant develop the software on his computer and then having the IT department install it on its network. You might also hire a consultant who is bonded or who can provide some other form of assurance or insurance to the IT department.

The situation at DSI is particularly puzzling, since the IT department consists of one employee. Recall the four primary responsibilities of an IT department: managing the 1) information technology, 2) data resource, and 3) systems applications and, in addition, 4) renewing the IT infrastructure), and consider that DSI is a $50-million-plus company. The IT job would seem too large for one individual to perform. Either (a) the sole IT person works 200 hours a week, or (b) users are performing some of the IT department's work, or (c) some tasks are not being done.

Clearly, the first is impossible, so either the users are performing the IT department's function or work is not being done. As you learned in Q3, the IS department has the responsibilities of maintaining and renewing the IT infrastructure. DSI runs successfully, so the operate-and-maintain function must be adequate, at least as far as the infrastructure is concerned. DSI uses only licensed software, so there is no need for in-house software development and testing. (An example of a custom-developed software application is provided in the *Case Study 10* at the end of this chapter. The case describes the development of a revenue management system called OneSystem.)

Systems that use only licensed software still require project management. One individual cannot perform that task, so users at DSI must be doing much of it. Similarly, the sole person cannot be doing much planning. He seems to be a technically oriented person, one who repairs hardware and installs network gear, so he probably does not have the interest or background to think about strategic uses of IT. Possibly, the DSI partners perform that function themselves.

Most likely, the "protect" function either is not being performed or is not performed adequately. No one at DSI will know that they have inadequate protection until a crime, natural disaster, or other problem occurs. At that point, actions that should have been done will be visible. Considerable loss is likely. We will consider this topic further in Chapter 12.

If you were an intern at DSI, you might realize that no one seems to be thinking strategically about the use of IS. The various proposals you developed in Part 3 of this text might be very well received. At least it would be worth advocating them. You might even mention the IT functions and wonder whether it's possible for one person to perform them all. You should use care, however, because such statements could be perceived as meddling or unwarranted criticism.

It is a delicate matter for you as an intern to raise the protection issue. You are a very junior, part-time person, who is under review for possible full-time employment. Your comments about inadequate security may not be appreciated. If my weight is endangering my health, I want my doctor, and not my summer intern, to tell me that. You might raise the possibility of improving security and then drop it if there's no positive response.

If you believe that DSI is not properly protecting its data, you should be careful about the data, especially personal data, you store on your work computer. Understand that it could find its way to a criminal by tomorrow.

Active Review

Use this Active Review to verify that you understand the material in the chapter. You can read the entire chapter and then perform the tasks in this review, or you can read the material for just one question and perform the tasks in this review for that question before moving on to the next one.

Q1 Why do you need to know about the IT department?

Describe two reasons why you need to know about the IT department. Summarize why Dee needed to know. Give an example of a business initiative that involves IT support. Explain why knowing the functions of IT will help you develop that initiative.

Q2 What should you know about IT operations and IT projects?

Describe the relationship between IT operations and IT projects. Where does the IT department create value for an organization? Explain why operations often takes the largest share of the IT budget. Explain why large IT projects are often funded outside of the IT department. How has the web changed the delivery of IT services?

Q3 What are the responsibilities of the IT department?

Name the two basic responsibilities of the IT department. Briefly describe the three areas that the IT department is charged with managing and protecting. How do these three areas differ? Explain how the web influences the responsibilities of the IT department.

Q4 How is the IT department organized?

Draw an organization chart for a typical IT department. Explain the functions of the CIO and the CTO. State reporting relationships of the IT department and the CIO. What positions require mostly technical skills? What positions require mostly business skills?

Q5 What IS-related job positions exist?

Name positions in the IT department that do not require a four-year degree. Name positions that do not require substantial knowledge of business. State your conclusions from these observations. Select two positions you're interested in. Describe what you think you could do to prepare yourself for these positions. Explain why a joint major of IS and another functional discipline may make sense.

Q6 How do organizations decide how much to spend on IT?

Explain the general principles that organizations use for justifying investments in information technology. Explain the difference between tangible and intangible benefits. Describe the problem of intangible benefits and one way of assessing projects that cannot be justified on their tangible benefits.

Q7 What are your rights and responsibilities?

Using Figure 10-4 as a guide, summarize the rights you have with regard to information systems and technology. Summarize the responsibilities you have toward the IT department as well.

Key Terms and Concepts

Business analysts 284
Chief information officer (CIO) 283
Chief technology officer (CTO) 284
Information Technology Infrastructure Library (ITIL) 280
Intangible benefit 289
IT Operations 278
IT Projects 278
Project management body of knowledge (PMBOK) 280
Systems analysts 284
Tangible benefit 289
Tuned 282

Using Your Knowledge

1. Explain Dee's mistake. Explain the mistake of her management. Describe what Dee should have done.

2. Explain how you can use the definition of the four major responsibilities of the IT department to bolster the proposal to develop one of the innovative information systems you considered in Part 3. Suppose DSI chooses to develop one of those systems; explain how the new system will impact DSI's current IT personnel.

3. Consider the information system that your university uses to schedule classes. List 10 benefits that might arise from using this system. For each, indicate whether it is a tangible or an intangible benefit. For the tangible benefits, briefly explain how you could compute their value. For the intangible ones, indicate why they are intangible.

4. Suppose you work for an organization that you believe does not adequately protect its data and IT assets. Assume you manage the telesales department and that you have raised your concerns several times with your management, all to no avail. Describe how you would protect yourself and your department.

5. Suppose you work for a company where the design and content for the website is the responsibility of the IT department. Explain why some of the responsibility for the site should be given to another department. Explain what you see as the IT department's role in the website. Write down the skills of someone who you think would make a good web designer.

6. Suppose you represent an investor group that is building software to integrate provincial hospitals into a unified system. List five potential problems and risks concerning information systems. How do you think IS-related risks compare to other risks in such an acquisition program?

Case Study 10

Marriott International, Inc.

Marriott International, Inc. operates and franchises hotels and lodging facilities throughout the world. Its 2005 revenue was just over $11.5 billion. Marriott groups its business into segments according to lodging facility. Major business segments are full-service lodging, select-service lodging, extended-stay lodging, and timeshare properties. Marriott states that its three top corporate priorities are profitability, preference, and growth.

In the mid-1980s the airlines developed the concept of *revenue management*, which adjusts prices in accordance with demand. The idea gained prominence in the airline industry because an unoccupied seat represents revenue that is forever lost. Unlike a part in inventory, an unoccupied seat on today's flight cannot be sold tomorrow. Similarly, in the lodging industry, today's unoccupied hotel room cannot be sold tomorrow. So, for hotels, revenue management translates to raising prices on Monday when a convention is in town and lowering them on Saturday in the dead of winter when few travellers are in sight.

Marriott had developed two different revenue-management systems: one for its premium hotels and a second one for its lower-priced properties. It developed both of these systems using pre-Internet technology; systems upgrades required installing updates locally. The local updates were expensive and problematic. Also, the two systems required two separate interfaces for entering prices into the centralized reservation system.

In the late 1990s Marriott embarked on a project to create a single revenue-management system that could be used by all of its properties. The new system, called OneSystem, was custom developed in-house. The IT professionals understood the importance of user involvement, and they formed a joint IT–business user team that developed the business case for the new system and jointly managed its development. The team was careful to provide constant communication to the system's future users, and it used prototypes to identify problem areas early. Training is a continuing activity for all Marriott employees, and the company integrated training facilities into the new system.

OneSystem recommends prices for each room, given the day, date, current reservation levels, and history. Each hotel property has a revenue manager who can override these recommendations. Either way, the prices are communicated directly to the centralized reservation system. OneSystem uses Internet technology so that when the company makes upgrades to the system, it makes them only at the web servers, not at the individual hotels. This strategy saves considerable maintenance cost, activity, and frustration.

OneSystem computes the theoretical maximum revenue for each property and compares actual results to that maximum. Using OneSystem, the company has increased the ratio of actual to theoretical revenue from 83 percent to 91 percent. That increase of 8 percentage points has translated into a substantial increase in revenues.

Questions

1. How does OneSystem contribute to Marriott's objectives?
2. What are the advantages of having one revenue-management system instead of two? Consider both users and the IT department in your answer.
3. At the same time it was developing OneSystem in-house, Marriott chose to outsource its human relations information system. Why would it choose to develop one system in-house but outsource the other? Consider the following factors in your answer.
   - Marriott's objectives
   - The nature of the systems
   - The uniqueness of each system to Marriott
   - Marriott's in-house expertise
4. How did outsourcing HR contribute to the success of OneSystem?

Visit MyMISLab at **www.pearsoned.ca/mymislab**. MyMISLab is a state-of-the-art, interactive, online solution that combines multimedia, tutorials, and quizzes. Use MyMISLab for *Experiencing MIS* to prepare for tests and exams, and go to class ready to learn!

What Do YOU Think?

Using the Corporate Computer

Suppose you work at a company that has the following computer-use policy:

Computers, email, and the Internet are to be used primarily for official company business. Small amounts of personal email can be exchanged with friends and family, and occasional usage of the Internet is permitted, but such usage should be limited and never interfere with your work.

Suppose you are a manager, and you learn that one of your employees has been engaged in the following activities:

1. Playing computer games during work hours
2. Playing computer games on the company computer before and after work hours
3. Responding to emails from an ill parent
4. Watching DVDs during lunch and other breaks
5. Sending emails to plan a party that involves mostly people from work
6. Sending emails to plan a party that involves no one from work
7. Searching the web for a new car
8. Reading the news on Canada.com
9. Checking the stock market over the Internet
10. Bidding on items for personal use on eBay
11. Selling personal items on eBay
12. Paying personal bills online
13. Paying personal bills online when travelling on company business
14. Buying an airplane ticket for an ill parent over the Internet
15. Changing the content of a personal website
16. Changing the content of a personal business website
17. Buying an airplane ticket for a personal vacation over the Internet

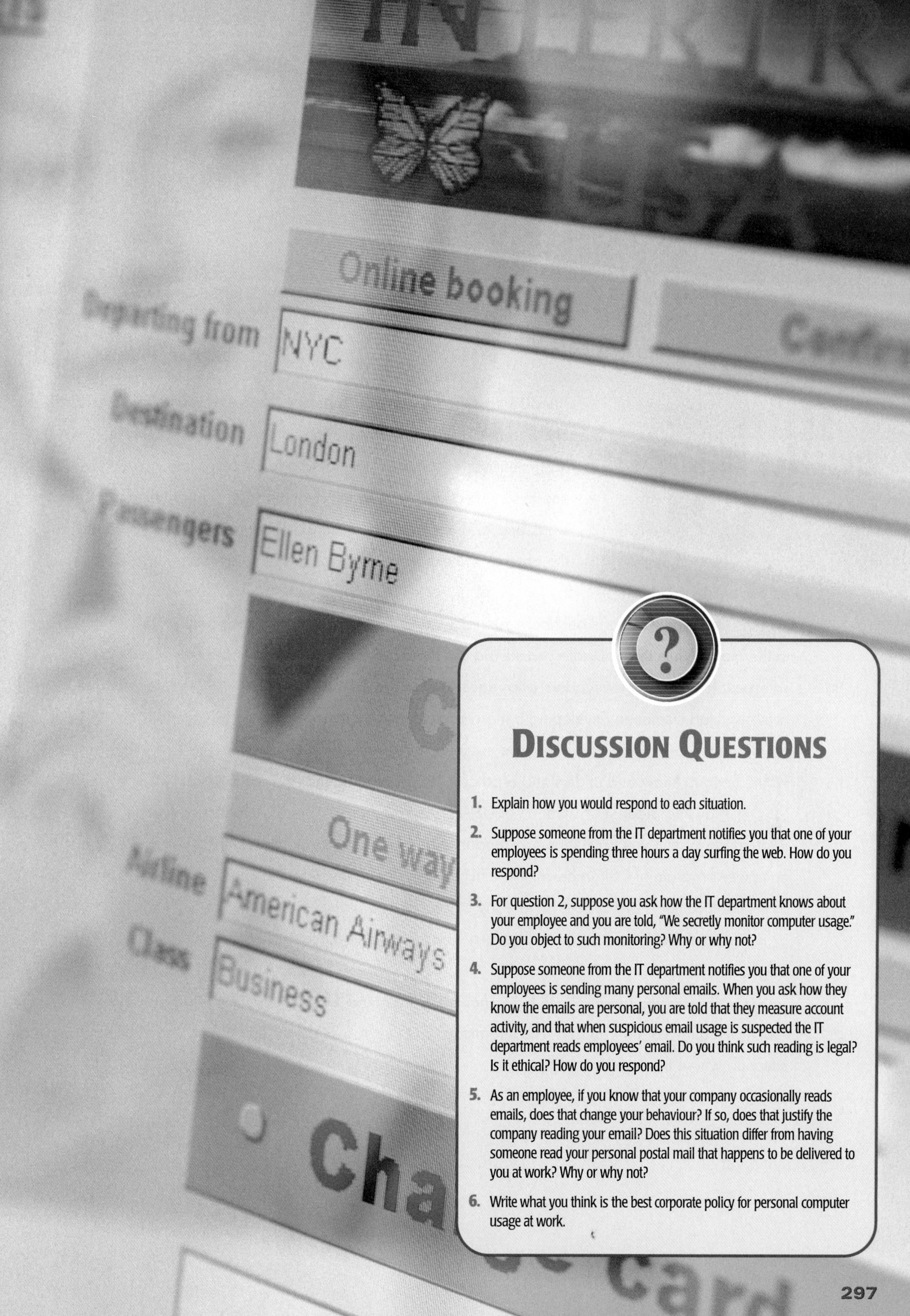

Discussion Questions

1. Explain how you would respond to each situation.
2. Suppose someone from the IT department notifies you that one of your employees is spending three hours a day surfing the web. How do you respond?
3. For question 2, suppose you ask how the IT department knows about your employee and you are told, "We secretly monitor computer usage." Do you object to such monitoring? Why or why not?
4. Suppose someone from the IT department notifies you that one of your employees is sending many personal emails. When you ask how they know the emails are personal, you are told that they measure account activity, and that when suspicious email usage is suspected the IT department reads employees' email. Do you think such reading is legal? Is it ethical? How do you respond?
5. As an employee, if you know that your company occasionally reads emails, does that change your behaviour? If so, does that justify the company reading your email? Does this situation differ from having someone read your personal postal mail that happens to be delivered to you at work? Why or why not?
6. Write what you think is the best corporate policy for personal computer usage at work.

11 IT Projects and Acquiring Information Systems

This
could happen
to you

Dee Clark wanted to develop a blog to communicate to her sales force. She had a focused goal and a short time frame. Her employer, Emerson, has extensive IT resources, including a large corporate network, and Dee needed to integrate her blog into that network. She proceeded by fits and starts and, with the help of her consultant, was successful. However, in the process she exposed her organization to an enormous security risk, as you will learn in Chapter 12.

Dee was successful only because her system was simple. She was the only person contributing to the blog. While the 450 salespeople did use the blog, they needed no training to do so. The salespeople were passive readers who required no more skill than the ability to read news on a browser. Had Dee been developing a more complicated system with more users and greater functionality, she could not have succeeded in proceeding as she did. She would need to know and understand a process for developing information systems.

Now, consider your situation at DSI as described in Chapter 9. Suppose you pitch the RFID information system you have in mind: Vendors place RFID tags on components they produce, and a computer program at DSI processes the RFID data to determine where to place the component into raw materials inventory. This system isn't nearly as simple as building a blog.

What would you do if Mr. Stratford says to you, "Great idea. Tell me how to proceed. What do we do next?"

How do you answer him? How *should* DSI proceed? Do you tell him to start buying RFID tags? Not likely. But what do you say? The information in this chapter should help if you find yourself in a situation where this happens to you.

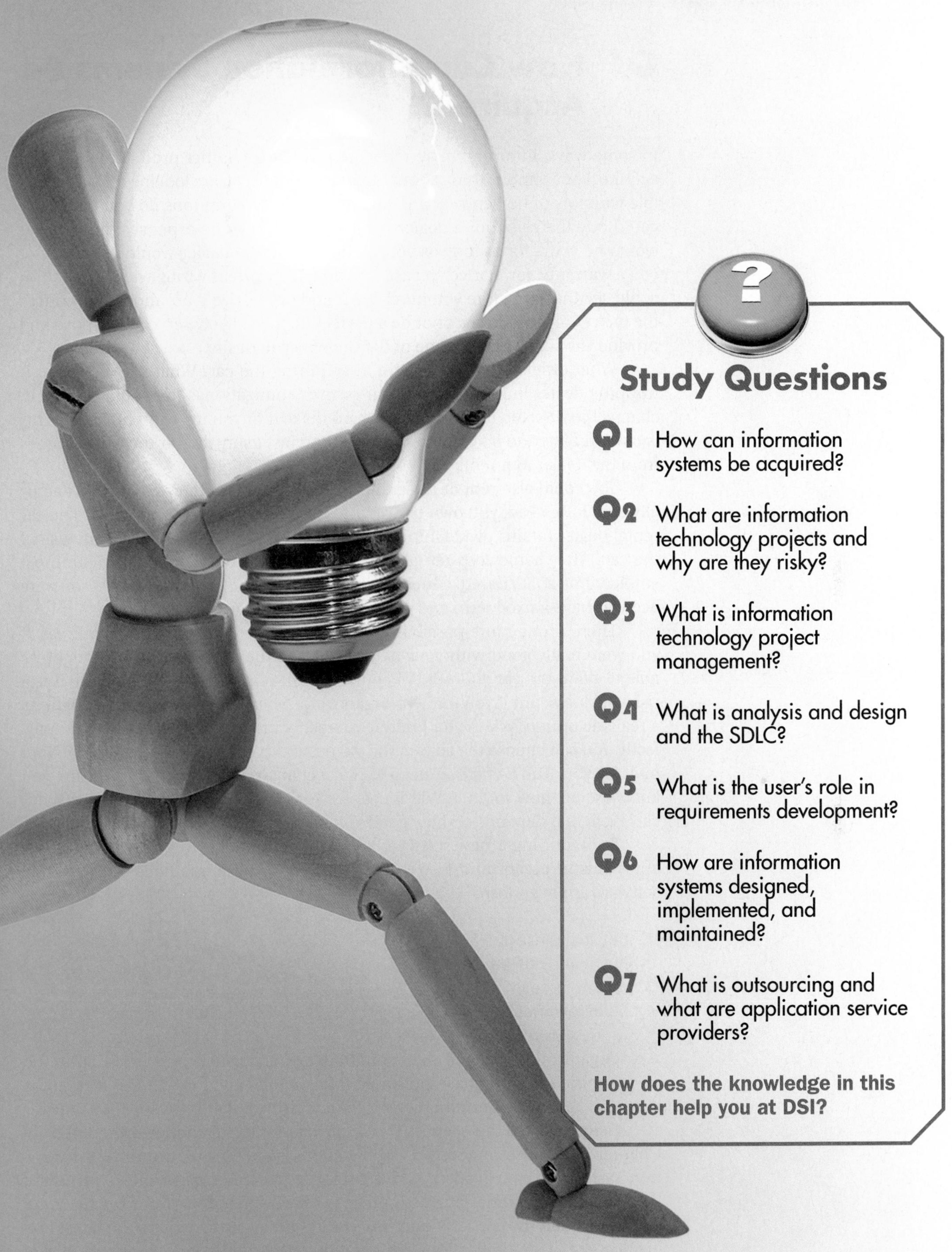

Study Questions

Q1 How can information systems be acquired?

Q2 What are information technology projects and why are they risky?

Q3 What is information technology project management?

Q4 What is analysis and design and the SDLC?

Q5 What is the user's role in requirements development?

Q6 How are information systems designed, implemented, and maintained?

Q7 What is outsourcing and what are application service providers?

How does the knowledge in this chapter help you at DSI?

Q1 How Can Information Systems Be Acquired?

In some ways, information systems are just like any other product we want to acquire. For example, think about buying a car. Say you are looking for a convertible with lots of horsepower and a great stereo. What options do you have? You could buy the car from a dealer. That would initially be expensive but the car would be yours for as long as you wanted it and the dealer would usually offer you a warranty, for a price, in case anything major went wrong with the car. You could see the car before you purchase it and even drive it around. That reduces the risk. While the car may not be a perfect fit, it will likely serve its purpose and provide you with at least some of the benefits you desire.

What other options are there in acquiring the car? What if you bought it from the dealer but then made your own customizations? You could repaint it, change the rims, upgrade the stereo, and make it fit you the way you like it. This is *customizing,* and it is more expensive than just using the car the way it comes from the dealer. But it fits you better.

You could also rent or lease the car. When you rent the car, you don't actually own it. Instead, you own the right to use the car for a specific time. The car rental dealer retains ownership and you pay the car rental dealer for the use of the car. While some software allows you to buy the application outright, most applications are licensed, which is similar in concept to renting. Some software licences have a fixed term and others have no fixed term.

There is one more possibility we should consider in acquiring your car. If you were really good with your hands and had the proper tools, you might be able to build the car yourself. Of course, if you've never done this before it is a risky business, but if you (or your organization) has built cars then this might be a realistic option. When you build it yourself you can make the car fit you perfectly. You can choose the colour, the stereo, and every other feature. It is custom built for you. And if you ever need to make changes or adapt it in the future, you know exactly how to do it. Will it cost less? Will it work better than the dealer's car? Well, that depends on how good you are at building cars.

So, acquiring a new software application is similar to buying a car. If we apply this to organizations, we can identify four basic methods for acquiring software applications:

1. buy it and use it
2. buy it and customize it
3. rent or lease it
4. build it yourself

Organizations use all these methods for acquisition; however, option 2, where companies purchase pre-built software and then customize it to some degree, is the most common method for acquiring larger software applications.

Before we end this section, it is important for us to reiterate our point from Chapter 1 that acquiring software applications is not equal to acquiring information systems. If you read the advertisements in trade magazines, you might believe that substantial business process improvements for your organization are just around the corner if only you could find a way to acquire the latest and greatest software applications. The reality is that there are a large number of tremendously powerful and effective software applications—but acquiring these applications does not come free (even if they are open source, as we will discuss later), and acquiring and integrating these systems does not come without risks.

The model of information systems we introduced in Chapter 1 suggested that information systems are the combination of hardware, software, data, procedures, and people. Acquiring an information system therefore involves more than just obtaining and installing software. It involves incorporating the software into the current technological infrastructure and integrating the software into the data and procedures people use to make things happen in an organization. This is shown in Figure 11-1. Acquiring new software is NOT the same as acquiring new information systems, because there is a lot more to think about in systems than just software.

As a future business manager, it is important for you to realize that even if the software is free, the organization will always face the cost of integrating the software with the current hardware, data, and procedures in the organization. These costs are often substantial and can exceed the costs of the software itself. Organizations that understand these costs before acquiring new applications are more likely to be successful in eventually integrating software than organizations that think software = systems. You know better than that now!

Q2 What Are Information Technology Projects and Why Are They Risky?

We learned in Chapter 10 that when an organization is considering acquiring an information system, the organization is embarking on a project. So what is a project? Projects often begin with a scope, or an objective. Projects usually have a start and an end date and temporarily use resources (such as people, office space, and computers) to accomplish the project. Projects also tend to be unique in that they do not happen over and over again, but rather only once. Perhaps most importantly, the objective of the project is to accomplish something new, so projects often represent change in an organization.

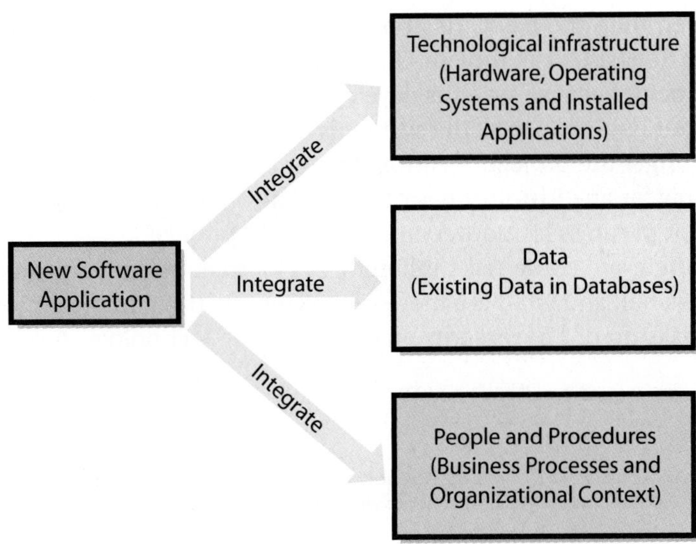

Figure 11-1
New Software Must Be Integrated into Existing Systems

Projects that have a large information technology (IT) component (in terms of budget or personnel) are often referred to as information technology projects. Installing a new email application, or a customer relationship management system, or an enterprise resource planning system are examples of IT projects. Projects that require some fundamental changes to business processes are often also referred to as IT projects because the new IT supports the change in business processes. What is important for a business student to recognize is that IT projects are never exclusively about technology. IT projects always include some impact on data, people, and procedures. This occurs because information systems include more than just software and hardware.

Any student of project management will tell you that all projects, no matter how small or how well defined, face some risks. There is some dispute as to how risky IT projects are. For example, the oft-quoted CHAOS Report created by the Standish Group (www.standishgroup.com) in 1994 suggested that only 16 percent of IT projects were delivered on time, on budget, and on scope, whereas more than 30 percent of IT projects were cancelled before delivering any benefits. In a later study, Sauer, Gemino, and Reich[1] (www.pmperspectives.org) indicated that the success rate of IT projects was roughly 2 out of 3, or 66 percent, with only 9 percent of projects cancelled. They also indicated, however, that IT projects faced a general failure rate of 25 percent regardless of size. Whatever the actual numbers are, it's clear that IT projects face significant risks.

So what makes IT projects so risky? Consider a construction project, such as building a bridge. The project begins with an architect who builds a scale model of the bridge. What does a scale model for an IT project look like? Have you ever seen one? Often it cannot easily be developed, so the lack of a good scale model becomes an important risk.

What about estimating costs for a project? The bridge uses steel, concrete, labour, and other industrial products. These components are stable, well known, and have been used for hundreds of years. In an IT project, however, the tools for building the project are constantly changing. Computers get cheaper and faster; programming languages, operating systems, and databases get more complex; and the web makes projects even more difficult to estimate. So good estimates for IT projects are difficult to develop because the technology is continually changing.

Assuming you can make some relatively accurate estimates, the next step in the bridge-building project is to start building the bridge. How can you tell how far the project has gone? Well, you just look at the bridge. If it's halfway across the river, then the bridge is about half complete. But what about an IT project? What does a half-complete IT project look like? It's hard to tell. It gets even more difficult because systems development often aims at a moving target. System requirements change as the system is developed, and the bigger the system and the longer the project, the more the requirements change. It is difficult to estimate how far an IT project has come and how far it needs to go. So, being able to monitor progress is another challenge for IT projects.

Clearly there are some risks inherent in IT projects. But how many risks should we consider, and what are these risks? The first thing to recognize is that the primary risks do not necessarily emerge from the technology. A good list of

[1] Sauer, C., A. Gemino, and B. H. Reich, "Managing Projects for Success: The Impact of Size and Volatility on IT Project Performance," accepted for publication and forthcoming in *Communications of ACM* 50, no. 11 (November 2007): 79–84.

the risks, 52 in total, is provided in an article by Wallace and Keil.[2] These risks include a lack of experience in the team, lack of support from top management, lack of participation from system users, unclear and uncertain project requirements, a high level of technical complexity, and changes in the project environment, along with many others. Many of the risks associated with IT projects have been summarized by researchers in a time-based (temporal) model of IT project performance[3] and are provided in Figure 11-2.

The model is read from left to right. The blue lines indicate positive relationships, and the red lines indicate negative relationships. The items on the left (knowledge resources and structural risk) are normally known when the project begins. The items in the middle of the graph represent the things that happen during a project. For example, volatility risks emerge, project management practices are used to drive the project forward and coordinate effort, and organizational support resources are realized. On the right-hand side of the model are the project outcomes. When the project ends we measure the project process performance, usually by measuring whether the project is on budget and on schedule. In addition, we consider whether what we produced added any business value. This is represented by project product performance.

The model shows us three things about **IT project risk.** It first shows that IT project performance has to be evaluated on not only whether the project was on budget and on time (project process performance), but also whether the expected benefits from the project were realized (project product performance). In addition, the model shows two pathways that the authors describe as the *"forces of evil"* and the *"forces of good"* in IT projects.

The forces of evil involve structural risk, volatility risk, and project process performance. When structural risk is high it means that the project is either large or technically complex (or both). High levels of structural risk are associated with high levels of volatility risk. When volatility risk is high, project process performance tends to be lower. So large, technically complex projects tend to be more

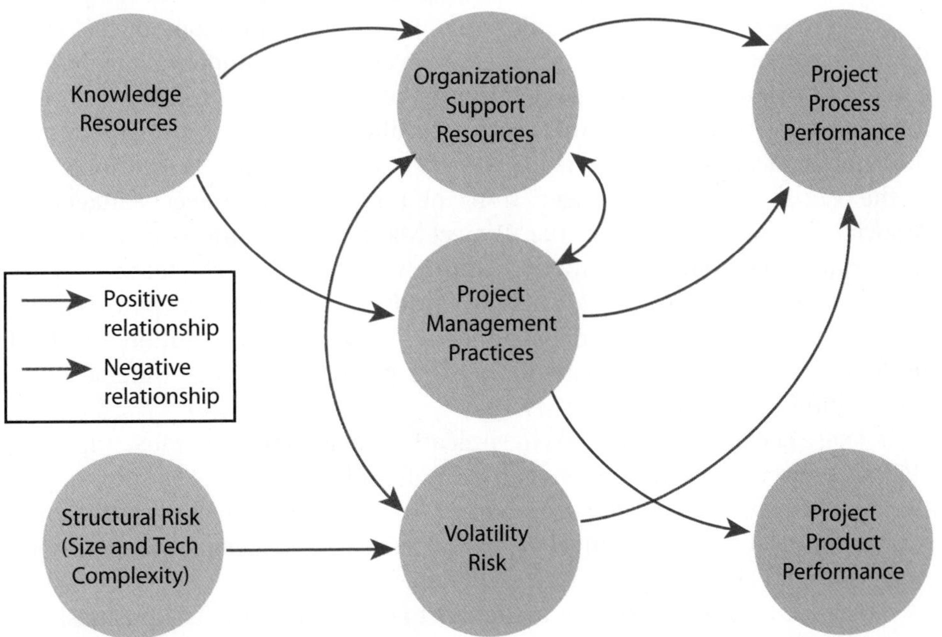

Figure 11-2
Impact of Risks on IT Projects

2. Wallace, L., and M. Keil, "Software Project Risks and Their Effect on Outcomes," Association for Computing Machinery, *Communications of the ACM* 47, no. 4 (2004): 68–73.
3. Gemino, A., B. Horner-Reich, and C. Sauer, "A Temporal Model for IT Project Management," *Journal of MIS* 24, no. 3 (Winter 2007–8): 9–44.

volatile and hence tend to lead to projects that are over budget and over schedule. Increased organizational support may help to reduce the volatility risk, but the forces of evil make hitting budget and schedule estimates difficult.

The forces of good involve knowledge resources, organizational support, project management practices, and both process and product performance. You will note that all the relationships among these items are positive. This suggests that when the team's knowledge resources are high, there is a tendency to observe higher levels of organizational support and higher levels of project management (PM) practice. Higher levels of organizational support and PM practices are correlated not only with increased levels of process performance, but also with increased levels of project product performance. The knowledge resources, which are part of the forces of good, help create a virtuous cycle of improved performance.

It is important to note that Figure 11-2 is just a model and not reality. Real IT projects are subject to many different effects. While the model may help us organize our thinking about IT project risk, the temporal model of IT project performance is a relatively recent development and will likely be adapted as we learn more about IT projects in the future.

Q3 What Is Information Technology Project Management?

Information technology project management (ITPM) is the collection of techniques and methods that project managers use to plan, coordinate, and complete IT projects. The tools of ITPM are basically the same tools used in any project management. These tools include planning tools such as work breakdown structures, budgeting methods, graphical scheduling methods such as PERT (Program Evaluation Review Technique) and Gantt charts, risk management techniques, communication planning, and high-tech team development.

A description of these techniques is well beyond the scope of this book; however, project management skills are relevant for any student considering a career in business. The increasing importance of IT projects has led to a rapid increase in the number of people seeking certification of PM skills. This surge in demand for IT project managers has led to the growth of PM certifications, such as the "Certified Project Manager" from the International Project Management Association (www.ipma.ch), or the "Project Management Professional" designation from the Project Management Institute (www.pmi.org). The number of certified members has grown dramatically worldwide, and a sizable percentage of these project managers work on IT projects. PM-certifying institutions establish professional standards, advocate for the PM profession, and provide access to information and resources for PMs.

These certifying institutions have clearly indicated that the most important skill for a successful project manager, in IT and other industries, is communication. While technical knowledge is an asset for an IT project manager, the ability to communicate with technical and business-oriented people about project objectives and challenges is the key skill for a successful PM.

The business environment continues to change rapidly. As a business student, one of the things you should realize is that this rapid pace of change suggests that organizations must improve their ability to adapt to changing conditions. As we noted earlier in this chapter, organizations adapt to changes through projects. Project management skills are therefore likely to become even more important skills for any manager in the future. Students should also recognize that most significant projects have some technology component. So, ITPM is central to the skills needed for organizations to adapt appropriately to an increasingly complex business environment.

An aside for those who are interested in this subject: Fred Brooks was a successful senior manager at IBM in the 1960s. After retiring from IBM, he wrote a classic book on IT project management called *The Mythical Man-Month.* Published by Addison-Wesley in 1975, the book is pertinent today and should be read by every IT or IS project manager. It's an enjoyable book, too.

Q4 What Is Analysis and Design and the SDLC?

Systems analysis and design, as it is sometimes called, is the process of creating and maintaining information systems. Notice that this process concerns *information systems,* not just computer programs. Building computer networks, writing computer programs, and implementing data models require technical skills. But there are many other non-technical skills required in systems analysis and design. Establishing the system's goals, setting up the project, determining requirements, interviewing users and understanding their view of the business, and designing procedures (especially those involving group action) require business knowledge and an understanding of group dynamics. In addition, developing job descriptions, staffing, and training all require human resource and related expertise. Thus, do not suppose that **systems development** is exclusively a technical task undertaken by programmers and hardware specialists. Rather, it requires coordinated teamwork of both specialists and non-specialists with business knowledge.

As a future business manager, you will likely play a key role in information systems development. In order to accomplish the goals of your department, you need to ensure that effective procedures exist for using the information system. You need to ensure that personnel are properly trained and are able to use the IS effectively. If your department does not have appropriate procedures and trained personnel, you must take corrective action. Although you might pass off hardware, program, or data problems to the IT department, you cannot pass off procedural or personnel problems to that department. Such problems are your problems. The single most important criterion for information systems success is for users to take ownership of their systems.

The IT industry has more than 50 years of experience acquiring and developing information systems, and over those years methodologies have emerged that successfully deal with these problems. In the next section we will consider the systems development life cycle (SDLC), the classic process for systems development. Many other development methods exist, including rapid application development (RAD), object-oriented systems development (OOD), and extreme programming (XP).

You might be wondering why there are so many methodologies. This occurs because no single process works for all organizational situations. The scale of information systems also varies widely. Personal systems support one person with a limited set of requirements. Workgroup systems support a group of people, normally with a single application. Enterprise systems support many workgroups with many different applications. Given the variety of possible systems, it is not surprising that there are different acquisition methodologies. Different methodologies are appropriate for different types of systems.

The Systems Development Life Cycle (SDLC)

The **systems development life cycle (SDLC)** is the classical process used to acquire information systems. The IT industry developed the SDLC in the "school of hard knocks." Many early projects met with disaster, and companies and systems developers sifted through the ashes of those disasters to determine what went wrong. By the 1970s, most seasoned project managers agreed on the basic tasks that need to be performed to successfully acquire and maintain information systems. These basic tasks are combined into phases of systems development.

Different authors and organizations package the tasks into different numbers of phases. Some organizations use an eight-phase process, others use a seven-phase process, and still others use a five-phase process. In this text, we will use the following five-phase process:

1. **System definition**
2. **Requirements analysis**
3. **Component design**
4. **Implementation**
5. **System maintenance**

Figure 11-3 shows how these phases are related. Acquisition begins when a business-planning process identifies a need for a new system. For now, suppose that management has determined in some way that the organization can best accomplish its goals and objectives by acquiring a new information system.

Developers in the first SDLC phase, system definition, use management's statement of the system needs in order to begin to define the new system. The resulting project plan is the input to the second phase, requirements analysis. Here, developers identify the particular features and functions of the new

Figure 11-3
Phases in the SDLC

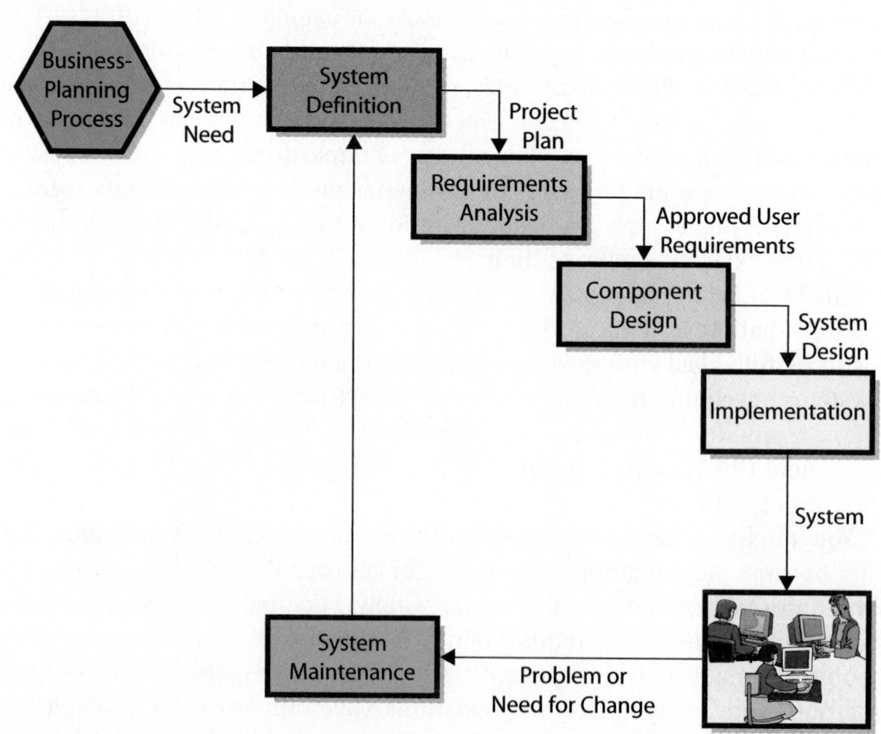

system. The output of that phase is a set of approved user requirements, which become the primary input used to design system components. In phase 4, developers implement, test, and install the new system. Over time, users will find errors, mistakes, and problems. They will also develop new requirements. The description of fixes and new requirements is input to a system maintenance phase. The maintenance phase starts the process all over again, which is why the process is considered a cycle.

Our discussion of the SDLC will focus on the first two phases of the SDLC, which are system definition and requirements analysis.

Step 1: System Definition

In response to the need for the new system, the organization will assign a few employees, possibly on a part-time basis, to define the new system, to assess its feasibility, and to plan the project. Typically, someone from the IS department leads the initial team, but the members of that initial team are both users and IS professionals.

Define System Goals and Scope

As Figure 11-4 shows, the first step is to define the goals and scope of the new information system. As you learned in Part 3, information systems exist to facilitate an organization's competitive strategy by supporting business processes or by improving decision making. At this step, the development team defines the goal and purpose of the new system in terms of these purposes.

Consider the materials inventory RFID system at DSI. What is the purpose of that system? It exists to reduce costs in two ways: First, it will lower labour costs by eliminating (or reducing) the number of times raw materials inventory needs to be reorganized to fit in parts and components. Second, it will reduce material costs by eliminating damage to materials and components incurred when items are moved in raw materials inventory.

Another task is to define the project's scope. For the DSI system, are all parts and components to be managed? Or are only major assemblies and components to be managed? How is *major* defined? By size? By cost? Is this system to be effective for all future projects or only certain future projects? Furthermore, which parts of the system are to be implemented at DSI, and which parts will be implemented at the suppliers and manufacturers?

In other systems, the scope might be delineated by specifying the users that will be involved, or the business processes that will be involved, or the plants, offices, and factories that will be involved. At Emerson, for example, Dee might

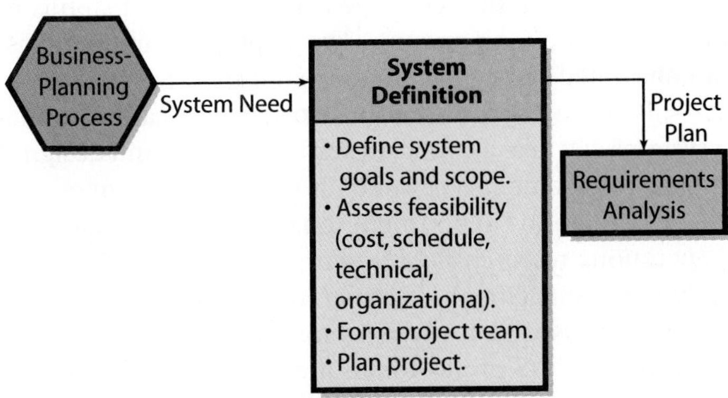

Figure 11-4
SDLC: System Definition Phase

have defined the scope of her blog to include only Nova Scotia salespeople, or only Nova Scotia salespeople who sell certain products.

A clear definition of project scope greatly simplifies requirements determination and other subsequent development work.

Assess Feasibility

Once we have defined the project's goals and scope, the next step is to assess feasibility. This step answers the question, "Does this project make sense?" The aim here is to eliminate obviously inappropriate projects before forming a project development team and investing significant labour.

Feasibility has four dimensions: **cost**, **schedule**, **technical**, and **organizational**. Because IS development projects are difficult to budget and schedule, cost and schedule feasibility can be only an approximate, back-of-the-envelope analysis. The purpose is to eliminate any obviously infeasible ideas as soon as possible.

For example, for the DSI system, you might investigate how much the hardware for RFID scanning costs. If the answer is a minimum of $30 000, then you can decide whether DSI can reasonably expect to receive benefits to justify this expense. If you do not expect sufficient benefits, DSI can cancel the project or agree to accomplish your goals using some other system.

Like cost feasibility, *schedule feasibility* is difficult to determine because it is difficult to estimate the time it will take to acquire the system. However, if, for example, you determine that it will take no less than six months to acquire the system and put it into operation, DSI can then decide if it can accept that minimum schedule. At this stage of the project, the company should not rely on either cost or schedule estimates; the purpose of these estimates is simply to rule out any obviously unacceptable projects.

Technical feasibility refers to whether existing information technology is likely to be able to meet the needs of the new system. At DSI, you might ask whether it is possible to use RFID to organize inventory. Is there sufficient regularity in the way inventory is accessed to determine where goods should be placed? You know that it's technically feasible to read RFID data. The question is, Can you do something useful with that data?

Finally, *organizational feasibility* concerns whether the new system fits within the organization's customs, culture, charter, or legal requirements. For example, if DSI has contracts that prohibit suppliers from providing the RFID data, the proposed system is organizationally infeasible. Or if the combined data violate antitrust law, the new system would be organizationally infeasible.

Step 2: Requirements Analysis

If the defined project is determined to be feasible, the next step is to form the project team and develop requirements. Developing requirements is a process that might be considered somewhat unique to the area of management information systems. This is why any student interested in a career in management information systems will take a course in system analysis and design. The development of project requirements is essentially the management of scope in an IT project. While the accounting department can teach us about maintaining budgets and the operations research department can focus on minimizing project schedules, only the management information systems area focuses on how to manage scope in projects. This is why systems analysis and design is a core skill in MIS. The reason why MIS professionals are focused on scope is likely due to the difficulty of conceptualizing just what an information system looks like and what it should do.

When developing requirements, the team normally consists of both IT personnel and user representatives. The project manager and IT personnel can be in-house personnel or outside contractors. Typical personnel on a development team are a manager (or managers, for larger projects), systems analysts, programmers, software testers, and users.

Systems analysts are IT professionals who understand both business and technology. They are active throughout the systems development process and play a key role in moving the project through the systems development process. Systems analysts integrate the work of the programmers, testers, and users. Depending on the nature of the project, the team may also include hardware and communications specialists, database designers and administrators, and other IT specialists.

The team composition changes over time. During requirements definition, the team will be heavy with systems analysts. During design and implementation, it will be heavy with programmers, testers, and database designers. During integrated testing and conversion, the team will be augmented with testers and business users.

User involvement is critical throughout the system development process. Depending on the size and nature of the project, users are assigned to the project either full or part time. Sometimes users are assigned to review and oversight committees that meet periodically, especially at the completion of project phases and other milestones. Users are involved in many different ways. *The important point is for users to have active involvement and to take ownership of the project throughout the entire development process.* DSI has only one person in its IT department, so the development team will consist, at least initially, of that person and users. As the project progresses, DSI will need to outsource for professional systems developers and programmers (or hire additional IT personnel).

Q5 What Is the User's Role in Requirements Development?

The primary purpose of the requirements analysis phase is to determine and document the specific features and functions of the new system. For most development projects, this phase requires interviewing dozens of users and documenting potentially hundreds of requirements. Requirements definition is, thus, expensive. It is also difficult, as you will see.

Determine Requirements

Determining the system's requirements is the most important phase in the systems development process. If the requirements are wrong, the system will be wrong. If the requirements are determined completely and correctly, then design and implementation will be easier and more likely to result in success.

Examples of requirements are the contents of a report or the fields in a data entry form. Requirements include not only what is to be produced, but also how frequently and how fast it is to be produced. Some requirements specify the volume of data to be stored and processed.

If you take a course in systems analysis and design, you will spend weeks on techniques for determining requirements. Here, we will just summarize that process. Typically, systems analysts interview users and record the results in some consistent manner. Good interviewing skills are crucial; users are notorious for being unable to describe what they want and need. Users also tend to focus on the tasks they are performing at the time of the interview. Tasks performed at the end of the quarter or end of the year are forgotten if the interview takes place mid-quarter. Seasoned and experienced systems analysts know how to conduct interviews so as to bring such requirements to light.

As listed in Figure 11-5, sources of requirements include existing systems as well as the forms, reports, queries, and application features and functions desired in the new system. Security is another important category of requirements.

If the new system involves a new database or substantial changes to an existing database, then the development team will create a data model. As you learned in Chapter 5, that model must reflect the users' perspective on their business and business activities. Thus, the data model is constructed on the basis of user interviews and must be validated by those users.

Sometimes, the requirements determination is so focused on the software and data components that other components are forgotten. Experienced project managers ensure consideration of requirements for all five IS components, not just for software and data. Regarding hardware, the team might ask: Are there special needs or restrictions on hardware? Is there an organizational standard governing what kinds of hardware may or may not be used? Must the new system use existing hardware? What requirements are there for communications and network hardware?

Similarly, the team should consider requirements for procedures and personnel: Do accounting controls require procedures that separate duties and authorities? Are there restrictions that some actions can be taken only by certain departments or specific personnel? Are there policy requirements or union rules that restrict activities to certain categories of employees? Will the system need to interface with information systems from other companies and organizations? In short, requirements need to be considered for all the components of the new information system.

These questions are examples of the kinds of questions that must be asked and answered during requirements analysis.

Figure 11-5
SDLC: Requirements Analysis Phase

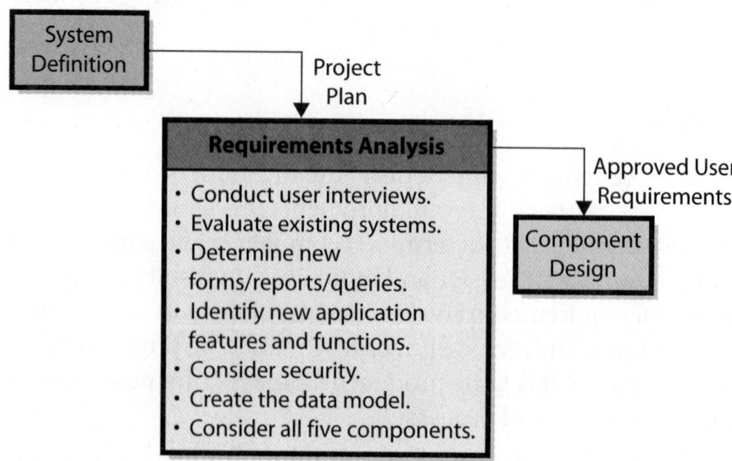

Approve Requirements

Once the requirements have been specified, the users must review and approve them before the project continues. The easiest and cheapest time to alter the information system is in the requirements phase. Changing a requirement at this stage is simply a matter of changing a description. Changing a requirement in the implementation phase may require weeks of reworking applications components and the database. Before going further, you might want to read about how estimates of budget and schedule are often created in the real world in the Exercise "The Real Estimation Process" at the end of the chapter. This Exercise will help you understand how difficult it can be to develop accurate estimates for IT projects.

Q6 How Are Information Systems Designed, Implemented, and Maintained?

Before we consider component design, we need to discuss the options we have for developing the system. Our previous discussion in this chapter suggested four ways to acquire information systems: buy, buy and customize, rent, or build it yourself. For the first three of these methods the information system is already built, so the organization does not have to do major development. This type of acquisition requires the organization to match its requirements with the capabilities of the software application that has already been built. Figure 11-6 summarizes this matching process.

When an organization works through the matching process, it will almost always find discrepancies between the requirements of the business and the capabilities of the software application. No application fits perfectly. When these discrepancies are identified, the organization faces one of three choices, as shown in Figure 11-6. These choices are to: (1) modify the software, (2) modify the organizational procedures and data, or (3) live with the problems. In reality,

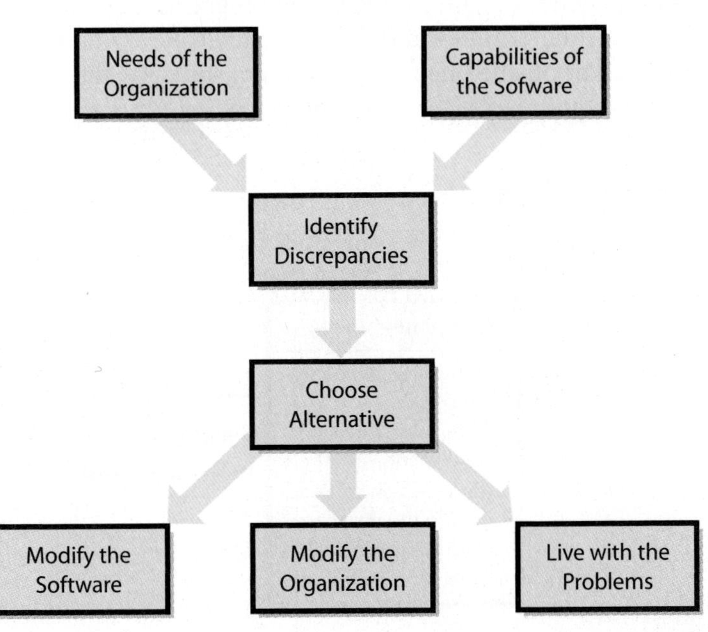

Figure 11-6
Matching Organizational Needs and COTS Software Capabilities

the final solution for the organization is likely a combination of these three choices.

As a future business manager, it is important for you to realize that **commercial-off-the-shelf (COTS)** software will never fit your organizational requirements exactly. So it is reasonable to expect and budget for some cost and some time before the software is successfully implemented in the organization. How long? For a large implementation like an ERP, it is reasonable to consider a span of 18 months before things settle down. For smaller systems this time will be significantly shorter.

In the rest of the chapter we will discuss the steps in the SDLC assuming that the organization will be building the system itself. What you should realize now is that regardless of whether you buy, rent, or build the information system, the basic steps for acquiring are all the same. You first have to understand your objectives and analyze your requirements. Then you design the system using either COTS or a custom design. Then you implement it and maintain it.

Step 3: Component Design

Each of the five components of an information system must be designed. Typically, the team designs each component by developing alternatives, evaluating each of those alternatives against the requirements, and then selecting among those alternatives. Accurate requirements are critical here; if they are incomplete or wrong, then they will be poor guides for evaluation. Figure 11-7 shows that design tasks pertain to each of the five IS components.

Hardware Design

For hardware, the team determines specifications for the hardware it wants to acquire. (The team is not designing hardware in the sense of building a CPU or a disk drive.) For the DSI system, the team would need to determine what hardware is required to read and write to the RFID devices. They also need to specify the computer and network connections that will process the RFID data and compute inventory locations for incoming components.

Software Design

Software design depends on the source of the programs. For off-the-shelf software, the team must determine candidate products and evaluate them against the requirements. For off-the-shelf with alteration software, the team identifies products to be acquired off-the-shelf and then determines the alterations

Figure 11-7
SDLC: Component Design Phase

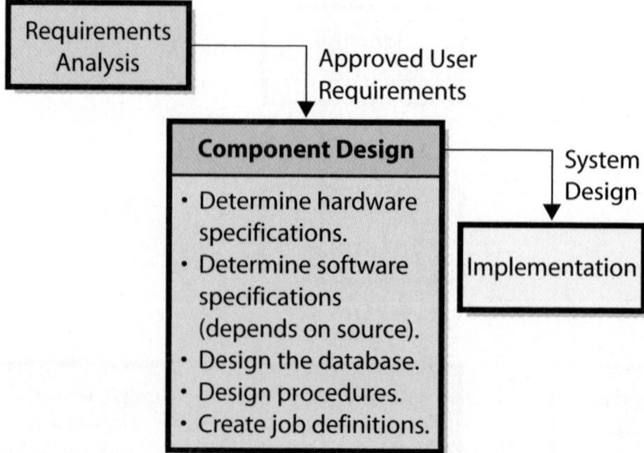

required. For custom-developed programs, the team produces design documentation for writing program code.

Database Design

If developers are constructing a database, then during this phase they convert the data model to a database design using techniques like those described in Chapter 5. If developers are using off-the-shelf programs, then little database design needs be done; the programs will handle their own database processing. There will likely be a need to integrate with existing databases.

Procedure Design

For a business information system, the system developers and the organization must also design procedures for both users and operations personnel. Procedures need to be developed for normal processing, backup, and failure recovery operations, as summarized in Figure 11-8. Usually, teams of systems analysts and key users design the procedures.

Design of Job Descriptions

With regard to people, design involves developing job descriptions for both users and operations personnel. Sometimes new information systems require new jobs. If so, the duties and responsibilities for the new jobs need to be defined in accordance with the organization's human resources policies. More often, organizations add new duties and responsibilities to existing jobs. In this case, developers define these new tasks and responsibilities in this phase. Sometimes the personnel design task is as simple as statements like, "Jason will be in charge of making backups." As with procedures, teams of systems analysts and users determine job descriptions and functions.

Step 4: Implementation

Once the design is complete, the next phase in the SDLC is implementation. Tasks in this phase are to build, test, and convert the users to the new system (see Figure 11-9). Developers construct each of the components independently. They

	Users	Operations Personnel
Normal processing	• Procedures for using the system to accomplish business tasks	• Procedures for starting, stopping, and operating the system
Backup	• User procedures for backing up data and other resources	• Operations procedures for backing up data and other resources
Failure recovery	• Procedures to continue operations when the system fails • Procedures to convert back to the system after recovery	• Procedures to identify the source of failure and get it fixed • Procedures to recover and restart the system

Figure 11-8
Procedures to Be Designed

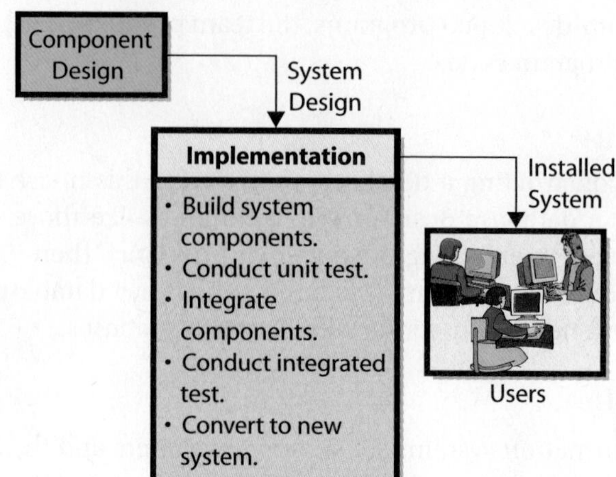

Figure 11-9
SDLC: Implementation Phase

obtain, install, and test hardware. They license and install off-the-shelf programs; they write adaptations and custom programs as necessary. They construct a database and fill it with data. They document, review, and test procedures, and they create training programs. Finally, the organization hires and trains needed personnel.

System Testing

Once developers have constructed and tested all the components, they integrate the individual components and test the system. So far, we have glossed over testing as if there is nothing to it. In fact, software and system testing are difficult, time-consuming, and complex tasks. Developers need to design and develop test plans and record the results of tests. They need to devise a system to assign fixes to people and to verify that fixes are correct and complete.

A **test plan** consists of sequences of actions that users will take when using the new system. Test plans include not only the normal actions that users will take, but also incorrect actions. A comprehensive test plan should cause every line of program code to be executed. The test plan should cause every error message to be displayed. Testing, retesting, and re-retesting consume huge amounts of labour. Often, developers can reduce the labour cost of testing by writing programs that invoke system features automatically.

Today, many IT professionals work as testing specialists. Testing, or **product quality assurance (PQA),** as it is often called, is an important career. PQA personnel usually construct the test plan with the advice and assistance of users. PQA test engineers perform testing, and they also supervise user test activity. Many PQA professionals are programmers who write automated test programs.

In addition to IT professionals, users should be involved in system testing. Users participate in the development of test plans and test cases. They can also be part of the test team, usually working under the direction of PQA personnel. Users have the final say on whether the system is ready for use. If you are invited to participate as a user tester, take that responsibility seriously. It will become much more difficult to fix problems after you've begun using the system in production.

Beta testing is the process of allowing future system users to try out the new system on their own. Software vendors like Microsoft often release beta versions of their products for users to try and to test. Such users report problems back to the vendor. Beta testing is the last stage of testing. Normally products in the beta test phase are complete and fully functioning; they typically have few serious errors. Organizations that are developing large new information systems sometimes use a beta-testing process just as software vendors do.

System Conversion

Once the system has passed integrated testing, the organization installs the new system. The term **system conversion** is often used for this activity because it implies the process of *converting* business activity from the old system to the new.

Organizations can implement a system conversion in one of four ways:

- Pilot
- Phased
- Parallel
- Plunge

IS professionals recommend any of the first three, depending on the circumstances. In most cases, companies should avoid "taking the plunge"!

With **pilot installation**, the organization implements the entire system on a limited portion of the business. An example would be for DSI to use the system for one or two component manufacturers. The advantage of pilot implementation is that if the system fails, the failure is contained within a limited boundary. This reduces exposure of the business and also protects the new system from developing a negative reputation throughout the organization(s).

As the name implies, with **phased installation** the new system is installed in phases across the organization(s). Once a given piece works, the organization installs and tests another piece of the system, until the entire system has been installed. Some systems are so tightly integrated that they cannot be installed in phased pieces. Such systems must be installed using one of the other techniques. DSI's RFID system falls into this category.

With **parallel installation**, the new system runs in parallel with the old one until the new system is tested and fully operational. Parallel installation is expensive because the organization incurs the costs of running both systems. Users must work double time, if you will, to run both systems. Then considerable work is needed to determine if the results of the new system are consistent with those of the old system.

However, some organizations consider the costs of parallel installation to be a form of insurance. It is the slowest and most expensive style of installation, but it does provide an easy fallback position if the new system fails.

The final style of conversion is **plunge installation** (sometimes called *direct* or *cutover installation*). With it, the organization shuts off the old system and starts the new system. If the new system fails, the organization is in trouble: Nothing can be done until either the new system is fixed or the old system is reinstalled. Because of the risk, organizations should avoid this conversion style if possible. The one exception is when the new system is providing a new capability that is not vital to the operation of the organization.

Figure 11-10 summarizes the tasks for each of the five components during the design and implementation phases. Use this figure to test your knowledge of the tasks in each phase.

	Hardware	Software	Data	Procedures	People
Design	Determine hardware specifications.	Select off-the-shelf programs. Design alterations and custom programs as necessary.	Design database and related structures.	Design user and operations procedures.	Develop user and operations job descriptions.
Implementation	Obtain, install, and test hardware.	License and install off-the-shelf programs. Write alterations and custom programs. Test programs.	Create database. Fill with data. Test data.	Document procedures. Create training programs. Review and test procedures.	Hire and train personnel.
	Integrated Test and Conversion				

Unit test each component (applies to the Implementation row)

Figure 11-10
Design and Implementation for the Five Components

Step 5: Maintenance

The last phase of the SDLC is system maintenance. Maintenance is a misnomer; the work done during this phase is either to *fix* the system so that it works correctly or to *adapt* it to changes in requirements. *MIS in Use 11* provides a glimpse into the difficult issues related to maintaining an information system.

Figure 11-11 shows tasks during the system maintenance phase. First, there needs to be a means for tracking both failures[4] and requests for enhancements to meet new requirements. For small systems, organizations can track failures and enhancements using word-processing documents. As systems become

Figure 11-11
SDLC: System Maintenance Phase

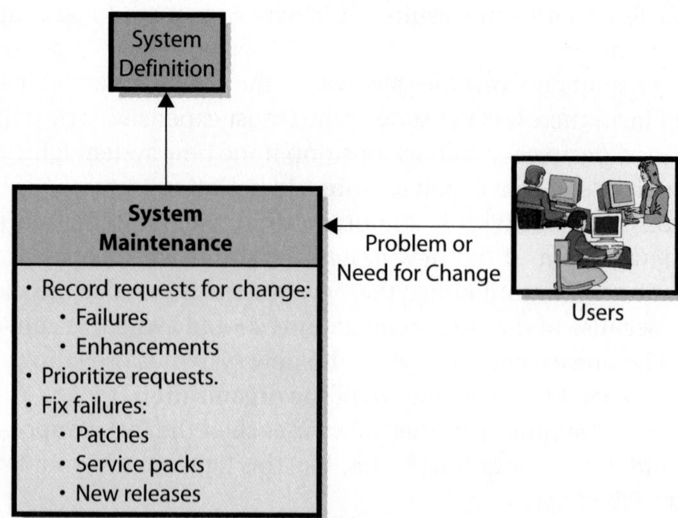

4. A *failure* is a difference between what the system does and what it is supposed to do. Sometimes you will hear the term *bug* used instead of *failure*. As a future user, call failures *failures*, for that's what they are. Don't have a *bugs list*, have a *failures list*. Don't have an *unresolved bug*, have an *unresolved failure*. A few months of managing an organization that's coping with a serious failure will show you the importance of this difference in terms.

Choice, Complexity, and Compatibility

Delivering Internet-based courses is an important part of the computing environment for Jim Cranston, chief information officer at British Columbia's Simon Fraser University—and one that has its share of challenges. Not only has his staff had to deal with a merger between the two main suppliers of the content delivery system, a difficult upgrade, and demands that have exceeded predictions, but they are also constantly aware that, while SFU IT has overall accountability for the availability of the system, they have little control of the components that are used to access the system.

Distance education—or, the delivery of education over distance—has been around since the development of the postal service. Initially adopted as a way for universities to expand beyond the physical reach of the campus, students corresponded and interacted with faculty and received lectures (usually audio tapes) and assignments by mail or telephone. Fast forward to the present, however, and it is clear that the Internet has changed everything. Instead of envelopes and audio tapes, students now watch video, listen to lectures, interact with their professors and other students, and complete or submit assignments and take tests and exams online. And it's not just about removing distance—while online education is still popular among geographically remote students, at many universities online education is routinely added to all courses. At SFU, online education was a part of more than 395 courses and used by almost 25 000 students, who accessed the system either remotely or while on campus. Consisting of two V245 application servers running SUN Solaris 10, SUN T2000 database servers, an F5 load balancer that equally distributed the workload, and 1.2 terabytes of mirrored disk space, the system was generally available 24 hours a day and at any given moment was in use by 1200–1500 students with occasional peaks of almost 2000 students during mid-terms and when the due dates for end-of-semester assignments approached.

What bothered Jim today was a troubling email he had received from one of the professors. It was the first week of the semester and the professor had written to Jim to alert him of a serious problem. Some students who were accessing the system were reporting that the online quizzes would sometimes freeze and not allow them to finish. If this wasn't bad enough, other students had found that quizzes would sometimes reset and display the same question two or three times. Jim and his team knew that part of the problem would be solved by a pending hardware upgrade scheduled for the following month (the support staff had intentionally kept the software and hardware upgrades separate to simplify problem diagnosis), but he wasn't sure if this was the only problem. Trying to find out what was causing the problem was difficult because it was intermittent and there seemed to be many variances. Not all students were affected, and it didn't happen at the same time of day. While there are tools in the system to help users check that they're using a supported configuration for which the eLearning system provider explicitly provides support—i.e., computers, operating systems, browsers, etc.—the university does not control and cannot manage the end-user environment. With students facing system problems that affected their grades, and professors receiving too many complaints, Jim's team knew they had to diagnose the problem and plan a solution in short order. At the same time it was hard to collect information. Where should they start?

Questions

1. Why is the distance education environment so complex? How many different types of problems could there be? (*Hint:* Identify the various pieces used to establish a connection, and locate which ones the university has control over and which ones can vary.)
2. How should SFU IT staff diagnose the problem? What information would you need to isolate the problem, and how hard would it be to collect? (*Hint:* As a student, how would you respond to a request for information and how it would be used?)
3. How common are intermittent types of problems? Why are they so much more difficult to identify and solve? (*Hint:* Compare this type of problem with having a flat tire.)
4. What role should the CIO play in diagnosing the problem and communicating to students and faculty?

larger, however, and as the number of failure and enhancement requests increases, many organizations find it necessary to develop a failure-tracking database. Such a database contains a description of each failure or enhancement. It also records who reported the problem, who will make the fix or enhancement, what the status of that work is, and whether the fix or enhancement has been tested and verified by the originator.

Typically, IS personnel prioritize system problems according to their severity. They fix high-priority items as soon as possible, and they fix low-priority items as time and resources become available.

With regard to the software component, software developers group fixes for high-priority failures into a **patch** that can be applied to all copies of a given product. As described in Chapter 4, software vendors supply patches to fix security and other critical problems. They usually bundle fixes of low-priority problems into larger groups called **service packs**. Users apply service packs in much the same way that they apply patches, except that service packs typically involve fixes to hundreds or thousands of problems.

By the way, you may be surprised to learn this, but all commercial software products are shipped with known failures. Usually vendors test their products and remove the most serious problems, but they seldom, if ever, remove all the defects they know about. Shipping with defects is an industry practice; Microsoft, Adobe, Oracle, RedHat, and many others all ship products with known problems.

Because an enhancement is an adaptation to new requirements, developers usually prioritize enhancement requests separately from failures. The decision to make an enhancement includes a business decision that the enhancement will generate an acceptable rate of return. Although minor enhancements are made using service packs, major enhancement requests usually result in a complete new release of a product.

Keep in mind that although we usually think of failures and enhancements as applying to software, they can apply to the other components as well. There can be hardware or database failures or enhancements. There can also be failures and enhancements in procedures and people, though the latter is usually expressed in more humane terms than failure or enhancement. The underlying idea is the same, however.

As stated earlier, note that the maintenance phase starts another cycle of the SDLC process. The decision to enhance a system is a decision to restart the systems development process. Even a simple failure fix goes through all the phases of the SDLC; if it is a small fix, a single person may work through those phases in an abbreviated form. But each of those phases is repeated nonetheless.

Problems with the SDLC

Although the industry has experienced notable successes with the SDLC process, there have been many problems with it as well. One of the reasons for these problems is the waterfall nature of the SDLC. Like a series of waterfalls, the process is supposed to operate in a sequence of nonrepetitive phases. For example, the team completes the requirements phase and goes over the waterfall into the design phase, and on through the process (look back to Figure 11-3). Unfortunately, systems development seldom works so smoothly. Often, there is a need to crawl back up the waterfall, if you will, and repeat work in a prior phase.

Another problem, especially on complicated systems, is the difficulty of documenting requirements in a usable way. One of the authors of this text once managed the database portion of a software project at Boeing in which we invested more than 70 labour-years into a requirements statement. The requirements document comprised 20-some volumes that stood more than two metres tall when stacked on top of one another.

When we entered the design phase, no one really knew all the requirements that concerned a particular feature. We would begin to design a feature only to find that we hadn't considered a requirement buried somewhere in the documentation. In short, the requirements were so unwieldy as to be nearly useless. Projects that spend so much time documenting requirements are sometimes said to be in **analysis paralysis.** These difficulties with the SDLC have led some companies to leave the job of designing, implementing, and maintaining systems to another organization. This option is explored in the next section.

Q7 What Is Outsourcing and What Are Application Service Providers?

Outsourcing is the process of hiring another organization to perform a service. Just about any business activity in the value chain can be outsourced, from marketing and sales to logistics, manufacturing, or customer service. The outsourced vendor can be domestic or international. When a vendor is overseas, outsourcing is referred to as *offshoring*. Offshoring has become an important consideration for IT services. Offshoring experience has shown that establishing clear requirements is the key to providing success in an offshoring agreement.

Many companies today have chosen to outsource portions of their information systems activities. Why? First, outsourcing can be an easy way to gain expertise. Suppose, for example, that an organization wants to upgrade its thousands of user computers on a cost-effective basis. To do so, the organization would need to develop expertise in automated software installation, unattended installations, remote support, and other measures that can be used to improve the efficiency of software management. Developing such expertise is expensive, and it is not in the company's strategic direction. Consequently, the organization might choose to hire a specialist company to perform this service.

Other common reasons for choosing to outsource concern cost reductions. In the case of offshoring, skilled programmers in other countries such as China, India, and Russia make as little as one-sixth the wage of an experienced programmer in North America. Even without this wage difference, organizations can obtain part-time services with outsourcing. An office of 25 lawyers does not need a full-time network administrator. It does need network administration, but only in small amounts. By outsourcing that function, the office of lawyers can obtain network administration in the small amounts needed.

Another reason for outsourcing might be to reduce development risk. Outsourcing can cap financial risk by setting specific prices on components of the system. In addition, outsourcing can reduce risk by ensuring a certain level of quality or avoiding the risk of having substandard quality. Organizations also choose to outsource IS in order to reduce implementation risk. Hiring an outside vendor can reduce the risk of picking the wrong hardware or the wrong software, using the wrong network protocol, or implementing incorrectly.

With so many advantages and with so many different outsourcing alternatives, you may wonder why any company has any in-house IS/IT functions. In fact, outsourcing presents significant risks, as listed in Figure 11-12.

The first risk of outsourcing is a loss of control. Outsourcing puts the vendor in the driver's seat. Each outsource vendor has methods and procedures for its service. Your organization and employees will have to conform to those procedures. For example, a hardware infrastructure vendor will have standard forms and procedures for requesting a computer, for recording and processing a computer problem, or for providing routine maintenance on computers. Once the vendor is in charge, your employees must conform.

In addition, the outsource vendor may change its pricing strategy over time. Initially, an organization obtains a competitive bid from several outsource vendors. However, as the winning vendor learns more about the business and as relationships develop between the organization's employees and those of the vendor, it becomes difficult for other firms to compete for subsequent contracts. The vendor becomes the de facto sole source and, with little competitive pressure, may increase its prices.

Another problem is that an organization can find itself paying for another organization's mismanagement, with little recourse. Over time, if the outsource vendor is mismanaged or suffers setbacks in other arenas, costs will increase.

The final category of outsourcing risk concerns ending the agreement. There is no easy exit. For one, the outsource vendor's employees have gained significant knowledge of the company. They know the server requirements in customer support, they know the patterns of usage, and they know the best procedures for downloading operational data into the data warehouse. Consequently, lack of knowledge will make it difficult to bring the outsourced service back in-house.

Application Service Providers

Application service providers (ASPs) are a special form of outsourcing. In an ASP agreement, an organization contracts with a vendor to "rent" applications from the vendor company on a fee-for-service basis. In traditional outsourcing the vendor often maintains the systems at the organization's location. But that is

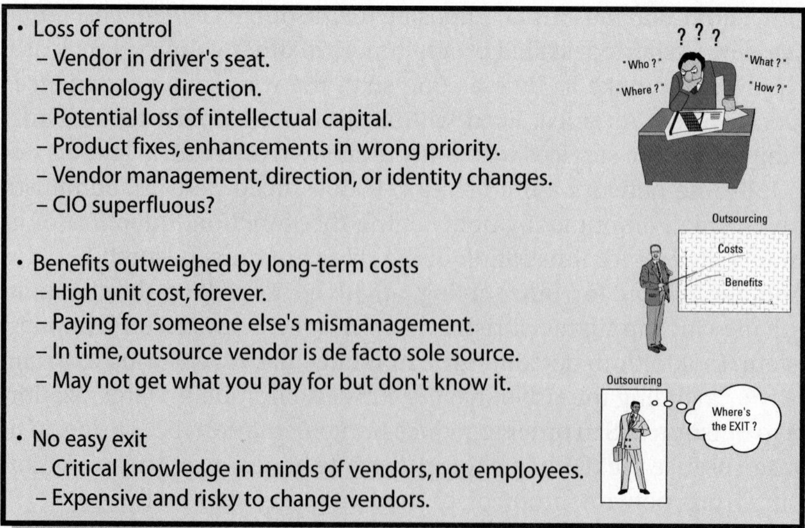

• Loss of control
– Vendor in driver's seat.
– Technology direction.
– Potential loss of intellectual capital.
– Product fixes, enhancements in wrong priority.
– Vendor management, direction, or identity changes.
– CIO superfluous?
• Benefits outweighed by long-term costs
– High unit cost, forever.
– Paying for someone else's mismanagement.
– In time, outsource vendor is de facto sole source.
– May not get what you pay for but don't know it.
• No easy exit
– Critical knowledge in minds of vendors, not employees.
– Expensive and risky to change vendors.
? ? ?
"Who?"
"What?"
"Where?"
"How?"
Outsourcing
Costs
Benefits
Outsourcing
Where's the EXIT?

Figure 11-12
Outsourcing Risks

not the case for ASP. In ASP the vendor maintains the system at its own web location and the client organization accesses the application on the vendor's website. The application software therefore does not have to be located with the client. The vendor can then offer standardized software to many companies while maintaining only a single site (where the actual application resides). This reduces the costs of supporting the application and theoretically reduces the cost associated with outsourcing. The payments are made either monthly or yearly and are often based on the number of employees or on the number of "users" of the software.

Some experts expect that ASP services will become an important acquisition alternative, not only for smaller companies with low budgets but also for larger companies. But the ASP model has some significant risks. For example, the client company loses physical control over some corporate data that are stored in the vendor's machines. In addition, any failure of the Internet means that the client company cannot operate even internally. Finally, there is the potential for "lock-in" of the ASP, which may not allow corporate data to be easily ported to competitor sites. Ownership of the data has to be very clearly stated in the ASP contract. These are significant risks, so the potential benefits of ASP must be weighed against these risks.

ASPs are just one type of outsourcing alternative. There are many other alternatives, and each type carries with it benefits and risks. Business managers need to be aware of the alternatives and be able to balance the benefits and risks associated with these alternatives. What is clear is that what works for one company may not work for another. It's most important to consider the fit between the client and vendor and to carefully develop the relationship between the two companies. Outsourcing deals are very close to partnership agreements. Companies that are successful with outsourcing have recognized the importance of establishing the relationship first before engaging in significant outsourcing arrangements.

How does the knowledge in this chapter help you at DSI?

Knowledge of the SDLC will be invaluable to you at DSI. When Mr. Stratford says, "Great idea, what do we do next?" you know exactly what to say. You can give him a quick summary of the phases of the SDLC and then describe tasks in the definition phase more specifically. You could also say that, as a summer intern, you'll have time to do work on the definition phase, but that if DSI wants to go forward beyond that, it will need to involve other personnel and probably professional systems developers. However, during the summer you should be able to gather the data to help DSI decide whether this project is cost (and otherwise) feasible.

If you get this far, we'd say the full-time job has to be yours. It would be very hard for any intern, niece or otherwise, to compare to this performance!

Active Review

Use this Active Review to verify that you understand the material in the chapter. You can read the entire chapter and then perform the tasks in this review, or you can read the material for just one question and perform the tasks in this review for that question before moving on to the next one.

Q1 How can information systems be acquired?

Explain the four ways that systems can be acquired. What is the most popular method for acquiring systems? Explain why buying software is different from acquiring information systems.

Q2 What are information technology projects and why are they risky?

Provide some examples of IT projects. What are some of the major risks associated with IT projects? Explain why IT projects tend to be risky. What does the temporal model of IT project performance tell us about risks?

Q3 What is information technology project management?

What is ITPM? What organization has established standards for performance in project management? What is the most important skill in IT project management?

Q4 What is analysis and design and the SDLC?

What is the objective of systems analysis and design? Why is systems analysis and design unique to management information systems? What are the five phases of the SDLC? Explain each of the phases.

Q5 What is the user's role in requirements development?

Explain why requirements development is not just for technical experts. What activities can a nontechnical business manager be expected to do in an IT project? Explain why developing good requirements is important for IT project success.

Q6 How are information systems designed, implemented, and maintained?

Summarize design activities for each of the five components of an information system. Name the two major tasks in systems implementation. Summarize the system testing process. Describe the difference between system and software testing. Name four ways of system conversion. Describe each way, and give an example of when each would be effective.

Q7 What is outsourcing and what are application service providers?

Define outsourcing. Explain why come companies choose to outsource. Explain what risks can be associated with outsourcing. Define what an application service provider is. Explain the benefits and risk of the ASP model.

Key Terms and Concepts

Analysis paralysis 319
Application service provider (ASP) 320
Beta testing 314
Commercial-off-the-shelf (COTS) 312
Component design phase 312
Cost feasibility 308
Implementation phase 313
Information technology project management (ITPM) 304
IT project risks 303
Maintenance phase 316
Organizational feasibility 308
Outsourcing 319
Parallel installation 315
Patch 318
Phased installation 315
Pilot installation 315
Plunge installation 315
Product quality assurance (PQA) 314
Requirements analysis phase 308
Schedule feasibility 308
Service pack 318
System conversion 315

Using Your Knowledge

1. Assume Mr. Stratford said to you, "Great idea, what do we do next?" with regard to the project to use RFID on arriving components to assess where to place those components in raw materials inventory.
   a. Develop a plan for this project using the SDLC.
   b. Specify in detail the tasks to accomplish during the system definition phase.

2. Using the knowledge you have gained from this chapter, summarize the roles that you think users should take during an information systems development project. What responsibilities do users have? How closely should they work with the IS team? Who is responsible for stating requirements and constraints? Who is responsible for managing requirements?

3. Consider the DSI project in Chapter 7 in which you were going to analyze tool repair data to determine if tool outages are causing substantial labour losses. Assume that these tools are kept in a centralized tool crib. The tool crib assigns a unique identifier to each tool and maintains records that indicate whether a tool is (a) checked out to an employee, (b) in repair, or (c) available and unused. Further assume that the records for each tool include a tool type, such as 10-inch grinder or 4-inch belt sander. Finally, assume you are to build a system that will produce a quarterly report that shows, for each tool and each tool type, the number of days in use, the number of days in repair, and the number of days available and unused. Further, for each type, your report should show the number of days that all tools of a given type were in repair.
   a. Describe the tasks that need to be accomplished for each phase of the SDLC to build such a system.
   b. Specify in detail the tasks to accomplish during the systems definition phase.

4. If you ask users why they did not participate in requirements specification, some of the common responses are the following:
   a. "I wasn't asked."
   b. "I didn't have time."
   c. "They were talking about a system that would be here in 18 months, and I'm just worried about getting the order out the door today."
   d. "I didn't know what they wanted."
   e. "I didn't know what they were talking about."
   f. "I didn't work here when they started the project."
   g. "The whole situation has changed since they were here; that was 18 months ago!"

   Comment on each of these statements. What strategies do they suggest to you as a future user and as a future manager of users?

5. Consider outsourcing of the following business functions:
   - Employee cafeteria
   - General ledger accounting
   - Corporate IT infrastructure (networks, servers, and infrastructure applications such as email)

   a. Compare the benefits of outsourcing for each business function.
   b. Compare the risks of outsourcing for each business function.
   c. Do you believe that the decision to outsource is easier for some of these functions than for others? Why or why not?

6. Read the Marriott International case at the end of Chapter 10.
   a. List the advantages of outsourcing the HR function.
   b. List the risks of outsourcing the HR function.
   c. How did outsourcing HR reduce the risk in developing OneSystem?

Case Study 11

Slow Learners, or What?

In 1974, when one of the authors of this textbook was teaching at Colorado State University, we conducted a study of the causes of information systems failures. We interviewed personnel on several dozen projects and collected survey data on another 50 projects. Our analysis of the data revealed that the single most important factor in IS failure was a lack of user involvement. The second major factor was unclear, incomplete, and inconsistent requirements.

At the time, I was a devoted computer programmer and IT techie, and frankly, I was surprised. I thought that the significant problems would have been technical issues.

I recall one interview in particular. A large sugar producer had attempted to implement a new system for paying sugar-beet farmers. The new system was to be implemented at some 20 different sugar-beet collection sites, which were located in small farming communities, adjacent to rail yards. One of the benefits of the new system was significant cost savings, and a major share of those savings occurred because the new system eliminated the need for local comptrollers. The new system was expected to eliminate the jobs of 20 or so senior people.

The comptrollers, however, had been paying local farmers for decades; they were popular leaders not just within the company, but in their communities as well. They were well liked, highly respected, important people. A system that caused the elimination of their jobs was, using a term from this chapter, *organizationally infeasible,* to say the least.

Nonetheless, the system was constructed, but an IS professional who was involved told me, "Somehow, that new system just never seemed to work. The data weren't entered on a timely basis, or they were in error, or incomplete; sometimes the data weren't entered at all. Our operations were falling apart during the key harvesting season, and we finally backed off and returned to the old system." Active involvement of system users would have identified this organizational infeasibility long before the system was implemented.

That's ancient history, you say. Maybe, but in 1994 the Standish Group published a now famous study on IS failures. Entitled "The CHAOS Report," the study indicated the leading causes of IS failure are, in descending order, (1) lack of user input, (2) incomplete requirements and specifications, and (3) changing requirements and specifications (www.standishgroup.com). That study was completed some 20 years after our study.

In 2004, Professor Joseph Kasser and his students at the University of Maryland analyzed 19 system failures to determine their cause. They then correlated their analysis of the cause with the opinions of the professionals involved in the failures. The correlated results indicate that the first-priority cause of system failure was "Poor requirements" and the second-priority cause was "Failure to communicate with the customer" (www.softwaretechnews.com/technews2-2/trouble.html).

In 2003, the IRS Oversight Board concluded that the first cause of the IRS BSM failure was "inadequate business unit ownership and sponsorship of projects. This resulted in unrealistic business cases and continuous project scope 'creep.'"

For over 30 years, studies have consistently shown that leading causes of system failures are a lack of user involvement and incomplete and changing requirements. Yet failures from these very failures continue to mount.

Sources: www.standishgroup.com; www.softwaretechnews.com/technews2-2/trouble.html.

Questions

1. Using the knowledge you have gained from this chapter, summarize the roles you think users should take during an information systems development project. What responsibilities do users have? How closely should they work with the IS team? Who is responsible for stating requirements and constraints? Who is responsible for managing requirements?
2. If you ask IS professionals why they did not obtain a complete and accurate list of requirements, common responses are:
   a. "It was nearly impossible to get on the users' calendars. They were always too busy."
   b. "The users wouldn't regularly attend our meetings. As a result, one meeting would be dominated by the needs of one group, and another meeting would be dominated by the needs of another group."
   c. "Users didn't take the requirement process seriously. They wouldn't thoroughly review the requirements statements before review meetings."
   d. "Users kept changing. We'd meet with one person one time and another person a second time, and they'd want different things."
   e. "We didn't have enough time."
   f. "The requirements kept changing."

   Comment on each of these statements. What strategies do they suggest to you as a future user and a future manager of users?
3. If it is widely understood that one of the principal causes of IS failures is a lack of user involvement, and if that factor continues to be a problem after 301 years of experience, does this mean that the problem cannot be solved? For example, everyone knows that you can maximize your gains by buying stocks at their annual low price and selling them at their annual high price, but doing so is very difficult. Is it equally true that although everyone knows that users should be involved in requirements specification, and that requirements should be complete, it just cannot be done? Why or why not?

PEARSON
myMISlab

What Do YOU Think?

The Real Estimation Process

"I'm a software developer. I write programs in an object-oriented language called C++. I'm a skilled object-oriented designer, too. I should be—I've been at it 12 years and worked on major projects for several software companies. For the last 4 years I've been a team leader. I lived through the heyday of the dot-com era and now work in the IT department of a giant pharmaceutical company.

"All this estimating theory is just that—theory. It's not really the way things work. Sure, I've been on projects in which we tried different estimation techniques. But here's what really happens: You develop an estimate using whatever technique you want. Your estimate goes in with the estimates of all the other team leaders. The project manager sums all those estimates together and produces an overall estimate for the project.

"By the way, in my projects, time has been a much bigger factor than money. At one software company I worked for, you could be 300 percent over your dollar budget and get no more than a slap on the wrist. Be two weeks late, however, and you were finished.

"Anyway, the project managers take the project schedule to senior management for approval, and what happens? Senior management thinks they are negotiating.

"'Oh, no,' they say, 'that's way too long. You can surely take a month off that schedule. We'll approve the project, but we want it done by February 1 instead of March 1.[2]

"Now, what's their justification? They think that tight schedules make for efficient work. You know that everyone will work extra hard to meet the tighter time frame. They know Parkinson's Law—'the time required to perform a task expands to the time available to do it.' So, fearing the possibility of wasting time because of too-lenient schedules, they lop a month off our estimate.

"Estimates are what they are; you can't knock off a month or two without some problem, somewhere. What does happen is that projects get behind, and then management expects us to work longer and longer hours. Like they said in the early years at Microsoft, 'We have flexible working hours. You can work any 65 hours per week you want.'

"Not that our estimation techniques are all that great, either. Most software developers are optimists. They schedule things as if everything will go as planned, and things seldom do. Also, schedulers usually don't allow for vacations, sick days, trips to the dentist, training on new technology, peer reviews, and all the other things we do in addition to writing software.

"So we start with optimistic schedules on our end, then management negotiates a month or two off, and voilà, we have a late project. After a while, management has been burned by late projects so much that they mentally add the month or even more back onto the official schedule. Then both sides work in a fantasy world, where no one believes the schedule, but everyone pretends they do.

"I like my job. I like software development. Management here is no better or worse than in other places. As long as I have interesting work to do, I'll stay here. But I'm not working myself silly to meet these fantasy deadlines."

Discussion Questions

1. What do you think of this developer's attitude? Do you think he's unduly pessimistic or do you think there's merit to what he says?
2. What do you think of his idea that management thinks they're negotiating? Should management negotiate schedules? Why or why not?
3. Suppose a project actually requires 12 months to complete. Which do you think is likely to cost more: (a) having an official schedule of 11 months with at least a 1-month overrun, or (b) having an official schedule of 13 months and following Parkinson's Law, having the project take 13 months?
4. Suppose you're a business manager and an information system is being developed for your use. You review the scheduling documents and see that little time has been allowed for vacations, sick leave, miscellaneous other work, and so forth. What do you do?
5. Describe the intangible costs of having an organizational belief that schedules are always unreasonable.
6. If this developer worked for you, how would you deal with his attitude about scheduling?
7. Do you think there's a difference between scheduling information systems development projects and scheduling other types of projects? What characteristics might make such projects unique? In what ways are they the same as other projects?
8. What do you think managers should do in light of your answer to question 7?

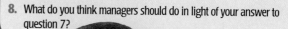

12 Managing Information Security and Privacy

This
could happen
to you

"One person?" That's what I asked myself when I met the one and only IT person at DSI. "How can one person perform the whole IT job for a company with $50 million-plus in sales?" Dee's division of Emerson sells about $800 million per year and is supported by an IT department with 200 people. Divide sales by the number of IT personnel, and Emerson supports $4 million of revenue per IT person. DSI supports $50 million or so with one person. Is Emerson inefficient, or is something out of whack at DSI?

I commented to DSI's IT person, Chris, that he must be pretty busy.

"Not really," he said. "Oh, sometimes, if one of our servers fails. But, most of the time, I work fairly regular hours."

I learned that DSI develops no software in-house; it uses only licensed software. I also found that John Stratford employs directors and project managers that are IT self-sufficient. Apparently, the only support users want from DSI's IT department is reliable infrastructure. The company has a wired/wireless LAN with two servers. One supports sales and marketing and includes the DSI website; the other supports design, inventory, and manufacturing. Seemingly, as long as the servers work, the users are happy.

As stated at the end of Chapter 10, one might bet that something is falling through the cracks at DSI. How secure is the company's system? How well is its data protected? How well is the data backed up? Is DSI prepared for a natural disaster like a flood or hurricane? What plan does it have to respond to a security incident?

As a summer intern, you probably cannot raise these issues yourself. But suppose that Mr. Stratford asked you about them. Or, suppose you work in accounting, and your boss asked you to help prepare for the annual audit. You know that security is part of that audit. What should DSI be doing about security? What are the risks, and what can the company do about them?

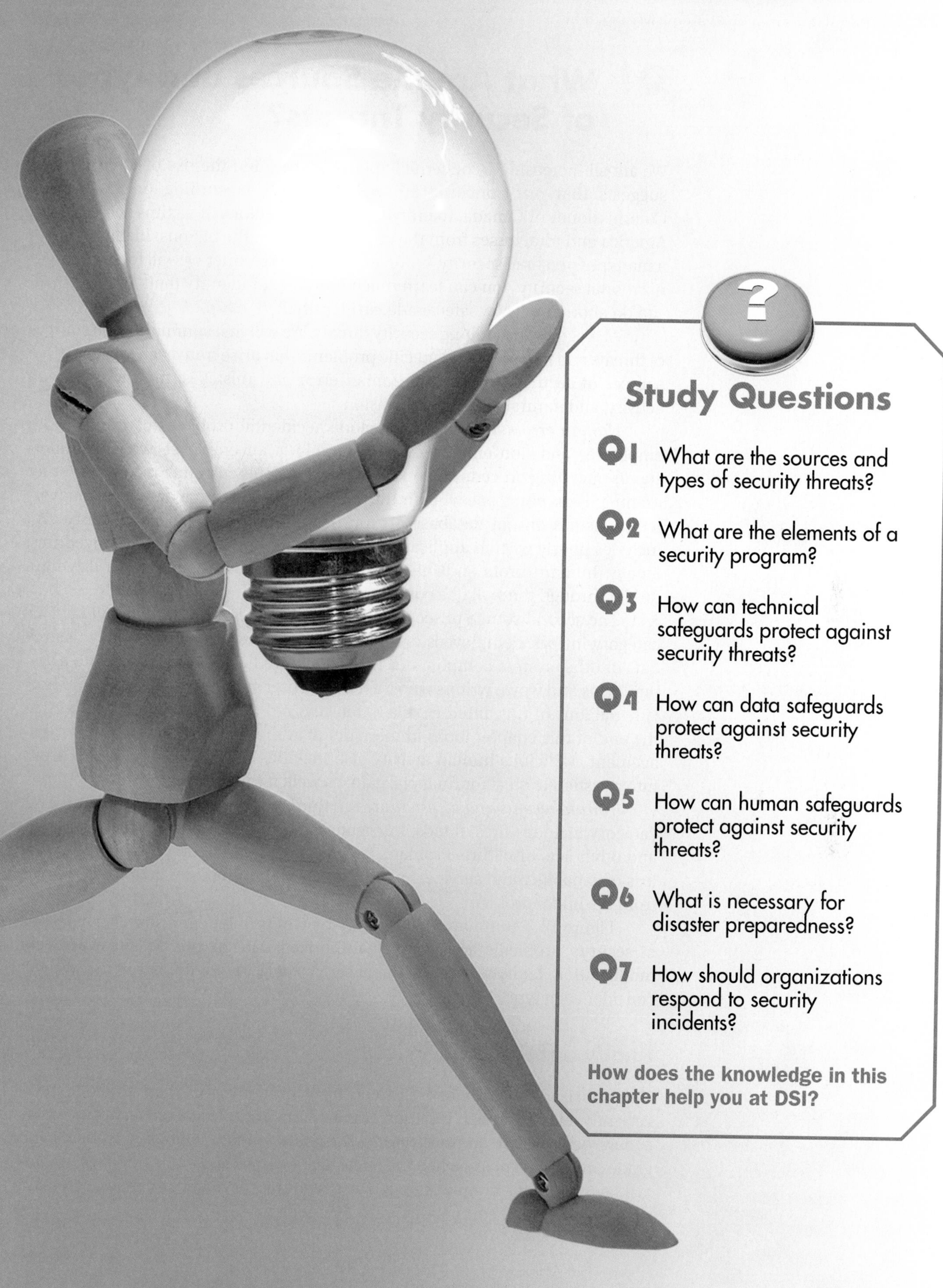

Study Questions

Q1 What are the sources and types of security threats?

Q2 What are the elements of a security program?

Q3 How can technical safeguards protect against security threats?

Q4 How can data safeguards protect against security threats?

Q5 How can human safeguards protect against security threats?

Q6 What is necessary for disaster preparedness?

Q7 How should organizations respond to security incidents?

How does the knowledge in this chapter help you at DSI?

Q1 What Are the Sources and Types of Security Threats?

We are all increasingly concerned about security, and the rise of **identity theft** suggests that our concerns are well founded[1]. According to the Privacy Commissioner of Canada, identity theft claims millions of victims across North America and total losses from the crime measure in the billions. Identity theft is a matter of personal security, however, and in this chapter we will focus on organizational security. You can learn much more about identity theft and what you can do about it at www.safecanada.ca/identitytheft_e.asp.

We begin by describing security threats. We will first summarize the sources of threats and then describe specific problems that arise from each source. Three sources of **security threats** are human error and mistakes, malicious human activity, and natural events and disasters.

Human errors and mistakes include accidental problems caused by both employees and non-employees. An example is an employee who misunderstands operating procedures and accidentally deletes customer records. Another example is an employee who, in the course of backing up a database, inadvertently installs an old database on top of the current one. This category also includes poorly written application programs and poorly designed procedures. Finally, human errors and mistakes include physical accidents like driving a forklift through the wall of a computer room.

The second source of security problems is *malicious human activity*. This category includes employees and former employees who intentionally destroy data or other system components. It also includes hackers who break into a system, virus and worm writers who infect computer systems, and people who provide millions of unwanted emails (often referred to as **spam**). *Case Study 12* at the end of this chapter looks in more detail at the issues related to spam management. Malicious human activity also includes outside criminals who break into a system to steal for financial gain; as well, it includes terrorism.

Natural events and disasters are the third source of security problems. This category includes fires, floods, hurricanes, earthquakes, tsunamis, avalanches, and other acts of nature. Problems in this category include not only the initial loss of capability and service, but also losses stemming from actions to recover from the initial problem.

Figure 12-1 summarizes threats by type of problem and source. Five types of security problems are listed: unauthorized data disclosure, incorrect data modification, faulty service, denial of service, and loss of infrastructure. We will consider each type.

Unauthorized Data Disclosure

Unauthorized data disclosure can occur by human error when someone inadvertently releases data in violation of policy. An example at a university would be a new department administrator who posts student names, numbers, and grades in a public place, when the releasing of names and grades violates provincial law. Another example is employees who unknowingly or carelessly release proprietary data to competitors or to the media.

[1] "Identity Theft- A Primer" from Privacy Commissioner of Canada, March 2007 (http://www.privcom.gc.ca/id/primer_e.asp).

		Source		
		Human Error	Malicious Activity	Natural Disasters
Problem	Unauthorized data disclosure	Procedural mistakes	Pretexting Phishing Spoofing Sniffing Computer crime	Disclosure during recovery
	Incorrect data modification	Procedural mistakes Incorrect procedures Ineffective accounting controls System errors	Hacking Computer crime	Incorrect data recovery
	Faulty service	Procedural mistakes Development and installation errors	Computer crime Usurpation	Service improperly restored
	Denial of service	Accidents	DOS attacks	Service interruption
	Loss of infrastructure	Accidents	Theft Terrorist activity	Property loss

Figure 12-1
Security Threats

The popularity and efficacy of search engines has created another source of inadvertent disclosure. Employees who place restricted data on websites that can be reached by search engines may mistakenly publish proprietary or restricted data over the web.

Of course, proprietary and personal data can also be released maliciously. **Pretexting** occurs when someone deceives by pretending to be someone else. A common scam involves a telephone caller who pretends to be from a credit card company and claims to be checking the validity of credit card numbers: "I'm checking your MasterCard number; it begins 5181. Can you verify the rest of the number?" All MasterCard numbers start with 5181; the caller is attempting to steal a valid number.

Phishing is a similar technique for obtaining unauthorized data that uses pretexting via email. The *phisher* pretends to be a legitimate company and sends an email requesting confidential data, such as account numbers, social insurance numbers, account passwords, and so forth. Phishing compromises legitimate brands and trademarks. The *MIS in Use* feature "Phishing for Credit Card Accounts" on pages 350–351 looks in more detail at some examples of phishing.

Spoofing is another term for someone pretending to be someone else. If you pretend to be your professor, you are spoofing your professor. The *MIS in Use* feature in this chapter provides an example of this. **IP spoofing** occurs when an intruder uses another site's IP address as if it were that other site. **Email spoofing** is a synonym for phishing.

Sniffing is a technique for intercepting computer communications. With wired networks, sniffing requires a physical connection to the network. With wireless networks, no such connection is required: **drive-by sniffers** simply take computers with wireless connections through an area and search for unprotected wireless networks. They can monitor and intercept wireless traffic at will. Even protected wireless networks are vulnerable, as you will learn. Spyware and adware are two other sniffing techniques discussed later in this chapter.

Other forms of computer crime include breaking into networks to steal data such as customer lists, product inventory data, employee data, and other proprietary and confidential data.

Finally, people may inadvertently disclose data during recovery from a natural disaster. Usually, during a recovery, everyone is so focused on restoring system capability that they ignore normal security safeguards. A request like, "I need a copy of the customer database backup" will receive far less scrutiny during disaster recovery than at other times.

Incorrect Data Modification

The second problem category in Figure 12-1 is *incorrect data modification.* Examples include incorrectly increasing a customer's discount or incorrectly modifying an employee's salary, earned days of vacation, or annual bonus. Other examples include placing incorrect information, such as incorrect price changes, on the company's website or company portal.

Incorrect data modification can occur through human error when employees follow procedures incorrectly or when procedures have been incorrectly designed. For proper internal control on systems that process financial data or that control inventories of assets like products and equipment, companies should ensure separation of duties and authorities and have multiple checks and balances in place.

A final type of incorrect data modification caused by human error includes *system errors.* An example is the lost-update problem discussed in Chapter 5.

Hacking occurs when a person gains unauthorized access to a computer system. Although some people hack for the sheer joy of doing it, other hackers invade systems for the malicious purpose of stealing or modifying data. Computer criminals invade computer networks to obtain critical data or to manipulate the system for financial gain. Examples are reducing account balances or directing a shipment of goods to unauthorized locations and customers.

Finally, faulty recovery actions after a disaster can result in incorrect data changes. The faulty actions can be unintentional or malicious.

Faulty Service

The third problem category, *faulty service,* includes problems that result because of incorrect system operation. Faulty service could include incorrect data modification, as just described. It could also include systems that work incorrectly by sending the wrong goods to the customer or the ordered goods to the wrong customer, incorrectly billing customers, or sending the wrong information to employees. Humans can inadvertently cause faulty service by making procedural mistakes. System developers can write programs incorrectly or make errors during the installation of hardware, software programs, and data.

Usurpation occurs when unauthorized programs invade a computer system and replace legitimate programs. Such unauthorized programs typically shut down the legitimate system and substitute their own processing. Faulty service can also result from mistakes made during the recovery from natural disasters.

Denial of Service

Human error in following procedures or a lack of procedures can result in **denial of service (DOS)**. For example, humans can inadvertently shut down a web server or corporate gateway router by starting a computationally intensive application. An OLAP application that uses the operational DBMS can consume so many DBMS resources that order-entry transactions cannot get through.

Denial-of-service attacks can be launched maliciously. A malicious hacker can flood a web server, for example, with millions of bogus service requests that so occupy the server that it cannot service legitimate requests. Computer worms can infiltrate a network with so much artificial traffic that legitimate traffic cannot get through. Finally, natural disasters may cause systems to fail, resulting in denial of service.

Loss of Infrastructure

Human accidents can cause *loss of infrastructure.* Examples are a bulldozer cutting a conduit of fibre-optic cables, or the floor buffer crashing into a rack of web servers.

Theft and terrorist events also cause loss of infrastructure. A disgruntled, terminated employee can walk off with corporate data servers, routers, or other crucial equipment. Terrorist events can also cause the loss of physical plants and equipment.

Natural disasters present the largest risk for infrastructure loss. A fire, flood, earthquake, or similar event can destroy data centres and all they contain. The devastation of the Indian Ocean tsunami in December 2004 and of hurricanes Katrina and Rita in the fall of 2005 are potent examples of the risks to infrastructure from natural causes.

You may be wondering why Figure 12-1 does not include viruses and worms. The answer is that viruses and worms are *techniques* for causing some of the problems in the figure. They can cause a denial-of-service attack, or they can be used to cause malicious, unauthorized data access or data loss.

Q2 What Are the Elements of a Security Program?

All the problems listed in Figure 12-1 are real and as serious as they sound. Accordingly, organizations must address security in a systematic way. A security program[2] has three components: senior management involvement, safeguards of various kinds, and incident response.

The first component, senior management, has two critical security functions: First, senior management must establish the security policy. This policy sets the stage for the organization's response to security threats. However, because no security program is perfect, there is always risk. Management's second function, therefore, is to manage risk by balancing the costs and benefits of the security program.

Safeguards are protections against security threats. A good way to view safeguards is in terms of the five components of an information system, as shown in Figure 12-2. Some of the safeguards involve computer hardware and software. Some involve data; others involve procedures and people. In addition to these safeguards, organizations must consider disaster recovery safeguards. An effective security program consists of a balance of safeguards of all these types.

The final component of a security program consists of the organization's planned response to security incidents. Clearly, the time to think about what to do is not when computers are crashing all around the organization. We will discuss incident response in the last section of this chapter.

2. Note that the word *program* is used here in the sense of a management program that includes objectives, policies, procedures, directives, and so forth. Do not confuse this term with *computer program*.

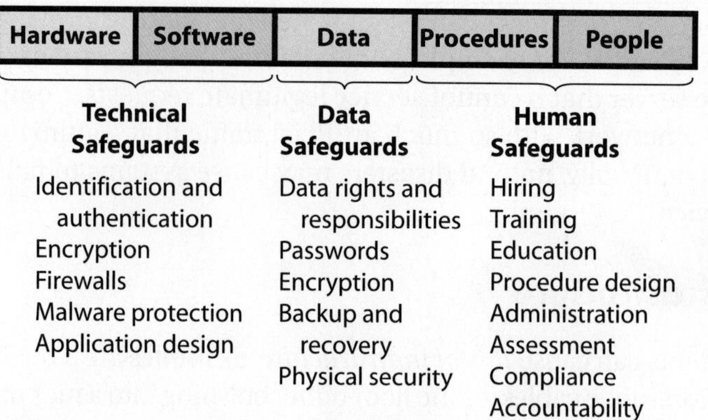

Figure 12-2
Security Safeguards as They Relate to the Five Components

Q3 How Can Technical Safeguards Protect against Security Threats?

Technical safeguards involve the hardware and software components of an information system. Figure 12-3 lists primary technical safeguards. We have discussed all of these in prior chapters. Here we will just supplement those prior discussions.

Identification and Authentication

Every information system today should require users to sign on with a user name and password. The user name *identifies* the user (the process of **identification**), and the password *authenticates* that user (the process of **authentication**). See the box on creating strong passwords and password etiquette later in this chapter (pages 345–346) for more on this topic.

Passwords have important weaknesses. For one, users tend to be careless in their use. Despite repeated warnings to the contrary, yellow sticky notes holding written passwords adorn many computers. In addition, users tend to be free in sharing their passwords with others. Finally, many users choose ineffective, simple passwords. With such passwords, intrusion systems can very effectively guess passwords.

These deficiencies can be reduced or eliminated using smart cards and biometric authentication.

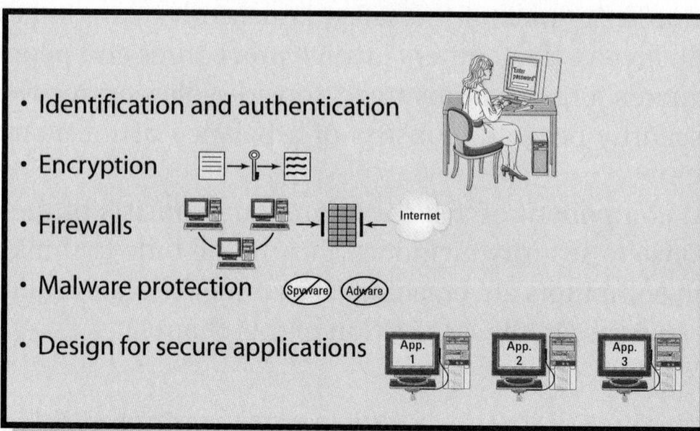

Figure 12-3
Technical Safeguards

Smart Cards

A **smart card** is a plastic card similar to a credit card. Unlike credit, debit, and ATM cards, which have a magnetic strip, smart cards have a microchip. The microchip, which holds far more data than a magnetic strip, is loaded with identifying data. Users of smart cards are required to enter a **personal identification number (PIN)** to be authenticated.

Biometric Authentication

Biometric authentication uses personal physical characteristics such as fingerprints, facial features, and retinal scans to authenticate users. Biometric authentication provides strong authentication, but the required equipment is expensive. Often, too, users resist biometric identification because they feel it is invasive.

Biometric authentication is in the early stages of adoption. Because of its strength, it will likely see increased usage in the future. It is also likely that legislators will pass laws governing the use, storage, and protection requirements for biometric data. For more on biometrics, visit http://searchsecurity.techtarget.com.

Note that authentication methods fall into three categories: what you know (password or PIN), what you have (smart card), and what you are (biometric).

Single Sign-On for Multiple Systems

Information systems often require multiple sources of authentication. For example, when you sign on to your personal computer, you need to be authenticated. When you access the LAN in your department, you need to be authenticated again. When you traverse your organization's WAN, you will need to be authenticated to even more networks. Also, if your request requires database data, the DBMS server that manages that database will authenticate you yet again.

It would be annoying to enter a name and password for every one of these resources. You might have to use and remember five or six different passwords just to access the data you need to perform your job. It would be equally undesirable to send your password across all these networks. The farther your password travels, the greater the risk it can be compromised.

Instead, today's operating systems have the capability to authenticate you to networks and other servers. You sign on to your local computer and provide authentication data; from that point on, your operating system authenticates you to another network or server, which can authenticate you to yet another network and server, and so forth.

Encryption and Firewalls

The next two categories of technical safeguards in Figure 12-3 are encryption and firewalls. In Chapter 6, firewalls were discussed briefly and encryption was noted in the discussion of VPNs. We will not repeat that discussion here. Just realize that they are very important technical safeguards.

Malware Protection

The next technical safeguard in our list in Figure 12-3 is malware protection. The term **malware** has several definitions. Here we will use the broadest one: *malware* is viruses, worms, spyware, and adware. We discussed viruses and worms in Chapter 4; you should review that material now if you have forgotten their definitions.

Spyware and Adware

Spyware programs are installed on the user's computer without the user's knowledge or permission. Spyware resides in the background and, unknown to the user, observes the user's actions and keystrokes, monitors computer activity, and reports the user's activities to sponsoring organizations. Some malicious spyware captures keystrokes to obtain user names, passwords, account numbers, and other sensitive information. Other spyware supports marketing analyses, observing what users do, websites they visit, products they examine and purchase, and so forth.

Adware is similar to spyware in that it's installed without the user's permission and resides in the background to observe user behaviour. Most adware is benign in that it does not perform malicious acts or steal data. It does, however, watch user activity and produce pop-up ads. Adware can also change the user's default window or modify search results and switch the user's search engine. For the most part it is just annoying, but users should be concerned any time they discover unknown programs on their computers that perform unrequested functions.

Figure 12-4 lists some of the symptoms of adware and spyware. Sometimes these symptoms develop slowly over time as more malware components are installed. Should these symptoms occur on your computer, remove the spyware or adware using anti-malware programs.

Malware Safeguards

Fortunately, it is possible to avoid most malware using the following malware safeguards:

1. *Install antivirus and antispyware programs on your computer.* Your IT department will have a list of recommended (perhaps required) programs for this purpose. If you choose a program for yourself, choose one from a reputable vendor. Check reviews of anti-malware software on the web before purchasing.
2. *Set up your anti-malware programs to scan your computer frequently.* You should scan your computer at least once a week and possibly more. When you detect malware code, use the anti-malware software to remove it. If the code cannot be removed, contact your IT department or anti-malware vendor.
3. *Update malware definitions.* **Malware definitions**—patterns that exist in malware code—should be downloaded frequently. Anti-malware vendors update these definitions continually, and you should install these updates as they become available.
4. *Open email attachments only from known sources.* Also, even when opening attachments from known sources, do so with great care. According to professor and security expert Ray Panko, about 90 percent of all viruses are spread

Figure 12-4
Spyware and Adware Symptoms

- Slow system start up
- Sluggish system performance
- Many pop-up advertisements
- Suspicious browser homepage changes
- Suspicious changes to the taskbar and other system interfaces
- Unusual hard-disk activity

by email attachments.[3] This statistic is not surprising, because most organizations are protected by firewalls. With a properly configured firewall, email is the only outside-initiated traffic that can reach user computers.

Most anti-malware programs check email attachments for malware code. However, all users should form the habit of *never* opening an email attachment from an unknown source. Also, if you receive an unexpected email from a known source or an email from a known source that has a suspicious subject, odd spelling, or poor grammar, do not open the attachment without first verifying with the known source that the attachment is legitimate.

5. *Promptly install software updates from legitimate sources.* Unfortunately, all programs are chock full of security holes; vendors are fixing them as rapidly as they are discovered, but the practice is inexact. Install patches to the operating system and application programs promptly.
6. *Browse only in reputable Internet neighbourhoods.* It is possible for some malware to install itself when you do nothing more than open a web page. Don't go there!

Malware Is a Serious Problem

America Online (AOL) and the U.S. National Cyber Security Alliance conducted a malware study using Internet users in 2004. They asked the users a series of questions and then, with the users' permission, scanned their computers to determine how accurately the users understood malware problems on their own computers. This fascinating study can be found online at www.staysafeonline.org/pdf/safety_study_v04.pdf.

Figure 12-5 shows a few important results from this study. Among the users, 6 percent thought they had a virus, but 19 percent actually did. Further, half of those surveyed did not know if they had a virus. Of those computers having viruses, an average of 2.4 viruses were found, and the maximum number of viruses found on a single computer was 213!

When asked how often they update their antivirus definitions, 71 percent of the users reported that they had done so within the last week. Actually, only one-third of the users had updated their definitions that recently.

Figure 12-5 shows similar results for spyware. The average user computer had 93 spyware components. The maximum number found on a computer was 1059. Note that only 5 percent of the users had given permission for the spyware to be installed.

Although the problem of malware will never be eradicated, you can reduce its size by following the six numbered safeguards listed in the previous subsection. You should take these actions as a habit, and you should ensure that employees you manage take them as well.

Design for Secure Applications

The final technical safeguard in Figure 12-3 concerns the design of applications. As a future IS user, you will not design programs yourself. However, you should ensure that any information system developed for you and your department includes security as one of the application requirements.

3. Panko, R., *Corporate Computer and Network Security* (Prentice Hall, 2004), p. 165.

Figure 12-5
Malware Survey Results

Source: AOL/NCSA Online Safety Study, October 2004, staysafeonline.info/news/safety_study_v04.pdf (accessed March 2005).

Question	User Response	Scan Results
Do you have a virus on your computer?	Yes: 6%	Yes: 19%
	No: 44%	No: 81%
	Don't know: 50%	
Average (maximum) number of viruses on infected computer		2.4 (213)
How often do you update your antivirus software?	Last week: 71%	Last week: 33%
	Last month: 12%	Last month: 34%
	Last 6 months: 5%	Last 6 months: 6%
	Longer than 6 months: 12%	Longer than 6 months: 12%
Do you think you have spyware or adware on your computer?	Yes: 53%	Yes: 80%
	No: 47%	No: 20%
Average (maximum) number of spyware/adware components on computer		93 (1,059)
Did you give permission to someone to install these components on your computer?	Yes: 5% No: 95%	

Q4 How Can Data Safeguards Protect Against Security Threats?

Data safeguards protect databases and other organizational data. Two organizational units are responsible for data safeguards. **Data administration** refers to an organization-wide function that is in charge of developing data policies and enforcing data standards. Data administration is a staff function to the CIO, as discussed in Chapter 10.

Database administration refers to a function that pertains to a particular database. The ERP and CRM databases each have a database administration function. Database administration ensures that procedures exist to facilitate orderly multiuser processing of the database, to control changes to the database structure, and to protect the database.

Both data and database administration are involved in establishing the data safeguards in Figure 12-6. First, data administration should define data policies such as "We will not share identifying customer data with any other organization" and the like. Then, data administration and database administration(s) work together to specify user data rights and responsibilities. Third, those rights should be enforced by user accounts that are authenticated at least by passwords.

- Define data policies
- Data rights and responsibilities
- Rights enforced by user accounts authenticated by passwords
- Data encryption
- Backup and recovery procedures
- Physical security

Figure 12-6
Data Safeguards

The organization should protect sensitive data by storing it in encrypted form. Such encryption uses one or more keys in ways similar to that described for data communication encryption. One potential problem with stored data, however, is that the key might be lost or that disgruntled or terminated employees might destroy it. Because of this possibility, when data are encrypted, a trusted party should have a copy of the encryption key. This safety procedure is sometimes called **key escrow.**

Another data safeguard is to periodically create backup copies of database contents. The organization should store at least some of these backups off premises, possibly in a remote location. Additionally, IT personnel should periodically practise recovery to ensure that the backups are valid and that effective recovery procedures exist. Do not assume that just because a backup is made, the database is protected.

Physical security is another data safeguard. The computers that run the DBMS and all devices that store database data should reside in locked, controlled-access facilities. If not, they are subject not only to theft, but also to damage. For better security, the organization should keep a log showing who entered the facility, when, and for what purpose.

In some cases, organizations contract with other companies to manage their databases. If so, all the safeguards in Figure 12-6 should be part of the service contract. Also, the contract should give the owners of the data permission to inspect the premises of the database operator and to interview its personnel on a reasonable schedule.

Q5 How Can Human Safeguards Protect against Security Threats?

Human safeguards involve the people and procedure components of information systems. In general, human safeguards result when authorized users follow appropriate procedures for system use and recovery. Restricting access to authorized users requires effective authentication methods and careful user account management. In addition, appropriate security procedures must be designed as part of every information system, and users should be trained in the importance and use of those procedures. In this section, we will consider the development of human safeguards first for employees and then for non-employee personnel.

Human Safeguards for Employees

Figure 12-7 lists security considerations for employees. The first is position definitions.

Position Definitions

Effective human safeguards begin with definitions of job tasks and responsibilities. In general, job descriptions should provide a separation of duties and authorities. For example, no single individual should be allowed both to approve expenses and to write cheques. Instead, one person should approve expenses, another should pay them, and a third should account for the payment. Similarly, in inventory, no single person should be allowed to authorize an inventory withdrawal and also to remove the items from inventory.

Given appropriate job descriptions, user accounts should be defined to give users the *least possible privilege* needed to perform their jobs. For example, users whose job description does not include modifying data should be given accounts with read-only privilege. Similarly, user accounts should prohibit users from accessing data that their job description does not require. Because of the

Figure 12-7
Security Policy for In-House Staff

- Position definition
  - Separate duties and authorities.
  - Determine least privilege.
  - Document position sensitivity.

"OK to pay this"

- Hiring and screening

"Where did you last work?"

- Dissemination and enforcement (responsibility, accountability, compliance)

"Lets talk security..."

- Termination
  - Friendly

"Congratulations on your new job"

  - Unfriendly

"We've closed your accounts. Goodbye"

problem of security, even access to seemingly innocuous data may need to be limited.

Finally, the security sensitivity should be documented for each position. Some jobs involve highly sensitive data (e.g., employee compensation, salesperson quotas, and proprietary marketing or technical data). Other positions involve no sensitive data. Documenting *position sensitivity* enables security personnel to prioritize their activities in accordance with the possible risk and loss. The *MIS in Use* feature "What Is My True Name?" provides an example of the need for position sensitivity.

Hiring and Screening

Security considerations should be part of the hiring process. Of course, if the position involves no sensitive data and no access to information systems, then screening for information systems security purposes will be minimal. When hiring for high-sensitivity positions, however, extensive interviews, references, and background investigations are appropriate. Note, too, that security screening applies not only to new employees, but also to employees who are promoted into sensitive positions.

Dissemination and Enforcement

Employees cannot be expected to follow security policies and procedures that they don't know about. Therefore, employees need to be made aware of the

What Is My True Name?

A professor at a large Canadian university, Howard Roark, would often log on to the websites of various textbook publishers to review or order copies of textbooks he was considering for his courses or to obtain access to restricted instructor materials such as test banks and sample exams.

Registering with a publisher was usually a relatively simple process of completing an online request form on the website with information such as name, university, and contact details. Once verified by the publisher (usually by email or telephone), login information (an ID and password) was then emailed back to the requestor.

However, as he read an email message from a publisher, Roark wondered if the existing processes were adequate.

The publisher had noticed that the email address used in a recent request for access did not match the email address on file for Roark, and so asked him to confirm that it was valid. Rather than the standard university address of Howard.Roark@universitydomain.com, a new account had been set up at a generic email service (such as Yahoo! or Hotmail) with the same name (i.e., Howard.Roark@). All other details on the request, such as address, title etc., were correct.

Roark was alarmed—was someone trying to impersonate him? What could he do about it?

Questions

1. Why do you think this has occurred? (*Hint*: Who could benefit?)
2. Who has been harmed (if anyone), or is this a "victimless" situation?
3. Are the registration procedures adequate? What changes, if any, would you recommend?
4. What action should be taken by Roark, the university, or the publisher? Does it matter where the request came from (i.e., if it was a student at Roark's university)?
5. Is this a case of identity theft?
6. Assuming that the individual is identified, what would be an appropriate penalty?

security policies, procedures, and responsibilities they will have. Employee security training begins during new-employee training, with the explanation of general security policies and procedures. That general training must be amplified in accordance with the position's sensitivity and responsibilities. Promoted employees should receive security training that is appropriate to their new position. The company should not provide user accounts and passwords until employees have completed required security training.

Enforcement consists of three interdependent factors: responsibility, accountability, and compliance. First, the company should clearly define the security *responsibilities* of each position. The design of the security program should be such that employees can be held *accountable* for security violations. Procedures should exist so that when critical data are lost, it is possible to determine how the loss occurred and who is accountable. Finally, the security program should encourage security *compliance*. Employee activities should be regularly monitored for compliance, and management should specify disciplinary action to be taken in light of noncompliance.

Management attitude is crucial: Employee compliance is greater when management demonstrates, both in word and deed, a serious concern for security. If managers write passwords on staff bulletin boards, shout passwords down hallways, or ignore physical security procedures, then employee security attitudes and employee security compliance will suffer. Note, too, that effective security is a continuing management responsibility. Regular reminders about security are essential.

Termination

Companies also must establish security policies and procedures for the termination of employees. Most employee terminations are friendly, and occur as the result of promotion, retirement, or when the employee resigns to take another position. Standard human resources policies should ensure that system administrators receive notification in advance of the employee's last day, so that they can remove accounts and passwords. The need to recover keys for encrypted data and any other special security requirements should be part of the employee's out-processing.

Unfriendly termination is more difficult because employees may be tempted to take malicious or harmful actions. In such a case, system administrators may need to remove user accounts and passwords prior to notifying the employee of his or her termination. Other actions may be needed to protect the company's information assets. A terminated sales employee, for example, may attempt to take the company's confidential customer and sales-prospect data for future use at another company. The terminating employer should take steps to protect those data prior to the termination.

The human resources department should be aware of the importance of giving IS administrators early notification of employee termination. No blanket policy exists; the information systems department must assess each case on an individual basis.

Human Safeguards for Non-Employee Personnel

Business requirements may necessitate opening information systems to non-employee personnel—temporary personnel, vendors, partner personnel (employees of business partners), and the public. Although temporary personnel can be screened, to reduce costs, the screening will be abbreviated from that for employees. In most cases, companies cannot screen either vendor or partner personnel. Of course, public users cannot be screened at all. Similar limitations pertain to security training and compliance testing.

In the case of temporary, vendor, and partner personnel, the contracts that govern the activity should call for security measures appropriate to the sensitivity of the data and IS resources involved. Companies should require vendors and partners to perform appropriate screening and security training. The contract should also mention specific security responsibilities that are particular to the work to be performed. Companies should provide accounts and passwords with least privilege and remove those accounts as soon as possible.

The situation differs with public users of websites and other openly accessible information systems. It is exceedingly difficult and expensive to hold public users accountable for security violations. In general, the best safeguard from threats from public users is to *harden* the website or other facility against attack as much as possible. **Hardening a site** means to take extraordinary measures to reduce a system's vulnerability. Hardened sites use special versions of the operating system, and they lock down or eliminate operating system features and functions that are not required by the application. Hardening is actually a technical safeguard, but we mention it here as the most important safeguard against public users.

Finally, note that the business relationship with the public, and with some partners, differs from that with temporary personnel and vendors. The public and some partners use the information system to receive a benefit. Consequently, safeguards need to protect such users from internal company security problems. A disgruntled employee who maliciously changes prices on a website potentially damages both public users and business partners. As one experienced IT manager put it, "Rather than protecting ourselves from them, we need to protect them from us."

Account Administration

The third human safeguard is account administration. The administration of user accounts, passwords, and help-desk policies and procedures is an important component of the security system.

Account Management

Account management concerns the creation of new user accounts, the modification of existing account permissions, and the removal of unneeded accounts. Information system administrators perform all these tasks, but account users are responsible for notifying the administrators of the need for these actions. The IT department should create standard procedures for this purpose. As a future user, you can improve your relationship with IS personnel by providing early and timely notification of the need for account changes.

The existence of accounts that are no longer necessary is a serious security threat. IS administrators cannot know when an account should be removed; it is up to users and managers to give such notification.

Password Management

Passwords are the primary means of authentication. They are important not just for access to the user's computer, but also for authentication to other networks and servers to which the user may have access. Because of the importance of passwords, the National Institute of Standards and Technology (NIST) recommends that employees be required to sign statements similar to that shown in Figure 12-8.

HOW CAN YOU CREATE A STRONG PASSWORD?

Whatever opportunities you find for using information systems in your career—and your life—one issue that will remain constant is security of those systems. Security is vitally important. As a user of information systems in a business organization, you will be given a user name and password. You will be instructed to create a strong password, and it is vitally important for you to do so. (In fact, you should now be using such passwords at your university.) So what is a strong password, and how do you create one?

Strong Passwords

Microsoft, a company that has many reasons to promote effective security, defines a strong password as one with the following characteristics:

- Has seven or more characters
- Does not contain your user name, real name, or company name
- Does not contain a complete dictionary word in any language
- Is different from previous passwords you have used
- Contains both upper- and lowercase letters, numbers, and special characters (such as ~ ! @ # $ % ^ & * ( ) _ + – = { } | [ ] \ : " ' < > ?,. /)

Examples of good passwords are:

- Qw37^T1bb?at
- 3B47qq<3>5!7b

The problem with such passwords is that they are nearly impossible to remember. And the last thing you want to do is write your password on a piece of paper and keep it near the workstation where you use it. Never do that!

One technique for creating memorable, strong passwords is to base them on the first letter of the words in a phrase. The phrase could be the title of a song or the first line of a poem or one based on some fact about your life. For example, you might take the phrase, "I was born in Calgary, Alberta, before 1990." Using the first letters from that phrase and substituting the character < for the word before, you create the password IwbiC,AB<1990. That's an acceptable password, but it would be better if all the numbers weren't placed at the end. So, you might try the phrase, "I was born at 3:00 a.m. in Calgary, Alberta." That phrase yields the password Iwba3:00AMiC,AB—a strong password that is easily remembered.

Password Etiquette

Once you have created a strong password, you need to protect it with proper behaviour. Proper password etiquette is one of the marks of a business professional. Never write down your password, and do not share it with others. Never ask others for their passwords, and never give your password to someone else.

But what if you need someone else's password? Suppose, for example, you ask someone to help you with a problem on your computer. You sign on to an information system, and for some reason, you need to enter that other person's password. In this case, say to the other person, "We need your password," and then get out of your chair, offer your keyboard to the other person, and look away while he or she enters the password. Among professionals working in organizations that take security seriously, this little "do-si-do" move—one person getting out of the way so that another person can enter a password—is common and accepted.

If someone asks for your password, do not give it out. Instead, get up, go over to that person's machine, and enter your own password yourself. Stay present while your password is in use, and ensure that your account is logged out at the end of the activity. No one should mind or be offended in any way when you do this. It is the mark of a professional.

Source: National Institute of Standards and Technology, *Introduction to Computer Security: The NIST Handbook*, Publication 800–812, p. 114.

I hereby acknowledge personal receipt of the system password(s) associated with the user IDs listed below. I understand that I am responsible for protecting the password(s), will comply with all applicable system security standards, and will not divulge my password(s) to any person. I further understand that I must report to the Information Systems Security Officer any problem I encounter in the use of the password(s) or when I have reason to believe that the private nature of my password(s) has been compromised.

Figure 12-8
Sample Account Acknowledgment Form

When an account is created, users should immediately change the password they are given to a password of their own. In fact, well-constructed systems require the user to change the password on first use.

Additionally, users should change passwords frequently thereafter. Some systems require a password change every three months or perhaps more frequently. Users grumble at the nuisance of making such changes, but frequent password changes reduce not only the risk of password loss, but also the extent of damage if an existing password is compromised.

Some users create two passwords and switch back and forth between them. This strategy results in poor security, and some password systems do not allow the user to reuse recently used passwords. Again, users may view this policy as a nuisance, but it is important.

Help-Desk Policies

In the past, help desks have been a serious security risk. A user who had forgotten his password would call the help desk and plead for the help-desk representative to tell him his password or to reset the password to something else. "I can't get this report out without it!" was (and is) a common lament.

The problem for help-desk representatives is, of course, that they have no way of determining that they're talking with the true user and not someone spoofing a true user. But they're in a bind: If they don't help in some way, the help desk is perceived to be the "unhelpful desk."

To resolve such problems, many systems give the help-desk representative a means of authenticating the user. Typically, the help-desk information system has answers to questions that only the true user would know, such as the user's birthplace, mother's maiden name, or last four digits of an important account number. Usually, when a password is changed, notification of that change is sent to the user in an email. Email, as you learned, is sent as plain text, however, so the new password itself ought not to be emailed. If you ever receive notification that your password was reset when you did not request such a reset, immediately contact IT security. Someone has compromised your account.

All such help-desk measures reduce the strength of the security system, and, if the employee's position is sufficiently sensitive, they may create too large a vulnerability. In such a case, the user may just be out of luck. The account will be deleted, and the user must repeat the account-application process.

System Procedures

Figure 12-9 shows a grid of procedure types—normal operation, backup, and recovery. Procedures of each type should exist for each information system. For example, the order-entry system will have procedures of each of these types, as will the web storefront, the inventory system, and so forth. The definition and use of standardized procedures reduces the likelihood of computer crime and

Figure 12-9
System Procedures

	System users	Operations personnel
Normal operation	Use the system to perform job tasks, with security appropriate to sensitivity.	Operate data centre equipment, manage networks, run web servers, and do related operational tasks.
Backup	Prepare for loss of system functionality.	Back up website resources, databases, administrative data, account and password data, and other data.
Recovery	Accomplish job tasks during failure. Know tasks to do during system recovery.	Recover systems from backed-up data. Perform role of help desk during recovery.

other malicious activity by insiders. It also ensures that the system's security policy is enforced.

Procedures exist for both users and operations personnel. For each type of user, the company should develop procedures for normal, backup, and recovery operations. As a future user, you will be primarily concerned with user procedures. Normal-use procedures should provide safeguards appropriate to the sensitivity of the information system.

Backup procedures concern the creation of backup data to be used in the event of failure. Whereas operations personnel have the responsibility for backing up system databases and other systems data, departmental personnel have the need to back up data on their own computers. Good questions to ponder are, "What would happen if I lost my computer (or PDA) tomorrow?" "What would happen if someone dropped my computer during an airport security inspection?" "What would happen if my computer were stolen?" Employees should ensure that they back up critical business data on their computers. The IT department may help in this effort by designing backup procedures and making backup facilities available.

Finally, systems analysts should develop procedures for system recovery. First, how will the department manage its affairs when a critical system is unavailable? Customers will want to order, and manufacturing will want to remove items from inventory even though a critical information system is unavailable. How will the department respond? Once the system is returned to service, how will records of business activities during the outage be entered into the system? How will service be resumed? The system developers should ask and answer these questions and others like them and develop procedures accordingly.

Security Monitoring

Security monitoring is the last of the human safeguards we will consider. Important monitoring functions are activity log analyses, security testing, and investigating and learning from security incidents.

Many information system programs produce *activity logs.* Firewalls produce logs of their activities, including lists of all dropped packets, infiltration attempts, and unauthorized access attempts from within the firewall. DBMS products produce logs of successful and failed log-ins. Web servers produce voluminous logs of web activities. The operating systems in personal computers can produce logs of log-ins and firewall activities.

None of these logs adds any value to an organization unless someone looks at them. Accordingly, an important security function is to analyze these logs for threat patterns, successful and unsuccessful attacks, and evidence of security vulnerabilities.

Additionally, companies should test their security programs. Both in-house personnel and outside security consultants should conduct such testing.

Another important monitoring function is to investigate security incidents. How did the problem occur? Have safeguards been created to prevent a recurrence of such problems? Does the incident indicate vulnerabilities in other portions of the security system? What else can be learned from the incident?

Security systems reside in a dynamic environment. Organization structures change. Companies are acquired or sold; mergers occur. New systems require new security measures. New technology changes the security landscape, and new threats arise. Security personnel must constantly monitor the situation and determine if the existing security policy and safeguards are adequate. If changes are needed, security personnel need to take appropriate action.

Security, like quality, is an ongoing process. There is no final state that represents a secure system or company. Instead, companies must monitor security on a continuing basis.

Q6 What Is Necessary for Disaster Preparedness?

A *disaster* is a substantial loss of computing infrastructure caused by acts of nature or crime. As stated several times, the best way to solve a problem is not to have it. The best safeguard against a disaster is appropriate location. If possible, place computing centres, web farms, and other computer facilities in locations not prone to floods, earthquakes, hurricanes, tornados, or avalanches. Even in those locations, place infrastructure in unobtrusive buildings, basements, backrooms, and similar locations well within the physical perimeter of the organization. Also, locate computing infrastructure in fire-resistant buildings designed to house expensive and critical equipment.

However, sometimes business requirements necessitate locating the computing infrastructure in undesirable locations. Also, even at a good location, disasters do occur. Therefore, some businesses prepare backup processing centres in locations geographically removed from the primary processing site.

Figure 12-10 lists major disaster preparedness tasks. After choosing a safe location for the computing infrastructure, the organization should identify all mission-critical applications. These are applications without which the organization cannot carry on and which, if lost for any period of time, could cause the organization's failure. The next step is to identify all resources necessary to run those systems. Such resources include computers, operating systems, application programs, databases, administrative data, procedure documentation, and trained personnel.

- Locate infrastructure in safe location.
- Identify mission-critical systems.
- Identify resources needed to run those systems.
- Prepare remote backup facilities.
- Train and rehearse.

Figure 12-10
Disaster Preparedness Guidelines

Next, the organization creates backups for the critical resources at the remote processing centre. So-called **hot sites** are remote processing centres run by commercial disaster-recovery services. For a monthly fee, they provide all the equipment needed to continue operations following a disaster. **Cold sites**, in contrast, provide office space but the customers themselves provide and install the equipment needed to continue operations.

Once the organization has backups in place, it must train and rehearse cutover of operations from the primary centre to the backup. Periodic refresher rehearsals are mandatory.

Preparing a backup facility is very expensive; however, the costs of establishing and maintaining that facility are a form of insurance. Senior management must make the decision to prepare such a facility by balancing the risks, benefits, and costs.

Q7 How Should Organizations Respond to Security Incidents?

- Have plan in place
- Centralized reporting
- Specific responses
  - Speed
  - Preparation pays
  - Don't make problem worse
- Practise!

Figure 12-11
Factors in Incident Response

The last component of a security plan we will consider is incident response. Figure 12-11 lists the major factors. First, every organization should have an incident-response plan as part of the security program. No organization should wait until some asset has been lost or compromised before deciding what to do. The plan should include how employees are to respond to security problems, whom they should contact, the reports they should make, and steps they can take to reduce further loss.

Consider, for example, a virus. An incident-response plan will stipulate what an employee should do when he notices the virus. It should specify whom to contact and what to do. It may stipulate that the employee should turn off his computer and physically disconnect from the network. The plan should also indicate what users with wireless computers should do.

Phishing for Credit Card Accounts

Before you read further, realize that the graphics in this case are fake. They were not produced by a legitimate business, but were generated by a phisher. A *phisher* is an operation that spoofs legitimate companies in an attempt to illegally capture credit card numbers, email accounts, driver's licence numbers, and other data. Some phishers even install malicious program code on users' computers.

Phishing is usually initiated via an email. Go to www.fraudwatchinternational.com/phishing to view several examples that appear to be email messages from legitimate senders but that are in fact fake. The most common phishing attack is initiated with a bogus email. For example, you might receive the email shown in Figure 12-12.

This bogus email is designed to cause you to click on the "See more details here" link. When you do so, you'll be connected to a site that will ask you for personal data, such as credit card numbers, card expiration dates, driver's licence number, social insurance number, or other data. In this particular case, you'll be taken to a screen that asks for your credit card number (see Figure 12-13).

Your Order ID: "17152492"
Order Date: "09/07/07"
Product Purchased: "Two First Class Tickets to Cozumel"
Your card type: "CREDIT"
Total Price: "$349.00"

Hello, when you purchased your tickets you provided an incorrect mailing address.
See more details here
Please follow the link and modify your mailing address or cancel your order. If you have questions, feel free to cortact with us account@usefulbill.com

Figure 12-12
Phishing Email

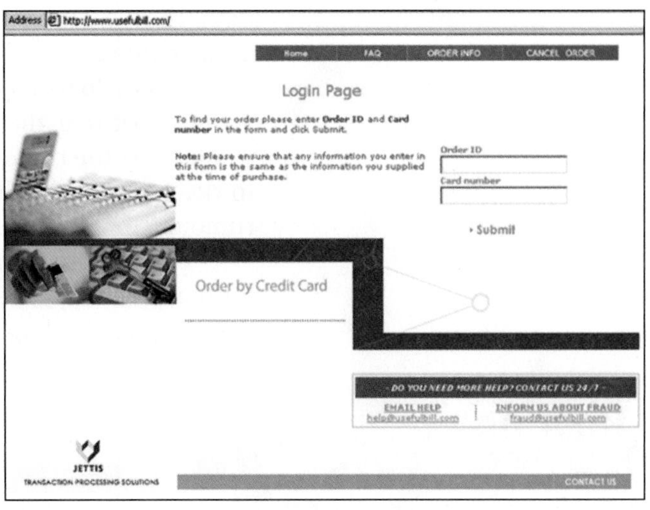

Figure 12-13
Phishing Screen

This web page is produced by a nonexistent company and is entirely fake, including the link "Inform us about fraud." The only purpose of this site is to illegally capture your card number. It might also install spyware, adware, or other malware on your computer.

If you were to get this far, you should immediately close your browser and restart your computer. You should also run anti-malware scans on your computer to determine if the phisher has installed program code on your computer. If so, use the anti-malware software to remove that code.

How can you defend yourself from such attacks? First, you know you didn't purchase two first class tickets to Cozumel. (Had you by odd circumstance just purchased airline tickets to Cozumel, you should contact the legitimate vendor's site *directly* to determine if there had been some mixup.) Because you haven't purchased such tickets, suspect a phisher.

Second, notice the implausibility of the email. It is exceedingly unlikely that you can buy two first-class tickets to any foreign country for $349. Additionally, note the misspelled word and the poor grammar ("cortact with us"). All these facts should alert you to the bogus nature of this email.

Third, do not be misled by legitimate-looking graphics. Phishers are criminals; they don't bother to respect international agreements on legitimate use of trademarks. The phisher might use names of legitimate companies like Visa, MasterCard, Discover, and AmericanExpress on the web page, and the presence of those names might lull you into thinking this is legitimate. The phisher is illegally using those names. In other instances, the phisher will copy the entire look and feel of a legitimate company's website.

Phishing is a serious problem. To protect yourself, be wary of unsolicited email, even if the email appears to be from a legitimate business. If you have questions about an email, contact the company directly (*not* using the addresses provided by the phisher!) and ask about the email. And above all, never give confidential data such as account numbers, social insurance numbers, driver's licence numbers, or credit card numbers in response to *any* unsolicited email.

The plan should provide centralized reporting of all security incidents. Such reporting will enable an organization to determine if it is under systemic attack or whether an incident is isolated. Centralized reporting also allows the organization to learn about security threats, take consistent actions in response, and apply specialized expertise to all security problems.

When an incident does occur, speed is of the essence. Viruses and worms can spread very quickly across an organization's networks, and a fast response will help mitigate the consequences. Because of the need for speed, preparation pays. The incident-response plan should identify critical personnel and their off-hours contact information. These personnel should be trained in where to go and what to do when they get there. Without adequate preparation, there is substantial risk that the actions of well-meaning people will make the problem worse. Also, the rumour mill will be alive with all sorts of nutty ideas about what to do. A cadre of well-informed, trained personnel will serve to dampen such rumours.

Finally, organizations should periodically practise incident response. Without such practice, personnel will be poorly informed on the response plan, and the plan itself may have flaws that become apparent only during a drill.

How does the knowledge in this chapter help you at DSI?

You can use the knowledge in this chapter at DSI in two ways. First, you can use it personally; you can act to limit DSI's exposure, and your own exposure, to security threats. First and foremost, you can create a strong password (page 346) and behave in a way to protect that password. If you work for longer than three months at DSI, you also should change your password.

Second, being aware of the problems in Figure 12-1, you can follow appropriate data procedures even if no DSI manager knows to state them. You can choose not to store sensitive data on your computer. If you have a portable computer, you can limit the data it contains to the absolute minimum you need when away from the office. You can also use all reasonable means to protect that computer from theft.

If you receive phishing attacks at work, you know not to respond to them, and you know to report any such attack at work to DSI's IT manager. You know to report any other suspicious activity as well.

With regard to helping the DSI organization with its security, as discussed at the end of Chapter 10, you are in a bind. You might send a copy of Figures 12-1 and 12-2 to your boss or to the IT manager and explain that you've learned about these issues in your MIS class. You might say something like, "I don't know if these issues are important to DSI or not, but I thought I'd raise them."

Later in your career, if you manage your own department, you can use the guidelines in Figure 12-7 to establish and maintain appropriate human safeguards in your department. Security issues are important. To you as a future manager, Figure 12-7 is one of the most important figures in this text!

That's it! You've reached the end of this text. Take a moment to reflect on how you will use all you have learned; then, turn to the Exercise "The Final, Final Word" to reflect on how this course might help you as you develop your business career.

Active Review

Use this Active Review to verify that you understand the material in the chapter. You can read the entire chapter and then perform the tasks in this review, or you can read the material for just one question and perform the tasks in this review for that question before moving on to the next one.

Q1 What are the sources and types of security threats?

Explain the differences among security threats, threat sources, and threat types. Give one example of a security threat for each cell in the grid in Figure 12-1. Describe a phishing attack. Explain the threat of phishing to individuals. Explain the threat of phishing to company and product brands.

Q2 What are the elements of a security program?

Define *technical, data,* and *human safeguards.* Show how these safeguards relate to the five components of an information system.

Q3 How can technical safeguards protect against security threats?

List five technical safeguards. Define *identification* and *authentication.* Describe three types of authentication. Define *malware,* and name five types of malware. Describe six ways to protect against malware. Summarize why malware is a serious problem.

Q4 How can data safeguards protect against security threats?

Define *data administration* and *database administration,* and explain their differences. List data safeguards.

Q5 How can human safeguards protect against security threats?

How do you create a strong password? Summarize human safeguards for each activity in Figure 12-7. Summarize safeguards that pertain to non-employee personnel. Describe three dimensions of safeguards for account administration. Explain how system procedures can serve as human safeguards. Describe security monitoring techniques.

Q6 What is necessary for disaster preparedness?

Define *disaster.* List major considerations for disaster preparedness. Explain the difference between a hot site and a cold site.

Q7 How should organizations respond to security incidents?

Summarize the actions that an organization should take when dealing with a security incident.

Key Terms and Concepts

Adware 338
Authentication 336
Biometric authentication 337
Cold site 350
Data administration 340
Data safeguards 340
Database administration 340
Denial of service (DOS) 334
Drive-by sniffer 333
Email spoofing 333
Hacking 334
Hardening 344
Hot site 350
Human safeguards 341
Identification 336
Identity Theft 332
IP spoofing 333
Key escrow 341
Malware 337
Malware definitions 338
Personal identification number (PIN) 337
Phishing 333
Pretexting 333
Security threat 332
Smart cards 337
Sniffing 333
Spam 332
Spoofing 333
Spyware 338
Technical safeguards 336
Unauthorized data disclosure 333
Usurpation 334

Using Your Knowledge

1. Search online to find the cheapest way possible to purchase your own credit report. Several sources to check are equifax.ca, experion.ca, and transunion.ca. Assume you can afford to purchase that report (and, if you can, do purchase it).
   a. You should review your credit report for obvious errors. However, other checks are appropriate. Search the web for guidance on how best to review your credit records. Summarize what you learn.
   b. What actions should you take if you find errors in your credit report?
   c. Define *identity theft*. Search the web and determine the best course of action for someone who has been the victim of identity theft.

2. Suppose you lose your company laptop at an airport. What should you do? Does it matter what data are stored on your disk drive? If the computer contained sensitive or proprietary data, are you necessarily in trouble? Under what circumstances should you now focus on updating your résumé?

3. Suppose you alert your boss to the security threats in Figure 12-1 and to the safeguards in Figure 12-2. Suppose he says, "Very interesting. Tell me more." In preparing for the meeting, you decide to create a list of talking points.
   a. Write a brief explanation of each threat in Figure 12-1.
   b. Explain how the five components relate to safeguards.
   c. Describe two to three technical, two to three data, and two to three human safeguards.
   d. Write a brief description of the safeguards in Figure 12-7.
   e. List security procedures that pertain to you, a temporary employee.
   f. List procedures that your department should have with regard to disaster planning.

4. Dee's consultant was given permission to install software on a server inside Emerson's network. Suppose he had been a computer criminal.
   a. Using Figure 12-1 as a guide, what might he have done?
   b. Suppose he maliciously deleted critical CRM data. What could Emerson do?
   c. Explain how Figure 12-11 pertains to this situation.
   d. In this circumstance, what is likely to happen to Dee? To the manager of the IT department? To the employee who authorized access to the consultant?

5. Suppose you need to terminate an employee who works in your department. Summarize security protections you must take. How would you behave differently if this termination were a friendly one?

6. Suppose DSI is located in a hurricane zone and that it has been given 36 hours' warning that a serious, category 4 hurricane is headed its way.
   a. List all the information systems assets that are in danger.
   b. For each asset in your list in (a), describe an appropriate safeguard.
   c. Suppose DSI has done little disaster preparedness planning. Summarize what you would do in that 36-hour period.
   d. Suppose DSI has a disaster preparedness plan. Summarize what you would do in that 36-hour period.

e. Compare your answers to (c) and (d). In your own words, state the advantages of a disaster preparedness plan.

Case Study 12

Spam Management

Steve Hillman, Senior Systems Administrator at Simon Fraser University, compares it to wrapping a needle in a haystack. Each day the 50 000 users of the university email system send and receive 500 000 email messages to each other or outside the university. Coming into the system, however, were one million messages per day, or 15 per second, of which somewhere between 90 and 95 percent were unsolicited and unwanted email or spam.

Sometimes called the cholesterol of the Internet, spam was threatening to overwhelm the university's computer resources and was a constant battle between the senders of email and systems administrators.

Although popularized in the explosive years of the Internet, electronic mail or email has been around since the 1970s, when the interconnection of computers facilitated the sharing of information and correspondence. A major difference between email systems and regular or "snail" mail systems is that each piece of regular mail requires its own postage stamp and has a direct cost that is borne by the sender. The cost structure of email, however, is reversed. Once a message has been composed, there is almost no difference in costs for the sender if the message is sent to one person or a thousand. The costs of the mail are passed on to the recipient and can quickly add up. In addition to the infrastructure costs to receive, process, and store the messages, other costs include sorting out the legitimate and real messages from those that were unwanted and unsolicited. For many people, more than half of the mail received by their computers is unsolicited and unwanted, costing them resources and time.

At Simon Fraser University, Steve oversees the mail system and manages a blacklist of known spam senders. All of the one million email messages sent every day to university recipients are automatically reviewed by the system and classified on a scale of 1 to 100 according to the probability that they are spam. Messages that are known to be fraudulent "get rich quick" schemes or that attempt to gain illegitimate confidential information (phishing) are given a rating above 90 and are instantly discarded and never delivered to the addressee. The remaining messages—approximately 100 000 a day—with a score between 1 (absolutely not spam) and 10 (probably spam) are delivered to the recipients, who are able to further refine their own filtering level and balance between messages incorrectly classified as spam or unwanted messages included in their mailbox.

Despite these measures, at times Steve still feels overloaded. Only 6 percent of the messages handled by the servers are valid, and the system continues to grow. Although the server configuration has been upgraded several times, it now has more than four terabytes of storage and will soon need to be expanded. Although the university faculty, staff, and students are generally satisfied, Steve faces a constant battle managing the lists. Recently he has begun to wonder if email should be outsourced or if the university needs to provide email to each of the three groups. While having a university email address is one way of identifying students, he has noticed that the majority of students already have other email accounts.

Questions

1. What are the direct and indirect costs associated with email and spam? Are there any that you think are surprising?
2. Can you think of any solutions to the problem of spam? For example, should email be taxed or changed to a system where the sender pays?
3. Is spam a problem or is it simply unsolicited "junk" mail that recipients can delete if they don't want it?
4. The spam filter tries to maintain a balance between categorizing a spam message as a valid email message and misidentifying a valid message as spam. Which has the greater risk and how should this be managed?
5. Should the university continue to provide email as a service to faculty, staff, and students? What are the implications of making a change?

Visit MyMISLab at **www.pearsoned.ca/mymislab**. MyMISLab is a state-of-the-art, interactive, online solution that combines multimedia, tutorials, and quizzes. Use MyMISLab for *Experiencing MIS* to prepare for tests and exams, and go to class ready to learn!

What Do YOU Think?

The Final, Final Word

Congratulations! You've made it through the entire book. With this knowledge you are well prepared to be an effective user of information systems. And with work and imagination, you can be much more than that. Many interesting opportunities are available to those who can apply information in innovative ways. Your professor has done what she or he can do, and the rest, as they say, is up to you.

We believe that, today, computer communications and data storage are free—or so close to free that the cost is not worth mentioning. What are the consequences? Our experience in the IT business makes us wary of predictions that extend beyond next year. But we know that free communication and data storage will cause fundamental changes in the business environment. When a company like Getty Images can produce its product at zero marginal cost, something's fundamentally different. Further, Getty Images is not the only such business; consider YouTube.

We suspect that the rate of technology development will slow in the next five years. Businesses are still digesting the technology that already exists. According to Harry Dent, technology waves always occur in pairs.* The first phase is wild exuberance, in which new technology is invented, its capabilities flushed out, and its characteristics understood. That first phase always results in overbuilding, but it sets the stage for the second phase, in which surviving companies and entrepreneurs purchase the overbuilt infrastructure for pennies on the dollar and use it for new business purposes.

The automotive industry, for example, proceeded in two stages. The irrational exuberance phase culminated in a technology crash; General Motors' stock fell 75 percent from 1919 to 1921. However, that exuberance led to the development of the highway system, the development of the petroleum industry, and a complete change in the conduct of commerce in the United States. Every one of those consequences created opportunities for business people alert to the changing business environment.

We believe we are poised today to see a similar second stage in the adoption of information technology. Businesses are configuring themselves to take advantage of the new opportunities. Dell builds computers to order and pays for the components days after the customer has paid Dell for the equipment. A customer begins using his or her new computer before Dell pays the supplier for the monitor.

Fibre-optic cable will come to our homes when telecom companies buy today's dark fibre for pennies on the dollar and light it up. With fibre-optic cable to your house, goodbye video store!

In 2005, bloggers stunned the mainstream media (MSM) with their commentary. A new age is coming to news as bloggers demolish the MSM monopoly and alter MSM news control. The readership of newspapers has fallen consistently for more than a decade;

*Harry Dent, *The Next Great Bubble Boom* (New York: The Free Press, 2004).

newsprint cannot last in an era of free data communications.

So as you finish your business degree, stay alert for new technology-based opportunities. Watch for the second wave and catch it. If you found this course interesting, take more IS classes. Enroll in a database class, a project management class, or a systems analysis and design class, even if you don't want to be an IS major. If you're technically oriented, take a data communications class or a security class. If you enjoy this material, become an IS major. If you want to program a computer, great, but if you do not, then don't. There are tremendous opportunities for nonprogrammers in the IS industry. Look for novel applications of IS technology to the emerging business environment. Hundreds of them abound! Find them and have fun!

Discussion Question

1. How will you further your career with what you've learned in this class? Give that question serious thought, and write a memo to yourself to read from time to time as your career progresses.

Glossary

Access A popular personal and small workgroup DBMS product from Microsoft. 103

Access control list (ACL) A list that encodes the rules stating which packets are to be allowed through a firewall and which are to be prohibited. 169

Access point (AP) A point in a wireless network that facilitates communication among wireless devices and serves as a point of interconnection between wireless and wired networks. The AP must be able to process messages according to both the 802.3 and 802.11 standards, because it sends and receives wireless traffic using the 802.11 protocol and communicates with wired networks using the 802.3 protocol. 162

Accounting functional systems Systems that support all of the organization's accounting activities. Such systems were some of the earliest calculation systems, and they have continued their importance as functional systems evolved. Examples are general ledger, financial reporting, accounts receivable, and accounts payable systems. Other important accounting systems include cost accounting, budgeting, cash management, and management of the organization's stocks and bonds, borrowings, and capital investments via treasury management. 207

Accurate information Information that is based on correct and complete data and that has been processed correctly as expected. 27

Activity The part of a business process that transforms resources and information of one type into resources and information of another type; can be manual or automated. 26

Advanced Research Projects Agency Network (ARPANET) The world's first operational packet switching network, which provided access to many research investigators who were geographically separated from the small number of large, powerful research computers available at the time. 172

Adware Programs installed on the user's computer without the user's knowledge or permission that reside in the background and, unknown to the user, observe the user's actions and keystrokes, modify computer activity, and report the user's activities to sponsoring organizations. Most adware is benign in that it does not perform malicious acts or steal data. It does, however, watch user activity and produce pop-up ads. 338

Alignment The ongoing, continually evolving challenge of fitting IT architecture to business objectives. 260

Alternatives formulation step A step in the decision-making process in which decision makers lay out various alternatives. 34

Analog signal A wavy signal. A modem converts the computer's digital data into analog signals that can be transmitted over dial-up Internet connections. 166

Analysis paralysis When too much time is spent documenting project requirements. 319

Antivirus programs Software that detects and possibly eliminates viruses. 86

Application service providers (ASPs) A special form of outsourcing in which an organization contracts with a vendor to "rent" applications from the vendor company on a fee-for-service basis. 320

Application software Programs that perform a business function. Some application programs are general purpose, such as Excel or Word. Other application programs are specific to a business function, such as accounts payable. 80

Asymmetric digital subscriber lines (ADSL) DSL lines that have different upload and download speeds. 167

Attribute (1) A variable that provides properties for an HTML tag. Each attribute has a standard name. For example, the attribute for a hyperlink is *href*, and its value indicates which web page is to be displayed when the user clicks the link. (2) Characteristics of an entity. Example attributes of *Order* would be *OrderNumber, OrderDate, SubTotal, Tax, Total,* and so forth. Example attributes of *Salesperson* would be *SalespersonName, Email, Phone,* and so forth. 121

Authentication The process whereby an information system approves (authenticates) a user by checking the user's password. 336

Automated system An information system in which the hardware and software components do most of the work. 29

Basic Input/Output System (BIOS) An important piece of firmware used when a computer is initially booted up: The first thing the computer does is to load BIOS from ROM and run through the commands provided by the firmware. BIOS checks to make sure the memory and input devices are functional. Once these are working, the operating system will be loaded. 82

Beta testing The process of allowing future system users to try out the new system on their own. Used to locate program failures just prior to program shipment. 314

Binary digits The means by which computers represent data; also called *bits*. A binary digit is either a zero or a one. 73

Biometric authentication The use of personal physical characteristics, such as fingerprints, facial features, and retinal scans, to authenticate users. 337

Bit The means by which computers represent data; also called *binary digit*. A bit is either a zero or a one. 73

Broadband Internet communication lines that have speeds in excess of 256 kbps. DSL and cable modems provide broadband access. 168

Browser A program that processes the HTTP protocol; receives, displays, and processes HTML documents; and transmits responses. 164

Budget Measures Act (Bill 198) Law enforcing compliance with standards for collecting, reporting, and disclosing information. 262

Bus Means by which the CPU reads instructions and data from main memory and writes data to main memory. 75

Business analysts Analysts who develop the business case for a newly proposed system and develop the requirements for the system. 284

Business intelligence (BI) system A system that provides the right information, to the right user, at the right time. A tool produces the information, but the system ensures that the right information is delivered to the right user at the right time. 243

Business process A network of activities, resources, facilities, and information that interact to achieve some business function; sometimes called a *business system.* 24

Business process design The creation of new, usually cross-departmental business practices during information systems development. With process design, organizations do not create new information systems to automate existing business practices. Rather, they use technology to enable new, more efficient business processes. 209

Business system Another term for *business process.* 24

Business-to-business (B2B) E-commerce sales between companies. 218

Business-to-consumer (B2C) E-commerce sales between a supplier and a retail customer (the consumer). 218

Business-to-government (B2G) E-commerce sales between companies and governmental organizations. 218

Byte (1) A character of data; (2) An 8-bit chunk. 75, 100

Cable modem A type of modem that provides high-speed data transmission using cable television lines. The cable company installs a fast, high-capacity optical fibre cable to a distribution centre in each neighbourhood that it serves. At the distribution centre, the optical fibre cable connects to regular cable-television cables that run to subscribers' homes or businesses. Cable modems modulate in such a way that their signals do not interfere with TV signals. Like DSL lines, they are always on. 167

Cache memory A file on a domain name resolver that stores domain names and IP addresses that have been resolved. Then, when someone else needs to resolve that same domain name, there is no need to go through the entire resolution process. Instead, the resolver can supply the IP address from the local file. 75

Calculation systems The very first information systems. The goal of such systems was to relieve workers of tedious, repetitive calculations. These systems were labour-saving devices that produced little information. 203

Central processing unit (CPU) The CPU selects instructions, processes them, performs arithmetic and logical comparisons, and stores results of operations in memory. 72

Certified Information Systems Auditor (CISA) A globally recognized certification earned by more than 50 000 professionals; members have job titles like IS auditor, consultant, IS security professional, regulator, chief information officer, and internal auditor. 264

Chief information officer (CIO) The title of the principal manager of the IT department. Other common titles are *vice president of information services, director of information services,* and, less commonly, *director of computer services.* 283

Chief technology officer (CTO) The head of the technology group. The CTO sorts through new ideas and products to identify those that are most relevant to the organization. The CTO's job requires deep knowledge of information technology and the ability to envision how new IT will affect the organization over time. 284

Choice step A step in the decision-making process in which decision makers analyze their alternatives and select one. 34

Clearinghouse An entity that provides goods and services at a stated price, prices and arranges for the delivery of the goods, but never takes title to the goods. 218

Clickstream data E-commerce data that describe a customer's clicking behaviour. Such data include everything the customer does at the website. 237

Client A computer that provides word processing, spreadsheets, database access, and usually a network connection. 77

Cluster analysis An unsupervised data-mining technique whereby statistical techniques are used to identify groups of entities that have similar characteristics. A common use for cluster analysis is to find groups of similar customers in data about customer orders and customer demographics. 248

Cold site A remote processing centre that provides office space, but no computer equipment, for use by a company that needs to continue operations after a natural disaster. 350

Columns Also called *fields,* or groups of bytes. A database table has multiple columns that are used to represent the attributes of an entity. Examples are *PartNumber, EmployeeName,* and *SalesDate.* 100

Commercial-off-the-shelf (COTS) Software that is purchased as-is and is not customized. 312

Competitive strategy The strategy an organization chooses as the way it will succeed in its industry. According to Michael Porter, there are four fundamental competitive strategies: cost leadership across an industry or within a particular industry segment, and product differentiation across an industry or within a particular industry segment. 51, 258

Component design phase The third phase in the SDLC, in which developers determine hardware and software specifications, design the database (if applicable), design procedures, and create job descriptions for users and operations personnel. 306

Computer hardware One of the five fundamental components of an information system. 6

Computer-based information system An information system that includes a computer. 6

Content management systems (CMS) An information system that tracks organizational documents, web pages, graphics, and related materials. 97

Control Objectives for Information and Related Technology (COBIT) A framework of best practices designed for IT management; provides board members, managers, auditors, and IT users with a set of generally accepted measures, indicators, processes, and best practices to assist in getting the best from organizational IT investments. 264

Cost feasibility One of four dimensions of feasibility. 308

Cross-departmental systems The third era of computing systems. In this era, systems are designed not to facilitate the work of a single department or function, but rather to integrate the activities of a complete business process. 203

Cross-functional systems Synonym for *Cross-departmental systems*. 203

Crow's foot A line on an entity-relationship diagram that indicates a 1:N relationship between two entities. 123

Crow's-foot diagram A type of entity-relationship diagram that uses a crow's foot symbol to designate a 1:N relationship. 123

Customer life cycle Taken as a whole, the processes of marketing, customer acquisition, relationship management, and loss/churn that must be managed by CRM systems. 212

Customer relationship management (CRM) system An information system that maintains data about customers and all their interactions with the organization. 212

Data Recorded facts or figures. One of the five fundamental components of an information system. 6

Data administration A staff function that pertains to *all* of an organization's data assets. Typical data administration tasks are setting data standards, developing data policies, and providing for data security. 340

Data channel Means by which the CPU reads instructions and data from main memory and writes data to main memory. 75

Data integrity problem In a database, the situation that exists when data items disagree with one another. An example is two different names for the same customer. 124

Data marts Facilities that prepare, store, and manage data for reporting and data mining for specific business functions. 246

Data mining The application of statistical techniques to find patterns and relationships among data and to classify and predict. 246

Data model A logical representation of the data in a database that describes the data and relationships that will be stored in the database. Akin to a blueprint. 120

Data resource challenge Occurs when data are collected in OLTP but are not used to improve decision making. 238

Data safeguards Steps taken to protect databases and other organizational data, by means of data administration and database administration. 340

Data warehouses Facilities that prepare, store, and manage data specifically for reporting and data mining. 244

Database A self-describing collection of integrated records. 100

Database administration The management, development, operation, and maintenance of the database so as to achieve the organization's objectives. This staff function requires balancing conflicting goals: protecting the database while maximizing its availability for authorized use. In smaller organizations, this function usually is served by a single person. Larger organizations assign several people to an office of database administration. 340

Database application A collection of forms, reports, queries, and application programs that process a database. 103

Database application system Applications, having the standard five components, that make database data more accessible and useful. Users employ a database application that consists of forms, formatted reports, queries, and application programs. Each of these, in turn, calls on the database management system (DBMS) to process the database tables. 103

Database management system (DBMS) A program used to create, process, and administer a database. 103

Data-mining system IS that processes data using sophisticated statistical techniques like regression analysis and decision-tree analysis to find patterns and relationships that cannot be found by simpler operations like sorting, grouping, and averaging. 243

DB2 A popular, enterprise-class DBMS product from IBM. 103

Decision support systems (DSS) Systems that focus on making data collected in OLTP useful for decision making. 239

Denial of service (DOS) Security problem in which users are not able to access an IS; can be caused by human errors, natural disaster, or malicious activity. 334

Device access router A generic term for a communications device that includes an access point, a switch, and a router. Normally the device access router provides DHCP and NAT services. 189

Dial-up modem A modem that performs the conversion between analog and digital in such a way that the signal can be carried on a regular telephone line. 167

Dirty data Problematic data. Examples are a value of *B* for customer gender and a value of *213* for customer age. Other examples are a value of *999-999-9999* for a North American phone number, a part colour of *gren*, and an email address of WhyMe@GuessWhoIAM.org. All these values are problematic when data mining. 236

Disintermediation Elimination of one or more middle layers in the supply chain. 219

Disruptive technologies Products that introduce a very new package of attributes from the accepted mainstream products. 53

Domain name system (DNS) A system that converts user-friendly names into their IP addresses. Any registered, valid name is called a domain name. 166

Drill down With an OLAP report, to further divide the data into more detail. 241

Drive-by sniffers People who take computers with wireless connections through an area and search for unprotected wireless networks in an attempt to gain free Internet access or to gather unauthorized data. 333

DSL (digital subscriber line) modem A type of modem. DSL modems operate on the same lines as voice telephones and dial-up modems, but they operate so that their signals do not interfere with voice telephone service. DSL modems provide much faster data transmission speeds than dial-up modems. Additionally, DSL modems always maintain a connection, so there is no need to dial in; the Internet connection is available immediately. 167

E-commerce The buying and selling of goods and services over public and private computer networks. 217

E-commerce auctions Applications that match buyers and sellers by using an e-commerce version of a standard auction. This e-commerce application enables the auction company to offer goods for sale and to support a competitive bidding process. 218

Electronic exchanges Sites that facilitate the matching of buyers and sellers; the business process is similar to that of a stock exchange. Sellers offer goods at a given price through the electronic exchange, and buyers make offers to purchase over the same exchange. Price matches result in transactions from which the exchange takes a commission. 218

Email spoofing A synonym for *phishing.* A technique for obtaining unauthorized data that uses pretexting via email. The *phisher* pretends to be a legitimate company and sends email requests for confidential data, such as account numbers, social insurance numbers, account passwords, and so forth. Phishers direct traffic to their sites under the guise of a legitimate business. 333

Enterprise architect Manages the company's complex information systems. 259

Enterprise DBMS A product that processes large organizational and workgroup databases. These products support many users, perhaps thousands, and many different database applications. Such DBMS products support 24/7 operations and can manage databases that span dozens of different magnetic disks with hundreds of gigabytes or more of data. IBM's DB2, Microsoft's SQL Server, and Oracle's Oracle are examples of enterprise DBMS products. 110

Enterprise resource planning (ERP) The integration of all the organization's principal processes. ERP is an outgrowth of MRP II manufacturing systems, and most ERP users are manufacturing companies. 214

Entity In the E-R data model, a representation of some thing that users want to track. Some entities represent a physical object; others represent a logical construct or transaction. 121

Entity-relationship (E-R) data model Popular technique for creating a data model, in which developers define the things that will be stored and the relationships among them. 121

Entity-relationship (E-R) diagrams A type of diagram used by database designers to document entities and their relationships to each other. 122

Ethernet Another name for the IEEE 802.3 protocol, Ethernet is a network protocol that operates at Layers 1 and 2 of the TCP/IP–OSI architecture. Ethernet, the world's most popular LAN protocol, is used on WANs as well. 161

Exabyte 10^{18} bytes. 234

Executive information system (EIS) An information system that supports strategic decision making. 33

Expert system Knowledge-sharing system that is created by interviewing experts in a given business domain and codifying the rules used by those experts. 244

Facilities Structures used within a business process. 26

Fields Also called *columns,* groups of bytes in a database table. A database table has multiple columns that are used to represent the attributes of an entity. Examples are *PartNumber, EmployeeName,* and *SalesDate.* 100

File A group of similar rows or records. In a database, sometimes called a *table.* 100

Firewall A computing device located between a firm's internal and external networks that prevents unauthorized access to or from the internal network. A firewall can be a special-purpose computer or it can be a program on a general-purpose computer or on a router. 168

Firmware Computer software that is installed into devices like printers, print services, and various types of communication devices. The software is coded just like other software, but it is installed into special, programmable memory of the printer or other device. 82

Five forces model A model proposed by Michael Porter that assesses industry characteristics and profitability by means of five competitive forces—bargaining power of suppliers, threat of substitution, bargaining power of customers, rivalry among firms, and threat of new entrants. 49

Five-component framework The five fundamental components of an information system—computer hardware, software, data, procedures, and people—that are present in every information system, from the simplest to the most complex. 6

Foreign keys A column or group of columns used to represent relationships. Values of the foreign key match values of the primary key in a different (foreign) table. 102

Form Data entry forms are used to read, insert, modify, and delete database data. 105

Functional systems The second era of information systems. The goal of such systems was to facilitate the work of a single department or function. Over time, in each functional area, companies added features and functions to encompass more activities and to provide more value and assistance. 203

Gigabyte (GB) 1024MB. 75

Global Positioning System (GPS) A collection of dozens of satellites orbiting the earth that transmit precise microwave signals. A GPS receiver can calculate its position by measuring the distance between itself and several of the satellites. 159

Governance Using a committee to decide on expectations for performance, to authorize appropriate resources and power to meet expectations, and perhaps eventually to verify whether expectations have been met. 261

Granularity The level of detail in data. Customer name and account balance is large granularity data. Customer name, balance, and the order details and payment history of every customer order is smaller granularity. 237

Hacking Occurs when a person gains unauthorized access to a computer system. Although some people hack for the sheer joy of doing it, other hackers invade systems for the malicious purpose of stealing or modifying data. 334

Hardening a site The process of taking extraordinary measures to reduce a system's vulnerability. Hardened sites use special versions of the operating system, and they lock down or eliminate operating systems features and functions that are not required by the application. Hardening is a technical safeguard. 344

Hardware Electronic components and related gadgetry that input, process, output, store, and communicate data according to instructions encoded in computer programs or software. 72

Horizontal-market application Software that provides capabilities common across all organizations and industries; examples include word processors, graphics programs, spreadsheets, and presentation programs. 80

Hot site A remote processing centre, run by a commercial disaster-recovery service, that provides equipment a company would need to continue operations after a natural disaster. 350

Human safeguards Steps taken to protect against security threats by establishing appropriate procedures for users to follow for system use. 341

Hypertext transfer protocol (HTTP) A Layer-5 protocol used to process web pages. 164

Identification The process whereby an information system identifies a user by requiring the user to sign on with a user name and password. 336

Identifier An attribute (or group of attributes) whose value is associated with one and only one entity instance. 121

IEEE 802.3 protocol This standard, also called *Ethernet,* is a network protocol that operates at Layers 1 and 2 of the TCP/IP–OSI architecture. Ethernet, the world's most popular LAN protocol, is used on WANs as well. 161

Implementation phase The fourth phase in the SDLC, in which developers build and integrate system components, test the system, and convert to the new system. 306

Implementation step A step in the decision-making process in which decision makers implement the alternative they have selected. 34

Industry standard processes Processes built into business applications from companies like Oracle or SAP. 210

Information (1) Knowledge derived from data, where *data* is defined as recorded facts or figures; (2) Data presented in a meaningful context; (3) Data processed by summing, ordering, averaging, grouping, comparing, or other similar operations; (4) A difference that makes a difference. 26

Information system (IS) A group of components that interact to produce information. 6

Information systems audit An audit focusing on information resources that are used to collect, store, process, and retrieve information. 263

Information Systems Audit and Control Association (ISACA) A key organization in developing knowledge and standards relating to IT audit and IT governance. 263

Information technology (IT) The products, methods, inventions, and standards that are used for the purpose of producing information. 8

Information Technology Infrastructure Library (ITIL) A well recognized collection of books providing a framework of best practice approaches to IT operations. ITIL provides a large set of management procedures that are designed to support businesses in achieving value from IT operations. 280

Information technology project management (ITPM) The collection of techniques and methods that project managers use to plan, coordinate, and complete IT projects. 304

Input hardware Hardware devices that attach to a computer; includes keyboards, mouse, document scanners, and barcode (Universal Product Code) scanners. 72

Instruction set The collection of instructions that a computer can process. 79

Intangible benefit A benefit of an IS for which it is impossible to compute a dollar value. 289

Intellectual property A form of creative endeavour that can be protected through a trademark, patent, copyright, industrial design, or integrated circuit topography. 96

Intelligence-gathering step The first step in the decision-making process in which decision makers determine what is to be decided, what the criteria for selection will be, and what data are available. 34

Internet/internet When spelled with a small *i*, as internet, a private network of networks. When spelled with a capital *I*, as Internet, the public network known as the Internet. 159

Internet service provider (ISP) An ISP provides a user with a legitimate Internet address; it serves as the user's gateway to the Internet; and it passes communications back and forth between the user and the Internet. ISPs also pay for the Internet. They collect money from their customers and pay access fees and other charges on the users' behalf. 163

Interorganizational system IS processing of routine transactions between two or more organizations. 203

IP address A series of dotted decimals in a format like 192.168.2.28 that identifies a unique device on a network or internet. With the IPv4 standard, IP addresses have 32 bits. With the IPv6 standard, IP addresses have 128 bits. Today, IPv4 is more common but will likely be supplanted by IPv6 in the future. With IPv4, the decimal between the dots can never exceed 255. 165

IP spoofing A type of spoofing whereby an intruder uses another site's IP address as if it were that other site. 333

Islands of automation The structure that results when functional applications work independently in isolation from one another. Usually problematic because data are duplicated, integration is difficult, and results can be inconsistent. 203

IT architecture The basic framework for all the computers, systems, and information management that support organizational services. 259

IT operations Service, maintenance, protection, and management of IT infrastructure. 278

IT projects Projects of all shapes and sizes that renew and adapt IT infrastructure. 278

Just-barely-sufficient information Information that meets the purpose for which it is generated, but just barely so. 28

Key (1) A column or group of columns that identifies a unique row in a table. (2) A number used to encrypt data. The encryption algorithm applies the key to the original message to produce the coded message. Decoding (decrypting) a message is similar; a key is applied to the coded message to recover the original text. 101

Key escrow A control procedure whereby a trusted party is given a copy of a key used to encrypt database data. 341

Kilobyte (K) 1024 bytes. 75

Knowledge management system (KMS) An information system for storing and retrieving organizational knowledge, whether that knowledge is in the form of data, documents, or employee know-how. 244

Licence Agreement that stipulates how a program can be used. Most specify the number of computers on which the program can be installed and sometimes the number of users that can connect to and use the program remotely. Such agreements also stipulate limitations on the liability of the software vendor for the consequences of errors in the software. 80

Linux A version of Unix that was developed by the open-source community. The open-source community owns Linux, and there is no fee to use it. Linux is a popular operating system for web servers. 79

Local area network (LAN) A network that connects computers that reside in a single geographic location on the premises of the company that operates the LAN. The number of connected computers can range from two to several hundred. 159

Lost-update problem An issue in multiuser database processing, in which two or more users try to make changes to the data but the database cannot make all the changes because it was not designed to process changes from multiple users. 109

MAC (media access control) address Also called *physical address.* A permanent address given to each network interface card (NIC) at the factory. This address enables the device to access the network via a Level-2 protocol. By agreement among computer manufacturers, MAC addresses are assigned in such a way that no two NIC devices will ever have the same MAC address. 160

MAC address filtering A security device for SOHO LANs that prevents unauthorized users from accessing the device access router and the LAN. 192

Mac OS An operating system developed by Apple Computer, Inc., for the Macintosh. The current version is Mac OS X. Macintosh computers are used primarily by graphic artists and workers in the arts community. Mac OS was developed for the PowerPC, but as of 2006 runs on Intel processors as well. 79

Macro virus Virus that attaches itself to a Word, Excel, PowerPoint, or other type of document. When the infected document is opened, the virus places itself in the startup files of the application. After that, the virus infects every file that the application creates or processes. 84

Main memory A set of cells in which each cell holds a byte of data or instruction; each cell has an address, and the CPU uses the addresses to identify particular data items. 72

Mainframes The first digital computing machines used in business and government. 69

Malware Viruses, worms, spyware, and adware. 337

Malware definitions Patterns that exist in malware code. Anti-malware vendors update these definitions continuously and incorporate them into their products in order to better fight against malware. 338

Management information system (MIS) An information system that helps businesses achieve their goals and objectives. 6, 32

Managerial decision Decision that concerns the allocation and use of resources. 32

Manual system An information system in which the activity of processing information is done by people, without the use of automated processing. 31

Manufacturing information systems Information systems that support one or more aspects of manufacturing processes, including planning, scheduling, integration with inventory, quality control, and related processes. 206

Many-to-many (N:M) relationships Relationships involving two entity types in which an instance of one type can relate to many instances of the second type, and an instance of the second type can relate to many instances of the first. For example, the relationship between Student and Class is N:M. One student may enroll in many classes and one class may have many students. Contrast with *one-to-many (1:N) relationships.* 123

Margin The difference between value and cost. 48

Market-basket analysis A data-mining technique for determining sales patterns. A market-basket analysis shows the products that customers tend to buy together. 244

Maximum cardinality The maximum number of entities that can be involved in a relationship. Common examples of maximum cardinality are 1:N, N:M, and 1:1. 123

Megabyte (MB) 1024KB. 75

Memory swapping The movement of programs and data into and out of memory. If a computer has insufficient memory for its workload, such swapping will degrade system performance. 76

Merchant companies In e-commerce, companies that take title to the goods they sell. They buy goods and resell them. 217

Metadata Data that describe data. 102

Minimum cardinality The minimum number of entities that must be involved in a relationship. 123

Modem Short for *modulator/demodulator,* a modem converts the computer's digital data into signals that can be transmitted over telephone or cable lines. 166

Moore's Law A law, created by Gordon Moore, stating that the number of transistors per square inch on an integrated chip doubles every 18 months. Moore's prediction has proved generally accurate in the 40 years since it was made. Sometimes this law is stated that the speed of a computer chip doubles every 18 months. While not strictly true, this version gives the gist of the idea. 15

Multiuser processing When multiple users process the database at the same time. 109

MySQL A popular open-source DBMS product that is licence-free for most applications. 103

Narrowband Internet communication lines that have transmission speeds of 56 kbps or less. A dial-up modem provides narrowband access. 168

Network A collection of computers that communicate with one another over transmission lines. 159

Network interface card (NIC) A hardware component on each device on a network (computer, printer, etc.) that connects the device's circuitry to the communications line. The NIC works together with programs in each device to implement Layers 1 and 2 of the TCP/IP–OSI hybrid protocol. 160

Neural networks A popular supervised data-mining technique used to predict values and make classifications, such as "good prospect" or "poor prospect." 248

Nonmerchant companies E-commerce companies that arrange for the purchase and sale of goods without ever owning or taking title to those goods. 217

Nonvolatile memory Memory that preserves data contents even when not powered (e.g., magnetic and optical disks). With such devices, you can turn the computer off and back on, and the contents will be unchanged. 77

Normal forms A classification of tables according to their characteristics and the kinds of problems they have. 126

Normalization The process of converting poorly structured tables into two or more well-structured tables. 124

Onboard NIC A built-in NIC. 160

One-of-a-kind application Software that is developed for a specific, unique need, usually for a particular company's operations. 80

One-to-many (1:N) relationships Relationships involving two entity types in which an instance of one type can relate to many instances of the second type, but an instance of the second type can relate to at most one instance of the first. For example, the relationship between Department and Employee is 1:N. A department may relate to many employees, but an employee relates to at most one department. 123

Online analytic processing (OLAP) A dynamic type of reporting system that provides the ability to sum, count, average, and perform other simple arithmetic operations on groups of data. Such reports are dynamic because users can change the format of the reports while viewing them. 239

Online transaction processing (OLTP) Collecting data electronically and processing transactions online. 237

Open-source community A loosely coupled group of programmers who mostly volunteer their time to contribute code to develop and maintain common software. Linux and MySQL are two prominent products developed by such a community. 79

Operating system (OS) A computer program that controls the computer's resources: It manages the contents of main memory, processes keystrokes and mouse movements, sends signals to the display monitor, reads and writes disk files, and controls the processing of other programs. 75

Operational decisions Decisions that concern the day-to-day activities of an organization. 32

Operations information systems Systems that maintain data on finished goods inventory and the movements of goods from inventory to the customer. 207

Optical fibre cable A type of cable used to connect the computers, printers, switches, and other devices on a LAN. The signals on such cables are light rays, and they are reflected inside the glass core of the optical fibre cable. The core is surrounded by a *cladding* to contain the light signals, and the cladding, in turn, is wrapped with an outer layer to protect it. 161

Oracle A popular, enterprise-class DBMS product from Oracle Corporation. 103

Organizational feasibility One of four dimensions of feasibility. 308

Output hardware Hardware that displays the results of the computer's processing. Consists of video displays, printers, audio speakers, overhead projectors, and other special-purpose devices, such as large flatbed plotters. 73

Outsourcing The process of hiring another organization to perform a service. Outsourcing is done to save costs, to gain expertise, and to free up management time. 319

Packet-filtering firewall A firewall that examines each packet and determines whether to let the packet pass. To make this decision, it examines the source address, the destination addresses, and other data. 169

Packet-switching network System in which messages are first disassembled into small packets, then sent through the network and reassembled at the destination. 172

Parallel installation A type of system conversion in which the new system runs in parallel with the old one for a while. Parallel installation is expensive because the organization incurs the costs of running both systems. 315

Patch A group of fixes for high-priority failures that can be applied to existing copies of a particular product. Software vendors supply patches to fix security and other critical problems. 86, 318

Payload The program code of a virus that causes unwanted or hurtful actions, such as deleting programs or data, or even worse, modifying data in ways that are undetected by the user. 84

People As part of the five-component framework, one of the five fundamental components of an information system; includes those who operate and service the computers, those who maintain the data, those who support the networks, and those who use the system. 6

Personal DBMS DBMS products designed for smaller, simpler database applications. Such products are used for personal or small workgroup applications that involve fewer than 100 users, and normally fewer than 15. Today, Microsoft Access is the only prominent personal DBMS. 110

Personal identification number (PIN) A form of authentication whereby the user supplies a number that only he or she knows. 337

Petabyte 10^{15} bytes. 234

Phased installation A type of system conversion in which the new system is installed in pieces across the organization(s). Once a given piece works, then the organization installs and tests another piece of the system, until the entire system has been installed. 315

Phishing A technique for obtaining unauthorized data that uses pretexting via email. The *phisher* pretends to be a legitimate company and sends an email requesting confidential data, such as account numbers, social insurance numbers, account passwords, and so forth. 333

Pilot installation A type of system conversion in which the organization implements the entire system on a limited portion of the business. The advantage of pilot implementation is that if the system fails, the failure is contained within a limited boundary. This reduces exposure of the business and also protects the new system from developing a negative reputation throughout the organization(s). 315

Plunge installation Sometimes called direct installation, a type of system conversion in which the organization shuts off the old system and starts the new system. If the new system fails, the organization is in trouble: Nothing can be done until either the new system is fixed or the old system is reinstalled. Because of the risk, organizations should avoid this conversion style if possible. 315

Port A number used to uniquely identify a transaction over a network. 168

Pretexting A technique for gathering unauthorized information in which someone pretends to be someone else. A common scam involves a telephone caller who pretends to be from a credit card company and claims to be checking the validity of credit card numbers. *Phishing* is also a form of pretexting. 333

Price elasticity A measure of the sensitivity in demand to changes in price. It is the ratio of the percentage change in quantity divided by the percentage change in price. 219

Primary activities In Michael Porter's value chain model, the fundamental activities that create value—inbound logistics, operations, outbound logistics, marketing/sales, and service. 48

Printer server A network interface card (NIC) that contains a special-purpose computer with firmware programs that enable the computers on a LAN to use a shared printer. 190

Procedures Instructions for humans. One of the five fundamental components of an information system. 6

Process blueprint In an ERP product, a comprehensive set of inherent processes for organizational activities. 215

Process-based systems The third era of computing systems. In this era, systems are designed not to facilitate the work of a single department or function, but rather to integrate the activities in an entire business process. 203

Product quality assurance (PQA) The testing of a system. PQA personnel usually construct a test plan with the advice and assistance of users. PQA test engineers perform testing, and they also supervise user-test activity. Many PQA professionals are programmers who write automated test programs. 314

Productivity paradox The lack of evidence of an increase in worker productivity associated with the massive increase in investment in information technology. 46

Project management body of knowledge (PMBOK) Provides project managers, sponsors, and team leaders with a large array of accepted project management techniques and practices. 280

Protocol A standardized means for coordinating an activity between two or more entities. 160

Pull production planning A manufacturing process whereby products are pulled through manufacturing by demand. Items are manufactured in response to signals from customers or other production processes that products or components are needed. 206

Push production planning A plan for producing products whereby the company analyzes past sales levels, makes estimates of future sales, and creates a master production schedule. Products are produced according to that schedule and pushed into sales (and customers). 206

Query A request for data from a database. 108

Radio frequency identification (RFID) tags A computer chip that transmits data about the container or product to which it is attached. RFID data include not just product numbers, but also data about where the product was made, what the components are, special handling requirements, and, for perishable products, when the contents will expire. RFID tags facilitate inventory tracking by signalling their presence to scanners as they are moved throughout the manufacturing facility. 207

Records Also called *rows*, groups of columns in a database table. 100

Regression analysis A type of supervised data mining that estimates the values of parameters in a linear equation. Used to determine the relative influence of variables on an outcome and also to predict future values of that outcome. 248

Relation The more formal name for a database table. 102

Relational database Database that carries its data in the form of tables and that represents relationships using foreign keys. 102

Relationship An association among entities or entity instances in an E-R model or an association among rows of a table in a relational database. 122

Relevant information Information that is appropriate to both the context and the subject. 28

Report A presentation of data in a structured, or meaningful context. 105

Reporting system A system that creates information from disparate data sources and delivers that information to the proper users on a timely basis. 243

Requirements analysis phase The second phase in the SDLC, in which developers conduct user interviews, evaluate existing systems, determine new forms/reports/queries, identify new features and functions, including security, and create the data model. 306

Resources Items of value, such as inventory or funds, that are part of a business process. 26

Review step The final step in the decision-making process, in which decision makers evaluate results of their decision, and if necessary repeat the process to correct or adapt the decision. 34

Router A special-purpose computer that moves network traffic from one node on a network to another. 163

Rows Also called *records*, groups of columns in a database table. 100

SAP R/3 A software product licensed by German company SAP that integrates business activities into *inherent processes* across an organization. 210

Sarbanes-Oxley (SOX) Act Law passed by the U.S. Congress in 2002 that governs the reporting requirements of publicly held companies. Among other things, it strengthened requirements for internal controls and management's responsibility for accurate financial reporting. 262

Schedule feasibility One of four dimensions of feasibility. 308

Security threat A problem with the security of an information or the data therein, caused by human error, malicious activity, or natural disasters. 332

Server A computer that provides some type of service, such as hosting a database, running a blog, publishing a website, or selling goods. Server computers are faster, larger, and more powerful than client computers. 77

Server farm A large collection of server computers that coordinates the activities of the servers, usually for commercial purposes. 77

Service pack A large group of fixes that solve low-priority software problems. Users apply service packs in much the same way that they apply patches, except that service packs typically involve fixes to hundreds or thousands of problems. 318

Smart card A plastic card similar to a credit card that has a microchip. The microchip, which holds much more data than a magnetic strip, is loaded with identifying data. Normally requires a PIN. 337

Sniffing A technique for intercepting computer communications. With wired networks, sniffing requires a physical connection to the network. With wireless networks, no such connection is required. 333

Software Instructions for computers. One of the five fundamental components of an information system. 6

SOHO (small office, home office) An acronym for small office/home office. 189

Spam Unwanted email messages. 332

Special function cards Cards that can be added to the computer to augment the computer's basic capabilities. 72

Spoofing When someone pretends to be someone else with the intent of obtaining unauthorized data. If you pretend to be your professor, you are spoofing your professor. 333

Spyware Programs installed on the user's computer without the user's knowledge or permission that reside in the background and, unknown to the user, observe the user's actions and keystrokes, modify computer activity, and report the user's activities to sponsoring organizations. Malicious spyware captures keystrokes to obtain user names, passwords, account numbers, and other sensitive information. Other spyware is used for marketing analyses, observing what users do, websites visited, products examined and purchased, and so forth. 338

SQL Server A popular enterprise-class DBMS product from Microsoft. 103

Storage hardware Hardware that saves data and programs. Magnetic disk is by far the most common storage device, although optical disks, such as CDs and DVDs, also are popular. 73

Strategic decision Decision that concerns broader-scope, organizational issues. 33

Structured decision A type of decision for which there is a formalized and accepted method for making the decision. 33

Structured Query Language (SQL) An international standard language for processing database data. 104

Supervised data mining A form of data mining in which data miners develop a model prior to the analysis and apply statistical techniques to data to estimate values of the parameters of the model. 248

Supplier relationship management (SRM) A business process for managing all contacts between an organization and its suppliers. 222

Supply chain A network of organizations and facilities that transforms raw materials into products delivered to customers. 221

Supply chain management (SCM) system An IS that integrates the primary inbound logistics business activity. 222

Support activities In Michael Porter's value chain model, the activities that contribute indirectly to value creation—procurement, technology, human resources, and the firm's infrastructure. 48

Sustaining technologies Changes in technology that maintain the rate of improvement in customer value. 52

Switch A special-purpose computer that receives and transmits data across a network. 160

Symmetrical digital subscriber lines (SDSL) DSL lines that have the same upload and download speeds. 167

System conversion The process of *converting* business activity from the old system to the new. 315

System definition phase The first phase in the SDLC, in which developers, with the help of eventual users, define the new system's goals and scope, assess its feasibility, form a project team, and plan the project. 306

System maintenance phase The fifth and final phase in the SDLC, in which developers record requests for changes, including both enhancements and failures, and fix failures by means of patches, service packs, and new releases. 306

Systems analysis and design The process of creating and maintaining information systems. It is sometimes called *systems development.* 305

Systems analysts IS professionals who understand both business and technology. They are active throughout the systems development process and play a key role in moving the project from conception to conversion and, ultimately, maintenance. Systems analysts integrate the work of the programmers, testers, and users. 284, 309

Systems development The process of creating and maintaining information systems. It is sometimes called *systems analysis and design.* 305

Systems development life cycle (SDLC) The classical process used to develop information systems. These basic tasks of systems development are combined into the following phases: system definition, requirements analysis, component design, implementation, and system maintenance (fix or enhance). 306

Table Also called a *file*, a group of similar rows or records in a database. 100

Tangible benefit A benefit of an IS that can be measured as a dollar value. 289

Technical feasibility One of four dimensions of feasibility. 308

Technical safeguards Safeguards that involve the hardware and software components of an information system. 336

10/100/1000 Ethernet A type of *Ethernet* that conforms to the IEEE 802.3 protocol and allows for transmission at a rate of 10, 100, or 1000 Mbps (megabits per second). 162

Terabyte (TB) 1024GB. 75

Test plan Groups of sequences of actions that users will take when using the new system. 314

Thick client A software application that requires programs other than just the browser on a user's computer—that is, that requires code on both a client and server computers. 82

Thin client A software application that requires nothing more than a browser and can be run on only the user's computer. 82

Timely information Information that is produced in time for its intended use. 27

Transaction processing system (TPS) An information system that supports operational decision making. 32

Tuned Adjusting information systems from time to time to changes in the workload. 282

Tunnel A virtual, private pathway over a public or shared network from the VPN client to the VPN server. 174

Unauthorized data disclosure Can occur by human error when someone inadvertently releases data in violation of policy, or when employees unknowingly or carelessly release proprietary data to competitors or the media. 333

Unified Modelling Language (UML) A series of diagramming techniques that facilitates OOP development. UML has dozens of different diagrams for all phases of system development. UML does not require or promote any particular development process. 121

Uniform resource locator (URL) A document's address on the Web. URLs begin on the right with a top-level domain, and, moving left, include a domain name and then are followed by optional data that locates a document within that domain. 165

Unix An operating system developed at Bell Labs in the 1970s. It has been the workhorse of the scientific and engineering communities since then. 79

Unshielded twisted pair (UTP) cable A type of cable used to connect the computers, printers, switches, and other devices on a LAN. A UTP cable has four pairs of twisted wire. A device called an RJ-45 connector is used to connect the UTP cable into NIC devices. 161

Unstructured decision A type of decision for which there is no agreed-on decision-making method. 33

Unsupervised data mining A form of data mining whereby the analysts do not create a model or hypothesis before running the analysis. Instead, they apply the data-mining technique to the data and observe the results. With this method, analysts create hypotheses after the analysis to explain the patterns found. 248

Usurpation Occurs when unauthorized programs invade a computer system and replace legitimate programs. Such unauthorized programs typically shut down the legitimate system and substitute their own processing. 334

Value chain A network of value-creating activities. 48

Vertical-market application Software that serves the needs of a specific industry. Examples of such programs are those used by dental offices to schedule appointments and bill patients, those used by auto mechanics to keep track of customer data and customers' automobile repairs, and those used by parts warehouses to track inventory, purchases, and sales. 80

Virtual private network (VPN) A WAN connection alternative that uses the Internet or a private internet to create the appearance of private point-to-point connections. In the IT world, the term *virtual* means something that appears to exist that does not exist in fact. Here, a VPN uses the public Internet to create the appearance of a private connection. 173

Virus A computer program that replicates itself; unchecked replication is like computer cancer by which ultimately the virus consumes the computer's resources. Many viruses also take unwanted and harmful actions. 84

Voice over Internet Protocol (VoIP) A technology that provides telephone communication over the Internet. 175

Volatile memory Data that will be lost when the computer or device is not powered. 76

Web crawler A software program that browses the web in a very methodical way. 176

Web storefront In e-commerce, a web-based application that enables customers to enter and manage their orders. 218

Wide area network (WAN) A network that connects computers located at different geographic locations. 159

Windows An operating system designed and sold by Microsoft. It is the most widely used operating system. 79

Wired Equivalent Privacy (WEP) A wireless security standard developed by the IEEE 802.11 committee that was insufficiently tested before it was deployed in communications equipment. It has serious flaws. 192

Wireless NIC (WNIC) Devices that enable wireless networks by communicating with wireless *access points.* Such devices can be cards that slide into the PCMA slot or they can be built-in, onboard devices. WNICs operate according to the 802.11 protocol. 162

Worm A virus that propagates itself using the Internet or some other computer network. Worm code is written specifically to infect another computer as quickly as possible. 84

Worth-its-cost information When an appropriate relationship exists between the cost of information and its value. 28

Wi-Fi Protected Access (WPA) An improved wireless security standard developed by the IEEE 802.11 committee to fix the flaws of the *Wired Equivalent Privacy (WEP)* standard. Only newer wireless hardware uses this technique. 192

WPA2 An improved version of WPA. 192

Zachman framework Conceived by John Zachman at IBM in the 1980s, divides systems into two dimensions: One is based on six reasons for communication (what—data, how—function, where—network, who—people, when—time, why—motivation), the other is based on stakeholder groups (Planner, Owner, Designer, Builder, Implementer, and Worker). The intersection of these two dimensions helps to provide a relatively holistic view of the enterprise. 259

INDEX

D

E

F

J

K

L

M

T

U

V

W

Y

Z